Excel Object Model, continued

C000174049

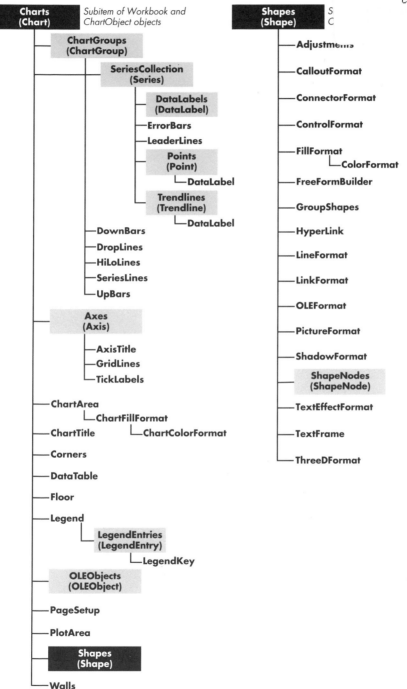

Charts (Chart) — *Subitem of Workbook and ChartObject objects*

- **ChartGroups (ChartGroup)**
  - **SeriesCollection (Series)**
    - **DataLabels (DataLabel)**
    - ErrorBars
    - LeaderLines
    - **Points (Point)**
      - DataLabel
    - **Trendlines (Trendline)**
      - DataLabel
  - DownBars
  - DropLines
  - HiLoLines
  - SeriesLines
  - UpBars
- **Axes (Axis)**
  - AxisTitle
  - GridLines
  - TickLabels
- ChartArea
  - ChartFillFormat
    - ChartColorFormat
- ChartTitle
- Corners
- DataTable
- Floor
- Legend
  - **LegendEntries (LegendEntry)**
    - LegendKey
- **OLEObjects (OLEObject)**
- PageSetup
- PlotArea
- **Shapes (Shape)**
- Walls

Shapes (Shape)

- Adjustments
- CalloutFormat
- ConnectorFormat
- ControlFormat
- FillFormat
  - ColorFormat
- FreeFormBuilder
- GroupShapes
- HyperLink
- LineFormat
- LinkFormat
- OLEFormat
- PictureFormat
- ShadowFormat
- **ShapeNodes (ShapeNode)**
- TextEffectFormat
- TextFrame
- ThreeDFormat

Continued

Microsoft®
Excel 97
Developer's
Handbook

Eric Wells,
Steve Harshbarger

Microsoft Press

PUBLISHED BY
Microsoft Press
A Division of Microsoft Corporation
One Microsoft Way
Redmond, Washington 98052-6399

Copyright © 1997 by Eric Wells and Micro Modeling Associates

All rights reserved. No part of the contents of this book may be reproduced or
transmitted in any form or by any means without the written permission of the publisher.

Library of Congress Cataloging-in-Publication Data
Wells, Eric, 1962–
    Microsoft Excel 97 developer's handbook / Eric Wells, Steve
Harshbarger.
        p.   cm.
    Includes index.
    ISBN 1-57231-359-5
    1. Microsoft Excel for Windows.   2. Business--Computer programs.
3. Electronic spreadsheets. 4. Computer software--Development-
-Software. I. Harshbarger, Steve. II. Title.
HF5548.4.M523W464 1997
005.369--dc21   97-8026
                                     CIP

Printed and bound in the United States of America.

3 4 5 6 7 8 9 WCWC 2 1 0 9 8

Distributed to the book trade in Canada by Macmillan of Canada, a division of Canada
Publishing Corporation.

A CIP catalogue record for this book is available from the British Library.

Microsoft Press books are available through booksellers and distributors worldwide. For further
information about international editions, contact your local Microsoft Corporation office. Or
contact Microsoft Press International directly at fax (206) 936-7329.

Microsoft, Microsoft Excel 97, Microsoft Press, PivotTable, PowerPoint, Win32, Windows, and
Windows NT are registered trademarks, and ActiveX, MSN, Outlook, Visual Basic, and Visual
C++ are trademarks of Microsoft Corporation. Other product and company names mentioned
herein may be the trademarks of their respective owners.

Acquisitions Editor: Casey Doyle
Project Editor: Victoria Thulman
Technical Editor: John Conrow

CONTENTS SUMMARY

TABLE OF CONTENTS

PART ONE   Introduction to Excel Objects and VBA

PART TWO   Developing Information Systems and Designing Custom Interfaces

Table of Contents

ACKNOWLEDGMENTS

Quite a bit of work goes into the creation of a book such as the *Microsoft Excel 97 Developer's Handbook*, and the many talented people involved are deserving of recognition. Thanks go to Casey Doyle, Victoria Thulman, John Conrow, and everyone else at Microsoft Press who worked on this book. They not only did an excellent job in pulling this project together, but they also exercised an exceptional degree of patience.

Many thanks also go to the talented people on the Microsoft Excel and Microsoft Office teams at Microsoft, all of whom have made significant contributions toward some of the best software ever developed for the personal computer. Special thanks go to Jon DeVaan, Ben Waldman, Russell Williams, Larry Tseng, PJ Hough, and Vinod Anantharaman for the parts they've played in making Microsoft Excel the powerful development tool it is today. Thanks also go to the Office Development Marketing Team—Michael Risse, Scott Horn, Neil Charney, and David Lazar—for their work in establishing Microsoft Office as a powerful solutions development platform.

Thanks also to the talented people at Micro Modeling Associates who have built hundreds of Excel-based solutions over the years. The sum of their knowledge and expertise gained through working with clients has helped direct the book's content at real-world problems. Special thanks to Roy Wetterstrom, Ken Heft, and Rob Erman for their support, input, and assistance.

Finally, we would like to thank Will Tompkins, Tom Chester, Chris Kinsman, Reed Jacobson, Don Baarns, and all of the other Excel consultants that we've had the pleasure of working with over the past four years. This group has been a driving force behind Microsoft Excel's success and an inspiration to our work with the product.

USING THE COMPANION CD

Contents of the CD

Bound into the back of this book is a companion CD-ROM that contains all the files referenced in the book and nine appendixes of critical reference material:

Appendix A: Additional VBA and Excel Development Topics

Appendix B: File and Directory Functions

Appendix C: Calling the Windows API and DLLs

Appendix D: Dynamic Data Exchange

Appendix E: Windows 95 Registry and EXCEL5.INI File Settings

Appendix F: Error Codes

Appendix G: New Development Features in Excel 97

Appendix H: Programming with Solver

Appendix I: Sources of Additional Information

Installing the Companion CD

The CD installation procedure you use depends on the operating system you have installed.

Microsoft Windows NT 3.x Users

1. Insert the CD into your CD-ROM drive.
2. In File Manager, choose Run from the File menu.
3. In the Run dialog box, enter *D:\SETUP.EXE.*
4. Respond to the on-screen prompts.

Microsoft Windows 95 and Microsoft Windows NT 4.x Users

1. Insert the CD into your CD-ROM drive.
2. Choose Run from the Start menu.
3. In the Run dialog box, enter *D:\SETUP.EXE.*
4. Respond to the on-screen prompts.

INTRODUCTION

In business, information is money. This book is about information—how to access it, analyze it, and give it meaning. The ability to rapidly convert raw data to useful information leads to better decision making, which ultimately leads to making more money.

In major corporations throughout the world, an enormous amount of raw data can be found—data on customers, markets, products, demographics, company finances, competitors, and so on. This is data that, in general, exists in electronic form in databases distributed throughout numerous departments and divisions. Yet, in any given market, the company that has access to the greatest amount of data does not necessarily enjoy a competitive advantage.

Effective Delivery of Meaningful Information

The value a company can derive from data lies not in the quantity of the data but in the ability to convert that data to meaningful information and to deliver the information to the company's decision makers. Doing so might sound easy enough, but delivering information effectively can be quite difficult. The difficulty arises not from the delivery process itself (anyone can do a print dump of a database and send a 10,000-page report through interoffice mail), but from the process of transforming data into meaningful information.

Because so many considerations are involved in transforming raw data into meaningful information, the task might appear to be daunting, if not impossible. Here are some of those considerations:

- How should the data be summarized? By week? By quarter? By year?

- Should the data be analyzed numerically or graphically?

- Which staff are analyzing the data? What decisions are they making, and what information do they need?

- Are those who are analyzing the data looking for trends? Do they want to perform some sort of advanced statistical analysis on the data?

- Should different decision makers be allowed to change data in a database? If so, what data should they be allowed to change?

Developing a computer-based information system that would take into account all of the above considerations and many others for every decision maker in a company would probably be impossible—or at least not cost effective. As soon as such a system were developed, the information needs of the decision makers would likely change because, in any market, conditions rarely remain static.

PC-Based Applications Alter Information Delivery

The 1980s saw the advent of personal computers, and with personal computers came general-purpose data analysis software, which found its primary form in spreadsheets. Although spreadsheets served as excellent general tools for basic numeric operations on small data sets, they were often too general and lacked the data-handling capabilities needed to perform specific analyses on large amounts of data. The beginning of the 1990s saw companies wanting to take greater advantage of the potential for effective data analysis that advances in computing technology provided, and millions of dollars were invested to develop large information systems using high-end development tools such as COBOL, C, and Pascal. Although such custom systems provided a way to analyze large amounts of data, they proved extremely costly to develop and difficult to maintain. They also tended to be either too narrow or too broad in scope—designed to deliver information in a specific manner to meet the needs of a few individuals or in a general manner to partially meet the needs of several individuals, but never fully meeting the needs of all.

Over time, efforts were made to build some of the capabilities of high-end development tools into spreadsheets by incorporating macro languages. Even through the early 1990s, however, spreadsheet macro languages were limited. Keystroke-based languages suffered from a lack of power, and function-based languages were difficult to work with. Efforts were also made to reduce the complexity of high-end development tools. The introduction of visual tools on PC-based systems simplified the development of applications that had in the past been created with high-end languages, greatly reducing the cost and effort involved in creating those applications. Yet, by this time, it had become apparent that the ideal tool for developing a PC-based information system would be one that leveraged the data analysis capabilities of spreadsheets, as well as the customization and data-handling capabilities offered by the newly introduced visual tools. Such a development tool would allow companies to design, implement, and maintain flexible and effective information systems in less time and at a lower cost.

Microsoft Excel as a Development Tool

Microsoft Excel is the first development tool to provide the advantages of both spreadsheets and visual programming tools. In fact, Excel is the first spreadsheet to offer a visual development language—Visual Basic for Applications, or VBA as it is more commonly known. VBA is actually an implementation of Microsoft's premier visual development tool, Visual Basic, embedded in the Excel spreadsheet (and other Microsoft Office applications). It provides the highest level of user-programmable access to data analysis functions ever available in a spreadsheet.

When you look at Excel as a development tool, it is important to understand that Excel is not merely a spreadsheet. Excel is also a powerful object library that includes over one hundred advanced data analysis objects. With VBA, developers can piece together Excel's objects to create powerful information systems. And because Excel's objects are general in scope, developers can add a high degree of flexibility to the information systems they create so that each system meets the needs of multiple users. Excel also supports OLE, as both an OLE Automation object and a controller. Such support of OLE allows developers to easily integrate Excel objects into systems based in other development environments.

Creating an Information System

Designing an information system requires careful consideration of the development tools to be used. Excel should be considered for any information system involving data analysis because Excel's data analysis objects are some of the most advanced available on the market. Microsoft uses some of the software industry's best computer scientists to design and create Excel's objects. By using these objects in your own applications, you can leverage the work of these computer scientists and actually incorporate their code in your applications, thus creating more powerful applications with less effort.

There are currently thousands of Excel-based information systems in use in corporations throughout the world. With the success of VBA in Excel, the demand for Excel-based applications is likely to continue to increase significantly over the next several years as more companies begin to discover that by using Excel, they can develop effective information systems with less investment of time and money.

Who Can Use This Book

This book provides an in-depth look at creating information systems using the Excel object model and VBA. Readers of this book should have some development experience, know at least one programming or macro language, and understand spreadsheets. Readers who know Visual Basic and are familiar with Excel will be best able to take advantage of the information in this book.

This book, a successor to *Developing Microsoft Excel 95 Solutions with Visual Basic for Applications,* includes development information for Excel version 8 for Microsoft Windows 95 and Microsoft Windows NT (or Microsoft Excel 97, as it is more commonly known). Appendix G, which you can find on the companion CD, includes a complete list of all new development features in Excel 97. The main features include the following:

- **New VBA Development Environment:** Starting with Microsoft Office 97, a truly common VBA development environment is shared between each Office application. The environment is nearly identical to the stand-alone VB product. Excel developers will appreciate a new full-featured forms tool (Microsoft Forms), improved editing and debugging tools, a new object browser, and the ability to host custom controls.

- **New Excel Event Model:** Excel now supports an expanded set of events for workbooks, worksheets, charts, and the Excel application itself. These events afford a much greater degree of control to the developer who needs to customize, control, or respond to the Excel environment. Excel event procedures are now written as "code behind documents" much like VB implements "code behind forms."

- **Full Microsoft VB 4.0 Language Compatibility:** Language extensions introduced in VB 4.0 are now available in VBA. These include class modules and conditional compilation.

- **On-Sheet Custom Controls:** Excel worksheets can now contain custom controls (ActiveX) and respond to their events. The new VBA environment exposes embedded custom controls' event procedures just like VB does.

- **Inter/Intranet Features:** Excel 97 implements new features that make Excel both a publishing and development tool for the Internet or internal corporate nets (intranets). These include hyperlinks and Internet queries.

- **Conditional Formatting:** Developers can now assign to cells conditional formats that fully control font, border, and fill attributes. Formats can be conditional on user-defined criteria and are evaluated whenever Excel recalculates.

- **Data Validation:** Cells can now enforce data validation rules when the user attempts to enter information into them. Data can be validated against a list, a data type, a range of values, a text length, or a custom validation rule. In addition, both custom input prompts and error messages can be associated with each validation.

- **Enhanced Worksheet Protection Properties:** New properties allow more granular control over the protection of worksheets and what the user is allowed to do. This greater control includes the ability to limit the scrollable area; disallow selection of cells; and disable the AutoFilter, PivotTable, Outlining, and Refresh Data features. In addition, AutoFilter listboxes can be programmatically hidden on a per-column basis. This new set of properties replaces and enhances the old data entry feature set.

- **Enhanced Charting:** The charting tool now provides a more intuitive interface for creating and manipulating charts as well as several new chart types. In addition, charts support an entire set of events that can be used to implement such things as "drill down" functionality. For example, developers can now hit-test to determine which point in a series the user clicks on. Finally, charts have their own set of protection properties, which allow a fine degree of control over what the user can and cannot do to the chart.

- **Enhanced Pivottables:** A number of enhancements are provided with pivottables in Excel 97. Perhaps the most significant enhancements are those that deal with server-based page fields and the new PivotCache object, which provides a means of manipulating certain aspects of the pivottable RAM memory cache. Additional new functionality is provided in the area of implementation of formulas on pivottable-based data. Full details are provided in Chapter 4.

- **New Drawing Tools:** A new set of common drawing tools called "Office Art" is available in Office 97. Office Art offers more shapes and more formatting options (e.g., 3D rendering and rotation) than Excel's old drawing tools. This functionality is programmable through a set of objects.

- **Commandbars:** Common to all Office 97 applications is a new user interface element called a commandbar. Commandbars combine and replace menus and toolbars. For the developer, a new CommandBar object is used for programmatic control.

- **Programmable Office Assistant:** Also new to Office 97 is the Office Assistant, an animated form of help for the user. Developers can tap into the Office Assistant to implement custom help through the Office Assistant's object model.

The Organization of This Book

This book is divided into four parts. Each part provides two or three chapters that introduce new development concepts and one chapter that steps through creating a VBA application using those concepts.

- **Part 1: Introduction to Excel Objects and VBA.** Chapters 1, 2, and 3 introduce Excel objects and their associated properties and methods and give an overview of Visual Basic for Applications, including the new VBA development environment. If you are already familiar with Excel objects and VBA, you might want to skim these chapters.

- **Part 2: Developing Information Systems and Designing Custom Interfaces.** Chapters 4, 5, and 6 begin to delve into more advanced topics, including creating Excel-based information systems and designing custom interfaces.

- **Part 3: Database Access, Messaging, and Built-In Excel Features.** Chapters 7, 8, and 9 cover database access, messaging, and the powerful features that are built into the Excel worksheet.

- **Part 4: Integrating with Other Applications, the Web, and Other Topics.** Chapters 10, 11, 12, and 13 examine incorporating objects from other Microsoft Office applications into an information system and building Internet applications. This section also takes a look at other Excel and VBA development topics.

Where Do You Go from Here?

After you read this book, you will know how to create VBA applications in Excel and will understand Excel's data analysis objects. This will enable you to use Microsoft Excel and Visual Basic for Applications to transform raw data into meaningful information—information that can be used by your company and your clients to make better decisions and, ultimately, more money.

PART

ONE

Introduction to Excel
Objects and VBA

1

Excel Objects

This chapter provides an overview of the Microsoft Excel object model. An object in Excel is something that can be programmed or, in essence, controlled. Excel's object model contains over 100 inherent objects and several objects that are shared by all Office applications. Shared objects include CommandBars, Data Access Objects (for both Jet and ODBCDirect databases), Forms (i.e., custom dialog boxes and controls), the Office Assistant, and FileSearch. In addition, hundreds of objects from other Microsoft Office and BackOffice applications can be used from within Excel. Excel can even use objects exposed by ActiveX controls. Excel's objects range from simple objects such as rectangles and textboxes to complicated objects such as pivottables and charts. Before you can create Excel applications, you must have not only a good understanding of the functionality that various Excel objects offer but also a firm knowledge of the structure of the Excel object model.

Excel objects are discrete entities that offer various pieces of data analysis functionality. You create applications in Excel by tying these objects together using Visual Basic for Applications (VBA), Excel's programming language. (Chapter 2 gives you a complete overview of the VBA language.) The end of this chapter focuses on showing you how to begin building custom applications with four commonly used Excel objects: Application, Workbook, Worksheet, and Range. Additional objects are discussed in detail throughout the course of this book. Note that all Excel objects are fully documented in the online VBA Help that comes with Excel.

Objects and Their Properties and Methods

All objects in Excel have what are known as "properties" and "methods." VBA is a tool through which you can control Excel objects by manipulating their properties and methods. To develop custom applications in Excel, you must understand the concepts of objects, properties, and methods as well as know the specific details about the properties and methods of Excel's objects.

> ### FYI
>
> **VBA Naming Conventions**
>
> In VBA code, the name of an object, a property, a method, or an event is written as one word (for example, the OptionButton object). In addition, all such names begin with a capital letter, and if a name consists of two concatenated words, the first letter of the second word is capitalized as well (for example, the HasPassword property or the PrintPreview method).

A Real-World Example

Let's look at a real-world example of an object and its properties and methods. Think of everything that you encounter in your daily life that can be controlled: your car, your phone, your television, your microwave, and your computer. Just about everything you encounter can be controlled in some way. Even the earth is subject to the gravitational control of the sun and other planets. These are all objects in the true definition of the word. In fact, every definable thing is an object. So, in essence, an object can be defined as any "thing."

In addition, all objects can be described. For each object, there is a set of associated adjectives that represent various measurable aspects of the object. A property is a measurable aspect of an object. Take a car as an example. It is an object that has properties of color (red), year (1990), make (Nissan), number of seats (two), top speed (145 mph), and numerous other measurable aspects. Properties represent all aspects of an object. If you measure all the properties of an object, you'll have a complete and accurate description of that object.

As properties are adjectives, methods are, in effect, verbs that represent actions that can be performed on or by an object. If we look again at the example of a car, the car's methods would include start, accelerate, decelerate, and stop.

Examples of Excel Workbook Properties

Excel objects are similar to real-world objects in the sense that each Excel object has a unique set of properties used to describe it and a unique set of methods representing the actions that can be performed on or by it. Let's take a look at the workbook as an example of an Excel object. Workbooks are simply Excel files. When describing a Workbook object, we're talking about the characteristics of an Excel file. At the top of the facing page is a partial list of the properties of an Excel Workbook object:

Author	The name of the person who created the workbook
Creator	A numeric code representing the application (Excel) that was used to create the workbook
HasPassword	True if the workbook has a password; False if it does not
Name	The name of the workbook
Path	The path that describes where the workbook is saved on disk
ReadOnly	True if the workbook has been saved as read-only; False if it has not

As we review this set of properties, a couple of important facts come to light. First, all properties have values associated with them—be they string values (as in Workbook Name), Boolean values (as in the Workbook HasPassword property), numeric values, or some other kind of value. Second, properties can be specific to a single object, or they can apply to several different objects. For example, the Workbook object is the only Excel object with a HasPassword property; it is also the only object with a ReadOnly property. On the other hand, most Excel objects have a Name property. In fact, Name is one of the most prevalent properties in Excel, which makes sense because most real-life objects have names.

Getting and Setting Properties

When dealing with properties using VBA in Excel, you can perform two types of actions: You can get a property setting, or you can set a property. When doing either, you must reference both the object name and the property name, separating the two with the dot operator (.). In addition, you get or set a property by using the equals operator (=). For example, to set the Author property of the workbook named BOOK1.XLS, you would use the following VBA syntax:

```
Workbooks("BOOK1.XLS").Author = "Jane Smith"
```

The five parts of the preceding line of code are as follows:

Object name	`Workbooks("BOOK1.XLS")`
Dot operator	`.`
Property name	`Author`
Equals operator	`=`
Property value	`"Jane Smith"`

When writing VBA code to set property values, you must include all of the elements just listed. The Workbook object here is specified using an index to the Workbook collection object. You'll find an explanation of this kind of reference in the section "Referencing Objects: Singular Objects vs. Objects in Collections," beginning on page 9. We'll go into more detail about each of the elements and the various ways you can reference them later in this book.

beginning on page 9.

NOTE To write an entire VBA subroutine that sets the Author property of the Workbook object, include the keyword Sub followed by the subroutine name on the first line of the subroutine and the keywords End Sub on the last line, as in the following example:

```
Sub SetAuthorName()
    Workbooks("BOOK1.XLS").Author = "Jane Smith"
End Sub
```

Getting property settings works in much the same way as does setting them except that the elements in the VBA command appear in the opposite order. Also, when getting a property setting, you usually use a variable to hold the value of the property. The following line of code assigns the value of the Author property of a Workbook object to a string variable named AuthorName:

```
AuthorName = Workbooks("BOOK1.XLS").Author
```

The parts of the line of VBA code used to get a property are similar to those used to set a property:

Variable	AuthorName
Equals operator	=
Object name	Workbooks("BOOK1.XLS")
Dot operator	.
Property name	Author

NOTE If you haven't yet saved your workbook, it has a default name assigned by Excel—such as Book1. If you don't specify a new name using the Save As command, Excel adds the file extension .XLS when it saves the file, and the name becomes BOOK1.XLS.

Examples of Excel Workbook Methods

Excel's Workbook object also has many methods that represent actions that can be performed on or by the workbook. Here are a few of these methods:

Activate	Activates the first window associated with the workbook
Close	Closes the workbook
PrintPreview	Displays a preview of the workbook as it would be printed
Protect	Protects a workbook with a password
Save	Saves the workbook
SendMail	Sends the workbook as an embedded object in an e-mail message
Unprotect	Unprotects the workbook

Calling Methods

The VBA syntax for calling a method differs from the syntax for setting or getting properties. All that is required for a method call is a reference to the object and the method. In addition, most methods in Excel have a set of "arguments," or additional pieces of information, that can be specified to indicate how the method is to be carried out. In VBA, many methods have optional arguments—that is, depending on how you want a particular method to be executed, you can specify all, some, or none of the method's arguments. For example, the Close method of the Workbook object has three optional arguments:

saveChanges	Either True (save changes to the file) or False (don't save changes)
fileName	The filename under which the workbook will be saved if saveChanges is True
routeWorkbook	Either True (route the workbook through e-mail) or False (don't route the workbook before closing)

Passing Arguments to Methods

Here is an example of the VBA syntax you would use to call the Close method without passing any arguments:

```
Workbooks("BOOK1.XLS").Close
```

If you call the Close method without passing any arguments, the arguments take on default values. For example, if you omit the first argument (saveChanges) and changes have been made to the file, Excel by default asks the user whether the file should be saved. The question comes in the form of a message box, as shown on the next page.

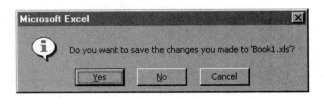

The default for the fileName argument is the file's current name, and the default for the routeWorkbook argument is False. This example shows the VBA syntax for calling the Close method while passing all three arguments:

```
Workbooks("BOOK1.XLS").Close True, "MYBOOK.XLS", False
```

When passing the arguments, you merely append them to the method call and separate multiple argument values with commas; however, be certain the arguments are in the proper order. For Close, for example, the appropriate order is saveChanges, fileName, and routeWorkbook. Also be aware that two different methods of passing arguments are available when you call a method. You can pass arguments "by name," or you can pass arguments "by order," as in the preceding example.

Passing arguments by name

When you pass an argument by name, you must specify three elements: the name of the argument (for example, saveChanges) followed by the colon-equals assignment operator (:=) and the value for the argument. The following example shows the appropriate VBA syntax for executing the Close method with all arguments being passed by name:

```
Workbooks("BOOK1.XLS").Close saveChanges:=True, _
    fileName:="BOOK1.XLS", routeWorkbook:=False
```

FYI

The Line Continuation Character in VBA

In VBA, the underscore character (_) at the end of a line indicates that the code is continued on the next line; you must precede the underscore with a space. One line of code can contain up to 1024 characters, but breaking up a line can make your code more readable. We'll use the line continuation character in this book to break up long lines of code in order to fit them on the page.

When you pass arguments by name in VBA, you need not pass them in order. For example, you can accomplish the same method call as the one we just looked at by passing the arguments by name in a different order:

```
Workbooks("BOOK1.XLS").Close routeWorkbook:=False, _
    saveChanges:=True, fileName:="BOOK1.XLS"
```

To call the Close method and pass only the first argument, saveChanges, you could pass the argument by order using the following:

```
Workbooks("BOOK1.XLS").Close True
```

Or you could pass the argument by name using the following:

```
Workbooks("BOOK1.XLS").Close saveChanges:=True
```

To pass the first and third arguments, you could do so by order by leaving a blank for the second argument:

```
Workbooks("BOOK1.XLS").Close True, , False
```

Or you could do so by name:

```
Workbooks("BOOK1.XLS").Close saveChanges:=True, routeWorkbook:=False
```

Performance considerations   Passing arguments by name has the advantage of making your code more readable. However, this advantage comes at a slight cost in performance. There is some overhead associated with interpreting the named arguments, even if you pass the named arguments in their natural order. In many cases, the difference will be negligible, but you should consider the trade-offs when performance is critical.

Referencing Objects:
Singular Objects vs. Objects in Collections

The preceding examples showed that when you reference a property or method of a particular object, you simply append the name of the property or method to the object reference using the dot operator (.). You can reference objects, though, in two different ways: You can reference the name of a single object directly, or you can reference an index in a collection of objects. To understand these two ways of referencing objects, you must have a clear understanding of collections. A collection, in its simplest definition, is a group of like objects. All Excel objects fall into two classes: singular objects and objects in a collection. Singular objects are referenced directly by name. Objects in a collection are referenced by an index in the collection. Approximately half of the objects in Excel are singular objects, and the other half are objects in collections.

NOTE Three objects in Excel—Range, Sheets, and Shapes—deviate slightly from this classification scheme. The Range object is classified as a singular object, yet it assumes characteristics of both a singular object and an object in a collection. Sheets and Shapes are both collections that contain collections of several other objects. Range and Shapes are discussed in the following sections: "The Range Object—An Exception," beginning on page 15; and "Shape Objects and the Shapes Collection," beginning on page 137 in Chapter 3.

Collections Are Also Objects

Although a collection contains groups of objects, a collection itself is also an object—a singular object. It is an object that contains a group of like objects. This concept might be difficult to grasp at first, but it will be easier to understand as you become more familiar with the Excel object model. An example would best illustrate the point.

The Worksheets collection contains multiple Worksheet objects. Each Worksheet object in the collection has properties and methods associated with it. It just so happens that the Worksheets collection also has a different set of properties and methods associated with it. You could say that there are three types of objects in Excel: singular objects, objects in collections, and collections. Technically speaking, collections are really singular objects, but we won't dwell on the point—simply remember that collections are objects themselves and as such are associated with their own set of properties and methods.

Which objects are singular, and which objects are in collections?

Of all the objects in Excel, you might wonder which are singular objects and which are objects in collections. You could memorize the names of all the objects as well as whether each object is singular or in a collection. Or you could apply two simple rules of intuition and avoid the work of memorization:

RULE 1 A singular object has only one instance in a given context. That is, it is a unique object—only one of this type of object exists in this object's context.

RULE 2 An object in a collection has multiple instances in a given context. That is, several of this type of object exist in the same context.

Applying these rules does require that you understand the objects in Excel, and you will likely understand them after you read this book. In the meantime, let's look at a few simple examples. Excel has an object named Application. The Application object is a singular object that represents the Excel application. It is singular because Excel has only one Application object. The Font object is another example of a singular object. For any given cell on an Excel worksheet, only one instance of the Font object exists. Although the Font object does have multiple properties, including Name (Courier, Times New Roman, Helvetica, and so on), Bold (True or False), Italic (True or False), and Size (the size of the font in points), a cell contains only one Font object. Therefore, Font is a singular object.

The Worksheet object, on the other hand, is an object in a collection. Any Excel workbook file can have multiple worksheets and, therefore, multiple instances of the Worksheet object. For example, if you open a new workbook file in Excel, by default three worksheets—or three instances of the Worksheet object—are included in the workbook file. Because the Worksheet object can exist in multiple instances within the same context, it is, by definition, an object in a collection. The Chart object provides another example. In an Excel workbook file, you can have multiple charts and, therefore, multiple instances of a Chart object. As such, the Chart object is an object in a collection. Figure 1-1 displays a collection of Chart objects.

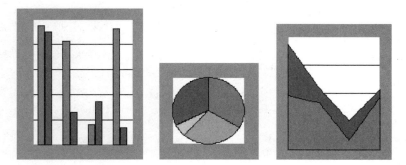

Figure 1-1. *A collection of Chart objects.*

Referencing Objects Directly or by Collection Index

As mentioned, singular objects are referenced directly, and objects in collections are referenced by specifying an index in the collection in which the object exists. Let's take a look first at an example of referencing a singular object. The Application object, which is singular, has several properties, including the following:

Caption	A string that is displayed in the application title bar
DisplayAlerts	True (allows display of built-in Excel alerts during subroutine execution) or False (prevents their display)
ScreenUpdating	True (Excel updates screen during subroutine execution) or False (Excel waits until subroutine completes before updating screen)

To set the Caption property, you reference the Application object directly:

```
Application.Caption = "My Custom Application"
```

Here is the result of setting the Caption property of the Application object:

Application caption

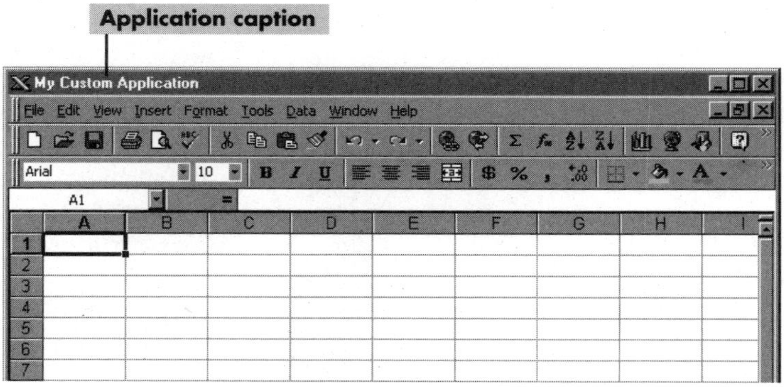

To turn off screen updating during the execution of a subroutine, you set the ScreenUpdating property to False, again referencing the Application object directly:

```
Application.ScreenUpdating = False
```

Now let's take a look at referencing an object in a collection. Because the Worksheet object is an object in a collection, you must reference the Worksheet object by specifying an index in the Worksheets collection. To set the Name property of the Worksheet object that corresponds to the first worksheet, for example, you use the following code:

```
Worksheets(1).Name = "My First Worksheet"
```

The following screen example shows the result of setting the Name property of the Worksheet object:

Worksheet name

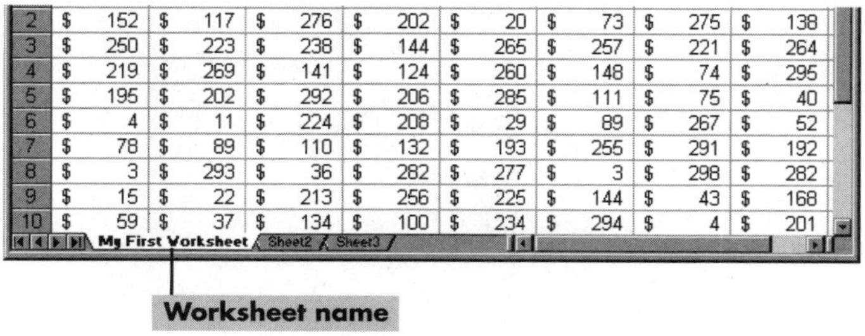

And to set the name of the third worksheet, you use the following VBA code:

```
Worksheets(3).Name = "My Third Worksheet"
```

NOTE   When you index the Worksheets collection to reference a specific Worksheet object, be sure to use the plural "Worksheets." You must use the plural for most collections in Excel with only two exceptions—Range and SeriesCollection.

Indexing Collections by Number or by Name

You can specify an index in a collection by number (as shown in the preceding examples) or by name. When writing VBA code, you'll encounter times when using one or the other indexing scheme is advantageous. For example, it is usually easiest to process the items in a collection one by one by using a numeric index. If you have a specific item (such as a "totals" worksheet), however, you can use a name index to jump directly to it without having to keep track of its numeric position in the collection.

Keep in mind when indexing by number that worksheets are numbered according to the order in which they are added to the workbook file. If you try to reference a Worksheet object by specifying an index number that is higher than the number of worksheets in the Worksheets collection, you will receive an error message at runtime. For example, if only 16 worksheets are present in the active workbook, any attempt to set the properties of or to call methods on Worksheets(17) will fail.

FYI

Collection Indexes Are 1-Based

Indexes for objects in collections in the Excel object model always start at 1. This is unlike indexes for array variables, which can start at 0, 1, or any other value.

If you don't know the index number for an object in a collection, you can reference it by name instead. Each Worksheet object in a Worksheets collection has a name associated with it; these names are displayed on the worksheet tabs at the bottom of the Excel screen. Let's assume you want to set the Visible property of a worksheet. The Visible property can take a value of True or False. If the Visible property is True, the worksheet is displayed; and if it is False, the worksheet is hidden from view. If the worksheet is named My Worksheet, for example, you might have no idea what numeric place that particular Worksheet object occupies in the Worksheets collection. Therefore, you could index the

Worksheets collection by name rather than by number, as in the following example:

```
Worksheets("My Worksheet").Visible = False
```

NOTE When indexing a collection by name, you must indicate the particular object name by enclosing it in double quotation marks within the parentheses. Also, VBA ignores case when indexing objects by name. For example, Worksheets("MY WORKSHEET") is the same as Worksheets("my worksheet").

FYI

Beware of Changing the Name Property

Take care when you set the Name property of objects in collections because the Name property affects the way in which an object is referenced when indexed by name. For example, when the following two lines of code are executed, the second line generates an error message:

```
Worksheets("My Worksheet").Name = "New Worksheet Name"
Worksheets("My Worksheet").Visible = False
```

It generates an error message because the first line changes the name of the My Worksheet worksheet to New Worksheet Name. When VBA attempts in the second line to index the Worksheets collection by name using the worksheet's old name, it cannot find any Worksheet object in the collection by that name, and execution fails.

Let's look at some other examples of indexing collections by name. The Chart object has a property named HasLegend that can take a value of True or False. If HasLegend is True, a legend appears on the chart; if it is False, no legend appears. The Chart object is an object in a collection. Therefore, if you have a chart sheet named Chart1 and you want to have a legend displayed on the chart, you index the Charts collection by name, as in the following code sample:

```
Charts("Chart1").HasLegend = True
```

This example is for a chart sheet—the code would be different for a chart embedded in a worksheet. The example chart on the facing page shows the result of setting the HasLegend property of the Chart object to True:

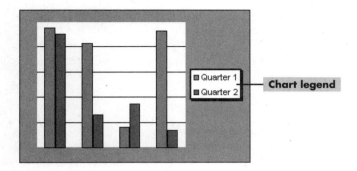

Chart legend

Let's suppose you have an application that opens and closes several Excel workbooks, one of which is named BOOK2.XLS. The Workbook object is an object in a collection. So to close BOOK2.XLS, you index the Workbooks collection by name and call the Close method, as in the following example:

```
Workbooks("BOOK2.XLS").Close
```

FYI

Referring to an Object Directly (Without Using a Collection)

New to Excel 97 is the ability to reference objects in code directly without going through a collection. This is accomplished through a new property named CodeName, which can be set by the developer only at design time. The Code-Name property is discussed in depth in the section titled "Referencing Controls and Other Objects Directly," beginning on page 144 in Chapter 3.

The Range Object—An Exception

We've seen the differences between referencing singular objects and referencing objects in collections, and we've looked at examples of how objects in collections can be indexed either by number or by name. One Excel object—the Range object—falls into the gray area between singular objects and objects in collections. The Range object is used to reference a cell or a group of cells on an Excel worksheet. It is, by definition, a singular object; however, it also exhibits some of the behavior of an object in a collection. For example, to reference a specific range on a worksheet, you must index the Range object by address or by name in a manner similar to the way in which you index an object in a collection.

Suppose you wanted to change the contents of a particular cell. Range has a property named Value that represents the value contained in a cell or a group of cells. In addition, each cell on an Excel worksheet has an address that is specified by combining the column letter displayed at the top of the worksheet and the row number displayed on the left side of the worksheet. For example, the address of the first cell in a worksheet is A1. To set the Value property of the first cell on a worksheet, you could index the Range object using an address, as in the following example:

```
Range("A1").Value = 1
```

Here you see the result of setting the Value property of the Range object corresponding to the address A1:

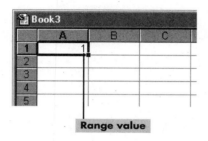

Range value

Worksheet ranges can also have names. You can therefore index the Range object using the name of a cell or group of cells instead of an address. In the following code example, the first line sets the Name property of the first cell, referencing the Range object by address. The second line sets the Value property of the same cell, this time referencing the Range object by name:

```
Range("A1").Name = "FirstCell"
Range("FirstCell").Value = 1
```

NOTE Cells that have names still retain their addresses. In the second line of code in the example above, an index to the Range object by address would still execute properly. You should be aware, though, that you cannot index the Range object by number. For example, the following code example generates an error message:

```
Range(1).Value = 1
```

When you set properties of or call methods on the Range object, you can use an address index that contains multiple cells. For example, the following code sets the Value property of all the cells that fall into the address A1:F20:

```
Range("A1:F20").Value = 1
```

The Excel Object Hierarchy

Of the 100-plus different objects in the Excel object library, not all exist on the same level—that is, some objects are contained within others. You can think of these levels as tiers in a hierarchy. (See Figure 1-2 on pages 19–21.) To reference Excel objects effectively in your VBA code, you need to understand this hierarchy and become familiar with the different tiers at which each object exists.

The Tiers of the Hierarchy

The topmost tier of the Excel object hierarchy is occupied by a single object: Application. The Application object represents Excel itself, and all other Excel objects fall under Application.

Fifteen objects are included in the second tier:

AddIn	An object representing an Excel add-in file (discussed in Chapter 13).
Assistant	An object used to control and manipulate the Office Assistant. This object is shared among all Office applications.
AutoCorrect	An object used to access Excel's AutoCorrect functionality.
CommandBar	An object representing both built-in and custom command bars (i.e., menus and toolbars). This object is shared among all Office applications (except Microsoft Outlook).
Debug	An object representing the Excel debug window.
Dialog	An object representing a built-in Excel dialog box.
FileFind	An object representing the functionality of the File Find dialog box (Macintosh only).
FileSearch	An object used to search for files. This object is shared among all Office applications (except Microsoft Outlook).
Name	An object representing a defined name for a range of cells.
ODBCError	An object used to represent errors encountered during an ODBC database operation.
RecentFile	An object representing a file in the list of most recently used files.
VBE	An object used to control the VBA editor. This object is shared among all Office applications (except Microsoft Outlook).

(continued)

continued

Window	An object used to access different windows in Excel.
Workbook	An object representing an Excel workbook file.
WorksheetFunction	An object used to execute worksheet functions from code.

The third, fourth, and fifth tiers of the hierarchy include a variety of additional objects used to access functionality that the second tier objects contain. The Excel object hierarchy has a treelike structure. For example, if we descend from the Workbook object on the second tier to the third tier of the hierarchy, we encounter these objects: Chart, CommandBar, CustomView, Datatable, DocumentProperty, Mailer, Name, PivotCache, RoutingSlip, Style, VBProject, Window, and Worksheet. Or if we descend from the Window object on the second tier to the third tier of the hierarchy, we encounter only one object, Pane.

Figure 1-2 shows the Microsoft Excel object model hierarchy. In the diagram, collections appear in boxes, and the names of the objects in the collection appear in parentheses. Although Excel has over 100 objects, a different number of nodes are shown in this diagram. That's because each collection can itself be treated as an individual object. Also, certain objects such as Font, Border, and Interior are repeated in several places. Finally, the diagram includes some shared Office objects that are not exclusive to Excel.

Refer to the object model diagram shown in Figure 1-2 when you need help with the hierarchy of Excel's objects. For example, if you are writing code to set a property of the Range object, you can see from the diagram that the Range object falls under the Worksheet object in the hierarchy, which in turn falls under the Workbook object, which itself falls under the Application object. Or if you are writing code to call a method on the Legend object of a chart sheet, you can see from the diagram that you have to descend from the Application object to the Workbook object and then to the Chart object before you finally reach the Legend object.

Using the Excel Object Hierarchy

How does the Excel object hierarchy affect the way you write VBA code? To manipulate the properties and methods of an object, you must sometimes reference all objects that lie on the hierarchical path to that object. You traverse that path down to a specific object by using the dot operator (.).

For example, let's suppose you are writing a VBA subroutine to set the Value property of a Range object that represents the first cell in the first worksheet of the first workbook in Excel. Using the full hierarchical path, the reference to Range appears as follows:

```
Application.Workbooks(1).Worksheets(1).Range("A1").Value = 1
```

Excel Object Model

Objects listed outside of boxes are singular objects; objects enclosed in boxes are objects in collections. Objects in black boxes are expanded in diagrams on the following page. The objects displayed in this diagram are the primary objects accessible in Excel 97. Several additional objects are not shown here but are accessible from Excel 97 for backward compatibility. For example, the DrawingObjects collection and the various drawing and control objects that were accessible in Excel 5 and Excel 95 are not shown here. (The drawing and control objects have been replaced by shape objects and ActiveX controls in Excel 97.) Additionally, the Microsoft Map object model is not shown here—information on the Microsoft Map object model can be found in the object browser and in online help.

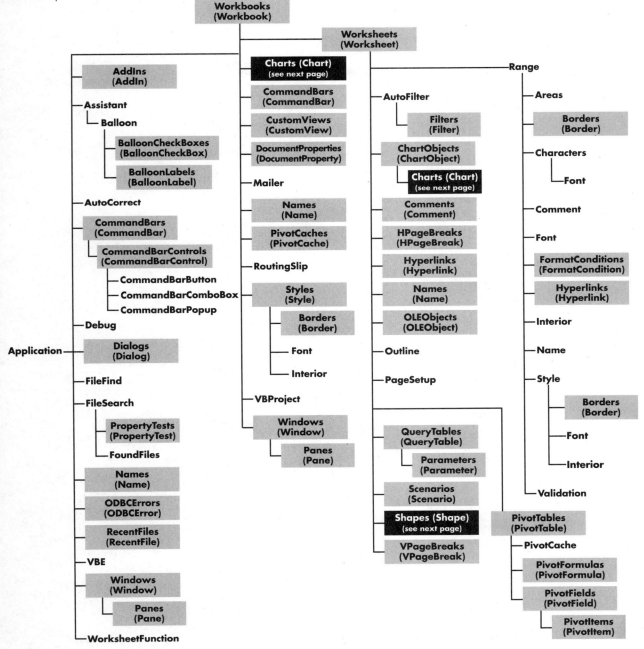

Figure 1-2. *The Excel object hierarchy.*

(continued)

Figure 1-2. *continued*

Excel Object Model, continued

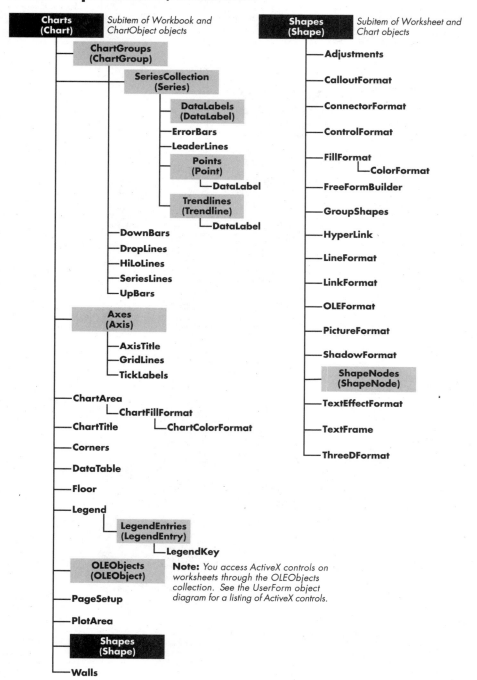

Figure 1-2. *continued*

DAO Object Model

UserForm Object Model

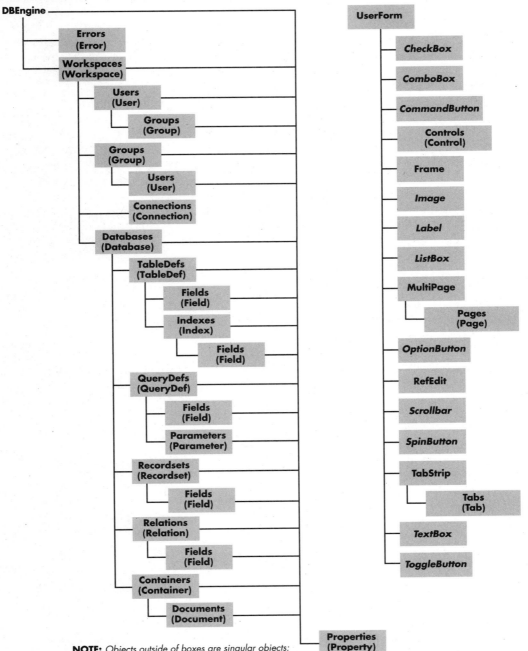

NOTE: *Objects outside of boxes are singular objects; objects enclosed in boxes are objects in collections. All objects except the Error object have a Properties collection. Objects contained within the UserForm object are ActiveX controls. Those ActiveX controls displayed in italic can be used on Excel worksheets.*

Although this code executes properly in Excel, it is not always necessary to traverse the entire hierarchical object path when setting a property of or calling a method on a particular object. How far from the top of the hierarchy you must begin depends on the context in which the property setting or method call is made.

Referencing the Application object implicitly

The preceding code example, which starts at Application and steps all the way down to Range, could be executed anywhere in Excel under any circumstances and will always assign 1 to the Value property of the Range("A1") object on the first worksheet in the first workbook (provided a workbook is open). If this code is executed in Excel (it typically would be), a reference to the Application object isn't necessary. Application refers to Excel, so in the absence of an explicit reference to the Application object—and as long as the code is executed inside Excel—VBA understands that the code is to be executed on Excel's Application object. Therefore, we can remove the reference to Application, as shown here:

```
Workbooks(1).Worksheets(1).Range("A1").Value = 1
```

Executing this line of code in Excel has the exact same effect as does executing the earlier line of code, which includes the reference to Application.

Referencing the active workbook implicitly

Excel can have several workbook files open at one time. However, only one workbook can be active at a time—that is, a user can enter or manipulate data in only one workbook at any given time. The active workbook is displayed in front of all other open workbooks so that the active workbook window is on top in the Excel work area; the inactive workbook windows are displayed behind the active workbook. The preceding line of code uses an index to the Workbooks collection to reference the first workbook in the collection. Let's assume that instead of setting the property in the first workbook, the goal is to set the property in the active workbook. To do so, you use a Workbook object reference named ActiveWorkbook.

Object references such as ActiveWorkbook and ThisWorkbook are explained thoroughly in the "FYI" titled "Accessing Objects Through Properties and Methods," beginning on page 25 in this chapter. For now, here is an example:

```
ActiveWorkbook.Worksheets(1).Range("A1").Value = 1
```

This code executes on the workbook that is currently active, which might not be the same as Workbooks(1).

NOTE You can also use ThisWorkbook to reference a Workbook object. ThisWorkbook, however, always refers to the workbook that actually holds the code being executed, which is not necessarily the active workbook.

If only one workbook is open and it's the workbook whose property you want to set, you don't have to include the workbook reference in the hierarchical object path. VBA infers that the property setting is to occur in the one open workbook. You could therefore eliminate the workbook reference and use the shortened code shown here:

```
Worksheets(1).Range("A1").Value = 1
```

NOTE If the code above executes while multiple workbooks are open, the property setting takes place in the active workbook.

Referencing the active sheet implicitly

In the same way that the ActiveWorkbook reference accesses the active workbook, a reference named ActiveSheet accesses the active sheet. If the property setting is to occur on the active worksheet, the preceding line of code could be changed to the following:

```
ActiveSheet.Range("A1").Value = 1
```

Here is the result of the altered line of code:

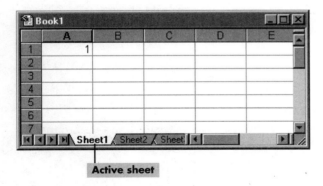

Active sheet

In addition, if the workbook has only one worksheet or if the context is such that the property setting is, by default, to occur on the active worksheet, the worksheet reference could be removed entirely:

```
Range("A1").Value = 1
```

This line of code sets the Value property of Range("A1") equal to 1 on the active worksheet. Note, though, that some objects in Excel have what is known as a "default property." Value is the default property of the Range object. That being the case, the line of code above could be shortened even further:

```
Range("A1") = 1
```

NOTE Although default properties can reduce the amount of code you need to write, specifying properties explicitly is better practice. Being explicit makes your code more readable to the next developer who maintains it (or to you long after you've written it). Thus,

```
Range("A1").Value = 1
```

is considered better programming practice than the functionally equivalent code:

```
Range("A1") = 1
```

As mentioned, ActiveWorkbook and ActiveSheet can be used to reference the active workbook and the active worksheet. The active range—those cells on the worksheet that have been selected—can also be referenced by using the Application object's Selection property. The Selection property, however, can refer to other objects in addition to the Range object. During execution, VBA evaluates Selection according to the type of object that has been selected. When using Selection, you should not rely on default properties, so if Selection is used to set the Value property of a Range object, a specific reference to the Value property should be included, as the following code example shows:

```
Selection.Value = 1
```

Executing this code assigns 1 to the Value property of the currently selected range, be it Range("A1") or Range("A1:Z256").

At Which Level Should Object References Begin?

Looking back at the preceding discussion, you can see that—assuming the proper context—each of the following lines of code produces the same result—assigning 1 to the Value property of the selected range:

```
Application.Workbooks(1).Worksheets(1).Range("A1").Value = 1
Workbooks(1).Worksheets(1).Range("A1").Value = 1
ActiveWorkbook.Worksheets(1).Range("A1").Value = 1
Worksheets(1).Range("A1").Value = 1
ActiveSheet.Range("A1").Value = 1
Range("A1").Value = 1
Range("A1") = 1
Selection.Value = 1
```

So at which level on the hierarchical object path should object references begin? If you were to play it safe, you would start all object references at the

Application object. By doing so, you would always be certain about the objects in the path, and your code would always execute without error (assuming your code had the proper syntax). You would also find yourself typing an enormous amount of code. You should, therefore, try to keep track of the context in which object references are made and traverse the hierarchical object path accordingly, using longer paths where needed to avoid any errors that might arise when you are unsure of the context in which the code will be executed. You can, however, abbreviate object references to take advantage of longer object references without having to type so much code; you do so by using object variables and With statements, both of which are covered in Chapter 2.

FYI

Accessing Objects Through Properties and Methods

Before moving on, it's important to clarify how objects are referenced using VBA. As mentioned, singular objects are referenced by name, and objects in collections are referenced by an index in the collection. When you reference a singular object by name, you are actually using a property that points to the singular object. For example, Legend is a singular object that is contained in the Chart object. The VBA reference to the Legend object in a chart appears as follows:

```
Charts(1).Legend
```

In the line of code above, Legend is actually a property of the Chart object—a property that can be used to reference the Legend object associated with that particular chart.

In Excel 97, when you specify an index in a collection to reference an object in a collection, you reference either a property or a method of a containing object. Note that in past versions of Excel, all collections were accessed through method calls. However, in Excel 97, some discrepancies exist: some collections are accessed through properties and some through methods (as indicated by the Object Browser and the online help). For the sake of consistency in this book, we have decided to stick to labeling collection accessors as methods. You therefore may see some discrepancies between this book and the Object Browser or online help. (For example, in this book, we talk of a Worksheets method, whereas in the Object Browser, Worksheets is listed as a property of the Workbook object.)

(continued)

Accessing Objects Through Properties and Methods, *continued*

In referencing the method that pertains to a collection, you pass an argument of either an integer or a string that corresponds to the object in the collection that you want returned. This example is used to reference the first worksheet in the first workbook:

```
Application.Workbooks(1).Worksheets(1)
```

Worksheets is actually a method of the Workbook object, while Workbooks is, in turn, a method of the Application object.

Note that references to ActiveWorkbook, ThisWorkbook, ActiveSheet, and Selection are all references to properties. For example, the Application object has a property named ActiveWorkbook that represents the currently active Workbook object. The following line of code calls the Close method on the active workbook:

```
ActiveWorkbook.Close
```

You could produce the same result using the full hierarchical object path:

```
Application.ActiveWorkbook.Close
```

When you use the ActiveWorkbook property and omit the reference to Application, VBA implicitly determines that the property is that of the Application object. The same holds true for ThisWorkbook, ActiveSheet, and Selection; for these as well, VBA determines the appropriate object by the context of the reference.

Online VBA Help

Full online help is available for all objects, properties, and methods in Excel. After you start writing code in VBA, you will find the online reference an invaluable tool.

You access VBA Help in Excel by selecting Contents And Index from the Help menu and then selecting Microsoft Excel Visual Basic Reference from the Contents Tab of the Help Topics dialog box. (You might need to install VBA Help from the Office installation CD if you haven't already done so.) In the Visual Basic Reference sections, you can list help topics on objects, properties, methods, statements, and functions. You can even view a diagram depicting the Excel object model. Additional help on VBA is also available in the Microsoft Office Visual Basic Reference and Microsoft Data Access Objects (DAO) sections. The Help Topics dialog box allows you to search for specific help topics in the Index tab and find all help topics related to a particular subject through the Find tab.

All Excel object help screens are structured in a similar manner. The top of the screen displays the name of the object; the body of the screen shows where the object lies in the Excel object hierarchy, and it provides a short description of the object as well as how to access the object. Under the name of the object at the top of the screen, the headings See Also, Example, Properties, Methods, and Events are displayed as shown in the following illustration:

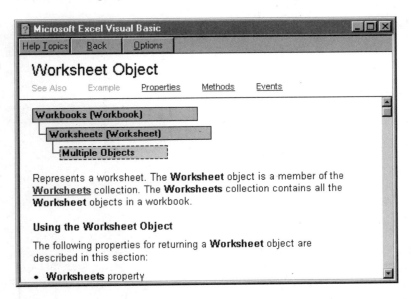

On your screen, the Properties, Methods, and Events headings (underlined in the illustration) appear in green. By clicking these headings, you can access lists of the properties, methods, and events for the displayed object. In the Properties, Methods, and Events lists, you can click a particular property, method, or event name to access a help screen. All property, method, and event help screens are structured in a similar manner, as shown on the next sample screen. The top of the screen displays the name of the property, method, or event, and the body of the screen is broken up into one or more of the following sections:

Description	Describes the property, method, or event
Syntax	Provides the appropriate syntax to be used when setting the property, calling the method, or handling the event (see the following sample screen)
Elements	Describes each of the syntactical elements of the property setting or method call; for a method, includes a full description of all arguments
Remarks	Provides additional information about how to use the property, method, or event and provides references to any associated properties, methods, or events

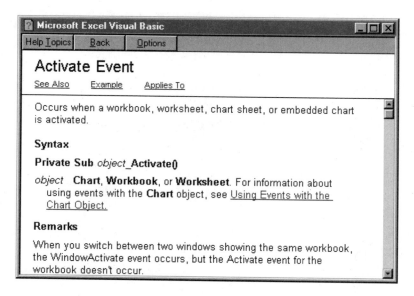

At the top of the help screen, under the property, method, or event name, you'll find three green labels: See Also, Example and Applies To. By clicking See Also, you can access other help topics related to the displayed property or method, and by clicking Example, you can view an example of syntactically correct code that shows the property being set, the method being called, or the event being used. Note that from the Example screen, you can copy and paste the code example directly to your VBA module. By clicking Applies To, you can obtain a listing of all objects to which the property, method, or event applies.

> **NOTE** The VBA editor itself (which is covered in detail in the next chapter) offers several features that complement the online help file. These include automatic keyword completion, QuickInfo (pop-up syntax hints), and on-demand lists of properties, methods, and constants for the current context.

The Application, Workbook, Worksheet, and Range Objects

The remainder of this book focuses on how to build custom applications using Excel objects. Although this book provides information about nearly every object in Excel, some objects are discussed at great length, and others (because of space constraints) are mentioned only briefly. Here we take a look at four Excel objects: Application, Workbook, Worksheet, and Range. These are four of the most commonly used objects in Excel, and gaining a basic understanding of them now will help you as you continue to read this book.

The following diagram shows the hierarchical structure of these four objects:

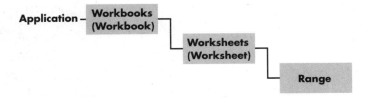

Figure 1-3 displays these four objects as they appear in Excel.

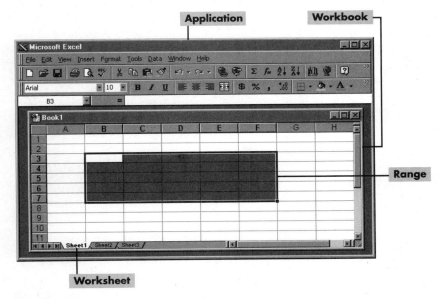

Figure 1-3. *The Application, Workbook, Worksheet, and Range objects as they appear in Excel.*

The Application Object

Application is the topmost object in the Excel object hierarchy and represents Excel itself. Because Excel VBA applications run in Excel, you can think of the Application object as representing the environment in which VBA applications run. Any property settings or method calls made on the Application object affect all of Excel and thereby also affect all VBA applications that run in the Excel environment.

The next two sections follow a format that is repeated for each object introduced here. A partial list of properties presents a short description of a property, the type of values the property can hold, information about whether the property is read/write or read-only, and a segment of VBA code that shows how the value of the property can be set or retrieved. A partial list of methods gives a description of the method, the arguments that can be passed to the method, and an example of how the method can be called.

Only a few of the more important properties and methods are listed here—the Application object actually has over 120 properties and over 40 methods. For a complete list of properties and methods or for more information about a particular property or method, see Excel's online VBA Help.

Properties of the Application object

Caption: The caption that is displayed in the Excel title bar. String; read/write.

```
Application.Caption = "My Custom Application"
```

DisplayAlerts: If DisplayAlerts is True, built-in Excel alerts are displayed during subroutine execution. If it is False, alerts are not displayed. True or False; read/write.

```
Application.DisplayAlerts = False
```

Path: The pathname of the directory in which Excel is installed. String; read-only.

```
ExcelPath = Application.Path
```

ScreenUpdating: If ScreenUpdating is True, Excel updates the screen display as subroutines execute. If it is False, the screen display is not updated during execution. This property is True by default; it remains set only during execution of the subroutine in which the setting is made. True or False; read/write.

```
Application.ScreenUpdating = False
```

WindowState: The state of the Application window. WindowState can take three different values:

xlNormal	Window in normal state
xlMaximized	Window maximized
xlMinimized	Window minimized

Read/write.

```
Application.WindowState = xlNormal
```

DisplayStatusBar: Shows or hides the status bar. If True, the status bar is displayed. If False, it is hidden. True or False; read/write.

```
Application.DisplayStatusBar = False
```

DisplayFormulaBar: Shows or hides the formula bar. If True, the formula bar is displayed. If False, it is hidden. True or False; read/write.

```
Application.DisplayFormulaBar = False
```

Methods of the Application object
Calculate: Forces all formulas in all worksheets in all open workbooks to be recalculated. Arguments: none.

```
Application.Calculate
```

Help: Displays a help topic from a specified help file. Arguments:

helpFile	String that represents the help filename, including the path to the file if necessary
helpContextId	Integer that represents context ID number for help topic

```
Application.Help helpFile:="MAINXL.HLP", helpContextId:=100
```

Quit: Closes the Excel application. Note that if the DisplayAlerts property is set to False when the Quit method is called, Excel does not prompt the user to save any open workbook files. Arguments: none.

```
Application.Quit
```

Run: Used to execute a VBA subroutine or XLM macro. XLM is the Excel 4 macro language. Arguments: The first argument of Run is a string that represents the name of the VBA subroutine or macro to be run. Run can take additional arguments; the number and type depend on the number and type of arguments that the VBA subroutine or XLM macro expects.

```
Application.Run macro:="OldMacro", arg1:=100, arg2:="Revenue"
```

The Workbook Object
The Workbook object falls directly below the Application object in the Excel object hierarchy and represents an Excel workbook file. In terms of application development, think of the Workbook object as the delivery mechanism, or the container, of any VBA application that you create in Excel. A VBA application can span more than one workbook. Generally speaking, however, a single

application can be characterized as existing in a single workbook. Any property setting or method call that you perform on the Workbook object affects your entire application.

A workbook can come in two forms: an .XLS file (or what is characterized as a standard Excel workbook) or an .XLA file (known as an Excel "add-in file"; .XLA files are fully compiled VBA applications). You can compile VBA code without creating an .XLA file; however, if you create an .XLA file, you will be certain that your code is, indeed, fully compiled. Also, .XLAs allow you to hide your code from users. Topics related to .XLA files are discussed in greater depth in Chapter 13. The following two sections describe some of the Workbook object's more commonly used properties and methods. For more information about these properties and methods, see Excel's online VBA Help.

Properties of the Workbook object

HasRoutingSlip: If HasRoutingSlip is True, a routing slip is added to the workbook. If it is False, any existing routing slips are removed from the workbook. A routing slip is used to route a workbook to several recipients through a MAPI-compatible e-mail network. True or False; read/write.

```
Workbooks("BOOK1.XLS").HasRoutingSlip = True
```

Name: The name of the workbook. Note that Name is a read-only property; to change the name of a workbook file, you must save the file with a new name using the SaveAs method. String; read-only.

```
WorkbookName = ThisWorkbook.Name
```

Path: The path to the workbook file. String; read-only.

```
WorkbookPath = ActiveWorkbook.Path
```

Saved: If Saved is True, no changes have been made to the workbook since it was last saved. If it is False, changes have been made to the workbook since it was last saved. True or False; read/write.

```
If Not(ActiveWorkbook.Saved) Then
    ActiveWorkbook.Save
End If
```

Methods of the Workbook object

Activate: Activates the first window associated with the workbook and makes the specified workbook active. Arguments: none.

```
Workbooks("MYAPP.XLS").Activate
```

Close: Closes the workbook. Arguments:

saveChanges	If True, workbook saved before closing; if False, workbook is not saved
fileName	If saveChanges argument is True, workbook is saved to the file represented by the fileName string
routeWorkbook	If True and workbook has routing slip, workbook is routed before it is closed

```
ActiveWorkbook.Close saveChanges:=False
```

Protect: Protects the workbook so that no changes can be made to it. Arguments:

password	String that represents password for workbook
structure	If True, worksheet structure of workbook is protected; if False, workbook structure is not protected
windows	If True, window structure of workbook is protected; if False, window structure is not protected

```
Workbooks(1).Protect "password", True, True
```

Save: Saves the workbook. Arguments: none.

```
ActiveWorkbook.Save
```

SaveCopyAs: Saves the workbook to a new file but leaves the existing workbook in memory intact with the original name. Arguments:

fileName	String that represents name of the file to which workbook will be saved

```
ActiveWorkbook.SaveCopyAs "BookCopy.xls"
```

The Worksheet Object

The Worksheet object is contained in the Workbook object and serves several purposes in a VBA application in Excel. Its most important purpose perhaps is as the basis for designing forms; the majority of custom forms in Excel are designed using the Worksheet object. Worksheets also provide a powerful grid that can be used to display and manipulate data. In addition, worksheets contain over 400 built-in Excel functions that can perform advanced numeric calculations at lightning speed. And worksheets can serve as miniature databases. Their tablelike structure makes them ideal for storing, summarizing, and even performing lookup functions on small data sets.

Here we discuss a few of the Worksheet object's more commonly used properties and methods. For more information about these properties and methods, see Excel's online VBA Help. Worksheets themselves are discussed in greater detail in Chapter 5, which provides information about designing forms. In addition, Chapter 8 covers the different ways in which you can handle data on a worksheet. Recall that a worksheet can be referenced either by an index in the Worksheets collection or by using the Application object's ActiveSheet property.

Properties of the Worksheet object

Index: The numeric index of the specified worksheet object in the Worksheets collection. Integer; read-only.

```
ActiveSheet.Name = "WkSheet" & ActiveSheet.Index
```

Name: This is the name of the worksheet. String; read/write.

```
Worksheets(1).Name = "My Worksheet"
```

UsedRange: Returns a Range object that references the range on the worksheet containing data. Range object; read-only.

```
Dim Range1 As Range
Set Range1 = Worksheets(1).UsedRange
```

Visible: If Visible is True, the worksheet is displayed. If Visible is False, the worksheet is hidden from view, but the user can restore the worksheet to view by choosing the Sheet command from the Format menu. If Visible is xlVeryHidden, the worksheet is hidden from view and can be restored to view only through a subroutine. True, False, or xlVeryHidden; read/write.

```
Worksheets("Main").Visible = xlVeryHidden
```

Methods of the Worksheet object

Activate: Activates the specified worksheet. Arguments: none.

```
Worksheets("My Worksheet").Activate
```

Calculate: Forces all formulas on the worksheet to be recalculated. Arguments: none.

```
Worksheets(1).Calculate
```

Delete: Deletes the worksheet from the workbook. Arguments: none.

```
Worksheets("My Worksheet").Delete
```

Protect: Protects the worksheet so that no changes can be made to it. Arguments:

password	String to be used as password for worksheet.
drawingObjects	If True, all graphical objects on worksheet are protected; if False, unprotected.
contents	If True, cells on worksheet are protected; if False, cells are unprotected.
scenarios	If True, scenarios on worksheet are protected; if False, unprotected.
userInterfaceOnly	If True, the worksheet is protected from any changes made through the user interface—that is, the worksheet can be altered through subroutines but not through the user interface. If False, the worksheet is protected from changes made through the user interface and through subroutines.

```
Worksheets("My Sheet").Protect "password"
```

The Range Object

The Range object is contained in the Worksheet object and is used to represent one or more cells on a worksheet. The Range object's primary purpose is to hold and display individual pieces of data: integers, strings, or formulas. The worksheet cells that a Range object represents actually possess a degree of intelligence. From a cell, you can access over 400 built-in Excel functions; you can call VBA functions; and you can even establish links to other cells that exist on the same worksheet, on other worksheets, or in other workbooks. Understanding the flexibility and power of the Range object allows you to tap into the power of Excel's built-in calculation engine and to create more powerful data analysis applications. We touch here on a few of the most commonly used properties and methods associated with the Range object, but we will deal with Range in greater detail in the section titled "Using the Range Object to Create Forms," beginning on page 232 in Chapter 5. For more information about these properties and methods, see Excel's online VBA Help.

Properties of the Range object

Count: The Count property is the number of cells in a range. Integer; read-only.

```
NumOfCells = Worksheets(1).UsedRange.Count
```

Dependents: Returns a range that contains all the dependents of the referenced range. Dependents are cells that reference the range in a formula. Range object; read-only.

```
Dim Range1 As Range
Set Range1 = Worksheets(1).Range("A1").Dependents
MsgBox Range1.Address
```

Name: The name of a range. String; read/write.

```
Worksheets(1).Range("A1").Name = "FirstCell"
```

Value: The value contained in a range. If the range contains multiple cells, the Value property is an array that contains values for all the cells. Boolean, Byte, Currency, Date, Double, Integer, Long, Single, or String; read/write.

```
Worksheets(1).Range("FirstCell").Value = 1
```

Formula: The formula contained in a range as a string (including the equals sign). If the range contains multiple cells, the Formula property is an array that contains formulas for all the cells. String; read/write.

```
Worksheets(1).Range("FirstCell").Formula = "=$A$4 + $A$10"
```

Text: The formatted value contained in a range as a string. For example, the Text property of a cell formatted as currency would return the string "$5.00" when the Value property returns the integer 5. If the range contains multiple cells, the Text property is an array that contains text for all the cells. String; read-only.

```
Worksheets(1).Range("FirstCell").Value = 1
MsgBox Worksheets(1).Range("FirstCell").Text
```

Methods of the Range object

Calculate: Forces all formulas in the range to be recalculated. Arguments: none.

```
Worksheets(1).Range("A1:F20").Calculate
```

ClearContents: Clears all values and formulas from the range but leaves the formatting. Arguments: none.

```
Worksheets(1).Range("A1:F20").ClearContents
```

Copy: Copies the values in the range either to another range of the same dimensions or to the clipboard. Argument:

destination   Range to which values are to be copied (if nothing passed for destination argument, values copied to clipboard)

```
Worksheets(1).Range("A1").Copy
```

SUMMARY

This chapter has covered the concepts of objects, properties, and methods. You'll want to remember these important points:

- Excel is made up of over 100 inherent and several shared objects. Each object represents a feature or a piece of functionality in Excel.

- Every Excel object has a unique set of properties and methods. You program Excel by using Visual Basic for Applications (VBA) to manipulate the properties and methods of Excel objects.

- A property represents a value or a setting that describes an object. VBA can be used to either get or set a property setting.

- A method represents an action that can be taken by or on an object. A method usually has a set of arguments associated with it that specify information about how the method is to be carried out. When using VBA to call a method, passing arguments is in most cases optional; you can pass all arguments, only some, or none. If arguments are used, however, they can be passed by order or by name.

- Objects come in two different forms: singular objects and objects in collections. A singular object is a unique object of which only one instance occurs in a given context. An object in a collection is an object of which multiple instances occur in the same context.

- You reference singular objects directly. You reference objects in collections by indexing the appropriate collection either by name or by number.

- The Range object is by definition a singular object, but it is referenced in a manner similar to that of a collection: by indexing the Range object by name or by address.

- Excel objects are arranged in a hierarchical structure; some objects are contained in others.

- When setting a property of or calling a method on an Excel object, you must sometimes specify the entire hierarchical path for the object. The starting position on the hierarchical object path, however, depends on the context in which the property setting or the method call is made, so the path can sometimes be shortened.

■ Full online VBA Help is available in Excel for all objects, properties, and methods. You access VBA Help in Excel by selecting Contents And Index from the Help menu and then selecting Microsoft Excel Visual Basic Reference on the Contents tab. Excel's online VBA Help is an excellent source of information about VBA, Excel objects, properties, and methods.

■ The Application object exists at the top of the Excel object hierarchy and represents the environment in which VBA applications are run.

■ The Workbook object is contained in the Application object. The Workbook object represents an Excel file and serves as the container or delivery mechanism for VBA applications.

■ The Worksheet object is contained in the Workbook object and serves as the basis for designing custom forms in Excel.

■ The Range object is contained in the Worksheet object and serves a variety of purposes that involve data handling and data display.

2

Visual Basic for Applications

The previous chapter introduced you to Microsoft Excel objects and illustrated how to set and get properties and call methods. This chapter focuses on the language that you use to manipulate Excel objects, called Microsoft Visual Basic for Applications (VBA). VBA is an implementation of Microsoft's award-winning visual programming tool Visual Basic, common to Microsoft Office 97. It is the glue that binds Excel objects together when you create custom applications. This chapter explains the most important VBA concepts, including subroutines, variables, data types, arrays, constants, functions, scoping, control structures, and VBA editing and debugging tools.

This chapter is comprehensive, and its explanation of VBA moves at a rapid pace. You won't necessarily learn everything about VBA, but you will have as much information as is necessary to create powerful applications in Excel. The rest of the book focuses on using VBA with Excel objects to create custom applications.

If You Already Know Visual Basic

If you are already familiar with Visual Basic, you might want to skim some of this chapter because the syntax constructs used in VBA are identical to those used in Visual Basic. If you are using VBA with Excel 5 or 95, however, you should note the following new VBA features in Excel 97.

■ **Editing and debugging tools:** Office 97 provides a common VBA integrated development environment called the Visual Basic Editor (VBE). This environment contains an improved set of editing, project browsing, object browsing, and debugging tools. Unlike previous versions of Excel, the Visual Basic Editor is hosted in a window separate from Excel.

- **New forms package:** Office 97 applications share a common forms development tool known as Microsoft Forms. These forms replace the dialogsheets found in Excel 5 and 95. (Forms will be covered in detail in Chapter 5, "Custom Interface Design.") Note that dialogsheets from existing Excel 5 and Excel 95 applications will continue to be supported in Excel 97.

- **Code behind documents:** VBA now supports code modules directly attached to workbooks, worksheets, and charts (much like code modules behind visual basic forms). These modules expose a rich set of Excel-specific events to which you can assign Visual Basic code.

- **Class modules:** As in Visual Basic (VB), you can write class modules that define the methods and properties of objects internal to your application. Unlike VB, VBA classes cannot be instantiated by external applications (i.e., you cannot build an OLE Server in VBA).

- **Handling application events via the WithEvents keyword:** To handle events raised by the Excel application object (or objects that do not exist at design time), you declare a variable of that object's type using the WithEvents keyword. This tells VBA to establish a set of event procedures for the object that is tied to the variable you declare.

- **Conditional compilation:** You can insert compiler directives into your code that cause portions of the code to be either compiled or excluded from compilation based on conditional compilation arguments.

> **NOTE** One feature of VB that is not available in VBA is control arrays, which enables you to place several controls with the same name on a form or document and then write one event procedure for the group.

VBA Subroutines

VBA code in Excel is contained in what is called a "VBA routine." There are two types of routines: subroutines and functions. We discuss VBA subroutines first in this chapter. VBA functions, which are subroutines that can return values, are discussed in detail in the section titled "Function Routines," beginning on page 79.

The VBA subroutine is the basic building block of all VBA applications. A subroutine is simply a stand-alone segment of code that holds a series of VBA commands. A VBA application can be defined as consisting of at least one VBA subroutine, although VBA applications generally consist of several subroutines (and functions).

NOTE The terms "routine," "subroutine," and "subprocedure" are often used interchangeably. All three terms refer to the same thing— a standalone segment of VBA code that begins with the keyword Sub and ends with the keywords End Sub. Throughout this book we will refer to VBA code segments as routines or subroutines.

Let's take a look at a simple VBA routine:

```
Sub Chap02aProc01_SetRangeValue()
    Workbooks(1).Worksheets(1).Range("A1").Value = 1
End Sub
```

In specifying a VBA subroutine, you must use certain keywords. In Proc01, for example, the word Sub on the first line and the words End Sub on the last line are the keywords that define the VBA subroutine. All VBA subroutines begin with Sub and end with End Sub.

FYI

Where to Find the VBA Code Examples

This book includes numerous examples of VBA code. You can find all of the code examples in the files on the companion CD. You might want to start Excel, open the appropriate file, and step through the code examples in the file as you read through the book. (For Chapter 2, the file is named CHAP02.XLS.) Note that the name of each routine in a file follows a predefined naming convention. For example, the first routine for this chapter is named Chap02aProc01_SetRange-Value. The name has three components:

- **Chap02a:** The name of the VBA module in which the routine resides in the CHAP02.XLS file

- **Proc01:** An indication of the sequential order of the routine in this chapter

- **_SetRangeValue:** A description of what the routine does

This naming convention helps you find a specific code example. Thus, the routine named Chap02gProc59_IfThenElse resides in the VBA module named Chap02g, is the 59th routine in the chapter, and demonstrates the use of the If-Then-Else control structure. In the text, we abbreviate routine names by using, for example, simply "Proc59."

NOTE The Sub and End Sub keywords in the example code on page 41 are formatted in boldface. In a VBA module, however, they usually appear on the screen in blue. (They appear in boldface in this book to make them stand out.) The Visual Basic Editor colors all keywords blue to show you as you write code that it recognizes the keywords you have entered. If you ever enter a keyword in a VBA module and the Editor does not color it blue, go back and check your spelling. Most likely, you have made an error in typing the keyword. You will find as you read this chapter that keywords are an integral part of the various features of VBA.

A subroutine in its simplest form can be defined as any segment of VBA code that contains the word Sub as the first word in the first line and the words End Sub in the last line. The Proc01 subroutine example on page 41 assigns the number 1 to the Value property of the upper left cell on the first worksheet of the first workbook. Let's look at a few other simple examples of VBA subroutines. The following subroutine closes the active workbook:

```
Sub Chap02aProc02_CloseWorkbook()
    ActiveWorkbook.Close
End Sub
```

The next subroutine sets the Name property of the first worksheet in the first workbook to "My First Worksheet" and then sets the Visible property of the same worksheet to False, which hides the worksheet from view:

```
Sub Chap02aProc03_SetWorksheetProperties()
    Workbooks(1).Worksheets(1).Name = "My First Worksheet"
    Workbooks(1).Worksheets("My First Worksheet").Visible = False
End Sub
```

Proc04 below resets the Visible property of the first worksheet to True:

```
Sub Chap02aProc04_SetVisibleProperty()
    Workbooks(1).Worksheets(1).Visible = True
End Sub
```

As Proc03 showed, VBA subroutines can contain multiple VBA commands or, in this case, property assignments; a single VBA subroutine can contain thousands of lines of VBA commands. It is a good idea, however, to keep VBA subroutines short and concise so that they are easy to edit and understand.

How do you create and use the preceding VBA routines in Excel? Before you can write VBA routines, you must understand how to launch the Visual Basic Editor and attach code to Excel workbook files. Let's deviate here from our discussion of VBA code to briefly cover these topics.

A Quick Look at the Visual Basic Editor

The Visual Basic Editor (VBE) provides all the tools you'll need to manage the components of your project, write code, create forms, and debug applications. While these topics will be covered in detail throughout the book, a quick tour of the VBE would be useful at this point. To display the VBE, do the following: from the Tools menu, select the Macro command, and then choose Visual Basic Editor (as shown in this example screen).

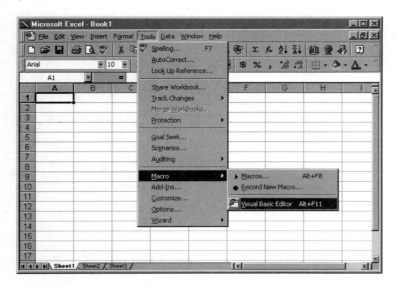

The Visual Basic Editor (VBE) window should appear, as shown in Figure 2-1 on page 45. (Your screen won't show all of the parts in the screen we show in Figure 2-1 because you haven't added a code module yet.) Note that unlike in Excel 5 or 95, the VBA environment in Excel 97 is in a window separate from Excel. This is what allows other Office 97 applications such as Microsoft Word and Microsoft PowerPoint to use this same editor.

The VBE contains the following major parts:

VBE Component	Description
Project window	The Project window contains a hierarchical list of the elements of your VBA project. This can include certain high-level Excel objects such as worksheets, charts, and ThisWorkbook (a reference to the workbook in which the project resides). It can also include modules, class modules (a special kind of module that lets you define your own objects), and userforms (i.e., custom dialog boxes).
Properties window	The Properties window lets you view and set properties of various objects in your project including the Excel objects displayed in the Project window. Properties can be displayed either alphabetically or in logical categories.
Code Editor window	The Code Editor window is where you enter and edit VBA code. The two drop-down listboxes at the top of this window help you navigate through the code. The Object Selector (on the left) lets you pick an object whose code you want to view. The Procedure Selector (on the right) lets you select a particular routine to view.
UserForm Editor window (not pictured)	The UserForm Editor window lets you create custom dialog boxes, place ActiveX controls on them, and test them. Userforms will be covered in detail in Chapter 5.
Object Browser window (not pictured)	The Object Browser window helps you find and use any objects needed by your application. Use the View Object Browser command to display it. It is covered in detail later in this chapter.
Immediate, Locals, and Watch windows (not pictured)	These windows are available to help you debug your code. Each can be shown using commands on the View menu. They will be covered in detail later in this chapter.

The Project, Properties, Immediate, Locals, and Watch windows can either dock to the VBE window like toolbars or be dragged outside of the VBE window. To undock any of them, drag them by their title bars. While they are docked, they can be resized by dragging their borders.

The remaining windows (Code Editor, UserForm Editor, and Object Browser) are normal MDI (multiple document interface) windows of the VBE. They can be maximized, restored, and minimized within the VBE window. You can also use the Window menu to switch between them. Note that you can have many Code Editor and UserForm Editor windows open simultaneously (one for each module or userform, respectively).

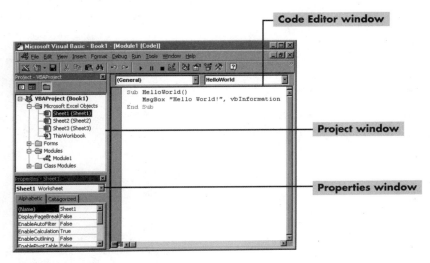

Figure 2-1. *The Visual Basic Editor window.*

Inserting a VBA Module

Now that we've taken a brief look at the VBE, let's insert a module and start learning about VBA code. From Excel, open a new, blank workbook and launch the Visual Basic Editor. Then insert a VBA module into your project as follows: from the Insert menu, choose the Module command.

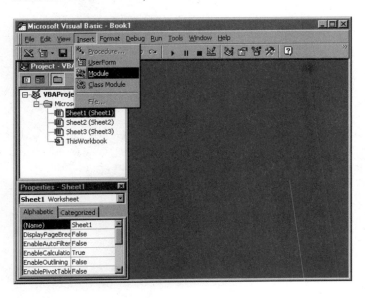

A new, blank module should appear in the Code Editor window (as shown below). Note that the name of the new module (Module1) is now reflected in the Project window as well (or in the VBE title bar if the Code Editor window is maximized).

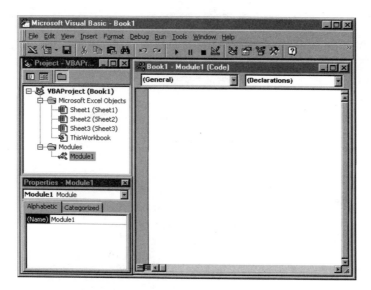

Entering and Executing VBA Routines

To enter a subroutine in a VBA module, begin typing at the top of the module. Remember that a VBA routine must begin with the keyword Sub and end with the keywords End Sub. Try entering the following routine:

```
Sub Chap02aProc05_DisplayMsgBox()
    MsgBox "Hello World"
End Sub
```

This routine uses a built-in VBA function named MsgBox, which displays a message box on the screen. The MsgBox function takes as its first argument a string that is displayed in the body of the message box. MsgBox can also take several other arguments that govern how the resulting message box is displayed (the types of buttons used, the title, and so forth); however, only the first argument is necessary to display a simple box that includes the message and an OK button. MsgBox is one of several built-in VBA functions that allow you to perform an action aside from manipulating properties and methods of Excel objects.

After you enter Proc05 in your VBA module, the next step is to execute it. You can execute a routine in one of five ways; these methods are described on the facing page. The first four ways are from the Visual Basic Editor window; the fifth way is from the Excel window:

From the VBE window

- Position the insertion point anywhere in the body of the routine, and choose the Run Sub/UserForm command from the Run menu.

- Position the insertion point anywhere in the body of the routine, and click the Run Sub/UserForm button on the Standard toolbar. (If the Standard toolbar is not displayed, choose the Toolbars command from the View menu, and then select Standard from the list of toolbars.)

- Position the insertion point anywhere in the body of the routine, and press the F5 key.

- From the Tools menu, select Macros. Next select the name of the routine you want to run from the list of available routines, and then click the Run button.

From the Excel window

- To use this method, switch back to Excel (using the Windows taskbar or any other method you prefer). From the Tools menu, choose the Macro command, and then choose Macros. Next select the name of the routine you want to run from the list of available routines, and then click the Run button.

Run Proc05. If the routine executes successfully, a message box is displayed in the middle of the screen. Clicking OK closes the message box and causes the routine to finish executing.

Now try entering and executing the following routine (Proc06):

```
Sub Chap02aProc06_SetRangeValue()
    Worksheets(1).Visible = True
    Worksheets(1).Range("A1:B1").Value = 1
    Worksheets(1).Select
End Sub
```

After you execute Proc06, the first worksheet of the active workbook is displayed, and the value 1 appears in the cells that correspond to the range A1:B1 on the worksheet. Now try making a minor change to the routine by specifying a new range address of A1:F20.

```
Sub Chap02aProc07_SetRangeValue()
    Worksheets(1).Range("A1:F20").Value = 1
    Worksheets(1).Select
End Sub
```

By running this routine, you can set the value of a block of cells in a worksheet in a single command.

TIP
When executing a routine from the Visual Basic Editor, you will likely need to switch back to the Excel window to see the results. If you have a high resolution monitor, try positioning the Excel and Visual Basic Editor windows side by side.

NOTE
You can also run a routine by referencing a VBA function in a spreadsheet formula. These topics are covered in the "FYI" titled "Executing a Function by Calling It from a Worksheet Cell" on page 81.

Locating Routines in a Module

The Visual Basic Editor provides two views of a module. The default view, called Procedure view, displays one routine at a time in the module window. To view another routine, you use the procedure selector dropdown listbox located at the top right corner of the module window.

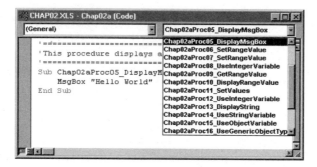

NOTE
You can also switch sequentially between routines using the key combinations Ctrl-PgDn and Ctrl-PgUp.

The other view, called Full Module view, displays all routines together much like Excel 5 and 95 module sheets did. To switch between the two views, use the small buttons located at the lower left corner of the module window.

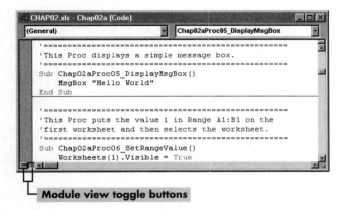

Module view toggle buttons

Variables

Variables are used to hold and manipulate values, or data, when a routine is executing. Using variables saves you time and effort in coding and makes your routines run faster. Variables can assume several different data types (see the next section), including various numeric types, strings, objects, variants, and user-defined types. Before you use a variable in your code, you should "dimension," or declare, the variable to set aside space in memory for holding the variable during execution. To dimension a variable, you include a simple statement at the top of your VBA routine, as explained in the section titled "Dimensioning a Variable," beginning on page 51.

Data Types for VBA Variables

The types of values that variables can hold are referred to as "data types." The following is a list of the data types that VBA variables can accommodate. For each data type, the amount of memory required to hold a single variable of that type is noted in parentheses.

Boolean: (2 bytes) True or False.

Byte: (1 byte) Unsigned integer between 0 and 255.

Currency: (8 bytes) Currency; useful for fixed-point calculations in which accuracy is imperative:
−922,337,203,685,477.5808 through 922,337,203,685,477.5807

Date: (8 bytes) Date and time values between January 1, 100, and December 31, 9999.

Double: (8 bytes) Double precision floating-point (real number):
Negative double numbers:
−1.79769313486231E308 through −4.94065645841247E−324
Zero.
Positive double numbers:
4.94065645841247E−324 through 1.79769313486231E308

Integer: (2 bytes) Integer between −32,768 and 32,767

Long: (4 bytes) Integer between −2,147,483,648 and 2,147,483,647

Object: (4 bytes) Object variable that can be used to refer to any Excel object.

Single: (4 bytes) Single precision floating-point (real number):
Negative single numbers: −3.402823E38 through −1.401298E−45
Zero.
Positive single numbers: 1.401298E−45 through 3.402823E38

String: (1 byte per character) String of text characters from 0 to over 2 billion characters.

Variant: (16 bytes + 1 byte for each character if the variant holds a string) Can be used to represent any VBA data type (except a user-defined type). Useful when you need to store a piece of data in a variable and are uncertain of the data's type.

User-defined: (Dependent on definition) Similar to data structures in other programming languages. User-defined types allow you to store multiple values of different data types in a single variable.

> **NOTE** In the Excel documentation you might see mention of a 12-byte "Decimal" data type. This is not a true data type but rather a subtype of Variant.

It's probably a good idea to know the names of the different data types listed above as well as the types of data they represent. For the numeric data types, however, you don't need to memorize the exact upper and lower bounds of the numbers they represent. Instead, you might want to remember these general definitions:

Integer	Medium-size integer numbers up to roughly 32,000
Long	Large integer numbers
Single	Very large floating-point numbers
Double	Very, very large floating-point numbers

Dimensioning a Variable

You dimension, or declare, a variable in a VBA routine to tell VBA to set aside extra memory in order to hold the variable while the routine executes. The amount of memory that VBA sets aside is determined by the variable's data type (as shown in the preceding list). You dimension a variable before it is used by placing a Dim statement for the variable at the beginning of a VBA routine or VBA module. Although you don't need to dimension variables before they are used, doing so can improve the performance of your routines and make them easier to debug. (You'll read more about the performance costs of undeclared variables in the section titled "The Pros and Cons of Using Variants," beginning on page 59.) Here is an example Dim statement for dimensioning a variable:

```
Dim Var1 As Integer
```

The above statement declares Var1 as a variable of the Integer data type and, by doing so, sets aside 2 bytes of memory for Var1. Three keywords are included in the statement: Dim, As, and Integer. Let's take a look at the components:

Dim	Keyword that indicates a variable declaration (abbreviation for "dimension")
Var1	Name of the variable
As	Keyword used as a qualifier to separate the variable name from the data type
Integer	Keyword that represents the name of the data type; can be any one of Boolean, Byte, Currency, Date, Double, Integer, Long, Object, Single, String, Variant, or user-defined types

Here are some other examples of variable declarations:

```
Dim Var2 As Double
Dim Var3 As Date
Dim Var4 As Currency
Dim Var5 As Variant
```

It is possible to declare more than one variable in a single Dim statement. For each variable that you declare, however, you must use the As keyword, specify the appropriate data type, and include a comma to separate one variable from the next. The following is an example:

```
Dim Var2 As Double, Var3 As Date, Var4 As Currency, Var5 As Variant
```

Using Variables in Routines

Now let's take a look at using a variable in a routine. Proc08 uses an Integer variable to set the Value property of a Range object:

```
Sub Chap02aProc08_UseIntegerVariable()
    Dim Num1 As Integer
    Num1 = 5
    Worksheets(1).Range("A1").Value = Num1
    Worksheets(1).Select
End Sub
```

This routine sets the Value property of range A1 on the first worksheet to the value stored in Num1, which in this case is 5. In the third line of the routine, an Integer value is assigned to the Num1 variable. Num1 then holds that value while the routine executes. In the fourth line of the routine, we use Num1 to set the Value property of the specified Range object. Let's look at an example (Proc09) in which a variable is assigned the value of a range:

```
Sub Chap02aProc09_GetRangeValue()
    Dim Num1 As Integer
    Num1 = Worksheets(1).Range("A1").Value
    MsgBox Num1
End Sub
```

Proc09 uses Num1 to get the setting of the Value property of the specified Range object. Assuming that Proc09 is run in the same workbook as the previous Proc08, the statement in the third line of Proc09 returns the value 5 and assigns it to the Num1 variable. Num1 then holds the value and is used again in the fourth line of the routine to display the value in a message box:

Proc09 merely displays in a message box the setting for the Value property of range A1 on the worksheet. The same result can be accomplished easily without using a variable, as the following example shows:

```
Sub Chap02aProc10_DisplayRangeValue()
    MsgBox Worksheets(1).Range("A1").Value
End Sub
```

Advantages of Variables

After reviewing the preceding example, you might be asking yourself, "Why use variables at all?" One good reason to use variables is that they simplify the writing of routines, particularly when you need to use a specific value numerous times. For example, let's say you need to write a routine that assigns the Value property of range A1 in the active workbook's second, third, and fourth worksheets to the same setting as the Value property of range A1 in the first worksheet. If you do not use variables, you must write the following routine:

```
Sub Chap02aProc11_SetValues()
    Worksheets(2).Range("A1").Value = Worksheets(1).Range("A1").Value
    Worksheets(3).Range("A1").Value = Worksheets(1).Range("A1").Value
    Worksheets(4).Range("A1").Value = Worksheets(1).Range("A1").Value
End Sub
```

If you use variables, however, you can write the same routine in fewer keystrokes and produce a routine that is easier to read and understand:

```
Sub Chap02aProc12_UseIntegerVariable()
    Dim Num1 As Integer
    Num1 = Worksheets(1).Range("A1").Value
    Worksheets(2).Range("A1").Value = Num1
    Worksheets(3).Range("A1").Value = Num1
    Worksheets(4).Range("A1").Value = Num1
End Sub
```

In addition to offering fewer keystrokes and code that's easier to read, using variables makes your code execute faster. Proc12, for example, executes faster than does Proc11. We will look further at speed issues later in this section. For now, however, remember that every property or method reference and every hierarchical object reference requires a certain amount of processing by Excel and therefore a certain amount of time. In Proc11 above, you can count the number of object and property references by counting the number of times the dot operator (.) is used. In lines 2, 3, and 4 of Proc11, the dot operator is used four times in each line, for a total of twelve times in the whole routine. In Proc12, the dot operator is used two times in each of lines 3, 4, 5, and 6 for a total of eight times in the routine. If we think of the dot operator as representing a unit of processing time, Proc12 should take roughly two-thirds the time to execute that Proc11 does, which is indeed the case. With routines this simple, you cannot see the speed difference on your computer. With larger and more complicated routines, however, the difference becomes apparent.

Let's look at another example (at the top of the following page), this time using a variable of a data type other than Integer.

```
Sub Chap02aProc13_DisplayString()
    Dim String1 As String
    String1 = "Hello World"
    MsgBox String1
End Sub
```

Proc13 assigns a value to the String variable String1 and then displays the value in a message box. And, in the following example, the routine transfers a value from a String variable to the Value property of the Range object:

```
Sub Chap02aProc14_UseStringVariable()
    Dim String1 As String
    String1 = "Important Data"
    Worksheets(1).Range("A1").Value = String1
    Worksheets(1).Select
End Sub
```

Object Variables

An object variable is a variable that is used to refer to an object. As you become a VBA expert, you will find that object variables are of tremendous use because they reduce the number of keystrokes required to write your VBA code. They make your code easier to read, and they improve the performance of your routines. Throughout the pages that follow, several examples demonstrate these advantages.

Setting an object variable

You declare and assign values to object variables slightly differently from the way you declare and assign values to other variables. Let's take a look at a code segment that shows how you make these declarations and assignments:

```
Dim Range1 As Object
Set Range1 = Worksheets(1).Range("A1")
```

Notice that the declaration statement in the first line above is much like declarations for other variables, although in the declaration for an object variable you can actually specify the type of object being declared. (We'll look at that later.) Focus on the second line, in which an object is assigned to the variable. Note that when you assign an object to an object variable, you must always use the Set keyword. If you look at the preceding example, for instance, the components of a statement that assigns an object variable are as follows:

Set	Keyword that indicates the assignment of an object variable
Range1	Name of the object variable
=	Assignment operator
Worksheets(1).Range("A1")	Object assigned to the variable

Using generic Object variables

What can you do with a variable of the Object data type? Let's take a look at an example. The following routine uses an Integer variable and an Object variable to set the Value property of a Range object:

```
Sub Chap02aProc15_UseObjectVariable()
    Dim Num2 As Long
    Num2 = 100000
    Dim Range1 As Object
    Set Range1 = Worksheets(1).Range("A1")
    Range1.Value = Num2
    MsgBox Range1.Value
End Sub
```

Proc15 shows that we can use the Object variable Range1 to set the Value property of the object Worksheets(1).Range("A1")—and then display the setting for that Value property in a message box:

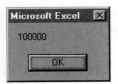

Using specific object variables

As mentioned, you can use the exact name of the type of object when you declare a variable. For example, it is possible to dimension a Range object in the following manner:

```
Dim Range1 As Range
```

In this example, we use the specific name of the object, "Range," as the type of the object variable as opposed to the generic Object type. Here are a few other examples of object variable declarations in which the names of the objects are used as types when the variables are declared:

```
Dim Workbook1 As Workbook
Dim MyWorksheet As Worksheet
Dim XL As Application
```

You might wonder how you will know the name of the type of object to use when declaring object variables. Object types are simply the names of the objects in Excel—the same names that appear in the Excel object model hierarchy diagram in Chapter 1 (Figure 1-2 on page 19–21) and the same names that are used for Excel objects throughout this book. After you become familiar with the objects in Excel, you will know their names well.

Note that you can make the same three object variable declarations we just looked at by using the generic Object type instead of the specific names of objects, as the following example shows:

```
Dim Workbook1 As Object
Dim MyWorksheet As Object
Dim XL As Object
```

So, if it's possible to use the generic Object type when declaring object variables, why bother with declaring variables by using specific object names? If you declare object variables by using specific object names, you see better performance in your routines than if you use the generic Object type. When VBA performs a property setting or a method call on an Excel object via an object variable, VBA must first determine the type of object that the variable represents. If the generic Object type is used to declare the variable, VBA must do some extra work to determine the specific object type to which the variable refers. If the object variable is declared by specifying the name of the object to which the variable refers, however, VBA does not have to do that extra work. For simple routines, either approach will do. But for large and complicated applications, you can see measurable improvements in performance if you use object names to declare object variables rather than the generic Object type.

Let's take a look at an example in which declaring an object variable as a specific object type improves performance. Proc16, which follows, uses two object variables that are declared with the generic Object type to exchange values between cells A1 and A2 on the first worksheet. The routine uses a For-Next loop to execute the operation 2000 times and the VBA Timer function to keep track of how much time is required for the routine to execute:

```
Sub Chap02aProc16_UseGenericObjectType()
    Dim Range1 As Object
    Dim Range2 As Object
    Dim StartTime As Variant
    Dim x As Integer
    Set Range1 = Worksheets(1).Range("A1")
    Set Range2 = Worksheets(1).Range("A2")
    StartTime = Timer
    For x = 1 To 2000
        Range1.Value = 5
        Range2.Value = Range1.Value
    Next
    MsgBox (Timer - StartTime) & " seconds."
End Sub
```

After you run Proc16, a message box indicates how much time it took the routine to execute:

You can rewrite the same routine using the Range type to declare the two Range object variables:

```
Sub Chap02aProc17_UseSpecificObjectType()
    Dim Range1 As Range
    Dim Range2 As Range
    Dim StartTime As Variant
    Dim x As Integer
    Set Range1 = Worksheets(1).Range("A1")
    Set Range2 = Worksheets(1).Range("A2")
    StartTime = Timer
    For x = 1 To 2000
        Range1.Value = 5
        Range2.Value = Range1.Value
    Next
    MsgBox (Timer - StartTime) & " seconds."
End Sub
```

Proc17 should run faster than Proc16 because VBA has to spend less time evaluating the types of objects to which the variables Range1 and Range2 refer. Here is the message box displayed by Proc17; when you compare the Proc16 and Proc17 times, it is apparent that Proc17 is faster:

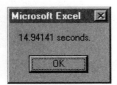

FYI

The Ampersand Operator (&)

In Proc16 and Proc17, we introduced the ampersand operator (&). Ampersands are used to concatenate the contents of variables with strings—or even strings with strings. In Proc16 and Proc17, VBA converts the elapsed time to a character string, and then combines it with the literal string to form a single string that is passed to the MsgBox function.

A closer look at the advantages of using object variables

As we've seen, using object variables cuts down on the time required to write code, makes code easier to read, and makes your routines run faster. You save time writing your code by using object variables because object variables allow you to represent hierarchical object references with a single word (the name of the variable). For example, the following routine sets the Value, RowHeight, and ColumnWidth properties of the Range object; displays the setting for the Value property in a message box; and then calls the ClearContents method. Hierarchical object references starting at the Worksheet object are used to access the properties and methods of the Range object in this example:

```
Sub Chap02aProc18_RangeObject()
    Worksheets(1).Range("A1").Value = 25
    Worksheets(1).Range("A1").RowHeight = 50
    Worksheets(1).Range("A1").ColumnWidth = 50
    MsgBox Worksheets(1).Range("A1").Value
    Worksheets(1).Range("A1").ClearContents
End Sub
```

You could rewrite this routine using an object variable to refer to the Range object, as the following example shows:

```
Sub Chap02aProc19_RangeObjectVariable()
    Dim Range1 As Range
    Set Range1 = Worksheets(1).Range("A1")
    Range1.Value = 25
    Range1.RowHeight = 50
    Range1.ColumnWidth = 50
    MsgBox Range1.Value
    Range1.ClearContents
End Sub
```

Proc19 appears to be more concise than Proc18, and, in fact, fewer keystrokes were required to write Proc19. Using object variables also makes code easier to read; when you look at the statements in Proc19, you can easily see that actions are being performed on the same object throughout.

Regarding the use of object variables to improve performance, object references take a certain amount of processing time in VBA, which you can approximate by counting the number of occurrences of the dot operator (.). Compare Proc19 with Proc18 above, and you will see that using an object variable results in fewer dot operators in Proc19 (six) than in Proc18 (ten). In fact, Proc19 runs roughly twice as fast as Proc18. Although it is difficult to measure the time differences between these two routines, such time differences become obvious, for example, when you are dealing with looping structures that execute hundreds of times.

Optional Variable Declaration and Variants

VBA has an interesting feature that is well appreciated by the renegade developer but scorned by those who are more organized in their code-writing habits. The feature is called "optional variable declaration." You've probably noticed that in all the routines presented in this section on variables, each variable used has first been declared with a Dim statement. In reality, however, Dim statements are optional. If you fail to use a Dim statement to declare a variable, VBA simply dimensions the variable for you. For example, let's look at one of the routines presented earlier:

```
Sub Chap02aProc13_DisplayString()
    Dim String1 As String
    String1 = "Hello World"
    MsgBox String1
End Sub
```

You can write this routine without the Dim statement; it executes in the same way as Proc13 even though the Dim statement for the variable String1 is omitted:

```
Sub Chap02aProc20_NoVariableDeclaration()
    String1 = "Hello World"
    MsgBox String1
End Sub
```

When a Dim statement for a variable is omitted, the variable assumes the default data type—in this case, it's the Variant data type. In essence, therefore, String1 in Proc20 is a variable of the Variant data type. Because variants can take on values of any data type, the routine runs without problem. In the following example, Proc20 has been rewritten to declare the variable explicitly as a variant:

```
Sub Chap02aProc21_UseVariant()
    Dim String1 As Variant
    String1 = "Hello World"
    MsgBox String1
End Sub
```

The Pros and Cons of Using Variants

When a value is assigned to a Variant variable, VBA evaluates the value and coerces the variable to match the value's data type. Because VBA's default data type is Variant, a variable assumes the Variant data type if you omit a Dim statement for that variable. (It is possible to change the default data type to a different type using a Def*Type* statement, as you'll see in the following pages.) Omitting Dim statements and assuming the default data type for variables reduces the number of keystrokes required to write your code. Some developers will appreciate being able to use a variable whenever and wherever they want without having to worry about whether it is properly declared.

Using a default Variant data type, however, presents three disadvantages, and programmers who are concerned about structure and organization are probably aware of these problems. First, the Variant data type requires more memory. If you look back to the section titled "Data Types for VBA Variables," beginning on page 49, you'll see that variables of the Variant type require more memory than variables of any other data type, with the possible exception of user-defined variables (covered later in this chapter). Variant variables require 16 bytes (plus 1 byte per character for strings)—at least twice as much memory as is required for the other data types that also demand lots of memory: Currency, Date, and Double. For small routines, the memory demands present little problem, but with large and complicated routines that have lots of variables, you could definitely see performance problems; your application might even eat up all available memory.

The second disadvantage also involves performance. VBA is required to coerce a variable of the Variant type to match the data type of any value being assigned to it. This process takes time. You see the results of these time demands most clearly when assignments to variants occur multiple times in a loop; each time the assignment occurs in each loop, VBA must perform the coercion.

The third disadvantage deals with keeping track of the data that variants contain. You can never be certain what type of data is contained in a Variant variable because a Variant can hold anything. Variants make debugging code and successfully implementing error-checking routines a cumbersome process. For example, if you always declare variables to be of specific data types, no question ever arises about the type of data a variable contains. If you use variants, however, you will often have to build checks into your code to determine whether the data held in the variant is of the proper type.

Let's take as an example a subroutine that performs a mathematical calculation on a variable. If the subroutine is called and an Integer variable is passed to the subroutine, no code need be implemented in the subroutine to determine that the data in the variable is numeric. If a Variant variable is passed to the same subroutine, however, error checking must be implemented to be sure that the variable contains numeric data and not a string, a date, or even an object reference. This error checking requires time and degrades performance further.

Despite the disadvantages mentioned here, variants do serve a purpose. In fact, variants are useful whenever you are uncertain about the type of data you are dealing with. For example, suppose you have written a subroutine that prompts a user to enter an integer. You can never be entirely certain that the user will actually enter an integer—perhaps the user will mistakenly enter a text string or a real number instead. Your subroutine must be able to accept the user's input and check the data before manipulating the data further. Variants are well suited to accepting user input because they can accept any type of input. Therefore, you would likely use a variant to accept the user input and then, after performing error checking, pass the value to another variable of the appropriate data type before manipulating the data further.

Forced Variable Declaration

VBA offers a feature called "forced variable declaration" that can keep you from inadvertently omitting variable declarations and thus protect you from the potential disadvantages of using variants. You can impose forced variable declaration in one of two ways. You can place the Option Explicit statement in the declarations section (that is, at the top) of each VBA code module. (This statement must be included at the top of the module, before any subroutines or function routines.) Or in the Visual Basic Editor, you can choose the Options command from the Tools menu and, in the Options dialog box, click the Editor tab and check the Require Variable Declaration check box. When this check box is checked, the Visual Basic Editor inserts the Option Explicit statement at the beginning of any new VBA module. Note that checking the Require Variable Declaration check box has no effect on existing VBA modules. The following illustration shows the Require Variable Declaration check box checked.

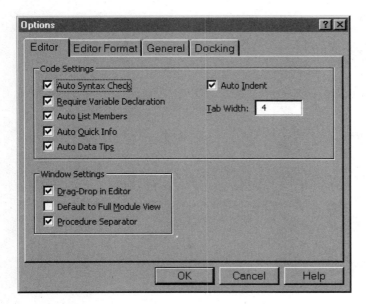

The following is an example of a module that includes the Option Explicit statement:

```
Option Explicit

Sub Chap02bProc22_UseString()
    Dim String1 As String
    String1 = "Hello World"
    MsgBox String1
End Sub
```

Again, the Option Explicit statement must reside in the Declarations section of the VBA module, before any subroutines.

If you remove the Dim statement but retain the Option Explicit statement, the Visual Basic compiler generates an error message when you attempt to run this routine:

```
Option Explicit

Sub Chap02cProc23_NoVariableDeclaration()
    String1 = "Hello World"
    MsgBox String1
End Sub
```

In Proc23, execution halts immediately, and VBA displays an error message:

You can circumvent this error message either by including a Dim statement for the String1 variable or by removing the Option Explicit statement.

Default Data Types

It is possible in VBA to change the default data type to something other than Variant. To do so, place a Def*Type* declaration at the beginning of a VBA module. For example, if you want all undeclared variables to default to an Integer data type, place the following statement at the beginning of a VBA module, before any subroutines:

```
DefInt A-Z
```

The arguments A–Z after the DefInt keyword indicate that all undeclared variables that have names starting with any letter from A through Z (irrespective of case) should assume the Integer data type. Because Def*Type* declarations take starting letters as arguments, different undeclared variables in a module can take different data types, depending on each variable's first letter. For example, the following statements at the beginning of a VBA module force all undeclared variables that begin with the letter "I" to assume an Integer data type, all that begin with the letter "S" to assume a String data type, and all that begin with the letter "C" to assume a Currency data type:

```
DefInt I
DefStr S
DefCur C
```

In the absence of any Def*Type* statements at the top of a VBA module, all undeclared variables assume the Variant data type by default.

NOTE You can place multiple VBA statements on a single line of code by separating the statements with a colon (:), as in the following example:

```
DefInt I: DefStr S: DefCur C
```

User-Defined Data Types

VBA allows you to create your own user-defined data types. Such user-defined data types are similar to structures found in other programming languages and can be defined simply as data types that form some combination of the other available data types in VBA. Using user-defined variables, you can group multiple values of different data types all in a single variable. Declaring a variable as a user-defined data type is a little more complicated than declaring a variable as another data type. Before you can declare a variable as a user-defined data type, you must first give a definition of the type. Definitions of user-defined types are always placed at the beginning of a VBA module.

```
Type PersonalData
    PName As String
    PAge As Integer
    PBirthDate As Date
End Type
```

Let's look at the different components of the above user-defined type definition:

Type	Keyword that indicates a user-defined data type definition
PersonalData	Name of the user-defined data type
PName **As String**	First element of the user-defined data type
PAge **As Integer**	Second element of the user-defined data type
PBirthDate **As Date**	Third element of the user-defined data type
End Type	Keywords that indicate the end of the user-defined data type definition

When placed at the top of a VBA module, the above user-defined data type definition creates a data type named PersonalData that contains three elements: a string represented by PName, an integer represented by PAge, and a date represented by PBirthDate. But how would you use a variable of the PersonalData type? Let's take a look at an example:

```
Type PersonalData
    PName As String
    PAge As Integer
    PBirthDate As Date
End Type

Sub Chap02dProc24_UserDefinedType()
    Dim User1 As PersonalData
    User1.PName = "Billijean"
    User1.PAge = 33
    User1.PBirthDate = #2/23/64#
    MsgBox User1.PName & ", Age " & User1.PAge & _
            ", Born " & User1.PBirthDate & "."
End Sub
```

In line 2 of Proc24, a variable named User1 is declared as type PersonalData. Then, in lines 3, 4, and 5, values are assigned to the different elements that are contained in the PersonalData type structure for User1: "Billijean" is assigned to PName, 33 is assigned to PAge, and #2/23/64# is assigned to PBirthDate. Line 6 of the routine then displays values of User1's elements in a message box:

Note that at the end of line 6 the line continuation character (_) is used to continue the statement on the next line.

FYI

Date Literals

The preceding code (Proc24) also introduces date literals. In line 5, an assignment is made to User1.PBirthDate by specifying a date that is enclosed in number signs (#). Number signs are required whenever you assign a literal date value to a Date variable. Literal dates are similar to literal strings—except that you enclose them in number signs instead of in double quotation marks.

Using VBA Arrays

VBA arrays offer a powerful approach to dealing with large amounts of data; you use VBA arrays much as you use arrays in other programming languages. An array is a variable that contains multiple values—in the simplest definition, it is an indexed group of values that all have the same data type. Whereas a non-array variable is useful in dealing with a single value of a particular data type, an array is useful in dealing with multiple values of a particular data type.

In reality, arrays are more complex than you might gather from the definition just given because they can be multidimensional. All dimensions of an array are indexed numerically. A one-dimensional array is simply a single, indexed list of values. The list has a starting point (the first item) and an ending point (the last item), and each item in the list falls in line between the starting and ending points; no two items overlap, so each item has a unique index.

A two-dimensional array is a bit more complicated and is a group of lists that are all the same length. Such a group of lists is more commonly known as a "table" or a "matrix." It contains rows and columns, much as a spreadsheet does, and each value in the table occupies a position that represents the intersection of a certain row with a particular column. Figure 2-2 shows a simple example of a two-dimensional array.

	Column		
	1	**2**	**3**
1	Billijean	33	2/23/64
2	Johann	85	3/21/12
·	·	·	·
·	·	·	·
·	·	·	·
10	Jane	36	3/31/61

Figure 2-2. *A two-dimensional array is commonly called a "table" or a "matrix."*

A three-dimensional array can be characterized as a group of tables in which each table has the same number of rows and the same number of columns. The concept of a three-dimensional array is similar to an Excel workbook, which contains multiple worksheets. You can access any value in a three-dimensional array by specifying three pieces of information: the row, the column, and the table.

Taking this discussion even further, we see that a four-dimensional array can be characterized as a larger group that contains groups of tables in which each group has the same number of tables and each table has the same number of rows and the same number of columns. Again using the Excel workbook example, a four-dimensional array is analogous to a directory of Excel workbook files: You can access any value in a four-dimensional array by specifying a row, a column, a table, and a file.

VBA arrays can have up to 60 dimensions. Consider the possibilities entailed in using 60-dimensional arrays, and you can come up with some very complex sets of data. For the most part, however, in VBA you use either one- or two-dimensional arrays; three-dimensional arrays are rare. Arrays of greater than three dimensions are extremely rare and, depending on their size, could require more memory than is usually available on a personal computer.

Declaring an Array

Arrays operate in much the same way as do variables. Before you use an array, you must first declare it and specify the data type for the values that the array is to hold. Note that an array can hold values only of a single data type. It is easy to get around this limitation, however, by declaring an array to be of the Variant data type, which allows the array to hold any type of data. Array data types are exactly the same as the variable data types discussed in the section titled "Data Types for VBA Variables," beginning on page 49. Let's take a look at an example of an array declaration, which declares a one-dimensional array of the Integer data type:

```
Dim NumberArray(10) As Integer
```

You'll notice that this array declaration is similar to the variable declarations discussed previously, with one exception: A number is enclosed in parentheses after the name used in the declaration. The number in parentheses indicates that this declaration is for an array and not for a single-value variable. The value (or values) enclosed in parentheses after the name provides information about the architecture of the array. In the example above, the presence of only one number indicates that NumberArray is a one-dimensional array, and the number 10 indicates that the size of the array is 10—or that the array can hold up to 10 integer values. That number actually refers to the upper bound of the array; when you state that the array can hold up to 10 values, it is assumed that the lower bound is 1.

A declaration for a two-dimensional array appears as follows:

```
Dim TableArray(10, 20) As String
```

TableArray consists of 10 rows and 20 columns, which means it is capable of holding a total of 200 string values. And here's one more example—the following is a declaration for a three-dimensional array of variants:

```
Dim BigArray(5, 50, 100) As Variant
```

FYI

The Option Base Statement

Note that VBA allows lower bounds of arrays to start at either 0 or 1 by default, as governed by an Option Base statement at the beginning of a VBA module. Option Base 0 makes the default lower bound of the array 0, and Option Base 1 makes the default lower bound of the array 1. In the absence of an Option Base statement, array lower bounds are 0 by default. For the sake of simplicity, the examples that follow assume Option Base 1. Option Base statements are discussed in greater detail in the section titled "Option Base and Array Bounds," beginning on page 70.

BigArray is composed of 5 tables, each of which consists of 50 rows and 100 columns, which means the array can hold up to 25,000 variants.

You can see from these examples that as you increase the number of dimensions of an array, its size (and therefore the number of values it can hold) grows quickly. After you declare an array, VBA sets aside enough memory to accommodate the array; how much memory must be allocated depends on the array's size and data type. Declaring a one-dimensional Integer array of size 10 requires 20 bytes because each Integer value occupies 2 bytes. BigArray declared above—the three-dimensional array of variants—requires at least 400,000 bytes (25,000 × 16). Take care if you plan to declare arrays of greater than two dimensions because they can eat up a lot of memory and negatively impact performance. The amount of memory that can be allocated for an array depends on the amount of RAM available on your computer. If you try to declare an array whose size will exceed the amount of available memory, you get an "Out of Memory" message.

Using an Array

After you declare an array, how exactly do you use it? Let's take a look at an example. Proc25 uses a three-element array of integers:

```
Option Base 1

Sub Chap02dProc25_IntegerArray()
    Dim Vals(3) As Integer
    Vals(1) = Int(100 * Rnd())
    Vals(2) = Int(100 * Rnd())
    Vals(3) = Int(100 * Rnd())
    MsgBox "Lottery Numbers: " & Vals(1) & ", " & _
            Vals(2) & ", " & Vals(3)
End Sub
```

In this routine, after the Vals array is declared in line 3 (a one-dimensional, three-element array of integers), assignments are made to the three elements in Vals in lines 4, 5, and 6. An assignment to an array element is similar to an assignment to a variable; however, for an array element, you must specify the index of the element to which the assignment is being made. In lines 4, 5, and 6, the index is specified in the parentheses that follow Vals.

Also notice an interesting formula that appears on the right side of the assignment statements in lines 4, 5, and 6. This formula uses two built-in VBA functions, Rnd and Int, to create a randomly generated integer between 0 and 100. The Rnd function generates real random numbers between 0 and 1. Rnd can take one argument, which can be used as a seed number. (See Excel's online VBA Help for details.) The Int function converts real numbers to integers by removing all numbers to the right of the decimal point (effectively, always rounding down). By multiplying the value returned by Rnd by 100 and then using the Int function to convert the product of this multiplication to an integer, we arrive at a random integer between 0 and 100. And by using the same formula three times to make assignments to the three elements of the Vals array, we end up with an array that contains three random integers. In line 7 of Proc25, you'll find a reference to each element by its index number, causing the values that the array contains to be displayed in a message box:

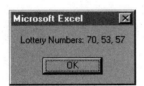

The next example shows the use of an array of variants:

```
Sub Chap02dProc26_VariantArray()
    Dim Data(3) As Variant
    Data(1) = "Johann"
    Data(2) = 85
    Data(3) = #3/21/1912#
    MsgBox Data(1) & ", age " & Data(2) & ", born " & Data(3)
End Sub
```

In this example, values of different data types have been assigned to the different elements of the array: a string to the first element, an integer to the second element, and a date to the third element. Because Data is an array of variants, values of any type can be assigned to any of its elements. Line 6 of Proc26 displays the values held by the elements of the array in a message box. We could extend the above example and create a two-dimensional array that might hold name, age, and birth date data for, say, 10 people:

```
Sub Chap02dProc27_2DVariantArray()
    Dim Data2(10, 3) As Variant
    Data2(1, 1) = "Johann"
    Data2(1, 2) = 85
    Data2(1, 3) = #3/21/1912#
    MsgBox Data2(1, 1) & ", age " & Data2(1, 2) & _
        ", born " & Data2(1, 3)
End Sub
```

If we look at the Data2 array in Proc27 as a table, the code assigns values to those elements in the first row of the table. Additional code could be written to provide data for nine more people. Note that we can rewrite Proc27 to take advantage of the PersonalData user-defined type explained earlier in this chapter. In fact, we can achieve the same functionality as that in Proc27 by using a one-dimensional array of the PersonalData type, as the following example shows. Remember, the user-defined type definition must occur at the top of the VBA module.

```
Type PersonalData
    PName As String
    PAge As Integer
    PBirthDate As Date
End Type

Sub Chap02dProc28_UserDefinedTypeArray()
    Dim Data3(10) As PersonalData
    Data3(1).PName = "Johann"
    Data3(1).PAge = 85
    Data3(1).PBirthDate = #3/21/1912#
    MsgBox Data3(1).PName & ", age " & Data3(1).PAge
End Sub
```

The message box displayed by Proc28 follows:

Dynamic Arrays

VBA actually provides two different types of arrays: dynamic arrays and fixed-size arrays. All of the examples we have looked at so far in this section have been fixed-size arrays, in which the size of the array is specified in the array's declaration statement. When you declare a dynamic array, the size of the array is not specified. In fact, the size of a dynamic array can be specified at any time the code is executing.

Dynamic arrays are useful when you know that the size of the array you are working with is going to change during code execution. If you are concerned about conserving memory, you can adjust the sizes of any arrays you use to meet your immediate needs; otherwise, you might have arrays in your code that are doing nothing but taking up memory, which can have a negative impact on performance. Let's take a look at a dynamic array. Proc29 which follows, uses the ReDim statement to dimension Data4 first as a one-dimensional, two-element array and then as a two-dimensional, thirty-element array:

```
Sub Chap02dProc29_UseDynamicArray()
    Dim Data4() As Variant
    ReDim Data4(2)
    Data4(1) = Int(100 * Rnd())
    Data4(2) = Int(100 * Rnd())
    MsgBox "Lottery Numbers: " & Data4(1) & ", " & Data4(2)
    ReDim Data4(10, 3)
    Data4(1, 1) = "Johann"
    Data4(1, 2) = 85
    Data4(1, 3) = #3/21/1912#
    MsgBox Data4(1, 1) & ", age " & Data4(1, 2) & _
        ", born " & Data4(1, 3)
End Sub
```

In line 2 of Proc29, we start by dimensioning an array, Data4, as a variant, without specifying the number of dimensions or the number of elements. This statement declares a dynamic array, yet it does not allocate any memory to the array. It is not until the ReDim statement in line 3 that memory is allocated for the array. The ReDim statement declares a one-dimensional, two-element array. Lines 4 and 5 are then used to assign random integer values to the two elements of the array; line 6 of the routine displays the values held by the elements of the array in a message box. In line 7, we use the ReDim statement again to change the array to a two-dimensional array that contains 30 elements. We then assign values to the elements in the first row of the array and display the values in a message box. This example shows how you can conserve memory during code execution by using dynamic arrays and the ReDim keyword to redimension arrays as the code executes. For more information about using ReDim and dynamic arrays, see the online VBA Help.

Option Base and Array Bounds

In the examples of arrays given so far, all numeric indexing of array dimensions has started at 1. As mentioned earlier, you can make numeric indexing for an array dimension start at 0, 1, or any number you choose. Many developers prefer to have array indexing start at 0, and some prefer 1. VBA makes it easy to choose either 0 or 1 as the basis for starting array indexing by using an Option Base statement at the beginning of a VBA module. If you don't specify Option Base at the beginning of a VBA module, VBA defaults to Option Base 0.

If you want array indexing to begin at a number other than 0 or 1, you must specify the lower and upper bounds of the index in the declaration of the array. Proc30, which follows, is an example:

```
Sub Chap02dProc30_UseArrayBounds()
    Dim Data5(4 To 5) As Integer
    Data5(4) = Int(100 * Rnd())
    Data5(5) = Int(100 * Rnd())
    MsgBox "Lottery Numbers: " & Data5(4) & ", " & Data5(5)
End Sub
```

In Proc30, Data5 is a one-dimensional, two-element array. In the declaration of the array, however, the numbers enclosed in parentheses after the array name specify the lower and upper bounds of the array. In essence, Data5 is a two-element array that has number indexing beginning at 4 and ending at 5.

Five Frequently Used Array Functions

Five functions are used often with arrays in VBA; these are Array, Erase, IsArray, LBound, and UBound. Let's take a brief look at each of these functions.

The Array function

The Array function allows you to create an array during code execution without having to first dimension the array, as Proc31 shows:

```
Sub Chap02dProc31_ArrayFunction()
    Data6 = Array("Johann", 85, #3/21/1912#)
    MsgBox Data6(1) & ", age " & Data6(2) & ", born " & Data6(3)
End Sub
```

Line 2 of Proc31 uses the Array function to create a fixed-size, one-dimensional, three-element array of variants. Well, that's not exactly correct, although it seems it should be. Data6 is not actually an array; it is a variant that contains an array—the array that the Array function returns. Even though Data6 is not really an array, it acts like one, so we won't bother getting caught up in the technical details here. Suffice it to say, the preceding code works. Note that the Array function always returns an array of variants and conforms to the numeric indexing specified by the Option Base statement at the beginning of the VBA module.

The Erase function

The Erase function can be used to erase the data that an array holds. With fixed-size arrays, Erase erases the values held by all the elements of the array without deallocating any memory that the array occupies. For a dynamic array, however, Erase not only erases values but also deallocates all of the memory assigned to the array. Proc32 (on the next page) is an example of using Erase to eliminate the values in a fixed-size array.

```
Sub Chap02dProc32_EraseFunction()
    Dim Data7(2) As Integer
    Data7(1) = Int(100 * Rnd())
    Data7(2) = Int(100 * Rnd())
    MsgBox "Lottery Numbers: " & Data7(1) & ", " & Data7(2)
    Erase Data7
    MsgBox "Lottery Numbers: " & Data7(1) & ", " & Data7(2)
End Sub
```

Proc32 assigns values to a one-dimensional, two-element array and then displays them in a message box. Then, by using the Erase function, the routine eliminates the values in the array. The second call to the MsgBox function in line 7 of the routine displays the value 0 for the elements of the array. Here Proc33 is an example of calling Erase on a dynamic array:

```
Sub Chap02dProc33_EraseDynamicArray()
    Dim Data8() As Integer
    ReDim Data8(2)
    Data8(1) = Int(100 * Rnd())
    Data8(2) = Int(100 * Rnd())
    MsgBox "Lottery Numbers: " & Data8(1) & ", " & Data8(2)
    Erase Data8
    MsgBox "Lottery Numbers: " & Data8(1) & ", " & Data8(2)
End Sub
```

Executing Proc33 results in a runtime error in Excel; the routine fails in line 8. When the Erase function is called in line 7, it wipes out all memory allocated to the dynamic array, Data8. After the array's memory is deallocated, VBA has no way to evaluate the array indices that are specified in the call to MsgBox in line 8, which causes the routine to fail and VBA to generate an error message.

When Proc33 causes an error, a VBA Error dialog box is displayed telling you which error occurred. The error in this case is "Subscript out of range." At this point, you can choose to take one of three actions: End the execution of Proc33 (choose End), access a help screen that describes the error and its probable cause (choose Help), or debug your code (choose Debug). If you choose Debug, the module is displayed in break mode, from which you can step through your code, examine the contents of variables, or even execute single VBA instructions. For more information about using break mode, see the section titled "The Quick Watch and Watch Window buttons," beginning on page 126.

The IsArray function

IsArray is a built-in VBA function that allows you to test a variable to determine whether it is indeed an array. IsArray takes one argument and returns either True (if it is an array) or False (if it is not). IsArray is useful when you call a function that is supposed to return an array; you can use IsArray to verify that the value returned is indeed an array. The following example demonstrates IsArray:

```
Sub Chap02dProc34_IsArrayFunction()
    Dim Data9(2) As Integer
    Dim ArrayBool As Boolean
    ArrayBool = IsArray(Data9)
    If ArrayBool = True Then
        MsgBox "Data9 is an array."
    End If
End Sub
```

Although this example is not practical in a real-world sense, it does demonstrate the functionality of IsArray. In line 2 of the routine, an array is declared, and in line 3, a Boolean variable (ArrayBool) is declared. IsArray is then used to make an assignment to ArrayBool (either True or False). An If statement next determines whether the value in ArrayBool is True; if it is True, a message is displayed in a message box. (The syntax of the If statement is covered in detail in the section titled "Altering Flow Using the If-Then-Else Control Structure," beginning on page 91.)

The LBound and UBound functions

You can use the LBound and UBound functions to determine the lower bound and upper bound indices of an array. Here's an example:

```
Sub Chap02dProc35_LBoundAndUBound()
    Dim Data10(4 To 15) As Integer
    MsgBox "The lower bound is " & LBound(Data10) & "."
    MsgBox "The upper bound is " & UBound(Data10) & "."
End Sub
```

NOTE   Using these functions on a variable which is not an array, or on a dynamic array which has not yet been sized with a redim statement, will cause a runtime error. You can use the IsArray function to ensure the variable is an array before calling UBound or LBound.

VBA Constants

A constant is a value that does not change during the execution of a routine. VBA constants are similar to constants found in other programming languages, and, in fact, constants represent exactly what their name implies: constant values. You use constants, therefore, when dealing with a value that you know will not change or that you do not want to change during the execution of a routine.

You declare constants in a manner that is similar to the way in which you declare variables, with one exception: Constants are assigned values in the same statement in which they are declared. After the declaration, constants cannot be changed. Any effort to change the value of a constant causes an error. Here's an example of a constant declaration:

```
Const MinVal As Integer = 1
```

As the example shows, you declare constants by using the Const keyword, followed by the name of the constant, the data type, and the value assigned to the constant. Constant data types are the same as those for variables, with one exception: You cannot declare a constant of a user-defined type. If you omit the data type for a constant in its declaration, the constant is given a data type that matches the value assigned to it. Note that expressions can also be used to assign values to constants, as in the following example:

```
Const TwoSquared As Integer = 2 * 2
```

You can also include multiple constant declarations in a single Const statement by separating the declarations with commas, as shown in the following example:

```
Const Con1 As Integer = 5, Con2 As Integer = 6, Con3 As Integer = 7
```

Constants do not come in the form of arrays, but you can use a constant in the same way you use a variable, provided you do not try to change the constant's value.

Calling One Routine from Another

In VBA, it's possible to call, or execute, one routine from another routine. This capability allows you to separate your code into logical segments. You gain two advantages by separating code into multiple subroutines:

■ If you want to use a VBA routine repeatedly, you need only write the code once and store it in a routine that can be called by any routine that requires it. Doing so also makes editing this shared routine easier because you have to make changes in only one place.

■ You can separate your VBA code into discrete, logical segments that are easy to code, debug, and maintain.

If you could not call one subroutine from another, your VBA routines would be extremely long and difficult to edit and debug.

Use logic, however, when breaking up your application into separate routines. A single routine should represent a single functional operation. Be careful not to go overboard in this respect; you could potentially write a separate routine for each VBA command in your application. Deciding when a particular operation should stand alone functionally is largely a matter of preference and experience. Let's take a look at an example. Proc36 calls the DisplayMessage routine to display a message:

```
Sub Chap02dProc36_CallSecondProc()
    Dim Range1 As Range
    Set Range1 = Worksheets(1).Range("A1")
    Range1.Value = 500
    DisplayMessage
End Sub

Sub DisplayMessage()
    MsgBox "Data has been entered."
End Sub
```

This routine enters data in range A1 of the first worksheet. Then, in line 5, the routine makes a call to the second routine, DisplayMessage. The DisplayMessage routine executes, displaying a message before returning control to Proc36.

The DisplayMessage routine above is perhaps not practical; the call to the MsgBox function could just as easily have been placed in the body of Proc36. If you had several routines that involved entering data in some way, however, and all of them displayed a message box that indicated that data was entered, you could see how the DisplayMessage routine would be useful—ensuring that all routines displayed the same message. Also, using the DisplayMessage routine simplifies the process of changing the message displayed. By including the message in only one routine, you have to change it only once, rather than having to make the change in several places.

Passing Data When You Call a Routine

When you call one routine from another, it's possible to pass variables or data to the routine being called. This capability gives you greater power in separating your code into multiple subroutines by allowing a single routine to act on different inputs. Take as an example the DisplayMessage routine. It displays a message box that states only "Data has been entered." Let's suppose you want the message box to display the actual value that has been entered instead—something like "The value 500 has been entered." The easiest way to do so is to specify an argument when calling the DisplayMessage routine. (You can pass a variable from one routine to another in two ways—see the next section.) Proc37 (at the top of the next page) calls and passes arguments to Display-Message2.

```
Sub Chap02dProc37_PassArgumentToProc()
    Dim Range1 As Range
    Set Range1 = Worksheets(1).Range("A1")
    Range1.Value = 500
    DisplayMessage2 Range1.Value
End Sub

Sub DisplayMessage2(Value1)
    MsgBox "The value " & Value1 & " has been entered."
End Sub
```

Two items of interest occur in the two routines we just examined. First, in Proc37, the call to DisplayMessage2 contains an argument: Range1.Value. Second, in line 1 of the DisplayMessage2 routine, Value1 appears in the parentheses that follow the routine name. In this case, Value1 serves as a variable. And, in fact, Value1 assumes the value of the argument that is specified when the call to DisplayMessage2 is made. Value1 is then used in DisplayMessage2 to display the appropriate value in the message box:

Proc38, which follows, shows another example of passing arguments when calling a routine. This routine passes elements of a user-defined type variable as arguments to DisplayMessage3:

```
Type PersonalData
    Dim PName As String
    Dim PAge As Integer
    Dim PBirthDate As Date
End Type

Sub Chap02dProc38_PassUserDefinedElements()
    Dim User2 As PersonalData
    User2.PName = "Jane"
    User2.PAge = 36
    User2.PBirthDate = #3/31/61#
    DisplayMessage3 User2.PName, User2.PAge
End Sub

Sub DisplayMessage3(UserName, UserAge)
    MsgBox UserName & ", Age " & UserAge & "."
End Sub
```

In Proc38, two values are passed to DisplayMessage3: User2.PName and User2.PAge. DisplayMessage3 then displays both of those values in a message box.

Passing a variable by reference or by value

You can pass a variable from one subroutine to another in two ways: by reference or by value. When a variable is passed by reference, the variable itself is actually passed to the routine that is called, and the called routine can change the variable. When a variable is passed by value, however, the variable's value—and not the variable itself—is passed to the routine that is called, and the called routine cannot change the variable.

How do you pass a variable by reference or by value? You do so by specifying either the ByRef or the ByVal keyword in the parentheses that follow the routine name in the routine that is being called.

NOTE If you fail to specify either the ByRef or the ByVal keyword, variables are by default passed by reference.

Proc39 below calls the ChangeName routine and passes the UserName variable by reference:

```
Sub Chap02dProc39_PassArgumentByReference()
    Dim UserName As String
    UserName = "Jeff"
    ChangeName UserName
    MsgBox UserName
End Sub

Sub ChangeName(ByRef UserName)
    UserName = "Dave"
End Sub
```

In the first line of the ChangeName routine above, the ByRef keyword and the name of the variable are specified in the parentheses that follow the routine name, indicating that the variable is being passed by reference—that is, the actual variable is being passed to the subroutine. In addition, a new value is assigned to the UserName variable in ChangeName. In fact, when the ChangeName routine finishes executing and returns to the calling routine, Proc39, the new value of UserName, which is "Dave", is displayed in a message box:

Note that in the preceding routines, the original name of the variable used in Proc39 is the same as that used in the ChangeName routine: UserName. You are not required, however, to use the same name in both instances. For example, the two routines that follow have the same effect even though they use two different variable names:

```
Sub Chap02dProc40_ByRefDifferentVariableNames()
    Dim UserName As String
    UserName = "Jeff"
    ChangeName2 UserName
    MsgBox UserName
End Sub

Sub ChangeName2(ByRef NewName)
    NewName = "Dave"
End Sub
```

Passing a variable by value does not involve passing the variable itself but rather the value of the variable. Therefore, changes to the variable in the called subroutine cannot affect the value of the variable in the calling routine. You pass a variable by value in the same manner as you pass a variable by reference except that you use the ByVal keyword:

```
Sub Chap02dProc41_PassArgumentByValue()
    Dim UserName As String
    UserName = "Jeff"
    ChangeName3 UserName
    MsgBox "Yet remains as " & UserName & " in the original proc."
End Sub

Sub ChangeName3(ByVal UserName)
    MsgBox "The original name is " & UserName & "."
    UserName = "Dave"
    MsgBox "The name is changed to " & UserName & _
        " in the called proc."
End Sub
```

The original value of UserName is passed to the ChangeName3 routine, and the value is displayed in a message box. ChangeName3 then changes the value of UserName and displays the new value in a second message box. Because the argument was passed to ChangeName3 by value, the UserName variable still retains its original value when ChangeName3 finishes executing and returns control to Proc41. The value is displayed in a message box in the last line of Proc41.

Specifying Optional and ParamArray arguments

Two additional keywords can be used when passing arguments from one routine to another: Optional and ParamArray. The argument list of a called routine uses the Optional keyword to specify those arguments that are optional. After you declare as optional an argument in an argument list, all remaining arguments must be declared optional as well. In addition, all optional arguments are evaluated as variants.

Here's an example of an argument list that uses the Optional keyword:

```
Sub OptionalExample(ByVal Arg1, Optional ByRef Arg2, _
                    Optional ByVal Arg3)
```

A ParamArray argument will accept an arbitrary number of arguments from the calling routine and package them into an array of variants. (In the absence of any Option Base statement, the array is base 0.) You can use ParamArray only with the last argument in an argument list. Here is an example of an argument list that uses the ParamArray keyword:

```
Sub ParamArrayExample(ByVal Arg1, ParamArray Arg2())
```

For more information about the Optional and ParamArray keywords, see the online VBA Help.

Function Routines

As mentioned, VBA uses two types of routines: subroutines and function routines. The first half of this chapter focused on subroutines; we'll look now at function routines.

Function routines are similar to subroutines; in fact, there are only three main differences between a function routine and a subroutine:

- All function routines begin with the Function keyword and end with the End Function keywords.

- Function routines can be called through formulas entered in worksheet cells.

- A function routine can return a value to the subroutine or formula expression that calls it.

Let's take a look at an example of a function that returns the product of two numbers:

```
Sub Chap02dProc42_CallFunction()
    Dim Var1 As Integer
    Dim Var2 As Integer
```

(continued)

continued

```
    Dim Var3 As Integer
    Var1 = 5
    Var2 = 10
    Var3 = Multiply(Var1, Var2)
    MsgBox Var3
End Sub

Function Multiply(ByVal Var1, ByVal Var2)
    Multiply = Var1 * Var2
End Function
```

The Multiply function shown here is a simple function that returns the product of its two arguments. Notice that in line 2 of the Multiply function, the product of the two arguments is assigned to the name of the function. Such a statement in a function routine—in which an assignment is made to the function name—specifies the return value of the function.

NOTE

You can specify the data type of each argument and of a function's return type, as in the following example:

```
Function Multiply (ByVal Var1 As Integer, _
                   ByVal Var2 As Integer) As Integer
```

Arguments and return types are variants by default if no data type is specified.

You might have noticed something interesting about the way in which Proc42 calls the Multiply function. The call is made by using an assignment statement in which a variable appears on the left side of the statement and the function name, along with a parameter list enclosed in parentheses, appears on the right side of the statement. This assignment statement calls the Multiply function with two arguments, Var1 and Var2, and assigns the return value of the Multiply function to the Var3 variable. In earlier examples of calling one subroutine from another, we saw that when arguments are passed to a subroutine, they are not enclosed in parentheses. You'd do well to remember the following general rules about passing arguments to functions or subroutines:

RULE 1

Because a function can return a value, you can use a function in an expression—that is, you can use a function anywhere that you might normally use a variable or a literal value. When a function is used in an expression on the right side of an assignment statement or as an argument to some other routine, you must enclose any arguments passed to that function in parentheses.

RULE 2   You can also call either a function or a subroutine using the Call keyword, in which case you must again enclose any arguments in parentheses. See the online VBA Help for more information about using the Call keyword.

RULE 3   If the function or subroutine is called by itself—not as part of an expression and without using the Call keyword—you must *not* enclose arguments in parentheses.

FYI

Executing a Function by Calling It from a Worksheet Cell

You can execute a function routine by calling it directly from a worksheet cell in the same way that you can call one of Excel's built-in worksheet functions. For example, by entering the Multiply function in a VBA module, you can access the function through a formula in a worksheet cell, as the following example shows:

```
=Multiply(50,100)
```

Also note that when calling a function routine from a cell formula, instead of passing values to the function, you can also pass range addresses. The function accepts the addresses as arguments and evaluates the values they contain. Here is an example:

```
=Multiply(A1,B1)
```

This call to Multiply returns the product of the values in cells A1 and B1.

Excel calls this function only when the values of cells A1 or B1 change. To force Excel to call the function whenever the value of any cell in the workbook changes, you would add the following statement at the top of the function:

```
Function Multiply(ByVal Var1, ByVal Var2)
    Application.Volatile True
    Multiply = Var1 * Var2
End Function
```

Volatile is a method of the Application object which "flags" the function as one that should recalculate just like a built-in Excel function. If Volatile is not called with the True keyword, the function will run only when its inputs (A1 or B1 in the example) are changed.

Scoping of Variables, Constants, Subroutines, and Functions

All VBA variables, constants, subroutines, and functions have what is called "scope," which refers to the area in the VBA application in which a specific variable, constant, subroutine, or function can be accessed. For example, let's suppose that you declare a variable named Var1 in a routine named Proc1. Then suppose you write a second routine named Proc2 in which you want to access the variable declared previously in Proc1—that is, Var1. If Var1 is declared in the body of Proc1 using the Dim keyword (shown in numerous examples in this chapter), Var1 has what is known as "procedure-level scope," which means that its scope is bounded by the procedure, or subroutine, in which it is declared. Therefore, you cannot access Var1 from Proc2 unless you expand the scope of Var1.

Let's take a different example—a function named Function1 that has been written in a VBA module named Module1. Suppose you want to call Function1 from a routine that resides in a different module—specifically, Module2. If Function1 was written using the Function keyword (as described in the previous section, titled "Function Routines"), Function1 has what is known as "project-level scope," meaning its scope is bounded by the workbook that contains the function. Because it has project-level scope, you can call Function1 from any routine in any VBA module in the workbook. If for some reason you wanted to prevent Function1 from being called by routines in other modules, you would have to limit the scope of Function1.

To get a more complete picture of scope, let's look at the scoping issues and at the ways you set scope for each of the main VBA elements we've discussed thus far: variables, constants, subroutines, and functions.

Scope of Variables

Although the scope of a variable refers to the area in your VBA application in which the variable can be accessed, the scope of a variable is also sometimes referred to as that area of the application in which the variable "stays alive" or retains the value that has been assigned to it. VBA provides three different levels of variable scope:

- Procedure-level scope
- Module-level scope
- Project-level scope

These levels apply to arrays as well as to single-value variables. Also note that by default, user-defined type definitions, which must occur in the Declarations section of a VBA module, have project-level scope. That is, after a user-defined type definition has been entered, you can declare a variable of that type anywhere in the project.

The following sections look at each of these levels of scope in more detail.

Variables: procedure-level scope

A variable has procedure-level scope if it is declared using the Dim keyword in the body of a subroutine. In this example, Var1 has procedure-level scope:

```
Sub Chap02eProc43_ProcedureLevelVariable()
    Dim Var1 As Integer
    Var1 = 55
    MsgBox Var1
End Sub
```

Any attempt to access Var1 from another routine will fail. Let's suppose that you write a second routine in the same module as Proc43 above and that in this second routine an attempt is made to access Var1. Let's also suppose that you change Proc43 by inserting a line at the end of the routine that calls this second routine. The resulting two routines would appear as follows:

```
Sub Chap02eProc43_ProcedureLevelVariable()
    Dim Var1 As Integer
    Var1 = 55
    MsgBox Var1
    Chap02eProc44
End Sub

Sub Chap02eProc44()
    MsgBox Var1
End Sub
```

Now, when you execute Proc43, the Var1 variable is declared and the value 55 is assigned to it and then displayed in a message box, as in the original routine. After the initial message box is displayed, however, the routine calls Proc44. Proc44 also attempts to display the value held by Var1 in a message box, but a blank message box is displayed instead of "55." Because Var1 has procedure-level scope, it does not retain its value outside of the routine (Proc43) in which it was declared. When Proc44 tries to access the value of Var1, VBA assumes that the Var1 variable referenced in Proc44 is an undeclared variant to which no value has been assigned and therefore displays an empty string in the message box. Figure 2-3 on the next page illustrates procedure-level scope.

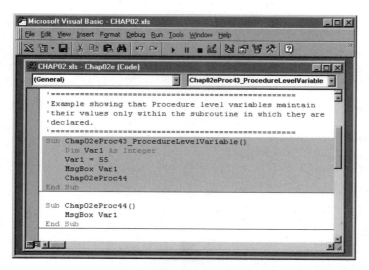

Figure 2-3. *Var1, declared with procedure-level scope, is available only in Proc43. The shaded area represents the scope of Var1.*

If you want to be able to access the original value of Var1 (55) from Proc44, you could do so in one of two ways: As already discussed, you could pass Var1 from Proc43 to Proc44. Or you could change Var1 to module-level scope, which is described in the next section.

Variables: module-level scope

A variable with module-level scope can be accessed by any subroutine or function routine that resides in the module in which the variable is declared. To declare a module-level variable, you place the declaration in the Declarations section of the VBA module, before any subroutines or function routines, as in this example:

```
Dim Var2 As String

Sub Chap02eProc45_ModuleLevelVariable()
    Var2 = "Hello World"
    Chap02eProc46
End Sub

Sub Chap02eProc46()
    MsgBox Var2
End Sub
```

In the example, Proc46 successfully accesses the correct value of Var2 as set in Proc45 because Var2 has been declared as a module-level variable and therefore retains its value throughout the VBA module. Figure 2-4 illustrates module-level scope.

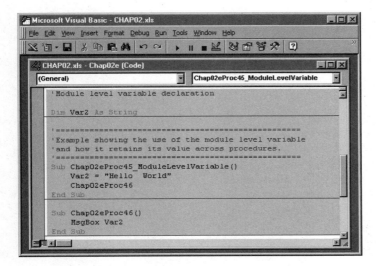

Figure 2-4. *Var2, declared with module-level scope, is available in all of module Chap02e. The shaded area represents the scope of Var2.*

The keyword Private explicitly declares a variable to have module-level scope, as in this example:

```
Private Var2 As String
```

However, since variables declared at the top of the module are module-level by default, the Private keyword is not required.

Let's consider another case, in which a module-level variable named Var3 is declared and assigned a value in Module1. Suppose, however, that you have a routine in Module2 that must have access to this variable. Because a module-level variable retains its value only in the module in which it is declared, you must change the scope of the variable to be able to access it from different modules, as the next section explains.

Variables: project-level scope

A variable that has project-level scope can be accessed from and retains its value in any module in the project in which it is declared. You declare variables of project-level scope by using the Public keyword; again, the declaration must occur at the Declarations section of any VBA module in the project, before any subroutines or function routines. Let's assume that we have two routines that exist in two different modules. One routine sets the value of a project-level variable, and the other displays the value in a message box. Here's an example:

```
Public Var3 As String

Sub Chap02fProc47()
    Var3 = "This variable was declared and set in module Chap02f."
End Sub

Sub Chap02eProc48_ProjectLevelVariable()
    Chap02fProc47
    MsgBox Var3
End Sub
```

In this example, Proc48 calls Proc47 in a separate module, which in turn sets the value of the project-level variable Var3. Proc48 then displays the value of Var3 in a message box. Figure 2-5 illustrates project-level scope.

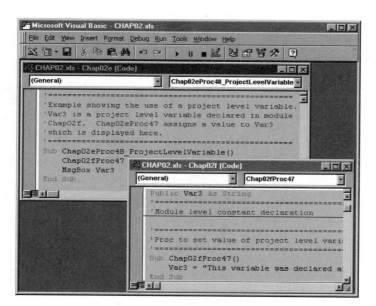

Figure 2-5. *Var3, declared with project-level scope, is available in all modules in the workbook. The shaded area represents the scope of Var3.*

Static Variables

We have seen how the Dim and Public keywords can be used to declare variables; however, the Static keyword can also be used to declare variables—at the procedure level only. Normally, if a procedure-level variable is declared with Dim, the variable ceases to retain its value after the subroutine in which it is declared finishes executing—when execution encounters the End Sub or End Function statement at the end of the routine. Declaring a variable as Static extends the life of the variable until execution of all routines, including the routine in which the variable is declared, is finished, as shown in this example:

```
Sub Chap02fProc49_StaticVariable()
    Chap02fProc50
    Chap02fProc50
End Sub

Sub Chap02fProc50()
    Static Var1 As String
    Dim Var2 As String
    If Var1 = "" Then
        Var1 = "Var1: Static Value"
        Var2 = "Var2: Non-Static Value"
    End If
    MsgBox Var1
    MsgBox Var2
End Sub
```

Proc49 calls Proc50 twice. The first time it calls Proc50, the routine declares Var1 as a static variable and Var2 as a non-static variable. Execution then flows into an If statement, which compares Var1 to an empty string. The If statement evaluates to True because no value has yet been assigned to Var1. In the If statement, strings are assigned to both Var1 and Var2, and before the routine finishes executing, the values of Var1 and Var2 are displayed in message boxes. Proc50 returns control to Proc49, which then calls Proc50 a second time. Because Var1 was declared as a static variable, this time it retains its value and continues to retain its value until execution stops. The If statement evaluates to False because Var1 has retained its value; consequently, the assignment statements in the If clause are not executed. Finally, the values of Var1 and Var2 are displayed in message boxes a second time. Because Var1 has retained its value, we see the value of Var1 displayed, but because Var2 is non-static, it has not retained its value from the first time Proc50 executed. Therefore, when Var2 is displayed in a message box, we see only an empty string.

FYI

**A Few Words About Project-Level
and Module-Level Variables and Compilation**

After an assignment is made to a project-level or module-level variable, that variable retains its value until a new assignment is made or until the user closes the Excel workbook file that contains the application. There is one other circumstance in which module-level and project-level variables lose the values they contain: when the VBA module in which those variables exist reaches an uncompiled state. A VBA module reaches an uncompiled state whenever a module-wide change is made—specifically, whenever a procedure is added or removed, or a change is made to the Declarations area of the module. The first time a routine in the affected module is executed, the whole module is compiled. After this first execution, the module remains in a compiled state until any module-wide changes are made to it. To ensure that all modules are compiled at the time you save and distribute a VBA application, choose Compile from the Debug menu in the Visual Basic Editor. These topics are discussed in greater detail later. For now, remember that if you make module-wide changes, data held by any module or project-level variables in that module is lost, and you will be forced to run code to re-initialize the variables.

Scope of Constants

Constants have the same three levels of scope as do variables: procedure, module, and project. The way in which constants are declared with each level, however, differs slightly from that of variables. Constants that have procedure-level scope can be accessed only from within the subroutine in which they are declared. The following is an example:

```
Sub Chap02fProc51_ProcedureLevelConstant()
    Const USCapitalCity As String = "Washington, D.C."
    MsgBox "The capital of the U.S. is " & USCapitalCity & "."
End Sub
```

You declare constants of module-level scope by using the Const keyword in the Declarations section of a VBA module, as shown in the following examples:

```
Const MoonLandingDate As Date = #7/20/69#
```

```
Sub Chap02fProc52_ModuleLevelConstant()
    MsgBox "People first walked on the moon on " & _
        MoonLandingDate & "."
End Sub
```

```
Sub Chap02fProc53_ModuleLevelConstant()
    MsgBox "I was in Los Angeles on " & MoonLandingDate & "."
End Sub
```

As the preceding examples show, module-level constants can be accessed by any routines that reside in the module. Note also that, as with module-level variables, a module-level constant can be declared with the keyword Private, as in the following example:

```
Private Const MoonLandingDate As Date = #7/20/69#
```

Using the Private keyword in a declaration of a module-level constant makes the constant available in that particular module only. All module-level constants are private by default, however, so you don't have to be concerned about including the Private keyword.

To declare project-level constants, you include the Public and Const keywords in the Declarations section of a VBA module, as in the following example:

```
Public Const ColorOfSky As String = "Blue"
```

You can access project-level constants from anywhere in the project in which they are declared.

Scope of Subroutines and Function Routines

Subroutines and function routines have only two levels of scope: module-level scope and project-level scope. Routines have, by default, project-level scope; they can be called by any routine in any module in the project. It is possible to declare a subroutine or a function by using a Public keyword, as in the following examples:

```
Public Sub Chap02fProc54_ProjectLevelProc()
    Dim Var1 As Integer
    Var1 = 1
    MsgBox AddOne(Var1)
End Sub

Public Function AddOne(ByRef Var1)
    AddOne = Var1 + 1
End Function
```

Because all routines by default have project-level scope, the only reason to use the Public keyword is to make those routines easily identifiable as being at the project level. Omitting the Public keyword, however, has no functional effect.

To make a routine module-level in scope, you use the Private keyword before the subroutine or function declaration. Note that declaring a routine by using the Private keyword makes it impossible for the routine to run stand-alone; private routines can be called only from other routines, as shown in the example code on the following page.

```
Sub Chap02fProc55_ModuleLevelProc()
    Var1 = GetRand
    Chap02fProc56 Var1
End Sub

Private Sub Chap02fProc56(ByVal Var1)
    MsgBox Var1 * GetRand
End Sub

Private Function GetRand()
    GetRand = Int(100 * Rnd())
End Function
```

In the example above, Proc55 first calls the GetRand function to get a random integer between 0 and 99 and then calls Proc56, passing the integer. Proc56 then multiplies its argument by the result of another call to GetRand before it displays the product in a message box.

Static Subroutines and Function Routines

You can declare subroutines and function routines as static, and when you do so, all variables in those subroutines and functions become static also. The following provides an example:

```
Sub Chap02fProc57_StaticProc()
    Chap02fProc58
    Chap02fProc58
End Sub

Static Sub Chap02fProc58()
    Dim Var1 As String
    If Var1 = "" Then
        Var1 = "Var1 is not yet proven to be static."
    Else
        Var1 = "Var1 is static."
    End If
    MsgBox Var1
End Sub
```

Var1 in the example above is declared and set in Proc58 and is static because Proc58 is static. When you run Proc57, it calls Proc58 twice and displays a message box both times, the second time confirming that Var1 is indeed static.

Control Structures

VBA provides several control structures that you can use to control the flow of execution of your routines. You will find that these control structures give you a great deal of power and flexibility in creating complex routines. These control structures are functionally equivalent to those generally found in other programming languages, with the exception of one structure unique to VB and VBA—the For-Each-Next structure. The following list describes the most commonly used VBA control structures:

If-Then-Else	Tests a condition and alters execution flow based on the results of the test
For-Next	Carries out a repetitive action a specific number of times
While-Wend	Carries out a repetitive action while a specific condition is True
Do-Loop	Carries out a repetitive action either while a specific condition is True or until a specific condition becomes True
Select Case	Branches to one of several possible code segments based on the value of a variable or the outcome of a specific test
For-Each-Next	Performs a repetitive action on each object in a collection or on each item in an array

The following sections take a closer look at each of these control structures.

Altering Flow Using the If-Then-Else Control Structure

You use the If-Then-Else control structure to alter the flow of execution based on the evaluation of what is referred to as a "test condition." The following code provides an example:

```
Sub Chap02gProc59_IfThenElse()
    Dim Num1 As Integer
    Num1 = GetRandomNumber
    If Num1 = 7 Then
        MsgBox "Congratulations! You received the winning " & _
            Num1 & "."
    Else
        MsgBox "I'm sorry; you lose. Your number was " & _
            Num1 & "."
    End If
End Sub

Function GetRandomNumber()
    GetRandomNumber = Int(10 * Rnd())
End Function
```

Proc59 starts by calling the GetRandomNumber function to set Num1 to a random integer between 0 and 9. The routine then uses an If statement to evaluate a test condition: Num1 = 7. If the test condition evaluates to True (Num1 is equal to 7), VBA executes the first MsgBox statement and displays a message announcing that the winning number has been received:

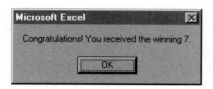

If the test condition in Proc59 evaluates to False (Num1 is not equal to 7), however, VBA executes the second MsgBox statement and displays a message stating that a losing number has been received.

Let's look at the individual elements that make up the above If-Then-Else statement:

If	A keyword that indicates the start of an If-Then-Else statement.
Num1 = 7	The test condition. The initial test condition always follows the If keyword and is used to determine the flow of execution through the If-Then-Else statement. The evaluation of the test condition can result in only one of two values—either True or False—and the execution flow is altered based on the result. If the test condition evaluates to True, execution flows to the line immediately after the If statement and continues until an Else statement is encountered. After the Else statement is encountered, execution jumps to the line that contains the End If keywords. If the test condition evaluates to False, execution jumps immediately to the line that contains the Else statement and continues until the End If statement is encountered.
Then	A keyword that signals the end of the test condition.
MsgBox "Congratulations! You received the winning " & Num1 & "."	The statement that is executed if the test condition (Num1 = 7) evaluates to True.

Else	A keyword that indicates where execution should stop if the test condition evaluates to True and where execution should start if the test condition evaluates to False.
MsgBox "I'm sorry; you lose. Your number was " & Num1 & "."	The statement that is executed if the test condition (Num1 = 7) evaluates to False.
End If	Keywords that indicate the end of the If-Then-Else control structure.

In an If-Then-Else statement, the Else keyword and the code segment that follows it are optional. If both are omitted and the test condition evaluates to False, execution flows immediately to the End If keywords and exits the If-Then-Else control structure.

Providing an alternative test condition by using ElseIf

As shown previously in Proc59, the If-Then-Else control structure is useful for executing statements selectively, depending on the evaluation of a test condition. Let's take a look at another example of If-Then-Else—one that contains the ElseIf keyword. Proc60 (which follows) prompts the user for a password. Depending on the password entered, the routine grants certain worksheet access and displays a message box that indicates the level granted:

```
Sub Chap02gProc60_IfThenElseIf()
    Dim Password As String
    Password = GetPassword
    If Password = "level1" Then
        For Each Sheet In ActiveWorkbook.Sheets
            Sheet.Visible = True
            Sheet.Unprotect
        Next
        MsgBox "You have read/write access to all sheets."
    ElseIf Password = "level2" Then
        ActiveWorkbook.Worksheets(1).Visible = True
        ActiveWorkbook.Worksheets(1).Unprotect
        MsgBox "You have read/write access to one worksheet."
    ElseIf Password = "level3" Then
        ActiveWorkbook.Worksheets(1).Visible = True
        MsgBox "You have read-only access to one worksheet."
    Else
        MsgBox "Password incorrect. Please try again."
    End If
End Sub

Function GetPassword()
    GetPassword = LCase(InputBox("Enter Password:", "Password"))
End Function
```

NOTE You can design an interface for password entry by placing a textbox on a userform and assigning a character to the PasswordChar property of the textbox. When a user enters data into such an editbox, the specified character is displayed to prevent the password from being seen. Textboxes are discussed in more detail in Chapter 5, "Custom Interface Design."

In Proc60, the If-Then-Else statement contains two instances of an ElseIf keyword followed by a condition. The ElseIf keyword provides an alternative test condition if the previous test condition evaluates to False. The first test condition in Proc60 comes immediately after the If keyword: *Password = "level1"*. If this initial test condition evaluates to False, execution jumps immediately to the first ElseIf keyword, at which point a new test condition is introduced: *Password = "level2"*. From here on, VBA ignores the original condition and concentrates solely on the new one. If the new test condition evaluates to False, execution again jumps to the next ElseIf keyword, where the process continues.

FYI

Using the LCase and InputBox Functions to Get Lowercase User Input

Line 3 of Proc60 (on page 93) calls a function named GetPassword, in which you might have noticed a few new items. Let's take a look at this function again:

```
Function GetPassword()
    GetPassword = LCase(InputBox("Enter Password:", "Password"))
End Function
```

GetPassword uses two built-in VBA functions—LCase and InputBox. LCase takes one string argument and returns the same string with all letters converted to lowercase. InputBox displays a box on the screen that requests input from the user. InputBox takes several optional arguments, although here we will concern ourselves with only the first two arguments. The first argument is a string that will be displayed to the user as a prompt in the body of the input box. The second argument is a string that will be displayed at the top of the input box in the title bar. When the InputBox function is called, an input box is displayed that includes the appropriate prompt string and title bar string as well as an empty edit box in which the user can type a value. If the user chooses OK in the input box, the string value that the user has entered is returned. (If the user chooses the Cancel button, however, an empty string is returned.) In the GetPassword function, the string is then passed to the LCase function, which converts it to lowercase.

Looking at Proc60, you might have noticed a few other items of interest. The segment that immediately follows the If statement includes a For-Each-Next loop. (For-Each-Next is discussed in greater detail in the section titled "Using VBA's For-Each-Next Control Structure," beginning on page 107.) The For-Each-Next loop in this routine goes through all the sheets in the active workbook and performs the same two actions on each sheet: it sets the Visible property of each sheet to True so that the user can see the sheets, and it calls the Unprotect method on each sheet. (Individual sheets in an Excel workbook can be password protected; calling the Unprotect method unprotects a sheet.) Unprotect takes a single argument—a string that represents a password. It is possible to protect a sheet without a password. Let's assume that the worksheets don't have a password in this example; therefore, no password argument is passed to Unprotect. As you look at the other code segments that follow the ElseIf keywords, you can see that, depending on the evaluation of each test condition, the Visible property of the first worksheet is selectively set to True, and the Unprotect method of the same worksheet is selectively called.

Using the For-Next Control Structure to Repeat an Action

The For-Next control structure lets you execute the same action a certain number of times. Let's take a look at an example in Proc61 below, which raises the number contained in the variable Base to the power of the number contained in the variable Power:

```
Sub Chap02gProc61_ForNext()
    Dim Base As Integer
    Dim Power As Integer
    Dim Result As Integer
    Dim Count1 As Integer
    Base = 4
    Power = 5
    Result = 1
    For Count1 = 1 To Power Step 1
        Result = Result * Base
    Next
    MsgBox Base & " raised to the " & Power & "th power = " & Result
End Sub
```

This routine determines the result of the value of 4 raised to the fifth power by using a For-Next loop. VBA has a built-in exponent operator (^) that can easily perform this calculation for you. To assign the value of 4 raised to the fifth power to variable Num2, you execute the following statement:

```
Num2 = 4 ^ 5
```

We are using the For-Next loop in this circumstance, however, as an example only. Proc61, which we just looked at, uses four integer variables to perform the calculation: Base, which holds the value 4; Power, which holds the value 5; Result, which holds the result of 4 raised to the fifth power; and Count1, which is used as the counter in the For-Next loop. Let's look at the individual components of the For-Next loop:

For	Keyword that indicates the start of the For-Next loop.
Count1 = 1 **To** Power	Expression that contains a counter variable as well as start and end values that determine the number of times the loop is executed. In this case, a variable named Count1 is used as the counter variable. The To keyword is used to separate the start value from the end value. With 1 as the start value and Power as the end value, the loop begins executing by setting the counter variable equal to 1.
Step 1	Keyword used to specify the value by which the counter variable is incremented or decremented with each loop execution. In the majority of For-Next loops, the step value is 1. It is possible, however, for the step value to be any integer, and it can even be a negative number (in which case the counter variable is decremented with each loop execution). At the beginning of every loop execution, the counter variable is compared with the end value. If the step value is positive and the counter variable is greater than the end value, execution flows out of the loop and on to the statements that follow the For-Next loop. On the other hand, if the step value is negative and the counter variable is less than the end value, execution also flows out of the loop. Specifying the Step keyword and the step value is optional; if you omit them, VBA assumes Step 1.
Result = Result * Base	Statement that is executed with each loop. The body of a For-Next loop can contain multiple statements.
Next	Keyword that indicates the end of the For-Next loop. Each time execution encounters the Next keyword, the step value is added to the counter variable, and execution flows back to the top of the For-Next loop. There the counter variable is once more compared with the end value to determine whether the loop should be executed again.

Proc62, which follows, includes another example of the For-Next loop. The routine uses the InputBox function to prompt the user to enter a number and then employs a For-Next loop, along with two nested If-Then-Else control structures, to calculate the factorial of the number. (The factorial of n is the product of all the integers from 1 to n; the factorial of 0 is defined as 1, and n must be greater than or equal to 0.)

```
Sub Chap02gProc62_ForNextIfThenElse()
    Dim NumberString As String
    Dim Num As Integer
    Dim Factorial As Double
    Dim Count1 As Integer
    NumberString = InputBox("Enter Number:", "Calculate Factorial")
    If IsNumeric(NumberString) Then
        Num = Val(NumberString)
        If Num >= 0 Then
            Factorial = 1
            For Count1 = 1 To Num
                Factorial = Factorial * Count1
            Next
            MsgBox "The factorial of " & Num & " is " & Factorial
        Else
            MsgBox "Factorials cannot be calculated on negative " _
                & "numbers."
        End if
    Else
        MsgBox "The factorial could not be calculated.  Please " _
            "try again."
    End If
End Sub
```

Again, we calculate the factorial as shown in Proc62 above for example purposes only. (Excel has a built-in worksheet function that calculates the factorial with much greater ease.) In Proc62, we combine two If-Then-Else statements with a For-Next loop. The test condition of the first If-Then-Else statement introduces a built-in VBA function—IsNumeric. The IsNumeric function takes a single argument and returns True if the argument is numeric or False if it is not. If the user enters a number, the test condition evaluates to True, and execution flows into the code segment that follows the If statement. Another built-in VBA function, Val, is included in the first line of the code segment after the If statement. The Val function takes a string, converts it to a number, and, in this case, assigns it to Num. The Val function is required here because the value that InputBox returns is always a string, and the string must be converted to a number before its factorial can be calculated.

Execution next flows into a second If-Then-Else statement, in which a test condition is used to determine whether the Num variable is greater than or equal to 0. If this second test condition evaluates to True, execution flows to the code segment after the second If statement and enters a For-Next loop in which the factorial is calculated and assigned to the Factorial variable. (Note that the factorial of 0 is indeed 1.) If the test condition of the second If statement evaluates to False, the routine displays a message to indicate that factorials cannot be calculated for negative numbers; if the user enters a nonnumeric string, the test condition of the first If statement evaluates to False, and a message box explains that the factorial could not be calculated and that the user should try again. But if the user enters a numeric value, a message displays its factorial:

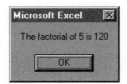

Although we have included two If-Then-Else statements in Proc62 to do some error checking, Proc62 will still, in some instances, break. For example, if the user enters a value greater than 170, Proc62 generates an "Overflow" error message because factorials of numbers greater than 170 exceed the upper bound of a Double variable (roughly 1.79E308). Proc62 also fails to check whether the user has entered a real number that contains values to the right of the decimal point. VBA automatically converts any numeric input to an integer if you assign the result of the Val function to an Integer variable, so Proc62 simply rounds off real number input and acts as if it had been given an integer.

Using the While-Wend Control Structure to Loop Based on a Test Condition

While-Wend is another VBA looping structure; it is similar in concept to the For-Next control structure. Instead of looping a set number of times, however, While-Wend loops as long as a specified test condition evaluates to True. Let's look at a simple example. Proc63 uses a While-Wend loop to obtain a specific number from the Rnd function:

```
Sub Chap02gProc63_WhileWend()
    Dim LotteryEntry As Integer
    LotteryEntry = 0
    While LotteryEntry <> 7
        LotteryEntry = Int(10 * Rnd())
        Beep
    Wend
    MsgBox "Your number is " & LotteryEntry & ". You Win!!"
End Sub
```

Proc63 provides a foolproof way of ensuring that the message box always displays a 7. The routine uses a While-Wend loop along with a test condition that causes the loop to continue executing until the value of the variable LotteryEntry is equal to 7. The test condition compares LotteryEntry with the integer 7 by using a not-equals operator (<>). You read the test condition statement, therefore, as "LotteryEntry not equal to 7." With each loop that is executed, a new random integer is assigned to LotteryEntry. You will also notice that the routine uses the VBA Beep function to tell the computer's internal speaker to beep every time the loop executes—this is purely for effect. If you run this routine multiple times on your computer, you hear a different number of beeps with each execution because the series of numbers generated by successive calls to the Rnd function is random.

TIP	Use the Randomize statement in your applications to force Rnd to generate a different sequence of random numbers each time the application is run. Otherwise, Rnd generates the same sequence of numbers each time you open the application's workbook file. For more information about random number sequences, see the topic titled "Rnd Function" in the online VBA Help.

Let's take a closer look at the elements of the While-Wend loop on the facing page:

While	Keyword that indicates the start of the While-Wend loop.
LotteryEntry <> 7	Test condition used to determine whether the loop should execute. If this condition is True, the loop executes. If it is False, execution flows to the Wend keyword at the end of the loop and continues with the rest of the routine.
LotteryEntry = Int(10 * Rnd( ))	First statement executed with each loop.
Beep	Second statement executed with each loop.
Wend	Keyword that signals the end of the While-Wend loop.

Using While-Wend in a geography quiz application

Proc64 on the following page shows a more realistic example of using While-Wend. The routine and the accompanying GeoQuiz function form the basis of a geography quiz application. Proc64 makes repetitive calls to the GeoQuiz function, which prompts the user to enter the name of the country that corresponds to a specified capital city.

```vba
Sub Chap02gProc64_GeographyApplication()
    Dim GeoResult As Boolean
    Dim GeoCount As Integer
    Dim GeoArray(3, 2) As String
    GeoArray(1, 1) = "Copenhagen"
    GeoArray(1, 2) = "Denmark"
    GeoArray(2, 1) = "Beijing"
    GeoArray(2, 2) = "China"
    GeoArray(3, 1) = "Cairo"
    GeoArray(3, 2) = "Egypt"
    GeoResult = True
    GeoCount = 1
    While GeoResult And GeoCount <= UBound(GeoArray, 1)
        GeoResult = GeoQuiz(GeoArray(GeoCount, 1), _
                            GeoArray(GeoCount, 2))
        GeoCount = GeoCount + 1
    Wend
    If GeoResult Then
        MsgBox "Congratulations.  All of your answers are correct."
    End If
End Sub


Function GeoQuiz(ByVal Capital, ByVal Country)
    Dim CountryName As String
    Dim PromptString As String
    PromptString = Capital & " is the capital of which country?"
    GeoQuiz = True
    While (CountryName <> UCase(Country)) And GeoQuiz
        CountryName = UCase(InputBox(PromptString, "GeoQuiz"))
        If CountryName = "" Then
            'User chose Cancel or OK with no input.
            GeoQuiz = False
        Else
            PromptString = CountryName & _
                " is not correct. Try again." & Chr(13) & Chr(13) & _
                Capital & " is the capital of which country?"
        End If
    Wend
    If GeoQuiz Then
        MsgBox Country & " is the correct answer."
    End If
End Function
```

Proc64 and the GeoQuiz function combine—in several ways—many of the components that this book has already discussed and also introduce several new items. Let's step through the routine and take a look at what it shows.

At the beginning of Proc64, two variables—GeoResult and GeoCount—and one array—GeoArray—are declared. GeoArray is a two-dimensional array that, if we look at it as a table, has two columns of data in each row: the name of a capital city in the first column and the name of the corresponding country in the second column. After the array is initialized, execution in Proc64 flows into the While-Wend loop. The loop has a test condition that evaluates two expressions that are joined by an And operator; both expressions must be True for the test condition to be True. GeoResult is a Boolean variable that is used to capture the return value from the GeoQuiz function. The first time the While-Wend loop executes, GeoResult is True. GeoCount is a counter that is used to loop through the array's rows. The test condition for the While-Wend loop checks for two items: that GeoResult is True and that GeoCount is less than or equal to the upper bound of the first dimension of GeoArray. If both expressions in the test condition evaluate to True, execution enters the loop's body.

A call is made in the body of the loop to the GeoQuiz function. The routine passes two arguments to GeoQuiz: a capital city name and a corresponding country name from GeoArray. Using GeoCount, we can specify which row of the array is current. In short, GeoQuiz takes the first argument (the capital city), displays it in an input box, and asks the user to enter the corresponding country:

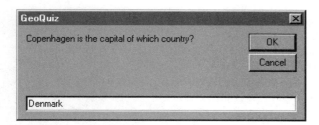

If the user enters the correct answer, GeoQuiz returns a value of True, which is assigned to GeoResult. The second statement in the While-Wend loop in Proc64 is used to increment GeoCount to move to the next row of the array. Execution then goes back to the beginning of the While-Wend loop, where the process begins again. If the user enters all country names correctly, GeoCount eventually becomes greater than the upper bound of GeoArray, causing the test condition to evaluate to False and execution to exit the loop. Execution then flows to the If statement at the end of Proc64, which displays the following message box at the top of the next page if all answers are correct:

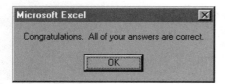

The GeoQuiz function takes two arguments: a capital city name and a corresponding country name. In the While-Wend loop in GeoQuiz, the InputBox function is first invoked; it displays the capital city's name and asks the user to enter the corresponding country. If the user chooses Cancel in the input box or leaves the edit box blank, the function's return value is set to False, causing the loop to end.

If the user enters a value in the input box and chooses OK, execution flows to the start of the While-Wend loop, where the test condition is evaluated again. If the user has entered the incorrect country, the test condition evaluates to True, and the loop executes again. If the user enters at least one character and chooses OK, the function return value retains the value of True. The test condition evaluates to False when the user enters the correct country, and execution flows to the end of the While-Wend loop. Because the function's return value is still True, a message box tells the user that the correct answer has been entered:

In the GeoQuiz function, review the assignment statement for the PromptString variable at the end of the While-Wend loop. The statement involves building a string that says something along the lines of "The country name you entered is not correct. Please enter another country name." At the end of the first line of the assignment statement, the line continuation character (_) is used to continue the statement on a second line. In addition, on the following line, we see a built-in VBA function called Chr. The Chr function takes one argument—a number from 0 through 255—and returns the ASCII character that corresponds to the argument. Chr(13) evaluates to a linefeed character, which, in GeoQuiz, causes the prompt displayed in the input box to wrap around to a new line. Calling Chr(13) twice inserts two linefeed characters in the prompt.

FYI

Comments in Code Listings

A comment begins with an apostrophe ('); everything to the right of the apostrophe is part of the comment. A comment can be on a line by itself, as in the GeoQuiz function, or it can be at the end of a line of code. If you use comments on the same lines as your code, use tabs to align the comments; comments should make your code more—not less—readable.

NOTE Chr(13) and Chr(10) produce a linefeed character when used with the MsgBox or InputBox function. To produce a linefeed in the text of a TextBox object, you must use Chr(10).

Proc64 and the GeoQuiz function are perhaps the most complicated routines encountered so far in this book. They could easily form the basis of a geography quiz application that could be used in a real-life educational setting. You would simply have to retrieve the names of all the countries in the world and their corresponding capital cities from a database or an Excel worksheet. And you would probably want to improve the user interface by using custom graphics and perhaps dialog boxes, which offer more flexibility than do input boxes. As this example shows, input boxes are limited. Chapter 5 includes a discussion of designing dialog boxes (also known as userforms in Excel 97). Because you can add many features to a dialog box, you can create a user interface that is custom designed.

The Do-Loop Control Structure Offers Two Additional Features

The Do-Loop control structure is similar to While-Wend. Do-Loop, however, provides two important features that While-Wend does not. First, Do-Loop lets you choose whether to specify the test condition at the beginning or at the end of the loop. With While-Wend, you can specify the test condition only at the beginning of the loop. Placing the test condition at the end of the loop, however, guarantees that the loop will always execute at least one time. Second, Do-Loop allows you to specify that execution of the loop should continue either while the test condition is True or until the test condition becomes True. This second feature, however, is achievable with While-Wend; by using the VBA Not operator, you can easily transform a test condition that allows execution while it is True into a test condition that executes until it is True.

Let's take a look at some examples. We saw that Proc63 (on page 98) employed While-Wend to retrieve random integers until a 7 was returned. Proc65 shows how the same routine would be written using Do-Loop:

```
Sub Chap02gProc65_DoWhileLoop()
    Dim LotteryEntry As Integer
    LotteryEntry = 0
    Do While LotteryEntry <> 7
        LotteryEntry = Int(10 * Rnd())
        Beep
    Loop
    MsgBox "Your number is " & LotteryEntry & ". You Win!!"
End Sub
```

If we compare Proc65 with Proc63, we see only two subtle differences: The keyword Do appears before the keyword While in Proc65, and the keyword Loop replaces the keyword Wend. We can rewrite the above routine in several different ways, however, using Do-Loop. In Proc66, which follows, the While keyword is replaced with the Until keyword, and the not-equals operator (<>) that compares the LotteryEntry variable to the value 7 is replaced with an equals operator (=):

```
Sub Chap02gProc66_DoUntilLoop()
    Dim LotteryEntry As Integer
    LotteryEntry = 0
    Do Until LotteryEntry = 7
        LotteryEntry = Int(10 * Rnd())
        Beep
    Loop
    MsgBox "Your number is " & LotteryEntry & ". You Win!!"
End Sub
```

By using Do-Loop, we can continue to make changes to this routine. For example, in Proc67, which follows, we keep the Do keyword at the top of the loop but move the Until keyword and the test condition to the end of the loop after the Loop keyword. Making this change ensures that the loop will execute at least one time because the test condition is not evaluated until the end of the loop. As a result, we no longer need to initialize LotteryEntry before entering the loop.

```
Sub Chap02gProc67_DoLoopUntil()
    Dim LotteryEntry As Integer
    Do
        LotteryEntry = Int(10 * Rnd())
        Beep
    Loop Until LotteryEntry = 7
    MsgBox "Your number is " & LotteryEntry & ". You Win!!"
End Sub
```

We can make one final change to show the last permutation of Do-Loop: substitute the While keyword for the Until keyword at the end of the loop. In doing so, we must change the equals operator (=) back to a not-equals operator (<>):

```
Sub Chap02gProc68_DoLoopWhile()
    Dim LotteryEntry As Integer
    Do
        LotteryEntry = Int(10 * Rnd())
        Beep
    Loop While LotteryEntry <> 7
    MsgBox "Your number is " & LotteryEntry & ". You Win!!"
End Sub
```

Using the Select Case Control Structure
to Selectively Alter the Flow of Execution

The Select Case control structure alters the flow of execution to one of several possible code segments, depending on the value of a variable or the evaluation of an expression. Using Select Case is similar to using multiple ElseIf statements to redefine a test condition in an If-Then-Else control structure. Earlier, Proc60 used an If-Then-Else statement to prompt a user for a password and then, depending on the password entered, provided a certain level of access privilege to an Excel workbook. Let's rewrite Proc60 using a Select Case statement:

```
Sub Chap02gProc69_SelectCase()
    Dim Password As String
    Dim Sheet As Object
    Password = LCase(InputBox("Enter Password:", "Password"))
    Select Case Password
        Case "level1"
            For Each Sheet In ActiveWorkbook.Sheets
                Sheet.Visible = True
                Sheet.Unprotect
            Next
            MsgBox "You have read/write access to all sheets."
        Case "level2"
            ActiveWorkbook.Worksheets(1).Visible = True
            ActiveWorkbook.Worksheets(1).Unprotect
            MsgBox "You have read/write access to one worksheet."
        Case "level3"
            ActiveWorkbook.Worksheets(1).Visible = True
            MsgBox "You have read-only access to one worksheet."
        Case Else
            MsgBox "Password incorrect. Please try again."
    End Select
End Sub
```

The following list describes the components of the Select Case control structure used above in Proc69:

Select Case	Keywords that indicate the beginning of the Select Case control structure.
Password	The test expression, which can be a variable or an expression. The test expression is evaluated, and execution flows to the Case statement that contains an expression equal to the test expression. If no such Case statement exists, execution flows to a Case Else statement. If no Case Else statement exists, execution flows to the End Select statement at the end of the control structure.

(continued)

continued

Case "level1" First Case expression. If the test expression is equal to the Case expression listed here, execution flows to the code segment that starts on the following line and continues until another Case statement is encountered, at which time execution flows to the End Select statement. If the test expression is not equal to the Case expression listed here, execution flows to the next Case statement.

Case "level2" Second Case expression—handled in the same way as Case "level1".

Case "level3" Third Case expression—handled in the same way as Case "level1".

Case Else Evaluates to True if all of the other Case expressions evaluate to False. If Case Else evaluates to True, execution flows to the code segment that follows the Case Else statement.

End Select Keywords that signal the end of the Select Case control structure.

Proc70, which follows, also uses a Select Case control structure, but the one it uses differs slightly from the original Select Case control structure we looked at in Proc69:

```
Sub Chap02gProc70_SelectCase()
    Dim Score As Integer
    Score = Int(100 * Rnd())
    Select Case Score
        Case 0 To 33
            MsgBox "Score: " & Score & Chr(13) & _
                "You're in the first third."
        Case 34 To 66
            MsgBox "Score: " & Score & Chr(13) & _
                "You're in the second third."
        Case 67 To 100
            MsgBox "Score: " & Score & Chr(13) & _
                "You're in the last third."
    End Select
End Sub
```

In Proc70, the Case expressions cover a range of values. Each Case expression specifies a starting value, followed by the To keyword, and then an ending value. If the test expression for the control structure is equal to a value that falls within one of the ranges specified, the appropriate Case expression evaluates to True, and the code segment that corresponds to that Case expression is executed.

Using VBA's For-Each-Next Control Structure

For-Each-Next is perhaps the most powerful looping control structure in VBA. In fact, few programming languages provide such a powerful control structure. For-Each-Next allows you to loop through all of the objects in a collection or all of the elements in an array and perform the same action on each object or element. The following is a simple example of the For-Each-Next control structure:

```
Option Base 1
Sub Chap02gProc71_ForEachNext()
    Dim CountryArray(5) As String
    Dim Country As Variant
    CountryArray(1) = "India"
    CountryArray(2) = "Peru"
    CountryArray(3) = "Greece"
    CountryArray(4) = "Canada"
    CountryArray(5) = "Kenya"
    For Each Country In CountryArray
        MsgBox Country
    Next
End Sub
```

Proc71 assigns country names to the five elements of the array CountryArray and then uses the For-Each-Next control structure to display the value of each element in the array in a message box:

Note that a loop is executed a certain number of times exactly as in the For-Next control structure. The benefit of For-Each-Next, however, is that you don't have to worry about trying to figure out how many times the loop should execute; it executes as many times as there are elements in the array (or objects in the collection). For example, we could rewrite Proc71 and use a standard For-Next loop, as shown in Proc72 here:

```
Sub Chap02gProc72_ForNext()
    Dim CountryArray(5) As String
    Dim Count1 As Integer
    CountryArray(1) = "India"
    CountryArray(2) = "Peru"
```

(continued)

continued

```
    CountryArray(3) = "Greece"
    CountryArray(4) = "Canada"
    CountryArray(5) = "Kenya"
    For Count1 = 1 To UBound(CountryArray)
        MsgBox CountryArray(Count1)
    Next
End Sub
```

With the For-Next loop in Proc72, however, we've had to use a counter variable—Count1—to count from 1 to the upper bound of the array. Note also that in the body of the For-Next loop we've had to index CountryArray to retrieve values from the array. The For-Each-Next loop in Proc71 did not require a counter variable; nor did it require that the array be indexed in the body of the loop. Let's take a look at the elements of the For-Each-Next loop shown in Proc71:

For Each	Keywords that indicate the start of a For-Each-Next loop.
Country	Variable to which all the elements in the group will be assigned. The group can be either an array or a collection of objects. If the group is an array, this variable must be of the Variant data type. If the group is a collection, this variable must be of the Variant data type, of the generic Object data type, or of the specific object data type that corresponds to the objects in the collection.
In	Keyword that separates the variable from the group.
CountryArray	The group, which can be either an array or a collection of objects. The loop executes as many times as there are items in the group. With the first loop, the variable is set to the value of the first item in the group; with each successive loop, the variable is set to the value of each successive item.
MsgBox Country	Action that is performed in the body of the loop.
Next	Keyword that indicates the end of the loop. After reaching Next, execution flows back to the start of the loop, where the For Each keywords appear. If, after reaching Next, the variable is equal to the last element of the group, execution breaks out of the loop and continues with the rest of the routine.

NOTE If the group in a For-Each-Next statement is an array, the values of the array elements can only be retrieved; you cannot use For-Each-Next to change the items in an array. If the group is a collection, however, you can use For-Each-Next to display or change the properties of the objects in the collection.

Using For-Each-Next with multidimensional arrays

Let's take a look at what happens when For-Each-Next is used with a two-dimensional array. Note how For-Each-Next allows access to each element in the array, regardless of dimension:

```
Sub Chap02gProc73_ForEachNext2DArray()
    Dim StudentNames(2, 2) As String
    Dim NameVar As Variant
    StudentNames(1, 1) = "Nancy"
    StudentNames(1, 2) = "Tim"
    StudentNames(2, 1) = "Margie"
    StudentNames(2, 2) = "Louie"
    For Each NameVar In StudentNames
        MsgBox NameVar
    Next
End Sub
```

For-Each-Next visits all elements in all dimensions in Proc73 above. Accomplishing the same using For-Next instead would require two For-Next loops—one nested in the other. Proc74, which follows, uses a For-Each-Next loop to go through all of the elements in a six-dimensional array, incrementing a counter with each element encountered.

```
Sub Chap02gProc74_ForEachNext6DArray()
    Dim BigArray(5, 5, 5, 5, 5, 5) As Boolean
    Dim Var1 As Variant
    Dim Var2 As Integer
    Var2 = 0
    For Each Var1 In BigArray
        Var2 = Var2 + 1
    Next
    MsgBox Var2
End Sub
```

Accessing every element of a multidimensional array using standard For-Next loops would be much more difficult.

Using For-Each-Next with collections

Although For-Each-Next loops are powerful with arrays, their real power comes when you use them with collections of objects. Let's take a look at a simple example on the following page.

```
Sub Chap02gProc75_ForEachNextWorksheet()
    Dim SheetVar As Worksheet
    For Each SheetVar In ActiveWorkbook.Worksheets
        MsgBox SheetVar.Name
    Next
End Sub
```

Proc75 above uses a For-Each-Next loop to access each Worksheet object in the ActiveWorkbook's Worksheets collection, displaying the value of the Name property for each worksheet in a message box:

It is possible to change the value of the Name property of each worksheet, as the following example shows:

```
Sub Chap02gProc76_ForEachNextWorksheet()
    Dim SheetVar As Worksheet
    For Each SheetVar In ActiveWorkbook.Worksheets
        SheetVar.Name = "Work" & SheetVar.Name
        MsgBox SheetVar.Name
    Next
End Sub
```

Proc76 changes the Name property of each worksheet in the workbook by attaching the string "Work" to the front of each name. To reinstate the names, you could use the following:

```
Sub Chap02gProc77_ForEachNextWorksheet()
    Dim SheetVar As Worksheet
    Dim x As Integer
    x = 1
    For Each SheetVar In ActiveWorkbook.Worksheets
        SheetVar.Name = "Sheet" & x
        x = x + 1
        MsgBox SheetVar.Name
    Next
End Sub
```

You can also use For-Each-Next to call methods on objects in a collection. Proc78 adds 10 new workbooks, arranges all the workbooks in a tiled fashion in the Excel work area, and then deletes all the workbooks except the workbook in which the code is being run:

```
Sub Chap02gProc78_ForEachNextWorkbook()
Dim x As Integer
Dim Book As Workbook
    For x = 1 To 10
        Workbooks.Add
    Next
    Windows.Arrange
    MsgBox "Workbooks have been arranged."
    For Each Book In Application.Workbooks
        If Book.Name <> ThisWorkbook.Name Then
            Book.Close
        End If
    Next
    ActiveWindow.WindowState = xlMaximized
End Sub
```

This routine first uses a For-Next loop to add 10 new workbooks; it does so by calling the Add method on the Workbooks collection. Then, by calling the Arrange method on the Windows collection, the routine arranges all of the workbooks in a tiled fashion on the screen. A message box pauses execution so that you can see the result:

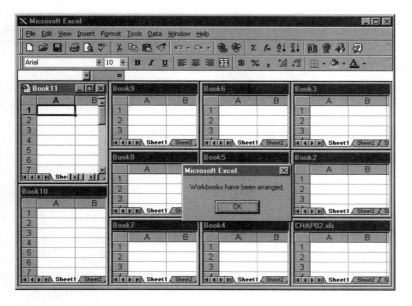

Next a For-Each-Next loop is used to test the value of each Workbook object's Name property. If the name does not match the name of ThisWorkbook, the Close method is called on the Workbook object. Last the routine sets the WindowState property of the ActiveWindow object to the constant xlMaximized, which adjusts the window size so that it fills the entire Excel work area.

Using For-Each-Next with the Range object

You might recall that the Range object can act like a collection of objects, so you can use the For-Each-Next loop to set properties and call methods on Range objects. Proc79 is an example:

```
Sub Chap02gProc79_ForEachNextRange()
    Dim SheetVar As Worksheet
    Dim Cell As Range
    For Each SheetVar In ActiveWorkbook.Worksheets
        SheetVar.Select
        For Each Cell In Range("A1:F20")
            Cell.Value = 25
        Next
    Next
End Sub
```

Proc79 uses a For-Each-Next loop nested in another For-Each-Next loop to set the Value property of all cells in Range("A1:F20") for each worksheet in the ActiveWorkbook object. The first For-Each-Next loop steps through all the worksheets in the Worksheets collection, calling the Select method on each worksheet object.

Proc79 can be made more interesting if you change it to set the ColorIndex property of each cell's Interior object. (Interior is an object that exists inside the Range object.) By setting the ColorIndex property of the Interior object to 15, for example, you can make the interior of each cell light gray:

```
Sub Chap02gProc80_ForEachNextRange()
    Dim SheetVar As Worksheet
    Dim Cell As Range
    For Each SheetVar In ActiveWorkbook.Worksheets
        SheetVar.Select
        For Each Cell In Range("A1:F20")
            Cell.Interior.ColorIndex = 15
        Next
    Next
End Sub
```

Previously, Proc79 set the Value property of each cell in Range("A1:F20") equal to 25. Let's use Proc81 to create a few minor deviations in this range of cells on the first worksheet:

```
Sub Chap02gProc81_SetDeviations()
    Worksheets(1).Select
    Range("B5") = 24
    Range("C2") = 26
    Range("D10") = 27
    Range("E18") = 22
End Sub
```

Looking at the range of cells that contains these minor deviations from 25, it is difficult to see which cells in the range differ. We need a routine that will go through the range, identify the cells that contain deviations, and make them stand out. Such a routine would be useful, for example, in a quality control application or in a financial application in which deviant values of grave importance must stand out. Proc82 accomplishes the task:

```
Sub Chap02gProc82_ForEachNextRange()
    Dim Cell As Range
    Worksheets(1).Select
    For Each Cell In Range("A1:F20")
        If Cell.Value <> 25 Then
            Cell.Font.Size = 18
            Cell.Font.Bold = True
            Cell.Interior.ColorIndex = 3
        End If
    Next
End Sub
```

This routine first calls the Select method on the first worksheet in the workbook. Then the routine uses a For-Each-Next loop to step through all of the cells in Range("A1:F20"). An If statement tests whether the Value property of each Range object is equal to 25. If the Value property is not equal to 25, the Size property of the Font object (in the Range object) is set to 18, the Bold property of the Font object is set to True, and the ColorIndex property of the Interior object (in the Range object) is set to 3 (equal to Red). Proc82 successfully identifies all of the Range objects in Range("A1:F20") on the first worksheet that have a Value property not equal to 25 and makes those objects stand out so that they are easily identifiable:

NOTE Similar results could have been obtained without writing VBA code by using Excel 97's new Conditional Formatting feature. However, this example still shows how to iterate through cells in a range and manipulate properties.

The With Statement

The With statement was introduced in VBA in Excel 5—it allows you to abbreviate object references. With statements provide three main advantages: they reduce the amount of code you have to type, make your code easier to read, and improve your code's performance. Perhaps the best way to see the advantages that With statements offer is to take a look at two different routines that accomplish the same task—one that does not use the With statement and one that does. Proc83 does not use With:

```
Sub Chap02hProc83_NonWith()
    ActiveWorkbook.Worksheets(2).Range("A1").Font.Bold = True
    ActiveWorkbook.Worksheets(2).Range("A1").Font.Italic = True
    ActiveWorkbook.Worksheets(2).Range("A1").Font.Size = 22
    ActiveWorkbook.Worksheets(2).Range("A1").Font.Name = "Times "New Roman"
    ActiveWorkbook.Worksheets(2).Range("A1").Font.ColorIndex = 3
    Worksheets(2).Select
End Sub
```

The above routine contains five statements that set five properties of the Font object contained in the second worksheet's cell A1. Approximately 360 keystrokes were required to write the routine. As it is currently written, Proc83 contains 21 object and property references (as indicated by the number of instances of the dot operator [.]), each one of which requires time to evaluate. The same routine can be rewritten using the With statement:

```
Sub Chap02hProc84_With()
    With ActiveWorkbook.Worksheets(2).Range("A1").Font
        .Bold = True
        .Italic = True
        .Size = 22
        .Name = "Times New Roman"
        .ColorIndex = 3
    End With
    Worksheets(2).Select
End Sub
```

Proc84 required 202 keystrokes and contains nine object and property references. That's roughly 56 percent of the keystrokes and 43 percent of the object and property references used in Proc83. You could argue that by using With, you can enter your code in half the time and make it run twice as fast. The example comparison that Proc83 and Proc84 provide is a fabrication; object references in Proc83 could have been shortened, improving performance and reducing keystrokes. But this fabrication clearly illustrates the advantages of using the With statement. Although not all code benefits from using With to as great a degree as is shown here, code benefits often enough that you should remember the following rule:

RULE Use the With statement whenever and wherever you can to shorten code, make code easier to read, and improve performance.

It probably doesn't make sense to use With when you are setting a single property or calling a single method; it does make sense to use With, however, if you are setting more than one property or calling more than one method. The following examples illustrate further:

```
Sub Chap02hProc85_NestedWith()
    With ActiveWorkbook.Worksheets(3)
        .Select
        .Unprotect
        With .Range("A1")
            MsgBox .Value
            .Value = 200
            .RowHeight = 60
            .ColumnWidth = 20
            .Font.Size = 20
            .Interior.ColorIndex = 3
        End With
    End With
End Sub
```

Proc85 above uses two With statements—one nested in the other. The routine first calls the Select and Unprotect methods on the third worksheet and then displays the setting of the Value property of Range("A1") in a message box. Next Proc85 changes the Value property to 200, sets the RowHeight and ColumnWidth properties, and then sets the Size property of the Font object and the ColorIndex property of the Interior object.

Proc86 uses a For-Next loop to slowly shrink the size of the active window, uses four additional For-Next loops to move the shrunken window along the four borders of the screen, and then restores the window to its normal size:

```
Sub Chap02hProc86_With()
    Application.Windows.Arrange
    With ActiveWindow
        For x = 1 To 25
            .Height = .Height - 10
            .Top = .Top + 5
```

(continued)

continued

```
            .Width = .Width - 20
            .Left = .Left + 10
        Next
        .Top = 0
        .Left = 0
        For x = 0 To 250 Step 5
            .Top = x
        Next
        For x = 0 To 400 Step 5
            .Left = x
        Next
        For x = 250 To 0 Step -5
            .Top = x
        Next
        For x = 400 To 0 Step -5
            .Left = x
        Next
    End With
    Application.Windows.Arrange
    ActiveWindow.WindowState = xlMaximized
End Sub
```

You can see in Proc86 that by using the With statement, you can abbreviate numerous property references throughout the body of the routine.

Other VBA Functions and Statements You'll Find Useful

Although this chapter has covered most of the functions and statements you will use to design applications in VBA, it is not possible or practical to cover in detail here all VBA functions and statements. A few additional VBA functions and statements deserve mention, however, and they are listed here:

Abs	Returns the absolute value of a number
CurDir	Returns the current MS-DOS path
Date	Returns the current system date
Exit Do	Causes execution to break out of a Do-Loop
Exit For	Causes execution to break out of a For-Next or For-Each-Next loop
Exit Function	Causes execution to break out of a function routine
Exit Sub	Causes execution to break out of a subroutine
Fix	Returns the integer portion of a number, rounding down positive numbers and rounding up negative numbers
Int	Returns the integer portion of a number, rounding down both positive numbers and negative numbers

IsArray	Returns True if an expression is an array
IsDate	Returns True if an expression is a date
IsEmpty	Returns True if no value has been assigned to a variable
IsError	Returns True if an expression is an error value
IsNull	Returns True if an expression evaluates to Null
IsNumeric	Returns True if an expression evaluates to a number
IsObject	Returns True if an expression represents an object
Len	Returns the length of a string or the number of bytes required to store a variable
Now	Returns the current date and time
Shell	Runs an executable program
Sqr	Returns the square root of a number
Str	Returns a string representation of a number
StrComp	Performs a string comparison
Time	Returns the current system time
TypeName	Returns the data type of a variable

For more information about other VBA functions and statements not covered here, see the online VBA Help.

VBA Editing and Debugging Tools

VBA comes with several advanced editing and debugging tools that will be of great help when you write code. You access most of the debugging tools from the Standard, Debug, and Edit toolbars, shown here. Let's take a look at the buttons on these toolbars and briefly discuss the functions they serve.

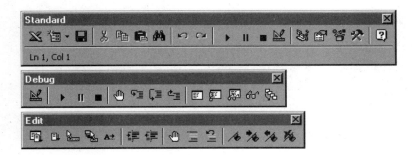

To display any of these toolbars, choose the Toolbars command from the View menu, and then choose the desired toolbar.

Buttons on the Standard Toolbar

The following sections briefly describe the buttons on the Standard toolbar.

The View Microsoft Excel button

The View Microsoft Excel button switches to the Excel window.

The Insert Object button

The Insert Object button inserts a new userform, module, class module, or procedure into your project.

In this chapter, we have been working only with modules. In Chapter 5, we will explore userforms (i.e., custom dialog boxes).

The Save Project button

The Save Project button saves the current project *and* the Excel workbook that hosts it.

Similarly, the Save button in Excel saves the current workbook *and* the project it contains. In other words, you can save from either Excel or the Visual Basic Editor and be assured that all your work is being saved.

The Find button

The Find button opens the Find dialog box, which enables you to search for text.

The Find dialog box offers you many options for controlling the scope of the search and allows you to perform search and replace operations.

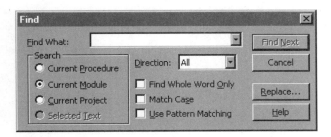

The Run Sub/UserForm button

If you select any routine in a VBA module and then click the Run Sub/UserForm button, the routine is executed. This button will also run a dialog box (userform) when selected. More on this in Chapter 5.

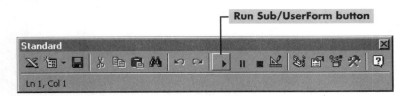

The Design Mode button

This button is used to prevent Excel from firing events that might run event procedures. It also prevents custom controls from responding to user actions. This tool will be explored fully in Chapter 5.

The Project Explorer button

This button displays the Project window.

The Project window (shown below) allows you to view the various elements of your VBA project.

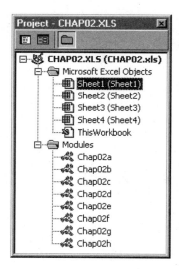

NOTE The Project window has some properties similar to a commandbar (i.e., toolbar) in that it will "dock" to the sides of the VBE window and can be dragged outside of the VBE window. In addition, it will dock to other dockable windows such as the Properties window. To prevent it from docking to the VBE window or other dockable windows, hold down the Ctrl key while dragging it around the screen.

The Properties button

This button displays the Properties window.

Properties button

The Properties window (shown below) allows you to directly manipulate the properties of various project objects including workbooks, worksheets, forms, and controls. Chapters 5 and 8 will cover in greater detail the use of this window.

The Object Browser button

Clicking the Object Browser button displays the Object Browser window.

Object Browser button

The Object Browser window (shown on the following page) shows you all of the programmable objects that are installed and registered on your system—along with their associated properties, methods, and events. You can also use the Object Browser window to browse the routines and module-level variables in your own VBA projects.

This window is divided into three main sections: the Project/Library drop-down listbox (in the top left-hand corner of the window), the Classes listbox, and the Members listbox. You can select different libraries or projects from the Project/Library drop-down listbox, such as the following: libraries that are installed on your system with Excel (including Excel, MSForms, VB, and VBA); all workbooks that are currently open in Excel; any add-in files for which you have established a reference; and any applications that expose OLE object models, including all Office 97 applications as well as Data Access Objects for which you have established a reference. (References are explained in Chapter 7, in the top sidebar on page 355.) The entry for <All Libraries> allows you to browse multiple sets of objects simultaneously.

Selecting Excel from the Project/Library drop-down listbox displays all Excel objects as well as an entry named <globals> in the Classes listbox. After you select an object in the Classes listbox, you can view all the properties, methods, events, and constants for that object in the Members listbox. Selecting an item in the Members listbox displays detailed information in the lower portion of the window. Objects in the hierarchical path above that item and collections of which that item is a member are displayed in green with underlines, indicating that you can click on them to jump directly to their definitions.

To see how the Members listbox works, select VBA from the Project/Library drop-down listbox, and then select Interaction from the Classes listbox—the Members listbox displays a list of interactive VBA functions, including InputBox and MsgBox. Now try selecting Constants from the Classes listbox—the Members listbox displays a list of VBA constants. Or select an Excel workbook from the Project/Library drop-down listbox to view all the modules in each open workbook and all the routines available in each module.

The Object Browser toolbar provides additional functionality as follows:

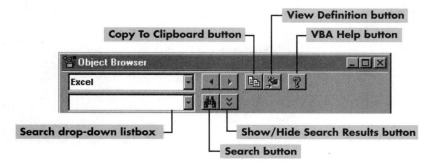

When browsing routines in a workbook, you can use the View Definition button to jump directly to a particular routine in its code module.

Any item you have selected in the Classes listbox or Members listbox can be copied to the clipboard with the Copy To Clipboard button. Click the Paste button on the Standard toolbar to paste the item directly into your code.

Clicking the question mark button displays an online VBA Help topic for the selected item.

You can also search for any Class or Member by entering a search string in the Search drop-down listbox and clicking the Search button. Search results can be shown or hidden using the Show/Hide Search Results button.

The Toolbox button

The Toolbox button is the rightmost button on the Standard toolbar. It displays a toolbox of controls that can be added to custom forms and dialog boxes. More details about this button are provided in Chapter 5.

Buttons on the Debug Toolbar

The following sections describe the buttons on the Debug Toolbar.

The Step Into, Step Over, Step Out, Reset, and Continue buttons

These buttons, shown on the following page, are used in conjunction with stepping through and debugging code.

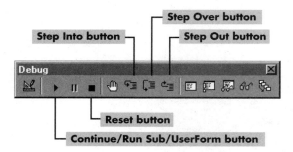

To execute a routine one statement at a time, click the Step Into button one time for each line of code. Clicking Step Into steps through a routine line by line, even stepping through subroutines or functions that the routine calls. Code whose execution is paused because of a line-by-line execution is said to be in "break mode."

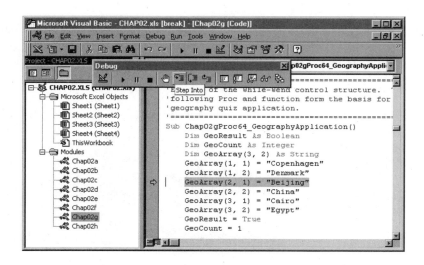

TIP   Pressing the F8 key on your keyboard has the same effect as clicking the Step Into button.

If you do not want to see the line-by-line execution of routines or functions that the original routine calls, you can click the Step Over button when those calls occur. Clicking the Step Over button executes called subroutines without stepping through them.

If you are stepping through a routine called by another routine and want to quickly finish executing the called routine, you can use the Step Out button. The Step Out button completes execution of the current routine and pauses on the next line of the calling routine.

If at any time while stepping through code you want to resume normal routine execution, click the Continue button (which is really the Run Sub/UserForm button). If you want to stop execution completely, click the Reset button.

The Toggle Breakpoint button

The Toggle Breakpoint button allows you to establish breakpoints in your code where execution will stop. Breakpoints are useful for investigating problems in your code; they allow you to stop code execution at a specific point and then step through the code line by line.

To establish a breakpoint in your code, place the insertion point anywhere in the line in the routine where you want the break to occur and then click the Toggle Breakpoint button, which highlights in red the selected line of code (in addition, a large red dot appears to the left of the breakpoint in the module window). When you execute the routine, execution breaks at the selected point. To remove a breakpoint, click the line that contains the breakpoint and then click the Toggle Breakpoint button again.

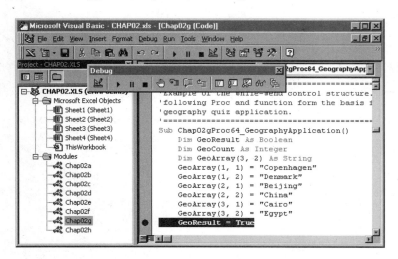

> **TIP** You can also set and remove breakpoints by clicking in the gray margin to the left of the code in the module window. You can remove all breakpoints from all VBA modules by choosing the Clear All Breakpoints command from the Debug menu.

The Quick Watch and Watch Window buttons

You use the Quick Watch and Watch Window buttons to establish and view Watch variables in your code.

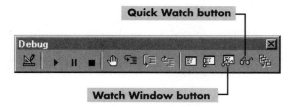

Watch variables, which are simply variables or expressions from your code that are added to the Watch window, are used in conjunction with break mode as powerful tools for debugging code. To specify a Watch variable, select any variable or expression in your code, and then click the Quick Watch button, which displays the Quick Watch dialog box. This dialog box displays the name of the routine, the selected expression, and the current value of the selected expression:

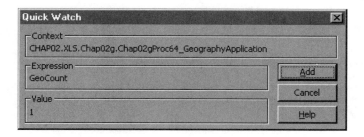

The Quick Watch dialog box includes an Add button; by choosing Add, you can add the selected expression to the Watch list, which is displayed in the Watches window. Let's use the following example routine to look at how you specify a Watch variable:

```
Sub Chap02hProc87_WatchVariables()
    Dim Num1 As Integer
    Dim x As Integer
    For x = 1 To 10
```

```
         Num1 = Num1 + x
     Next
End Sub
```

Before you execute Proc87, add the variable Num1 to the Watch list by high-lighting the variable in Proc87, clicking the Quick Watch button on the Debug toolbar, and then choosing the Add button in the Quick Watch dialog box. The Watches window is displayed (note that this is a dockable window so you can change its size and position as desired):

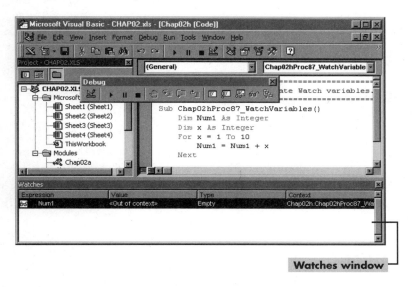

Watches window

Now debug the routine by placing the cursor in Proc89 and clicking the Step Into button, which puts the module in break mode.

Click the Step Into button to begin stepping through the routine. Continue to click the Step Into button to see the routine execute line by line; you see the value of the Num1 Watch variable change in the Watches window. As you loop through the code, the value of Num1 grows with increasing speed. You can add more Watch variables while in break mode by selecting the appropriate expression, clicking the Quick Watch button, and then choosing the Add button. For example, try adding the variable x to the Watch list. You can now watch both variables change as you step through the routine. To remove a Watch variable from the Watch list, select the line for that variable in the Watches window and then press the Delete key on your keyboard.

NOTE If you close the Watch window, you can show it again at any time by clicking the Watch Window button.

TIP You can also view the value of a variable using the Value Tip feature. To use this, position the cursor over any variable while in break mode and a window will pop up showing the value of the variable. You can even select a variable or expression and drag it from your code into the Watches window to add it to the Watch list!

The Locals Window button

The Locals Window button displays the Locals window, which is just like the Watches window except that it automatically contains all the variables within a few lines of the current line of code.

Locals Window button

The Locals window is a very useful tool for watching variables without having to explicitly add them to the Watch list. To explore the Locals window, locate the Proc88 routine and place a breakpoint on the last line (the MsgBox line):

```
Type tEmployee
    Name As String
    Pay As Currency
    Birthdate As Date
End Type

Sub Chap02hProc88_LocalsExample()
    Dim x As Integer
    Dim TotalPay As Currency
    Dim Employees(3) As tEmployee

    Employees(1).Name = "Joe"
    Employees(1).Birthdate = #11/11/66#
    Employees(1).Pay = 30000

    Employees(2).Name = "Mary"
    Employees(2).Birthdate = #12/30/56#
    Employees(2).Pay = 50000

    Employees(3).Name = "Jude"
    Employees(3).Birthdate = #1/5/44#
    Employees(3).Pay = 55000
```

```
For x = 1 To 3
    TotalPay = TotalPay + Employees(x).Pay
Next x

MsgBox "Total pay is " & TotalPay & "."

End Sub
```

Run the routine, and when the breakpoint is encountered, click the Locals Window button. The Locals window will be displayed showing each variable in the routine. Note that arrays and user-defined types can be expanded and collapsed using the plus (+) and minus (-) controls that appear next to them. (This is a feature of the Watches window as well.)

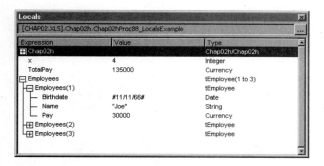

The Immediate Window button

The Immediate Window button displays the Immediate window.

In the Immediate window, you can type VBA statements directly so that they can be executed on a stand-alone basis in real time. For example, display the Immediate window, type in the following statement, and press Enter:

```
MsgBox "Hello World"
```

The statement is executed in real time, and you see a message box that displays the message "Hello World." You can also use the Immediate window to change the values of variables as your code executes.

TIP
Here are a few hints for using the Immediate window: The Immediate window can be very useful for debugging. To set a variable to a new value, just type in <variable> = <value> and press Enter. For example:

```
x = 7
```

To check the value of a variable or expression, type in ?<expression> and press Enter. For example:

```
?x
?Case(Employees(3).Name)
```

The Immediate window can process only one line at a time, but you can enter multiple statements on a line by separating them with colons. The following example runs a loop:

```
For x = 1 to 10: MsgBox x: Next x
```

Keep in mind that you cannot declare variables in the Immediate window using the Dim keyword, but you can create and use new variables by assigning values to them. Variables created in this manner will be of the Variant type.

Editing Tools on the Edit Toolbar

The Visual Basic Editor provides a number of tools to make writing, editing, and navigating through code easy. These tools are located on the Edit toolbar (shown in Figure 2-6). The first five show themselves automatically as you type, which you've probably noticed by now. The following table describes these tools.

Button	Function
List Properties/Methods	Displays a popup that lists the properties and methods available for the object that precedes the period (.).
List Constants	Displays a popup that lists the constants that are valid choices for the property preceding the equals sign (=).
Quick Info	Displays the syntax for a function, method, or procedure your cursor is in.
Parameter Info	Displays information about parameters for the function, method, or procedure currently to the left of the cursor.
Complete Word	Displays a popup of Visual Basic keywords appropriate for the given context. If you select one and press Enter, the keyword is added to whatever you're typing.
Indent	Indents the current line or selected lines.

Button	Function
Outdent	Outdents the current line or selected lines.
Comment Block	Comments out the current line or selected lines by adding an apostrophe at the beginning of the line(s).
Uncomment Block	Uncomments the current line or selected lines by removing the apostrophe from the beginning of the line(s).
Toggle Bookmark	Adds or removes a bookmark (indicated by a blue mark in the left margin) at the current line. Once bookmarks are added, you can use the next two buttons to jump between bookmarked lines.
Next Bookmark	Jumps to the next bookmark in the project.
Previous Bookmark	Jumps to the previous bookmark in the project.
Clear All Bookmarks	Clears all bookmarks.

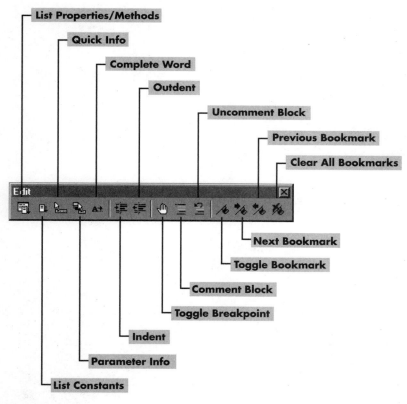

Figure 2-6. *Buttons on the Edit toolbar.*

NOTE   Many of the features available on the Edit toolbar are automatically on by default. For example, the List Properties/Methods feature will automatically pop up its list as you type without you having to request it. These features can be turned on and off using Environment Options, which are described on page 135.

In addition to these tools, one more editing feature enables you to jump to the definition of a variable, method, subroutine, function, or object by using the right mouse button and the Definition command. Just position the cursor on the desired item, right-click it, and choose the Definition command from the pop-up menu. If you used this tool with a variable, for example, you would jump to the Dim statement that declares the variable.

The Record Macro Feature

From the Excel Tools menu, you can select Macro and choose Record New Macro to start the Excel macro recorder.

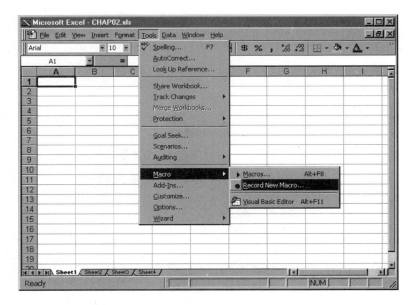

Using the macro recorder can help you to learn VBA and to become familiar with Excel objects, properties, and methods. If you don't know what objects are involved in performing a certain action in Excel, for example, you can turn on the macro recorder, perform the action manually, and then look at the recorded code.

When you record a routine, Excel records all of your actions and writes VBA code that corresponds to those actions. Excel continues to record your actions until you turn off the macro recorder.

Let's experiment by recording one routine. First start the macro recorder and display the Record Macro dialog box. Type a name for your routine in the Macro Name box. (The routine name must be one contiguous string of characters.) In the Description box, replace the default description with this text: *This routine enters data in Range("A1")*.

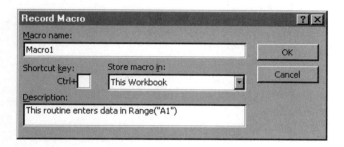

You can assign a shortcut key for the routine by entering a letter in the Shortcut Key edit box. In the Store Macro In box, you can specify where you would like the recorded routine to be placed—in your Personal Macro Workbook, in the current workbook, or in a new workbook.

NOTE The Personal Macro Workbook is a hidden workbook that holds routines that are loaded each time you start Excel. It is saved in Excel's startup directory as PERSONAL.XLS.

For our example, select This Workbook, and then click OK. A Stop Macro toolbar appears in the middle of the screen, and if the status bar is displayed, "Recording" appears at the bottom of the screen.

Now let's record entering data in Range("A1") of Worksheets("Sheet1"). First click the Sheet1 tab at the bottom of the screen to display Sheet1, and then click cell A1. Type the value *100* in the cell, and then press Enter. Click the Stop Macro button to turn off the macro recorder. If you now select the module in which Excel has stored the recorded routine, you see something similar to Proc89:

```
'
' Chap02hProc89_Proc
' This routine enters data in Range("A1").
'
'
Sub Chap02hProc89_RecordedProc()
    Sheets("Sheet1").Select
    Range("A1").Select
    ActiveCell.FormulaR1C1 = "100"
    Range("A2").Select
End Sub
```

When Proc89 is run, it performs the same actions that you performed while the macro recorder was on. You have probably noticed that the code the macro recorder generates is not necessarily the most efficient code possible. For example, the most efficient way to set the Value property of Range("A1") on Worksheets("Sheet1") to 100 is as follows:

```
Sub Chap02hProc90_EfficientProc()
    Worksheets("Sheet1").Range("A1").Value = 100
End Sub
```

> **TIP**
>
> Excel's macro recorder often goes a bit overboard in recording code—it records every property setting for an object, for example, even if only one property setting was changed while the macro recorder was on. That being the case, you'll want to be careful about incorporating recorded code directly in your VBA applications. If you do so, ensure optimal performance by editing the code to remove any unnecessary statements.

Other VBA Editing Tools and Features

In addition to the tools described so far, VBA provides several other editing tools and features that will help you write code efficiently. We'll take a brief look at those here.

VBA Online Help

As mentioned in Chapter 1, complete online help is available for VBA in Excel. You access VBA Help in Excel or the Visual Basic Editor by selecting Contents/Index from the Help menu (in Excel you must then select Microsoft Excel Visual Basic Reference from the Contents tab of the Help dialog box). Note, however, that you can also jump immediately to VBA Help by pressing the F1 key while a VBA module is active. In fact, if you select any VBA keyword, function, object, method, or property in a VBA module and press F1, the help topic for the selected item is displayed immediately. From VBA Help, you can access lists of Excel objects, methods, and properties as well as information about VBA functions, statements, and keywords. To search quickly for help on a specific topic, enter a topic in the search box at the top of the Index tab in the Help Topics dialog box.

> **TIP**
>
> Help topics for all properties and methods provide code examples to demonstrate how to set each property and call each method correctly. If you want, you can copy and paste these code examples directly into a VBA module to incorporate them in your own routines.

Syntax Checking

If you are typing VBA code as you read this chapter, you might have already encountered VBA's syntax checking feature, which checks your syntax as you type keywords for variable declarations, constant declarations, control structures, and functions. If your code's syntax is not correct, VBA alerts you by displaying an error message. If you ignore the error and keep on typing, VBA colors the erroneous code red to signal that it has been entered incorrectly.

VBA also recognizes object, property, and method names as you type them. If you enter such names correctly, VBA follows a standard capitalization scheme to format these names for you. The first letter of object, property, and method names is always capitalized, and if a property or method name is formed from two words, the first letter of the second word is capitalized as well (as in ReadOnly). All other letters are lowercase. Because VBA formats your object, property, and method names as you type them, you can check the accuracy of your code as you work. For example, if you enter a property name and VBA does not capitalize the first letter, you have likely misspelled the name and will need to go back and correct it.

Environment Options

By choosing the Options command from the Tools menu, you can access several option settings that affect the way code in VBA modules is entered, executed, and displayed. Under the General tab, you can specify options for grid size on forms, breaking on errors, and compilation methods. Under the Editor tab, you can set tab and indent widths, control automatic editor features such as syntax checking, and require variable declaration. Under the Editor Format tab, you can select the font and font size for your VBA code. You can also select the foreground and background colors for various components of VBA code, including keywords, comments, erroneous code, and plain code. By default, keywords are displayed in blue, comments in green, breakpoints in white on a red background, and erroneous code in red.

SUMMARY

Visual Basic for Applications is a powerful programming language. This chapter has briefly summarized the language, introducing you to its basic components. The rest of this book builds from the material introduced here by explaining how you can use VBA to control Excel objects.

Let's quickly summarize the main aspects of the VBA language before you move on to Chapter 3 and begin learning about using objects to create applications. Review the list on the next page.

- VBA supports variables of numerous data types: Boolean, Byte, Integer, Long, Single, Double, Currency, Date, Object, String, Variant, and user-defined.

- VBA supports arrays, which are single-dimensional or multidimensional groups of data that are all of the same data type.

- VBA constants are used to hold constant values during routine execution.

- VBA provides two different types of routines: subroutines, which can run on a stand-alone basis, and functions, which can return values.

- VBA variables, constants, and routines can have different levels of scope: variables and constants can have procedure-level, module-level, or project-level scope; routines can have module-level or project-level scope.

- VBA offers several powerful control structures, including If-Then-Else, For-Next, While-Wend, Do-Loop, Select-Case, and For-Each-Next.

- The VBA With statement is a powerful tool that you use to abbreviate object references.

- VBA offers numerous debugging and editing tools, including a Project Window, an Object Browser, breakpoints, Watch variables, an interactive break mode, and full online help.

After mastering the material in this chapter, you are now ready to move on and learn more about Excel objects. VBA is often referred to as the "glue" by which Excel objects are attached to one another in creating VBA applications. You have learned most of what there is to know about the glue. Now comes the task of learning how to apply the glue to the objects.

3

Sample Application 1: West Coast Airways

In this chapter, we learn about a few more objects and VBA features, and we use the concepts addressed in the first two chapters to examine an application built in Microsoft Excel.

Objects and Techniques Used in the Sample Application

In Chapter 1, we looked briefly at the purpose and function of a few Excel objects: Application, Workbook, Worksheet, and Range. The West Coast Airways application uses all of these objects plus a few others. In the next few sections, we'll cover the following new objects and topics:

- Shape objects

- Controls and event procedures

- The CodeName property (which enables you to reference objects without going through a collection)

Shape Objects and the Shapes Collection

The Shape object represents any graphical object placed "on top" of a worksheet or chart. All Shape objects on a particular sheet are represented by the Shapes collection. A Shapes collection can include such diverse objects as bitmaps and other kinds of pictures, rectangles, lines, text boxes, WordArt, and even controls (which we'll discuss in the next section). With the exception of controls, the user can create and manipulate most Shape objects by using the OfficeArt Drawing toolbar. OfficeArt is common among most Microsoft Office 97 applications, and the Shape object hierarchy in these applications is nearly identical. (Differences exist only because each Office application implements custom additions to the basic model.)

NOTE The Shapes collection replaces the DrawingObjects collection and associated objects in previous versions of Excel. The Drawing-Objects collection is still supported, however, for backward compatibility with applications developed in previous versions of Excel.

Each type of Shape object has a unique set of properties and methods. Note, however, that all Shape objects also have many properties and methods in common. Listed below are the properties and methods shared by all Shape objects and the Shapes collection object.

Shape object properties

Left, Top, Width, and Height: Determine the position and size of a Shape on the worksheet or chart that contains it.

Name: A text string used to identify the Shape object. It can be used as an index in the Shapes collection when referencing the Shape object in code. The name property can be assigned manually by selecting the Shape object, typing its name into Excel's Name Box on the Formula bar, and pressing Enter.

Type: A constant that identifies the type of Shape object (e.g., msoLine, msoAutoShape, msoPicture). Lists of constants can be found in VBA Help and the Object Browser.

Fill: Returns a FillFormat object that itself contains properties to control the color, patterns, and interior texture of the Shape object.

Line: Returns a LineFormat object that contains properties to control the color, weight, and borderline pattern of the Shape object.

Shadow: Returns a ShadowFormat object that contains properties to control the shadow effect of the Shape object.

TextFrame: Returns a TextFrame object that contains subobjects to control the content and formatting of text displayed in the Shape object.

Visible: Determines whether the Shape object can be seen by the user.

OnAction: Stores the name of a VBA routine that will run when the Shape object is clicked at runtime.

Shape object methods

Copy: Copies the Shape object to the clipboard.

Cut: Copies the Shape object to the clipboard and deletes it from the worksheet or chart that contains it.

Flip: Flips a Shape object either horizontally or vertically.

Delete: Deletes the Shape object from the worksheet or chart.

IncrementLeft: Moves a Shape object horizontally a specified number of points. A positive number moves the shape right; a negative number moves it left.

IncrementTop: Moves a Shape object vertically a specified number of points. A positive number moves the shape down; a negative number moves it up.

IncrementRotation: Rotates a Shape object a specified number of degrees in a specified direction.

Shapes collection methods

The Shapes collection has a series of Add methods designed to add different types of shapes. Here are a few examples:

AddShape: Adds an AutoShape object.

AddPicture: Adds a picture-type Shape object.

AddLabel: Adds a label-type Shape object.

The ShapeRange object

One other important object related to shapes is the ShapeRange object. The ShapeRange object represents any group of shapes. It is analogous to a multiple selection of shapes in the user interface, but a ShapeRange object can represent any group of Shape objects, whether the objects are selected or not. In this way, it acts as a collection object.

This object is useful for manipulating many objects as a group or for iterating through a group of related objects. The ShapeRange object has most of the same properties and methods as a Shape object—however, such properties and methods apply to the group of shapes as a whole rather than to a specific individual shape.

The ShapeRange object can be created from the Shapes collection by calling the Range method and passing an array of Shape object names:

```
Dim MyShapeRange As ShapeRange
Set MyShapeRange = ActiveSheet.Shapes.Range ( _
    Array("Utah","California","Idaho"))
```

Once the ShapeRange object is created, you can manipulate it as a single Shape object. For example, the following moves all the Shape objects in the ShapeRange object 10 points to the right.

```
MyShapeRange.IncrementLeft 10
```

You can also iterate through the Shape objects in the ShapeRange object using a For Each Next loop:

```
For Each StateShape in MyShapeRange
    MsgBox StateShape.Name
Next StateShape
```

Controls and Event Procedures

Controls are special types of objects that you can place on worksheets, charts, and custom dialog boxes (userforms). For example, the command buttons in the West Coast Airways sample application (in file CHAP03.XLS) are controls. In addition to having properties and methods, controls have a predefined set of events. An event is some type of action (e.g., a user action, such as clicking a mouse button); an "event procedure" is the code, or routine, that creates the response to the action. For example, the command buttons in the sample application have "Click" events; whenever a button is clicked, it triggers the event procedure to respond to the Click event for that button. Although controls will be covered in depth in Chapter 5, we will learn the basics here to understand the West Coast Airways sample application.

Placing controls on a sheet

To place controls on a sheet (worksheet or chart), you need to use the Control Toolbox toolbar. Start by opening a new, blank workbook in Excel. Display the Control Toolbox by selecting the View Toolbars menu in Excel and then selecting Control Toolbox.

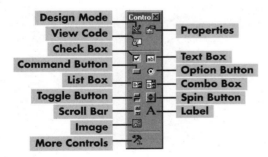

The Control Toolbox toolbar provides a set of standard common controls, such as command buttons, option buttons, list boxes, text boxes, and others, for use in Office 97 applications. Go ahead and try placing a command button on a worksheet: click the Command button on the Control Toolbox, and then click the worksheet to place the button.

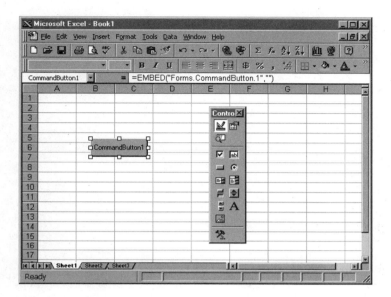

NOTE In Excel 97, controls are available both on the Control Toolbox toolbar and on the Forms toolbar. The controls available on the Control Toolbox toolbar are all ActiveX controls that come with several events for which VBA procedures can be written; these controls can be used on worksheets and userforms. The controls on the Forms toolbar are "standard Excel worksheet controls" that originated in Excel version 5; these controls really have only one event—the Click event—which is set by assigning a subroutine to the OnActive property. The controls on the Forms toolbar can be used on worksheets and charts (as well as on dialogsheets for applications created in past versions of Excel).

Setting control properties

Once a control is placed, you generally need to customize its property settings. In the case of a command button, the first property you will want to set is its Caption property, which is the text displayed on the button. To set control properties without writing code, use the Properties window. First make sure the control is selected. Then click the Properties button on the Control Toolbox toolbar. The Properties window will appear. Now change the Caption property of your button to "Knock, knock".

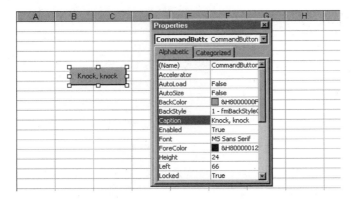

Writing event handling code for controls

Once you've set key properties for the control, you'll need to write code to respond to its events. A control typically has many events that are triggered by various user actions and system actions. For example, a command button has events for when the control is clicked with the mouse, when the control gets or loses focus for user input, when the mouse button is depressed while the mouse pointer is placed over the control, when the mouse cursor is moved or released while over the control, and when a drag-and-drop operation involving the control is performed with the mouse.

Before we write code for the button's Click event, we need to view the control's event procedures. Select the control, and then click the View Code button on the Control Toolbox toolbar. This activates the Visual Basic Editor and opens a code module containing predefined routines, or event procedures, that respond to the control's events. The Procedure Selector lists the available event procedures for the command button control.

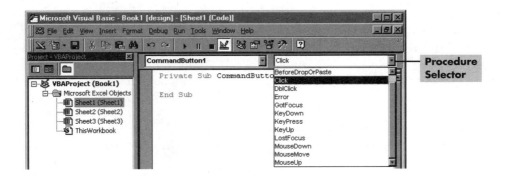

Notice that the code module is called "Sheet1". This means that the module of code is for a specific sheet in the workbook. Every Excel object (workbooks, worksheets, and charts) listed in the Project window has a code module behind it. If you are familiar with VB, this is analogous to "code behind forms;" in Office development, you can think of it as "code behind documents." Look in the Object Selector for this module (next to the Procedure Selector) and you will see the relationship between a control and the object in which it resides. Your command button is listed here along with "Worksheet" (a representation of the worksheet and its events) and "(General)" (the area of the module for defining module-level variables and constants).

If you placed additional controls on this sheet, they would also appear in the Object Selector. VB developers will appreciate the similarity between this representation and the way controls on forms are represented in code modules.

Write the following code, which will create a response to the command button's Click event:

```
Private Sub CommandButton1_Click()
    MsgBox "Who's there?"
End Sub
```

Running event handling code

After writing the code, switch back to Excel and click the command button. The button is selected, but no Click event occurs. So how can you test the code you just wrote? The answer lies in a new mode of operation for Excel 97. When you are placing a control and writing code, Excel enters what is called "design mode." In design mode, events do not fire and controls can be selected by clicking them. (A depressed Design Mode button on the Control Toolbox toolbar indicates that you are in design mode.) To run your code, you have to exit design mode by clicking the Design Mode button.

Once you've exited design mode, click the new control button again to run your code and produce the following message box:

Referencing Controls and Other Objects Directly (Without Going Through a Collection)

Let's examine one final topic before jumping into the sample application. Up to this point in the book, we've been referring to objects in code by indexing the collection to which they belong. For example, if we wanted to reference Sheet1, we would write the following code:

```
Application.Workbooks(1).Worksheets("Sheet1")
```

How would we reference a control on a sheet if we wanted to display its caption? As it turns out, controls are members of the OLEObjects collection, which is itself a property of Worksheet and Chart objects. To determine the caption of our command button, we could write the following code (the Object property of the OLEObject gets us "inside" the control):

```
MsgBox ActiveSheet.OLEObjects("CommandButton1").Object.Caption
```

You probably noticed that the control's name, CommandButton1, was available in its Property window as "(Name)". This represents a read-only property called CodeName. You use the CodeName to refer to a control directly in code without going through a collection object. For example, switch Excel back to design mode and modify your command button's Click event handler, as follows:

```
Private Sub CommandButton1_Click()
    MsgBox "Who's there?"
    CommandButton1.Caption = "Bill"
End Sub
```

This code references the button through its CodeName, CommandButton1, rather than through the OLEObjects collection. Exit design mode and click the button. The caption changes to "Bill." Referencing the control in this way can be very convenient. (The concept of referencing controls using a CodeName comes from VBA.)

This ability to reference an object using a CodeName applies not only to controls but also to Excel objects—such as worksheets, charts, and the workbook itself—that have code modules attached to them and therefore appear in the VBE Project window. To demonstrate this, modify the Click routine one more time, as follows:

```
Private Sub CommandButton1_Click()
    MsgBox "Who's there?"
    CommandButton1.Caption = "Bill"
    With Sheet2
        .Activate
```

```
            .Range("A1").Value = "Bill who?"
      End With
End Sub
```

Run this routine and observe what happens. We're manipulating Sheet2 by referring to it directly through its CodeName. Note that Sheet2 is the CodeName of the sheet whose Name property also happens to be Sheet2. To see this, click the Properties button of the Control Toolbox toolbar while Sheet2 is active. A list of properties for the sheet appears. You'll notice that Sheet2 is the value of the "(Name)" entry at the top of this list (the CodeName property) and the "Name" entry near the end of the list (the Name property).

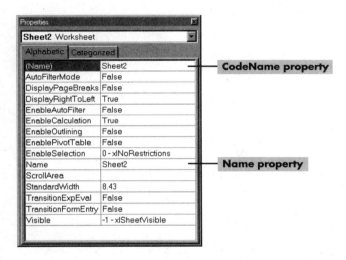

<table>
<tr><td>Properties</td><td></td></tr>
<tr><td colspan="2">Sheet2 Worksheet</td></tr>
<tr><td colspan="2">Alphabetic | Categorized</td></tr>
<tr><td>(Name)</td><td>Sheet2</td><td>— CodeName property</td></tr>
<tr><td>AutoFilterMode</td><td>False</td><td></td></tr>
<tr><td>DisplayPageBreaks</td><td>False</td><td></td></tr>
<tr><td>DisplayRightToLeft</td><td>True</td><td></td></tr>
<tr><td>EnableAutoFilter</td><td>False</td><td></td></tr>
<tr><td>EnableCalculation</td><td>True</td><td></td></tr>
<tr><td>EnableOutlining</td><td>False</td><td></td></tr>
<tr><td>EnablePivotTable</td><td>False</td><td></td></tr>
<tr><td>EnableSelection</td><td>0 - xlNoRestrictions</td><td></td></tr>
<tr><td>Name</td><td>Sheet2</td><td>— Name property</td></tr>
<tr><td>ScrollArea</td><td></td><td></td></tr>
<tr><td>StandardWidth</td><td>8.43</td><td></td></tr>
<tr><td>TransitionExpEval</td><td>False</td><td></td></tr>
<tr><td>TransitionFormEntry</td><td>False</td><td></td></tr>
<tr><td>Visible</td><td>-1 - xlSheetVisible</td><td></td></tr>
</table>

NOTE   Changing a control's Name property also changes its CodeName. For workbooks, worksheets, and charts, however, Name and CodeName are independent of each other. Changing the Name property of one of these objects does not change its CodeName. The only way to change the CodeName of a workbook, worksheet, or chart is by switching to design mode and editing the contents of the "(Name)" field of the Property window.

Control Scope

When referring to controls by CodeName, keep in mind that controls have scope only within the objects that contain them. You will need to qualify the control name with its container name if you are referring to the control outside of its container's code module. For example, to refer to CommandButton1 from a module other than Sheet1's module, you would need to refer to it as follows:

```
Sheet1.CommandButton1.Caption = "Bill"
```

Referring to an object via its CodeName can make your code more readable. Referring to an object via its collection is also useful when you need to be more explicit. You will probably find yourself using both referencing methods in your VBA applications.

A Look at the West Coast Airways Sample Application

If you have access to a computer as you read, start Excel and open the file named CHAP03.XLS on the companion CD packaged with this book.

The sample application we're looking at uses as its subject a fictitious airline named West Coast Airways. West Coast Airways does business in the western United States, serving Arizona, California, Colorado, Idaho, Montana, Nevada, Oregon, Utah, Washington, and Wyoming. The application was developed solely in Excel and is used by the company and specifically by its president to track summary financial data for each West Coast Airways sales office—the company has one sales office in each state in which it does business. The application presents revenue and profit data in various formats for analysis. An example of how such data is presented for the state of Washington is shown here.

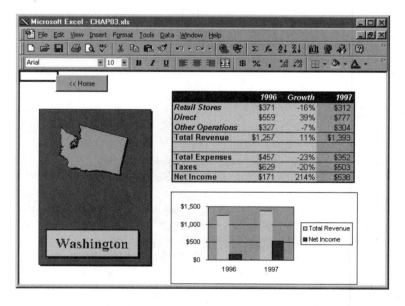

Users move from one form, or Excel sheet, to another by clicking buttons. (The pictures and maps you see on these forms were created in drawing programs and imported as bitmaps.)

The Splash Form

As soon as CHAP03.XLS is opened, Excel displays the main form of the application, the Splash form. The Splash form is used to access the various other forms in the application and has three main elements: a title box, graphics, and buttons on a blue background.

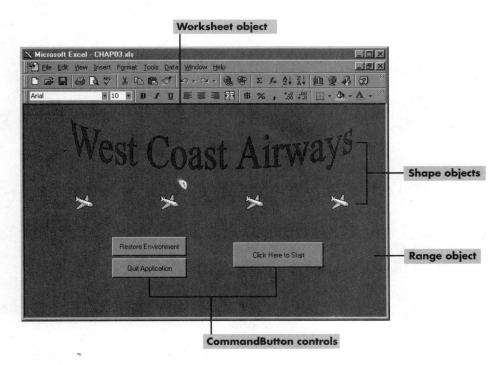

Here is a list of the objects used to create the elements on the Splash form.

Worksheet object: Serves as the basis for the form; the whole area that makes up the form is an Excel worksheet.

Shape objects: The title at the top of the screen, "West Coast Airways," is an Excel Shape object (or more specifically, a WordArt object). The four airplanes are Shape objects as well (specifically, bitmap images).

CommandButton controls: Three CommandButton controls appear on the screen: Click Here To Start, Restore Environment, and Quit Application. The user can choose these buttons to view the Home form, restore the Excel environment, or quit the application. Notice that the Click Here To Start button flies the planes before activating the Home form.

Range object: It isn't obvious, but the Range object has been used to design this form. The blue background is a range of worksheet cells that have been colored blue so that the screen looks like a form instead of a spreadsheet.

The Home Form

On the Splash form, choose the Click Here To Start button to display the Home form. The Home form shows a color-coded map of the western United States, which gives the user a quick view of how West Coast Airways is doing throughout the region. The Home form contains these objects:

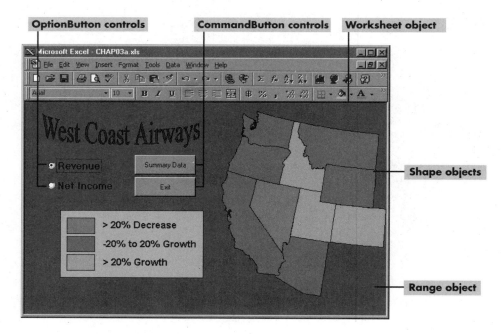

Following is a description of the objects on the Home form.

CommandButton controls: Clicking the Summary Data button activates the SummaryData form. Clicking the Exit button takes you back to the Splash form.

Shape objects: The map is made up of ten Shape objects. These objects are bitmaps; each depicts a state in which West Coast Airways does business. Each state Shape object is connected to a VBA routine that runs when the shape is clicked. The routine that is run is connected to the Shape object via its OnAction property. The logo and legend are also made up of Shape objects.

TIP The OnAction property can be set by right-clicking the Shape object, and then selecting the Assign Macro command. Once the macro is assigned, you'll need to hold down the Ctrl key to select the Shape object without activating the routine. Note that this mechanism for attaching code to an object is very different from responding to events in a control. This is because Shape objects are not controls—they are graphical objects in the workbook. You can use the Caller property of the Application object within an OnAction subroutine to determine the name of the object that was clicked to force execution of the subroutine. See the GotoStateForm subroutine in the sample application to see this technique in action.

OptionButton controls: Two OptionButton controls—Revenue and Net Income—are displayed on the left side of the form.

Range object: A range of gray cells that lies behind the other objects.

Worksheet object: The basis for the Home form.

The Home form gives the user an immediate impression of how the company is doing in the different states—in terms either of revenue or net income (profit). By selecting either the Revenue or the Net Income optionbutton, the user launches a routine that updates the map with the appropriate data. The routine retrieves the numbers for percentage changes in revenue (growth) or net income from the state forms and colors the individual states appropriately. Try selecting the Revenue and Net Income optionbuttons, and notice how the states change color. The user can choose the Summary Data button to activate the SummaryData form or click any of the individual states on the map to activate the state form for the selected state. Try clicking some of the states on the map form to activate the respective state forms. Recall that you can return to the Home form from a state form by clicking the Home button. After viewing data in the Home form and various state forms, click the Home button to return to the Home form.

NOTE Although Excel provides mapping technology (the DataMap object) that allows you to create geographical maps for displaying data, our sample application is more appropriately implemented using simple bitmaps. The maps used in the West Coast Airways application were created using a third-party graphics mapping package.

The SummaryData Form

The first button on the Home form is the Summary Data button. Click this button now to run a routine that activates the SummaryData form, which summarizes data for all states served by the company. The SummaryData form contains a number of objects.

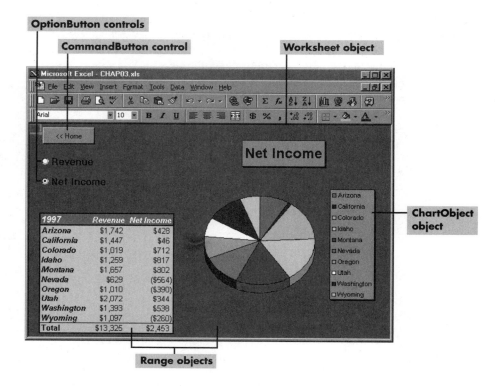

A description of the objects follows.

CommandButton control: Choosing the Home button activates the Home form.

OptionButton controls: The Revenue and Net Income OptionButton controls determine which type of data is displayed on the chart.

Range objects: Comprises the cells in the table, which summarizes the data for the whole company. The table contains formulas that are linked to the individual state forms; if the data on one of the state forms changes, Excel automatically updates the table on the SummaryData form. A range of gray cells also lies behind the other objects.

ChartObject object: Beside the table is a ChartObject object—or what is known as an on-sheet chart. As mentioned earlier, Excel uses two types of objects for charts: a chart that floats as a graphical object on a sheet, known as a ChartObject object; and a chart that exists on a separate sheet by itself, known as a Chart object. The on-sheet chart on the SummaryData form displays the data from the table in the form of a three-dimensional pie chart. The chart includes a legend and a title and is automatically updated if the table changes.

Worksheet object: The basis for the SummaryData form.

Selecting either the Revenue or Net Income optionbutton changes the data displayed in the chart. The ChartObject object linked to the data in the table displays either "Revenue" or "Net Income" in the title above the chart. Notice the number formatting applied to the data in the table—all numbers are formatted as currency, and negative numbers are enclosed in parentheses.

The State Forms

Each state form shows summary financial information about a specific state. To display a state form, click a state on the map on the Home form. Clicking Utah, for example, runs a VBA routine that activates the Utah form. A state form contains several Excel objects:

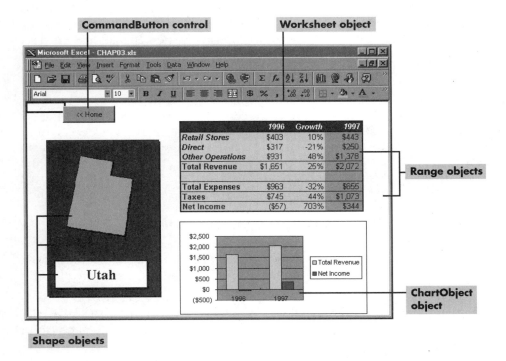

A description of these objects follows.

CommandButton control: The button at the top of the sheet is the Home button; clicking it activates the Home form.

Shape objects: Each state form includes a map of the selected state in the form of an imported bitmap. There is also a gray rectangular Shape object behind the state map and a Shape object with the text name of the state beneath the map.

Range objects: In the upper right portion of the screen, a table displays financial data specific to the selected state. This table is a range of cells in which data has been entered; the cells have been formatted using various colors and special effects to make them visually appealing. Note that a range of cells lies behind the other objects on the form; the gridlines have been removed to give the cells the appearance of plain white space.

ChartObject object: The on-sheet chart graphically displays the data from the range of cells above it and is linked to the cells. If the data in the cells changes, the ChartObject object is automatically updated.

Worksheet object: The basis for the State form.

The Utah form shows summary financial data for West Coast Airways business in the state of Utah. You'll notice that the table in the upper right portion of the form displays data for 1996 and 1997, along with the percentage difference for various values between those two years. The chart in the lower right portion of the form is linked to the table. The map of Utah and the text under the map indicate for which state the data is being displayed. Notice that the map is color coded based on the percentage change in revenue from 1996 to 1997. If the revenue decreases by more than 20 percent, the map is red; if the change is between −20 percent and 20 percent, the map is blue; if the increase is greater than 20 percent, the map is green. After reviewing the data for Utah, you can click the Home button to run a routine that activates the Home form. On the Home form, try clicking on some of the other states on the map. You'll see that each of the state forms is constructed in the same manner.

Flaws in the West Coast Airways Application

Because the West Coast Airways application is so simple, it would probably serve best as a prototype rather than as an actual information system. Looking at the application critically reveals several flaws that would limit its use in a real-world setting. Let's look at its flaws and some alternatives.

First, that the application only allows for manual entry of data. However, the application could be set up so that the manager for each state's operation could enter data in the separate state forms and then forward the forms to the company's Finance Department via e-mail. There the forms could be combined with the rest of the data for the West Coast Airways system or the state forms could use database queries that would import data from a corporate database directly into the state forms.

The second flaw involves protection of data. The application has not been designed to protect the data in the forms or the individual objects that reside on the forms. In the tables on the various state forms or on the SummaryData form, any user can enter any data in any of the cells. A real-world application, on the other hand, would use different levels of protection. Some elements of the application would be fully protected, and other elements would allow for different levels of access so that only certain users could change or enter certain values.

The application's third flaw lies in some of the Excel interface artifacts that are displayed on the screen. For example, unless you've changed your menu and toolbar settings manually, the standard Excel menubar with all the standard menus is displayed at the top of the Excel screen, and some Excel toolbars are visible. A professional application would not allow these or any other Excel artifacts to be displayed in order to give the impression that a true stand-alone application—not an Excel routine—is being used.

The fourth flaw in the application is that it does not provide any mechanism for printing or distributing data. The user could choose the Print command from the Excel File menu and print any screen; however, this possibility might not be obvious to a user who is not familiar with Excel. A professional application would provide a simple interface to allow the user to print data and might also allow the user to distribute the data over e-mail.

All of these flaws are easily eliminated by taking advantage of Excel's more advanced objects—objects that deal with database access, control of user input, interaction with e-mail systems, and the Excel environment. We won't fix these flaws here, but in later chapters we examine the more advanced Excel objects that allow you to build a fully functional information system.

Exploring the West Coast Airways Application

Thus far, we've taken a look at the functionality of the West Coast Airways application and reviewed some of the development techniques used to create the application. Take some time and explore the code and objects used to construct the application. To get you started, here's a description of the modules included in the application.

Module	Description
Module1	Contains the majority of routines for the application, many of which are called by event procedures connected to command buttons and option buttons.
	One variable in this module worthy of note is the public variable gsrMaps, which is found in the declarations section of Module1. This variable refers to a ShapeRange object containing each of the 10 state maps that constitute the large map on the Home form. This ShapeRange object is used extensively to manage the format of and interaction with the large map.

(continued)

continued

Module	Description
wsSplash	This module contains event procedures for each of the three command button controls on the related Splash form.
wsHome	This module contains event procedures for each command button and option button control on the related Home form.
wsSummaryData	This module contains event procedures for each command button and option button control on the related SummaryData form.
wsState*Name*	This module, one instance of which exists for each State form, contains event procedures for the command button on the related State form. (The italicized portion of the name refers to a variable.)

FYI

Naming Conventions

The code in this and subsequent sample applications uses a naming convention for variables, constants, and routines that makes the code more maintainable by teams of developers. In a nutshell, the convention adds prefixes to names used in code to indicate both scope and data type. Examples of prefixes used in the code for this chapter include the following:

Scope	Prefixes
g	Public or global
m	Module
none	Local

Data Type	Prefixes
n	Integer
s	String
b	Boolean
rng	Range
ws	Worksheet
vnt	Variant
obj	Object

The two types of prefixes are added next to each other so that a Boolean variable of module scope, for example, would get the prefix "mb". This prefix lets developers know that they should use caution when setting this variable to a value since it could be used throughout the module, and that they should assign only a True or False value to the variable. You might want to consider using your own naming conventions for any serious VBA development efforts you undertake.

Looking Ahead

If you have taken the time to understand the West Coast Airways application, congratulations! Although it isn't really suitable as a full-fledged information system, the concepts it illustrates are critical, and if you have mastered those covered in this chapter you are well on your way to building powerful information systems in Excel.

The rest of the chapters in this book cover more advanced topics associated with more complicated Excel objects, including database access, data flow, control of user input, and e-mail integration. Mastering these advanced topics and the more complicated objects in Excel will allow you to transform applications such as West Coast Airways into full-fledged information systems. The discussion of such advanced topics begins with the next chapter, "Building Information Systems with Pivottables and Charts."

SUMMARY

This chapter introduced Shape objects and the Shapes collection, the use of controls on sheets, the concept of event procedures, and the use of the CodeName property to refer to controls and other objects in code. The following list summarizes the key points.

- The Shapes collection represents all the graphical objects, or Shape objects, residing on a particular sheet or chart. The ShapeRange object can be used to manipulate a group of Shape objects as a single object.

- Controls are special objects that can be placed on worksheets, charts, and userforms.

- You can set a control's properties manually by using the Properties window.

- Controls initiate events that you can write code to respond to. This code resides in special routines called event procedures.

- Excel's design mode enables you to place controls and write event-handling code without needing to worry about the events actually firing.

- Certain Excel objects such as worksheets and charts have code modules behind them. These code modules contain event-handling code for that object and any controls placed on it.

- Both controls and Excel objects with code modules can be referred to directly in code using the CodeName property.

- Shape objects do not provide events as controls do, but they do have an OnAction property that allows them to run a routine when clicked.

- Routines called by an OnAction property can determine the object that called them using the Application.Caller property.

- Adopting a naming convention for development efforts can promote more maintainable code.

Developing Information
Systems and Designing
Custom Interfaces

4

Building Information Systems with Pivottables and Charts

This chapter describes how best to use Microsoft Excel objects to build the data analysis components of information systems. We take an in-depth look at two of the most powerful objects in Excel used for this purpose—pivottables and charts—and examine their major properties. We review numerous example routines that show you how to use Microsoft Visual Basic for Applications (VBA) to manipulate these two objects. The example routines for this chapter can be found in the CHAP04-1.XLS and CHAP04-2.XLS files on the companion CD packaged with this book.

We combine the concepts introduced in this chapter with those in Chapter 5 to construct the second sample application in Chapter 6.

Using Excel to Create Data Analysis Tools

Excel is an ideal development platform for creating data analysis tools that can be used with information systems. Although most people probably think of Excel as "just a spreadsheet," it is actually a large set of programmable data analysis objects. In fact, Excel offers what is probably the richest and most powerful library of data analysis objects available in any development platform. Excel objects themselves are extremely powerful, and the manner in which they are connected to one another and to other components of an information system is a vital part of their utility in a system.

Corporations throughout the world have access to almost limitless amounts of data—for example, corporate databases and other sources contain data on sales, demographics, trends, competitive products, and so forth. Yet most corporations cannot effectively convert this data to useful information. How many corporate managers, for example, can easily determine the sales level of one of their products in a particular region? Can they access this information with a couple of mouse clicks, or does gathering the information require several people working for hours or even days? Such data certainly exists somewhere (most likely in a database); however, the speed at which the data can be converted to useful information depends on the information system that the company uses. Companies with systems that allow employees to communicate and analyze information rapidly enjoy a competitive advantage in the marketplace. By using Excel objects, you can develop data analysis tools that are capable of analyzing large amounts of data in less time and give users greater access to information—thereby increasing the likelihood that they will make better decisions.

Data analysis applications developed in Microsoft Excel 97 tend to take on a basic architecture. A flow diagram of such an information system in Excel is shown in Figure 4-1.

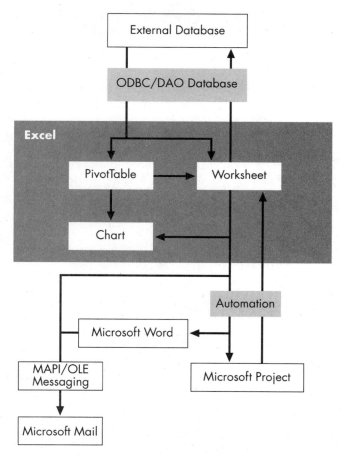

Figure 4-1. *The flow of data through an Excel information system.*

In data analysis applications developed in Excel 97, data is usually read from an external database into a pivottable or a worksheet range and then displayed in a chart. The user is then given the option of changing the data and even distributing it in various ways—for example, via e-mail or in a printed report.

The rest of this chapter concentrates on the components shown in the "Excel" box in Figure 4-1 and focuses in particular on the PivotTable and Chart objects. Other components in the diagram are explained briefly.

Excel's Data Analysis Objects

At the core of Excel's data analysis capabilities are two objects: PivotTable and Chart. These objects, along with several others contained in them, are the basic building blocks for creating the data analysis components of information systems. You must understand these objects if you are to incorporate them effectively in your applications, so we will look in detail at these two objects and the objects they contain.

The PivotTable Object

A PivotTable object is a table that resides on an Excel worksheet and is used to display large amounts of data in almost any configuration and any form that you choose—without you having to write code for querying and handling the data. The pivottable is one of the most advanced data analysis tools available in any software product or development environment. You can use a PivotTable object to perform lightning-fast queries from large data sets; the data sets can originate from an external database or from a range on an Excel worksheet.

When developers write applications that query databases, they often have problems with querying, data handling, and speed. Pivottables, however, address all three of these problems in the following manner:

- **Querying:** Pivottables do much of the work of generating queries. The structure of the pivottable often allows you to perform complex queries using only a single statement.

- **Data handling:** After data is queried from a database, it must be placed somewhere. The dynamic structure of the pivottable enables the table to adjust its size automatically to accommodate the data that has been queried, relieving you of the task of writing code to calculate the space needed to display data.

- **Speed:** Pivottable queries are many times faster than queries performed directly from a disk-based database. Pivottables achieve this speed advantage because they query data sets that are stored in RAM rather than on disk.

A pivottable can be created in one of two ways:

- Manually, by choosing the PivotTable Report command from the Data menu and stepping through the PivotTable Wizard

- By using the PivotTableWizard method of the Worksheet object in a VBA routine

If you have never worked with a pivottable before, step through the manual process first so that you can see all of the setup options available.

FYI

The PivotTable Object Is for Importing Data Only

The PivotTable object can be used only for importing data; you cannot enter data in a pivottable and save it with the table or export it back to the source database. If you try to enter data in a pivottable, Excel displays the error message "Cannot change this part of a PivotTable."

Excel does, however, offer ways of getting around this unidirectional flow of data in the pivottable. For example, you can copy data out of a pivottable to a range on a worksheet, make changes, export the data back to the source database directly, and then call the RefreshTable method on the pivottable to cause the new data to appear in the table. Chapter 7 discusses external database access in detail, and the sample application in Chapter 9 shows how to update the source data of a pivottable.

Creating a Pivottable Manually by Using the PivotTable Wizard

Let's walk through the process of using the PivotTable Wizard to manually create a pivottable on a worksheet using an external database. A Microsoft Access 97 database named BIKEDATA.MDB is included on the companion CD; it contains data for a company that manufactures and sells bicycles and bicycle accessories throughout the world. If you have not already done so, copy the BIKEDATA.MDB file to a directory on your hard drive.

To create a pivottable from this database, follow these steps:

1. Start Excel and select cell B8 on the first worksheet.

2. From the Data menu, choose the PivotTable Report command. You see the PivotTable Wizard, which is a step-by-step guide to constructing a pivottable. The PivotTable Wizard's first dialog box lets you choose among four different data sources for building your pivottable.

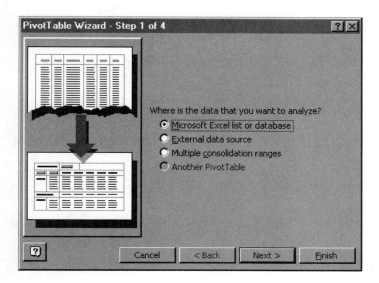

The options are as follows:

■ Option 1: To build a pivottable from a database that exists on a single Excel worksheet.

■ Option 2: To use any external database that supports Open Database Connectivity (ODBC), such as Access, FoxPro, SQL Server, DEC RDB, ORACLE, dBASE, and Paradox. (For more information about ODBC, see the "FYI" titled "ODBC Eases Importing and Exporting Database Data" on page 168. ODBC is also discussed in greater detail in Chapter 7.)

■ Option 3: To build a pivottable from data that's been consolidated from several Excel worksheets. (All worksheets in the consolidation must be formatted with similar data labels.)

■ Option 4: To build a pivottable using the same database source as that of an existing pivottable.

3. Because you are building a pivottable from an Access database, select the second option—External Data Source. Then click the Next button.

4. On the second dialog box of the PivotTable Wizard, click the Get Data button. This launches Microsoft Query, an Excel add-in application that you use to query external databases.

NOTE   In order to build a pivottable from an external data source, Microsoft Query and the required ODBC drivers must be installed from the Microsoft Office 97 installation CD.

The first dialog box you see in Query is Choose Data Source.

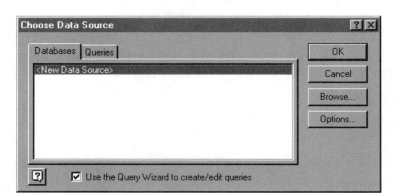

If you have used Query before, this dialog box lists some existing data sources. If this is the first time you have used the BikeData database, no ODBC data source is yet available for it.

5. Select <New Data Source> and click OK to establish a data source for the file BIKEDATA.MDB. You now see the Create New Data Source dialog box.

6. Fill out items 1 and 2 in this dialog box as pictured here. The name of the datasource is BikeData and the driver is Microsoft Access Driver.

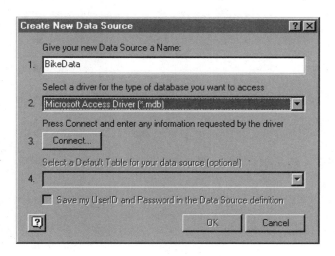

7. Click Connect to display the ODBC Microsoft Access Setup dialog box.

8. Click the Select button in the Database section of the dialog box to bring up the Select Database dialog box. Here you specify the exact location of the BIKEDATA.MDB file on your hard drive.

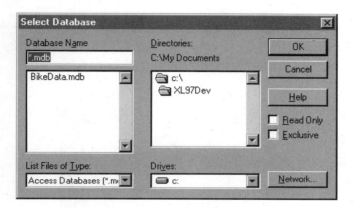

9. Select the file, and then click OK. You're now back at the ODBC Microsoft Access Setup dialog box. Click OK again.

At this point, you have successfully added an ODBC data source named BikeData to your system and have returned to the Create New Data Source dialog box.

10. In step 4 of the Create New Data Source dialog box, select Sales from the drop-down listbox as your default table and click OK. This returns you to the Choose Data Source dialog box.

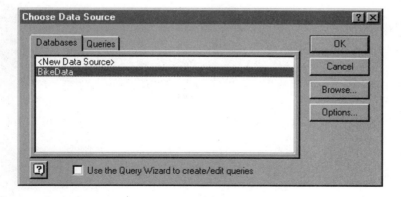

11. Make sure the Use The Query Wizard To Create/Edit Queries checkbox is *not* checked, and then select BikeData. Click OK. The main window in Query is displayed.

The main window in Query (shown in the next step) is broken down into two sections: a Table area in the upper portion of the window that displays the fields of the selected tables in the database and a Data area in the lower portion of the window that displays data sets that result from queries. In the Sales table in the upper portion of the window, the first field is represented by an asterisk (*). This asterisk is a label that represents all fields in the table.

12. Double-click the asterisk in the table in the upper portion of the window. Doing so queries the entire database and displays it in the Data area.

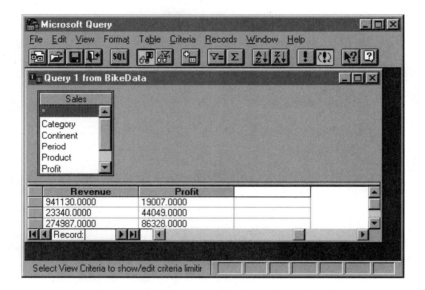

Seven fields appear in this database; you will use them to construct the pivottable.

13. From the File menu, choose the Return Data To Microsoft Excel command to return the data set to Excel. Now you are back to step 2 of the PivotTable Wizard. Click Next to continue.

Excel reads the data from the database you selected into an internal RAM cache, which the pivottable will query directly. (The amount of RAM in your system limits the size of the cache. Later in this chapter, you'll learn how to get around RAM limitations when using pivottables—see the sections titled "Managing large amounts of data in pivottables" beginning on page 199 and "Server-Based Page Fields" on pages 200–201.) The dialog box for step 3 of the PivotTable Wizard is then displayed.

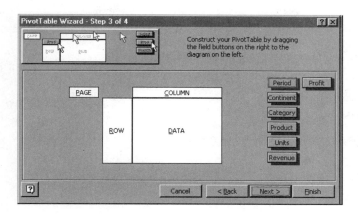

The right side of the lower portion of the dialog box shows a list of all the database fields from the Access database, and the left side of the dialog box displays an empty skeleton for the pivottable. You construct the pivottable by dragging these database field labels to different sections of the pivottable skeleton.

NOTE The skeleton shows that the pivottable consists of four component parts—the Row, Column, Data, and Page areas. The Row, Column, and Data areas make up the standard components of a two-dimensional matrix. The Page area adds a third dimension to the table; any database fields that are placed in this area will be displayed in drop-down list boxes above the final pivottable.

14. Drag the Period field into the Row area, the Continent and Category fields into the Page area (you can have multiple fields in a single pivottable area), the Product field into the Column area, and the Revenue field into the Data area.

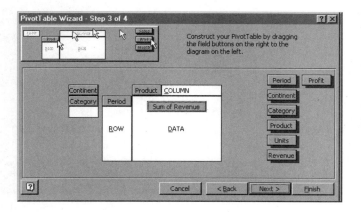

Click Next to display step 4 of the PivotTable Wizard.

In this dialog box, you can specify the range on the current worksheet in which the pivottable will reside or place the pivottable on a new worksheet. Using the Options button, you can also set various advanced options. This process will be described later in this chapter.

FYI

ODBC Eases Importing and Exporting Database Data

Excel uses ODBC, or Open Database Connectivity—a standard developed by Microsoft for querying, importing, and exporting database data in a common way from various data sources. With ODBC, the user does not have to know the format of the specific database being accessed.

All databases that are to be accessed using ODBC must have what is known as an "ODBC data source," which provides a data source name (DSN) as well as summary information about the type of database and the ODBC driver to be used when accessing the database. Be aware that ODBC data source information can be stored in one of two places—in the Windows Registry or in a DSN file. When a user creates an ODBC data source using Microsoft Query in Excel 97, the data source information is stored in a DSN file on the hard disk. To create ODBC data sources that are stored in the Registry, you must access the ODBC Data Source Administrator in the Windows Control Panel and add a System DSN (also note that Registry-based data sources can be created programmatically using DAO). When working with ODBC data sources and pivottables, keep in mind that in the initial release of Excel 97, users can access only DSN files when using Microsoft Query to build pivottables. It is possible, however, to use VBA to programmatically access ODBC data sources in both the Registry and DSN files.

15. Keep the default settings in step 4 of the PivotTable Wizard, and click the Finish button. A pivottable is now displayed on the selected worksheet.

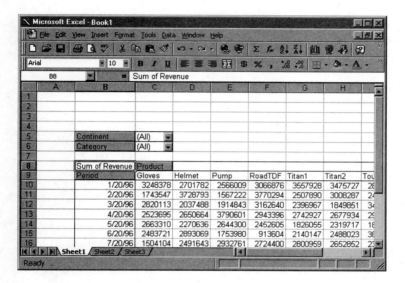

In the pivottable, the Continent and Category fields are in the Page area, the Product field is in the Column area, the Period field is in the Row area, and the Revenue field is in the Data area.

Now that you have created a pivottable manually, let's take a look at how you can create a pivottable through VBA by calling the PivotTableWizard method on the Worksheet object.

Creating a Pivottable Through VBA

You rarely have to create a pivottable using a routine in Excel. Most custom Excel applications contain pivottables that were manually designed and created when the application was built. Although you won't generally need to build pivottables during code execution, you should understand how to manipulate the component objects of a pivottable through VBA. Knowing how to control these objects will greatly enhance what you can do using pivottables.

NOTE Before you run the routines in this section, be sure you have set up a pivottable manually as outlined in the previous section. Steps 4 through 6, on pages 163–164, set up the BikeData data source, which must be available for the following routines to execute successfully.

To create a pivottable through VBA, you call the PivotTableWizard method on the Worksheet object. Note that this method is called on the Worksheet object—not on the PivotTable object—because the pivottable being created will reside on the worksheet. The PivotTableWizard method has the following arguments, all of which are optional.

sourceType: One of four Excel constants that represent the four data sources that can be used to create a pivottable:

- xlDatabase (an Excel list or database)
- xlExternal (an external database)
- xlConsolidation (a consolidation of two or more Excel worksheet ranges)
- xlPivotTable (the same data source as that of an existing pivottable)

sourceData: An argument that specifies the source of the data, depending on the sourceType:

- For xlDatabase, a range
- For xlExternal, an array of strings that contains an ODBC connect string and a SQL statement
- For xlConsolidation, an array of ranges
- For xlPivotTable, the name of an existing pivottable

> **NOTE** SQL (usually pronounced "sequel") stands for Structured Query Language, an industry standard language for querying databases.

tableDestination: A range in which the pivottable will be placed.

tableName: A name to be assigned to the pivottable.

rowGrand: If True, totals for the rows of the pivottable are displayed; if False, totals are not displayed. Defaults to True.

columnGrand: If True, totals for the columns of the pivottable are displayed; if False, totals are not displayed. Defaults to True.

saveData: If True, the internal RAM cache that contains the data set for the pivottable is saved with the table in the workbook file; if False, the cache is not saved. Defaults to True.

hasAutoFormat: If True, Excel reformats the pivottable when it changes. Defaults to True.

autoPage: Used only if the sourceType is xlConsolidation. If True, Excel automatically creates a pagefield; if False, no pagefield is created. Defaults to True.

Reserved: Reserved for future use. Leave blank.

backgroundQuery: If True, Excel executes the query to populate the pivottable asynchronously (in the background). If False, the user must wait for the query to execute before continuing work. Defaults to True.

optimizeCache: Used to optimize the performance of pivottables with very large or complex data sets. Optimization slows the initial querying and construction of the cache. If True, enables optimization; if False, disables. The default setting for optimizeCache is False.

pageFieldOrder: Used to determine the physical orientation of pagefields on the sheet. The constant xlDownThenOver "stacks" the pagefields vertically; xlOverThenDown arranges them across a row horizontally. Use pageFieldOrder in conjunction with the next property, pageFieldWrapCount, to arrange pagefields in multiple rows or columns. Default is xlDownThenOver.

pageFieldWrapCount: Determines the number of pagefields at which a new row or column starts (depending on the value of pageFieldOrder). A value of 0 prevents wrapping; any other value sets the threshold. Defaults to 0.

readData: If True, data is read into pivot cache from the external database; if False, reading data is deferred until needed. Defaults to True.

Connection: Used to specify an ODBC data source, a URL data source, or the name of a file containing a query.

Let's take a look at an example of code that could be used to create a pivottable:

```
Sub Chap04aProc01_CreatePivot1()
    Dim QArray As Variant
    Dim Range1 As Range
    Dim ConnectString As String
    Dim PivotName As String
    Set Range1 = Worksheets(1).Range("B8")
    ConnectString = "ODBC;" & _
        "DBQ=" & ThisWorkbook.Path & "\BIKEDATA.MBD;" & _
        "Driver={Microsoft Access Driver (*.mdb)};"
    QArray = Array(ConnectString, "SELECT * FROM Sales")
    PivotName = "Pivot1"
    Worksheets(1).PivotTableWizard xlExternal, QArray, _
                                    Range1, PivotName
End Sub
```

When the PivotTableWizard method is called on the Worksheet object in Proc01, arguments are passed by order and not by name. Also, only the first four arguments are passed; because nothing is specified for the remaining arguments, they all assume their default values.

One of the most important aspects of the call to the PivotTableWizard method in Proc01 is the second argument, QArray, which is a two-element array of strings that contains an ODBC connect string and a SQL query statement. In its simplest form, the syntax for specifying the ODBC data source can be a string such as "FileDSN=BikeData", in which DSN stands for "data source name." The specification for the data source can be more complicated in structure, however, depending on the database being used and the access privileges to the database. For example, it might be necessary to specify a logon ID as well as a password. The connect string in Proc01 accesses the BikeData data source regardless of whether it's been set up in a file or in the Registry. The second element of the array for the sourceData argument contains the SQL query string that is used for querying the external database to obtain the data for the pivottable. The syntax for the SQL string is governed by standard ODBC SQL. In Proc01, "SELECT * FROM Sales" retrieves all records from the Sales table. You might on occasion be unsure of the exact syntax to use for both the ODBC connect string and the SQL query string elements of the sourceData array. To be certain of using the proper syntax, you can always turn on the macro recorder and create a pivottable manually. Excel records the call to the PivotTableWizard method, specifying the appropriate ODBC connect string as well as the proper SQL query string.

When you run Proc01, Excel reads the data from the BikeData data source into an internal RAM cache and creates a pivottable on the first worksheet. What you see on the worksheet, however, looks nothing like a pivottable:

	Total
Total	

You get this sparse-looking table because the PivotTableWizard method causes Excel to read data into the internal RAM cache and allocate space on the worksheet for the pivottable. None of the code in Proc01 tells Excel which database fields to place in each area of the pivottable, and until such code is executed, no data will be displayed on the worksheet.

To write the code that specifies which database fields go in which areas of the pivottable, you must understand the architecture of the pivottable and the objects that are included in it. A pivottable consists of the Row, Column, Data, and Page areas where database fields can be placed. The PivotTable object also has a collection named PivotFields. The PivotFields collection is used to hold each database field in the pivottable, and you can access each field by indexing this collection—either by the name of the database field or by number. For example, for the pivottable created in Proc01, the database field named Product can be accessed in the following manner:

```
Worksheets(1).PivotTables("Pivot1").PivotFields("Product")
```

By using the PivotFields collection, you can place the various fields in the different areas of the pivottable. Proc02 (which follows) presents a new version of Proc01, with additional code for placing the pivotfields in the pivottable's areas. Note the use of the BackgroundQuery argument to the PivotTableWizard method. By default, Excel performs queries to populate the cache asynchronously, meaning it does this in the background to allow the user to keep working during the query operation. If we allow Excel to do this for Proc02, however, execution will continue past the PivotTableWizard line *before* the cache is actually populated. This will cause a runtime error when attempting to set the orientation of the PivotFields (because they don't exist yet!). To prevent this from happening, we set BackgroundQuery to False. This makes Excel wait until the cache is populated before the next line of the routine executes.

```
Sub Chap04aProc02_CreatePivot2()
    Dim QArray As Variant
    Dim Range1 As Range
    Dim ConnectString As String
    Dim PivotName As String
    Dim Pivot1 As PivotTable

    PivotName = "Pivot1"
    Worksheets(1).Select
    Set Range1 = Worksheets(1).Range("B8")
    ConnectString = "ODBC;" & _
        "DBQ=" & ThisWorkbook.Path & "\BIKEDATA.MDB;" & _
        "Driver={Microsoft Access Driver (*.mdb)};"
    QArray = Array(ConnectString, "SELECT * FROM Sales")
    PivotName = "Pivot1"
    Worksheets(1).PivotTableWizard sourceType:=xlExternal, _
        SourceData:=QArray, tableDestination:=Range1, _
        tablename:=PivotName, BackgroundQuery:=False

    Set Pivot1 = Worksheets(1).PivotTables(PivotName)
    With Pivot1
        .PivotFields("Continent").Orientation = xlRowField
        .PivotFields("Category").Orientation = xlColumnField
        .PivotFields("Period").Orientation = xlPageField
        .PivotFields("Product").Orientation = xlPageField
        .PivotFields("Revenue").Orientation = xlDataField
    End With
End Sub
```

FYI

Limitations on the sourceData Argument

Be aware that Excel limits to 255 characters all strings that are passed to any Excel object. (You can have longer strings in VBA, but they can't be passed as method arguments or property settings to an Excel object.) Therefore, take care when passing a SQL string as the second element in the array for the PivotTableWizard method's sourceData argument—you must limit the string to 255 characters.

You can get around this limitation, however, by passing additional SQL strings in the array; in other words, it is possible for the sourceData array to contain more than two elements. Excel treats all elements of the sourceData array after the first element as SQL strings to be used to query the external database. In fact, Excel concatenates all the strings and treats them as one big SQL statement, giving you a way around the 255-character limit. No element of the array can be more than 255 characters long, but the number of characters of all the elements added together can be about as long as you want it to be (up to around 65,000 characters). To use extremely long SQL strings with the sourceData argument of the PivotTableWizard method, you start one string, close it at 255 characters or less, and immediately start the second string where you left off in the previous string.

Proc03 shows an example of passing multiple SQL strings in the array for the sourceData argument:

```
Sub Chap04aProc03_CreatePivot3()
    Dim QArray As Variant
    Dim Range1 As Range
    Dim Pivot1 As PivotTable
    Dim ConnectString As String
    Dim SQLString1 As String
    Dim SQLString2 As String
    Set Pivot1 = Worksheets(1).PivotTables("Pivot1")
    Set Range1 = Pivot1.DataLabelRange
    ConnectString = "ODBC;" & _
        "DBQ=" & ThisWorkbook.Path & "\BIKEDATA.MDB;" & _
        "Driver={Microsoft Access Driver (*.mdb)};"
    SQLString1 = "SELECT * FROM Sales "
    SQLString2 = "WHERE (Sales.Revenue > 500000)"
    QArray = Array(ConnectString, SQLString1, SQLString2)
    Worksheets(1).Select
    Range1.Select
    Worksheets(1).PivotTableWizard xlExternal, QArray
End Sub
```

By using the Orientation property of the PivotField object, as was done in Proc02, you can place any of the pivotfields in any of the areas of the pivottable itself. The resulting pivottable appears as follows:

Product	(All)			
Period	(All)			
Sum of Revenue	Category			
Continent	Accessories	Racing Bikes	Touring Bikes	Grand Total
Africa	17922851	16528025	19593723	54044599
Asia	15792606	14988839	21620611	52402056
Europe	18180315	15254466	19483602	52918383
North America	17849613	17679685	19068914	54598212
South America	17867977	18647185	18311934	54827096
Grand Total	87613362	83098200	98078784	268790346

The PivotCache Object

As the previous examples have shown, the pivottable and the RAM cache are really two separate entities. The cache contains the raw data retrieved from the data source in RAM, and the pivottable displays data in the cache in various ways.

Before getting into the details of the PivotTable object, let's spend a few minutes on the PivotCache object. The PivotCache object, of course, represents the RAM cache. It is accessed as a property of the PivotTable object like this:

```
Worksheets(1).PivotTables("PivotTable1").PivotCache
```

The PivotCache object has several useful properties, many of which are also exposed by the PivotTableWizard object. Following is a description of a few of these properties.

BackgroundQuery: If True, Excel executes the query to populate the cache asynchronously (in the background). If False, the user must wait for the query to execute before continuing work. Defaults to True.

OptimizeCache: Used to optimize the performance of the cache with very large or complex data sets. Optimization will slow the initial querying and construction of the cache. Set to True to enable optimization; False to disable. Defaults to False.

MemoryUsed: Stores the number of bytes of RAM currently used by the cache. Read-only.

RecordCount: Stores the number of records currently held in the cache. Read-only.

RefreshDate: Stores the last date and time that the cache was refreshed. Read-only.

RefreshName: Stores the name of the user who performed the last refresh. Read-only.

The PivotCache object also provides one method, Refresh, that requeries the data source to refresh the cache. This method has the same effect as the RefreshTable method of the PivotTable object.

Proc04, which follows, shows an example of code that obtains information about the cache using the PivotCache object, then refreshes it using the Refresh method:

```
Sub Chap04aProc04_PivotCache()
    Dim sMsg As String
    With Worksheets(1).PivotTables("Pivot1").PivotCache
        sMsg = ""
        sMsg = sMsg & "Memory Used: " & .MemoryUsed & Chr(13)
        sMsg = sMsg & "Record Count: " & .RecordCount & Chr(13)
        sMsg = sMsg & "Refresh Date: " & .RefreshDate & Chr(13)
        sMsg = sMsg & "Refresh Name: " & .RefreshName & Chr(13)
        sMsg = sMsg & "Background Query: " & .BackgroundQuery
        MsgBox sMsg
        .Refresh
    End With
End Sub
```

The PivotTable Structure

The following diagram shows the structure of a pivottable:

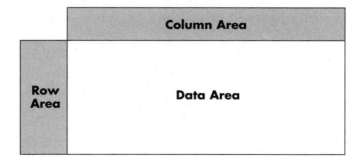

You can place a pivotfield in any of the areas of the pivottable by setting the Orientation property of the PivotField object to one of the following five constants:

xlColumnField	Puts the pivotfield in the Column area of the pivottable
xlDataField	Puts the pivotfield in the Data area of the pivottable
xlHidden	Hides the pivotfield from view (not displayed in any area of the pivottable)
xlPageField	Puts the pivotfield in the Page area of the pivottable
xlRowField	Puts the pivotfield in the Row area of the pivottable

You can completely change the structure of the pivottable that was originally created in Proc01 on page 171 by using the following routine:

```
Sub Chap04aProc05_ChangePivot()
    Dim Pivot1 As PivotTable
    Set Pivot1 = Worksheets(1).PivotTables("Pivot1")
    Worksheets(1).Activate
    With Pivot1
        .PivotFields("Continent").Orientation = xlPageField
        .PivotFields("Category").Orientation = xlPageField
        .PivotFields("Product").Orientation = xlColumnField
        .PivotFields("Period").Orientation = xlRowField
        .PivotFields("Sum of Revenue").Orientation = xlHidden
        .PivotFields("Profit").Orientation = xlDataField
    End With
End Sub
```

Proc05 takes the Continent and Category pivotfields out of the Row and Column areas and places them in the Page area. The routine then takes the Product and Period pivotfields out of the Page area and places them in the Column and Row areas, respectively. Finally the routine removes the Sum Of Revenue pivotfield from the Data area (by setting its Orientation property to xlHidden) and places Profit in the Data area instead. Note that if a pivotfield is already hidden, any attempt to set its Orientation property to xlHidden produces an error message. Under such circumstances, therefore, you should use an If statement to determine whether the pivotfield is already hidden. The resulting pivottable appears as follows:

Category	(All)									
Continent	(All)									
Sum of Profit	Product									
Period	Gloves	Helmet	Pump	RoadTDF	Titan1	Titan2	TourItalia	Triathlete	VeloTron	Grand Total
1/20/96	144077	127432	110550	109809	222402	298820	150823	182425	15256	1361594
2/20/96	59918	188268	52657	156204	181031	221692	102188	85762	175112	1222832
3/20/96	151163	32805	96770	205503	82469	94043	263253	167098		1093104
4/20/96	151650	176205	257248	87782	164816	99284	132376	83780	76526	1229667
5/20/96	24573	114941	178316	192207	122953	52004	95967	53299	50809	885069
6/20/96	137599	267858	33696		117302	184658	164231	129134		1034478
7/20/96	76295	175684	128181	94102	225243	167466	208881	99138	185231	1360221
8/20/96	36252	148667	232640	196440	160655	95435	191102	14112	237970	1313273
9/20/96	82898	128305	60847	148827	163959	98231	115313	180691		979071
10/20/96	136973	86350	53314	92512	239129	18601	108637	118044	196563	1050123
11/20/96	41322	81315	147075	268929	206599		160480	138981	98909	1143610
12/20/96	61043		144659	165138	99296	109406	107466	88482	169435	944925
Grand Total	1103763	1527830	1495953	1717453	1985854	1439640	1800717	1340946	1205811	13617967

The PivotTable object consists of a hierarchy of objects:

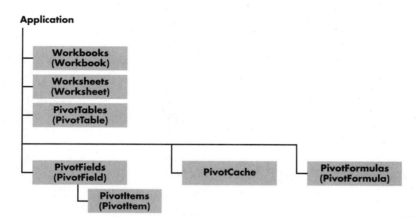

The PivotTable object represents the pivottable itself. A PivotField object is used to represent a particular database field from the underlying data source for the table; the pivottable is constructed by placing pivotfields in the various areas of the table. A PivotItem object is used to represent a unique piece of data in a pivotfield; by being able to access unique data, you can exercise a high degree of control over how data is displayed in the table.

Each of these objects, except for the PivotCache object, falls into the category of "object in a collection"; Excel includes PivotTables, PivotFields, PivotItems, and PivotFormulas collections that enable you to access objects in those collections. The next few sections of this chapter take a look at the properties and methods of these objects, with primary focus given to the PivotTable, PivotField, and PivotItem objects. Several code samples are also provided to show how these objects can be used to control the display of data.

PivotTable Properties and Methods

The PivotTable object has numerous properties and methods that you can use to manipulate the structure and display of data in a pivottable.

Pivottable properties

Several PivotTable properties return Range objects, on which further property settings or method calls can be made by using Range properties and methods. The following PivotTable properties return Range objects.

ColumnRange: A range that encompasses the Column area (e.g., the column headers) of the pivottable.

RowRange: A range that encompasses the Row area (e.g., the row headers) of the pivottable.

PageRange: A range that encompasses the Page area of the pivottable.

DataBodyRange: A range that encompasses the Data area of the pivottable.

DataLabelRange: A range that holds the name(s) of the pivotfield(s) in the Data area.

TableRange1: A range of the pivottable that includes the Row, Column, and Data areas (but not the Page area).

TableRange2: A range of the pivottable that includes the Row, Column, Data, and Page areas (e.g., the entire pivottable).

Under certain circumstances, you might find it extremely useful to obtain a Range object for part of a pivottable. For example, let's assume that you want to apply one of Excel's built-in autoformats to the pivottable that you created using Proc03 on page 174. The AutoFormat method applies to the Range object, so you must obtain a range from the pivottable before you call the AutoFormat method. In addition, you probably do not want to apply an autoformat to the entire pivottable but instead only to the range that encompasses the Row, Column, and Data areas of the table—specifically, to TableRange1. Proc06 applies the xlClassic3 AutoFormat in such a way.

```
Sub Chap04aProc06_FormatTable()
    Dim Pivot1 As PivotTable
    Set Pivot1 = Worksheets(1).PivotTables("Pivot1")
    Worksheets(1).Activate
    Pivot1.TableRange1.AutoFormat Format:=xlClassic3
End Sub
```

To delete a pivottable from a worksheet, you must call the Clear method on the Range object that represents the entire pivottable—TableRange2. Proc07 uses the PivotTables collection to delete each pivottable on the first worksheet. Then the first worksheet is activated, a message box is displayed, and Proc02 and Proc06 are called to construct and format a new pivottable:

```
Sub Chap04aProc07_DeletePivotTable()
    Dim PivotTableVar As PivotTable
    For Each PivotTableVar In Worksheets(1).PivotTables
        PivotTableVar.TableRange2.Clear
    Next
    Worksheets(1).Activate
    MsgBox "PivotTable deleted."
    Chap04aProc02_CreatePivot2
    Chap04aProc06_FormatTable
End Sub
```

The resulting pivottable appears as follows:

Product	(All)			
Period	(All)			

Sum of Revenue	Category			
Continent	*Accessories*	*Racing Bikes*	*Touring Bikes*	*Grand Total*
Africa	17922851	16528025	19593723	54044599
Asia	15792606	14988839	21620611	52402056
Europe	18180315	15254466	19483602	52918383
North America	17849613	17679685	19068914	54598212
South America	17867977	18647185	18311934	54827096
Grand Total	87613362	83098200	98078784	268790346

The PivotTable object has the following additional properties, all of which are read/write except for RefreshDate, RefreshName, and SourceData.

ColumnGrand: If True, totals for columns are displayed; if False, totals are not displayed.

RowGrand: If True, totals for rows are displayed; if False, totals are not displayed.

HasAutoFormat: If True, Excel reformats the pivottable when it changes; if False, Excel does not reformat the table.

Name: The name of the pivottable. The Value property also returns the name of the pivottable.

RefreshDate: The date and time that the internal RAM data set for the pivottable was last refreshed. (You can refresh the data by calling the RefreshTable method on the PivotTable object.)

RefreshName: The name of the registered user who last refreshed the pivottable.

SaveData: If True, the internal RAM cache is saved with the pivottable; if False, the cache is not saved.

SourceData: The source of the data in the pivottable. This can be an Excel worksheet range; an array of worksheet ranges (for a consolidation data source); or, for an external database, a two-element array of strings, the first of which is the ODBC connect string and the second of which is the SQL query string used to extract the data. For a pivottable whose data source is another pivottable, SourceData returns the source of the data of the original pivottable.

DisplayErrorString: If True, the pivottable displays the value of the ErrorString property in place of error values in cells that contain errors.

ErrorString: The custom error string to display in place of error values in cells that contain errors if DisplayErrorString is True.

DisplayNullString: If True, the pivottable displays the value of the NullString property in cells that contain null values.

NullString: The string to display in cells that contain null values if Display-NullString is True.

ManualUpdate: If True, the pivottable view does not update when manipulated. (It allows multiple VBA statements to execute without redrawing.)

> **NOTE** The PivotTable object has more properties in addition to those just listed; for a complete list of PivotTable properties and methods, see Excel's online VBA Help.

Proc08 shows an example of setting the ColumnGrand and RowGrand properties of the PivotTable object to False:

```
Sub Chap04aProc08_TurnOffTotals()
    Dim Pivot1 As PivotTable
    Set Pivot1 = Worksheets(1).PivotTables("Pivot1")
    Worksheets(1).Activate
    With Pivot1
        .ColumnGrand = False
        .RowGrand = False
    End With
End Sub
```

Pivottable methods

The PivotTable object also has several methods, most of which return pivotfields that reside in various areas of the pivottable. Such methods include the following.

ColumnFields: Returns all the pivotfields in the Column area (e.g., the column labels).

DataFields: Returns all the pivotfields in the Data area.

PageFields: Returns all the pivotfields in the Page area.

RowFields: Returns all the pivotfields in the Row area (e.g., the row labels).

PivotFields: Returns all the pivotfields in the table.

VisibleFields: Returns all the pivotfields that are displayed in the table (in the Row, Column, Data, and Page areas).

HiddenFields: Returns all the pivotfields that are not displayed in the table.

CalculatedFields: Returns all the pivotfields that are calculated fields.

Proc09 uses the PageFields method to display the name of each pivotfield in the Page area in a message box:

```
Sub Chap04aProc09_DisplayPageFields()
    Dim FieldVar As PivotField
    Dim Pivot1 As PivotTable
    Set Pivot1 = Worksheets(1).PivotTables("Pivot1")
    For Each FieldVar In Pivot1.PageFields
        MsgBox FieldVar.Name
    Next
End Sub
```

You can provide either a name or a numeric index to any of the pivottable methods that return a pivotfield. Proc10 passes a numeric index to the DataFields method to hide the first pivotfield in the Data area and then replace it with the pivotfield named Profit:

```
Sub Chap04aProc10_AddProfit()
    Dim Pivot1 As PivotTable
    Set Pivot1 = Worksheets(1).PivotTables("Pivot1")
    Worksheets(1).Activate
    Pivot1.DataFields(1).Orientation = xlHidden
    Pivot1.PivotFields("Profit").Orientation = xlDataField
End Sub
```

Here are three additional methods belonging to the PivotTable object.

AddFields: Used to add pivotfields to the Row, Column, and Page areas of the pivottable. Only pivotfields that have an orientation of xlHidden can be used with AddFields. AddFields has four arguments: rowFields, columnFields, pageFields, and addToTable. The rowFields, columnFields, and pageFields arguments can each take either a string or an array of strings that represents the name of one or more pivotfields to be added to the particular area of the table. The addToTable argument can be either True or False. If it is True, the new fields are added to the fields that already exist in the appropriate area. If it is False, the specified pivotfields replace any existing pivotfields in that area. Be careful when setting addToTable to False because doing so completely rebuilds the Row, Column, and Page areas of the pivottable.

RefreshTable: Used to refresh the data set in the internal RAM cache for the pivottable.

ShowPages: Used to create a separate pivottable for each data item in the specified PageField, with each new pivottable residing on a new worksheet.

Proc11 uses the AddFields method of the PivotTable object to reconstruct a pivottable. Notice that the last line of the routine makes a call to the RefreshTable method to update the data in the RAM cache.

TIP If the status bar is displayed at the bottom of your screen, you can see Excel's progress as the refresh takes place. To display the status bar, choose the Status Bar command from the View menu.

```
Sub Chap04aProc11_RebuildPivotTable()
    Dim Pivot1 As PivotTable
    Dim FieldVar As PivotField
    Dim PageArray As Variant
    Dim ColumnArray As Variant
    Dim RowArray As Variant
    Set Pivot1 = Worksheets(1).PivotTables("Pivot1")
    PageArray = Array("Period", "Product")
    ColumnArray = Array("Category")
    RowArray = Array("Continent")
    Worksheets(1).Activate
    For Each FieldVar In Pivot1.PivotFields
        If FieldVar.Orientation <> xlHidden Then
            FieldVar.Orientation = xlHidden
        End If
    Next
    With Pivot1
        .AddFields PageFields:=PageArray, _
                   ColumnFields:=ColumnArray, _
                   RowFields:=RowArray, _
                   addToTable:=True
        .DataFields(1).Orientation = xlHidden
        .PivotFields("Revenue").Orientation = xlDataField
        .RefreshTable
    End With
End Sub
```

PivotField Properties and Methods

The PivotField object is used to represent the different database fields that hold the data that populates the pivottable. By manipulating various properties and methods of the PivotField objects in a pivottable, you can exercise a great degree of control over the way in which data is displayed in the different areas of the pivottable. Different pivotfield properties and methods become available depending on the area of a pivottable—Row, Column, Page, or Data—that is occupied by the pivotfield, and on whether the field has been grouped. (Fields are grouped using the Group method and are useful for combining related sets of data.) It is best to categorize pivotfield properties and methods, therefore, according to the area of the pivottable to which they apply and according to whether the field has been grouped.

Properties of pivotfields in the Row, Column, and Page areas

The following properties apply only to pivotfields that reside in the Row, Column, and Page areas of the pivottable.

CurrentPage: Applies only to pivotfields in the Page area. The CurrentPage property corresponds to the item displayed for the pivotfield in the Page drop-down list box. The following example, Proc12, scrolls through all items for the Continent pivotfield in the Page drop-down list box:

```
Sub Chap04aProc12_ShowContinentPages()
    Dim Pivot1 As PivotTable
    Set Pivot1 = Worksheets(1).PivotTables("Pivot1")
    Worksheets(1).Activate
    With Pivot1
        .PivotFields("Continent").Orientation = xlPageField
        .PivotFields("Period").Orientation = xlRowField
    End With
    With Pivot1.PivotFields("Continent")
        .CurrentPage = "Africa"
        MsgBox "Africa"
        .CurrentPage = "Asia"
        MsgBox "Asia"
        .CurrentPage = "Europe"
        MsgBox "Europe"
        .CurrentPage = "North America"
        MsgBox "North America"
        .CurrentPage = "South America"
        MsgBox "South America"
        .CurrentPage = "(All)"
        MsgBox "(All)"
    End With
End Sub
```

Subtotals: Provides a way to calculate up to 11 types of subtotals in the pivottable. Although subtotals can be set for pivotfields in the Row, Column, and Page areas, they are displayed only for pivotfields in the Row and Column areas. The Subtotals property takes a 12-element Boolean array, with the elements representing the following subtotals in this order:

Automatic
Sum
Count
Average
Max
Min
Product
Count Nums (number of numeric values)
StdDev

StdDevp (standard deviation for which underlying data is the entire
population)
Var
Varp

If the element in the array that corresponds to Automatic is set to True, all other
Array elements are ignored and Excel determines a type of subtotal appropriate
for the data (usually Sum). Also note that you can calculate such subtotals for
pivotfields in the Data area by using the Function property on the Subtotals
method.

NOTE The Subtotals property is missing from VBA Help and the Object
Browser in the initial release of Excel 97.

Proc13 places the Continent pivotfield in the Row area and sets it to the first
position in the Row area's ordering of pivotfields. The routine then turns on the
Column and Row grand totals and, last, calculates all 11 subtotal values for the
Continent pivotfield by assigning a 12-element array to the Subtotals property:

```
Sub Chap04aProc13_ShowAllSubtotals()
    Dim Pivot1 As PivotTable
    Set Pivot1 = Worksheets(1).PivotTables("Pivot1")
    Worksheets(1).Activate
    With Pivot1
        .PivotFields("Continent").Orientation = xlRowField
        .PivotFields("Continent").Position = 1
        .ColumnGrand = True
        .RowGrand = True
        .PivotFields("Continent").Subtotals = _
            Array(False, True, True, True, True, True, _
                True, True, True, True, True, True)
    End With
    Range("A1").Select
End Sub
```

Proc14, which follows, can be used to restore the pivottable to its previous configuration. It sets the Continent pivotfield to display Automatic subtotals by assigning a 12-element array, of which only the first element is True, to the
Subtotals property:

```
Sub Chap04aProc14_ResetSubtotals()
    Dim Pivot1 As PivotTable
    Set Pivot1 = Worksheets(1).PivotTables("Pivot1")
    Worksheets(1).Activate
    With Pivot1.PivotFields("Continent")
        .Subtotals = Array(True, False, False, False, False, _
            False, False, False, False, False, False, False)
```

(continued)

continued

```
        .Orientation = xlPageField
    End With
    Range("A1").Select
End Sub
```

TIP You can set Subtotals manually by double-clicking the pivotfield label and selecting various subtotals in the PivotTable Field dialog box. There is also a Subtotals method that allows you to turn on and off individual subtotal types.

PivotField properties that deal with groups

Four of the PivotField properties can be used only with pivotfields that have been grouped. Grouped pivotfields can exist only in the Row, Column, and Page areas. Note that the Group method is actually a method of the Range object. Therefore, to call the Group method and apply it to data in a pivotfield, you must obtain a range for the pivotfield by using the DataRange property. (DataRange is discussed under "Properties of all pivotfields" on page 193.)

You can group data in a pivotfield in two ways: by automatic grouping (Excel sets up the group for you) or by manual grouping (you set up the group yourself). Both ways use the Group method; however, automatic grouping requires that certain values be passed to the arguments of the Group method, and manual grouping requires no arguments. In addition, automatic grouping can be performed only on pivotfields that contain date/time or numeric data.

Proc15 takes the Period pivotfield in the Row area and calculates two groups—one based on months and one based on quarters. The result is the breakdown of the Period pivotfield into two separate pivotfields: one labeled "Period" (which displays months) and one labeled "Quarters". Here is Proc15:

```
Sub Chap04aProc15_AutoGroup()
    Dim Pivot1 As PivotTable
    Set Pivot1 = Worksheets(1).PivotTables("Pivot1")
    Worksheets(1).Select
    With Pivot1
        .PivotFields("Period").DataRange.Rows(1).Group _
            start:=True, End:=True, _
            periods:=Array(False, False, False, False, _
                        True, True, False)

        .PivotFields("Quarters").Subtotals = _
            Array(True, False, False, False, False, False, _
                False, False, False, False, False, False)
    End With
    Range("A1").Select
End Sub
```

The resulting pivottable appears as follows:

Continent	(All)			
Product	(All)			
Sum of Revenue		Category		
Quarters	Period	Accessories	Racing Bikes	Touring Bikes	Grand Total
Qtr1	Jan	8516169	8434013	8464510	25414692
	Feb	7039562	8278071	9695973	25013606
	Mar	6772444	5019475	9532922	21324841
Qtr1 Total		22328175	21731559	27693405	71753139
Qtr2	Apr	8964960	8178945	8829652	25973557
	May	7578246	5647414	6577985	19803645
	Jun	7130770	5024416	7020738	19175924
Qtr2 Total		23673976	18850775	22428375	64953126
Qtr3	Jul	6928508	8143865	6955922	22028295
	Aug	6750719	7980298	8360849	23091866
	Sep	7488224	6206130	7859366	21553720
Qtr3 Total		21167451	22330293	23176137	66673881
Qtr4	Oct	7021606	6409764	7970004	21401374
	Nov	6908621	6602607	8429619	21940847
	Dec	6513533	7173202	8381244	22067979
Qtr4 Total		20443760	20185573	24780867	65410200
Grand Total		87613362	83098200	98078784	268790346

Note that the Group method is called on PivotTables("Pivot1").PivotFields-("Period").DataRange.Rows(1)—this corresponds to the cell in the top row of the DataRange of the Period pivotfield. As you recall, the Group method must be called on a Range object; in addition, for automatic grouping to take effect, Group must be called on a range that contains only one cell in the DataRange. Group has four arguments (but only three are passed in the preceding example).

Start: The value at which the group starts. If True, the group starts at the first value in the field.

End: The value at which the group ends. If True, the group ends at the last value in the field.

By: The unit of measure to group by.

Periods: A seven-element Boolean array that specifies a choice of seven built-in date/time periods: Seconds, Minutes, Hours, Days, Months, Quarters, and Years.

If the Start and End arguments are both set to True, Excel applies the grouping to all items in the table's DataRange. Proc15 uses the built-in Months and Quarters groups to break down the Period data on a monthly and quarterly basis. After the grouping is implemented, Excel treats the two resulting pivotfields as regular pivotfields on which property settings and method calls can be made. In the next statement in the routine, the Subtotals property of the new Quarters pivotfield is set to display automatic subtotaling.

TIP You can group pivotfields manually by clicking the Group button on the PivotTable toolbar as shown on the following page.

Proc16 calls the Ungroup method to remove the grouping that was implemented previously in Proc15:

```
Sub Chap04aProc16_UnAutoGroup()
    Dim Pivot1 As PivotTable
    Set Pivot1 = Worksheets(1).PivotTables("Pivot1")
    Worksheets(1).Select
    Pivot1.PivotFields("Quarters").DataRange.Ungroup
End Sub
```

Because Ungroup (like Group) is a Range method, Ungroup in the preceding example is called on the DataRange for the Quarters pivotfield. After the Ungroup method is called, Quarters ceases to exist as a pivotfield.

> **TIP** You can ungroup pivotfields manually by using the Ungroup button on the PivotTable toolbar.

Manual grouping is similar to automatic grouping, except that for manual grouping, when calling the Group method, no values are passed as arguments. Because no arguments are passed, none of the built-in date/time group periods are available. You must, therefore, specify an entire range that is to be segmented into a single group. Proc17 calls the Group method twice on the DataRange for the Period pivotfield, breaking the DataRange into two 6-month groups.

```
Sub Chap04aProc17_ManualGroup()
    Dim Pivot1 As PivotTable
    Set Pivot1 = Worksheets(1).PivotTables("Pivot1")
    Worksheets(1).Select
    Pivot1.PivotFields("Period").DataRange.Select
    With Selection.Resize(6, 1)
        .Group
        .Offset(6, 0).Group
```

```
    End With
    Pivot1.PivotFields("Period2").Subtotals = Array(True, _
        False, False, False, False, False, False, False, _
        False, False, False, False)
    Range("A1").Select
End Sub
```

The resulting pivottable appears as follows:

Sum of Revenue		Category			
Continent	(All)				
Product	(All)				
Period2	Period	Accessories	Racing Bikes	Touring Bikes	Grand Total
Group1	1/20/96	8516169	8434013	8464510	25414692
	2/20/96	7039562	8278071	9695973	25013606
	3/20/96	6772444	5019475	9532922	21324841
	4/20/96	8964960	8178945	8829652	25973557
	5/20/96	7578246	5647414	6577985	19803645
	6/20/96	7130770	5024416	7020738	19175924
Group1 Total		46002151	40582334	50121780	136706265
Group2	7/20/96	6928508	8143865	6955922	22028295
	8/20/96	6750719	7980298	8360849	23091866
	9/20/96	7488224	6206130	7859366	21553720
	10/20/96	7021606	6409764	7970004	21401374
	11/20/96	6908621	6602607	8429619	21940847
	12/20/96	6513533	7173202	8381244	22067979
Group2 Total		41611211	42515866	47957004	132084081
Grand Total		87613362	83098200	98078784	268790346

In Proc17, the Resize and Offset properties, which are Range properties, are used to select the appropriate ranges in the DataRange of the Period pivotfield to establish two 6-month groups. In line 5 of the routine, the entire DataRange is selected. The next line uses the Resize property to select only the first six rows of the data range. (The two arguments for Resize are rowSize and columnSize.) The Group method is then called from inside the With statement. The Offset property moves the selection down six rows (the two arguments of Offset are rowOffset and columnOffset) to select the rows that correspond to months seven through twelve and the rows on which the Group method is called a second time. The result of the two calls to the Group method is a pivotfield named Period2 that contains two 6-month groups. The Subtotals property of the Period2 group is then set to automatic.

TIP After a group has been established for a pivotfield in the pivottable, you can expand or contract the level of detail in the group by double-clicking the group item name.

Proc18 on the following page is used to call the Ungroup method in order to eliminate the manual grouping previously implemented.

```
Sub Chap04aProc18_UnManualGroup()
    Dim Pivot1 As PivotTable
    Set Pivot1 = Worksheets(1).PivotTables("Pivot1")
    Worksheets(1).Select
    Pivot1.PivotFields("Period2").DataRange.Ungroup
    Range("A1").Select
End Sub
```

Following are the properties you can use with grouped pivotfields.

ChildField: Can be used only on manually grouped pivotfields. The ChildField property returns the pivotfield that corresponds to the direct subset of the group. For example, in Proc17 on pages 188–189, two 6-month groups were created from the Period pivotfield; the resulting groups were contained in a new pivotfield named Period2. After the grouping, Period is the ChildField of Period2 because it is a subset of Period2.

ParentField: Can be used only on manually grouped pivotfields. This property acts in a manner opposite to that of the ChildField property, returning the pivotfield that is a superset of the specified pivotfield. In Proc17, Period2 is the ParentField of Period.

GroupLevel: Meaningful only for manually grouped pivotfields. GroupLevel returns the numeric level of the pivotfield in the group. After you run Proc17, Period2 has a GroupLevel of 1, and Period has a GroupLevel of 2.

TotalLevels: Can be used with both manually or automatically grouped pivotfields. TotalLevels returns the total number of pivotfields in the group. After you run Proc17, TotalLevels returns 2 because the grouping has only two fields—Period and Period2.

Properties of pivotfields in the Data area

The following properties apply only to pivotfields that reside in the Data area of the pivottable.

NumberFormat: Takes a string that can be used to set the number format of the pivotfield in the Data area. Excel has numerous built-in formats for currency, dates, scientific notation, percentages, and so on; you can also create your own number formats.

> **TIP**
>
> You can view all of Excel's number formats in the Number tab of the Format Cells dialog box. To do so, select any cell on a worksheet, choose the Cells command from the Format menu, and click the Number tab. You can also find an explanation of the format codes in Excel's online VBA Help topic titled "User-Defined Numeric Formats (Format Function)."

Proc19 changes the pivotfield in the Data area of the pivottable to a currency format:

```
Sub Chap04aProc19_ChangeNumberFormat()
    Dim Pivot1 As PivotTable
    Set Pivot1 = Worksheets(1).PivotTables("Pivot1")
    Worksheets(1).Activate
    Pivot1.DataFields(1).NumberFormat = "$#,##0_);($#,##0)"
End Sub
```

Calculation: Can be used to break down in various ways the values in the pivotfield in the Data area. Calculation provides nine ways of displaying data:

xlDifferenceFrom	The absolute difference between the value in the pivotfield and a specified value (BaseItem) in a specified pivotfield (BaseField) is displayed. This form of calculation provides a single reference point from which all values can be evaluated.
xlIndex	An index is calculated for each value using the following formula:

$$index = \frac{(value\ in\ cell) \times (grand\ total)}{(grand\ row\ total) \times (grand\ column\ total)}$$

xlNormal	Data is displayed as normal—that is, without any calculations applied.
xlPercentDifferenceFrom	This form of calculation is similar to xlDifferenceFrom, except that the field's percentage difference, rather than its absolute difference from a BaseItem in a BaseField, is displayed.
xlPercentOf	The pivotfield's percentage of a BaseItem in a BaseField is displayed.
xlPercentOfColumn	Percentages are calculated going down the columns of the table, with all the values in a single column adding up to 100 percent.
xlPercentOfRow	Percentages are calculated going across the rows of the table, with all the values in a single row adding up to 100 percent.
xlPercentOfTotal	Percentages are calculated throughout the table, with all the values in the table adding up to 100 percent.
xlRunningTotal	Going down the rows of the table, a running total is kept of all the displayed values.

Proc20 changes the Calculation property of the pivotfield in the Data area to xlPercentOfRow:

```
Sub Chap04aProc20_ChangeCalculation()
    Dim Pivot1 As PivotTable
    Set Pivot1 = Worksheets(1).PivotTables("Pivot1")
    Worksheets(1).Activate
    Pivot1.DataFields(1).Calculation = xlPercentOfRow
End Sub
```

BaseItem: The BaseItem property sets or returns the pivotfield item used in the Calculation property's xlDifferenceFrom, xlPercentDifferenceFrom, and xlPercentOf settings.

BaseField: The BaseField property sets or returns the pivotfield used in the Calculation property's xlDifferenceFrom, xlPercentDifferenceFrom, and xlPercentOf settings.

Function: Through the Function property, Excel provides several functions that can be applied to the underlying data of a pivotfield's Data area. The Function property can take any of the following values:

xlAverage	Displays the average of the underlying data
xlCount	Displays the number of underlying records
xlCountNums	Displays the number of underlying records that are numeric
xlMax	Displays the largest value in the underlying data
xlMin	Displays the smallest value in the underlying data
xlProduct	Displays the product of all the underlying data
xlStDev	Displays the standard deviation, for which the underlying data is a sample of the population
xlStDevP	Displays the standard deviation, for which the underlying data is the entire population
xlSum	Displays the sum of the underlying values
xlVar	Displays the variance, for which the underlying data is a sample of the population
xlVarP	Displays the variance, for which the underlying data is the entire population

Proc21 sets the Function property of the pivotfield in the Data area to xlAverage, causing averages of the underlying data to be displayed:

```
Sub Chap04aProc21_DisplayAverage()
    Dim Pivot1 As PivotTable
    Set Pivot1 = Worksheets(1).PivotTables("Pivot1")
    Worksheets(1).Activate
```

```
With Pivot1.DataFields(1)
    .Calculation = xlNormal
    .Function = xlAverage
    .NumberFormat = "$#,##0_);($#,##0)"
End With
End Sub
```

NOTE Applying a function to a pivotfield in the Data area causes the Name property of the pivotfield to change. When you run Proc21 while the Revenue pivotfield is displayed in the Data area, the pivotfield name is changed to Average Of Revenue. To access this pivotfield by name, you must use PivotFields("Average of Revenue"). Also, when you place any pivotfield in the Data area, Excel applies a function (usually xlSum) and immediately changes the name of the pivotfield—for example, to "Sum of Pivotfield Name."

Properties of all pivotfields

The following properties apply to all pivotfields in a pivottable, regardless of the area of the table in which they reside.

DataRange: The worksheet range that is occupied by the data displayed in the pivotfield. For pivotfields in the Data area, use the DataBodyRange property of the PivotTable object to include any grand total rows or columns in the range.

LabelRange: The worksheet range that is occupied by the label that displays the name of the pivotfield. To get this range for pivotfields in the Data area, you can also use the DataLabelRange property of the PivotTable object.

Name: Returns the name of the pivotfield as it is displayed in the pivottable. Because this property is read/write, you can change the displayed name of any pivotfield.

SourceName: Returns the original name of the pivotfield. This property is read-only; it returns the name of the field in the underlying data source of the table.

Orientation: Used to place a pivotfield in a particular area of the pivottable. This property can take the values of xlPageField, xlRowField, xlColumnField, xlDataField, and xlHidden. If the Orientation property of a pivotfield is set to xlHidden, the pivotfield is removed from display in the table.

Position: Used to get or set the numeric position of the pivotfield in a particular area of the pivottable. For example, if the Page area contains two pivotfields, numbering starts from the bottom, and the lowest drop-down list box has a position of 1.

Value: Synonymous with the Name property.

DataType: Read-only; can be used to get the data type of a pivotfield. DataType returns one of three values: xlText (a text data type), xlNumber (a numeric data type), or xlDate (a date data type). Note that when getting the DataType property, you should compare the DataType property to the appropriate *xl-* constant rather than trying to read and make sense of the value of the DataType property directly. (The same could be said for all properties that are set to *xl-* constants.) This is done in the Select Case control structure in Proc22:

```
Sub Chap04aProc22_DisplayDataTypes()
    Dim FieldVar As Variant
    Dim FieldType As String
    Dim Pivot1 As PivotTable
    Set Pivot1 = Worksheets(1).PivotTables("Pivot1")
    For Each FieldVar In Pivot1.PivotFields
        Select Case FieldVar.DataType
            Case xlText
                FieldType = "xlText"
            Case xlNumber
                FieldType = "xlNumber"
            Case xlDate
                FieldType = "xlDate"
        End Select
        MsgBox FieldVar.Name & ", " & FieldType
    Next
    Pivot1.DataFields(1).Function = xlSum
End Sub
```

PivotField methods

The following is a list of pivotfield methods. All of these methods apply only to pivotfields in the Row, Column, and Page areas of a pivottable.

PivotItems: Returns the names of all the unique items in the pivotfield. (These correspond to Row and Column headings as well as to items in the Page drop-down list boxes.)

VisibleItems: Returns those pivotitems that are currently visible. For example, in a Page drop-down list box, where only one item can be visible at a time, VisibleItems returns the name of that one item.

HiddenItems: Returns the pivotitems that are not currently visible. For example, because only one pivotitem can be displayed at a time in a Page drop-down list box, HiddenItems provides a method for accessing the other items in the drop-down list box.

ChildItems: Applies only to Row, Column, or Page pivotfields that have been grouped manually. ChildItems returns the pivotitems in the pivotfield to which grouping has been applied.

ParentItems: Applies only to Row, Column, or Page pivotfields that have been grouped manually. ParentItems returns the new group items that have been formed by grouping the various ChildItems.

PivotItem Properties and Methods

The PivotItem object is used to represent unique items in a pivotfield. Because Excel can generate a list of unique items from a database field, you save a tremendous amount of work dealing with database data. The PivotItem object has only a few properties and methods; the next two sections review the more important ones. Notice that several PivotField properties and methods also apply to PivotItem objects.

PivotItem properties

DataRange: Applies only to pivotitems of pivotfields in the Row, Column, and Page areas of the pivottable. DataRange returns a Range object that represents the range in the table's Data area corresponding to the specified pivotitem.

LabelRange: Applies only to pivotitems of pivotfields in the Row and Column areas of a pivottable. LabelRange returns a Range object that corresponds to the labels for the specified pivotitem in the pivottable.

Name: Returns either the name of the pivotitem or the actual value associated with the pivotitem. The Name property is read/write. When you change the name of a pivotitem, the pivottable retains the new name until the pivotitem is removed from the table, for example, by a new query specified through the PivotTableWizard method (which replaces the data in the RAM cache). Proc23 displays the pivotitem names in the drop-down list boxes in the Page area of the pivottable:

```
Sub Chap04aProc23_DisplayPageItems()
    Dim MessageString As String
    Dim FieldVar As PivotField
    Dim ItemVar As PivotItem
    Dim Pivot1 As PivotTable
    Set Pivot1 = Worksheets(1).PivotTables("Pivot1")
    With Pivot1
        .PivotFields("Category").Orientation = xlPageField
        .PivotFields("Product").Orientation = xlColumnField
    End With
    For Each FieldVar In Pivot1.PageFields
        MessageString = FieldVar.Name & " PivotItems:" & Chr(13)
        For Each ItemVar In FieldVar.PivotItems
            MessageString = MessageString & ItemVar.Name & Chr(13)
        Next
        MsgBox MessageString
    Next
End Sub
```

ParentItem: Applies only to pivotitems in manually grouped pivotfields in the Row, Column, and Page areas. As you recall, when a pivotfield is manually grouped, its items are represented as a group by items in a new pivotfield. The ParentItem property applies only to a pivotitem that is a childitem in a group. The ParentItem property returns the name of the group to which the childitem belongs. This property is read-only.

ShowDetail: A read/write property that pertains to pivotitems in manually grouped pivotfields in the Row, Column, and Page areas of a pivottable. ShowDetail can be set only for pivotitems that are considered parentitems of a grouped pivotfield. It can take a True or False value. If ShowDetail for a parentitem is True, all detail for the group is displayed. If ShowDetail is False, no childitems of the parentitem are displayed; only the total for the group is displayed. Proc24 (which follows) calls Proc17 (discussed on pages 188–189) to apply manual grouping to the pivottable. It then sets the ShowDetail property for the parentitems of the two resulting groups to False in order to hide all detail regarding the childitems:

```
Sub Chap04aProc24_HideParentItemDetail()
    Dim ItemVar As PivotItem
    Dim Pivot1 As PivotTable
    Set Pivot1 = Worksheets(1).PivotTables("Pivot1")
    Chap04aProc17_ManualGroup
    For Each ItemVar In Pivot1.PivotFields("Period2").PivotItems
        ItemVar.ShowDetail = False
    Next
    With Pivot1.PivotFields("Period2")
        .PivotItems(1).Name = "First Six Months"
        .PivotItems(2).Name = "Last Six Months"
    End With
End Sub
```

The resulting pivottable appears as follows. (Note that the right portion of the pivottable is not displayed here.)

Category	(All)					
Continent	(All)					
Sum of Revenue		Product				
Period2	Period	Gloves	Helmet	Pump	RoadTDF	Tita
First Six Months		$15,482,764	$16,282,432	$14,236,955	$16,309,415	$15,171,9
Last Six Months		$11,428,272	$12,333,407	$17,849,532	$17,090,914	$15,769,7
Grand Total		$26,911,036	$28,615,839	$32,086,487	$33,400,329	$30,941,6

By calling Proc18 (discussed on page 190), Proc25 resets the pivottable to its original state:

```
Sub Chap04aProc25_ResetDetail()
    Chap04aProc18_UnManualGroup
End Sub
```

ParentShowDetail: A read-only property that can be True or False and pertains only to pivotitems in manually grouped pivotfields in the Row, Column, and Page areas. ParentShowDetail is a property of the childitem. If ParentShowDetail is True, all detail regarding the parent pivotitem is displayed—that is, all the childitems in the group are displayed. If ParentShowDetail is False, no detail is displayed.

Position: Can be used to get or set the numeric ordering of a pivotitem relative to all the pivotitems in the corresponding pivotfield. This property pertains only to pivotitems in the Row, Column, and Page pivotfields.

SourceName: A read-only property that holds the name of the pivotitem as it exists in the original data source. (As mentioned, pivotitem names can be changed. Excel remembers the names and keeps them even when the architecture of the pivottable is changed.)

Value: Synonymous with the Name property.

Visible: Can be True or False and pertains only to pivotitems in pivotfields in the Row, Column, and Page areas. You can hide pivotitems from display (by setting the Visible property to False) without actually removing them from the pivottable. Proc26 uses the Visible property to hide the first six pivotitems in the Period pivotfield:

```
Sub Chap04aProc26_ShowLast6Months()
    Dim IntVar As Integer
    Dim Pivot1 As PivotTable
    Set Pivot1 = Worksheets(1).PivotTables("Pivot1")
    Worksheets(1).Activate
    With Pivot1.PivotFields("Period")
        For IntVar = 1 To 6
            .PivotItems(IntVar).Visible = False
        Next
    End With
End Sub
```

Proc27 uses the collection of pivotitems returned by the HiddenItems method to restore the table so that all Period pivotitems are displayed:

```
Sub Chap04aProc27_ResetPeriod()
    Dim ItemVar As PivotItem
    Dim Pivot1 As PivotTable
    Set Pivot1 = Worksheets(1).PivotTables("Pivot1")
    Worksheets(1).Select
    For Each ItemVar In Pivot1.PivotFields("Period").HiddenItems
        ItemVar.Visible = True
    Next
End Sub
```

PivotItem method

ChildItems: Returns one pivotitem or a collection of pivotitems that are child-items to the specified parentitem of a grouped pivotfield.

Calculated Fields and Items

New in Excel 97 is the ability to define calculated fields and items. Calculated fields are simply new PivotFields defined by some formula. The formula can refer to other PivotFields and/or cell references and can use most Excel functions. Once defined, the calculated field is maintained in the cache just like any other PivotField.

Calculated fields are defined by calling the Add method of the CalculatedFields object. This method takes two parameters—a name for the new field and a formula to define it. Proc28 demonstrates adding a calculated field called "Expenses" and displaying it in the data area of the pivottable:

```
Sub Chap04aProc28_AddCalculatedField()
    With Worksheets(1).PivotTables("Pivot1")
        .CalculatedFields.Add "Expenses", "=Revenue-Profit"
        .DataFields(1).Orientation = xlHidden
        .PivotFields("Expenses").Orientation = xlDataField
    End With
End Sub
```

Similar to calculated fields are calculated items, represented by the CalculatedItem object. Calculated items also have a name and formula, and are defined by calling the Add method of the CalculatedItems object. Once defined, they are treated like any other PivotItem object. For more information on calculated items, refer to the online VBA Help.

> **NOTE** To determine whether a PivotField or PivotItem is calculated, you can use the IsCalculated property of each of these objects. It will be set to True for calculated fields and items.

The Two Levels of Pivottable Queries

Pivottable queries operate at two levels. At the first level, a query is used to bring data from the underlying data source into the internal RAM cache of the pivottable, represented by the PivotCache object. The second level does not involve structured queries in the strictest sense but rather queries from the internal RAM cache that affect how the data is displayed in the table. You perform such second-level queries by manipulating the various properties and methods of the PivotTable, PivotField, and PivotItem objects. For example, setting the CurrentPage property of a pivotfield in the Page area to display a new pivotitem generates a new second-level query; this process requires only a single simple command. If you were to try to perform the same query by reading directly from an external database and placing data directly in a grid, you would have to do a tremendous amount of additional work.

The real power of the pivottable comes into play with second-level queries, which enable the pivottable to perform all the data-handling work for you. You can use simple, English-language–like syntax to generate these second-level queries, and because data is queried from a RAM-based data set, second-level queries are performed significantly faster than queries from disk-based databases.

Managing large amounts of data in pivottables

How much data can be stored in the internal RAM cache is a rather complicated issue because it depends on the amount of RAM on your system as well as on the structure and type of data in the database being queried. Some Excel developers have successfully pulled databases that have more than 100,000 records and over 10 fields per record into a RAM cache—this on Pentium/120 systems with 32 megabytes of RAM. When such large data sets are involved, however, performance suffers—primarily at the time when the data is read into the RAM cache. Reading such a large data set into the RAM cache on such a system could take up to 20 minutes.

FYI

Saving Space in RAM by Querying Portions of the Database

You can explicitly control what data gets read into the cache by manipulating the query that builds it. By using ODBC SQL query statements, you can bring selected portions of the database into the table. Therefore, to reduce the size of the data set in the RAM cache, you might want to call the PivotTableWizard method at various points in your application to change the data in the cache. Proc03 (discussed earlier in this chapter) showed how to do this. Let's take another look at that routine:

```
Sub Chap04aProc03_CreatePivot3()
    Dim QArray As Variant
    Dim Range1 As Range
    Dim Pivot1 As PivotTable
    Dim ConnectString As String
    Dim SQLString1 As String
    Dim SQLString2 As String
    Set Pivot1 = Worksheets(1).PivotTables("Pivot1")
    Set Range1 = Pivot1.DataLabelRange
    ConnectString = "ODBC;" & _
        "DBQ=" & ThisWorkbook.Path & "\BIKEDATA.MDB;" & _
        "Driver={Microsoft Access Driver (*.mdb)};"
```

(continued)

Saving Space in RAM by Querying Portions of the Database, *continued*

```
        SQLString1 = "SELECT * FROM Sales "
        SQLString2 = "WHERE (Sales.Revenue > 500000)"
        QArray = Array(ConnectString, SQLString1, SQLString2)
        Worksheets(1).Select
        Range1.Select
        Worksheets(1).PivotTableWizard xlExternal, QArray
End Sub
```

Proc03 calls the PivotTableWizard method to repopulate the RAM cache only with records that have Revenue values greater than $500,000. You can build complicated first-level queries by using ODBC SQL statements. (Chapter 7 covers such statements in greater detail.) Also, when calling the PivotTableWizard method on a pivottable that already exists, be sure to select the DataLabelRange property for the pivottable before you make the call to the PivotTableWizard. (Proc03 does so in the statement Range1.Select.) If you do not, Excel might attempt to create a new pivottable over the existing one, which often generates an error message.

This negative impact on performance is witnessed only when a program calls the PivotTableWizard method or the RefreshTable method; these are the only methods that read data into the RAM cache. Because you can save cached data with the pivottable in the workbook file, you can design your pivottables up front and save them along with the cached data to a workbook file for distribution. In such a case, the only real drain on performance comes when calls to the RefreshTable method are made to refresh the cache. Note that after data is in the RAM cache, performance no longer suffers. Excel is again able to perform lightning-fast second-level queries.

TIP Trial and error is probably the best approach for determining how much data to bring into the RAM cache in an application. Try testing data sets of different sizes on a system similar to your users', and then determine how long a period of time is reasonable to wait for the RefreshTable method to execute.

Server-Based Page Fields

Excel provides a feature called "server-based page fields" to help developers manage larger data sets in pivottables. When this feature is turned on, Excel only reads data into the cache for the currently displayed page field(s). When the user selects another item in the page field, the data source is queried again and the cache is rebuilt for the new page. This approach has the advantage of allowing pivottables to operate on data sets larger than the cache can hold, but it comes with trade-offs—you'll experience a delay when switching between items in the page field while Excel requeries the data source. Also, the ability to display the "(All)" item for page fields is lost.

Proc29 demonstrates how to set up server-based page fields. The ServerBased property of the PivotField object is used to turn this feature on. This property is ignored for PivotFields that do not have an xlPageField orientation:

```
Sub Chap04aProc29_ServerBasedPageFields()
    Dim PivotFieldVar As PivotField
    Dim Pivot1 As PivotTable
    Set Pivot1 = Worksheets(1).PivotTables("Pivot1")
    For Each PivotFieldVar In Pivot1.PageFields
        PivotFieldVar.ServerBased = True
    Next PivotFieldVar
End Sub
```

After running this routine, try selecting different items from the page fields. Note that Excel requeries the data source after each selection, and that the choices for "(All)" no longer appear in the page field item lists.

To return the page field behavior to normal, run Proc30:

```
Sub Chap04aProc30_ServerBasedPageFieldsReset()
    Dim PivotFieldVar As PivotField
    Dim Pivot1 As PivotTable
    Set Pivot1 = Worksheets(1).PivotTables("Pivot1")
    For Each PivotFieldVar In Pivot1.PageFields
        PivotFieldVar.ServerBased = False
    Next PivotFieldVar
End Sub
```

Display Area Limitations

The display area of a pivottable can be no larger than an Excel worksheet, which is limited to 65,536 rows and 256 columns. If you try to build a pivottable that exceeds this worksheet size, Excel displays an error message to give you the choice of either abandoning the procedure or continuing. (If you continue, you get a table that is only partially displayed.) In addition, when you call the Clear method on a large range on a worksheet (for example, if you use the Clear method on a large pivottable) Excel displays a warning message. You can avoid the display of this message by setting the DisplayAlerts property of the Application object to False (Application.DisplayAlerts = False).

PivotTable Protection Properties

Excel 97 adds a variety of properties to pivottable objects that enable the developer to tightly control what a user can and cannot do with a pivottable. Each of these properties takes a Boolean (True/False) value to enable or disable the associated feature. The properties on the following page apply to the PivotTable object, thereby affecting the pivottable as a whole.

EnableDrillDown	Allows/disallows the ability to perform drill down
EnableFieldDialog	Allows/disallows user access to the PivotTable Field dialog box
EnableWizard	Allows/disallows user access to the PivotTable Wizard

The following property applies to the PivotCache object, which also affects the pivottable as a whole:

| EnableRefresh | Allows/disallows the user's ability to refresh the pivottable |

These properties apply to individual PivotField objects within the pivottable:

DragToColumn	If False, field cannot be dragged to column area
DragToHide	If False, field cannot be dragged off the pivottable
DragToPage	If False, field cannot be dragged to page area
DragToRow	If False, field cannot be dragged to row area

Using Multiple Pivotfields in the Data Area

Earlier in this chapter, you saw that it is possible to use multiple pivotfields in any area of the pivottable. When you use multiple pivotfields in the Data area, Excel creates a new pivotfield named Data. This pivotfield is specially designed to hold multiple pivotfields in the Data area. You can set the Orientation property of the Data field to xlRowField or xlColumnField so that the labels for the multiple pivotfields in the Data area are displayed either going down the rows or across the columns. This feature is a useful one, especially when you work with databases that are structured to incorporate dates into database field names. When using such a database, you can construct a pivottable that displays dates across the columns by placing multiple date fields in the Data area and then setting the Data pivotfield orientation to xlColumnField. Proc31 provides an example of using the Data pivotfield to show expenses, revenue, profit, and unit totals for each product:

```
Sub Chap04aProc31_AddDataFields()
    Dim Pivot1 As PivotTable
    Set Pivot1 = Worksheets(1).PivotTables("Pivot1")
    Worksheets(1).Activate
    With Pivot1
        .PivotFields("Revenue").Orientation = xlDataField
        .PivotFields("Profit").Orientation = xlDataField
        .PivotFields("Units").Orientation = xlDataField
    End With
    Pivot1.PivotFields("Data").Orientation = xlColumnField
End Sub
```

The resulting pivottable appears as follows. (Note that only a portion of the pivottable is displayed here.)

Category	Accessories				
Continent	Africa				
	Product	Data			
	Gloves				
Period	Sum of Expenses	Sum of Revenue	Sum of Profit	Sum of Units	Sum of
1/20/96	831929	930296	98367	23257	
2/20/96	129162	222046	92884	5551	
3/20/96	389063	392202	3139	9805	
4/20/96	536706	556051	19345	13901	
5/20/96	151879	166677	14798	4166	
6/20/96	532029	546373	14344	13659	
7/20/96	-78602	12085	90687	302	
8/20/96	570524	606776	36252	15169	
9/20/96	534922	617820	82898	15445	
10/20/96	672323	684850	12527	17121	
11/20/96	504875	546197	41322	13654	
12/20/96	393816	446830	53014	11170	
Grand Total	5168626	5728203	559577	143200	

In Proc31, the Data pivotfield is created when the Revenue, Profit, and Units pivotfields are all added to the Expenses field in the Data area of the table. The Orientation property of the Data field is then set to xlColumnField so that the labels for the four pivotfields are displayed across the columns. Proc32 resets the table to its original configuration:

```
Sub Chap04aProc32_ReconstructPivotTable()
    Dim Pivot1 As PivotTable
    Set Pivot1 = Worksheets(1).PivotTables("Pivot1")
    Worksheets(1).Activate
    With Pivot1
        .PivotFields("Data").Orientation = xlHidden
        .PivotFields("Revenue").Orientation = xlDataField
    End With
End Sub
```

The Chart Object

The Chart object is Excel's second most powerful data analysis object and one of the most powerful charting engines available in any applications program or development environment. You can display data from any Excel worksheet range using any of 73 different chart types—14 main types and numerous subtypes.

Virtually every aspect of the Chart object can be controlled or manipulated in some fashion using the approximately 70 separate objects contained in the Chart object. Figure 4-2 shows the Excel object hierarchy under the Chart object.

203

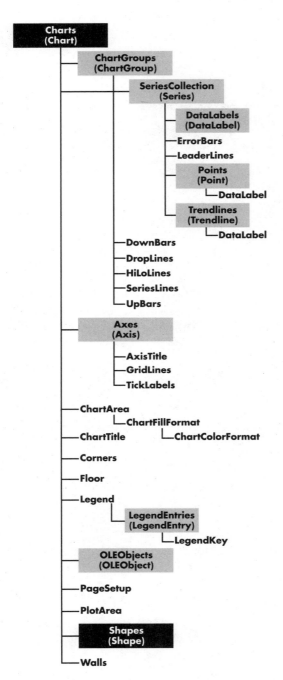

Figure 4-2. *The hierarchy of the Chart object.*

We'll take a look at each of the objects shown in Figure 4-2 and at their associated properties and methods. Figure 4-3 shows many of these objects as they appear in a chart.

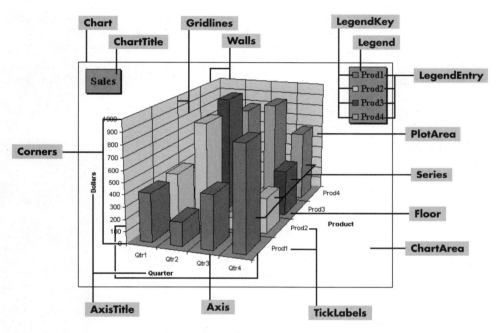

Figure 4-3. *The parts of a chart as represented by selected objects in the Chart object hierarchy.*

The Chart object can be used to access either charts that exist on their own separate sheets or ChartObject objects, which are floating graphical images of charts that exist on worksheets. (You'll read more about this topic in the coming pages.) Following are brief descriptions of many of the objects that fall under the Chart object's hierarchy.

ChartGroup: The ChartGroup object is used mostly in two-dimensional charts in which the different data series in the chart are plotted with different chart types. Such charts are known as "combination charts." For example, in a single two-dimensional chart you would be able to plot one data series as a line chart, another data series as a column chart, and still another data series as an area chart. A chartgroup is simply a group of data series that are all formatted with the same chart type. If you have a chart that has two data series formatted as line charts, for example, and two data series formatted as column charts, that chart consists of two chartgroups—one chartgroup that represents the data series formatted as lines and the other chartgroup that represents the data series formatted as columns. Charts that have data series plotted with only one chart type have only a single ChartGroup object.

The ChartGroup object includes several subobjects that are described here briefly: DownBars, UpBars, SeriesLines, DropLines, and HiLoLines. DownBars and UpBars may be used only with 2-D line charts and are most commonly found in High-Low-Close charts (line charts that have high, low, and close marks), although they can be applied to other line charts as well. When implementing UpBars and DownBars, Excel plots a bar between the first and last series at each data point. If the first series value is greater than the last series value at the given point, a DownBar is plotted (displayed in black), and if the last series value is greater than the first series value, an UpBar is plotted (displayed in white). HiLoLines are also used exclusively with 2-D line charts. HiLoLines display a vertical line between the highest and lowest values for a data point and are most often found in High-Low-Close stock charts. The following chart displays HiLoLines, UpBars, and DownBars:

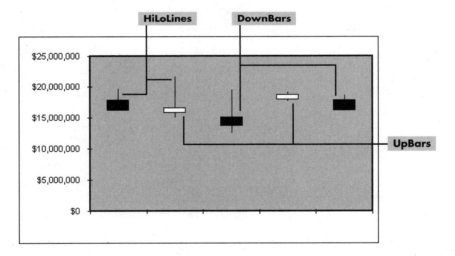

DropLines can be used in area, 3-D area, line, and 3-D line charts. DropLines are simply vertical lines that drop from a plotted point down to the x axis, as shown in the following chart:

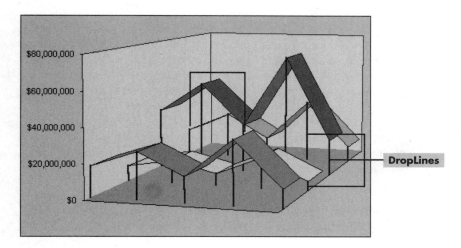

Last, SeriesLines can be used with stacked and 100-percent–stacked bar and column charts. They connect data ranges that correspond to the same data series in a stack. The following chart shows an example:

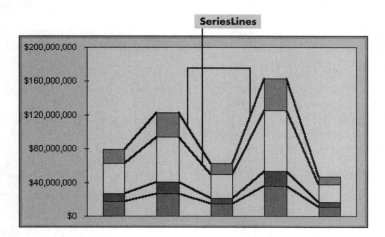

Series: In the Chart object hierarchy, the Series object falls under both the Chart and the ChartGroup objects. (See Figure 4-2 on page 204.) The Series object represents a data series that is plotted on the chart. It is an object in a collection; the name of the Series collection is SeriesCollection (because the plural of Series is also Series).

The Series object contains several subobjects that we discuss here only briefly: ErrorBars, Point, Trendline, and DataLabel. ErrorBars can be used on two-dimensional area, line, bar, column, and xy-scatter charts. They allow you to display an error range for every point in a data series (absolute, percentage, standard deviation, standard error, or custom). The Point object is used to represent the plotted points in a data series, and the Points collection contains all the data points in a data series. The Trendline object is used exclusively with two-dimensional line, bar, column, and xy-scatter charts. Trendlines are calculated by Excel automatically and can be based on one of six types of regression equations. (See Excel's online Help for more information.) The DataLabel object falls under three different objects: Series, Point, and Trendline. A DataLabel is simply a text box next to a point on a chart that displays the value of the point, the name of the data series, or a text string. Under the Point and Trendline objects, the DataLabel object represents a single label specific to a single point. Under the Series object, the DataLabels collection contains all the DataLabel objects for every point in the series.

ChartTitle: A text box that displays the title of the chart.

Legend: Represents the legend of the chart.

LegendEntry: Contained in the Legend object and represents an entry in the Legend. LegendEntries is a collection of all the LegendEntry objects in a Legend. Little can be done with the LegendEntry object—you cannot change the name of a data series in the legend through the LegendEntry object. You must instead use the Name property of the Series object to change a data series name.

LegendKey: Contained in the LegendEntry object. LegendKey's main purpose is to provide a way to change the color and style of the data point marker that is used in line, xy-scatter, and radar charts.

Axis: Represents the various axes of the Chart object: the category (x), value (y), and series (z) axes. The Axes collection represents all axes on a chart. Axis has numerous properties that mostly involve formatting of the axis. You cannot use the Axis object to change the values displayed on an axis. (These values represent the data being charted.)

AxisTitle: A subobject of the Axis object. It represents the title of the axis.

Gridlines: A subobject of the Axis object; its main function is to provide a way to format the gridlines on a chart. The only way to access the Gridlines object is through the MinorGridlines or MajorGridlines property of the Axis object (for example, Charts(1).Axes(1).MinorGridlines or Charts(1).Axes(1).MajorGridlines).

TickLabels: The TickLabels object is contained in the Axis object and provides a way to set the number format, font, and alignment of the various Axis labels. You cannot use the TickLabels object to change the values displayed on the axes.

ChartArea: The ChartArea object is contained in the Chart object and represents the entire area encompassing all elements of the chart (including the plotarea, legend, and charttitle).

DataTable: Contained in the Chartobject. It allows you to include a table of the chart's data inside the chart.

OLEObject: Applies only to charts that exist on their own sheets. It allows you to add ActiveX controls and linked or embedded OLE objects to your charts.

PlotArea: Contained in the Chart object. It represents the area occupied by the actual chart plot.

Floor: Represents the floor of the chart. (See Figure 4-3 on page 205.)

Walls: Represents the walls of the chart. (See Figure 4-3.)

Corners: Represents the corners of the chart. It applies only to 3-D charts. You cannot change chart corners; you can only select them. When corners are selected, the user can rotate the chart.

PageSetup: Represents all the page setup attributes associated with printing the chart.

Shapes: Represents all graphical objects and controls that are drawn on a chart.

Building and Formatting a Chart

As mentioned, two objects can represent charts in Excel:

■ **The ChartObject object:** The Chartobject object is a floating graphical image of a chart that can exist on a worksheet. Chartobjects are linked to worksheet ranges; whenever the numbers in the range to which a chartobject is linked are updated, the chartobject is updated as well.

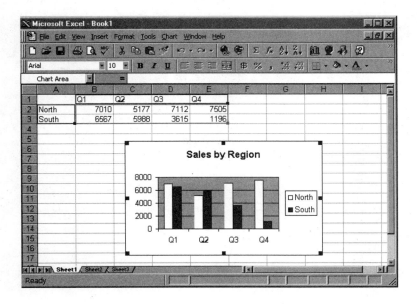

■ **The Chart object:** The Chart object exists on a separate sheet by itself. Charts are linked to ranges in the same manner as chartobjects.

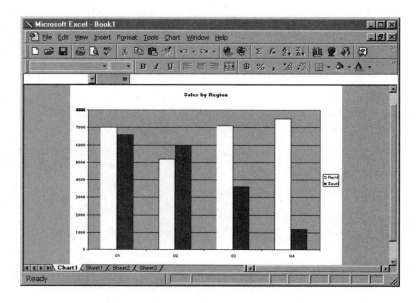

The important distinction here is that a ChartObject object is really just a container for a Chart object. For example, a chart on a separate sheet can be referred to in code as follows:

```
Workbooks(1).Charts(1)
```

A chart embedded on a worksheet, however, is referenced as follows:

```
Workbooks(1).Worksheets(1).ChartObjects(1).Chart
```

The ChartObject object actually *contains* a Chart object. To see this in practice, consider this example. To display a legend for a chart on a separate sheet, you would write this code (HasLegend is a property of the Chart object):

```
Workbooks(1).Charts(1).HasLegend = True
```

To do the same for a chart embedded on a worksheet, the following code would be used:

```
Workbooks(1).Worksheets(1).ChartObjects(1).Chart.HasLegend = True
```

The ChartObject object has its own set of properties that generally control the position and appearance of the chartobject on the sheet. Left, Top, Height, and Width are examples of these properties.

Creating a chart

Most charts used in Excel applications are created manually during the design phase. To create a chart, you must first have a range of data. Once you've got your data, follow these steps:

1. Select the entire range of data to be charted.

2. From the Insert menu, choose the Chart command. (You can also click the ChartWizard button on the Standard toolbar.)

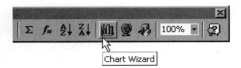

This launches Excel's ChartWizard, which steps you through four dialog boxes that help you to design a chart. The ChartWizard method is the main tool for creating a chart through VBA; it is actually a method of the Chart object. Before you can use the ChartWizard method, you must first have either a Chart object or a ChartObject object on which to call it.

3. Specify the various elements of your chart (i.e., type, format, data series, axes, legend, charttitle, and axistitle) in the first three dialog boxes.

4. The fourth dialog box asks you if you want to place the chart on a new sheet or as an object in a worksheet. These choices correspond to a Chart object and a ChartObject object, respectively.

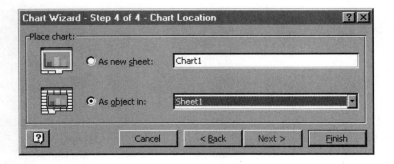

Let's take a look at two routines that create a single chart from the data in the pivottable you used earlier in this chapter. The first routine, Proc33 in module Chap04b, rebuilds the pivottable and then uses the DataBodyRange property of the pivottable, along with the Offset method of the Range object, to obtain the exact range of data to be charted. It then assigns this range to the ChartRange variable. Next the routine calls the Add method on the Charts collection to add a blank chart sheet and then makes a call to Proc34, passing the ChartRange and Chart1 variables. Proc34 uses the ChartWizard method to build and format the chart. Notice that numerous arguments that specify various elements of the chart are passed to the ChartWizard method. (All of these arguments are detailed in Excel's online VBA Help.)

```
Sub Chap04bProc33_CreateChart()
    Dim ChartRange As Range
    Dim PivotVar As PivotTable
    Dim Pivot1 As PivotTable
    Dim Chart1 As Chart
    'Remove all existing pivottables
    For Each PivotVar In Worksheets(1).PivotTables
        PivotVar.TableRange2.Clear
    Next
    'Re-create the sample pivottable
    Chap04aProc02_CreatePivot2
    Chap04aProc06_FormatTable
    Set Pivot1 = Worksheets(1).PivotTables("Pivot1")
    Worksheets(1).Activate
    Pivot1.DataBodyRange.Select
    'Include labels in the selected range
    Selection.Offset(-1, -1).Select
    Set ChartRange = Selection
    'Add and then format the chart
    Set Chart1 = Charts.Add
    Chap04bProc34_CallChartWizard ChartRange, Chart1
    Chart1.SizeWithWindow = True
End Sub

Sub Chap04bProc34_CallChartWizard(ChartRange As Range, _
                                  ChartVar As Object)
    ChartVar.ChartWizard _
            Source:=ChartRange, _
            gallery:=xl3DColumn, _
            Format:=6, _
            PlotBy:=xlColumns, _
            categoryLabels:=1, _
            seriesLabels:=1, _
            HasLegend:=True, _
            Title:="Sales"
End Sub
```

Run Proc33, and you see this chart on a separate sheet:

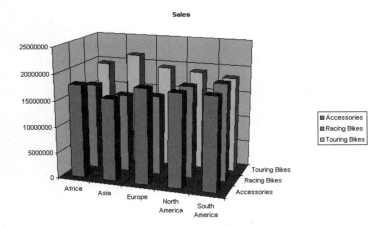

You create an on-sheet chart in a similar way, but instead of calling the Add method on the Charts collection, you call the Add method on the ChartObjects collection. When you call the Add method, you must pass four arguments that specify the Left, Top, Width, and Height properties of the on-sheet chart. Proc35 adds a chart on the second worksheet and then calls Proc34 to invoke the ChartWizard method to build and format the chart:

```
Sub Chap04bProc35_CreateChartObject()
    Dim ChartRange As Range
    Dim Pivot1 As PivotTable
    Dim ChartObject1 As ChartObject
    Dim Chart1 As Chart
    Set Pivot1 = Worksheets(1).PivotTables("Pivot1")
    Worksheets(1).Activate
    Pivot1.DataBodyRange.Select
    'Include labels in the selected range, remove totals
    Selection.Offset(-1, -1).Select
    Set ChartRange = Selection
    Worksheets(2).Activate
    'Add, then format the chart
    Set ChartObject1 =
        Worksheets(2).ChartObjects.Add(10, 10, 400, 200)
    Set Chart1 = ChartObject1.Chart
    Chap04bProc34_CallChartWizard ChartRange, Chart1
    Worksheets(2).Activate
End Sub
```

Proc36 changes the chart type of the chartobject on Sheet2 once for each series and changes the colors of a different series each time.

> **NOTE** In previous versions of Excel, you had to activate a ChartObject object before you could programmatically manipulate the properties of the Chart it contained. This limitation no longer exists in Excel 97.

```
Sub Chap04bProc36_ChangeChartObject()
    Dim SeriesVar As Series
    Dim ColorNum As Integer
    Dim OriginalColor As Integer
    Dim ChartTypeArray As Variant
    Dim ChartTypeVar As Integer
    ChartTypeArray = Array(xl3DArea, xl3DLine, xl3DColumn)
    ChartTypeVar = 0
    Worksheets(2).Activate
    With ActiveSheet.ChartObjects(1).Chart
        For Each SeriesVar In .SeriesCollection
            .Type = ChartTypeArray(ChartTypeVar)
            ChartTypeVar = ChartTypeVar + 1
            OriginalColor = SeriesVar.Interior.ColorIndex
            For ColorNum = 3 To 10
                SeriesVar.Interior.ColorIndex = ColorNum
                DoEvents
            Next
            SeriesVar.Interior.ColorIndex = OriginalColor
        Next
    End With
End Sub
```

Note the use of the DoEvents statement inside the For Next loop in this routine. DoEvents yields control of the computer back to Windows briefly to let it catch up on any pending operations. In the case of this routine, using the DoEvents statement lets Windows redraw the screen to reflect the new graph type and colors. Without it, the changes happen too fast to see.

The remainder of this chapter focuses on the first chart added to a separate sheet, Chart 1, using Proc33. All of the property settings and method calls that we will make on this chart can also be performed on the on-sheet chart that resides on Sheet2.

Chart Properties and Methods

The Chart object has numerous properties and methods, some of which you might never use when programming with VBA. Most of the Chart object's properties and methods are used to access either objects or collections that are contained in the chart (such as Legend, ChartTitle, PlotArea, Axes, and SeriesCollection). In addition, most of the properties and methods of the entire Chart object hierarchy deal primarily with formatting the chart; we cover such properties and methods only briefly here. For more information about the chart object's properties and methods (and about the objects contained in the Chart object), see Excel's online VBA Help.

Chart properties

The following list explains the chart properties and methods that you will use most often.

ChartTitle: Returns the ChartTitle object. To change the value displayed in the ChartTitle object, set the Text property (for example, Charts(1).ChartTitle.Text = "New Title").

Legend: Returns the Legend object, which you can use to format the chart legend.

ChartArea: Returns the ChartArea object, which you can use to format the chart's background.

PlotArea: Returns the area of the chart that contains the plotted data. It is often useful to format the size of the PlotArea without formatting the size of the other objects on the chart (legend, title, and so on).

Walls: Returns the Walls object of the chart, allowing you to format the chart's walls.

Floor: Returns the Floor object of the chart, allowing you to format the chart's floor.

Rotation: Available only for three-dimensional charts. It can be used to get or set the rotation of the chart (from 0 through 44 degrees for bar charts; from 0 through 360 degrees for other 3-D charts).

Elevation: Available only for three-dimensional charts. Elevation can be used to get or set the elevation of the chart (from 0 through 44 degrees for bar charts; from -90 through 90 degress for other 3-D charts).

ChartType: Used to get or set the type of the chart. Excel offers 73 chart types, including xlBarClustered, xlBarStacked, xl3DAreaStacked, xlCylinderCol, xlConeCol, xlLineMarkers, xlSurface, xlPieExploded, and xlStockHLC. For a complete list of chart types, refer to the online help or object browser.

SizeWithWindow: If set to True, Excel automatically resizes the Chart object to conform to the size of the window that contains the chart. This property applies only to charts that are on a separate sheet by themselves.

Chart methods

The following list describes Chart methods.

Axes: Returns a collection of Axis objects in the chart. You use the Axis objects to manipulate various axis properties as well as to format the AxisTitle, Gridlines, and TickLabels objects.

SeriesCollection: The SeriesCollection method returns a collection of the Series objects in the chart. Using the Series objects, you can format the display of the chart's data series.

ChartGroups: Provides access to the individual ChartGroup objects in a chart.

ChartWizard: Used to change the source data for the entire chart as well as perform many formatting functions.

Proc37 uses many of the properties and methods just described to format the chart that was created previously using Proc33. Some of the statements in this routine might cause flashing on your monitor's screen, depending on the type of monitor and graphics card installed on your system.

```
Sub Chap04bProc37_FormatChart()
    Dim AxisVar As Axis
    Dim RotateVar As Integer
    Dim ElevateVar As Integer
    Charts(1).Activate
    With Charts(1)
        MsgBox "Setting ChartTitle properties"
        With .ChartTitle
            .Text = "1996 Sales"
            .Font.Size = 18
            .Left = 5
            .Top = 10
            .Interior.ColorIndex = 15
            .Border.Weight = xlMedium
            .Shadow = True
        End With
        MsgBox "Setting Legend properties"
        With .Legend
            .Top = 10
            .Left = 390
            .Interior.ColorIndex = 15
            .Shadow = True
        End With
        MsgBox "Setting ColorIndex property of Interior of " _
                & "ChartArea object"
        .ChartArea.Interior.ColorIndex = 16
        MsgBox "Setting PlotArea properties"
```

```
With .PlotArea
    .Left = 5
    .Top = 0
    .Height = 250
    .Width = 450
End With
MsgBox "Setting Axis properties: Font of TickLabels " _
        & "and ColorIndex of the Border of Gridlines"
For Each AxisVar In .Axes
    With AxisVar.TickLabels.Font
        .Size = 8
        .Bold = True
        .Name = "Times New Roman"
    End With
    AxisVar.TickLabels.NumberFormat = "$#,##0_):($#,##0)"
    AxisVar.MajorGridlines.Border.ColorIndex = 5
Next
MsgBox "Setting the ColorIndex of the Interior of the Walls"
.Walls.Interior.ColorIndex = 15
MsgBox "Setting the ColorIndex of the Interior of the Floor"
.Floor.Interior.ColorIndex = 15
MsgBox "Setting the ColorIndex of the Interior of the " _
        & "Series in the Chart"
.SeriesCollection(1).Interior.ColorIndex = 3
.SeriesCollection(2).Interior.ColorIndex = 4
.SeriesCollection(3).Interior.ColorIndex = 5
MsgBox "Setting the Rotation property of the Chart"
For RotateVar = 30 To 120 Step 10
    .Rotation = RotateVar
Next
MsgBox "Setting the Elevation property of the Chart"
For ElevateVar = 10 To 80 Step 10
    .Elevation = ElevateVar
Next
For ElevateVar = 80 To 10 Step -10
    .Elevation = ElevateVar
Next
MsgBox "Setting the Type property of the Chart"
.Type = xl3DArea
MsgBox "3-D Area Chart"
.Type = xl3DColumn
MsgBox "3-D Column Chart"
.Type = xl3DLine
MsgBox "3-D Line Chart"
.Type = xl3DSurface
MsgBox "3-D Surface Chart"
.Type = xl3DPie
```

(continued)

continued

```
        MsgBox "3-D Pie Chart"
        .Type = xl3DBar
        MsgBox "3-D Bar Chart"
        .Type = xlArea
        MsgBox "2-D Area Chart"
        .Type = xlBar
        MsgBox "2-D Bar Chart"
        .Type = xlColumn
        MsgBox "2-D Column Chart"
        .Type = xlDoughnut
        MsgBox "Doughnut Chart"
        .Type = xlLine
        MsgBox "Line Chart"
        .Type = xlPie
        MsgBox "2-D Pie Chart"
        .Type = xlRadar
        MsgBox "Radar Chart"
        .Type = xlXYScatter
        MsgBox "XY-Scatter Chart"
        .Type = xl3DColumn
        .RightAngleAxes = False
        MsgBox "Showing data table."
        .HasDataTable = True
    End With
End Sub
```

After Proc37 executes successfully, you see the following chart:

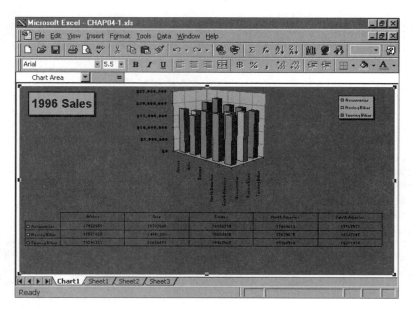

Changing the Data on a Chart

One of the most useful things that you can do with a chart in VBA is change the data that is plotted on the chart. You can do this in two ways:

- You can change the entire data range that the chart is based on by using the ChartWizard method.

- You can change the range of data that is plotted by an individual data series by setting the Values property of the Series object.

Proc38 below creates a new data range on the third worksheet in the workbook and then uses the ChartWizard method to change the data source for the entire chart:

```
Sub Chap04bProc38_NewChartData()
    Dim DataRange As Range
    Worksheets(3).Activate
    Range("C3").Select
    Range("C3").Value = "Q1"
    Range("C3").AutoFill Range("C3:F3"), xlFillDefault
    Range("B4").Value = "Prod1"
    Range("B4").AutoFill Range("B4:B11"), xlFillDefault
    Range("C4:F11").Formula = "=INT(1000*RAND())"
    Range("C4:F11").Copy
    Range("C4:F11").PasteSpecial xlValues
    Set DataRange = Range("C3").CurrentRegion
    DataRange.Select
    Charts(1).Select
    Charts(1).ChartWizard Source:=DataRange, _
                          categoryLabels:=1, _
                          seriesLabels:=1
End Sub
```

Proc39 displays only two data series on the chart. By setting the Values property of the second data series to different ranges on the worksheet, however, you can change the data that is plotted in the second data series.

```
Sub Chap04bProc39_ChangeChartSeriesData()
    Dim DataRange As Range
    Dim Q2Data As Range
    Dim Q3Data As Range
    Dim Q4Data As Range
    Worksheets(3).Activate
    Set Q2Data = Range("C3").CurrentRegion.Resize(8, 1).Offset(1, 2)
    Set Q3Data = Q2Data.Offset(0, 1)
    Set Q4Data = Q3Data.Offset(0, 1)
```

(continued)

continued
```
      Set DataRange = Range("C3").CurrentRegion.Resize(9, 3)
      With Charts(1)
          .Activate
          .ChartWizard source:=DataRange, _
                      categoryLabels:=1, _
                      seriesLabels:=1
          MsgBox "Chart currently displays Q1 and Q2 data"
          .SeriesCollection(2).Values = Q3Data
          .SeriesCollection(2).Name = "Q3"

          MsgBox "Chart currently displays Q1 and Q3 data"
          .SeriesCollection(2).Values = Q4Data
          .SeriesCollection(2).Name = "Q4"
          MsgBox "Chart currently displays Q1 and Q4 data"
      End With
  End Sub
```

Linking a chart to a pivottable

When a chart uses a pivottable as a data source and the source range corresponds to the TableRange1 property of the pivottable, the chart continues to display TableRange1 data no matter what structure the pivottable assumes. This feature is useful because it allows you to create one chart that will always be linked to the entire data area of the pivottable. In Excel, such charts are referred to as "pivot charts."

Proc40 creates a new chart sheet from TableRange1 of the pivottable on the first worksheet. (Notice how the RowGrand and ColumnGrand properties of the pivottable are set to False before the chart is created. This prevents "Grand Total" from appearing as a data series in the chart.) If you link the chart to TableRange1, the chart will always display all the data in the pivottable:

```
Sub Chap04bProc40_LinkChartToPivotTable()
    Dim ChartRange As Range
    Dim Pivot1 As PivotTable
    Dim Chart2 As Chart
    Set Pivot1 = Worksheets(1).PivotTables("Pivot1")
    Pivot1.RowGrand = False
    Pivot1.ColumnGrand = False
    Set ChartRange = Pivot1.TableRange1
    Worksheets(1).Select
    Set Chart2 = Charts.Add
    Chap04bProc34_CallChartWizard ChartRange, Chart2
End Sub
```

Take care when you link charts to TableRange1 of a pivottable, especially when you are working with pivottables that contain many rows and columns. Charts based on large pivottables tend to appear crowded. In such cases, you might want to control the data range on which your chart is based (by using the Offset and Resize methods to select a range directly).

Chart protection properties

Excel 97 adds a variety of properties to chart objects to let the developer tightly control what a user can and cannot do with a chart. Each of these properties takes a Boolean (True/False) value that enables or disables the associated feature. Note that these properties only affect end user actions—VBA code that is performing operations on charts will not be hindered or affected by setting these properties to True.

The following properties apply to the Chart object (either on a separate sheet or contained in a ChartObject object).

ProtectData	Setting to True prevents the user from modifying what data the chart is linked to
ProtectFormatting	Setting to True prevents access to all formatting commands associated with the chart
ProtectGoalSeek	Setting to True prevents direct manipulation of data points on charts that normally allow it (e.g., bar and column charts)
ProtectSelection	Setting to True prevents the selection of chart elements and the creation of new shapes or drawing objects on the chart

The following property applies only to the ChartObject object (i.e., the floating container for a Chart object embedded on a sheet).

ProtectChartObject	Setting to True prevents the user from moving, resizing, or deleting the ChartObject object

Take some time to experiment with these properties. You can set most of them manually using the Properties window. To do this, select the Chart2 sheet you just created using Proc40. Next, display the Control Toolbox toolbar (discussed in Chapter 3), and click the Properties button. The Properties window will appear and let you manipulate chart properties directly. The Properties window is shown on the following page.

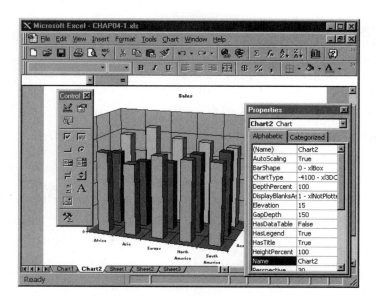

Note that for ChartObject objects, you'll need to set these properties in code; the Properties window is only available for Chart objects that exist on separate chart sheets.

Chart events

Also new to Excel 97 are a full set of events for charts. These events enable you to establish detailed responses to a user's interaction with a chart. You could, for example, implement "drill down" functionality so that when a user clicks on a particular series, a detailed breakdown of the data that makes up the series is shown. Chart events, which are handled by event procedures similar to those discussed for controls in Chapter 3, can be categorized into two groups: those intended to react to the chart as a whole and those intended to react to specific chart elements. In addition, the chart provides a special method that can be used in conjunction with events to implement manual hit testing.

Events for the chart as a whole

The following chart events react to manipulation of the chart as a whole.

Activate and Deactivate: Fire when a chart is activated (by clicking it) and deactivated (by clicking something other than the chart).

Arguments: None.

Resize: Fires when a ChartObject (an embedded chart) is resized or when the window containing a Chart object (a separate sheet) is resized. The Chart.SizeWithWindow property must be true for this event to fire.

Arguments: None.

Calculate: Fires when the chart recalculates because its underlying data is changing or new data is being added to the chart.

Arguments: None.

MouseDown, MouseUp, and MouseMove: MouseDown and MouseUp fire when the primary or secondary mouse buttons are pressed or released, respectively, over the chart. MouseMove fires continuously as the mouse pointer is moved over the chart.

Arguments: The button argument (MouseDown and MouseUp) indicates whether the primary or secondary mouse button fired the event. The shift argument (MouseDown and MouseUp) indicates the state of the Shift, Ctrl, and Alt keys during the event. The X and Y arguments specify the x and y coordinates of the mouse pointer in relation to the upper left-hand corner of the chart.

DoubleClick: Fires when the user double-clicks the chart.

Arguments: None.

BeforeRightClick: Fires before the shortcut menu that is activated by right-clicking a chart element appears. By setting the cancel argument of this event to True, you can, for example, suppress the default menu and show your own custom menu, or you can activate any other response you want.

Arguments: If set to True, the cancel argument prevents the default behavior (showing of a shortcut menu) from occurring.

DragOver, DragPlot: DragOver fires when a cell range is dragged over a chart. DragPlot fires when the cell range is actually dropped into the chart.

Arguments: None.

Events for chart elements

The following chart events react to the selection or manipulation of individual chart elements. Although they are technically events of the Chart object, each provides arguments that let you determine which chart element will be selected when the event fires.

Select: Fires when the user selects a particular chart element by clicking it.

Arguments: elementID, arg1, and arg2. (See the table on page 224 for details.)

BeforeDoubleClick: Fires just before the default action that occurs when a user double-clicks a particular chart element.

Arguments: elementID, arg1, arg2, and cancel. (See the following table for details about the first three.) If set to True, cancel cancels the default behavior associated with the double-click (usually the display of a format dialog box).

The following table describes the arguments that the Select chart event and BeforeDoubleClick chart event have in common:

elementID	Determines the chart element that fired the event. The chart element can be any one of the following constants: xlAxis, xlAxisTitle, xlChartArea, xlChartTitle, xlCorners, xlDataLabel, xlDataTable, xlDownBars, xlDropLines, xlErrorBars, xlFloor, xlHiLoLines, xlLeaderLines, xlLegend, xlLegendEntry, xlLegendKey, xlMajorGridlines, xlMinorGridlines, xlNothing, xlPlotArea, xlRadarAxisLabels, xlSeries, xlSeriesLines, xlShape, xlTrendLine, xlUpBars, xlWalls, xlXErrorBars, xlYErrorBars.
arg1	Provides different information depending on the value of elementID.
	Provides a seriesIndex argument, which is an index to a selected member of the chart's SeriesCollection collection, when elementID is one of the following: xlSeries, xlDataLabel, xlTrendLine, xlErrorBars, xlXErrorBars, xlYErrorBars, xlLegendEntry, and xlLegendKey.
	Provides an axisIndex argument, which is an index to a selected member of the chart's Axes collection, when elementID is one of the following: xlAxis, xlAxisTitle, xlMajorGridlines, xlMinorGridlines.
	Provides a groupIndex argument, which is an index to a selected member of the chart's ChartGroups collection, when elementID is one of the following: xlUpBars, xlDownBars, xlSeriesLines, xlHiLoLines, xlDropLines, xlRadarAxisLabels.
	Provides a shapeIndex argument, which is an index to a selected member of the chart's Shapes collection, when elementID is xlShape.
	For all other types of chart elements, arg1 is not used.
arg2	Provides additional information about arg1 depending on the value of elementID.
	Provides a pointIndex argument, which is an index to a selected member of the Points collection, when elementID is one of the following: xlSeries, xlDataLabel. A value of -1 indicates that all data points are selected.
	Provides a trendLineIndex argument, which is an index to a selected member of the TrendLines collection within a series, when elementID is xlTrendLine.

Provides an axisType argument (0=category, 1=value, 2=series) when elementID is one of the following: xlAxis, xlMajorGridlines, xlMinorGridlines, xlAxisTitle.

For all other types of chart elements, arg2 is not used.

SeriesChange: This event fires when the user directly manipulates a data point by selecting and dragging it on the chart.

Arguments: SeriesIndex and PointIndex. (See the preceding table for a description of these arguments.)

Manual Hit Testing

The Chart object also provides a method to let you perform manual hit testing. Hit testing means determining what was clicked given the x and y coordinates of the mouse pointer. Using the Chart.GetChartElement method, you can perform a hit test. Here's how hit testing works. GetChartElement takes the following five arguments: X, Y, elementID, arg1, arg2. X and Y are the coordinates of the mouse pointer, which you pass into the method call. You pass variables of the Long data type as the remaining three arguments. The method then returns information about the chart element through the elementID, arg1, and arg2 arguments, which are identical to those described for the Select and BeforeDouble-Click events.

Chart events example

To see some of these chart events in action, open the sample file CHAP04-2.xls. This workbook contains a chart sheet with event procedures written for the following chart events:

- Activate
- BeforeDoubleClick
- BeforeRightClick
- Calculate
- Deactivate
- Resize
- Select

Activate the chart by clicking the Chart1 tab and try to make these events fire by interacting with the chart. For example, to fire the Select event, click an element of the chart. A message box will appear with information about that element, as shown in the illustration on the following page.

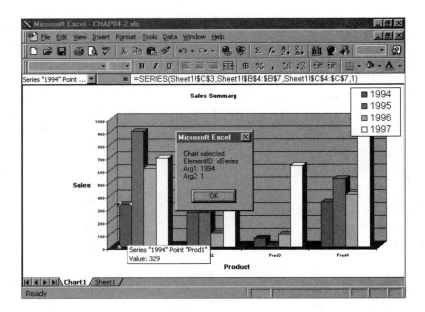

To view the code, you'll need to look at the code module for the Chart1 chart sheet. (Recall from Chapter 3 that Excel worksheets and charts can have code modules that contain their event procedures behind them.) You can get to this code module from the Project window in the Visual Basic Editor:

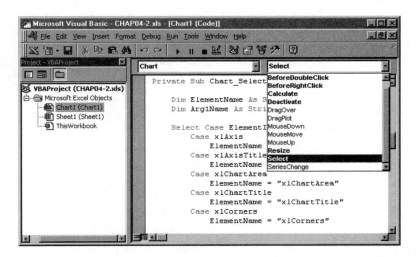

SUMMARY

This chapter described information systems and took an in-depth look at the two main building blocks for creating information systems that use Excel: the PivotTable and Chart objects. These are the main points covered in Chapter 4.

- Any information system that provides a mechanism for accessing large data sets so that users can quickly ask and get answers to complicated questions helps users make better decisions.

- Pivottables provide a tool for displaying data in different dynamic views, allowing the user to analyze data from various perspectives.

- Pivottables provide a number of ways for the user to apply mathematical functions to data, to group data, and to break down data on a percentage basis.

- All of the data analysis features provided by pivottables operate at a very high level of performance because the pivottable operates using data stored in a RAM cache.

- Using Excel's Chart object in conjunction with pivottables gives you even greater capability to analyze data. Charts and pivottables together allow you to graphically display the various data permutations a pivottable generates. When the Chart object is broken down into a hierarchy of different objects, almost every aspect of the chart can be manipulated through VBA.

- Charts provide a complete set of events and protection properties, which allows tight control of and response to user interaction with charts.

5

Custom Interface Design

The extent to which you customize an application that you develop in Microsoft Excel is a matter of preference. If you are writing a simple subroutine that will be used with some basic, built-in aspect of Excel, you might not need to create a custom menu or dialog box for it. If you are creating an application that will serve as a major information system, however, and you would like to limit the Excel environment to the functionality of your application, you might need to implement a high level of customization—eliminating all of Excel's menus and toolbars, for example, and using worksheet-based forms and dialog boxes extensively.

You can take customization to the ultimate level—at which no aspect of the Excel environment is visible to suggest to the user that your application is running in a spreadsheet program. That level of customization is, indeed, possible and is not all that difficult to implement. When you customize the Excel interface to that extent, however, take care to always return Excel to its original state after your application finishes running. Quite often, your users still need to use their copy of Excel as a stand-alone spreadsheet outside of your application, so your application shouldn't interfere with their other uses of Excel.

This chapter gives you an overview of how to create custom interfaces in Excel. You'll find information here about designing and implementing forms, working with control objects, handling dialog boxes, customizing command bars, and manipulating various Excel interface elements via the Application object. At the end of the chapter, you'll also find a brief discussion on the implementation of these interface elements.

Excel provides several control objects that allow you to easily transform a worksheet into an interactive form. With this functionality at the worksheet level, you are not limited to using menus, toolbars, and dialog boxes as the sole means of navigating through an application. Keep in mind, though, that to do a good job of designing an application, you must make a trade-off between having all features readily accessible to the user and designing an interface that avoids clutter. For example, too many buttons on a worksheet can be confusing, yet placing commands deep within a menu tree often ensures that they will never be used. Designing applications well is an art. But this chapter gives you some concrete direction by showing you various approaches to design and explaining how to manipulate Excel's user-interface aspects. This chapter also includes a number of sample routines. You can find these in the CHAP05-1.XLS file on the companion CD packaged with this book.

Designing and Creating Worksheet-Based Forms

The Excel Worksheet object serves as the base for designing and creating forms in Excel. Note that in Excel, a distinction is made between worksheet-based forms and custom dialog boxes. A form is based on a worksheet, and a dialog box is implemented with a userform in the Visual Basic Editor. In this section, we look exclusively at worksheet-based forms; dialog boxes are discussed in the section titled "Creating Custom Dialog Boxes," beginning on page 280.

NOTE Because the various controls provided by VBA can exist on worksheets or on userforms, the section titled "Working with Controls," beginning on page 261, pertains to both forms and dialog boxes.

A form in Excel is merely a specially formatted worksheet. Unformatted, a worksheet looks like a standard grid; it contains hundreds of thousands of cells, with column and row headings along its top and left sides, respectively. Each cell in a worksheet can contain text, numeric data, or formulas. Each cell also has associated aspects that can be manipulated to greatly enhance the appearance of the worksheet's contents. You can manipulate these aspects on the group of cells that constitute a worksheet to make the worksheet look like a form, as shown here.

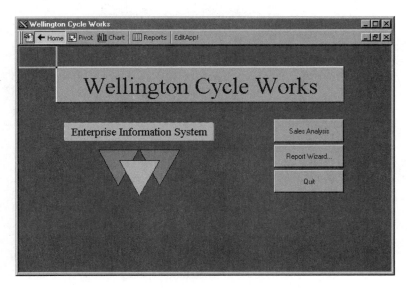

This form was built on top of a spreadsheet grid, yet no visual cues indicate to the user that a spreadsheet actually lies behind the form. Notice the custom buttons and graphics on the screen and the customized Excel title bar and menubar.

You usually design and create forms in Excel manually when you design an application. You format ranges to transform a worksheet into a form using the Format Cells dialog box. To access this dialog box, you either choose the Cells command from the Format menu or select Format Cells from the shortcut menu that appears when you right-click a cell or range of cells.

In the sections that follow, we look at the objects you use to design and create forms. These objects, as well as their associated properties and methods, are discussed in terms of how you use them in a VBA application. Although designing forms is primarily a manual process, you should be familiar with the objects that lie behind these forms. You will also often find it useful to format certain aspects of a form using VBA code, either during design so that you can automate repetitive tasks, or at runtime so that you can accentuate certain aspects of a form dynamically.

Objects Used to Design and Create Forms

To design and create forms, you most often use the following seven objects.

Range: Contained in the Worksheet object and used to reference worksheet cells.

Font: Contained in the Range object and used to format the font of cell entries.

Interior: Contained in the Range object and used to format the colors and patterns of cells.

Border: Contained in the Range object and used to format the style, color, and thickness (weight) of cell borders. The Border objects in a given range are accessible through the Borders collection.

Style: Contained in the Range object and used to hold groups of property settings for the Font, Interior, and Border objects; these groups make up what is known as a "style." You can also access the Font, Interior, and Border objects via the Style object.

Worksheet: Contained in the Workbook object and used to reference Excel worksheets. Worksheet objects are accessible through the Worksheets collection.

Window: Contained in the Application object (and also in the Workbook object) and used to format many of the various aspects of application or worksheet windows. Window objects are accessible through the Windows collection.

NOTE The Style, Font, Interior, and Border objects are also contained in many other Excel objects. Refer to the online VBA Help for a complete list.

Figure 5-1 shows the hierarchical ordering of these seven objects. Note that we do not look at the Application and Workbook objects in this section; they are displayed in Figure 5-1 only to show how the Window object is related to the other objects.

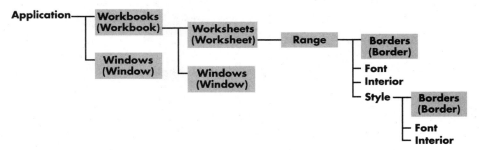

Figure 5-1. *The hierarchy of the objects you use most often to design and create forms.*

Using the Range Object to Create Forms

Our discussion of form design begins with an overview of the formatting properties of the Range object and then moves on to the Font, Interior, Border, and Style objects. We then examine the Worksheet and Window objects.

Because an Excel form is actually an Excel worksheet, the background of every form you design will contain a set—or a range—of worksheet cells. You can format these cells using the properties and methods of both the Range object and the objects that the Range contains. The Range object has quite a few properties and methods; we'll take a look at those that are most important in designing forms.

Range properties used with forms

Column: Number of the first column in the specified range. Read-only.

ColumnWidth: Width of the worksheet column or columns in the specified range; one ColumnWidth unit is equal to the width of one character in the Normal style.

CAUTION Do not confuse the ColumnWidth property with the Width property. Width is a read-only property of the Range object. It returns the width of the entire range in points (a point is $1/72$ inch). ColumnWidth sets or returns the width of an individual column or a set of columns in characters. If columns in the range are different widths, ColumnWidth returns Null.

Proc01 uses a For-Next loop to adjust the width of the first column in the first worksheet:

```
Sub Chap05aProc01_AdjustColumnWidth()
    Dim WidthVar As Integer
    Worksheets(1).Select
    With Range("A1")
        For WidthVar = .ColumnWidth To .ColumnWidth + 50
            .ColumnWidth = WidthVar
        Next
    End With
End Sub
```

EntireColumn: Returns the entire column(s) for the range. For example, the EntireColumn property of Range("B2") returns a Range object that consists of all the cells in Column B. Read-only.

EntireRow: Returns the entire row(s) for the range. Read-only.

Font: Returns the Font object for the range. The Font object is used to format various aspects of the font of the cell entries in a range. Font is discussed in greater detail in the section titled "Using the Font Object to Format Values in a Range," beginning on page 243. Read-only.

FormulaHidden: If True and the range contains a formula, the formula is hidden (i.e., not displayed in the formula bar) when the worksheet is protected.

Height: Height of the specified range in points ($1/72$ inch). Read-only.

Hidden: If True, the entire row or column of the specified range is hidden. When setting this property, you must specify an entire row or column as the Range object.

Proc02 uses the AutoFill method of the Range object to enter values in the first 30 cells in the first column of the worksheet and then uses the EntireColumn property to hide the entire column.

NOTE When setting the Hidden property to hide entire rows or columns, you must use the EntireRow and EntireColumn properties of the Range object.

```
Sub Chap05aProc02_HideColumn()
    Worksheets(1).Select
    Range("A1").Value = "Quarter1"
    Range("A1").AutoFill Range("A1:A30")
    MsgBox "Data is entered in the first 30 cells of Column A."
    Range("A1").EntireColumn.Hidden = True
    MsgBox "Column A is hidden."
End Sub
```

Proc03 can be used to reveal the column and restore its proper width:

```
Sub Chap05aProc03_RestoreColumn()
    Worksheets(1).Select
    Range("A1").EntireColumn.Hidden = False
    MsgBox "The Hidden property of Column A is set to False."
    Range("A1").UseStandardWidth = True
    Range("A1").CurrentRegion.ClearContents
    MsgBox "ClearContents is called to clear Column A data."
End Sub
```

HorizontalAlignment: Horizontal alignment of the entries in a range. This can be one of seven values:

xlGeneral	Normal alignment for the entry—that is, alignment depends on the data type
xlCenter	Entry is centered
xlRight	Entry is right-justified
xlLeft	Entry is left-justified
xlJustify	Entry is left-justified and, if required, broken up into multiple lines, with each full line both left- and right-justified
xlCenterAcrossSelection	Entry is centered across the specified range, all in the same row—if the range contains multiple entries, each entry is centered across a range up to the next entry
xlFill	Entry is repeated to fill the entire width of the column

Proc04 enters a text string in a cell and then goes through all the possible values for HorizontalAlignment:

```
Sub Chap05aProc04_SetHorizontalAlignment()
    Worksheets(1).Select
    With Range("A1")
        .UseStandardWidth = True
        .Value = "A computer is no better than its program."
        .HorizontalAlignment = xlGeneral
        MsgBox "HorizontalAlignment = xlGeneral"
        .ColumnWidth = 50
        .HorizontalAlignment = xlCenter
        MsgBox "HorizontalAlignment = xlCenter"
        .HorizontalAlignment = xlRight
        MsgBox "HorizontalAlignment = xlRight"
        .HorizontalAlignment = xlLeft
        MsgBox "HorizontalAlignment = xlLeft"
```

```
            .UseStandardWidth = True
            .HorizontalAlignment = xlJustify
            MsgBox "HorizontalAlignment = xlJustify"
            Range("A1:H1").HorizontalAlignment = xlCenterAcrossSelection
            MsgBox "HorizontalAlignment =" & _
                "xlCenterAcrossSelection: A1 to H1"
            .Value = "Computer"
            .ColumnWidth = 50
            .HorizontalAlignment = xlFill
            MsgBox "HorizontalAlignment = xlFill"
            .UseStandardWidth = True
            .ClearContents
            Range("A1:H1").HorizontalAlignment = xlGeneral
    End With
End Sub
```

The following example shows a text entry that has been entered in cell A1, with the HorizontalAlignment property of the range A1:H1 set to xlCenterAcross-Selection.

IndentLevel: Sets the level of indentation for the range in units based on the width of characters in the current font. This causes entries in cells to be indented from the left edge of the cell. The IndentLevel property can range from 0 through 15, where 0 means no indentation and 15 means maximum indentation. This property is meaningful only when the HorizontalAlignment property is set to xlLeft; if HorizontalAlignment is set to some other value, IndentLevel resets it to xlLeft before setting the indentation.

Interior: Returns the Interior object of the range. You use the Interior object to format various aspects of a range's background color and pattern. The Interior object is discussed in greater detail in the section titled "Using the Interior Object to Format the Interior of a Range," beginning on page 245.

Locked: If True, the contents of the range cannot be changed when protection is set for the worksheet contents. (This property is True by default.)

NumberFormat: Formatting style for the numbers that appear in the range.

235

NOTE For more information about number formatting styles, refer to Excel's online Help (see the "Formatting Numbers, Dates, and Times" topic under Formatting Worksheets).

Proc05 goes through some of the number format codes that are available in Excel:

```
Sub Chap05aProc05_ApplyNumberFormats()
    Dim RangeVar As Variant
    Worksheets(1).Select
    Range("A1:F1").ColumnWidth = 15
    For Each RangeVar In Range("A1:F20")
        RangeVar.Value = (1000 * Rnd) -500
    Next
    With Range("A1:F20")
        .NumberFormat = "#,##0.00_);[Red](#,##0.00)"
        MsgBox "Standard Number Format"
        .NumberFormat = "$#,##0.00_);[Red]($#,##0.00)"
        MsgBox "Currency Format"
        .NumberFormat = _
            "_($* #,##0_);_($* (#,##0);_($* "" - ""_);_(@_)"
        MsgBox "Accounting Format"
        .NumberFormat = "@"
        MsgBox "Numbers as Text"
        .NumberFormat = "0.00E+00"
        MsgBox "Scientific Notation"
        .NumberFormat = "0.00%"
        MsgBox "Percentage Format"
        .NumberFormat = "# ??/??"
        MsgBox "Fractions"
        .Clear
        .UseStandardWidth = True
    End With
End Sub
```

The following example shows a series of numbers that were formatted by setting the NumberFormat property to the "$#,##0.00_);[Red]($#,##0.00)" currency format.

	A	B	C	D	E
1	$205.55	$33.42	$79.52	($210.44)	($198.05)
2	($485.98)	$260.72	$314.49	$209.04	($454.65)
3	$362.62	$290.48	($126.46)	$461.95	$371.45
4	$449.56	($135.98)	$24.87	$267.11	($446.50)
5	($31.30)	($201.83)	$122.70	$147.82	($236.21)
6	$329.80	$324.60	$89.16	$486.09	$410.96
7	$195.12	$480.00	($256.07)	$33.87	($393.63)
8	$176.18	($484.30)	$75.18	($399.95)	($396.98)
9	($215.52)	($454.35)	($204.23)	($117.99)	($199.03)
10	$479.83	($98.63)	($221.72)	($339.56)	($337.18)
11	($89.93)	($87.23)	$212.73	($173.79)	$133.18
12	($313.99)	$83.36	($419.29)	($42.03)	$405.73

CHAP05-1.xls

Orientation: Orientation of a value in a range. This can be either an angle in degrees (ranging from -90° through 90°) or one of four predefined values:

xlDownward	Value aligned sideways going down the range (corresponds to -90°)
xlHorizontal	Value displayed horizontally (corresponds to 0°)
xlUpward	Value aligned sideways going up the range (corresponds to 90°)
xlVertical	Value displayed vertically (does not correspond to any angle)

Orientation has no effect when IndentLevel is non-zero. Proc06 shows the various settings for the Orientation property:

```
Sub Chap05aProc06_SetOrientation()
    Worksheets(1).Select
    With Range("A1")
        .Value = "All the world's a stage."
        .Orientation = xlHorizontal
        MsgBox "Orientation = xlHorizontal"
        .Orientation = xlVertical
        MsgBox "Orientation = xlVertical"
        .Orientation = xlUpward
        MsgBox "Orientation = xlUpward"
        .Orientation = xlDownward
        MsgBox "Orientation = xlDownward"
        .Orientation = 30
        MsgBox "Orientation = 30 degrees"
        .Orientation = -78
        MsgBox "Orientation = -78 degrees"
        .Clear
    End With
End Sub
```

This example shows a text entry in cell A1; the Orientation property of Range("A1") has been set to 30.

Row: Returns the number of the range's first row.

RowHeight: Sets or returns the height of all the rows in the specified range in points ($1/72$ inch). If the rows are of different heights, RowHeight returns Null.

> **CAUTION**   Don't confuse the RowHeight property with the Height property. RowHeight is used to set or return the height of each row in a range, and Height is a read-only property used to return the total height of all rows in a range.

ShrinkToFit: Causes a cell to automatically adjust the point size of its font to fit its contents within the width of the cell. The point size will automatically decrease as the contents get too large to display horizontally in the cell and increase if the length of the contents are later reduced. In no case will the point size grow larger than the originally formatted size.

Proc07 shows the effect of this property as a cell's contents grow and shrink in length:

```
Sub Chap05aProc07_ShrinkToFit()
    With Range("C2")
        .Font.Size = 12
        .ColumnWidth = 16
        .ShrinkToFit = True
        MsgBox "About to enter text."
        .Value = "Plenty of room."
        MsgBox "About to enter more text."
        .Value = "It's getting a little crowded."
        MsgBox "About to enter even more text."
        .Value = "It's getting more than a little crowded."
        MsgBox "About to remove text."
        .Value = "Much better."
        MsgBox "All done."
        .Clear
        .UseStandardWidth = True
    End With
End Sub
```

Style: Returns the Style object for the range. The Style object can be used to format the Font, Interior, and Borders objects as a group. The Style object is discussed in greater detail in the section titled "Using the Style Object," beginning on page 250.

UseStandardHeight: If True, the row height of the specified range is set to the StandardHeight (a property of the worksheet). If rows in the range are of differing heights, this property returns Null.

UseStandardWidth: If True, the column width of the specified range is set to the StandardWidth (a property of the worksheet).

NOTE The StandardHeight and StandardWidth properties are determined by the size and style of the worksheet's standard font (the
font specified in the Normal style). In addition, StandardWidth
can be changed through the Format Column menu.

VerticalAlignment: Vertical alignment of entries in the cells of a range. Alignment can be one of four values:

xlBottom	Entries at the bottom of the cells
xlCenter	Entries centered vertically
xlJustify	Entries of multiple lines distributed vertically within the cells
xlTop	Entries at the top of the cells

Proc08 sets the VerticalAlignment property to various values:

```
Sub Chap05aProc08_VerticalAlignment()
    Worksheets(1).Select
    With Range("A1")
        .RowHeight = 50
        .ColumnWidth = 20
        .Value = "An application is no better than its object model."
        .VerticalAlignment = xlCenter
        MsgBox "VerticalAlignment = xlCenter"
        .VerticalAlignment = xlBottom
        MsgBox "VerticalAlignment = xlBottom"
        .VerticalAlignment = xlTop
        MsgBox "VerticalAlignment = xlTop"
        .VerticalAlignment = xlJustify
        MsgBox "VerticalAlignment = xlJustify"
        .Clear
        .UseStandardHeight = True
        .UseStandardWidth = True
    End With
End Sub
```

The following shows an example of setting the VerticalAlignment property of
Range("A1") to xlCenter:

239

Width: The width of the specified range in points ($1/72$ inch).

WrapText: If True, Excel wraps the text within each cell in the range and distributes the text over multiple lines within the width setting of the columns, expanding the row heights as necessary to accommodate the text.

Range methods used with forms

AutoFormat: Provides access to one of the most powerful formatting features of the Range object. By calling the AutoFormat method, you can apply one of 16 built-in formats to a table of data within a range or remove existing formatting from the range. AutoFormat takes seven arguments. The first argument—format—is a constant value representing the type of AutoFormat to be implemented. The last six arguments—number, font, alignment, border, pattern, and width—can be set to either True or False to selectively implement certain aspects of the format.

Proc09 creates a table of data on the first worksheet and then applies all of Excel's built-in formats to the table, one format at a time:

```
Option Base 1
Sub Chap05aProc09_ApplyAutoFormats()
    Dim FormatArray As Variant
    Dim FormatName As Variant
    Dim y As Integer
    Worksheets(1).Select
    Range("B5") = "1996 Sales"
    Range("C5").Value = "Quarter1"
    Range("C5").AutoFill Range("C5:F5")
    Range("G5").Value = "Total"
    Range("B6").Value = "Product1"
    Range("B6").AutoFill Range("B6:B9")
    Range("B10").Value = "Total"
    With Range("C6:F9")
        .Formula = "=INT(1000*RAND())"
        .Copy
        .PasteSpecial xlValues
    End With
    Range("C10:F10").FormulaR1C1 = "=SUM(R[-4]C:R[-1]C)"
    Range("G6:G10").FormulaR1C1 = "=SUM(RC[-4]:RC[-1])"
    Range("B5").CurrentRegion.NumberFormat = "$#,##0"
    FormatArray = Array(xlClassic1, xlClassic2, xlClassic3, _
                    xlAccounting1, xlAccounting2, _
                    xlAccounting3, xlAccounting4, xlColor1, _
                    xlColor2, xlColor3, xlList1, xlList2, _
                    xlList3, xl3DEffects1, xl3DEffects2, _
                    xlSimple, xlNone)
```

```
FormatName = Array("xlClassic1", "xlClassic2", "xlClassic3", _
                "xlAccounting1", "xlAccounting2", _
                "xlAccounting3", "xlAccounting4", _
                "xlColor1", "xlColor2", "xlColor3", _
                "xlList1", "xlList2", "xlList3", _
                "xl3DEffects1", "xl3DEffects2", "xlSimple", _
                "xlNone")
Range("A1").Select
For y = 1 To UBound(FormatArray)
    Range("B5").AutoFormat Format:=FormatArray(y)
    MsgBox "format:=" & FormatName(y)
Next
Range("B5").CurrentRegion.Clear
Range("B5").UseStandardWidth = True
End Sub
```

For this table, the AutoFormat method has been called to apply the xlClassic3 format:

1996 Sales	Quarter1	Quarter2	Quarter3	Quarter4	Total
Product1	$635	$615	$912	$54	$2,216
Product2	$607	$646	$852	$814	$2,919
Product3	$409	$676	$62	$125	$1,272
Product4	$881	$165	$533	$998	$2,577
Total	$2,532	$2,102	$2,359	$1,991	$8,984

TIP You can manually apply one of Excel's built-in formats to any range of data by choosing AutoFormat from the Format menu.

BorderAround: Places a border around the specified range. BorderAround takes these arguments: lineStyle, weight, colorIndex, and color.

Borders: Returns a collection of borders for the range. Each range has up to eight borders—xlEdgeTop, xlEdgeBottom, xlEdgeRight, xlEdgeLeft, xlInsideHorizontal, xlInsideVertical, xlDiagonalUp, and xlDiagonalDown—and each border can be formatted using the properties of the Border object. The Border object is explained in detail in the section titled "Using the Border Object to Format Range Borders," beginning on page 247.

NOTE Single-cell ranges do not have xlInsideHorizontal and xlInsideVertical borders. Furthermore, single-row ranges do not have an xlInsideHorizontal border and single-column ranges do not have an xlInsideVertical border.

Columns: Returns a collection of columns for the specified range.

Justify: Evenly distributes a text entry vertically in a range. If necessary, the Justify method distributes text that is too wide for the given range among cells below it.

Merge and UnMerge: Microsoft Excel 97 adds a new feature called cell merging that allows you to combine any rectangular range of adjacent and contiguous cells into one cell. You would refer to the newly combined cell using the name of its upper left child cell. For example, if cells B4:D4 were merged into one cell, the single merged cell would be referred to as B4 (cells C4 and D4 would no longer exist on their own).

Merged cells can be very useful when designing forms. For example, they can be used to create input fields of different widths on different rows in the same column. Once cells are merged, the single cell behaves as any normal cell. It can have formats applied to it, contain formulas, etc.

Proc10 demonstrates merging cells (using the Merge method) and Proc11 demonstrates unmerging cells (using the UnMerge method):

```
Sub Chap05aProc10_MergeCells()
    Range("B2:D2").Select
    With Selection
        .Merge
        .HorizontalAlignment = xlCenter
        .Value = "I'm a merged cell."
        MsgBox "Cells have been merged."
    End With
End Sub


Sub Chap05aProc11_UnmergeCells()
    Worksheets(1).Select

    ' Note that the merged cell is referred to by its original
    ' upper left corner
    With Range("B2")
        .UnMerge
        .Value = "I'm no longer merged."
    End With
    MsgBox "Cells have been unmerged."
    Range("B2").ClearContents
    Range("A1").Select
End Sub
```

Rows: Returns a collection of rows for the specified range.

Using the Font Object to Format Values in a Range

To format entries in a range, you use the Font object, which is a subobject of the Range object. By setting the properties of Font, you can control how text strings, values, and formulas are displayed in a range.

The following list shows the most important Font properties for designing and creating forms. (Note that the Font object has no methods.) All of the Font properties listed can be set either manually or via a subroutine.

TIP To set Font properties manually, use the Font tab of the Format Cells dialog box.

Font properties used with forms

Bold: True or False; if True, the font is bold.

Color: RGB color of the font. Font has two properties that can be used to set color: Color and ColorIndex. To set the Color property, you must pass the result of the RGB function. RGB takes three arguments—red, green, and blue—and a number from 0 through 255 can be passed for each argument. RGB takes the three arguments and forms a number that corresponds to the appropriate color.

Proc12 uses the RGB function and three random integers from 0 through 255 to set the Color property 10 times:

```
Sub Chap05aProc12_ChangeFontColor()
    Dim x As Integer
    Dim RedColor As Integer
    Dim GreenColor As Integer
    Dim BlueColor As Integer
    Worksheets(1).Select
    Range("A1").Value = "Fourscore and seven years ago..."
    With Range("A1").Font
        .Size = 18
        .Bold = True
        For x = 1 To 10
            RedColor = Int((255 * Rnd) + 0)
            GreenColor = Int((255 * Rnd) + 0)
            BlueColor = Int((255 * Rnd) + 0)
            .Color = RGB(RedColor, GreenColor, BlueColor)
            MsgBox "Color = RGB(" & RedColor & ", " & _
                    GreenColor & ", " & BlueColor & ")"
        Next
    End With
    Range("A1").Clear
End Sub
```

ColorIndex: Second property that can be used to set font color. You can set ColorIndex to any integer from 0 through 56; these numbers correspond to the 56 colors on Excel's built-in color palette, which you can view in the online VBA Help for ColorIndex. (Setting ColorIndex to 0 applies the automatic color, which is defined in the Windows Control Panel.)

TIP   To view Excel's color palette in the user interface, click the Font tab in the Format Cells dialog box.

FontStyle: Can be used to set the Bold and Italic properties of the Font by using a string. FontStyle can take one of four values: "Regular", "Italic", "Bold", or "Bold Italic".

Italic: True or False; if True, the font is italicized.

Name: Name of the font as a string.

Size: Integer that represents the point size of the font.

Strikethrough: True or False; if True, the font has a horizontal line running through it.

Subscript: True or False; if True, the font is subscripted.

Superscript: True or False; if True, the font is superscripted.

Underline: Can take one of five values: xlNone, xlSingle, xlDouble, xlSingle-Accounting, or xlDoubleAccounting.

Proc13 shows how to set many of the Font properties we just reviewed:

```
Sub Chap05aProc13_FormatFont()
    Worksheets(1).Select
    With Range("A1")
        .Value = "Mr. Watson, come here."
        With .Font
            .Bold = True
            .Italic = True
            .Name = "Times New Roman"
            .Size = 26
            MsgBox "Times New Roman, Bold, Italic, 26"
            .Subscript = True
            MsgBox "Subscript = True"
            .Superscript = True
            MsgBox "Superscript = True"
            .Superscript = False
            .Strikethrough = True
            MsgBox "Strikethrough = True"
```

```
        .Strikethrough = False
        .Underline = xlSingle
        MsgBox "Underline = xlSingle"
        .Underline = xlDouble
        MsgBox "Underline = xlDouble"
      End With
      .Clear
    End With
End Sub
```

This example shows a text string that has been formatted as Times New Roman, bold, italic, point size 26, and double-underlined:

Using the Interior Object to Format the Interior of a Range

The Interior object, which is contained in the Range object, is used to format the interior of a range. By setting the ColorIndex and Pattern properties of a range's interior, you can change the color and texture of worksheet cells to make the worksheet look more like a form.

Interior properties used with forms

Color: Used in the same way as the Color property of the font to set the RGB color of a range's interior.

ColorIndex: Used to set the interior color ranges to one of the 56 colors in Excel's built-in color palette. Setting ColorIndex to 0 applies the automatic color.

Pattern: Used to set the background pattern of the range's interior. The pattern can be set to one of 20 *xl-* constants.

NOTE	See the "Pattern Property" topic in Excel's online VBA Help for information about the *xl*-constants used for the 20 possible settings of the Interior object's Pattern property.

PatternColor: Used to set the RGB color of the background pattern of a range's interior.

PatternColorIndex: Used to set the background pattern color of a range's interior to one of the 56 colors in Excel's built-in color palette. Setting Pattern-ColorIndex to 0 applies the automatic color.

Proc14 uses random integers to set the Pattern, PatternColorIndex, and Color-Index properties of Range("A1:J21") of the first worksheet:

```
Sub Chap05aProc14_FormatInterior()
    Dim PatArray As Variant
    Dim PatString As Variant
    Dim IntPattern As Integer
    Dim IntPatternColorIndex As Integer
    Dim IntColorIndex As Integer
    Dim x As Integer
    PatArray = Array(xlAutomatic, xlChecker, xlCrissCross, _
                     xlDown, xlGray16, xlGray25, xlGray50, _
                     xlGray75, xlGray8, xlGrid, xlHorizontal, _
                     xlLightDown, xlLightHorizontal, xlLightUp, _
                     xlLightVertical, xlNone, xlSemiGray75, _
                     xlSolid, xlUp, xlVertical)
    PatString = Array("xlAutomatic", "xlChecker", "xlCrissCross", _
                      "xlDown", "xlGray16", "xlGray25", "xlGray50", _
                      "xlGray75", "xlGray8", "xlGrid", _
                      "xlHorizontal", "xlLightDown", _
                      "xlLightHorizontal", "xlLightUp", _
                      "xlLightVertical", "xlNone", "xlSemiGray75", _
                      "xlSolid", "xlUp", "xlVertical")
    Worksheets(1).Select
    For x = 1 To 20
        IntPattern = Int(20 * Rnd) + 1
        IntPatternColorIndex = Int(56 * Rnd)
        IntColorIndex = Int(56 * Rnd)
        With Range("A1:J21").Interior
            .Pattern = PatArray(IntPattern)
            .PatternColorIndex = IntPatternColorIndex
            .ColorIndex = IntColorIndex
        End With
        MsgBox "Pattern = " & PatString(IntPattern) & Chr(13) & _
               "PatternColorIndex = " & IntPatternColorIndex & _
               Chr(13) & "ColorIndex = " & IntColorIndex
    Next
    Range("A1:J21").Interior.Pattern = xlNone
End Sub
```

Using the Border Object to Format Range Borders

The Border object, accessible through the Borders collection, represents the border outline of each cell on a worksheet. Through the Border object, you can format various properties of range borders, such as Color, LineStyle, and Weight. The Border object has no methods.

Border properties used with forms

Color: Used to set the RGB color of a range's border.

ColorIndex: Used to set the color of a range's border to one of the 56 colors in Excel's built-in color palette. Setting ColorIndex to 0 applies the automatic color.

LineStyle: Used to set the line style of a border. You can set LineStyle to one of eight *xl*-constants.

Weight: Used to set the line thickness of a border. This property can be one of four values: xlHairline, xlThin, xlMedium, or xlThick.

> **NOTE**
>
> The LineStyle and Weight properties are used together to represent the 13 border styles available from the Format Cells dialog box. The next sample routine we look at (Proc15) demonstrates all the valid combinations.

Proc15 sets the LineStyle, Weight, and ColorIndex properties of each Border object in a range. Note that you obtain the Border object by calling the Borders method on the Range object. The Borders method takes an index as an argument to indicate which border to return. The following indexes can be used:

xlEdgeLeft, xlEdgeRight, xlEdgeTop, xlEdgeBottom	Represent the left, right, top, and bottom outer edges of a range. For multiple-cell ranges, these indexes correspond to the *outer* edges only.
xlInsideHorizontal, xlInsideVertical	Represent the interior horizontal and vertical borders of a range. Not applicable to single-cell ranges or one-dimensional ranges (e.g., single-row ranges do not have interior horizontal borders, and single-column ranges do not have interior vertical borders).
xlDiagonalUp, xlDiagonalDown	Represent diagonal borders on the interior of each individual cell in a range. The "up" diagonal extends from the lower left to the upper right of the cell, and the "down" diagonal extends from the upper left to the lower right.

NOTE When both diagonal borders are set to a LineStyle other than
xlNone, setting the properties of the up diagonal border affects
both borders; setting the properties of the down diagonal has
no effect.

```
Sub Chap05aProc15_FormatBorder()
    Dim aRange As Range
    Set aRange = Range("B2:E6")
    MsgBox "About to cycle through border styles."
    Chap05aProc16_CycleThruBorderFormats aRange
    aRange.ClearFormats
End Sub

Sub Chap05aProc16_CycleThruBorderFormats(aRange As Range)
    Dim BorderArray As Variant
    Dim x As Variant
    BorderArray = Array( _
        xlEdgeLeft, _
        xlEdgeRight, _
        xlEdgeTop, _
        xlEdgeBottom, _
        xlInsideHorizontal, _
        xlInsideVertical, _
        xlDiagonalDown, _
        xlDiagonalUp)
    For Each x In BorderArray
        With aRange.Borders(x)
            .LineStyle = xlContinuous
            .Weight = xlHairline
            .ColorIndex = 1
        End With
    Next
    MsgBox "Hairline"
    For Each x In BorderArray
        With aRange.Borders(x)
            .LineStyle = xlDot
            .Weight = xlThin
            .ColorIndex = 1
        End With
    Next
    MsgBox "Dot"
    For Each x In BorderArray
        With aRange.Borders(x)
            .LineStyle = xlDashDotDot
            .Weight = xlThin
            .ColorIndex = 3
        End With
```

```
Next
MsgBox "DashDotDot (Thin)"
For Each x In BorderArray
    With aRange.Borders(x)
        .LineStyle = xlDashDot
        .Weight = xlThin
        .ColorIndex = 4
    End With
Next
MsgBox "DashDot (Thin)"
For Each x In BorderArray
    With aRange.Borders(x)
        .LineStyle = xlDash
        .Weight = xlThin
        .ColorIndex = 5
    End With
Next
MsgBox "Dash (Thin)"
For Each x In BorderArray
    With aRange.Borders(x)
        .LineStyle = xlContinuous
        .Weight = xlThin
        .ColorIndex = 6
    End With
Next
MsgBox "Thin"
For Each x In BorderArray
    With aRange.Borders(x)
        .LineStyle = xlDashDotDot
        .Weight = xlMedium
        .ColorIndex = 7
    End With
Next
MsgBox "DashDotDot (Medium)"
For Each x In BorderArray
    With aRange.Borders(x)
        .LineStyle = xlSlantDashDot
        .Weight = xlMedium
        .ColorIndex = 8
    End With
Next
MsgBox "SlantDashDot (Medium)"
For Each x In BorderArray
    With aRange.Borders(x)
        .LineStyle = xlDashDot
        .Weight = xlMedium
        .ColorIndex = 9
```

(continued)

continued

```
            End With
        Next
        MsgBox "DashDot (Medium)"
        For Each x In BorderArray
            With aRange.Borders(x)
                .LineStyle = xlDash
                .Weight = xlMedium
                .ColorIndex = 10
            End With
        Next
        MsgBox "Dash (Medium)"
        For Each x In BorderArray
            With aRange.Borders(x)
                .LineStyle = xlContinuous
                .Weight = xlMedium
                .ColorIndex = 11
            End With
        Next
        MsgBox "Medium"
        For Each x In BorderArray
            With aRange.Borders(x)
                .LineStyle = xlContinuous
                .Weight = xlThick
                .ColorIndex = 12
            End With
        Next
        MsgBox "Thick"
        For Each x In BorderArray
            With aRange.Borders(x)
                .LineStyle = xlDouble
                .Weight = xlThick
                .ColorIndex = 0
            End With
        Next
        MsgBox "Double"
End Sub
```

Using the Style Object

The Style object is an object in a collection that has many of the same format-ting properties as the Range object: FormulaHidden, HorizontalAlignment, IndentLevel, Locked, NumberFormat, Orientation, ShrinkToFit, VerticalAlign-ment, and WrapText. Style also contains the Font, Interior, and Border objects, and has a Name property that you can use to specify the name of a style.

Proc17 creates a new Style object by calling the Add method on the Styles collection. One argument is passed to Add; this is "NewStyle", which is the name of the new Style object. Several property assignments are then made to the NewStyle object and to the Font, Interior, and Borders objects within NewStyle. Next some text is entered into Range("A1") through the Value property, and the Style property for the same range is set to "NewStyle", which applies NewStyle to the range:

```
Sub Chap05aProc17_CreateNewStyle()
    Dim NewStyle As Style
    ActiveWorkbook.Styles.Add ("NewStyle")
    Set NewStyle = ActiveWorkbook.Styles("NewStyle")
    With NewStyle
        .HorizontalAlignment = xlCenter
        .NumberFormat = "$#,##0_);($#,##0)"
        .Orientation = 0
        With .Font
            .Name = "Times New Roman"
            .Size = 12
            .Bold = True
            .Italic = True
        End With
        With .Interior
            .ColorIndex = 3
        End With
        With .Borders
            .LineStyle = xlDouble
            .ColorIndex = 4
        End With
    End With
    Worksheets(1).Select
    Range("A1").Value = "Test"
    Range("A1").Style = "NewStyle"
End Sub
```

FYI

Using the Style Object to Simplify Assigning Property Settings

You can assign to a single Style object a group of formatting property settings for range, font, pattern, and border. Then you can assign this Style object to the Style property of the range in order to apply this group of property settings to the range. Taking this approach saves you the extra work of specifying each property setting for the range.

When a Style object is added by calling the Add method on the Styles collection, the added style is saved with the workbook when it is saved. Once the Style object has been added, you can use it repeatedly to apply the formatting properties it contains to different ranges. Proc18 provides an example. It sets the Value property of all of the cells in Range("A1:I12") to random integers and then sets the Style property of the same cells to NewStyle (the style added in Proc17 on page 251). Last, Proc18 resets the Style property of each of the cells to Normal and calls the ClearContents method to clear the values from the cells:

```
Sub Chap05aProc18_ApplyNewStyle()
    Dim CellVar As Range
    Worksheets(1).Select
    For Each CellVar In Range("A1:I12")
        CellVar.Value = Int((999 * Rnd) + 100)
    Next
    For Each CellVar In Range("A1:I12")
        CellVar.Style = "NewStyle"
    Next
    MsgBox "New style applied."
    For Each CellVar In Range("A1:I12")
        CellVar.Style = "Normal"
        CellVar.ClearContents
    Next
End Sub
```

The following example shows the result of applying the Style object created in Proc18 to a range of data:

To delete a Style object from the Styles collection, you simply call the Delete method, as Proc19 shows:

```
Sub Chap05aProc19_DeleteNewStyle()
    ActiveWorkbook.Styles("NewStyle").Delete
End Sub
```

Using the Worksheet Object to Design Forms

Although forms in Excel are based on worksheets, you actually use only a few properties and methods of the Worksheet object to design forms. Several properties that are important to forms design appear to belong to the Worksheet object but actually belong to the Window object. These properties are DisplayGridlines, DisplayHeadings, DisplayHorizontalScrollBar, DisplayVerticalScrollBar, and DisplayWorkbookTabs. (These are discussed in the section titled "Using the Window Object to Design Forms," beginning on page 255.) Here we concern ourselves only with those worksheet properties and methods that are related to protecting and activating worksheets. By calling the Protect method, you can establish different levels of protection for the cells, shapes, and scenarios on a worksheet.

Worksheet properties used with forms

The following worksheet properties are important in designing forms:

Name: Name of the worksheet as a string.

ProtectContents: If True, the contents (cells) of the worksheet are protected. Read-only.

ProtectDrawingObjects: If True, the shapes on the worksheet are protected. Read-only.

ProtectionMode: If True, the worksheet has been protected from changes made only by the user—that is, VBA code can still be used to make changes to the worksheet. If False, the worksheet is protected from changes made by VBA code as well as any made by the user. Read-only.

ProtectScenarios: If True, the worksheet scenarios are protected. (Worksheet scenarios are discussed in Chapter 8 in the section titled "The Scenario Object," beginning on page 439.) Read-only.

Visible: Used to hide or display the worksheet. Visible can be assigned one of three values:

True	The worksheet is visible.
False	The worksheet is not visible, but the user can make the worksheet visible by choosing the Sheet command from the Format menu and then selecting Unhide.
xlVeryHidden	The worksheet is not visible, and the user cannot make the worksheet visible—in this case, the worksheet can be made visible only by setting the Visible property to True with VBA code.

Worksheet methods used with forms

The majority of the worksheet methods are used for data handling or to access the various collections that the Worksheet object contains, including the collections of graphical objects contained in the Shapes collection (refer to Chapter 2 for an overview of the Shapes collection). Five worksheet methods, however, are important in designing forms:

Activate: Activates the worksheet. This method brings the worksheet to the front of the active window. Either the Activate method or the Select method can be used to switch focus from one form to another.

Protect: Protects the worksheet so that changes cannot be made to it. By preventing users from making any changes to a form, the Protect method maintains the form's integrity. Protect has five arguments:

password	A string used as a password; if a password is specified, it is impossible to unprotect the worksheet without the password.
drawingObjects	If True, the shapes on the worksheet are protected.
contents	If True, the contents of the cells in the worksheet are protected.
scenarios	If True, the scenarios on the worksheet are protected. (Worksheet scenarios are discussed in Chapter 8 in the section titled "The Scenario Object," beginning on page 439.)
userInterfaceOnly	If True, the worksheet is protected from changes made only by the user—that is, VBA code can still be used to make changes to the worksheet. If False, the worksheet is protected from changes made by VBA code as well as any made by the user.

Select: Activates the worksheet. This method brings the worksheet to the front of the active window. Either the Select method or the Activate method can be used to switch focus from one form to another.

SetBackgroundPicture: The SetBackgroundPicture method takes one argument—fileName—a string that is the path to a graphic file that will be used as a tiled background for the worksheet. Note that the SetBackgroundPicture method is also available for the Chart object.

Unprotect: Unprotects the worksheet. Unprotect takes one argument—a string that represents a password. A password is required only if a password was specified when the Protect method was called on the worksheet.

Using the Window Object to Design Forms

The Window object is important in designing forms because it has several properties that affect the way a worksheet appears. Most of the properties discussed here can be set manually in the Window Options section under the View tab in the Options dialog box. (To get to this dialog box, choose the Options command from the Tools menu.) In addition, after these Window properties are set, they are saved with the workbook file when it is saved, which means that you can set the properties once during design time and then not worry about them at runtime.

Although many of the Window properties described in this section can be set no matter what type of sheet is currently active (worksheet or chart), here we look at these properties from the viewpoint of the Worksheet object only. Note also that some of the Window property settings are specific to individual worksheets. For example, settings made for the DisplayGridlines and Display-Headings properties are implemented only on the active worksheet. However, other Window property settings—such as DisplayWorkbookTabs, Display-HorizontalScrollBar, and DisplayVerticalScrollBar—affect all worksheets in a workbook. Let's take a look at these Window properties. (You generally don't use any methods of the Window object in designing a form.) Two lists of Window properties are presented below: those that affect individual worksheets and those that affect an entire workbook.

Window properties that affect individual worksheets

DisplayFormulas: If True, underlying formulas are displayed in cells on the worksheet; if False, values—that is, the results of such formulas—are displayed. This property is False by default.

DisplayGridlines: If True, gridlines are displayed on the worksheet.

DisplayHeadings: If True, row and column headings are displayed along the left side and across the top of the worksheet.

DisplayZeros: If True, zero values are displayed; if False, zero values are not displayed. This property is True by default.

ScrollColumn: Number of the worksheet column that appears at the far left of the window.

ScrollRow: Number of the worksheet row that appears at the top of the window.

Window properties that affect an entire workbook

Caption: The Window caption displayed in the title bar. By default, the Caption property holds the name of the active workbook. To restore the default caption of the Window object, set its Caption property to ActiveWorkbook.Name.

DisplayHorizontalScrollBar: If True, a horizontal scroll bar is displayed along the bottom edge of the worksheet.

DisplayVerticalScrollBar: If True, a vertical scroll bar is displayed along the right edge of the worksheet.

DisplayWorkbookTabs: If True, tabs for each of the sheets in the workbook are displayed along the bottom edge of the workbook.

Height: Height of the window in points (1/72 inch).

Left: Distance from the left edge of the window to the left edge of the Excel workspace in points (a point is 1/72 of an inch). A value of less than zero means that the left edge of the window is beyond the left edge of the Excel workspace.

Top: Distance from the top edge of the window to the top edge of the Excel workspace in points (1/72 inch). A value of less than zero means that the top edge of the window is higher than the top edge of the Excel workspace.

Width: Width of the window in points (1/72 inch).

WindowState: State of the window. WindowState can take one of three values:

xlNormal	Window neither maximized nor minimized; window size governed by the Height and Width properties
xlMaximized	Window maximized to fill the entire workspace area
xlMinimized	Window minimized and displayed as an icon in the workspace area

Proc20 sets many of the Window properties just listed as an example of how various aspects of the Excel worksheet can be altered to make the worksheet more closely resemble a blank form. Specifically, the routine turns off gridlines, row and column headings, horizontal and vertical scroll bars, and the workbook tabs. The routine also sets the Caption, WindowState, Height, Width, Top, and Left properties before it restores the active window to a more typical state:

```
Sub Chap05aProc20_FormatWorksheet()
    Dim oldCaption As String
    Worksheets(1).Activate
    With ActiveWindow
        .DisplayGridlines = False
        MsgBox "ActiveWindow.DisplayGridlines = False"
        .DisplayHeadings = False
        MsgBox "ActiveWindow.DisplayHeadings = False"
        oldCaption = .Caption
        .Caption = "Application File"
        MsgBox "ActiveWindow.Caption = ""Application File"""
        .DisplayHorizontalScrollBar = False
```

```
      MsgBox "ActiveWindow.DisplayHorizontalScrollBar = False"
      .DisplayVerticalScrollBar = False
      MsgBox "ActiveWindow.DisplayVerticalScrollBar = False"
      .DisplayWorkbookTabs = False
      MsgBox "ActiveWindow.DisplayWorkbookTabs = False"
      .WindowState = xlNormal
      MsgBox "ActiveWindow.WindowState = xlNormal"
      .Height = 150
      MsgBox "ActiveWindow.Height = 150"
      .Width = 150
      MsgBox "ActiveWindow.Width = 150"
      .Top = 0
      MsgBox "ActiveWindow.Top = 0"
      .Left = 0
      MsgBox "ActiveWindow.Left = 0"
      .WindowState = xlMaximized
      .DisplayGridlines = True
      .DisplayHeadings = True
      .Caption = oldCaption
      .DisplayHorizontalScrollBar = True
      .DisplayVerticalScrollBar = True
      .DisplayWorkbookTabs = True
   End With
End Sub
```

Following is the worksheet window after Proc20 runs. Notice that all evidence of Excel has been eliminated and that the window displays a custom caption:

Creating a Worksheet-based Form

Now that we've looked at many of the objects used to design forms, let's create a worksheet-based form. Proc21 on the following page uses the properties and methods we've just discussed to transform a blank worksheet into a form for a fictitious company named Wellington Cycle Works.

```vba
Sub Chap05aProc21_CreateAForm()
    Worksheets(1).Select
    With ActiveWindow
        .WindowState = xlMaximized
        .DisplayGridlines = False
        .DisplayHeadings = False
        .Caption = ""
        .DisplayHorizontalScrollBar = False
        .DisplayVerticalScrollBar = False
        .DisplayWorkbookTabs = False
    End With
    Range("A1:Z5").Interior.ColorIndex = 16
    With Range("A6:Z6").Borders(xlEdgeTop)
        .LineStyle = xlContinuous
        .Weight = xlThick
        .ColorIndex = 1
    End With
    Range("A6:Z100").Interior.ColorIndex = 5
    With Range("A2")
        .Value = "Wellington Cycle Works"
        With .Font
            .Name = "Times New Roman"
            .Size = 36
            .Bold = True
            .ColorIndex = 6
        End With
    End With
    Range("A2:J2").Select
    With Selection
        .Merge
        .HorizontalAlignment = xlCenter
    End With
    With Worksheets(1)
        .Shapes.AddShape(msoShapeUpRibbon, 170, 125, _
            300, 50).Select
        With Selection
            .ShapeRange.Fill.ForeColor.SchemeColor = 54
            .Characters.Text = "Enterprise Information System"
            .HorizontalAlignment = xlCenter
            .VerticalAlignment = xlCenter
            With .Font
                .Name = "Arial"
                .FontStyle = "Regular"
                .Size = 12
                .Bold = True
                .ColorIndex = 2
            End With
        End With
    End With
```

```
        End With
        Range("A1").Select
End Sub
```

Following is the form that is displayed when you run Proc21:

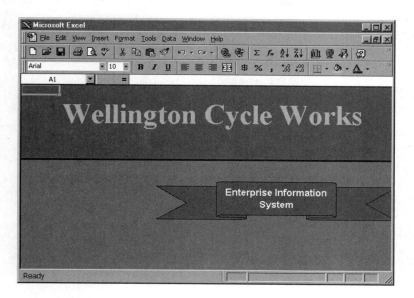

To restore the workspace to standard settings, you can use Proc22. (To run Proc22, choose the Macro command from the Tools menu, click Macros to display the Macro dialog box, select Chap05aProc22_ResetWorkSpace, and click Run.)

```
Sub Chap05aProc22_ResetWorkSpace()
    Worksheets(1).Select
    With ActiveWindow
        .WindowState = xlMaximized
        .DisplayGridlines = True
        .DisplayHeadings = True
        .Caption = ThisWorkbook.Name
        .DisplayHorizontalScrollBar = True
        .DisplayVerticalScrollBar = True
        .DisplayWorkbookTabs = True
    End With
    With Worksheets(1)
        .Range("A1:Z100").Clear
        .Shapes(1).Delete
    End With
End Sub
```

FYI

Removing the Window Control Menu

In Microsoft Excel 97 for Windows, both the Workbook window and the Application window contain a control menu that is accessed through a small icon in the upper left corner of the window. You eliminate the control menu from the workbook window by calling the Protect method on the Workbook object and passing True for the Windows argument:

```
ActiveWorkbook.Protect Windows:=True
```

The Workbook control menu can be restored by calling the Unprotect method. Eliminating the control menu from the Application window is a little more difficult because doing so actually requires that you call a Windows API function. The RemoveControlMenu and RestoreControlMenu routines (which follow) can be used to remove and restore the Control menu of the Application window in Excel 97. Note that the Declare statements listed must be present at the top of the VBA module in which these functions are used.

```
Declare Function FindWindowA Lib "USER32" ( _
    ByVal lpClassName As Any, _
    ByVal lpWindowName As Any) As Long
Declare Function GetWindowLongA Lib "USER32" ( _
    ByVal hWnd As Integer, _
    ByVal nIndex As Integer) As Long
Declare Function SetWindowLongA Lib "USER32" ( _
    ByVal hWnd As Integer, _
    ByVal nIndex As Integer, _
    ByVal dwNewLong As Long) As Long
Global Const GWL_STYLE = (-16)
Global Const WS_SYSMENU = &h80000

Sub RemoveControlMenu()
    Dim WindowStyle As Long
    Dim hWnd As Long
    Dim WindowName As String
    WindowName = Application.Caption
    hWnd = FindWindowA(0&, ByVal WindowName)
    WindowStyle = GetWindowLongA(hWnd, GWL_STYLE)
    WindowStyle = WindowStyle And (Not WS_SYSMENU)
```

```
        result = SetWindowLongA(hWnd, GWL_STYLE, WindowStyle)
End Sub

Sub RestoreControlMenu()
    Dim WindowStyle As Long
    Dim hWnd As Long
    Dim WindowName As String
    WindowName = Application.Caption
    hWnd = FindWindowA(0&, ByVal WindowName)
    WindowStyle = GetWindowLongA(hWnd, GWL_STYLE)
    WindowStyle = WindowStyle Or WS_SYSMENU
    result = SetWindowLongA(hWnd, GWL_STYLE, WindowStyle)
End Sub
```

Working with Controls

As we've seen, the Range, Font, Interior, Border, Style, Worksheet, and Window objects are used to format various aspects of a worksheet in order to create a form. To give forms functionality, you use controls. Controls can range in complexity from a simple command button to a multimedia control capable of playing video and sound. If you are familiar with Visual Basic, you already know about the many built-in controls provided by Excel 97 (text boxes, command buttons, listboxes, etc.), but you can also add any number of custom controls from Microsoft or third parties, and you can add controls you build yourself using C++. Both built-in and custom controls are called ActiveX controls. (ActiveX controls have been identified by several names in the past including OLE Controls and OCXs.) No matter what the name, the idea is the same: controls let you extend the functionality of your application by inserting pre-built components. Excel 97 now fully supports the ActiveX Control architecture. Controls, like other objects, have associated sets of properties, methods, and events. Controls can exist on worksheets, charts, or custom dialog boxes. (Note that the new ActiveX controls made available through the Control Toolbox can be used only on userforms and worksheets. You can implement controls on charts by using the controls available through the old Forms toolbar.) The same set of common controls is shared among all Microsoft Office 97 applications, VBA, and Microsoft Visual Basic 5.0. In this section, we'll take a look at the core set of common controls by using them on worksheets. The section titled "Creating Custom Dialog Boxes" on page 280 discusses using these controls on dialog boxes.

Placing Controls on Sheets

You usually create a control on a worksheet or dialog box when you first design an application; you use the Control Toolbox toolbar to create the control. To access the Control Toolbox, choose the Toolbars command from the View menu, and select Control Toolbox. On the Control Toolbox toolbar, you will find buttons that correspond to most of the common control objects, as well as a few additional buttons to manipulate them. This is the Control Toolbox toolbar:

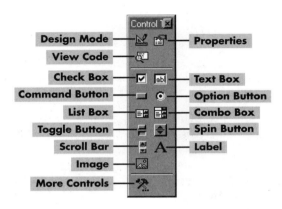

NOTE Excel 97 provides a series of new ActiveX controls that are made available through the Control Toolbox toolbar. These new ActiveX controls provide rich functionality and powerful event models, but they can be used only on userforms and worksheets—they cannot be used on charts. For backward compatibility reasons, Excel 97 still provides a set of "older" Excel controls through the old Forms toolbar. Although these older controls are not as flexible as their ActiveX counterparts, they can be used on charts (as well as on worksheets). You should also note that the ActiveX Frame control cannot be used on a worksheet. To group controls on a worksheet, you should use the Group Box control from the old Forms toolbar.

To place a control object on a sheet, click the corresponding button on the Control Toolbox toolbar and use the mouse to draw the control on the sheet. After you place a control object on a sheet, you can adjust the control's size by clicking any of the sizing handles on its border and then dragging the mouse. At the top of the facing page, the screen shows a command button control placed on a worksheet.

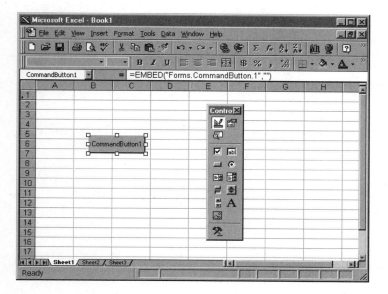

Design mode

In order to effectively manage controls during development, Excel 97 introduces the concept of "design mode" to the Excel environment. (This topic was briefly discussed in Chapter 3.) If you are familiar with Visual Basic or Microsoft Access development, you know that in design mode you can select and format controls, enter code, and otherwise "write" your application. When Excel 97 is in design mode, you will find similar functionality—you can select and resize controls and change their properties. This mode also prevents the controls' events from firing (more on this later in this chapter). To turn design mode on and off, use the design mode button on the Control Toolbox toolbar:

Setting control properties

To set a control's properties manually at design time, select the control and click the Properties button on the Control Toolbox toolbar:

Clicking the button displays the Properties window for the control. This window is very similar to the one available in Visual Basic. It provides one tab that lists the control's properties alphabetically and a second tab that categorizes the properties into logical groups. Here is the Properties window for a Command-Button control:

You can also use the Format Control command to govern how Excel treats the embedded control. For example, in the Properties tab of the Format Control dialog box, you determine whether the control can be moved or sized with cells. These options are not true properties of the control, but they do specify how the control is treated within the Excel environment.

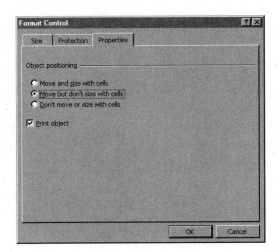

Writing code for control events

Controls typically have one or more events to which you can assign VBA sub-routines. CommandButton controls, for example, have (among others) a Click event that is fired when the user clicks the button. To view the event handlers for a control, select the control and click the View Code button on the Control Toolbox toolbar:

Clicking this button activates the Visual Basic Editor and takes you to the module containing event handlers for the control. For a more complete discussion of attaching event-handling code to controls on worksheets, refer to the section titled "Writing event handling code for controls" on page 142 in Chapter 3.

Common Properties and Events of Control Objects

Although all control objects have their own unique sets of properties, methods, and events, a common set of properties and events applies to all control objects. In the following sections, we'll examine these common properties and events. Then we'll move on to look at each control object individually.

Common properties

These are some common properties of control objects.

Name: The name of the control as you will reference it in code. This property is also referred to as CodeName. It can be set manually at design time or through code by changing the Name property.

AutoSize: If True, the control will reduce itself to the smallest possible size required to display its contents. This property does not apply to listboxes, scrollbars, or spinbuttons.

Enabled: If True, the user can interact with the control. If False, the control is protected and cannot receive focus.

> **NOTE** When a control or any other object in the Windows environment is ready to receive input from the mouse or keyboard, it is said to have "focus." Only one object has focus at any given time.

Font: The font name, size, and style used to display text in the control. This property does not apply to scrollbars or spinbuttons.

Left, Top, Width, and Height: The position and size of the control, expressed in points ($1/72$ of an inch).

Locked: If True and worksheet protection for objects is on, the user cannot edit the control in design mode.

Placement: Applies only to control objects on worksheets. Can be one of three values shown on the next page (use the constant in VBA code, the number in the Properties window).

xlMoveAndSize (1)	Object moves and resizes with the cells underneath it
xlMove (2)	Object moves but does not resize with the cells underneath it
xlFreeFloating (3)	Object neither moves nor resizes with the cells underneath it

PrintObject: If True, the object is printed when the user prints the sheet. If False, the object is not printed.

Visible: If True, the object is displayed at runtime. If False, the object is hidden.

Common events

Most controls share the following common events.

Click: Occurs when the user clicks and releases the mouse button over the control.

DblClick: Occurs when the user double-clicks the mouse button over the control.

KeyPress: When the control has focus, occurs whenever an ANSI key is pressed. (An ANSI key is any key on the keyboard except cursor movement keys, function keys, and control keys—Ctrl, Shift, and Alt.)

GotFocus, LostFocus: Occurs when the control gets and loses input focus, respectively.

MouseDown, MouseMove, and MouseUp: Used to detect the individual actions of depressing a mouse button, moving the mouse, and releasing the mouse button. By using these events, you can determine the exact location of the mouse cursor on screen, which mouse button was used, and whether any control keys (Ctrl, Shift, or Alt) were pressed when the event occurred.

BeforeDragOver, BeforeDropOrPaste: Used to implement drag-and-drop functionality with the control.

Error: Used to notify your application that an error related to the control has occurred. This event provides information about the error which your code can respond to accordingly.

The CommandButton Control

The CommandButton control is typically used to let the user run a routine quickly with a single click of the mouse. Following are the most common properties and events used with this control. It has no common methods.

Commonly used CommandButton properties

Caption: Determines the text displayed in the button.

Picture: Used to display a graphic image on the button.

TakeFocusOnClick: If False, the button will not accept focus. Whatever had focus (a sheet or other control) when the button was clicked will retain it.

TIP

It is a good idea to set the TakeFocusOnClick property to False for command buttons on worksheets and chart sheets. This is because many properties and methods of other Excel objects cannot be accessed from code while a command button on a sheet has focus.

Commonly used CommandButton events

Click: In almost all cases, you will use the Click event to respond to the user clicking the button.

Sample code

To explore sample code for the CommandButton control, refer to the CommandButton sheet in CHAP05-1.XLS and its associated code module in the Visual Basic Editor.

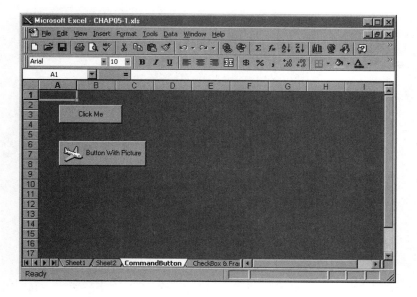

The CheckBox Control

The CheckBox control is typically used to let the user indicate a choice. Checkboxes usually have two possible states—checked and not checked—that correspond to the values True and False, respectively, but can be configured to have three states (checked, not checked, and indeterminate).

Commonly used CheckBox properties

Caption: Determines the text displayed next to the CheckBox control.

TripleState: If True, the checkbox can have three states corresponding to the three values True, False, and Null. If False, it has only two states.

Value: Sets or returns the state of the checkbox. True indicates checked; False indicates not checked; and Null indicates indeterminate.

LinkedCell: Lets you automatically store the Value property of the checkbox in a cell. Every time the state of the checkbox changes, so does the value in the cell. Conversely, when the cell value is modified, the state of the checkbox changes. The property is a text string that evaluates to a cell reference. It can be either a cell address (e.g., B5, or Sheet3!Q5) or a range name (e.g., MyCell).

Commonly used CheckBox events

Click: You will likely use the Click event to respond to the user clicking a checkbox. You can write event handling code for it or simply check its value in code when necessary.

Sample code

To explore sample code for the CheckBox control, refer to the CheckBox sheet in CHAP05-1.XLS and its associated code module in the Visual Basic Editor. You will see that there is no code written for the Click events of checkboxes 4 through 6. These checkboxes display their values in linked cells.

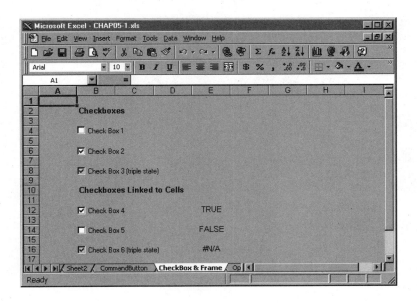

The OptionButton Control

The OptionButton control is similar in functionality to the CheckBox control; however, optionbuttons allow the user to choose one of several mutually exclusive options. Optionbuttons are usually displayed in groups—for example, you might design an interface that asks the user to choose only one of three optionbuttons (so that when one optionbutton is selected, the other optionbuttons are automatically deselected).

You can design your interface so that it enables users to select more than one optionbutton by dividing the optionbuttons on the worksheet into groups. All optionbuttons on a worksheet belong to the same group by default, but you can create separate groups of optionbuttons by setting the GroupName property of the OptionButton object. (You can either set this manually through the Properties box or programmatically). For example, let's assume that on a worksheet you want the user to be able to select two of four optionbuttons. Using the Properties box, you divide the optionbuttons into two groups of two by setting the GroupName property of the first two optionbuttons to "Group1" and setting the GroupName property of the second two optionbuttons to "Group2". By breaking up the four optionbuttons into two groups, the user can select one optionbutton from Group1 and one optionbutton from Group2. Note that optionbuttons have only two states—checked (True) or not checked (False).

Commonly used OptionButton properties

Caption: Determines the text displayed next to the OptionButton.

GroupName: A string that identifies the mutually exclusive group to which an optionbutton belongs. If you want to group optionbuttons, set their GroupNames to the same string. Optionbuttons placed on a worksheet are automatically grouped together with their GroupName properties set to the Name property of the worksheet.

TripleState: Not meaningful for optionbuttons.

Value: Sets or returns the state of the optionbutton. True indicates checked; False indicates not checked.

LinkedCell: This property lets you automatically store the Value property of the optionbutton in a cell. Every time the state of the optionbutton changes, so does the value in the cell. Conversely, when the cell value is modified the state of the optionbutton changes. The property is a text string that evaluates to a cell reference. It can be either a cell address (e.g., B5, or Sheet3!Q5) or a range name (e.g., MyCell).

Commonly used OptionButton events

Click: You will likely use the Click event to respond to the user clicking an optionbutton. You can write event-handling code or simply check its value in code when necessary.

Sample code

To explore sample code for the OptionButton control, refer to the OptionButton sheet in CHAP05-1.XLS and its associated code module in the Visual Basic Editor.

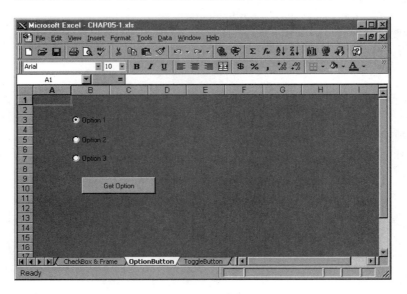

The ToggleButton Control

The ToggleButton control is functionally identical to the CheckBox control but indicates its states in a different visual manner. In a two-state mode, the control can look like it is in either the up position or depressed position. In a three-state mode, the control can also look indeterminate.

Commonly used ToggleButton properties

Caption: Determines the text displayed on the ToggleButton control.

TripleState: If True, the ToggleButton control can have three states—up, depressed, or indeterminate. If False, it has only two.

Value: Sets or returns the state of the ToggleButton control. True indicates depressed; False indicates up; and Null indicates indeterminate.

Picture: Used to display a graphic image on the toggle button.

LinkedCell: This property lets you automatically store the Value property of the togglebutton in a cell. Every time the state of the togglebutton changes, so does the value in the cell. Conversely, when the cell value is modified the state of the togglebutton changes. The property is a text string that evaluates to a cell reference. It can be either a cell address (e.g., B5, or Sheet3!Q5) or a range name (e.g., MyCell).

Commonly used ToggleButton events

Click: You will likely use the Click event to respond to the user clicking a ToggleButton control. You can write event-handling code or you can simply check its value in code when necessary.

Sample code

To explore sample code for the ToggleButton control, refer to the ToggleButton sheet in CHAP05-1.XLS and its associated code module in the Visual Basic Editor.

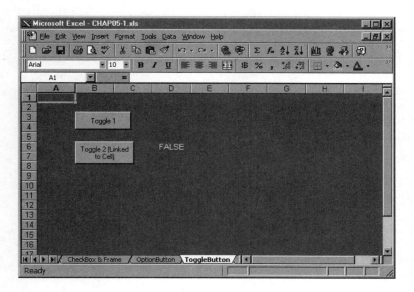

The ListBox Control

The ListBox control enables the user to select one or more items from a list. The ListBox control can contain thousands of items, but you can size the box to regulate how many items are displayed in the list at one time. The user can access the entire list by using the scroll bar, which runs along its right side.

Because a ListBox object can hold data, it is a little different from the control objects we have already looked at. As a result, the ListBox object has various properties and methods that get data in and out of the listbox.

NOTE   Excel has two basic styles of ListBox objects: single-select and multi-select. With a single-select listbox, the user can select only one item at a time from the listbox. With a multi-select listbox, the user can select multiple items. The setting of the MultiSelect property determines the type of selection a listbox offers.

Commonly used ListBox properties

List: Array of strings that represents the list. Each element in the array represents an item in the list. The List property is used when listbox items exist in the ListBox object rather than in a range on the worksheet.

When you store values in a ListBox control by setting the List properties, such values are not saved with the control when the Excel workbook file containing the control is saved. For example, suppose that on a worksheet you have a listbox that contains list items established through the setting of the List property. When you save, close, and then reopen the workbook, you will find that the items in the ListBox control were not saved with the file. (The listbox will be blank when you reopen the file.) If you want to populate the listbox when you open the file, you should incorporate (in the Open Event subroutine for the workbook) statements that can be used to populate listboxes in the workbook. Note that comboboxes exhibit this same behavior. Also note that this behavior is not exhibited with the "older" either listbox and drop-down controls available on the old Forms toolbar. (Lists stored in these controls are actually saved with the control when the workbook file is saved.)

ListCount: Number of items in the list.

ListFillRange: Range on a worksheet to which the list in the listbox is linked. When using a listbox control, you have a choice of storing the contents of the listbox within the control itself, or storing the contents on a worksheet range and then linking the listbox to the range. By assigning a range address to the ListFillRange property, you can link a listbox to a worksheet range. Note that when you set the ListFillRange property, any list contents stored within the listbox control will be automatically deleted. If you wish to store list contents directly in the listbox control rather than link the listbox to a range, you can do so by assigning an Array to the List property or by adding string values using the AddItem method. (Note that you can populate a combobox control in the same manner—by using the ListFillRange property to link to a range, by setting the List property, or by adding items with the AddItem method.)

LinkedCell: Range on a worksheet to which the Value property (text of the currently selected item in the list) is linked. Used in conjunction with the ListFillRange and List properties. The LinkedCell property can be used only with listboxes for which the MultiSelect property has been set to 0 (single-selection).

ListIndex: Index of the currently selected item in the listbox. The ListIndex property can be used only with listboxes for which the MultiSelect property has been set to 0 (single-selection).

ListStyle: Set to fmListStylePlain to display a normal listbox. Set to fmListStyleOption to display a column of checkboxes or optionbuttons at the left side of the list.

MatchEntry: Determines how typing into the listbox will automatically "jump" to list entries. FmMatchEntryFirstLetter matches each letter typed only to the first word in the list starting with that letter. FmMatchEntryComplete matches all the letters typed. FmMatchEntryNone disables the matching feature.

MultiSelect: Can take any of the following three values, which govern the way items can be selected in a listbox:

fmMultiSelectSingle	Single-item selection; only one item can be selected at a time.
fmMultiSelectMulti	Simple multiple-item selection or simple multi-select; multiple items can be selected by clicking one item at a time.
fmMultiSelectExtended	Extended multiple-item selection or extended multi-select; multiple items can be selected only by holding down the Shift key or the Ctrl key during selection.

Note that when the MultiSelect property is set to fmMultiSelectMulti or fmMultiSelectExtended, any attempt to use the LinkedCell, ListIndex, or Value property fails. (LinkedCell, ListIndex, and Value can be used only with single-select listboxes.)

Selected: An array of Boolean values, each value representing the selection state of the corresponding item in the list. The Selected property is useful when you deal with listboxes for which the MultiSelect property has been set to multi-selection or extended multi-selection. If an item in the listbox is selected, the corresponding value in the Selected array is True; if a listbox item is not selected, the corresponding value in the Selected array is False. You can use the Selected property with listboxes for which the MultiSelect property has been set to single-item selection; however, using the Value property or ListIndex property under such circumstances is much simpler.

Value: Text of the currently selected item in the listbox. As with ListIndex, Value can be used only with single-select listboxes.

Commonly used ListBox methods

Three of the ListBox object's many methods are used to add data to or remove data from a list. (These methods do not work on a list that is populated from a worksheet range through the ListFillRange property.)

AddItem: Adds items to the listbox one at a time. AddItem has two arguments: pvargText (the text string that represents the item) and pvargIndex (the index in the list after which the item is to be added; use 0 to add the item to the top of the list).

Clear: Removes all items from the list, resulting in an empty listbox.

RemoveItem: Removes one or more items from the list. RemoveItem takes one argument—pvargIndex (the index of the first item of the list to be removed). Rows are numbered starting at 0.

Commonly used ListBox events
Click: Use this event to respond to the selection of an item via a mouse click.

Three ways to populate a list in a listbox
Excel offers three ways to populate a list in a listbox:

- **Setting the List property**—By assigning an array of values to the List property, you can add a group of items to the list all at once.

- **Calling the AddItem method**—By using the AddItem method, you can add items to the list one at a time.

- **Setting the ListFillRange property**—By assigning a range to the ListFillRange property, you can link a ListBox object to a range on a worksheet. If you do so, the values in the listbox change whenever the values on the worksheet change.

Determining the selected item in a list
Determining the selected item in the list is simple for single-select listboxes. The Value property returns the text of the selected item in the list.

Determining the selected values of multi-select listboxes
Determining the selected values of multi-select listboxes is a bit more difficult. Instead of using the Value property, you must use the Selected property. Selected holds a Boolean array; the number of elements in the array corresponds to the number of items in the list. If an array element's value is True, the corresponding list item is selected; if an array element's value is False, the corresponding list item is not selected. To determine the text strings that correspond to the items selected from the list, you must, therefore, compare the array held by the List property (or the worksheet range held by the ListFillRange property) with the Boolean array held by the Selected property.

Sample code
To explore sample code for the ListBox control, refer to the Listbox sheet in CHAP05-1.XLS and its associated code module in the Visual Basic Editor.

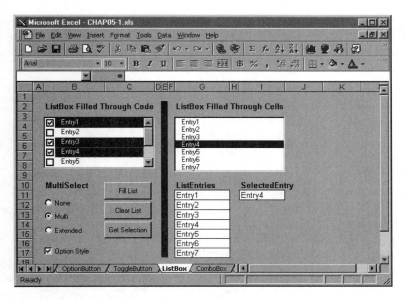

The ComboBox Control

The ComboBox control is similar in function to the ListBox control—it enables a user to select an item from a list. A ComboBox object, however, displays only one list item at a time—the selected item. In addition, the ComboBox object is always a single-select list; that is, you cannot have a multi-select combobox. Located on the right side of the combobox is a drop button, which can be one of four styles: blank, a down-pointing arrow, an ellipsis, or a minimize symbol. Clicking the drop button causes the list of items to appear below the combobox; the user can then select one item from this list. After the selection is made, the list disappears and the combobox returns to displaying only the selected item.

Drop-down list style vs. drop-down combo style

ComboBox controls come in two styles; styles are determined by the Style property. Setting the Style property to fmStyleDropDownList causes the ComboBox to behave exactly like a listbox (except that the list itself can drop down). Setting the Style property to fmStyleDropDownCombo, however, alters things a bit by letting the user type an entry into the visible portion of the control—an entry which does not necessarily exist in the list. The typed entry does not become a part of the list, but is assigned to the Value property of the combobox.

Using the ComboBox control

The ComboBox object has many of the same properties as the ListBox object, including List, ListCount, ListFillRange, ListIndex, and Value. One property is unique to the ComboBox object: ListRows. ListRows takes an integer value that indicates the number of items that are displayed in the drop-down list after the user accesses the list by clicking the down arrow. A scrollbar allows the user to see any additional items in the list.

The ComboBox object also has some of the same methods as the ListBox object, including AddItem, Clear, and RemoveItem.

To populate a list in a ComboBox object, you can use one of the same three approaches you use to populate a listbox list: setting the List property, calling the AddItem method, or setting the ListFillRange property. You can determine the selected item in a ComboBox object in only one way, however—by using the Value property.

Sample code

To explore sample code for the ComboBox control, refer to the ComboBox sheet in CHAP05-1.XLS and its associated code module in the Visual Basic Editor.

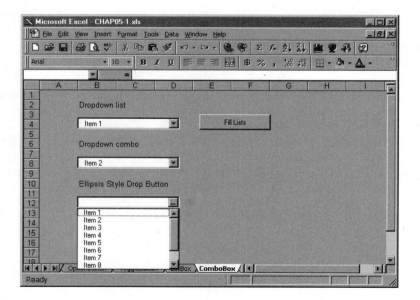

The ScrollBar and SpinButton Controls

The ScrollBar and SpinButton controls are similar in function—they both provide a graphical interface for adjusting numeric values. The user can change the value of a scrollbar in three ways: by clicking the arrows at the ends of the scrollbar, by clicking in the body of the scrollbar, or by using the mouse to move the scrollbar slider. The value of a spinbutton can be changed only by clicking the spinner arrows. (Essentially, a spinbutton is a scrollbar without a slider.)

Commonly used ScrollBar and SpinButton properties

The following properties are important when you work with ScrollBar and SpinButton objects.

Max: Maximum value of the scrollbar or spinner. This property must be a positive integer or zero.

Min: Minimum value of the scrollbar or spinner. This property must be a positive integer or zero. The value assigned to the Min property must be less than the value assigned to the Max property.

SmallChange: Negative or positive integer that represents the change in value of the scrollbar or spinner when the user clicks one of the arrows.

LargeChange: Negative or positive integer that represents the change in value of the scrollbar when a user clicks in the body of the scrollbar. This property is not available for the SpinButton object.

<table>
<tr><td>**TIP**</td><td>The SmallChange and LargeChange properties of the ScrollBar and SpinButton objects cannot be fractional values. You can work around this limitation, however, by dividing the value of the scrollbar or spinner by a constant—you achieve the same result as having a fractional value for SmallChange or LargeChange. In addition, the Value property of ScrollBar and SpinButton cannot evaluate to a negative number. You can work around this limitation by subtracting a constant from the resulting Value property in your code.</td></tr>
</table>

Value: Indicates the current value of the ScrollBar or Spinbutton.

LinkedCell: A range to which the Value property of the control is linked.

Commonly used ScrollBar and SpinButton event

Change: Occurs when the value of the control changes.

Sample code

To explore sample code for the ScrollBar and SpinButton controls, refer to the ScrollBar & SpinButton sheet in CHAP05-1.XLS and its associated code module in the Visual Basic Editor.

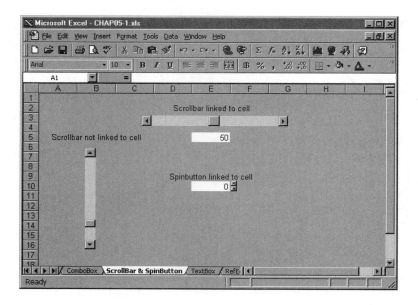

The TextBox Control

The TextBox control lets the user type text into a predefined area. Textboxes can be used to collect simple one-line entries or can be used as scaled-down word processors with multiple lines and word-wrap functionality.

Commonly used ToolBox properties

Text: Sets or returns the text contained in the control.

MultiLine: If True, the control will display multiple lines of text.

MaxLength: An integer used to set the maximum number of characters the control will accept. Set to 0 to allow any number of characters.

PasswordChar: A single character used to mask the entry of passwords. If a character is assigned to PasswordChar, this character will be displayed instead of the actual text entered into the control.

LinkedCell: This property lets you automatically store the text property of the textbox into a cell every time the text changes (or vice versa).

Sample code

To explore sample code for the TextBox control, refer to the TextBox sheet in CHAP05-1.XLS and its associated code module in the Visual Basic Editor. This sample illustrates many other properties of the textbox not discussed here as well as many of the other controls previously discussed.

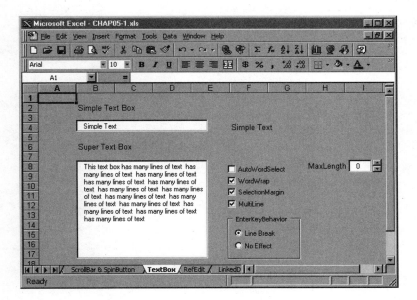

The Label, Image, and Frame Controls

The three remaining standard controls are the Label, Image, and Frame controls. The Label control is used to display static text. Its most important property is Caption, which is used to set the displayed text. The Image control is used to display a graphic (bitmap, metafile, icon, etc.). It has many properties that control how an image is displayed (e.g., clipped, stretched, tiled, etc.). The Frame control is used to visually group controls on a worksheet or userform. Note, however, that the Frame control available through the Control Toolbox toolbar can be used only on userforms—it cannot be used on worksheets. A control very similar to the Frame control that you can use to visually group controls on worksheets and charts is the Group Box control, which is on the old Forms toolbar.

> ### FYI
>
> **Performance Considerations**
> **when Linking Controls to Worksheets**
>
> In the earlier discussion of control objects, we looked at several examples of entering data in controls that were linked to worksheet ranges. As you consider approaches to using controls, you should be aware that linking control objects to worksheet ranges through the LinkedCell and ListFillRange properties can have a negative impact on the performance of the control. To achieve better performance, store values and lists directly in control objects rather than using links to worksheets. Excel takes more time to update a link between a worksheet range and a control than to handle data in RAM that's allocated for a control's properties. This performance difference might not be obvious when you work with simple applications, but it can be measurable when you work with larger, more complicated applications.
>
> Keep in mind however, that data stored in an ActiveX control on either a worksheet or a userform is not saved with the control when the workbook file is saved, so you must reinitialize the control when the workbook is opened. (This can be accomplished through using a workbook Open event subroutine.)

Creating Custom Dialog Boxes

Software applications commonly use dialog boxes when a limited amount of information is required from the user in order for the application to perform a particular task. You can create a custom dialog box from a userform that you create in the Visual Basic Editor. Userforms can contain the exact same controls we just learned about, plus a few more that don't apply to worksheets. Throughout this section, we'll be using the terms userform and dialog box interchangeably.

> **NOTE**   Custom dialog boxes in Excel are modal; when a custom dialog box is displayed, the user is limited to performing actions within that dialog box. However, you can let the user make selections on a worksheet while a custom dialog box is displayed by placing a RefEdit control on the userform (more on this later in the chapter).

Creating Your First UserForm

Let's start by creating a simple userform from scratch to get a feel for how the process works. Start by creating a blank workbook in Excel, and then switching to the Visual Basic Editor. Next, choose the Insert UserForm command. Your screen should look similar to this:

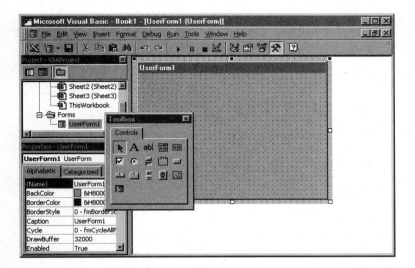

You should notice four things. First, the userform itself appears in its own window. Second, a Toolbox similar to the Control Toolbox appears. This contains the controls you can place on a userform. Third, the Properties window shows properties of the userform. Finally, the userform is listed in the Project window.

You can place controls on the userform by clicking the desired button on the toolbox, and then clicking and dragging in the userform to create the control. Once a control is created, you can change the control's properties by selecting it and then using the Properties window. Try adding a label, a textbox, and a commandbutton to this userform. Change the caption of the button to OK. When you're finished, your userform should look like this:

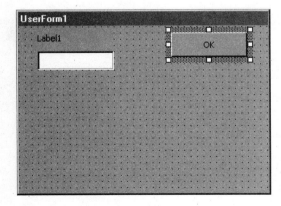

You can test the userform at any time by clicking the Run Sub/UserForm button on the toolbar. Go ahead and run the userform now.

Displaying and Closing a UserForm from Code

To display a userform from a VBA routine, call the Show method of the userform. Switch back to CHAP05-1.XLS and look at Proc23 in the Chap05b module. This routine calls the Show method of UserForm1. The subroutine then checks to see whether the userform was closed using the OK or Cancel button by checking the value of the userform's Tag property (more on the Tag property later in this chapter):

```
Sub Chap05bProc23_DisplayDialog()
    UserForm1.Show
    If UserForm1.Tag = vbOK Then
        MsgBox "OK clicked"
    Else
        MsgBox "Cancel clicked"
    End If
End Sub
```

To close a userform, you can call its Hide method from a control on the userform itself. Note that due to the modal nature of userforms, it is not possible to both show and hide a userform from a single subroutine. For example, let's assume you write a subroutine that calls the Show method on a userform. As soon as the Show method is called, execution of that subroutine halts until the userform is dismissed. It is therefore not possible to dismiss an instance of a userform from the same subroutine that created the instance of the userform by calling the Show method. Rather, the userform can be dismissed by executing code contained in a button on the userform. Such code would include a call to the Hide method in order to dismiss the userform. Userforms, like Excel worksheets and charts, have code modules behind them that can specify event procedures for the userforms and the controls they contain. To display UserForm1's code module, select UserForm1 and choose the View Code command.

> **TIP** You can quickly view a userform's code or any control's code in the Visual Basic Editor by double-clicking the userform or control.

In UserForm1's code module, you will find event procedures for each of the two commandbuttons' Click events. Note that both procedures call the Hide method. Note further that the OK button (CommandButton1) sets the Tag property of the form to the constant vbOK. The Cancel button, on the other hand, sets it to the constant vbCancel. Recall that in Proc23, we checked the value of the Tag property after the dialog box was closed to determine which button closed it. These two Click event procedures are the key to making this work.

```
Private Sub CommandButton1_Click()
    Me.Hide
    Me.Tag = vbOK
End Sub

Private Sub CommandButton2_Click()
    Me.Hide
    Me.Tag = vbCancel
End Sub
```

NOTE

Note the use of the Me keyword (Me.Hide). Me is a reserved keyword that refers to the object that owns the code currently running. In this case, Me refers to UserForm1 since the reference to Me is contained within the code module for UserForm1. (We could have also used the syntax UserForm1.Hide, but Me is shorter and prevents you from having to modify your code if the name of the userform is changed.)

The Tag property   You might be wondering at this point what the Tag property is. It's really just a blank property you can use to store any useful information about the form (in fact, most controls have a Tag property as well). Using it to store information about how a dialog box is closed is one very common use. Note that this technique is not limited to determining whether OK and Cancel buttons were clicked; you can store in a Tag property information about any number of events that cause a dialog box to close.

Getting and Setting Values of Controls on a UserForm

So far, we've been able to show a userform as well as determine the user-driven event that closes a userform (clicking either the OK or Cancel button). For a userform to be useful, we not only need to be able to retrieve values from the userform's controls after the userform is displayed but we need to be able to set those values before the userform is displayed to the user—for example, when setting default values. It turns out that this is very easy to accomplish. You simply refer in code to the properties of the controls on the dialog box using this syntax:

```
<UserFormName>.<ControlName>.<Property>
```

Proc24, which follows, shows how to set default values for UserForm1 before it is displayed and retrieve those values when the user clicks the OK button to close the form.

```
Sub Chap05bProc24_SetAndGetValues()
    Dim Msg As String
    With UserForm1
        .TextBox1.Text = "Steve"
        .OptionButton2.Value = True
        .Show
        If .Tag = vbOK Then
            Msg = "Name: " & .TextBox1.Text & Chr(13)
            If .OptionButton1.Value Then
                Msg = Msg & "Age: " & .OptionButton1.Caption
            ElseIf .OptionButton2.Value Then
                Msg = Msg & "Age: " & .OptionButton2.Caption
            Else
                Msg = Msg & "Age: " & .OptionButton3.Caption
            End If
            MsgBox Msg
        End If
    End With
End Sub
```

The result after clicking OK should look similar to this:

UserForm Properties, Methods, and Events

Now that we know the basics of creating and using userforms, let's backtrack and learn about some of their key properties, methods, and events.

UserForm properties

Here are some useful properties of the UserForm object. (Refer to online VBA Help for a complete list.)

Name: Also known as the CodeName property, this is the name you use to refer to the userform in code. Can only be set manually at design time.

BackColor: The color of the userform surface.

Caption: The text displayed in the userform's title bar.

Left, Top, Height, and Width: The position and size of the userform, expressed in points ($\frac{1}{72}$ of an inch).

Picture: Specifies the image displayed as a background for the userform. You must pass the result of the LoadPicture function to the Picture property. Use with the PictureAlignment, PictureSizeMode, and PictureTiling properties to control how the image is displayed.

StartUpPosition: Used to center the userform automatically. Can be one of three values:

1 - CenterOwner	Centers the userform over its parent window, in this case Microsoft Excel
2 - CenterScreen	Centers the userform on the screen
3 - None	No automatic centering (defaults to the upper left corner of the screen)

UserForm methods

Here are three useful methods of the UserForm object. (Refer to online VBA Help for a complete list.)

Show: Displays the userform modally.

Hide: Closes the userform.

PrintForm: Prints an image of the userform.

UserForm events

Here are three useful events of the UserForm object. (Refer to online VBA Help for a complete list.)

QueryClose: Fires just before the userform closes. By setting the cancel argument of the event procedure to True, you can prevent the userform from closing.

Initialize: Fires when the userform is about to be displayed.

Terminate: Fires after the userform is closed.

Using Controls on UserForms

As stated previously, you use the same controls on userforms that you use on worksheets. However, some additional controls can be used only on userforms, and some properties of many of these controls only apply to controls on userforms.

CommandButton controls

CommandButton controls work the same way on userforms as they do on worksheets. Two additional properties are available for commandbuttons on userforms.

Default: Setting this property to True makes the button a default button, meaning the Enter key will activate the button as if the button were clicked (as long as no other control has the focus). Most OK buttons are default buttons.

Cancel: Setting this property to True makes the button a cancel button, meaning the Esc key will activate the button as if the button were clicked. Most cancel buttons are labeled with the "Cancel" caption.

Frame and OptionButton controls

On a worksheet, optionbuttons that are meant to form a mutually exclusive group of choices might be presented in a group box, but it is not the group box that groups them functionally. To make the optionbuttons act as a group, you must set the GroupName property of each one to the same value—being in the same group box does not activate group behavior.

On a userform, the Frame control plays a bigger role. Optionbuttons placed inside a frame on a userform will act as a group regardless of whether their GroupName properties are the same value. Conveniently, when you move a frame, the optionbuttons inside it move, too.

> **NOTE** Whenever you move a frame, all controls inside it move, too.

The MultiPage control

The MultiPage control—available only on userforms—is used to implement tabbed dialog boxes. You can place controls on each tab so that clicking a tab displays only those controls associated with that tab.

At design time, you can insert, delete, rename, and reorder the pages (tabs) by right-clicking the control, and then selecting a command from the menu. To place controls on a page, select the page by clicking its tab, and then drop the controls onto the page.

Proc25 displays UserForm2, an example of the MultiPage control:

```
Sub Chap05bProc25_MultiPage()
    UserForm2.Show
End Sub
```

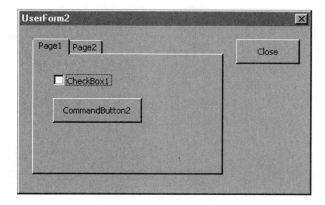

The Difference Between the MultiPage and TabStrip Controls

You might have noticed another tab control, called TabStrip, which is available on the Toolbox. This control can be used to implement tabbed dialog boxes, but the process is a bit more complicated. Since TabStrip cannot contain other controls, you must write code to show and hide controls for each page of the TabStrip in order to respond to an event that fires when the user switches pages. The advantage is that you have more control over how the TabStrip looks—for example, it can be configured to look like a strip of buttons instead of tabs. For most purposes, however, you will find the MultiPage control far easier to use for custom dialog boxes in Excel. If you want to learn more about the TabStrip control, refer to the online VBA Help.

The RefEdit control

The RefEdit control is unique to userforms created in Excel. This control lets you point at cells behind a modal dialog box for purposes of selecting a range. It also has a small button on its right side that will temporarily hide the dialog box or let the user see the entire sheet. You'll see this feature in many dialog boxes throughout Excel.

You can open the RefEdit sheet in CHAP05-1.XLS to see an example of a RefEdit control—just click the button on the sheet to display the dialog box. Using this dialog box, you can select a range of cells and specify a value to place in those cells.

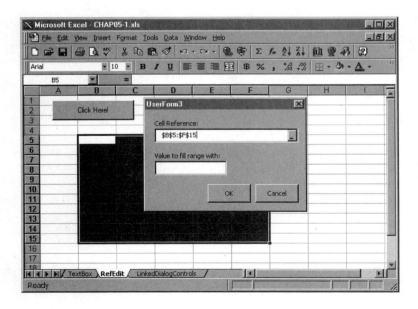

When you close the dialog box by clicking the OK button, the range you se-lected will be filled with the value you specified.

Proc26 does the work of displaying the dialog box and using the information it collects. Note that the range selected with the RefEdit control is in the form of a text string, which you can use to create a Range object and fill in the values accordingly.

```
Sub Chap05bProc26_RefEdit()
    On Error Resume Next
    With UserForm3
        .RefEdit1.Text = Selection.Address
        .Show
        If .Tag = vbOK Then
            Range(.RefEdit1.Text) = .TextBox1.Text
        End If
    End With
End Sub
```

Linking controls to worksheet cells

Like controls on worksheets, controls on userforms can be linked to worksheet cells. However, the properties you use to do this are different. Controls on userforms that allow the user to enter or set values have a ControlSource property that can be set to an Excel reference or single-cell range name. This is analogous to the LinkedCell property of controls on worksheets. ListBoxes and ComboBoxes also have a RowSource property, which is analogous to the ListFill-Range property used when these controls appear on worksheets.

The LinkedDialogControls sheet in CHAP05-1.XLS demonstrates how to link controls on dialog boxes to cells. Note that by using this technique, you eliminate the possibility of canceling changes made in the dialog box before the cells in the sheet are updated. All changes are linked as they occur. Figure 5-2 on the facing page is a userform that uses the ControlSource property to derive values for its textboxes.

Setting the tab order

Tab order refers to the order in which controls on a dialog box will become active as you press the Tab key. Users expect the tab order to be logical and natural—not random—so you should take the time to set tab order properly on all your custom dialog boxes.

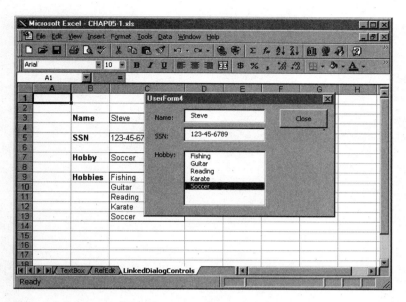

Figure 5-2. *A userform that uses the ControlSource property.*

To set the tab order, select the View Tab Order command in the Visual Basic
Editor for the userform you are interested in. The Tab Order dialog box appears
with the current tab order. Select the control you want to move and then click
the desired button to move it.

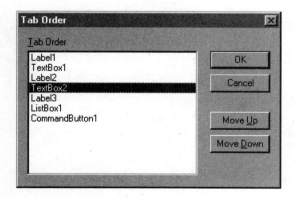

Implementing a Wizard

Let's end our discussion of userforms with an example of how to build a Wizard, which is a custom dialog box with many steps. You'll see examples of Wizards throughout Excel, Office, and Windows. Our example is a Travel Wizard that contains four steps, shown in the following four screens:

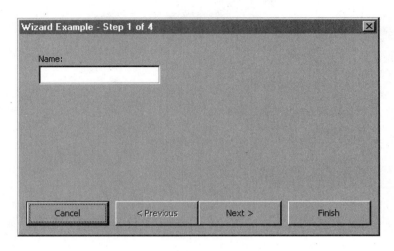

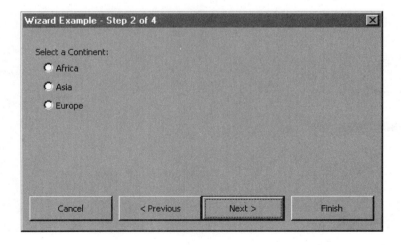

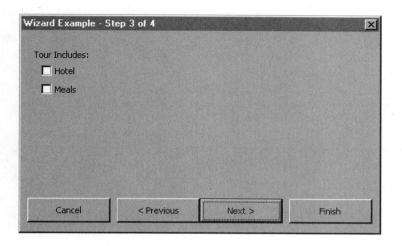

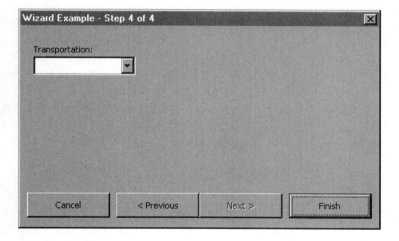

Proc27 displays the Wizard and retrieves the values of the controls after the Wizard closes. This routine looks very similar to Proc24 (on page 284). Code that is used to implement the Wizard is contained in Proc27 (on the following page) as well as in several subroutines that are contained in the code module for the WizardForm userform. The subroutines in this code module execute in response to events of the WizardForm and events of the controls that are contained on the WizardForm.

```
Sub Chap05bProc27_Wizard()
    Dim Msg As String
    With WizardForm
        .Show
        If .Tag = vbOK Then
            Msg = "Name: " & .txtName.Text & Chr(13)
            Msg = Msg & "Continent: "
            If .optAfrica.Value Then
                Msg = Msg & "Africa" & Chr(13)
            ElseIf .optAsia.Value Then
                Msg = Msg & "Asia" & Chr(13)
            Else
                Msg = Msg & "Europe" & Chr(13)
            End If
            Msg = Msg & "Package: "
            If .chkHotel.Value Then
                Msg = Msg & "Hotel "
            End If
            If .chkMeals.Value Then
                Msg = Msg & "Meals"
            End If
            Msg = Msg & Chr(13)
            Msg = Msg & "Transporation: " & _
                    .cboTransportation.Value
            MsgBox Msg
        End If
    End With
End Sub
```

Before looking at the Wizard-specific code, you should understand how the Wizard panels and controls themselves are represented. In the Visual Basic Editor, open the WizardForm userform. It may not be immediately apparent, but each panel of the Wizard is really a Frame control. The frames are named Frame1 through Frame4, and are "stacked" on top of one another. Furthermore, to make the frames themselves appear invisible, the following properties have been set:

- **Caption:** Set to a blank string

- **Border:** Set to fmBorderStyleNone

- **SpecialEffect:** Set to fmSpecialEffectFlat

Each frame contains the controls it displays. You can view each frame by choosing it in the Object Selector of the Properties window while the userform is selected. This causes the frame outline to appear. Right-click the frame outline and choose the Bring Forward command from the shortcut menu. You might need to repeat the Bring Forward command once or twice before the desired frame is on top.

Now that we know how the frames are implemented, let's find out how we navigate among them. In the WizardForm's code module (which you can view by right-clicking the userform and choosing the View Code command from the shortcut menu), we have declared a module-level variable (CurrentPanel) to keep track of which panel to display. We also have two constants to identify the first and last panels:

```
Option Explicit

Dim CurrentPanel As Integer

Const FIRST_PANEL = 1
Const LAST_PANEL = 4
```

A routine (ShowPanel) in that module will display the panel number identified by the CurrentPanel variable. It hides every panel by setting its Visible property to False, then shows the proper panel by setting only that panel's Visible property back to True:

```
Sub ShowPanel()
    Frame1.Visible = False
    Frame2.Visible = False
    Frame3.Visible = False
    Frame4.Visible = False
    Select Case CurrentPanel
        Case 1
            Frame1.Visible = True
        Case 2
            Frame2.Visible = True
        Case 3
            Frame3.Visible = True
        Case 4
            Frame4.Visible = True
```

(continued)

continued

```
        Case Else
            Beep
    End Select
    Me.Caption = "Wizard Example - Step " & CurrentPanel & _
        " of " & LAST_PANEL
End Sub
```

With the variable and routine in place, all we need to do is set the value of CurrentPanel at the appropriate times and call ShowPanel to display the correct panel—we need to do this in three places. The first place is where the Wizard is initially displayed via the Initialize event of the userform (which sets the CurrentPanel to 1):

```
Private Sub UserForm_Initialize()
    CurrentPanel = 1
    ShowPanel
    With cboTransportation
        .AddItem "Plane"
        .AddItem "Train"
        .AddItem "Boat"
    End With
End Sub
```

The other two times are when the CurrentPanel variable is set in the Click event procedures for the Next and Previous buttons on the WizardForm. Note the code that checks to see whether the current panel is the first or last panel in the series and disables the Next or Previous button accordingly:

```
Private Sub cmdNext_Click()
    CurrentPanel = CurrentPanel + 1
    ShowPanel
    cmdPrevious.Enabled = True
    If CurrentPanel = LAST_PANEL Then
        cmdNext.Enabled = False
    Else
        cmdNext.Enabled = True
    End If
End Sub

Private Sub cmdPrevious_Click()
    CurrentPanel = CurrentPanel - 1
    ShowPanel
    cmdNext.Enabled = True
    If CurrentPanel = FIRST_PANEL Then
        cmdPrevious.Enabled = False
    Else
        cmdPrevious.Enabled = True
```

```
    End If
End Sub
```

Finally, the Finish and Cancel buttons use code we've seen before to close the form and set the Tag property:

```
Private Sub cmdFinish_Click()
    Me.Hide
    Me.Tag = vbOK
End Sub

Private Sub cmdCancel_Click()
    Me.Tag = vbCancel
    Me.Hide
End Sub
```

Displaying Built-In Excel Dialog Boxes

Not only does Excel let you design and display custom dialog boxes, it also allows you to display any of its built-in dialog boxes from a VBA routine. To do so, you use the Dialogs collection. Each built-in dialog box in Excel has an associated constant that you can use as an index to the Dialogs collection. Proc28 displays Excel's built-in Print dialog box by using the xlDialogPrint constant when calling the Show method:

```
Sub Chap05bProc28_DisplayPrint()
    Application.Dialogs(xlDialogPrint).Show
End Sub
```

Following is Excel's built-in Print dialog box, as displayed when you run Proc28:

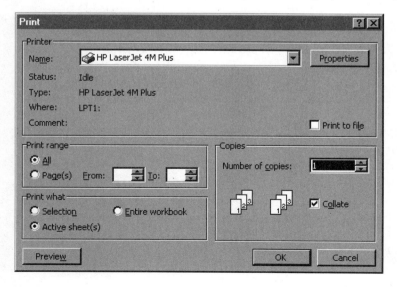

TIP

Excel has roughly 200 built-in dialog boxes and corresponding constants. The quickest way to determine which constant to use is to access the Auto List Members feature of the Visual Basic Editor (available on the Editor tab of the Options dialog box through the Tools Options command). If this feature is on, a list of constants appears automatically as you type *Dialogs* into the code window. If the feature is disabled, you can use the Edit List Constants command to force the Visual Basic Editor to display the list.

When calling the Show method on the Dialog object, you can pass arguments to built-in Excel dialog boxes. Proc29 uses the xlDialogOpen constant to display Excel's built-in Open dialog box. If you pass the string "*.*" as the first argument to the Show method, the File Name edit box in the Open dialog box displays all the files in the current directory:

```
Sub Chap05bProc29_DisplayOpen()
    Application.Dialogs(xlDialogOpen).Show "*.*"
End Sub
```

The following shows the Open dialog box as it is displayed by Proc29:

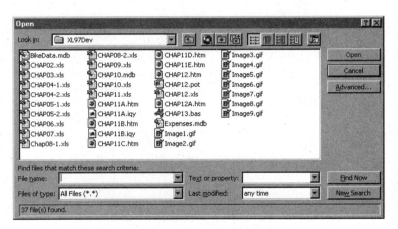

FYI

Finding Documentation on Arguments Passed to Dialog Boxes

You might be wondering where to find documentation on the arguments that can be passed to Excel's built-in dialog boxes when the dialog boxes are displayed by calling the Show method on the Dialog object. In Excel 97, you can access this information in online VBA Help under the topic "Built-In Dialog Box Argument Lists."

Commandbars: Creating Custom Menus & Toolbars

As you've probably already noticed, Excel 97 menus can now float and dock like toolbars. They can also contain graphic button images and textual menu items (as in the Microsoft Office Art toolbar). Why? The toolbars and menus have been unified into a single entity called the commandbar, which is represented programmatically as the CommandBar object. Some commandbars look very much like menus and others look very much like toolbars, but because toolbars and menus are now represented by the same entity—the commandbar—you create, manipulate, and modify both menus and toolbars in the same manner.

This section explains how to create custom commandbars for an application. You can customize many commandbar features using the Tools Customize command in the Excel user interface. Other customizations are best handled using the CommandBar object model.

CommandBar Object Model Overview

As Figure 5-3 shows, the Application contains the CommandBars collection. Each CommandBar object, in turn, contains a collection of CommandBarControl objects. A CommandBarControl can be one of three types: CommandBarButton, CommandBarComboBox, or CommandBarPopUp. A CommandBarButton object represents either a button or a menu item that executes a command or calls a routine. A CommandBarComboBox represents an editbox, drop-down listbox, or combobox. A CommandBarPopUp displays menus and submenus. (In fact, the menu or submenu is itself another CommandBar object contained by the CommandBarPopUp.)

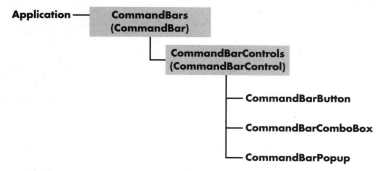

Figure 5-3. *The Office 97 CommandBar object hierarchy.*

Proc30 on the following page loops through the collection of CommandBar objects and displays the name of each one that is currently visible.

```
Sub Chap05cProc30_ListVisibleCommandBars()
    Dim CB As CommandBar
    For Each CB In Application.CommandBars
        If CB.Visible Then
            MsgBox CB.Name
        End If
    Next CB
End Sub
```

Proc31 is more complicated but illustrates the nature of the CommandBar object model hierarchy well. It first displays a dialog box with a list of all commandbars. When the user selects one and clicks OK, the routine writes to a worksheet information about every CommandBarControl for the selected CommandBar object, including the control's Caption and Type (CommandBarButton, CommandBarPopUp, or CommandBarComboBox). If the type is CommandBarPopUp (note the use of the TypeName function to determine the type), the routine cycles through all the CommandBarControls on the popup as well. In fact, the subroutine executes recursively for every level of submenu in the CommandBar.

```
Sub Chap05cProc31_DisplayCommandBarStructure()
    Dim CB As CommandBar
    Dim ItemNum As Integer
    Dim CBName As String
    UserForm5.Show
    If UserForm5.Tag = vbOK Then
        CBName = UserForm5.ListBox1.Value
        If CBName <> "" Then
            Set CB = Application.CommandBars(CBName)
            Worksheets("Sheet2").Activate
            With Range("A1")
                .Select
                .CurrentRegion.Clear
            End With
            Chap05cProc31a_EnumerateCommandBar CB, Selection, _
                ItemNum, 0
        End If
    End If
End Sub


Sub Chap05cProc31a_EnumerateCommandBar(CB As CommandBar, _
    WriteRange As Range, ItemNum As Integer, Level As Integer)
    Dim CBControl As CommandBarControl
    Dim CBControlType As String
    For Each CBControl In CB.Controls
        CBControlType = TypeName(CBControl)
```

```
        WriteRange.Offset(ItemNum, Level).Formula = _
            CBControl.Caption & " (" & CBControlType & ")"
        ItemNum = ItemNum + 1
        If CBControlType = "CommandBarPopup" Then
            Chap05cProc31a_EnumerateCommandBar _
                CBControl.CommandBar, WriteRange, _
                ItemNum, Level + 1
        End If
    Next CBControl
End Sub
```

Here is the result of running this routine for the Worksheet Menu Bar:

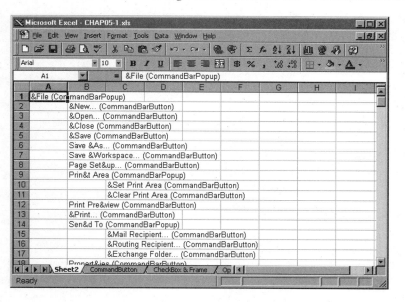

Now that we have a basic understanding of commandbars, let's take a more detailed look at each object in the CommandBars collection hierarchy.

The CommandBars Collection Object

You can use the Add method of the CommandBars collection object to create a new commandbar in code. The Add method takes the following arguments:

name
The name of the new commandbar. Can be used as an index in the CommandBars collection.

position
Position on the screen where the commandbar should be added and what its appearance will be. See online VBA Help for a list of constants to use for this argument.

(continued)

continued

menuBar	Boolean value. If True, the commandbar replaces the active menu box; if False, it acts as a toolbar.
temporary	Boolean value. If True, the commandbar will be deleted when Excel is closed. Very useful for customized menus you want deleted when your application is not running.

The CommandBar Object

The CommandBar object has many properties and methods. Some of the more common ones are described here.

CommandBar object properties

Visible: If True, the commandbar is visible. If False, it is hidden.

Position: A constant indicating where the commandbar appears on the screen (e.g., floating or docked). See the object browser or online VBA Help for a list of possible values.

Controls: Returns the collection of CommandBarControls, which are items contained in the commandbar.

CommandBar object methods

Delete: Deletes the commandbar. Cannot be used on built-in commandbars.

Reset: Resets a built-in commandbar to its original (default) state.

ShowPopup: Displays a popup commandbar.

The CommandBarControls Collection Object

You can use the Add method of the CommandBarControls collection object to create a new CommandBarControl in code (recall that the Controls property of the CommandBar object returns this collection). The Add method takes the following arguments:

type	The type of CommandBarControl to add. For user-defined controls, use one of the following:
	msoControlButton (a button or menu item)
	msoControlComboBox
	msoControlDropdown
	msoControlEdit
	msoControlPopup (a submenu)
ID	Used to identify a built-in control. Leave blank for user-defined controls.
parameter	Typically left blank for user-defined controls.

before	Index of the control before which the control is added (either by number or name). If left blank, the control is added to the end of the commandbar.
temporary	Boolean value. If True, the control will be deleted when Excel is closed. Very useful for customized menus you want deleted when your application is not running.

The CommandBarControl Object

The CommandBarControl object has dozens of properties and methods. Some of the more common ones are described here. Unless indicated otherwise, these properties and methods apply to all three types of CommandBarControl objects (CommandBarButton, CommandBarPopup, CommandBarComboBox).

CommandBarControl properties

Caption: String that is the text displayed in the control. Use the ampersand character (&) to create an accelerator key for the control.

CommandBar (CommandBarPopUp only): A CommandBar object that is the menu or submenu beneath the popup control.

Enabled: If True, the control can be selected by the user. If False, it is grayed out and cannot be accessed.

FaceID: ID number of a standard built-in icon, which is displayed on the face of the control.

OnAction: The name of a VBA routine that will run when the control is activated by the user.

Style (CommandBarButton only): Determines whether the button appears as text, as an icon, or as a combination of text and icon. Values are msoButtonAutomatic, msoButtonCaption, msoButtonIcon, and msoButtonIconAndCaption.

ToolTipText: Text that displays on a ToolTip for the control.

Visible: If True, the control can be seen. If False, it is hidden from view.

CommandBarControl methods

Reset: Resets the control to its original (default) function and appearance.

Creating a New Toolbar Using Code

Let's put some of these objects to work and build a custom toolbar using VBA code. Proc32 adds a new commandbar to the CommandBars collection. Note that the MenuBar argument is set to False, which will make the new commandbar behave like a toolbar. Once the commandbar is added to the collection, we use the Visible and Position properties to display it as docked on the left side of the application window. Then we use the Add method of the CommandBarControls collection (accessed through the Controls property of the new commandbar) to add a number of buttons. Each button gets a caption, an icon (by using its FaceID property), and a routine to run (by using its OnAction property). Note also that setting the BeginGroup property on the last button forces the button into a new group.

```
Sub Chap05cProc32_AddToolbar()
    With Application.CommandBars.Add("CustomToolbar", , False, True)
        .Visible = True
        .Position = msoBarLeft
        With .Controls
            With .Add(msoControlButton)
                .Caption = "Button1"
                .FaceId = 12
                .OnAction = "Chap05cProc34_MenuRoutine"
            End With
            With .Add(msoControlButton)
                .Caption = "Button2"
                .FaceId = 13
                .OnAction = "Chap05cProc34_MenuRoutine"

            End With
            With .Add(msoControlButton)
                .Caption = "Button3"
                .FaceId = 14
                .BeginGroup = True
                .OnAction = "Chap05cProc34_MenuRoutine"
            End With
        End With
    End With
End Sub
```

Pictured here is the custom toolbar resulting from Proc32:

Creating a New Menu Using Code

Proc33 creates a new menubar, complete with cascading submenus. It starts by adding a new commandbar to the CommandBars collection. Note that the MenuBar argument is set to True, which will make the new commandbar behave like a menubar and replace the active menu. Then we use the CommandBarControls collection's Add method (accessed through the Controls property of the new commandbar) to add pop-up controls. Each popup has its own MenuBar object; to create the submenu, we add buttons and another popup to the object.

```
Sub Chap05cProc33_AddMenu()
    On Error Resume Next
    With Application.CommandBars.Add("CustomMenu", , True, True)
        .Visible = True
        With .Controls
            With .Add(msoControlPopup)
                .Caption = "&Popup1"
                With .Controls
                    With .Add(msoControlButton)
                        .Caption = "Button&1"
                        .OnAction = "Chap05cProc34_MenuRoutine"
                    End With
                    With .Add(msoControlPopup)
                        .Caption = "Popup&3"
                        With .Controls
                            With .Add(msoControlButton)
                                .Caption = "Button&5"
                                .OnAction = _
                                    "Chap05cProc34_MenuRoutine"
                            End With
                            With .Add(msoControlButton)
                                .Caption = "Button&6"
                                .OnAction = _
                                    "Chap05cProc34_MenuRoutine"
                            End With
                        End With
                    End With
                End With
            End With
            With .Add(msoControlPopup)
                .Caption = "P&opup2"
                With .Controls
                    With .Add(msoControlButton)
                        .Caption = "Button&3"
                        .OnAction = "Chap05cProc34_MenuRoutine"
                    End With
                    With .Add(msoControlButton)
```

(continued)

303

continued

```
                                .Caption = "Button&4"
                                .OnAction = "Chap05cProc34_MenuRoutine"
                        End With
                    End With
                End With
            End With
        End With
End Sub
```

Pictured here is the custom menu resulting from Proc33:

All buttons created on the menu and toolbar call Proc34. Proc34 demonstrates calling a routine from a custom commandbar:

```
Sub Chap05cProc34_MenuRoutine()
    MsgBox "Test routine."
End Sub
```

Manipulating CommandBar Objects

You can also use CommandBar objects to manipulate menus and toolbars at runtime. Proc35 demonstrates a number of techniques including how to disable, hide, and delete a control, and how to reset a menu. You can execute this next routine by pressing Alt-F8 and selecting Proc35 from the list.

```
Sub Chap05cProc35_ManipulateCommandBars()
    Dim CBControl As CommandBarControl
    On Error Resume Next
    With Application.CommandBars("CustomMenu")
        .Visible = False
        .Delete
    End With
    With Application.CommandBars("Worksheet Menu Bar")
        With .Controls("&Tools")
            .Enabled = False
            .Visible = True
            DoEvents
            MsgBox "Tools menu has been disabled."
```

```
            .Enabled = True
            .Visible = False
            MsgBox "Tools menu has been hidden."
            .Visible = True
        End With
        For Each CBControl In .Controls
            CBControl.Delete
            DoEvents
        Next CBControl
        MsgBox "All popups on the menu have been deleted."
        .Reset
        MsgBox "Menu restored."
    End With
End Sub
```

Creating and Modifying CommandBars Manually

At this point you're probably thinking: "It sure takes a lot of code to create custom menus and toolbars." That would be a fair statement. Fortunately, Excel provides commands in the User Interface that enable you to create and modify commandbars without writing code. While the techniques demonstrated in Proc35 are best left to code, creating a custom menu or toolbar is better accomplished manually.

To do this, you use the Tools Customize command to activate the Customize dialog box. From the Toolbars tab on the dialog box, you can create new commandbars, delete ones you have created, and reset built-in ones to their defaults.

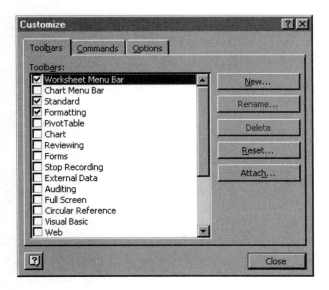

Clicking the New button prompts you for a name for a new bar and then displays a blank bar. The commands tab enables you to drag built-in commands as well as custom commands onto the bar. Selecting the Macros category provides the choices Custom Menu Item and Custom Button, which you can place on the bar and define to run your own routines.

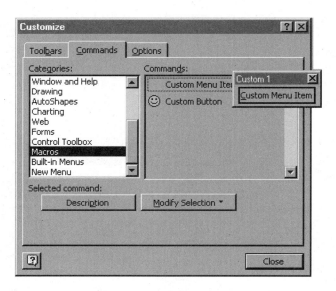

After you have dragged a button onto the new bar, right-click it to display a popup menu. On this menu, you can set the button name, image, and style.

Use the Assign Macro command on the pop-up menu to bring up the Assign Macro dialog box. Here you can assign a VBA routine to the button.

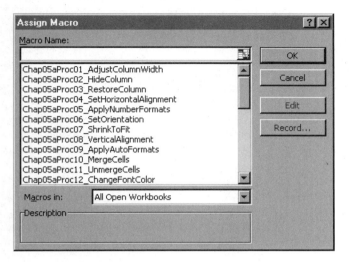

It's generally best practice to assign only macros stored in "This Workbook" because, in the future, you might not be able to locate macros created in other workbooks.

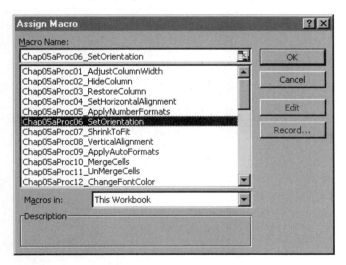

Once you have designed your commandbar, you can attach it to your workbook so that it will be available when your application is distributed. To do this, click the Attach button on the Toolbars tab of the Customize dialog box to bring up the Attach Toolbars dialog box. The Copy command copies the toolbar definition that you select in the left half of the dialog box into the current workbook area on the right. (See illustration on the following page.)

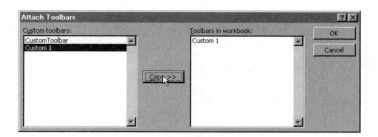

Once you have attached a commandbar to a workbook and saved the workbook, you can actually remove the commandbar from the Excel workspace while keeping it attached to your workbook. This means that your user will be able to access the custom commandbar when the workbook file containing your custom VBA application is loaded into memory; however, once that workbook is closed, the custom commandbar will no longer be accessible to the user. You can ship the custom commandbar with your application and have it displayed when the application starts up, or hide it and use code like the following to display it at any other time (note that attached commandbars appear in the Workbook object's own CommandBars collection):

```
ThisWorkbook.CommandBars("MyCommandBar").Visible = True
```

Additional Excel Interface Elements: The Application Object

One other area to consider when creating custom interfaces in Excel involves manipulating the Excel environment in which your application will run. For example, you could set a custom caption in the Excel title bar and hide the formula and status bars. Aspects of the Excel environment that can be modified are represented by the properties and methods of the Application object. Note that you cannot save the environment settings with the workbook file that contains your application. You must adjust these aspects of the Excel environment using a routine at runtime. (You can easily accomplish this by using the Workbook's Open event, which will fire every time the workbook is opened. This process is described in the next section.) Let's take a look at the pertinent Application properties and methods.

Application Properties

Calculation: Determines Excel's calculation mode. Can be xlCalculation-Automatic, xlCalculationManual, and xlCalculationSemiAutomatic (which corresponds to the Automatic Except Tables calculation option in the Excel User Interface). Note that if you attempt to set this property when no workbooks are open, a runtime error will be generated.

Caption: Caption displayed in the form of a string in the Excel title bar. Note that when the active window is maximized, both the Caption property of the Application object and the Caption property of the Window object that corresponds to the active window appear in the Application title bar. Setting the caption property to Empty returns the caption to the default "Microsoft Excel."

Cursor: Cursor takes one of four values that can be used to set a custom cursor:

xlNormal, xlDefault	Default pointer (as set in the Windows Control Panel)
xlWait	Hourglass pointer
xlNorthwestArrow	Northwest-arrow pointer
xlIBeam	I-beam pointer

Note that cursor settings remain in place after routine execution ends. Therefore, always set the cursor back to xlNormal before routine execution ends.

DisplayAlerts: If False, built-in Excel alerts are not displayed during routine execution. The default setting is True. At the end of routine execution, the DisplayAlerts property automatically reverts to its default setting of True. Therefore, you must reset this property to False in every routine in which you do not want built-in alerts displayed.

DisplayFormulaBar: If False, the formula bar at the top of the Excel workspace is not displayed.

DisplayStatusBar: If False, the status bar at the bottom of the Excel workspace is not displayed.

Height: Height of the Application window in points ($1/72$ inch).

Left: Distance in points ($1/72$ inch) from the left edge of the Application window to the left edge of the screen.

OperatingSystem: Read-only property that returns a text string corresponding to the operating system under which Excel is running. This property is useful in modifying interface components at runtime in order to accommodate different operating systems (Microsoft Windows 95, Microsoft Windows NT, Microsoft Windows 3.11, and Macintosh).

ScreenUpdating: If False, the screen display is not updated during routine execution. The default setting is True. At the end of routine execution, the ScreenUpdating property automatically reverts to its default setting of True. Therefore, you must reset this property to False in every routine in which you want to disable screen updating.

StatusBar: Text that is displayed in the status bar at the bottom of the Excel workspace. Setting this property provides a useful way to communicate messages to the user during routine execution. Because Excel also uses the StatusBar property to display messages, you must set the StatusBar property to False to give control of the status bar back to Excel.

Top: Distance in points ($\frac{1}{72}$ inch) from the top edge of the Application window to the top edge of the screen.

Version: Read-only property that returns the version number of Excel. The Version property is useful in modifying interface components that are dependent on the version of Excel running the application.

Width: Width of the Application window in points ($\frac{1}{72}$ inch).

WindowState: State of the Application window. WindowState can take one of three values:

xlNormal	Window is neither maximized nor minimized. (Window size is governed by the Height and Width properties.)
xlMaximized	Window is maximized to fill the entire screen.
xlMinimized	Window is minimized and displayed as an icon.

Application Methods

The most common Application method used when you implement a custom interface in Excel is the Quit method. Quit closes down Excel entirely. By calling the Quit method on the Application object when your application finishes running, you can close Excel completely to leave the impression of running a stand-alone application rather than a routine in a spreadsheet. If your application calls the Quit method after changes have been made to a workbook file, Excel prompts the user to save the changes to the file. If you set the DisplayAlerts property of the Application object to False before calling Quit, the display of this Excel prompt is eliminated, and the application quits immediately. Take care, however, when calling Quit while DisplayAlerts is set to False, because all changes made to the workbook file will be lost.

> **NOTE** You can also save changes before calling Quit by first calling the Save method on the Workbook object.

Proc36, which we examine next, takes advantage of several of the Application properties we've mentioned to manipulate various aspects of the Excel interface. The routine first sets the Caption property and then turns off the formula and status bars. It then turns the status bar back on and assigns a string to the StatusBar property to display a custom message. The routine sets ScreenUpdating to False and completely changes the position and size of the Application window by setting the WindowState, Height, Width, Top, and Left properties. Screen-Updating is then set back to True to display the application window in its new configuration. At the end of the routine, the Caption property is set to Empty, and control of the status bar is given back to Excel. Notice at the end of the routine that statements for setting the DisplayAlerts property and calling the Quit method have been commented out. Executing these two statements would result in Excel quitting without prompting the user to save any changes made to the workbook.

```vba
Sub Chap05dProc36_SetApplicationProperties()
    Worksheets(1).Activate
    With Application
        If UCase(Left(.OperatingSystem, 3)) <> "MAC" Then
            .Caption = "Custom Application"
            MsgBox "Application.Caption = ""Custom Application"""
        End If
        .DisplayFormulaBar = False
        MsgBox "Application.DisplayFormulaBar = False"
        .DisplayStatusBar = False
        MsgBox "Application.DisplayStatusBar = False"
        .DisplayStatusBar = True
        MsgBox "Application.DisplayStatusBar = True"
        .StatusBar = "Custom Status Bar Message"
        MsgBox "Application.StatusBar = " _
            & """Custom Status Bar Message"""
        .ScreenUpdating = False
        If UCase(Left(.OperatingSystem, 3)) <> "MAC" Then
            .WindowState = xlNormal
            .Height = 200
            .Width = 200
            .Top = 100
            .Left = 100
            .ScreenUpdating = True
            MsgBox "Application.ScreenUpdating = False" & Chr(13) & _
                "Application.WindowState = xlNormal" & Chr(13) & _
                "Application.Height = 200" & Chr(13) & _
                "Application.Width = 200" & Chr(13) & _
                "Application.Top = 100" & Chr(13) & _
                "Application.Left = 100" & Chr(13) & _
                "Application.ScreenUpdating = True"
            .WindowState = xlMaximized
            MsgBox "Application.WindowState = xlMaximized"
            .Caption = Empty
        End If
        .DisplayFormulaBar = True
        .StatusBar = False
        '.DisplayAlerts = False
        '.Quit
    End With
End Sub
```

Workbook and Worksheet Events

As mentioned, you might want to automatically set the Application object's properties whenever your workbook is opened. The key to doing this is using Workbook and Worksheet object events. Workbook and Worksheet events can fire in response to user interaction or to other stimuli.

Worksheet Events

Worksheet event procedures are exposed through the code module behind each workbook. To view them, select the Worksheet object in the module's Object Selector, and then view each event procedure with the Procedure Selector. Worksheets support the following events.

Activate: Fires when the sheet is activated.

BeforeDoubleClick: Fires after the user double-clicks the sheet but before the default Excel behavior occurs. A Range object representing the cell that was double-clicked is passed into the procedure as an argument called target. By setting the cancel argument to True, you can prevent the default behavior from occurring.

BeforeRightClick: Fires after the user right-clicks the sheet but before the default Excel behavior occurs. A Range object representing the cell that was right-clicked is passed into the procedure as an argument called target. By setting the cancel argument to True, you can prevent the default behavior from occurring. (The default is usually the display of a shortcut menu.)

Calculate: Fires after the sheet is recalculated.

Change: Fires when data changes on the sheet. The target argument is a Range object representing the cells that have changed.

Deactivate: Fires when the sheet is deactivated.

SelectionChange: Fires when the selection changes. The target argument is a Range object representing the new selection.

Workbook Events

Workbook event procedures are exposed through the code module behind the This Workbook object found in the Project window.

Workbook-specific events

AddinInstall: Fires when the workbook is installed as an add-in through the Add-in manager. (Further explanation is provided in Chapter 13.)

AddinUninstall: Fires when the workbook is uninstalled through the Add-in manager. (Further explanation is provided in Chapter 13.)

BeforeClose: Fires before the workbook closes. The cancel argument can be set to True to prevent it from closing. This event replaces the old Auto_Close macro in previous versions of Excel.

BeforePrint: Fires before the workbook prints (or the print preview is displayed). The cancel argument can be set to True to prevent it from printing.

BeforeSave: Fires before the workbook saves. The cancel argument can be set to True to prevent it from saving.

NewSheet: Fires when a new sheet is inserted into the workbook. The argument Sh is a sheet object representing the new sheet.

Open: Fires when the workbook opens. This event replaces the old Auto_Open macro in previous versions of Excel.

Other workbook events

Activate: Fires when the workbook is activated.

Deactivate: Fires when the workbook is deactivated.

WindowActivate: Fires when the workbook window is activated. Differs from the Activate event when more than one window is open on the same workbook. In this case, switching windows fires the WindowActivate event but not the Activate event.

WindowDeactivate: Fires when the workbook window is deactivated. Differs from the Deactivate event when more than one window is open on the same workbook. In this case, switching windows fires the WindowDeactivate event but not the Activate event.

WindowResize: Fires when the workbook window is resized (maximized, minimized, restored, or sized manually).

Workbook-level sheet events

The following workbook events respond to Sheet events, but unlike event handlers for specific sheets, workbook-level sheet events react to events for all sheets. Workbook-level sheet events function identically to their Sheet-event counterparts except that an additional argument, Sh, is passed to workbook event procedures. Sh is a sheet object representing the sheet that generated the event. Use workbook-level sheet events when you want to create identical responses to sheet events on all sheets in the workbook. Note that these events even fire for sheets created at runtime.

To find out more about the following events, see the online VBA Help:

SheetActivate
SheetBeforeDoubleClick
SheetBeforeRightClick
SheetCalculate
SheetChange
SheetDeactivate
SheetSelectionChange

Exploring Workbook and Worksheet Events

To explore these events further, open the file CHAP05-2.XLS on the companion CD. The file demonstrates most of the events described in the preceding section. Try to fire all of them by interacting with the workbook.

One thing worthy of note: pay attention when you activate and deactivate Sheet1. Sheet1 has its own sheet-level Activate event handler, but the workbook also has a SheetActivate handler. Examine the manner and the order in which the two Activate event handlers are fired.

Implementing a Custom Interface Effectively

This chapter has looked closely at customizing interfaces in Excel. The questions to ask now are "Which objects should I use?" and "How should I use those objects to design the most effective user interface—one that will require little user training and that will allow the user to rapidly access information provided by the application?" These are difficult questions to answer because numerous factors come into play:

- The expected number of users of the application

- The technical ability of the users

- The complexity of the tasks that the application performs

- The time and resources available for creating the application

Although this chapter cannot cover all possible cases, we can make a few recommendations here about good application design. Designing applications well is an art, and each developer has his or her own preferences. Some developers prefer to use menus and dialog boxes extensively, and others like using toolbars. Still others like to use only control objects on worksheets. Consider the following recommendations only to the degree to which you believe they will ultimately benefit your users by helping them make better use of the applications you create. Remember that these recommendations are based on the opinions of the authors, and as a result, you will most certainly encounter situations in which these recommendations will not apply.

Recommendations for Designing a User Interface

Some of the following recommendations are self-evident but worth mentioning. Others deal with less obvious issues related to using Excel—issues that often can be well understood only after years of experience. All of these recommendations were followed in designing the sample application in Chapter 6.

1. **Use a main control form in your application.** A main control form is the form that the user first encounters when running your application. The form should clearly display the name of the application, the purpose of the application, and a means of navigating to the various component parts of the application.

2. **Break up your application into at most four or five main logical components, and build separate forms for accessing each component.** By breaking up an application into logical components, you give more structure to your application. If users associate one main task with one form, the application appears more intuitive, and users learn the application more quickly. (Grouping several unrelated tasks on a single form can often be confusing to a novice user.)

3. **Make the navigation path through your application clear to the user.** The user should never have to wonder how to access a form or a major component of an application; the design of the interface should make this information obvious. Perhaps the best way to achieve this clarity is to place large and intuitive buttons on your application's forms—buttons that allow users to access the various component parts. Take care in using menus or toolbars as a means of navigating through an application because menu items and toolbar buttons are not as readily visible to the user as are control objects placed on a form. For example, users might not know to look in a certain menu to access a certain screen.

4. **Make your application as graphical as possible.** The more graphical the presentation of information, the better your user will understand it. For example, if you are creating an application to display sales data, go beyond simply displaying numeric data—display the data graphically in charts or even in geographical maps. Doing so will make the data much easier to understand.

5. **Format numeric data to make it easier to read.** When you create applications that involve the display of numeric data in tables, take advantage of Excel's built-in automatic formats, which are designed to make data easier to read.

6. **Avoid clutter on forms.** A form should contain no more than 7 to 10 controls, with 5 probably the optimal number. Putting too many controls on a form usually makes it confusing.

7. **For data-centric routines, use control objects on sheets.** For example, if you have a table of data on a worksheet and you've written a routine that manipulates the data in some fashion, attach the routine to a control that's close to the data table. With the control near the data that it affects, the control's function is more obvious to the user. In such situations, using a control on a sheet is better than using a menu or a dialog box.

8. **Use control objects on sheets whenever you can.** At the risk of sounding redundant, we'll mention again that you should use control objects directly on worksheets or charts whenever doing so makes sense. Some developers have a tendency to use controls only in dialog boxes, making the user complete an extra step to display a dialog box and then access a control. This extra step is not required when the control exists directly on the worksheet or chart.

9. **Create Wizards for multi-step processes.** By breaking up complicated tasks into logical component parts and placing them in Wizards (similar to the Wizard we looked at earlier in this chapter), you will greatly simplify such tasks for your users.

10. **Use custom menus only when control objects on sheets and dialog boxes are not appropriate.** Placing a command for a routine deep within a menu might make it difficult for the user to discover it. Control objects on worksheets, on the other hand, are much more intuitive and readily accessible. Of course, there are times when using menus is appropriate.

11. **Use the Tools Customize command to design custom commandbars (menus and toolbars).** You can then attach them to your workbook and distribute them with your application. Use VBA code to manipulate commandbars further at runtime.

12. **Eliminate all evidence of Excel from your application.** The ultimate goal is to make users think they are running your application and not Excel. If your application does not require Excel's menus, hide them. (Displaying Excel's menus along the top of the screen might be distracting to users while they are running your application.) You should also hide all built-in Excel toolbars and customize the Application and ActiveWindow captions. If your application does not require the user to interact with any standard built-in Excel functionality, take whatever steps are necessary to prevent the user from breaking out of your application and accessing Excel.

13. Use the Workbook Open event handler to make environment settings when your application first starts, and use the Workbook Close event handler to restore environment settings when your application has finished executing. The Open event is fired when you open your workbook, and the Close event is fired when you close it. If your application sets any properties of environment objects (Application, CommandBar, Window, and so on), be sure to restore the original values of those properties after your application has finished executing. Use the Open event to read the settings of all of the environment properties that will be changed and store such settings in variables. The Open event can then make the necessary changes to the properties, and the Close event can use these variables to restore the environment properties to their original state. Using Open and Close events in this way ensures that your users will still be able to use Excel as a stand-alone spreadsheet application without being affected by any environment settings left over from running your application.

SUMMARY

The user interface is one of the most important aspects of a custom application; it governs how the user interacts with the application. This chapter covered numerous objects, properties, and methods that can be used to design custom interfaces in Excel. Here are the main points covered in this chapter:

- Worksheets can serve as the basis for forms in Excel. When you are transforming a worksheet into a form, you use the Range, Font, Interior, Border, Style, Worksheet, and Window objects.

- Controls give forms functionality. By using controls on forms, you give users the ability to execute routines in a variety of ways.

- Dialog boxes can also be used to hold controls and are designed as userforms by using the Visual Basic Editor. A dialog box is displayed by calling the Show method on the UserForm object. By using dialog boxes, you can limit the user's interaction with Excel interface elements.

- Excel's commandbars (menus and toolbars) are fully customizable—either through the Tools Customize command or by using the CommandBar and CommandBarControl objects.

- The Application object has several properties that control the various aspects of the Excel environment. Because these properties cannot be saved in a workbook file, they must be set at runtime.

- The Workbook and Worksheet objects have a series of other events that you can write code to respond to. The Workbook object provides both its own events and a set of Workbook-level sheet events that respond to *every* sheet in the workbook.

- Use the workbook's Open event handler to store the user's interface configuration prior to the loading of your application as well as to establish the interface for your application. Use the workbook's Close event handler to return Excel to the user's original configuration when your application closes.

6

Sample Application 2: Wellington Cycle Works

Many of the objects discussed in Chapters 4 and 5 are used in the sample information system we look at in this chapter. This information system was developed for a fictitious company named Wellington Cycle Works that sells racing bikes, touring bikes, and bicycle accessories throughout the world. The Wellington system is designed to provide a way for managers in the company to analyze sales data.

You can find the completed sample application in the file named CHAP06.XLS on the companion CD packaged with this book. The application uses the BikeData database that was used in Chapter 4. To run the Wellington Cycle Works application in CHAP06.XLS, the BIKEDATA.MDB database file and the CHAP06.XLS file must be in the same folder on your hard drive—the code in the CHAP06.XLS file is written to look for the BIKEDATA.MDB file in the same folder.

The Wellington Cycle Works Application

After you start Microsoft Excel and load the CHAP06.XLS file, you see the Home form for the Wellington Cycle Works application (Figure 6-1 on the following page).

The Wellington Cycle Works application consists of three main forms and a Wizard. A custom commandbar is used to both navigate among forms and manipulate data on forms. We'll look at each of these components in detail shortly. For now, here's a brief description of the application components:

■ **Home form:** Main form of the application, which displays the company name and buttons for navigating to the "Sales Analysis" Pivot form, starting the Report Wizard, and quitting the application.

- **Pivot form:** Displays a pivottable. The commandbar contains several controls to manipulate the display of data in the pivottable. Data for the pivottable originates from the BikeData database.

- **Chart form:** Displays a chart that is linked to the pivottable. The commandbar contains several controls to manipulate the data presented on the chart. Other controls on the Chart form change the display of the chart itself.

- **Report Wizard:** Consists of a series of four dialog boxes that allows the user to take data out of the pivottable and place it on a standard Excel worksheet for further analysis. When the user creates a report using the Report Wizard, a new worksheet is added to the workbook —in essence, a new form is added. The Report Wizard can be used either to create new reports or to access existing ones.

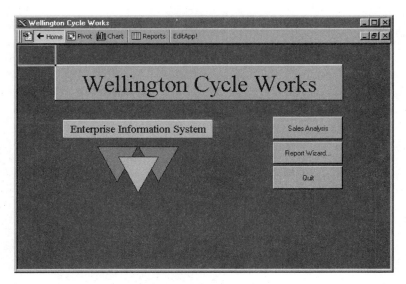

Figure 6-1. *The Home form of the Wellington Cycle Works sample application.*

TIP You might want to take a few minutes now to use the Wellington Cycle Works application on your own. Explore using the various controls on the different forms, and try to determine how the routines that are attached to the controls achieve the results that you see.

Navigating Through the Wellington Cycle Works Application

You navigate through the application in two ways: by using the buttons on the forms and by using the commandbar at the top of the window. The buttons on the forms take the user to selected areas of the application. From the Home form, the user can click the Sales Analysis button to go to the Pivot form to analyze numeric data in a pivottable, or the user can click the Report Wizard button to generate a report to manipulate the data further or to distribute the data. From a report and from the Pivot form, the user can move back to the Home form by clicking the Home button on the commandbar.

Whereas the buttons on the forms provide access to selected features, the buttons on the custom toolbar give the user access to any form in the application as well as to the Report Wizard. The next three sections take a closer look at each of the forms that make up the Wellington Cycle Works application.

NOTE	You will notice that on the custom commandbar of the Wellington application, there is a button labeled "EditApp!" When you click this button, a subroutine is run that restores all Excel interface artifacts that were displayed before the Wellington application was loaded (including commandbars, the status bar, the formula bar, and worksheet tabs). Clicking EditApp! essentially places the Wellington application into Edit mode, allowing the developer to edit the various aspects of the application. Also notice that when the Wellington application is placed into Edit mode, a commandbutton labeled "Restore App" appears on the Excel worksheet commandbar. When you click this button, a routine is run that places the application back into run mode. Placement of these buttons on the commandbars makes it easy for a developer to toggle back and forth between edit mode and run mode.

The Home Form

In Figure 6-2 on the following page, the Home form is displayed with labels for the Excel objects that make up the form. This Home form is an example of how Excel can be fully customized; the form retains no visual indications of Excel.

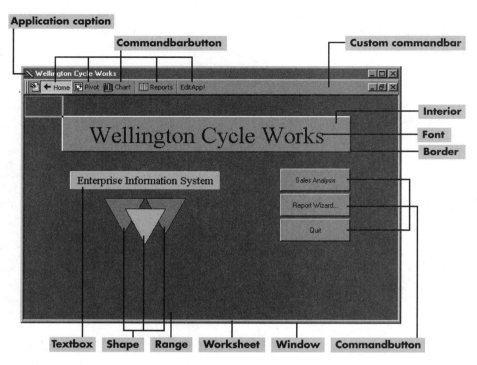

Figure 6-2. *The objects that make up the Home form.*

Let's take a brief look at the objects that were used to create this form.

Worksheet: Although the form exists on a worksheet, few worksheet properties and methods were used to create the form. However, several objects contained in the Worksheet object were used.

Range: The Value property of the Range object was used to display the title "Wellington Cycle Works" in the upper portion of the form. Range was also used to access the Font, Interior, and Border objects to format other aspects of the form.

Font: The Font object was used to format the text entries in the upper portion of the form as well as the text in the textbox that displays "Enterprise Information System."

Interior: The ColorIndex property of the Interior object was set to give the Wellington Cycle Works cell a light gray background and the rest of the form a blue background.

Border: The Border object was used to create the 3D effect surrounding Wellington Cycle Works text.

CommandButton: Three CommandButton controls appear on the right side of the form; they provide a way to navigate to selected portions of the application.

Shape: A textbox Shape object appears in the middle of the form and displays the text "Enterprise Information System." Three triangular Shape objects are used to display the company logo below the textbox.

In addition, several other objects (described below) have been used to customize Excel as displayed in Figure 6-2. Some of the property settings for these objects are maintained with the workbook that contains the Wellington Cycle Works application, and others represent aspects of the Excel workspace.

CommandBar: A custom commandbar was created using VBA code.

CommandBarButton: The Home, Pivot, and Chart buttons are CommandBarButton objects. Note that they are programmed to act as toggle buttons that switch you from form to form. This is accomplished by manipulating their State properties through code.

The Reports and EditApp! buttons are also CommandBarButton objects. They do not toggle, however, but merely call routines. The Reports button displays a UserForm object and the EditApp! button restores the Excel environment.

CommandBarComboBox: (See Figure 6-3 on the following page.) Several CommandBarComboBox objects have been added to allow the user to manipulate the pivottable and chart contents. These objects are disabled when the Home form is active.

Application: Various properties of the Application object have been set in order to hide all indications of Excel; among these are Caption ("Wellington Cycle Works"), DisplayStatusBar (False), and DisplayFormulaBar (False). Because none of these property settings can be saved with the workbook, they are set during the execution of the Workbook_Open event procedure by a call to the SetEnvironment routine.

Window: Recall from Chapter 5 that certain Window properties apply to individual worksheets, whereas others apply to the whole workbook. Both types of Window properties affect the display of the form shown in Figure 6-2 on page 322 and include the following:

Property	Setting
DisplayGridlines	False
DisplayHeadings	False
Caption	"" (an empty string)
DisplayHorizontalScrollBar	False
DisplayVerticalScrollBar	False
DisplayWorkbookTabs	False

To move to the Pivot form, the user clicks the Sales Analysis button on the Home form. The next section describes the Pivot form.

The Pivot Form

Figure 6-3 shows the Pivot form and the objects that make up the form.

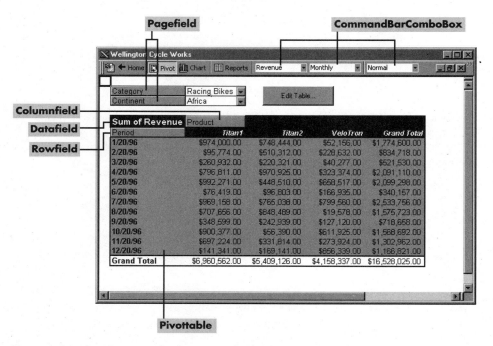

Figure 6-3. *The objects that make up the Pivot form.*

The focus of the Pivot form is the PivotTable object. The pivottable was created from data in the BikeData database and has the following default configuration:

PageFields	Category and Continent
RowField	Period (month)
ColumnField	Product
DataField	Revenue

Notice that a currency number format has been applied to the currency data in the Data area of the table and that the xlClassic3 AutoFormat has been applied to the range that corresponds to TableRange1. The user is free to manipulate the pivottable in any fashion—by dragging the pivotfield labels to different positions or by selecting different values from the pagefield drop-down listboxes.

Three CommandBarComboBox controls on the custom commandbar make it easy for the user to manipulate the pivottable. The first combobox, Data Item, allows the user to easily control which pivotfield is displayed in the table's Data area. When the user selects one of the three items, a routine is executed that removes whatever pivotfield currently exists in the Data area and replaces it with the pivotfield that corresponds to the item selected from the combobox. Which number formatting is applied to the table's Data area depends on the pivotfield being displayed—if the user selects either Revenue or Profit, a currency format is applied, and if the user selects Units from the combobox, a standard number format is applied.

The second combobox, Time Series, lets the user select either a Monthly or Quarterly grouping of data. If the user selects Quarterly, a routine is executed that calls the Group method on the Period pivotfield to group the period data by quarters. If the Period pivotfield is not in the Row area of the pivottable when an item is selected from the Time Series combobox, a message box is displayed informing the user that the Period pivotfield must be in the Row area in order to consolidate data on a quarterly basis.

The last combobox, Calculation, displays four options for the Calculation property of the pivotfield in the table's Data area. When the user selects an item from the combobox, a routine is executed that sets the Calculation property to a constant that corresponds to the item selected: xlNormal, xlPercentOfRow, xlPercentOfColumn, or xlPercentOfTotal. By default, the data is displayed with the Calculation property set to xlNormal.

The following shows the pivottable after each of the comboboxes has been changed (to display profit grouped quarterly as a percent of the column):

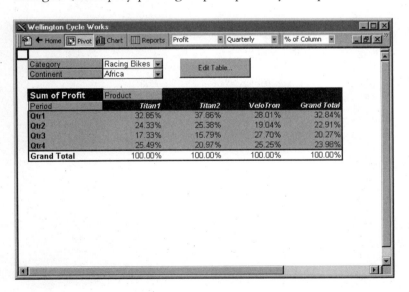

The Pivot form also contains one commandbutton control labeled Edit Table. This button's Click event calls a routine that displays a userform called frmEditTable. This custom dialog box, shown on the following page, allows the user to either rebuild the original pivottable or launch the PivotTable Wizard. It also allows the user to refresh the data in the pivottable.

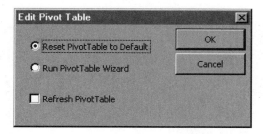

The dynamic nature of the pivottable lets the user change any aspect of the pivottable—the user can even delete the table. The Edit PivotTable dialog box, thankfully, lets the user backtrack. With this dialog box, the user can reconstruct the original pivottable if, for example, the table has been changed so much that it cannot be returned to its original configuration manually (for example, if the user deleted a pivotfield by dragging it out of the Table area). Giving the user access to the PivotTable Wizard through this dialog box allows the user to take advantage of this powerful built-in functionality of Excel. And with the Refresh Table checkbox, the user can ensure—without having to exit and restart the application—that the data being analyzed is current.

You might have noticed that many of the property settings that affect the display of the workspace while the Home form is displayed are also in effect while the Pivot form is displayed—properties associated with the Application and Window objects. Note, however, that on the Pivot form the horizontal and vertical scroll bars are displayed so that the user can navigate around the worksheet containing the pivottable. These scroll bars are activated by the routine that takes the user from the Home form to the Pivot form. (The routine sets the Window object's DisplayHorizontalScrollBar and DisplayVerticalScrollBar properties to True.)

Now let's move on to the Chart form described in the next section. Click the Chart button on the custom commandbar.

The Chart Form

The Chart form shows in a graphical manner the data that the pivottable contains. Figure 6-4 shows the objects that make up the Chart form.

The chart on the Chart form is linked to the pivottable on the Pivot form. When the structure of the pivottable changes, the chart changes as well, reflecting the new pivottable data. In fact, the chart shown in Figure 6-4 on page 327 was created from the pivottable range that corresponds to the TableRange1 property. As a result, the chart remains linked to the TableRange1 range—no matter what structure or size the pivottable takes on. Each of the CommandBarComboBox controls on the custom commandbar that change the structure and data in the pivottable automatically alters the display of the chart as well. The Calculation combobox is not visible on the Chart form since the Calculation property cannot be charted.

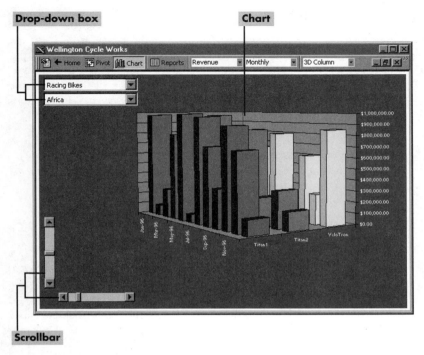

Drop-down box

Chart

Scrollbar

Figure 6-4. *The objects that make up the Chart form.*

One additional CommandBarComboBox control gives the user a choice of chart type. When the user selects one of the four options, a routine is executed that sets the Type property of the Chart object to one of four values: xl3DColumn, xlSurface, xl3DArea, or xl3DLine.

Drop-Down Control

The two controls at the top of the Chart form are actually drop-down controls, created using the drop-down button on the Forms toolbar. Note that these controls are not combobox controls from the new Control Toolbox toolbar—unfortunately, the controls accessible from the Control Toolbox toolbar cannot be used on chart sheets. Thus, dropdowns from the Forms toolbar are used in this case. Drop-down controls function in much the same manner as ComboBox controls. The main difference between the two is the fact that drop-down controls have only one event—a click event (which is assigned by setting the OnAction property of the DropDown object). The items that populate the two drop-down controls on the Chart form are identical to the pivotitems in the Continent and Category pivotfields in the pivottable's Page area. By selecting a value from one of the two drop-down controls on the Chart form, the user can launch a routine that changes the corresponding pagefield drop-down listbox on the pivottable and thus display the selected item. (The routine does so by setting the CurrentPage property.)

Note that the drop-down controls on the Chart form are dynamic; they always reflect the pagefield drop-down listboxes that are on the pivottable. (See the "FYI" titled "Keeping the Controls on the Chart Form and the Pivot Form in Sync" on page 331.) Regardless of what the pivottable's pagefields are, the dropdowns on the Chart form always conform. In fact, if the architecture of the pivottable is changed so that no pivotfields are displayed in the pagefields, no dropdowns appear on the Chart form.

> **NOTE** The drop-down controls on the Chart form can handle up to two pivotfields in the Page area of the pivottable. If you have modified the pivottable to have more than two pivotfields in the Page area, only the first two pivotfields will be available through the drop-down controls on the Chart form.

ScrollBars

The two ScrollBar controls that occupy the lower left portion of the Chart form were created using the Forms toolbar. As stated previously, the controls accessible from the Control Toolbox toolbar cannot be used on Chart sheets. The vertical scrollbar is used to set the Elevation property of the Chart object to any value from −90 through 90, and the horizontal scrollbar is used to set the Rotation property of the Chart object to any value from 0 through 360.

The following screen shows the chart as displayed for the following options: Category "Accessories", Continent "(All)", 3D surface chart type, monthly grouping, and the rotation/elevation altered.

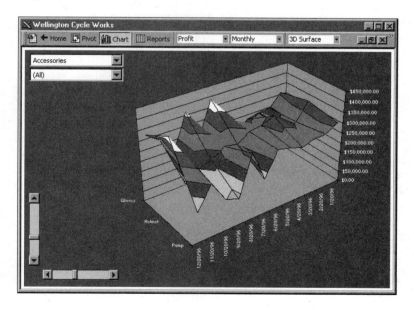

When you finish looking at the Chart and Pivot forms, make your way back to the Home form to take a look at the Report Wizard, which the next section describes.

Issues to Consider When Using ActiveX Controls in Workbooks

When using ActiveX Controls in a workbook, there are a few important issues to consider.

First, if you are planning to view the workbook inside Internet Explorer (IE), you will not be able to interact with the embedded controls. They will simply be disabled. This issue has to do with what can be referred to as "in-situ in-situ" activation. Basically, Excel is activated "in-situ" within IE; likewise, a control in a workbook is activated within Excel. Since Excel doesn't support nesting of in-situ activation, the control is disabled when the workbook is viewed in IE. (This is also why, for example, you can't place an ActiveX OptionButton control inside an ActiveX Frame control on a sheet—this is also "in-situ in-situ" activation, which Excel does not support.) The solution is to use the old Excel 5 and Excel 95 controls, which can be found on the Forms toolbar. All the standard controls (buttons, comboboxes, scrollbars, etc.) are available and work in a manner similar to the ActiveX controls.

Second, ActiveX controls cannot be placed on a chart—including a separate chart sheet and a chart embedded in a worksheet. If controls must be used on a chart, the solution again is to use the old controls.

Third, when you do you use ActiveX controls on worksheets, be aware that many Excel object properties and methods cannot be addressed while the control has the input focus. If you attempt to reference one of these properties or methods in code, a runtime error will occur. For example, you cannot change the Rotation property of a Chart object while a control has the focus. You have several options for dealing with this issue. With CommandButton controls, you can set the TakeFocusOnClick property to False. This will prevent the button from ever getting the focus and should prevent any runtime errors. For other controls, it may be possible at times to set focus back to the worksheet in code before attempting an operation that would cause an error. For example, you could use Range("A1").Select to force focus back to the sheet. You could also elect to use the old controls. Because you won't need to worry about setting focus, using old controls may be more convenient when you don't need the extra functionality ActiveX controls provide. In some cases, it may be necessary since setting the focus back to the sheet may be impractical or cause other side effects in your application.

The Report Wizard

The Report Wizard consists of four dialog boxes that step the user through building a simple report that contains data from the pivottable. This Wizard allows the user to take data out of the pivottable and transfer it to a standard Excel worksheet so that the user can analyze the data using all of Excel's built-in functionality. When the Report Wizard creates a new report, it actually adds a worksheet to the workbook; for each report that is added, a new worksheet is added.

The Report Wizard's first dialog box displays a list of all existing user-created reports. The user can then use the Report Wizard to navigate from the Wellington Cycle Works application to the user-created reports. Also, when a user-created report is displayed, all of the menus on the Excel worksheet commandbar are enabled, giving the user full access to the functionality of Excel. When the user goes back to the forms of the Wellington Cycle Works application, however, the Wellington-specific menus are restored in order to limit the user's access to Excel functionality.

To access the Report Wizard, the user either clicks the Reports button on the Home form or clicks the Reports button on the custom commandbar. The user then sees the Report Wizard's first dialog box:

The first dialog box gives the user few choices. If user-created reports existed, the left portion of the dialog box would show a listbox that displayed the names of all of the reports. In addition, the Go To Report and Delete Report buttons would be enabled, allowing the user to either go to or delete an existing report. Because no reports yet exist, the user can only click the Next button to create a report or click the Cancel button to exit the Report Wizard. If the user clicks the Next button, the second Report Wizard dialog box is displayed:

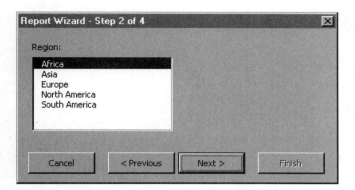

In this second dialog box, the user can select the region of the world for which to generate a report. The regions displayed in the listbox are taken directly from the pivotitems in the Continent pivotfield of the pivottable. After the user selects a region and clicks the Next button, the third Report Wizard dialog box is displayed (see the following page).

FYI

Keeping the Controls on the Chart Form and the Pivot Form in Sync

Because the chart is linked to the pivottable, the controls that manipulate data presented in the pivottable need to remain in sync on the Pivot and Chart forms. For all fields but the pagefields, this is accomplished by placing comboboxes directly on the custom commandbar. Thus, the user can directly manipulate the pivottable and chart from one place (as opposed to placing redundant controls on each form). The pagefields on the pivottable are represented as drop-down controls on the Chart form. When the chart form is activated, these drop-down controls are initialized to match the pagefields on the pivottable. Since these drop-down controls are connected to routines that change the pivottable, the pivottable's pagefields remain in sync automatically while the chart is active.

This type of chart interface in Excel is commonly referred to as an "electronic chart book." Thousands of different charts can be displayed in this single form simply by manipulating the various controls and changing the architecture of the pivottable. An electronic chart book provides a powerful interface for viewing data graphically. By combining the PivotTable and Chart objects with several control objects, we have created a powerful interface for an information system—one that will allow the user to analyze an extremely large amount of data with little effort.

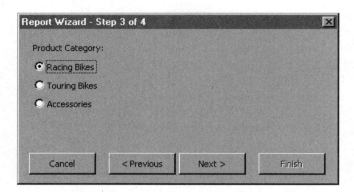

This dialog box prompts the user to select a product category. Although the product categories listed correspond to the pivotitems in the Category field on the pivottable, they are hardcoded into the design of the dialog box. A more flexible design decision would have been to dynamically fill a listbox with values from the pivottable as was done in the second dialog box. After the user selects a product category and clicks the Next button, the fourth and last Report Wizard dialog box is displayed, as shown here:

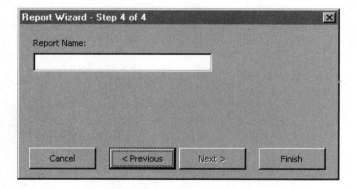

The fourth dialog box prompts the user to enter a name for the report. The report name entered will be assigned to the Name property of the worksheet that is created to hold the report. This name will also appear in the listbox in the Report Wizard's first dialog box. After the user enters a name and clicks the Finish button, the Report Wizard creates the report that corresponds to the user's entries, as shown on the facing page (in this example, the report name was entered as "My Report"):

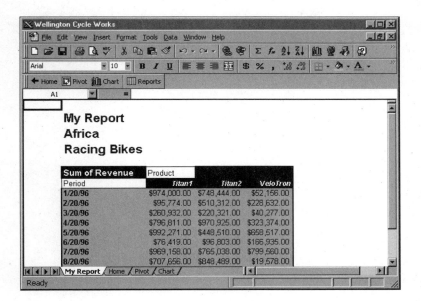

The report that the Report Wizard creates is a standard Excel worksheet that contains data from the pivottable; this data corresponds to the entries for the region and the product category that the user specified in steps 2 and 3 of the Report Wizard.

Quitting the Application

After analyzing data with the application, the user can click the Quit button on the Home form to exit the application. Clicking the Quit button runs a routine that restores all Excel workspace settings to their original values. This routine also restores the menus and deletes the custom commandbar that was placed in the user's workspace when the Wellington Cycle Works application was opened. With the original workspace restored, the user can then use Excel in the normal manner, without any changes to the environment left over by the application.

Exploring the Wellington Cycle Works Application

At this point, you have an overview of what the sample application does and all the concepts and techniques used to create it. Take some time and explore the code and objects used to construct the application. To get you started, look at the description of sheets, modules, and userforms that constitute the application on the following page.

Sheet, Module, or Userform	Description
cApplicationState	This class module defines the data and code that are used to save and restore the Excel workspace when the application starts and quits.
frmEditTable	This userform is the Edit Table dialog box. Its code module contains a routine (in the OK button's Click event) to perform the requested task.
frmReportWizard	This userform implements the Report Wizard.
mMain	This module contains routines to initialize the application, create the custom commandbar, and set the Excel environment as well as reset it upon exit.
mNavigation	This module contains the bulk of the routines that make up the application, including routines to navigate between forms and change pivottable and chart options.
mReports	This module contains routines to display the Report Wizard dialog box and create and display reports.
ThisWorkbook	Event procedures for the Open and Close events call routines in mMain to initialize and reset the application.
wsChart	The ScrollBar and drop-down controls on the Chart form call routines in the mNavigation module.
wsHome	Event procedures for the CommandButton controls on the Home form call routines in other code modules.
wsPivot	An Event procedure for the Edit Table button on the Pivot form opens the frmEditTable dialog box.

SUMMARY

In this chapter, we've taken a detailed look at the Wellington Cycle Works information system, which is not overly complicated or difficult to create. Here are key points to keep in mind:

- An application can provide a tremendous amount of power and flexibility for use in analyzing data by combining the PivotTable and Chart objects and various controls.

- Perhaps the most powerful aspect of the Wellington Cycle Works application is the electronic chart book as described in the "FYI" titled "Keeping the Controls on the Chart Form and the Pivot Form in Sync" on page 331. The electronic chart book is provided on the application's Chart form and gives the user a simple interface for viewing thousands of charts—all from a single screen.

- The Wellington Cycle Works application uses almost all of the custom interface elements available in Excel, including forms, commandbars, and dialog boxes.

Database Access,
Messaging, and
Built-In Excel Features

7

Database Access and Messaging

This chapter covers getting data in and out of Microsoft Excel via databases and messaging systems (electronic mail, or e-mail). Excel offers a number of ways to import data from or export data to external databases. In programmatic terms, the most important database feature in Excel 97 is Microsoft Data Access Objects (DAO), the shared Microsoft Office 97 object model for accessing databases. The latest version of DAO (version 3.5) adds the ability to differentiate between Jet databases (accessed through the Microsoft Access database engine) and ODBCDirect databases (accessed directly through Open Database Connectivity, or ODBC). We look at the difference between these two database access methods later in this chapter.

Using Excel, you can retrieve data from or export data to any database that supports the ODBC standard. (ODBC databases include Microsoft Access, Microsoft FoxPro, SQL Server, dBASE, Paradox, ORACLE, DEC RDB, and many others.) As explained in Chapter 4, ODBC provides a common standard for transferring data between databases and application software. This standard allows you to use one common set of functions to execute queries from any database that supports ODBC technology.

Excel also provides support for Microsoft's Messaging Application Programming Interface (MAPI), a standard for exchanging data with e-mail systems. Because of Excel's support for MAPI, you can exchange data between Excel and any MAPI-compliant e-mail system. You can use Excel 97 with Microsoft Exchange to access MAPI functionality through an OLE Automation interface. Over the course of this chapter, we'll cover Excel's support for these technologies in detail.

You can find the sample routines provided in this chapter in the CHAP07.XLS file on the companion CD. The routines follow the same naming convention used previously: the module name and the word "Proc," followed by an index number and a string that describes what the routine does. Also note that the routines in this chapter make use of the BikeData database used in earlier chapters. It might be helpful to run the sample routines as you read through the chapter.

Accessing External Data from Excel

The following list describes four ways of accessing external data from Excel:

- **DAO:** DAO 3.5, which ships with Office 97, provides an object model that lets you perform operations against Access .MDB files or any ODBC database either through the Jet database engine or directly through ODBC. Such operations include issuing select queries; adding, updating, and deleting records; performing seek and find operations; creating databases, tables, query definitions, and table relationships; and connecting to remote data sources. To access DAO, you must first establish a reference to the Microsoft DAO 3.5 Object Library in the Visual Basic Editor.

- **MS Query and the QueryTable Object:** The QueryTable object represents queries constructed and executed with MS Query. Using the QueryTable object, you can define and run queries that are embedded directly in worksheets.

- **Pivottables:** As explained in Chapters 4 and 6, a pivottable can be used to retrieve data directly from a database that supports ODBC.

- **Direct database access:** By using the Open command on the File menu, you can open dBASE and FoxPro database files directly. You can also save Excel files in dBASE format by using the Save As dialog box.

You can use Microsoft Query, pivottables, and DAO with any database that supports ODBC. Many commercial databases support ODBC; here are some of the more popular ones:

- DB2
- dBASE
- DEC RDB
- FoxPro
- Microsoft Access
- ORACLE
- Paradox
- SQL Server
- Sybase

FYI

You Need a Database-Specific ODBC Driver

To use Excel to access an external database, you must have an ODBC driver specific to the database (with the exception of Access .MDB files accessed through DAO). Several ODBC drivers ship with Office and are automatically configured when you install Office (provided you select the Data Access options during Office installation). These drivers include: Microsoft Access, dBASE, FoxPro, Paradox, and SQL Server. Additional ODBC drivers are available through the Microsoft ODBC Driver Pack. (In the United States, call Microsoft at 1-800-360-7561; outside the United States, contact your local Microsoft office.) The driver pack can also be downloaded from the Microsoft BBS at (206) 936-6735 and from the Microsoft Knowledge Base website at http://www.microsoft.com/kb. Look for the file name WX1220.

This chapter looks at each of the ways of accessing external databases listed above, with particular focus on DAO.

NOTE   Another method of database access, the XLODBC.XLA add-in, does exist in Excel. Prior to the availability of DAO in Excel 95, XLODBC was the only programmatic interface to external database data available to Excel developers. In Excel 97, XLODBC is included for backward compatibility purposes only. It is recommended that you use DAO, not XLODBC.XLA, for new development efforts. This chapter does not cover database access with XLODBC.XLA.

Which Method of Database Access Should Be Used?

Before attempting to master the four methods of accessing external data from Excel, you should take a step back and understand what it is you want to achieve with external data access in the Excel applications that you are developing. Understanding your goals will help you to identify the appropriate data access method for your applications and save you time in learning how to use the different methods of database access. The following guidelines will help you determine which of Excel's four methods of external data access are appropriate under different conditions:

■ For applications that bring data into Excel for analysis or viewing but that do not require any updates or changes to the underlying data, use pivottables. They are the most advanced tool for retrieving data into Excel for analysis.

- For applications that import data to and export data from Excel, use DAO.

- For applications that import data to and export data from Excel as well as analyze data extensively, use pivottables to bring data into Excel for analysis and viewing, and then use DAO to export data back to the external data source.

FYI

Designing an Interface that Allows Users to Change Pivottable Data

NOTE Pivottables can be used only for viewing data—not for updating external data. In fact, it is not possible for a user to make changes to data directly in a pivottable. (Excel displays an error message when a user attempts to enter data in a pivottable.) Because of the unidirectional flow of data in a pivottable, if you want to create an application that allows users to change pivottable data, you must design an interface that uses a four-step process to govern data flow:

1. Data is brought into the pivottable (through ODBC), where the user can view and analyze it.

2. If the user wants to change any of the pivottable data, the data must be copied out of the pivottable to a worksheet range or a userform control, where the user can then make changes.

3. After the user makes changes to the data, DAO is used to export the changes back to the external database.

4. The pivottable cache is refreshed (by calling the RefreshTable method on the PivotTable object) so that the pivottable reflects the user's changes.

In Chapter 9, you'll see an example of an application that uses this four-step process to change pivottable data.

Using Data Access Objects

DAO serves as the common database access interface for Office 97. (DAO is also accessible through Microsoft Access, Microsoft Word, Microsoft PowerPoint, Microsoft Project, and Microsoft Visual Basic.) Version 3.5 of DAO and the Jet database engine ship with the initial release of Office 97. You access DAO from VBA through OLE Automation, but you must first establish a reference to the Microsoft DAO 3.5 Object Library in the Visual Basic Editor before you can use DAO objects. When you use DAO, you can do the following:

- Issue Select and Action queries
- Perform seek and find operations
- Create databases, tabledefs (table definitions), querydefs (query definitions), and relations (table relationships)
- Connect to remote data sources

All of these operations are performed through the DAO object model, which consists of 33 objects.

This section focuses on how to use DAO to perform the most general external database operations from Excel—operations that include retrieving, updating, and deleting external data. Many advanced operations that you can perform with DAO will be covered only briefly here. Such operations include creating databases, creating tabledefs and relations, and establishing and modifying database security. If you want more in-depth information on these advanced operations, you might consider obtaining a copy of Microsoft Access as well as the Microsoft Office Developer's Edition (ODE). Microsoft Access and the ODE provide numerous tools for advanced operations.

The DAO Object Model

As mentioned earlier, when you establish a reference to the Microsoft DAO 3.5 Object Library in the Visual Basic Editor, you gain access to the 33 objects that make up the DAO object model. Of these objects, 16 are objects in collections, 16 are collections (which are objects in their own right), and 1 is a singular object, DBEngine. DBEngine sits at the top of the DAO object model hierarchy and is used to reference the database engine as a whole. Note that the DAO object model hierarchy exists by itself—it does not fall under the Excel Application object, as do other objects in Excel. Therefore, when you reference DBEngine, you do not need to go through the Excel Application object. (In fact, doing so will result in an error.)

The DAO object model is based on a seven-tier hierarchy. DBEngine exists on the first (top) tier, with all other DAO objects falling under DBEngine. The second tier consists of the Error object (and the Errors collection); and the Workspace object (and the corresponding Workspaces collection), which is used primarily for database security in multi-user applications. The object of primary importance on the third tier is the Database object, which is used to reference a Microsoft Access database file or another external database represented by an ODBC data source. On the fourth tier are the TableDef, QueryDef, Relation, and Container objects, all of which are used to reference components of the Database object—tables, queries, relations, and documents (saved objects). Also on the fourth tier is the Recordset object, which provides the primary interface for retrieving, adding, editing, and deleting records from a database. Figure 7-1 on the following page displays the hierarchical structure of the DAO object model. In the pages that follow, we will look at DAO objects in detail.

DAO Object Model

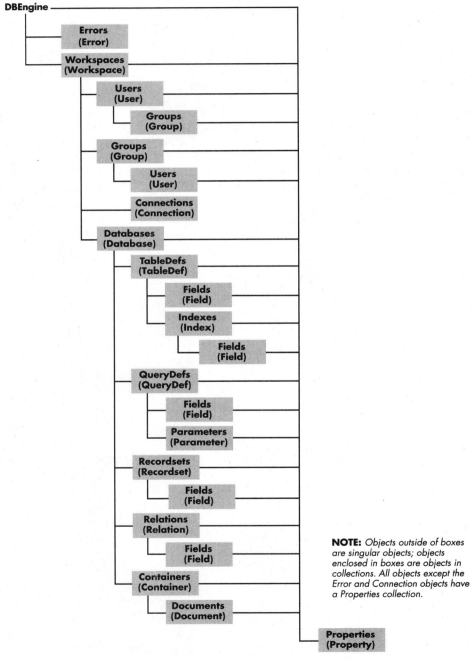

Figure 7-1. *The DAO object model hierarchy.*

NOTE: *Objects outside of boxes are singular objects; objects enclosed in boxes are objects in collections. All objects except the Error and Connection objects have a Properties collection.*

Notice in the diagram that there are fewer than 33 nodes displayed, suggesting that there are fewer than 33 objects. Keep in mind that, as with other object model diagrams that appear in this book, each node that is surrounded by a rectangle represents an object in a collection. All objects in collections have two objects associated with them: the object itself and the collection to which it belongs. Also notice that some of the objects are duplicated in different areas of the hierarchy (User, Group, and Field). Taking these points into account, you can see that there are 33 objects in the DAO object model hierarchy.

Each DAO object, except for the Error object and the Connection object, has a Properties collection associated with it. The Properties collection contains a separate object for each property of the DAO object that is referenced. For example, the DBEngine object has seven properties associated with it. Therefore, the Properties collection for DBEngine consists of seven Property objects, each representing a different property of DBEngine. Additionally, you can add Property objects to a Properties collection, allowing you to define your own custom properties specific to a DAO object. (You can create custom properties only for the Database, Field, Index, QueryDef, and TableDef objects.)

NOTE   Collections of DAO objects are always indexed starting from 0 (not from 1, as are other collections in Excel). Take care—especially when using For-Next loops—to always start indexing DAO objects from 0.

FYI

Jet vs. ODBCDirect Data Access Objects

As stated in the introduction to this chapter, DAO 3.5 adds the ability to access data through either the Jet database engine or ODBC directly. Let's examine the difference between these two methods.

The Jet database engine is Access's own internal database engine; it ships with Visual Basic and is included with Office 97. Jet allows you to access both local Access databases as well as other ODBC-compliant data sources such as SQL Server and Oracle. Beyond this, Jet adds two important capabilities:

- It can combine data from different types of data sources within the same query (e.g., a local Access table and a DB2 table on a mainframe).

- It provides an object model for changing the structure (tables, indexes, fields, and relationships) and security (users, groups, and permissions) of a database (although the extent to which this can be done with a server-based database is determined by that database).

(continued)

Jet vs. ODBCDirect Data Access Objects, *continued*

These two extra capabilities come with an overhead cost, especially when accessing server-based data sources such as SQL Server, Sybase, or Oracle. The overhead includes both the size of the Jet engine and a performance hit, because Jet uses ODBC to communicate with these back-end databases. Database operations, therefore, go through two layers—Jet and ODBC.

This is where ODBCDirect can be very useful in certain situations. ODBCDirect bypasses Jet entirely and talks to ODBC directly. It still provides a simple object model for programmers to use (which is, in fact, virtually identical to the Jet DAO model). ODBCDirect is faster and smaller than Jet when you are accessing a back-end server database.

In order to summarize when to use Jet vs. ODBCDirect Data Access Objects, let's consider the following points:

■ If you are accessing a desktop data source such as Access, dBASE, Paradox, or FoxPro, use Jet DAO.

■ If you need to manipulate the database structure, use Jet DAO.

■ If you need to combine data from two or more types of databases, use Jet DAO.

■ If you are accessing a server-based database such as SQL Server, Oracle, or Sybase exclusively, use ODBCDirect DAO.

Due to book space constraints and the similarity between Jet and ODBCDirect Data Access Objects, we will not cover ODBCDirect DAO in detail here. If you want more detail on ODBCDirect, read the online VBA Help topic titled "Data Access Objects Overview."

An Overview of DAO

Before launching into a detailed look at each DAO object, let's look at an overview of DAO, the Access database format, and where the various DAO objects fit. On the surface, DAO objects provide a simple representation of a database structure, providing different objects for databases, tables, relations, and queries. However, in reality, the interface to DAO can be quite complex, with such complexity directly linked to the power that DAO provides. Operations that you perform with DAO can be divided into three categories:

■ **Query operations:** These operations involve importing data from or exporting data to a database and include retrieving, adding, editing, and deleting records.

- **Operations that involve DAO database security in multi-user environments:** These operations involve creating Workspaces under different user names and using the User and Group objects in establishing and referencing users and groups.

- **Operations that alter database structure:** These operations include creating, altering, or deleting databases, tabledefs, querydefs, fields, indexes, and relations. Depending on the type of external database you are using in your application, you might be limited in performing some of these operations.

Our discussion of DAO will focus primarily on the first category, query operations. However, we will spend some time looking at operations in the two other categories as well.

The Database object and the Access .MDB database file

The Database object in the DAO object model hierarchy can be used to refer either to a Microsoft Access database file residing on a local or network drive or to a database represented by an ODBC data source (such as FoxPro, SQL Server, and so on). The Access .MDB database file provides the primary database format for DAO, the MDB acronym being derived from the three-character extension of Microsoft Access files. (Think of "MDB" as standing for "Microsoft database.") Already in widespread use, the .MDB file serves as the database file format for Microsoft Access and Microsoft Visual Basic. An .MDB file can be used as an actual database file, containing data tables (TableDef objects), queries (QueryDef objects), and relations (Relation objects). Additionally, an .MDB file can store links to tables in external ODBC databases. (This is accomplished through the process of "linking" or "attaching" to a table in an external database.) In summary, there are three ways to access data through the Database object:

- In tables contained in an Access .MDB file.

- In another external database through a linked table in an Access .MDB file.

- In an external database directly through an ODBC data source. This involves accessing the external data source directly, without going through a persistent table in an Access .MDB file.

The method you use to access external data is highly dependent on the format of the database for which you will be building your Excel application. If you are building an application for an existing Microsoft Access or Microsoft Visual Basic database, the database already conforms to the Access .MDB format. If you are creating a new database for your application and the database is to be used in a single-user environment or a multi-user environment with at most 20 users at a time, you might want to consider using the Access .MDB file format for your new database. However, if you are building your application to access data in non-.MDB format, you must decide whether to use an Access .MDB file and link to the external database or to access the external database directly through ODBC. When you establish a link to an external database table, DAO stores information regarding fields and indexes in the .MDB file. This results in increased speed of query execution, especially when accessing network databases—having table and index information stored locally reduces the amount of information that has to be exchanged with the server when issuing a query. Under certain circumstances, you will actually see a performance decrease when accessing a network database directly through ODBC as opposed to linking the data source to an Access .MDB file through a linked table.

> **NOTE** Using ODBCDirect DAO may be more appropriate for accessing server-based data sources. For more details, see the FYI on pages 345–346 titled "Jet vs. ODBCDirect Data Access Objects."

Using Microsoft Access to create an .MDB database file

If you are creating a new database for your application and the number of users that will access the database at any given time will not exceed 20, it is highly recommended that you use the .MDB format for your database. It is possible to create an .MDB file, along with the tables, queries, and relationships that make up the file, by using VBA and the programmatic DAO interface that is available in Excel 97. However, programmatic creation of .MDB database files is not recommended. Microsoft Access provides numerous graphical tools that aid in the design and creation of tables, queries, and table relationships. Using the tools in Microsoft Access provides a more intuitive and easier-to-use interface for designing .MDB files. Additionally, if you are creating a very complex database, consisting of numerous tables and relationships, you might want to consider a structured approach. Numerous books have been written on the subject of database design, and there are established methodologies that database developers use. Commercial software products are also available to aid in database design, including InfoModeler by Asymetrix. InfoModeler steps you through the process of designing tables and establishing relationships and then actually builds the resulting .MDB database file for you.

Relational vs. flat databases

Through use of the .MDB file format, you can create relational databases. If you are new to the world of databases, you should be aware of the differences between "relational" and "flat" databases as well as the benefits that relational databases offer. A flat database is essentially a single two-dimensional table consisting of columns that represent database fields and rows that represent database records. For most data sets, flat databases suffer from one fundamental flaw: unnecessary duplication of data. Such duplication of data can have a negative impact on the performance of database queries and can also result in the database occupying more disk space than is necessary. Let's take a look at a simple example of a flat database. The following illustration displays a flat database that is used to track customer orders:

CusNo	Name	Address	City	State	Zip	Product	Units	Amount
1	John Smith	221 Main St.	New York	NY	08842	Television	1	$500
2	William Chin	43 1st Ave.	Redmond	WA	98332	Refrigerator	1	$800
3	William Chin	43 1st Ave.	Redmond	WA	98332	Toaster	1	$80
4	Marta Dieci	2 West Ave.	Reno	NV	92342	Television	1	$500
5	Marta Dieci	2 West Ave.	Reno	NV	92342	Radio	1	$40
6	Marta Dieci	2 West Ave.	Reno	NV	92342	Stereo	1	$200
7	Peter Melinkoff	53 NE Redmond	Miami	FL	18332	Computer	1	$1,500
8	Martin Sengali	1234 5th St.	Boston	MA	03423	Television	1	$500
9	Martin Sengali	1234 5th St.	Boston	MA	03423	Stereo	1	$200
10	Martin Sengali	1234 5th St.	Boston	MA	03423	Radio	1	$40
11	Martin Sengali	1234 5th St.	Boston	MA	03423	Refrigerator	1	$800

When we look at this flat database, the data redundancy is obvious—address information for William Chin, Marta Dieci, and Martin Sengali appears multiple times. If we create a relational structure for this database, such data redundancy can be eliminated, resulting in faster query performance and reduced disk space requirements for storing the data. The most obvious approach to creating a relational database from this flat database is to break the flat table into two separate tables—a customer table and an orders table—and then to relate the two tables by a common field. Here's what the resulting relational structure would look like:

Customer table

CusNo	Name	Address	City	State	Zip
1	John Smith	221 Main St.	New York	NY	08842
2	William Chin	43 1st Ave.	Redmond	WA	98332
3	Marta Dieci	2 West Ave.	Reno	NV	92342
4	Peter Melinkoff	53 NE Redmond	Miami	FL	18332
5	Martin Sengali	1234 5th St.	Boston	MA	03423

Orders table

CusNo	Product	Units	Amount
1	Television	1	$500
2	Refrigerator	1	$800
2	Toaster	1	$80
3	Television	1	$500
3	Radio	1	$40
3	Stereo	1	$200
4	Computer	1	$1,500
5	Television	1	$500
5	Stereo	1	$200
5	Radio	1	$40
5	Refrigerator	1	$800

As shown in this figure, by implementing a relational structure, we have been able to create two tables that actually occupy less disk space than the initial single table. This was accomplished by removing all of the redundant customer information. With the new relational structure, one record exists for each customer in the Customer table and one or more records exist for each customer in the Orders table. Both tables are linked by a field: the CusNo field (representing the customer number). By retrieving the value from the CusNo field for a particular order in the Orders table, the user can look up the corresponding value in the Customer table and identify to whom the order belongs. The two tables are said to be "related" by the CusNo field that exists in each table. This relationship is represented graphically by the arrow that points from the CusNo field in the Customer table to the CusNo field in the Orders table. In this case, we are dealing with what is known as a "one-to-many" relationship—that is, one customer record corresponds to potentially many order records. (For example, there is one record for Martin Sengali in the Customer table, and there are four records that correspond to Martin Sengali in the Orders table—records that are linked by the value 5 in the CusNo field in each table.)

Table relationships, such as the one established between the CusNo fields in the two sample tables, form the basis for the term "relational database." In addition to the benefits of improved query performance and reduced disk space requirements provided by relational databases, there are other benefits, such as general ease of updating data and maintaining data integrity. For example, let's take the case of the four orders that have been entered for the customer Martin Sengali. Let's assume that after entering all four orders, we discover that the wrong street address has been entered for the customer. Correcting the mistake using a flat database, as in the first figure, requires that the customer's address be re-entered in four separate records. However, if we use the relational structure, the address must be corrected in only one record in the Customer table. A relational structure not only simplifies the process of updating data, but it also provides a foundation for better managing data and maintaining data integrity.

Creating a relational database

As mentioned, if you are planning to create a new database for your application, you should invest in a copy of Microsoft Access so that you can take advantage of its graphical tools for designing tables and establishing relationships when creating an .MDB database file. If you already have data in a flat database, you might consider converting your flat database to a relational database. Microsoft Access 97 provides a feature named the Table Analyzer Wizard that will convert a flat database to a relational database for you. If your flat database is in the form of an Excel spreadsheet, you can easily import your Excel spreadsheet directly into Microsoft Access 97. Then you can use the Table Analyzer Wizard to convert the spreadsheet to a relational database.

Although the .MDB file provides a very powerful relational database format for multi-user access by 20 or fewer users at a time, your application might require a more powerful database, one that supports queries from hundreds of users at a time. For such applications, you should consider using an enterprise server database such as Microsoft SQL Server. Microsoft SQL Server running on Microsoft Windows NT Server can support queries from more than 200 users at a time, depending on the type, amount, and frequency of database transactions required. Microsoft offers a product called the Access Upsizing Tools, which allows you to easily convert an Access .MDB file to a SQL Server database.

For information about Access Upsizing Tools, in the United States, call Microsoft Developer Services at 1-800-426-9400. Outside the United States, contact your local Microsoft office.

DAO Objects

This section provides detailed information about the objects that make up the DAO object model. In reading about DAO objects, keep in mind that two basic types of objects are defined by the DAO object model: persistent and non-persistent objects. Persistent objects can be saved in an Access .MDB file (or a system database file) and include the following: User, Group, Database, TableDef, QueryDef, Field, Parameter, Relation, and Property. (Note that the Container and Document objects are not really persistent objects but are used to access persistent objects—namely, objects representing saved databases, tables, queries, and relationships.)

Non-persistent objects are not saved in files and include the following: DBEngine, Error, Workspace, Connection, and Recordset. (Note that Field objects of a Recordset are not persistent and that any properties of non-persistent objects are non-persistent as well.)

When you access a DAO object in an application, you usually either "create" the object or reference the object through a collection that contains the object. (Note that with the Database object, you can also "open" the database, which effectively adds the database to the Databases collection.) It is always the case with a non-persistent object that the object must be created before it can be referenced through a collection.

For example, in a given application, you must open a Recordset before you can access the Recordset—Recordsets are not stored in .MDB files, and as such, they are not persistent. (The OpenRecordset method creates a new Recordset.) On the other hand, a TableDef object is persistent, and therefore in an application you do not always need to create a TableDef object before you access it. This is because a TableDef object can be saved in an .MDB file and is therefore persistent.

Note that you can create persistent objects in a manner similar to the way in which non-persistent objects are created. After a persistent object is created, in most cases it does not actually become persistent until it is "appended" to its corresponding collection. (Note that QueryDef objects become persistent upon creation and do not require that you append them to the QueryDefs collection.) For example, from within a routine you can create and use a TableDef object even though the object is not actually persistent. The TableDef object becomes persistent once it is appended to the TableDefs collection (by calling the Append method). The Append method, in effect, saves the object to the .MDB file. (There is one exception: you can append a Workspace object to the Workspaces collection, but the Workspace object remains non-persistent.) You will see numerous examples throughout this chapter that demonstrate the differences between persistent and non-persistent objects. Having an understanding of the difference between these types of objects up front will aid in your learning of DAO.

Following are brief descriptions of DAO objects; each object is identified as either persistent or non-persistent. In the next section, we'll look at these objects in more depth.

Connection (Connections collection): Used to refer to an ODBC data source in using ODBCDirect for accessing external data. *Non-persistent object.*

Container (Containers collection): Used to access collections of saved objects that represent databases, tables, queries, and relationships. *Non-persistent object.*

Database (Databases collection): Used to refer to an Access database (an .MDB file) or external ODBC data source. *Persistent object.*

DBEngine: Object at the top of the DAO hierarchy. *Non-persistent object.*

Document (Documents collection): Used to access individual saved objects representing databases, tables, relationships, and other objects within corresponding container objects. *Non-persistent object.*

Error (Errors collection): Used for accessing and tracking DAO error messages. *Non-persistent object.*

Field (Fields collection): A field within a TableDef, Index, QueryDef, Recordset, or Relation object. *Persistent object for TableDef, Index, QueryDef, and Relation objects.*

Group (Groups collection): A group of users within a Workspace (used for security). Group objects are stored in the system database (usually either SYSTEM.MDA or SYSTEM.MDB). *Persistent object.*

Index (Indexes collection): Used to represent a single field or multiple fields for sort or search operations (often used to form a unique identification for each record in establishing relationships). *Persistent object.*

Parameter (Parameters collection): A parameter of a query represented by a QueryDef object. *Persistent object.*

Property (Properties collection): Used to access properties of an object. Persistent for persistent objects, and non-persistent for non-persistent objects.

QueryDef (QueryDefs collection): A query statement. For Jet workspaces, QueryDefs are stored in .MDB files. (The statement can include parameters.) *Persistent object.*

Recordset (Recordsets collection): Used for retrieving, adding, editing, and deleting records in a database. There are three types of recordsets: Table (read/write), Dynaset (read/write), and Snapshot (read-only). *Non-persistent object.*

Relation (Relations collection): Represents a link between two tables, with the link established on one or more fields in each table. (Such fields are often defined by an index.) *Persistent object.*

TableDef (TableDefs collection): A table within an .MDB database file. *Persistent object.*

User (Users collection): A user within a Workspace (used for security). User objects are stored in the system database (usually SYSTEM.MDW). *Persistent object.*

Workspace (Workspaces collection): Defines how the application interacts with the database—via either Jet or ODBCDirect. Used in conjunction with User and Group objects for security purposes. *Non-persistent object.*

The DAO structure diagram in Figure 7-2 on the following page shows the physical structure of DAO objects. If you are new to DAO, the diagram might appear rather complicated and difficult to grasp at first. However, as you read through the detailed descriptions of DAO objects on the pages that follow, refer to the diagram to see how the objects relate to one another.

In the DAO structure diagram, the Database object represents a physical .MDB file that is saved on disk. Within this file are stored TableDef, QueryDef, and Relation objects as well as associated Field and Parameter objects. The diagram depicts a second file—the system database file, usually named SYSTEM.MDW.

The system file is a database file, much like the .MDB file represented by the Database object, except that the system file stores Group and User objects. The non-persistent Workspace object employs User and Group objects in the system file when establishing security for a database session. Also notice in the diagram the presence of three non-persistent Recordset objects—Table, Dynaset, and Snapshot. Recordset objects can be created either from local or linked TableDefs or QueryDefs or through the use of query statements. (See the section on the Recordset object beginning on page 365 for details.) Although not depicted in Figure 7-2, the DBEngine object provides access to the DAO structure. Also note that the Error, Container, Connection, Document, and Property objects are not depicted in the figure.

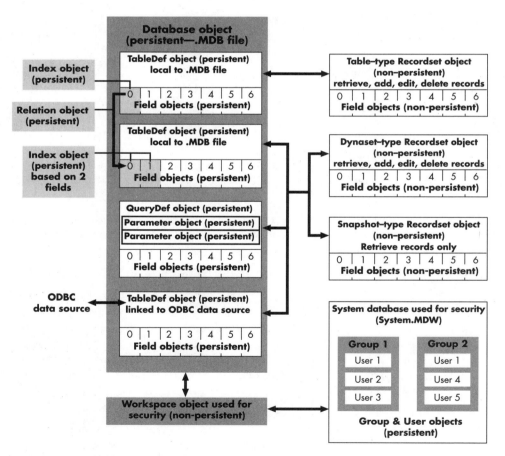

Figure 7-2. *The physical structure of DAO objects.*

FYI

Establishing a Reference to the Microsoft DAO 3.5 Object Library

Before you can access any DAO objects through Excel, you must first establish a reference to the Microsoft DAO 3.5 Object Library. References are established in the Visual Basic Editor by selecting References from the Tools menu and then selecting Microsoft DAO 3.5 Object Library from the list of available references. Note that you must have installed Excel 97 with Database Access options in order to successfully establish a reference to the Microsoft DAO 3.5 Object Library. Also be aware that if you are running Excel 97 on a system with Microsoft Access 97 installed, you will see an entry in the references list that reads "Microsoft DAO 2.5/3.5 Compatibility Library." You should not select this reference when you are using DAO objects in Excel; instead, you should select "Microsoft DAO 3.5 Object Library." After a reference is established, the reference can be saved with the workbook file. When a user on another system opens the workbook file, the reference will remain intact provided the user is running Excel 97 and has installed Excel 97 with Database Access options. (OLE references are maintained through the Microsoft Windows 95 Registry and as such do not require applications to know absolute directory paths to re-establish references.)

FYI

Using the Object Browser to View DAO Objects

After you establish a reference to the Microsoft DAO 3.5 Object Library, you can view DAO objects, properties, and methods from the Object Browser. To do so, click the Object Browser button on the Visual Basic Editor's Standard toolbar and select DAO from the Project/Library drop-down listbox. This will display all DAO objects and associated properties and methods.

In the pages that follow, we'll discuss each of the 33 DAO objects. Note, however, that some objects are discussed in greater detail than others. Because of space limitations in this book, only the DBEngine, Error, Workspace, Database, Recordset, QueryDef, and Parameter objects are discussed in detail. Other DAO objects (User, Group, Connection, TableDef, Field, Index, Relation, Container, Document, and Property) are introduced but not discussed in detail. You can find more information about these objects in the DAO online help that ships with Excel 97. Information provided for each object includes a summary description of the object, an explanation of how to access the object, a listing of the collections that can be accessed from the object, and listings of properties and methods associated with the object.

The DBEngine Object

The DBEngine object sits at the top of the DAO hierarchy and is used to represent the Jet engine itself. Various properties and methods of DBEngine are used to compact and repair databases, set up ODBC data sources, and create Workspace objects.

Accessing the DBEngine object

Once you establish a reference to the Microsoft DAO 3.5 Object Library, you can access the DBEngine object directly in a VBA module. Proc01 displays the version of the installed DBEngine object:

```
Sub Chap07aProc01_DBEngineVersion()
    MsgBox DBEngine.Version
End Sub
```

> **NOTE** You can use version 3.5 of DAO to access .MDB files created with DAO 3.5 in Microsoft Access 97 as well as .MDB files created with earlier versions (1.0, 2.0, and 95) of Microsoft Access.

Collections under DBEngine

Collections are Errors, Workspaces, and Properties. Proc02, which follows, displays the Name and Value properties of all Property objects in the DBEngine Properties collection.

```
Sub Chap07aProc02_DisplayProperties()
    Dim Prop As Property
    On Error Resume Next
    With DBEngine
        For Each Prop In .Properties
            MsgBox Prop.Name & ": " & _
                    Prop.Value
        Next Prop
    End With
End Sub
```

DBEngine properties

DefaultType: Sets the type of workspace (Jet or ODBCDirect) to be used by the next workspace object that is created.

DefaultPassword (write-only property): Sets the password of the default user for the Jet database engine when it is initialized. If the user and password are not set by a call to CreateWorkspace, DefaultPassword and DefaultUser should be established before any data access functions are called.

DefaultUser (write-only property): Sets the default user for the Jet database access engine when it is initialized. If the user and password are not set by a call to CreateWorkspace, DefaultPassword and DefaultUser should be established before any data access functions are called.

IniPath (read/write property): References the Windows Registry key containing the path for the SYSTEM.MDW file.

LoginTimeout (read/write property): The number of seconds before an error message is displayed when logging on to an ODBC database.

Version (read-only property): Returns the version number of DAO.

DBEngine methods
Following are selected methods of the DBEngine object.

CompactDatabase: Copies and compacts a database. This process defragments the database file to improve performance. (Used with .MDB files only.)

CreateWorkspace: Creates a Workspace object.

Idle: Suspends data processing, allowing the Jet database engine to complete any pending tasks.

RegisterDatabase: Enters ODBC connection information for a database in the Windows Registry.

RepairDatabase: Attempts to repair a corrupted .MDB file. A database can be corrupted by an incomplete write operation resulting from a power outage or a computer hardware problem.

The Error Object
Whenever an error is encountered in performing an operation with a DAO object, a series of Error objects describing errors in the operation is created and placed in the Errors collection. When a subsequent operation generates an error, the Errors collection is cleared and replaced with new Error objects that describe errors from the most recent operation. A new collection of Error objects is created with each operation that provides information regarding errors in the operation. Information that can be accessed through an Error object includes a description of the error, a help topic ID, and the name of a Windows help file that can be used to reference information about the error and the name of the object that generated the error. If an operation generates no errors, the Errors collection will contain no objects.

Accessing an Error object

You access an Error object by indexing the Errors collection. Proc03, which follows, attempts to open a database named NODATA.MDB residing in the root directory on the Z drive. Assuming this database does not exist, Error objects that describe the operation will be added to the Errors collection. Note that without the On Error GoTo statement, execution will break when the error is encountered.

```
Sub Chap07aProc03_DisplayErrors()
    Dim DB1 As Database
    Dim dbErr As Error
    On Error GoTo ErrorHandler:
    Set DB1 = OpenDatabase(Name:="Z:\NODATA.MDB")
    DB1.Close
    Exit Sub
ErrorHandler:
    With DBEngine
        For Each dbErr In .Errors
            MsgBox dbErr.Number & ": " & _
                    dbErr.Description
        Next dbErr
    End With
End Sub
```

Collections under Error

None.

Error properties

Description (read-only property): Text string describing the error.

HelpContext (read-only property): Help Context ID number for the help topic explaining the error.

HelpFile (read-only property): Name of the Help file containing the help topic explaining the error.

Number (read-only property): Number representing the error.

Source (read-only property): Name of the object that served as the source of the error.

Error methods

None.

The Workspace Object

For the Jet database engine, the Workspace object is used primarily for security purposes. DAO security is established through the creation of a "workgroup," which is governed by the presence of a SYSTEM.MDW file. (The system file can have other names as well.) You must have a copy of Microsoft Access to create a SYSTEM.MDW file and establish a workgroup, which is accomplished through the Access Workgroup Administrator. Through the Workspace object, you can create and access User and Group objects that represent various users and groups with different access permissions as established in the current workgroup. If no system database file is referenced, a default Workspace object for the Admin user is available. This Workspace object has no password. (Note that you establish a reference to a system database file by setting the IniPath property of the DBEngine object.)

Accessing a Workspace object

You access a Workspace object by indexing a Workspaces collection or by creating a new Workspace object by calling the CreateWorkspace method on the DBEngine object. (Remember that a Workspaces collection is not persistent.) When you create a Workspace object, you pass a workspace name, a user name, and a password for the workgroup. (If a system database file has been referenced, the user name and password will be compared against the user and group information in the system file.) Note that in the absence of a system database file, it is not necessary to create a Workspace object because all access to DAO objects will be accomplished through the Admin user. After a Workspace object has been created, you can append it to a Workspaces collection. (You can simultaneously access multiple workspaces.)

Proc04, which follows, first creates a new Workspace object under the Admin user name and then appends the Workspace to the Workspaces collection. The routine then uses a For-Each loop to display the names of all current Workspace objects. Note that DAO supplies a default Workspace named #Default Workspace#. When you run Proc04, the For-Each loop at the end of the routine will display both "#Default Workspace#" and the name of the newly appended Workspace. Remember that Workspace objects are not persistent: if you run this routine multiple times, changing the name of the created Workspace object each time, the appended Workspace objects will not remain in the collection between subsequent calls to the routine. In essence, the newly appended Workspace object disappears once the routine ends execution.

```
Sub Chap07aProc04_CreateWorkspace()
    Dim WS1 As Workspace
    Dim WS As Workspace
    With DBEngine
        MsgBox "Initial Workspaces: " & .Workspaces.Count
        Set WS1 = .CreateWorkspace(Name:="Workspace1", _
                                    UserName:="Admin", _
                                    Password:="")
        .Workspaces.Append WS1
```

(continued)

continued

```
        For Each WS In .Workspaces
            MsgBox "Workspace :" & WS.Name
        Next WS
    End With
    WS1.Close
End Sub
```

Collections under Workspace

Collections are Users, Groups, and Properties. Proc05 creates a new Workspace object and then displays message boxes indicating the number of users and groups contained within the workgroup represented by the Workspace object. Note that in the absence of a system database file, there will be 0 users and 0 groups. Also note the setting of the IniPath property of the DBEngine object. IniPath is set to a string that represents a Windows 95 Registry key containing information about the location of the system file. In this example, if the RegKey variable contains a string value named Systemdb, which points to a path for a system file, the call to the CreateWorkspace method will result in the establishment of a workgroup to which User and Group objects can be added and accessed. However, this routine assumes that no such system file exists, and specifies a dummy value for the RegKey variable, which returns 0 for the number of users and groups.

```
Sub Chap07aProc05_DisplayUsersAndGroups()
    Dim WS1 As Workspace
    Dim RegKey As String
    Dim x As Integer
    RegKey = "HKEY_LOCAL_MACHINE\SOFTWARE\Microsoft\MyApp"
    With DBEngine
        .IniPath = RegKey
        Set WS1 = .CreateWorkspace(Name:="Workspace1", _
                                   UserName:="Admin", _
                                   Password:="")
        .Workspaces.Append WS1
        MsgBox .Workspaces(1).Users.Count & " users."
        MsgBox .Workspaces(1).Groups.Count & " groups."
    End With
    WS1.Close
End Sub
```

Workspace properties

Following are selected properties of the Workspace object.

IsolateODBCTrans (read/write property): In certain applications, you might be required to have multiple simultaneous transactions pending against the same ODBC data source through multiple Workspace objects. Some server databases (such as SQL Server) do not allow simultaneous transactions against a single database. Under these circumstances, you must set the IsolateODBC-Trans property of each Workspace object to True to keep transactions isolated.

Name (read/write property): The name of the workspace. The Name property becomes read-only after the Workspace object is appended to the Workspaces collection.

UserName (read/write property): The name of the user who owns the workspace. The UserName property becomes read-only after the Workspace object is appended to the Workspaces collection.

Workspace methods
Following are selected methods of the Workspace object.

BeginTrans: Begins a new transaction. (Proc19, discussed later in this chapter, provides an example of a transaction.)

Close: Closes the workspace.

CommitTrans: Commits a transaction to the database.

CreateDatabase: Creates a Database object.

CreateGroup: Creates a Group object.

CreateUser: Creates a User object.

OpenDatabase: Opens a Database object.

Rollback: Rolls back a transaction so that it is not committed to the database.

The Database Object

The Database object lies at the heart of the DAO object model. The Database object represents an open database against which various operations can be carried out. (The database can be either an Access .MDB file or another external database represented by an ODBC data source.) The majority of DAO operations will occur through the Database object and the objects on the DAO object hierarchy that reside under the Database object. Common operations on the Database object include creating Recordsets, TableDefs, QueryDefs, and Relations.

Accessing a Database object
You access a Database object by indexing the Databases collection, or by creating a new Database object by calling either the CreateDatabase or the OpenDatabase method on the Workspace object. Proc06 first creates and appends a new Workspace object and then uses the OpenDatabase method to open the BIKEDATA.MDB database. BIKEDATA.MDB must be in the same directory as the current workbook for this routine to work. A For-Each loop is then employed to display values of properties associated with the Database object.

```
Sub Chap07aProc06_OpenDatabase()
    Dim WS1 As Workspace
    Dim DB1 As Database
    Dim DatabaseName As String
    Dim Prop As Property
    On Error Resume Next
    DatabaseName = ThisWorkbook.Path & "\BIKEDATA.MDB"
    With DBEngine
        Set WS1 = .CreateWorkspace(Name:="Workspace1", _
                                   UserName:="Admin", _
                                   Password:="")
        .Workspaces.Append WS1
    End With
    Set DB1 = WS1.OpenDatabase(Name:=DatabaseName, _
                               ReadOnly:=False)
    With DB1
        For Each Prop In .Properties
            With Prop
                MsgBox Prompt:="Property" & Chr(13) & _
                       "Name: " & .Name & Chr(13) & _
                       "Value: " & .Value & Chr(13) & _
                       "Type: " & .Type & Chr(13) & _
                       "Inherited: " & .Inherited, _
                       Title:="Database Properties"
            End With
        Next Prop
    End With
    DB1.Close
    WS1.Close
End Sub
```

In Proc06, a Workspace object was first created and then appended to the Workspaces collection before a call was made to the OpenDatabase method. Note that you can call OpenDatabase directly, without referencing a Workspace object, as shown in Proc07, which follows. (When no Workspace object is referenced, the database is opened against the default workspace.)

```
Sub Chap07aProc07_OpenDatabase2()
    Dim DB1 As Database
    Dim DatabaseName As String
    On Error Resume Next
    DatabaseName = ThisWorkbook.Path & "\BIKEDATA.MDB"
    Set DB1 = OpenDatabase(Name:=DatabaseName, _
                           ReadOnly:=False)
    MsgBox DB1.Name
    DB1.Close
End Sub
```

You can also use the OpenDatabase method to establish a connection to a non-ISAM (indexed sequential access method) network server database (such as SQL Server). When connecting to such a database through the OpenDatabase method, pass the database name as the Name argument and the ODBC connection string as the Connect argument. Required elements of the ODBC connection string are determined by the network server database being accessed. In most cases, at least three elements are required: DSN (data source name), UID (user identification), and PWD (password). Proc08 demonstrates how OpenDatabase can be used to access a SQL Server database. Note that if you pass an empty string for the Name argument, DAO will display the ODBC data sources dialog box, allowing you to select an ODBC data source. If no SQL Server is available when Proc08 is run, the For-Each loop at the end of the routine will display one or more appropriate error messages:

```
Sub Chap07aProc08_OpenDatabase3()
    Dim DB1 As Database
    Dim DatabaseName As String
    Dim ConnectionStr As String
    Dim dbErr As Error
    On Error GoTo ErrorHandler
    DatabaseName = "SQLForecast"
    ConnectionStr = "DSN=SQLForecast;UID=sa;PWD="
    Set DB1 = OpenDatabase(Name:=DatabaseName, _
                        Connect:=ConnectionStr)
    MsgBox DB1.Name
    DB1.Close
    Exit Sub
ErrorHandler:
    With DBEngine
        For Each dbErr In .Errors
            MsgBox dbErr.Description
        Next dbErr
    End With
End Sub
```

One other method of accessing a Database object involves using the CreateDatabase method in creating a new database. Proc09 shows an example of this method. Note that an If statement is used in combination with the VBA Dir function to check for the existence of the database. If the database already exists, the VBA Kill function is used to delete the database before CreateDatabase is called:

```
Sub Chap07aProc09_CreateDatabase()
    Dim DB1 As Database
    Dim DatabaseName As String
    On Error Resume Next
    DatabaseName = ThisWorkbook.Path & "\DATA1.MDB"
```

(continued)

continued

```
    If Dir(DatabaseName) <> "" Then
        If MsgBox(Prompt:="Delete database?", _
                  Buttons:=vbYesNo, _
                  Title:="Database already exists.") = vbYes Then
            Kill DatabaseName
        Else
            MsgBox "Proc execution halted."
            End
        End If
    End If
    Set DB1 = CreateDatabase(Name:=DatabaseName, _
                             Locale:=dbLangGeneral)
    MsgBox DB1.Name
    DB1.Close
End Sub
```

Collections under Database

Collections are TableDefs, QueryDefs, Recordsets, Relations, Containers, and Properties.

Database properties

Following are selected properties of the Database object.

CollatingOrder (read-only property): Specifies the sequence of the sort order in text for purposes of string comparison or sorting. CollatingOrder is set initially when a database is created through the Options argument of the Create-Database method.

Connect (read-only property): Used to set or get ODBC data source information for a non-ISAM database. This property is set initially through the Connect argument of the OpenDatabase method.

Name (read-only property): The name of the database.

QueryTimeout (read/write property): The number of seconds DAO will wait before timing out on a query submitted to a non-ISAM ODBC database.

RecordsAffected (read-only property): The number of database records affected by the most recent query issued through calling the Execute method.

Transactions (read-only property): If True, the database supports transactions (BeginTrans, CommitTrans, and Rollback). Proc19 on page 380 provides an example of using transactions.

Updatable (read-only property): If True, the database can be updated.

Version (read-only property): Version number of Jet used to create the database.

Database methods

Following are selected methods of the Database object.

Close: Closes the database. You should always take care to close a database when it is no longer needed.

CreateProperty: Creates a Property object.

CreateQueryDef: Creates a QueryDef object.

CreateRelation: Creates a Relation object.

CreateTableDef: Creates a TableDef object.

Execute: Used to issue SQL or QueryDef Action queries to a database. Note that with Execute, you can use only Action queries (queries that create, update, or delete records, or that alter database structure). Using Execute to issue Select queries that return records will result in an error.

MakeReplica: If you are using a replicable .MDB database, the MakeReplica method will make a replica of the database. Note that you must have a copy of Microsoft Access 97 in order to create a replicable database. Also be aware that replication operations, including MakeReplica, can be issued through DAO only if a copy of Microsoft Access 97 is installed on the same computer on which the copy of Excel issuing the replication operation resides. In other words, you cannot use MakeReplica unless you have a copy of Microsoft Access 97 on your machine and are using a replicable .MDB database created with Microsoft Access 97.

OpenRecordset: Opens a new Recordset object for reading, adding, updating, or deleting records from a database table. For Jet databases, you can open four different types of Recordset objects: Table, Dynaset, Snapshot, and Forward-only (a kind of Snapshot recordset). Each offers different functionality depending on the type of queries you are issuing. Note that the OpenRecordset method can be called from a number of different objects, including Database, TableDef, QueryDef, and Recordset. The different types of Recordset objects are described in the next section.

Synchronize: Synchronizes two replicable databases in the same replica set. As with other operations that involve replication, in order to use this method, Microsoft Access 97, as well as a replicable database created in Microsoft Access 97, must be installed on your machine.

The Recordset Object

Through the Recordset object, you can retrieve, add, update, and delete single records from a single table or related records from multiple tables. Each of the recordset types available for Jet databases is well suited for a different type of operation.

Types of recordsets

Table recordsets: Used to access records in a table stored in an .MDB file. With Table recordsets, you can retrieve, add, update, and delete records in a single table. Table recordsets are best for operations that involve sorting, indexing, or seeking.

Dynaset recordsets: Used to access records in a table stored in or linked to an .MDB file. Dynasets are also used to access records returned from executing a query. With Dynasets, you can retrieve, add, update, and delete records from either a single table or multiple tables as defined by a query.

Snapshot recordsets: Snapshots are similar to Dynasets in that they are used to access records from a local table, a linked table, or a query. However, Snapshots are used for reading data only—you cannot perform Action queries with a Snapshot (adding, updating, or deleting records). A Dynaset contains indirect references to records in tables, but a Snapshot actually contains a copy of the records. For unidirectional scrolling through a set of records, forward-only Snapshots offer the highest level of performance.

Accessing a Recordset object

You access a Recordset object by calling the OpenRecordset method on the Database, TableDef, QueryDef, or Recordset object. You can also access Recordset objects by indexing the Recordsets collection of the Database object; however, since recordsets are non-persistent, all Recordset objects within the Recordsets collection cease to exist after routine execution ends. When referencing a recordset, always declare a Recordset object variable and assign the return value of the OpenRecordset method to that object variable. When called on the Database object, the OpenRecordset method takes four arguments.

name: A string representing the source of the recordset. This can be one of three types of values:

- The name of a TableDef object. (For Table-type recordsets, you must specify a TableDef for the Name argument.)
- The name of a QueryDef object.
- A SELECT SQL string.

type: One of three possible values: dbOpenTable (Table-type recordset), dbOpenDynaset (Dynaset-type recordset), or dbOpenSnapshot (Snapshot-type recordset).

options: The sum of one or more constants, which defines characteristics of the Recordset object. (See the online VBA Help for details.)

lockedits: One of five constant values that determines the lock status of the recordset. (See the online VBA Help for details.)

You have already seen some examples of creating and using Recordset objects in this chapter. Proc10 provides three examples of using the OpenRecordset method. Note that at the beginning of Proc10, a call is made to the Populate-Tables function (which is not displayed here—the objects employed by this routine are described throughout the chapter). PopulateTables fills the Customer and Orders tables of the DATA1.MDB database with fictitious data. The function uses a random selection routine to add 20 records to the Customer table and 500 records to the Orders table (maintaining referential integrity). After the tables are populated, Proc10 first creates a Table-type recordset from the Customer table. You are then asked whether you want to see all of the properties for the new recordset. Next Proc10 creates a Dynaset-type recordset by issuing a SQL statement ("Select * From Orders") to select all of the records from the Orders table. Finally, Proc10 creates a Snapshot-type recordset by issuing a rather complicated SQL statement that, in effect, creates a join between the Customer and Orders tables. (SQL syntax will be covered in detail in the next section, "The QueryDef Object.")

```
Sub Chap07aProc10_CreateRecordsets()
    Dim DB1 As Database
    Dim RS1 As Recordset
    On Error Resume Next
    Chap07a_PopulateTables
    Set DB1 = OpenDatabase(ThisWorkbook.Path & "\DATA1.MDB")
    Set RS1 = DB1.OpenRecordset(Name:="Customer", _
                                Type:=dbOpenTable, _
                                options:=dbDenyWrite + dbDenyRead)
    If MsgBox("Display properties for Table type recordset" & _
        " created from database object?", vbYesNo) = vbYes Then
        Chap07a_DisplayObjProperties RS1
    End If
    Set RS1 = DB1.OpenRecordset(Name:="Select * From Orders", _
                                Type:=dbOpenDynaset, _
                                options:=dbAppendOnly)
    If MsgBox("Display properties for Dynaset type recordset" & _
        " created from database object?", vbYesNo) = vbYes Then
        Chap07a_DisplayObjProperties RS1
    End If
    Set RS1 = DB1.OpenRecordset(Name:="SELECT Customer.*, " & _
        "Orders.* FROM Customer, Orders WHERE Orders.CusNo " & _
        "= Customer.CusNo", _
                                Type:=dbOpenSnapShot, _
                                options:=dbForwardOnly)
    If MsgBox("Display properties for Snapshot type recordset" & _
        " created from database object?", vbYesNo) = vbYes Then
        Chap07a_DisplayObjProperties RS1
    End If
    DB1.Close
End Sub
```

Navigating a Recordset

The most common operations that you will perform with Recordset objects include retrieving, adding, editing, and deleting records. Before you can perform these operations, however, you must understand how to navigate through a Recordset object. When you are working with Recordset objects, it is important to understand that Recordset objects operate in much the same manner as two-dimensional arrays: each column of a Recordset object represents a database field (or a field created through a query), and each row represents a record. Table-type and Dynaset-type Recordset objects store references to underlying data (such as TableDefs in .MDB files) in RAM. When operations are performed on such Recordset objects, the references are used to access the underlying data. Snapshot-type Recordset objects, however, store a copy of the data in RAM but provide no direct access to the underlying data.

All Recordset objects have a "current record." (Think of a cursor that points to only one record within the Recordset object at a given time.) When you first open a Recordset object, the cursor points to the first record—the first record is the current record. To move to subsequent records, you call the MoveNext method. The MovePrevious method will move the cursor to the previous record; the MoveFirst and MoveLast methods will move the cursor to the first and last records. Note that if the cursor is pointing to the last record and you call the MoveNext method, the cursor will move off the last record to an area known as EOF (or end of file) and set a property of the Recordset object named EOF to True. Note that if you call the MoveNext method while the EOF property is True, a DAO error is generated. (You cannot move past the end of the file.) Likewise, if you call the MovePrevious method when the cursor is pointing to the first record, the cursor moves to an area known as BOF (or beginning of file), and under such conditions, the BOF property of the Recordset object becomes True. If you call MovePrevious while the BOF property is True, a DAO error is generated. Proc11, which follows, demonstrates use of the MoveNext, MovePrevious, MoveFirst, and MoveLast methods as well as the EOF and BOF properties.

```
Sub Chap07aProc11_MoveRecordsetCursor()
    Dim DB1 As Database
    Dim RS1 As Recordset
    On Error GoTo ErrorHandler
    Set DB1 = OpenDatabase(ThisWorkbook.Path & "\DATA1.MDB")
    Set RS1 = DB1.OpenRecordset("Customer", dbOpenDynaset)
    With RS1
        MsgBox "When recordset is opened, cursor is at: " & _
            .AbsolutePosition
        .MoveNext
        MsgBox "After calling MoveNext, cursor is at: " & _
            .AbsolutePosition
```

```
            .MovePrevious
            MsgBox "After calling MovePrevious, cursor is " & _
                "again at: " & .AbsolutePosition
            .MoveLast
            MsgBox "After calling MoveLast, cursor is at: " & _
                .AbsolutePosition
            .MoveNext
            MsgBox "When MoveNext is called after MoveLast, " & _
                "cursor is at: " & .AbsolutePosition & _
                Chr(13) & "and the EOF property becomes: " & _
                .EOF
            MsgBox "Calling MoveNext again generates an error."
            .MoveNext
            .MoveFirst
            MsgBox "After calling MoveFirst, cursor is at: " & _
                .AbsolutePosition
            .MovePrevious
            MsgBox "When MovePrevious is called after " & _
                "MoveFirst, cursor is at: " & .AbsolutePosition & _
                Chr(13) & "and the BOF property becomes: " & _
                .BOF
            MsgBox "Calling MovePrevious again generates " & _
                "an error."
            .MovePrevious
        End With
        DB1.Close
        Exit Sub
ErrorHandler:
        Chap07a_ErrorRoutine
        Resume Next
End Sub
```

There are additional ways to navigate through a Recordset object, such as by using the FindFirst, FindLast, FindNext, or FindPrevious method with Dynaset and Snapshot recordsets or by using the Seek method with Table-type recordsets. You can also use the Bookmark property to obtain a unique identification for a specific record that can be used for returning to that record at any time. All of these methods of navigating through Recordset objects are discussed in the sections on Recordset properties (beginning on page 374) and Recordset methods (beginning on page 381), and examples are provided in Proc17 (on pages 375–376) and Proc20 (on pages 382–383).

Adding, editing, and deleting records

You can add, edit, or delete records with only Table-type and Dynaset-type Recordset objects. (Snapshot-type Recordset objects can be used only for retrieving data.)

Adding a record: Adding a record to a Recordset object is a four-step process.

1. Open the Recordset object by calling the OpenRecordset method.

2. Call the AddNew method on the Recordset object.

3. Set values for all required Field objects. (A Field object is required if its Required property is set to True.)

4. Call the Update method on the Recordset object. Always call the Update method when adding or editing a record—if you do not call Update, new records or changes to existing records will not be saved.

Proc12 provides an example of adding a new record to the Customer table. Note that when you add a new record, the new record does not become the current record. Instead, whichever record was current prior to adding the new record remains current after the new record is added. (Think of the new record as being added to the end of the table while the cursor remains in its current position.)

```
Sub Chap07aProc12_AddRecord()
    Dim DB1 As Database
    Dim RS1 As Recordset
    On Error GoTo ErrorHandler
    Set DB1 = OpenDatabase(ThisWorkbook.Path & "\DATA1.MDB")
    Set RS1 = DB1.OpenRecordset(Name:="Customer", _
                                Type:=dbOpenDynaset)
    With RS1
        .AddNew
        .Fields("CusNo").Value = 21
        .Fields("Name").Value = "Name1"
        .Fields("Address").Value = "Address1"
        .Fields("City").Value = "New York"
        .Fields("State").Value = "NY"
        .Fields("Zip").Value = "01234"
        .Update
        MsgBox "One record added to Customer table."
    End With
    DB1.Close
    Exit Sub
ErrorHandler:
    Chap07a_ErrorRoutine
    DB1.Close
End Sub
```

Editing a record: Editing a record in a Recordset object is a five-step process.

1. Open the Recordset object by calling the OpenRecordset method.

2. Locate the record to be edited. When working with Table-type Record-set objects, you must use the Seek method in combination with a table index to locate a record that meets your criteria. When working with Dynaset-type and Snapshot-type recordsets, you can use the FindFirst, FindLast, FindNext, and FindPrevious methods to locate a record that meets your criteria.

3. Call the Edit method on the Recordset object.

4. Change values for Field objects. (Note that all required Field objects must have a non-Null value.)

5. Call the Update method on the Recordset object. Always be sure to call the Update method when adding or editing a record. If you do not call Update, new records or changes to existing records will not be saved.

Proc13 opens a Dynaset-type Recordset object and then calls the FindFirst method to find the first record that contains a value of 21 in the CusNo field. The routine then calls the Edit method and proceeds to assign new values to the Name, Address, City, State, and Zip fields before calling the Update method.

```
Sub Chap07aProc13_EditRecord()
    Dim DB1 As Database
    Dim RS1 As Recordset
    On Error GoTo ErrorHandler
    Set DB1 = OpenDatabase(ThisWorkbook.Path & "\DATA1.MDB")
    Set RS1 = DB1.OpenRecordset(Name:="Customer", _
                                Type:=dbOpenDynaset)
    With RS1
        .FindFirst "[CusNo]=21"
        .Edit
        .Fields("Name").Value = "NewName"
        .Fields("Address").Value = "NewAddress"
        .Fields("City").Value = "NewCity"
        .Fields("State").Value = "NewState"
        .Fields("Zip").Value = "NewZip"
        .Update
        MsgBox "One record changed in Customer table."
    End With
    DB1.Close
    Exit Sub
ErrorHandler:
    Chap07a_ErrorRoutine
    Resume Next
End Sub
```

Deleting a record: Deleting a record in a Recordset object is a three-step process.

1. Open the Recordset object by calling the OpenRecordset method.

2. Locate the record to be deleted. When working with Table-type Recordset objects, you must use the Seek method in combination with a table index in order to locate a record that meets your criteria. When working with Dynaset-type and Snapshot-type recordsets, you can use the FindFirst, FindLast, FindNext, and FindPrevious methods to locate a record that meets your criteria.

3. Call the Delete method on the Recordset object.

Proc14 opens a Table-type Recordset object and uses the Seek method to locate the first instance of a record that contains a value of 21 in the CusNo field. Note that before you call Seek, the Index property of the Recordset object must be set to the table index that defines the CusNo field as an index. In this case, the name of the index is Index1, as set in the CreateRel function which was called by the PopulateTables routine. After the Seek method moves the cursor to the first record that meets the criteria, the Delete method is called to delete the record.

```
Sub Chap07aProc14_DeleteRecord()
    Dim DB1 As Database
    Dim RS1 As Recordset
    On Error GoTo ErrorHandler
    Set DB1 = OpenDatabase(ThisWorkbook.Path & "\DATA1.MDB")
    Set RS1 = DB1.OpenRecordset(Name:="Customer", _
                                Type:=dbOpenTable)
    With RS1
        .Index = "Index1"
        .Seek "=", 21
        .Delete
    End With
    MsgBox "One record deleted from Customer table."
    DB1.Close
    Exit Sub
ErrorHandler:
    Chap07a_ErrorRoutine
    DB1.Close
End Sub
```

Retrieving records

You can retrieve data from a Recordset object in the following three ways.

- Individual field values can be obtained directly by indexing a field within the current record.

- A block of records can be copied out of the Recordset object into a VBA array using the GetRows method.

- Recordset data can be copied directly to a worksheet range by calling the CopyFromRecordset method on the Range object.

The GetRows method is called on the Recordset object and takes one argument, numRows, which is the number of rows to be copied to the array. The rows that are copied to the array begin at the current row. Proc15 provides an example of how GetRows can be used to copy records from a recordset to a VBA array. Also notice that after copying the records to an array, the routine assigns the array to a worksheet range by setting the Value property of the range. (The Excel Transpose function is used to change the dimensions of the array.)

```
Sub Chap07aProc15_GetRows()
    Dim DB1 As Database
    Dim RS1 As Recordset
    Dim Array1 As Variant
    Dim x As Long
    On Error GoTo ErrorHandler
    Set DB1 = OpenDatabase(ThisWorkbook.Path & "\DATA1.MDB")
    Set RS1 = DB1.OpenRecordset(Name:="Orders", _
                                Type:=dbOpenDynaset)
    With RS1
        .MoveLast
        x = .RecordCount
        .MoveFirst
    End With
    Array1 = RS1.GetRows(x)
    MsgBox "Recordset copied to " & UBound(Array1, 1) + 1 & _
            " by " & UBound(Array1, 2) + 1 & " array."
    With Worksheets(1)
        .Range("A1").CurrentRegion.Clear
        .Range("A1:E" & x).Value = _
            Application.Transpose(Array1)
        .Select
    End With
    MsgBox "Array copied to the first worksheet."
    DB1.Close
    Exit Sub
ErrorHandler:
    Chap07a_ErrorRoutine
    DB1.Close
End Sub
```

The CopyFromRecordset method of the Range object can be used to copy data from a Recordset object directly to a worksheet range. CopyFromRecordset takes three arguments:

- data: an object variable representing a Recordset object.

- MaxRows: the maximum number of records (rows) to be copied from the Recordset. (If maxRows is omitted, all records are copied.)

- MaxColumns: the maximum number of fields (columns) to be copied from the Recordset. (If maxColumns is omitted, all fields are copied.)

Proc16 provides an example of using CopyFromRecordset.

```
Sub Chap07aProc16_CopyFromRecordset()
    Dim DB1 As Database
    Dim RS1 As Recordset
    On Error GoTo ErrorHandler
    Set DB1 = OpenDatabase(ThisWorkbook.Path & "\DATA1.MDB")
    Set RS1 = DB1.OpenRecordset(Name:="Orders", _
                                Type:=dbOpenDynaset)
    With Worksheets(1)
        .Range("A1").CurrentRegion.Clear
        .Range("A1").CopyFromRecordset RS1
        .Select
    End With
    MsgBox "Recordset copied to the first worksheet."
    DB1.Close
    Exit Sub
ErrorHandler:
    Chap07a_ErrorRoutine
    DB1.Close
End Sub
```

Collections under Recordset
Collections are Fields and Properties.

Recordset object properties
The Recordset object has numerous properties and methods. Certain properties and methods are applicable for certain types of recordsets. (We will take only a brief look at selected Recordset object properties and methods here. You'll find additional information in the online VBA Help for DAO objects.) Note that each property and method discussed in this section is marked with some combination of the letters "T," "D," and "S." These letters indicate whether the property or method is supported by Table-type, Dynaset-type, and Snapshot-type recordsets, respectively. For example, a property marked "TDS" is supported by

all three types of Recordset objects. A property marked "TD," for example, is supported by only Table-type and Dynaset-type Recordset objects.

AbsolutePosition (read/write property—DS): Used to set the current record of Dynaset-type or Snapshot-type recordsets based on a numeric position within the recordset.

BOF (read-only property—TDS): If True, the cursor is at the beginning of the recordset, before the first record.

Bookmark (read/write property—TDS): Each record in a Recordset object has a unique bookmark that can be used for locating that record. To obtain a bookmark for a record, move the cursor to the record, and then assign the value of the Bookmark property of the Recordset object to a variant variable. If you then move the cursor from the record, you can return to the record at any time by setting the Bookmark property to the value held by the variant variable. Bookmarks are supported by Recordset objects based on tables stored in .MDB files. Recordset objects representing non-.MDB tables might not support bookmarks. You can determine whether a Recordset object supports bookmarks by checking the Bookmarkable property. (If this property is True, bookmarks are supported.) Proc17 provides an example of using a bookmark.

```
Sub Chap07aProc17_Bookmark()
    Dim DB1 As Database
    Dim RS1 As Recordset
    Dim BkMrk1 As Variant
    On Error GoTo ErrorHandler
    Set DB1 = OpenDatabase(ThisWorkbook.Path & "\DATA1.MDB")
    Set RS1 = DB1.OpenRecordset(Name:="Customer", _
                                Type:=dbOpenTable)
    With RS1
        .Index = "Index1"
        .Seek "=", 10
        If .Bookmarkable Then
            BkMrk1 = .Bookmark
            MsgBox "The bookmark is set at the record " & _
                    "for: " & .fields("Name")
            .MoveLast
            MsgBox "The MoveLast method moves the " & _
                    "cursor to the record for: " & .Fields("Name")
            .Bookmark = BkMrk1
            MsgBox "By setting the Bookmark property, " & _
                    "the cursor moves back to: " & .fields("Name")
        End If
    End With
    DB1.Close
    Exit Sub
```

(continued)

continued

```
ErrorHandler:
    Chap07a_ErrorRoutine
    DB1.Close
End Sub
```

Bookmarkable (read-only property—TDS): If True, the Recordset object supports bookmarks. (Bookmarks are not supported by Snapshot-type Recordset objects that are created with the option dbForwardOnly.)

CacheSize (read/write property—D): Sets or returns a value that specifies the number of records in a local Dynaset cache for a non-.MDB ODBC data source. (See the online VBA Help for details.)

CacheStart (read/write property—D): Sets or returns a value that specifies a bookmark of the first record in the Dynaset-type Recordset object to be cached.

DateCreated (read-only property—T): The date and time that the underlying table of a Table-type Recordset object was created.

EditMode (read-only property—TDS): Returns the edit state of the Recordset object. (See the online VBA Help for details.)

EOF (read-only property—TDS): If True, the cursor is at the end of the file.

Filter (read/write property—DS): Sets or returns a string expression that is used to filter a Dynaset-type or Snapshot-type Recordset object. When setting Filter, use a string representing a SQL WHERE clause (without the WHERE keyword). When assigning a filter string, enclose the Recordset object field names in brackets. Here are a few examples of valid filter strings:

- Filter for records that have a value of 50 in the CusNo field:

  ```
  [CusNo]=50
  ```

- Filter for records that have Television in the Product field:

  ```
  [Product] LIKE 'Television'
  ```

- Filter for records that have a value less than 300 in the Amount column:

  ```
  [Amount]<300
  ```

- Filter for records that have either Television or Computer in the Product field and a value less than 20 in the Units field:

  ```
  [Product] IN ('Television', 'Computer') AND [Units] < 20
  ```

- Filter for records in which the product of the values in the Units field and the Amount field is greater than 7000:

```
[Units]*[Amount]>7000
```

In order for the filter to take effect after you set it, you must open a new Recordset object based on the Recordset object to which the filter was applied. Assuming that you set a filter for Recordset RS1, the filter takes effect when you call the OpenRecordset method on RS1. Proc18 provides an example:

```
Sub Chap07aProc18_RecordsetFilter()
    Dim DB1 As Database
    Dim RS1 As Recordset
    Dim NumRecs As Long
    Dim CustNumber As Long
    On Error GoTo ErrorHandler
    Set DB1 = OpenDatabase(ThisWorkbook.Path & "\DATA1.MDB")
    Set RS1 = DB1.OpenRecordset(Name:="Orders", _
                                Type:=dbOpenDynaset)
    With RS1
        .MoveLast
        MsgBox .RecordCount & " records in Orders table."
        .MoveFirst
        CustNumber = .Fields("CusNo").Value
        .Filter = "[CusNo]=" & CustNumber
    End With
    Set RS1 = RS1.OpenRecordset()
    With RS1
        .MoveLast
        MsgBox .RecordCount & " records for customer " & _
            CustNumber & "."
    End With
    DB1.Close
    Exit Sub
ErrorHandler:
    Chap07a_ErrorRoutine
    DB1.Close
End Sub
```

Index (read/write property—T): Sets the name of an Index for a Table-type Recordset object; this allows the use of the Seek method to locate records that meet your criteria within the Recordset object. See Proc14 on page 372 for an example.

LastModified (read-only property—TD): Returns a bookmark for the last modified record in the Recordset object.

LastUpdated (read-only property—T): The date and time of the most recent change to the TableDef object that serves as a source for the Recordset object. Note that this property represents the date and time of the last structural change to the TableDef object, not the last query operation (adding, updating, or deleting records). To track the last date and time of the most recent query operation on a TableDef object, you must add a custom property.

LockEdits (read/write property—TD): Sets or returns a value that represents the type of locking that is in effect during editing. If True, Pessimistic locking is in effect. When Pessimistic locking is in effect and the Edit method is called, a 2 KB page containing the record being edited is locked, and the page remains locked until the Update, Close, or CancelUpdate method is called. If the LockEdits property is False, Optimistic locking is in effect. When Optimistic locking is in effect, the 2 KB page containing the record being edited is locked only while the record is updated using the Update method. (The page is not locked when the Edit method is called.) When used with Dynasets based on non-.MDB ODBC data sources, LockEdits is always set to False.

Name (read/write property—TDS): The name of the table or QueryDef or the first 256 characters of the SQL string on which the Recordset object is based. The Name property is set by calling the OpenRecordset method. The Name property becomes read-only after it is set by calling OpenRecordset.

NoMatch (read-only property—TDS): If True, a find (Dynaset-type or Snapshot-type Recordset object) or seek (Table-type) operation has failed to return a record that meets your criteria.

PercentPosition (read/write property—TDS): Sets or returns the current record based on percent position within a Recordset object.

RecordCount (read-only property—TDS): For Table-type Recordset objects, RecordCount returns the total number of records in the Recordset object. For Dynaset-type or Snapshot-type Recordset objects, RecordCount returns the number of records visited in the Recordset object. To obtain the total number of records in a Dynaset-type or Snapshot-type Recordset object, you must first call the MoveLast method to move the cursor to the end of the Recordset object before obtaining a value from RecordCount.

Restartable (read-only property—TDS): If True, you can call the Requery method on the Recordset object to requery the underlying data. Restartable is always False for Table-type Recordset objects.

Sort (read/write property—DS): Sets or returns the sort order for records in the Recordset object. When setting Sort, use a string representing a SQL ORDER BY clause (without the ORDER BY keywords). When assigning a sort string, enclose Recordset object field names in brackets. You can specify sort order based on one or multiple fields. The following are a few examples of valid sort strings:

- Sort records by CusNo field in ascending order:

  `[CusNo]`

- Sort records by CusNo field in ascending order. (This example accomplishes the same as the one immediately above, but it uses the optional keyword ASC.)

  `[CusNo] ASC`

- Sort records by Amount field in descending order:

  `[Amount] DESC`

- Sort records first by OrdNo in ascending order and then by Product in descending order:

  `[OrdNo] ASC, [Product] DESC`

- Sort records first by OrdNo in descending order and then by the product of the values in the Units and Amount fields in ascending order:

  `[OrdNo] DESC, [Units] * [Amount] ASC`

In order for the sort order to take effect after you set Sort, you must open a new Recordset object based on the Recordset object to which the sort was applied. Assuming that you set the Sort property for Recordset object RS1, the sort takes effect when you call the OpenRecordset method on RS1. Sorting Recordset object records by specifying an ORDER BY clause in a SQL string for the Name argument of the OpenRecordset method is often faster than sorting the Recordset object records by setting the Sort property.

Transactions (read-only property—TDS): If True, the Recordset object supports transactions. The Transactions property is always False for Snapshot-type Recordset objects. Transactions are supported by Table-type and Dynaset-type Recordset objects based on tables stored in .MDB files. Note, however, that Recordset objects representing non-.MDB tables might not support transactions. By using transactions, you can designate a set of Recordset object transactions to occur all at the same time. You begin a transaction by calling the BeginTrans method on the Workspace object. You can commit a transaction by calling the CommitTrans method or roll back a transaction by calling the Rollback method. Both methods are called on the Workspace object. Note that within a single workspace, you can have multiple databases open, and you can carry out transactions against multiple databases. Proc19 provides an example of executing a transaction. In this example, no Workspace object is specified when calling the BeginTrans, CommitTrans, and Rollback methods. When no Workspace object is specified with these methods, the default workspace is used.

```
Sub Chap07aProc19_Transactions()
    Dim DB1 As Database
    Dim RS1 As Recordset
    Dim x As Integer
    Dim TempName As String
    Dim NameString As String
    On Error GoTo ErrorHandler
    Set DB1 = OpenDatabase(ThisWorkbook.Path & "\DATA1.MDB")
    Set RS1 = DB1.OpenRecordset(Name:="Customer", _
                                Type:=dbOpenTable)
    With RS1
        If .Transactions = True Then
            BeginTrans
            For x = 1 To 5
                .Edit
                TempName = .Fields("Name").Value
                .Fields("Name").Value = "New" & TempName
                .Update
                .MoveNext
            Next
            If MsgBox(Prompt:="Commit Transaction?", _
                    Buttons:=vbYesNo) = vbYes Then
                CommitTrans
            Else
                Rollback
            End If
            .MoveFirst
            For x = 1 To 5
                NameString = NameString & _
                    .Fields("Name") & Chr(13)
                .MoveNext
            Next
            MsgBox "Top 5 Customers:" & Chr(13) & _
                Chr(13) & NameString
        End If
    End With
    DB1.Close
    Exit Sub
ErrorHandler:
    Chap07a_ErrorRoutine
    DB1.Close
End Sub
```

Type (read-only property—TDS): The type of Recordset object (dbOpen-Table, dbOpenDynaset, or dbOpenSnapshot). This property is set initially when you call the OpenRecordset method. Type becomes read-only after Open-Recordset is called.

Updatable (read-only property—TDS): If True, the Recordset object can be updated. This property is always False for Snapshot-type Recordset objects. For Table-type or Dynaset-type Recordset objects, this property is False only if no fields in the Recordset object can be updated. (If some fields can be updated, Updatable is True.)

ValidationRule (read-only property—TDS): The validation rule associated with the underlying data. Supported by Recordset objects based on tables in .MDB files only.

ValidationText (read-only—TDS): The validation text associated with the underlying TableDef object. Supported by Recordset objects based on tables in .MDB files only.

Recordset methods

Following are selected methods of Recordset objects.

AddNew (TD): Used to add a new record to a Recordset object. See Proc12 on page 370 for an example.

CancelUpdate (TD): Cancels a pending update operation (initiated through either the AddNew or the Edit method).

Clone (TDS): Creates a clone of a Recordset object, allowing you to have multiple copies of a single Recordset object, each with different current records. Bookmarks established in a source or clone Recordset object are shared across the source and all clones. See the online VBA Help for more details.

Close (TDS): Closes a Recordset object.

CopyQueryDef (DS): Returns a copy of the QueryDef object that serves as a source for the Recordset object. CopyQueryDef can be used only with Dynaset-type or Snapshot-type Recordset objects created from QueryDef objects.

Delete (TD): Deletes the current record in the Recordset object. See Proc14 on page 372 for an example.

Edit (TD): Copies the current record of the Recordset object to the copy buffer for editing. See Proc13 on page 371 for an example.

FillCache (D): Fills all or part of a local cache for a Recordset object that represents a non-.MDB ODBC data source. See the online VBA Help for details.

FindFirst (DS): Moves the cursor to the first occurrence of a record that meets your criteria. FindFirst takes one argument, criteria, which is a string representing a SQL WHERE clause without the WHERE keyword (similar to strings used for the Filter property). On the following page are examples of valid criteria strings.

■ Find the first record in which the value in the CusNo field is 50:

```
[CusNo]=50
```

■ Find the first record in which the value in the Product field is Television and the value in the Amount field is greater than 100:

```
[Product] LIKE 'Television' AND [Amount] > 100
```

■ Find the first record in which the value in the Product field is Computer or Radio and the product of the values in the Units and Amount columns exceeds 100:

```
[Product] IN ('Radio', 'Computer') AND [Units] * [Amount] > 100
```

Proc20 (listed under FindPrevious) provides an example of FindFirst.

FindNext (DS): Finds the next occurrence of a record meeting your criteria. (See the description of FindFirst for details.) Proc20 (listed under FindPrevious) provides an example of FindNext. (This method is not supported by Snapshot-type Recordset objects that are created with the option dbForwardOnly.)

FindLast (DS): Finds the last occurrence of a record meeting your criteria. (See the description of FindFirst for details.) Proc20 (listed under FindPrevious) provides an example of FindLast.

FindPrevious (DS): Finds the previous occurrence of a record meeting your criteria. (See the description of FindFirst for details.) Proc20 provides an example of FindPrevious.

```
Sub Chap07aProc20_FindFirstNextLastPrevious()
    Dim DB1 As Database
    Dim RS1 As Recordset
    Dim CriteriaString As String
    On Error GoTo ErrorHandler
    Set DB1 = OpenDatabase(ThisWorkbook.Path & "\DATA1.MDB")
    Set RS1 = DB1.OpenRecordset(Name:="Orders", _
                                Type:=dbOpenDynaset)
    CriteriaString = "[Units] * [Amount] > 5000"
    With RS1
        .FindFirst CriteriaString
        MsgBox "The FIRST order to exceed $5,000 " & _
            "is order number " & .Fields("OrdNo") & "."
        .FindNext CriteriaString
        MsgBox "The NEXT order to exceed $5,000 " & _
            "is order number " & .Fields("OrdNo") & "."
        .FindLast CriteriaString
        MsgBox "The LAST order to exceed $5,000 " & _
            "is order number " & .Fields("OrdNo") & "."
```

```
        .FindPrevious CriteriaString
        MsgBox "The PREVIOUS order to exceed $5,000 " & _
            "is order number " & .Fields("OrdNo") & "."
    End With
    DB1.Close
    Exit Sub
ErrorHandler:
    Chap07a_ErrorRoutine
    DB1.Close
End Sub
```

GetRows (TDS): Retrieves multiple rows from a Recordset object into an array. The number of rows is specified by the numRows argument. Proc15 on page 373 provides an example of using GetRows.

Move (TDS): Moves the record pointer a certain number of rows forward or backward from the current position. The Move method takes two arguments. The first argument, rows, is a positive or negative long integer indicating the number of rows to be moved forward or backward. (For Snapshot-type recordsets created with the dbForwardOnly option, rows can only be positive.) The second argument, start, is a bookmark indicating the record at which the move will start. (This argument is optional. If the start argument is not specified, the record pointer moves from its current position.)

MoveFirst (TDS): Moves to the first record in the Recordset object. See Proc11 on pages 368–369 for an example.

MoveLast (TDS): Moves to the last record in the Recordset object. See Proc11 on pages 368–369 for an example.

MoveNext (TDS): Moves to the Next record in the Recordset object. See Proc11 on pages 368–369 for an example.

MovePrevious (TDS): Moves to the Previous record in the Recordset object. See Proc11 on pages 368–369 for an example.

OpenRecordset (TDS): Opens a new Recordset object that is based on the existing Recordset object.

Requery (DS): Updates the data in a Recordset object by re-executing the query on which the Recordset object's data is based.

Seek (T): Used with Table-type Recordset objects to find the first occurrence of a record that matches your criteria. (Criteria are based on an index established for the table.)

Update (TD): Used to update the underlying data source with any new records or edited records residing in the copy buffer. (A record is placed in the copy buffer when either the AddNew or the Edit method is called.)

The QueryDef Object

The QueryDef object is a persistent object that is used to store a query statement in an .MDB database. Such queries include either Select queries, which allow you to retrieve data from one or more tables or from an external ODBC data source, or Action queries, which allow you to add, edit, or delete records in database tables. When you create a new QueryDef object and append it to the QueryDefs collection, the QueryDef is compiled and stored in an .MDB file. When a query string is required by a method for a DAO object (such as the OpenRecordset method), it is always faster to pass a QueryDef object than to pass a query string. Queries contained within QueryDef objects are stored in a compiled state, allowing them to execute at a faster speed than queries passed as text strings.

Accessing a QueryDef object

You access a QueryDef object either by indexing the QueryDefs collection of the Database object (by name or by number) or by calling the CreateQueryDef method on the Database object. CreateQueryDef takes two arguments. The first argument, name, is the name of the QueryDef. The second argument, SQLText, is a string specifying a SQL statement. Calling CreateQueryDef automatically appends the new QueryDef object to the QueryDefs collection and saves it in the .MDB file. Proc21 provides an example of creating a QueryDef object using the CreateQueryDef method.

```
Sub Chap07aProc21_CreateQueryDef()
    Dim DB1 As Database
    Dim QRY1 As QueryDef
    Dim QueryString As String
    On Error GoTo ErrorHandler
    QueryString = "SELECT * FROM Customer"
    Set DB1 = OpenDatabase(ThisWorkbook.Path & "\DATA1.MDB")
    Set QRY1 = DB1.CreateQueryDef(Name:="Query1", _
                            SQLText:=QueryString)
    Chap07a_DisplayObjProperties QRY1
    DB1.Close
    Exit Sub
ErrorHandler:
    Chap07a_ErrorRoutine
    DB1.Close
End Sub
```

Query syntax

To take full advantage of QueryDef objects, you need to understand the syntax of query strings that can be assigned to QueryDef objects. The query statement of any existing QueryDef object can be set through the SQL property, allowing you to change QueryDef objects in code. The query syntax supports most syntactical elements defined by ANSI SQL. However, DAO provides additional functions that are not supported by ANSI SQL. The following pages provide a brief overview of DAO query syntax by way of example. For a thorough source of information about DAO query syntax, as well as a useful tool for building QueryDef objects, you need a copy of Microsoft Access. In the following discussion, query syntax is broken down into these categories:

- Select queries
- WHERE clauses
- ORDER BY statements
- JOIN statements
- Insert queries
- Update queries
- Delete queries
- Query functions

These categories by no means represent a comprehensive set of actions that can be performed through a DAO query. However, the categories do cover the most common actions that are executed through queries. Additional information about query statements can be found in documentation provided with Microsoft Access. Keep in mind that queries tend to fall into one of two major categories: select queries, which include the SELECT keyword and are used to retrieve records from a database, and Action queries, which include the INSERT, UPDATE, or DELETE keyword and are used to insert, update, or delete records.

Each of the example query strings provided can be executed by running Proc22 in the Chap07a module in the CHAP07.XLS sample file. (Proc 22 is not displayed here.) Proc22 displays a dialog box containing a listbox with every query statement found on the following pages. When you select a statement and then click OK, a QueryDef object is created with its SQL property set to the selected string, the statement is executed, and the results of the query are copied to the Worksheet Sheet1 using the CopyFromRecordset method.

Select queries   Select queries are used to retrieve records from a database table and are characterized by the SELECT and FROM keywords. The most basic form of Select query has the following syntax:

```
SELECT Field FROM Table
```

On the following page are examples of Select queries. In these examples, keywords are presented in capital letters.

- This query selects all fields for all records from the Customer table. Note that the asterisk (*) can be used as a wildcard character to represent all fields:

```
SELECT * FROM Customer
```

- Each of the following three queries generates the same result. Each selects the Product field from the Orders table. (All three syntactical ways of referring to the Product field are acceptable.)

```
SELECT Orders.Product FROM Orders
SELECT Product FROM Orders
SELECT [Product] FROM Orders
```

- This query selects the Product, Units, and Amount fields from the Orders table:

```
SELECT [Product], [Units], [Amount] FROM Orders
```

WHERE clauses   WHERE clauses are used with Select, Insert, Update, and Delete queries to specify criteria that determine which records the query will affect. Below is the general syntax of a Select query that uses a WHERE clause. (Note that the keyword LIKE can be substituted for the equals (=) operator.)

```
SELECT Field FROM Table WHERE Field = Value
```

The following are examples of Select queries that use WHERE clauses.

- The following two queries return the same result—they select from the Orders table all records that have a value of 10 in the CusNo field:

```
SELECT * FROM Orders WHERE [CusNo] = 10
SELECT * FROM Orders WHERE [CusNo] LIKE 10
```

- The following query selects from the Orders table the Product, Units, and Amount fields for all records that have the value Television in the Product field:

```
SELECT [Product], [Units], [Amount] FROM Orders WHERE [Product]
  LIKE 'Television'
```

- The following query selects from the Customer table all fields for all records that have the value CA or NY in the State field. (Notice the use of the keyword IN when comparing a field to multiple values.)

```
SELECT * FROM Customer WHERE [State] IN ('CA', 'NY')
```

- The following query selects from the Customer table all distinct values in the State field. (Notice the use of the DISTINCT keyword.)

```
SELECT DISTINCT [State] FROM Customer
```

- The following query selects from the Orders table all fields for all records that have the value Television or Computer in the Product field and that have a value greater than 5 in the Units field. Note the use of the AND statement and the greater than (>) comparison operator.

```
SELECT * FROM Orders
  WHERE [Product] IN ('Television','Computer') AND [Units] > 5
```

- The following query selects from the Orders table all fields for all records that have the value Radio in the Product field or that have a value less than 300 in the Amount field. Note the use of the OR statement and the less than (<) comparison operator.

```
SELECT * FROM Orders
  WHERE [Product] LIKE 'Radio' OR [Amount] < 300
```

- The following query selects from the Orders table the Product, Units, and Amount fields as well as a fourth column, which represents a calculated field ([Units] * [Amount]), for all records for which the product of the values in the Units field and the Amount field exceeds 4000:

```
SELECT [Product], [Units], [Amount], [Units] * [Amount]
  AS Total FROM Orders WHERE [Units] * [Amount] > 4000
```

ORDER BY statements   ORDER BY statements are used to sort records returned by a query. ORDER BY statements are used with a single field or some combination of fields in conjunction with the ASC and DESC keywords, which specify an ascending or a descending sort. ORDER BY statements take the following general form:

```
SELECT Field FROM Table ORDER BY Field ASC
```

The following are examples of Select queries that use ORDER BY statements.

- The following two queries select all records from the Customer table and arrange the records in ascending order based on the CusNo field. (Note that if no order is specified, the order is ascending by default.)

```
SELECT * FROM Customer ORDER BY [CusNo]
SELECT * FROM Customer ORDER BY [CusNo] ASC
```

- The query on the following page selects from the Orders table all fields for all records and sorts them by the OrdNo field in descending order.

```
SELECT * FROM Orders ORDER BY [OrdNo] DESC
```

- The following query selects all fields as well as a calculated field ([Units] * [Amount]) for all records in the Orders table that have the value Television in the Product field and for which the product of the values in the Units and Amount fields exceeds 2000. The records are sorted in descending order according to the product of the values in the Units and Amount fields:

```
SELECT *, [Units] * [Amount] AS Total FROM Orders
  WHERE [Product] LIKE 'Television' AND [Units] * [Amount] > 2000
  ORDER BY [Units] * [Amount] DESC
```

JOIN statements   JOIN statements let you establish relationships between two tables within a query. Three types of JOIN statements can be used in a query statement:

- **INNER JOIN:** Used to combine records from two tables whenever there are matching values in the specified field in each table.

- **LEFT JOIN:** Includes all the records from the first table (to the left of the JOIN statement) and all the matching records from the second table. (Records match when they have equal values in the specified fields.)

- **RIGHT JOIN:** Includes all the records from the second table (to the right of the JOIN statement) and all the matching records from the first table. (Records match when they have equal values in the specified fields.)

The following is the general syntax for a Select query that uses a JOIN statement:

```
SELECT Field1, Field2, FROM Table1
  INNER JOIN Table2 ON Table1.Field1 = Table2.Field2
```

The following are examples of Select queries that use JOIN statements.

- The following query selects from the Orders and Customer tables all fields for all records for which the values in the CusNo field in both tables are equal:

```
SELECT Orders.*, Customer.* FROM Orders
  INNER JOIN Customer ON Orders.CusNo = Customer.CusNo
```

- The following query returns the same result as the preceding query but uses a WHERE statement in place of the INNER JOIN statement:

```
SELECT Orders.*, Customer.* FROM Orders, Customer
  WHERE Orders.CusNo = Customer.CusNo
```

■ The following query selects from the Orders table all fields for all records and from the Customer table all fields of records that have a matching value in the CusNo field of both tables:

```
SELECT Orders.*, Customer.* FROM Orders
  LEFT JOIN Customer ON Orders.CusNo = Customer.CusNo
```

■ The following query selects from the Customers table all fields for all records and from the Orders table all fields of records that have a matching value in the CusNo field of both tables:

```
SELECT Orders.*, Customer.* FROM Orders
  RIGHT JOIN Customer ON Orders.CusNo = Customer.CusNo
```

Insert queries   You can use an Insert query to add a new record to a database. Although the recommended method for adding records to a database is the AddNew method of a Recordset object, you can execute an Insert query statement instead. To execute an Insert query statement, assign the query string to the SQL property of a QueryDef object, and then call the Execute method on the QueryDef object. The following is the general syntax for an Insert query:

```
INSERT INTO Table ([Field]) VALUES (Value)
```

The following example inserts a new record into the Customer table. If you execute this query using Proc22, the routine will copy all of the records from the Customer table to worksheet Sheet1. After the Insert query is executed, a new record, Customer22, is in the Customer table. (Notice that strings within a SQL string are enclosed in single quotation marks.)

```
INSERT INTO Customer ([CusNo], [Name], [Address], [City],
  [State], [Zip]) VALUES (22, 'Customer 22', 'Address 22',
  'Las Vegas', 'NV', 98030)
```

Update queries   You can use an Update query to change fields for a single record or for multiple records in a table. (This can also be accomplished by using the Edit and Update methods of the Recordset object.) To execute an Update query statement, assign the query string to the SQL property of a QueryDef object, and then call the Execute method on the QueryDef object. The following is the general syntax for an Update query:

```
UPDATE Table SET [Field] = Value WHERE [Field] = Value
```

The example on the following page updates in the Customer table the record that has a value of 22 in the CusNo field, by setting the Name field to New Customer Name. If you execute this query using Proc22, the routine will copy all of the records from the Customer table to worksheet Sheet1. After the Update query is executed, the name of customer 22 is New Customer Name.

```
UPDATE Customer SET [Name] = 'New Customer Name'
  WHERE [CusNo] = 22
```

Delete queries   You can use a Delete query to delete a single record or multiple records from a database. (You can also accomplish this by calling the Delete method on the Recordset object.) To execute a Delete query statement, assign the query string to the SQL property of a QueryDef object, and then call the Execute method on the QueryDef object. The following is the general syntax for a Delete query:

```
DELETE FROM Table WHERE [Field] = Value
```

The following example deletes from the Customer table the record that has a value of 22 in the CusNo field. If you execute this query using Proc22, the routine will copy all of the records from the Customer table to worksheet Sheet1. After the Delete query is executed, the record for customer 22 no longer exists in the table.

```
DELETE FROM Customer WHERE [CusNo] = 22
```

Query functions   You can use certain functions such as SUM, MAX, or MIN within query statements. Information about all available functions can be found in Microsoft Access online help. Here are three simple examples:

- The following example returns the sum of the product of the values in the Units and Amount fields for all records in the Orders table:

```
SELECT SUM([Units] * [Amount]) AS TotalSum FROM Orders
```

- The following example returns the maximum product of values in the Units and Amount fields in all rows of the Orders table:

```
SELECT MAX([Units] * [Amount]) AS TotalMax FROM Orders
```

- The following example returns the minimum product of the values in the Units and Amount fields in all rows of the Orders table:

```
SELECT MIN([Units] * [Amount]) AS TotalMin FROM Orders
```

Parameter queries

With a Parameter query, you can establish and use a variable within a query string in a QueryDef object. Parameter queries are very useful in applications that require multiple calls to the same Select statement with differing WHERE clauses. You create a PARAMETER query by first creating a query string that includes the PARAMETERS keyword (and other appropriate syntactical elements), and then assigning the string to the SQL property of a QueryDef object. The following is the general syntax for a Parameter query:

```
PARAMETERS [Param1] DATATYPE; SELECT [Field] FROM Table
  WHERE [Field] = [Param1]
```

The following are three examples of Parameter queries.

■ The following query selects from the Orders table all records that have
   a value in the CusNo column equal to the value of the parameter Param1:

```
PARAMETERS [Param1] Integer; SELECT * FROM Customer
  WHERE [CusNo] = [Param1]
```

■ The following query selects from the Orders table all records for which
   the product of values in the Units and Amount fields exceeds the value
   of the parameter Param1:

```
PARAMETERS [Param1] Integer; SELECT * FROM Orders
  WHERE [Units] * [Amount] > [Param1]
```

■ The following query deletes from the Customer table all records for
   which the value in the CusNo field is equal to the value of the parameter Param1. (Brackets are required around the parameter name only
   if the name contains spaces. In the examples, brackets are optional.)

```
PARAMETERS Param1 Integer; DELETE FROM Customer
  WHERE [CusNo] = Param1
```

Before executing a Parameter query, you must first assign a value to the parameter. You accomplish this by indexing the Parameters collection of the QueryDef
object (by name) and setting the Value property of the Parameter object. To then
execute the query, you can call the OpenRecordset method on the QueryDef
object if the query is a Select query, or you can call the Execute method on the
QueryDef object if the query is an Action query.

Proc23 demonstrates a Parameter query. The routine uses an input box to
prompt the user for a customer number, issues the entered number as a parameter as part of a WHERE clause in a Select query, and then displays the
name of the corresponding customer in a message box. (Only values from 1
through 20 will return a customer name, as there are only 20 records in the
Customer table.)

```
Sub Chap07aProc23_ParameterQuery()
    Dim DB1 As Database
    Dim RS1 As Recordset
    Dim QRY1 As QueryDef
    Dim QueryString As String
    On Error GoTo ErrorHandler
```

(continued)

continued

```
    QueryString = "PARAMETERS [Param1] Integer; " & _
            "SELECT * FROM Customer WHERE [CusNo] = [Param1]"
    Set DB1 = OpenDatabase(ThisWorkbook.Path & "\DATA1.MDB")
    If DB1.QueryDefs.Count < 1 Then
        Set QRY1 = DB1.CreateQueryDef("Query1", QueryString)
    Else
        Set QRY1 = DB1.QueryDefs("Query1")
        QRY1.Sql = QueryString
    End If
    QRY1.Parameters("Param1") = InputBox("Enter customer number.")
    Set RS1 = QRY1.OpenRecordset(dbOpenDynaset)
    With RS1
        .MoveFirst
        MsgBox "Customer's name is " & .Fields("Name") & "."
    End With
    DB1.Close
    Exit Sub
ErrorHandler:
    Chap07a_ErrorRoutine
    DB1.Close
End Sub
```

Collections under QueryDef
Collections are Parameters, Fields, and Properties.

QueryDef properties
Following are selected properties of the QueryDef object.

Connect (read/write property): Used to set a string representing connection information for an external ODBC data source. You use the Connect property in executing a SQL pass-through query—that is, a query that is not executed by DAO but that is passed through to the external ODBC database. (See the online VBA Help for full details on syntax for the Connect property.)

DateCreated (read-only property): Returns the date and time that the QueryDef object was created.

LastUpdated (read-only property): Returns the date and time of the most recent change made to the QueryDef object.

LogMessages (read/write property): If LogMessages is True, DAO will create a table that stores ODBC messages returned from external ODBC data sources. Note that this property must first be created using the CreateProperty method. (See the online VBA Help for details.)

Name (read/write property): The name of the QueryDef object.

ODBCTimeout (read/write property): Sets or returns the number of seconds that the Jet database engine waits before a time-out error occurs on a query issued against an external ODBC data source.

RecordsAffected (read-only property): Returns the number of records affected by the query issued through the most recently invoked Execute method.

ReturnsRecords (read/write property): Sets or returns a value that indicates whether a SQL pass-through query to an external ODBC data source returns records.

SQL (read/write property): Sets or returns the SQL statement that defines the query executed by the QueryDef object.

Type (read-only property): The type of query. (See the online VBA Help for details.)

Updatable (read-only property): If True, the QueryDef object can be changed.

QueryDef methods
Following are selected methods of the QueryDef object.

CreateProperty: Creates a custom property for the QueryDef object.

Execute: Used to execute an Action query defined by a QueryDef.

OpenRecordset: Returns a resulting Recordset from a Select query defined by a QueryDef object.

> **NOTE** You delete a QueryDef object by calling the Delete method on the QueryDefs collection and passing the name of the QueryDef to be deleted.

The Parameter Object
The Parameter object is used to represent parameters that are passed to Parameter queries defined by QueryDef objects. A Parameter object exists for a QueryDef if the QueryDef defines a SQL statement that contains a Parameters clause declaring one or more parameters. If a QueryDef SQL statement has no Parameters clause, no Parameter objects exist for that QueryDef.

Accessing a Parameter object
You access a Parameter object by indexing the Parameters collection of a QueryDef object. Note that the only way to create a Parameter object is to assign a SQL string containing a Parameters clause to the SQL property of a QueryDef object. Proc23 on pages 391–392 provides an example.

Collection under Parameter
Properties is the only collection under Parameter.

Parameter properties
Following are selected properties of the Parameter object.

Name (read-only property): The name of the parameter.

Type (read-only property): The data type of the parameter.

Value (read/write property): The value of the parameter.

Parameter methods
None.

Other Data Access Objects

Several other Data Access Objects are available to either alter the database struc-
ture or manage security in multi-user environments. These are the User, Group,
TableDef, Field, Index, Relation, Container, Document, and Property objects.
Additionally, the Connection object is used to access external data sources using
ODBCDirect. A brief overview of each object is provided. In addition, sample
routines that demonstrate the use of most of these objects are included in
CHAP07.XLS. For more information on these objects, refer to online Help.

The User object
The User object lets you establish individual user accounts for your application.
User information is stored in the system database file. (You must have a copy
of Microsoft Access to create a system file through the Access Workgroup Administrator.) With a User object, you can establish various access permissions
for the different components of your database and set and change passwords
for the user. Proc24 in CHAP07.XLS demonstrates the User object. This procedure uses a typical value for the Registry key that indicates the path to the system database file; you might need to edit this value to match the actual Registry
key value on your system.

The Group object
A Group object represents a group of user accounts that have common access
permissions within a specific Workgroup object (as defined by a system database file). Each group can contain one or more users and, as is the case with
the User object, information about groups is stored in the system file. (You must
use the Workgroup Administrator in Microsoft Access to create a system file.)
With a Group object, you can establish certain permissions for the group and
then add users. Each user added to the group will assume the permissions
granted to the whole group.

The TableDef object

The TableDef object is used to reference tables within a Database object—either local tables stored in an .MDB file or linked tables in external databases. TableDef is used for altering the structure of existing tables in a database, not for actually reading or changing data within tables. (The Recordset object is used for these purposes.) Through the TableDef object, you can create Fields and Indexes, refresh links to linked tables from external databases, set validation rules for Fields as they are added to a table, and determine the number of records in a table. Proc25, Proc26, and Proc27 in CHAP07.XLS demonstrate the TableDef object. Proc26 requires the presence of BIKEDATA.MDB in the same directory as the workbook file.

The Field object

The Field object is used to refer to fields contained within TableDef, QueryDef, Index, Relation, and Recordset objects. With TableDef, Index, and Relation objects, the Field object is used in establishing or altering the structure of tables, as well as in establishing indexes and relations. With the Recordset object, the Field object is used to retrieve and update a particular field for a record in a data set. Proc28 in CHAP07.XLS demonstrates the Field object.

The Index object

The Index object is used to specify the order of records in TableDef objects and to specify whether duplicate records can be entered. Additionally, use of Index objects can increase the speed of query execution. Index objects are used by DAO when joining tables in creating Recordset objects from multiple tables. You should note that an index affects the sorting of records only in Table-type Recordset objects. (Index objects do not affect the sorting of records in Dynaset or Snapshot Recordset objects.) Also note that although an index will affect the sorting of records retrieved through a Table-type recordset, an index has no effect on the actual ordering of records in the TableDef object. (Records are ordered according to the sequence in which they are entered in the TableDef object.) You are not required to specify an index with a TableDef object but doing so will increase the speed of seek operations and the execution of queries. (This is especially true for tables that have an index designated as a "primary key" or an index for which each record has a unique value.) Keep in mind that too many indexes within a table can actually decrease the speed of query execution. An Index object can be made up of one or more fields—and for Index objects defined as unique, values for each record within an Index object must be unique. Proc29 in CHAP07.XLS demonstrates the Index object.

The Relation object

The Relation object is used to establish relationships between two database tables. As discussed earlier in this chapter, there are many benefits to breaking up data sets into multiple tables that are related through specific fields. Relationships, in essence, allow you to join two tables through established related fields. Joining tables through related fields lets you treat fields in separate tables as though they were the same field. This allows you to maintain integrity between tables, and in the case of one-to-many relationships, allows you to cascade updates or deletions from a single record in a primary table to one or more records in a foreign table. This can save you a lot of work when you execute Action queries. Proc30, Proc31, Proc32, and Proc33 in CHAP07.XLS demonstrate the Relation object.

The Container object

The Container object is used to access collections of saved objects representing databases, tables, queries, and relationships. Although you can use the Databases, TableDefs, QueryDefs, and Relations collections to access open objects of their respective types, you can use a Container object to access collections of saved objects—objects that aren't necessarily open but that are saved in an .MDB file. A single Container object actually holds a collection of Document objects, with each Document object representing an object of the particular container type—database, table (which includes queries), and relationships. For example, the Container object representing tables contains a collection of Document objects, and each Document object represents a table or query in the database. Container objects are often used for establishing permissions for the Document objects they contain. Proc34 in CHAP07.XLS demonstrates the Container object.

The Document object

A Document object represents a database, table, query, or relationship saved in an .MDB file. Each Container object contains a collection of Document objects. For a given database, three Container objects exist—one for each group of databases, tables (including queries), and relationships. Each of these Container objects contains a Documents collection, and each Document object in the collection represents a single object (database, table/query, or relationship). Document objects are used primarily for obtaining or setting permissions for a user or group in regard to the object that the Document object represents. Proc35 in CHAP07.XLS demonstrates the Document object.

The Property object

The Property object is used to represent built-in properties for DAO objects. For a given DAO object, one Property object represents each property of the object. You can create custom Property objects using the CreateProperty method with the Database, Index, QueryDef, TableDef, and Field objects. (Custom properties can be created only for Field objects contained in TableDefs and QueryDefs.) Proc36 in CHAP07.XLS demonstrates the Property object.

The Connection object

The Connection object is a non-persistent object that is used in much the same manner as the Database object—however, the Connection object is used for accessing ODBC databases via ODBCDirect. To use a Connection object, you must first create an ODBCDirect workspace, which is a workspace created using the dbUseODBC option. (The Connection object is not discussed in detail here. You can find information on the Connection object in the DAO online Help that ships with Excel 97.)

Other Ways to Access External Databases

As mentioned previously, in addition to using DAO, you can access external data from Microsoft Excel in three ways: using Microsoft Query, using a pivottable, or using direct database access. Let's look briefly at each of these approaches.

Using Microsoft Query and the QueryTable Object to Access External Data

Microsoft Query is an Excel add-in application that lets users access external databases through ODBC. Query is accessed by choosing Get External Data from the Data menu and then by choosing the Create New Query command. By using Query, the user can bring data from an external database into Excel through ODBC. By embedding a series of queries into a worksheet, you could create a report that retrieves various pieces of data from external sources. The report could be refreshed as necessary simply by refreshing the queries.

TIP	When you use Query to retrieve data from a database and bring the data into Excel, you can save the query definition along with the table of retrieved data on the Excel worksheet. If you elect to save the query definition, you can easily refresh the query by choosing the Refresh Data command on the Data menu—the saved query is automatically executed.

Each Worksheet object contains a QueryTables collection that represents the set of queries embedded on that sheet by MS Query. This collection contains one QueryTable object for each query.

The QueryTable object

You can use the QueryTable object to both create and run MS Query queries, although it is more likely you will create the queries manually and use the QueryTable object merely to run them. If you do need to create a query programmatically, you would create the query by using the Add method of the QueryTables collection object. Refer to the online help for more information about this method.

QueryTable properties   The following are the more commonly used properties of the QueryTable object.

BackgroundQuery: If True, the query will execute in the background asynchronously. If False, Excel will wait for the query to finish execution before the user can interact with Excel. Note that this setting can be overridden by the backgroundQuery argument of the Refresh method, which is described under QueryTable Methods.

Destination: A range object describing where the resulting data will be placed.

EnableEditing: If True, the user can edit the query definition using MS Query. If False, the query cannot be edited.

EnableRefresh: If True, the user can refresh the query using the Refresh Data command. If False, the query cannot be refreshed.

FieldNames: If True, field names of the result set are included and placed into the Destination range.

FillAdjacentFormulas: If True, Excel updates any formulas based on the incoming data in columns adjacent to the Destination range.

Name: The name of the QueryTable object. Can be used as an index in the QueryTables collection.

Parameters: A collection of parameter objects that can be used for passing parameters into the query.

Refreshing: A Boolean value used to determine if an asynchronous query is still executing. Will be set to True while the query is executing and back to False when execution is complete. Read-only.

RefreshStyle: Determines how data is inserted into the worksheet. Can be one of three values:

xlInsertDeleteCells	Cells are inserted or deleted to accommodate the incoming data.
XlInsertEntireRows	Entire rows are inserted or deleted to accommodate the incoming data.
XlOverwriteCells	Incoming data overwrites existing cells.

SavePassword: If True, the username and password are saved with the query definition.

SQL: The SQL statement that defines the data to be returned by the query.

QueryTable methods   The following are the more commonly used methods of the QueryTable object.

Refresh: Refreshes the query. One argument, backgroundQuery, determines whether the query runs asynchronously. Set to True to run asynchronously; False to return control to the routine only after the query is finished running.

CancelRefresh: For asynchronous queries, CancelRefresh can be called to cancel a query that has not yet completed running.

Proc37, a portion of which follows, displays properties from a QueryTable object on Sheet 2, and then runs the query.

```
Sub Chap07aProc37_QueryTables()
Sheets("Sheet2").Select
    With ActiveSheet.QueryTables("SalesByContinent")
        MsgBox "Name: " & .Name & Chr(13) & _
               "SQL: " & .Sql & Chr(13) & _
               "Destination: " & .Destination.Address _
                    & Chr(13) & _
               "FieldNames: " & .FieldNames & Chr(13) & _
               "FillAdjacentFormulas: " _
                    & .FillAdjacentFormulas & Chr(13) & _
               "BackgroundQuery: " & .BackgroundQuery
        If MsgBox("Do you want to run this query?", vbYesNo) = _
            vbYes Then
            .Connection = "ODBC;" & _
                "DBQ=" & ThisWorkbook.Path & "\BIKEDATA.MDB;" & _
                "Driver={Microsoft Access Driver (*.mdb)};"
            .Refresh False
            . . .
```

Using Pivottables to Access External Data

Pivottables let the user view large amounts of data—originating either from an external database or from an Excel worksheet—dynamically. Pivottables were discussed at length in Chapter 4 and so are mentioned only briefly here.

The user can create a pivottable in two ways:

■ By using the PivotTable Wizard, which is accessed by choosing the PivotTable command from the Data menu.

■ Through VBA, by using the PivotTableWizard method of the Worksheet object.

To create a pivottable from an external database using the PivotTableWizard method, you pass the constant xlExternal as the first argument of the method and a two-element array as the second argument; the array contains the ODBC data source name for the database and a SQL string.

NOTE   Pivottables are unidirectional. That is, you can read data from any ODBC database into a pivottable, but you cannot export data from the pivottable back to the database.

A pivottable can execute a query directly from an external database, reading the resulting data into an internal RAM cache. The data is kept in the cache as the pivottable is used, and you have the option of saving the cache with the workbook file. How much data can be read into a pivottable is not subject to the constraints imposed by the spreadsheet's 65,536-row and 256-column structure but rather is solely dependent on the amount of RAM on the user's machine. Because a pivottable resides on a worksheet, however, how much data can be displayed by a pivottable is subject to the limitation of 65,536 rows and 256 columns. For more information about pivottables, see the section in Chapter 4 titled "The PivotTable Object," beginning on page 161, or take a look at Excel's online VBA Help topics titled "PivotTableWizard Method" and "PivotTable Object."

FYI

The Text Import Wizard Helps with Text Files

Excel has a special feature, known as the Text Import Wizard, for dealing with text files. If you try to open a text file directly in Excel, the Text Import Wizard opens automatically to prompt you for more information about the text file—such as whether the file is delimited or fixed width, the starting row for the data to be imported, the delimiter (if delimited), and the data type of the columns that make up the file. (Note that when you open text files in Excel, you are subject to the limitation of 65,536 rows and 256 columns imposed by the worksheet.)

A text file can be opened through VBA by using the OpenText method of the Workbooks collection object. OpenText takes several arguments that correspond to the information prompted for by the Text Import Wizard. Here is the second dialog box of the Text Import Wizard.

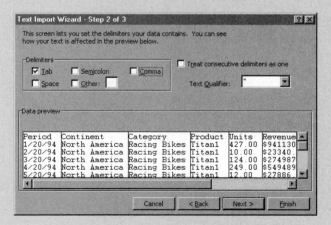

For more information about the OpenText method, see Excel's online VBA Help.

Using Direct Database Access to Access External Data

You can open dBASE and FoxPro database files directly in Excel by choosing the Open command from the File menu. You can do the same through VBA by using the Open method on the Workbooks object. Be sure that the dBASE or FoxPro file that you are opening is not larger than the Excel worksheet—65,536 rows and 256 columns.

You can also save Excel files to dBASE (.DBF) format by choosing the Save As command from the File menu, and then selecting one of the .DBF formats from the Save File As Type drop-down listbox. Through VBA, you can do the same by using the SaveAs method of the Workbook object. Notice in the Open and Save As dialog boxes that Excel can either read or save to a number of other file formats.

Messaging

Excel offers various degrees of access to Microsoft Mail, Microsoft Exchange, and Lotus Vendor Independent Messaging (VIM). With Microsoft Exchange as well as with Microsoft Mail under Windows, you can use VBA to embed an Excel workbook in an e-mail message and then send it or to route an Excel workbook to a list of users, either sequentially or in parallel. With Microsoft Exchange only, you can post a workbook to a public folder. With Lotus VIM, you can use only VBA to embed an Excel workbook and send it in a single e-mail message.

In the pages that follow, you will look at using VBA to send a workbook in a single e-mail message (Microsoft Exchange, Microsoft Mail, and Lotus VIM), posting to a public folder (Microsoft Exchange), and routing a workbook (Microsoft Exchange and Microsoft Mail). When you use Excel 97 under Windows 95 or Windows NT, you can access additional messaging functionality through OLE Automation. The OLE Messaging interface is only covered briefly in this chapter. More information about the OLE Messaging interface is available through the Microsoft Exchange Software Development Kit. (For information, in the United States, contact Microsoft Developer Services at 1-800-426-9400; outside the United States, contact your local Microsoft office.) The routines in this section are contained in the Chap07b module of CHAP07.XLS.

> **NOTE** To execute the routines in the Chap07b module properly, you need an e-mail system; a MAPI-compliant system (preferably Microsoft Exchange) works best. If you have no e-mail system installed, you will not be able to execute these routines.

Determining Whether an E-Mail System Is Installed

By using the MailSystem property of the Application object, you can use VBA to determine whether a Microsoft Mail system is installed. Unfortunately, Excel does not provide a method for determining whether a Lotus VIM system is installed.

If Microsoft Mail is installed, the MailSystem property is set to the value represented by the constant xlMAPI. Proc38 uses a Select Case statement to determine the e-mail system installed.

```
Sub Chap07bProc38_CheckMailInstallation()
    Select Case Application.MailSystem
        Case xlMAPI
            MsgBox "Microsoft Mail installed."
        Case xlPowerTalk
            MsgBox "Apple PowerTalk Mail installed."
        Case xlNoMailSystem
            MsgBox "No e-mail system installed."
    End Select
End Sub
```

Sending a Workbook in a Single E-Mail Message

Sending a workbook in a single e-mail message is a simple process.

- If you are using a MAPI e-mail system (such as Microsoft Mail for Windows), you can use the SendMail method of the Workbook object.

- If you are using a Lotus VIM system, you can call the Show method of the Dialogs(xlDialogSendMail) object.

Using the Send Mail method

The SendMail method that is used with MAPI systems takes the following three arguments.

recipients: Single string or array of strings that lists the recipients.

subject: Single string for the subject of the e-mail message.

returnReceipt: If True, a return receipt is sent through the e-mail system after the recipient opens the message.

NOTE   When using the SendMail method, Excel automatically starts a MAPI session, which continues to run even after the routine finishes executing. To end the MAPI session, call the MailLogoff method of the Application object.

Proc39 shows how to use the SendMail method; notice the use of MailLogoff at the end of the routine. Also note that if you specify a recipient not registered in the e-mail system, the SendMail method fails, generating an error message. (Take care to edit the e-mail names in Proc39 before running it.)

```
Sub Chap07bProc39_SendMail()
    Dim RecipArray As Variant
    RecipArray = Array("Harshbarger, Steve", _
                       "Heft, Jennifer", _
                       "Bonta, Tony")
    If Application.MailSystem <> xlNoMailSystem Then
        ActiveWorkbook.SendMail _
            Recipients:=RecipArray, _
            Subject:="Fiscal Year Budget Forecast", _
            returnReceipt:=True
        Application.MailLogoff
    Else
        MsgBox "No mail system installed."
    End If
End Sub
```

Using the Show method

To send e-mail on a Lotus VIM system, you must call the Show method on the Dialogs(xlDialogSendMail) object. Proc40 provides an example:

```
Sub Chap07bProc40_xlDialogSendMail()
    If Application.MailSystem <> xlNoMailSystem Then
        Application.Dialogs(xlDialogSendMail).Show
    Else
        MsgBox "No mail system installed."
    End If
End Sub
```

If you are using a MAPI system, you can pass arguments when you call the Show method on xlDialogSendMail. The arguments correspond to the same three arguments used for the SendMail method.

NOTE	With a MAPI system, when you call the Show method on xlDialog-SendMail, an e-mail message is not sent immediately. The message is first displayed in a Mail Message edit box for editing. After finishing the editing, the user can send the message by clicking the Send button.

Proc41 calls the Show method on the Dialogs(xlDialogSendMail) object. Three arguments are passed to the method; they correspond to the recipients, subject, and return receipt arguments of the SendMail method.

```
Sub Chap07bProc41_xlDialogSendMailWithArguments()
    If Application.MailSystem <> xlNoMailSystem Then
        Application.Dialogs(xlDialogSendMail).Show _
```

(continued)

continued

```
            arg1:="Miles Takahashi", _
            arg2:="Budget Forecast", _
            arg3:=True
        Application.MailLogoff
    Else
        MsgBox "No mail system installed."
    End If
End Sub
```

This is the Microsoft Mail message box that results from Proc41:

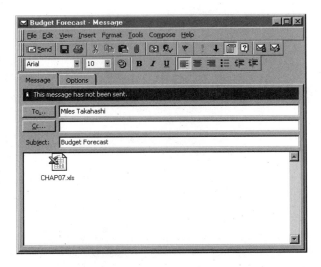

Using the RoutingSlip Object to Route a Workbook

Excel offers a feature called "routing" that lets you send a workbook to multiple users, either sequentially or in parallel. When it is routed sequentially, the workbook goes to a list of users, one user at a time; when one user finishes reviewing the workbook, he or she forwards it to the next user on the routing list. When it is routed in parallel, the workbook goes to a group of users all at once. Routing is available only for Microsoft Mail systems.

If Microsoft Mail is installed, the user can access the routing feature by choosing Send To from the File menu and then choosing the Routing Recipient command. (Send To does not appear on the File menu if Microsoft Exchange or Microsoft Mail is not installed.) An example of a completed Routing Slip dialog box is shown on the facing page.

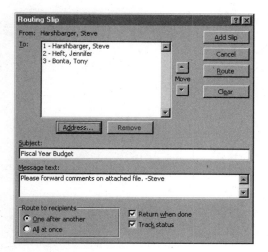

The RoutingSlip object, which is a singular object that is contained in the Workbook object, can be used to route a workbook using VBA. Before a RoutingSlip object can be accessed, a routing slip must be added to the workbook by setting the HasRoutingSlip property of the Workbook object to True.

NOTE Each workbook can have only one routing slip.

After you set the RoutingSlip object's properties, you must call the Route method of the Workbook object to route the workbook.

The following properties of the RoutingSlip object are important to the routing process.

Delivery: The way in which the workbook will be routed. Delivery can have one of two values:

xlOneAfterAnother	The workbook is routed in a sequential fashion.
xlAllAtOnce	All users on the routing list receive the workbook at the same time.

Message: String that represents the text to be included in the e-mail message in which the routed workbook is embedded.

ReturnWhenDone: If True, the workbook is returned to the originator after it has been routed to all recipients.

Status: Routing status of a workbook file. Status is a read-only property that can have one of the three values at the top of the next page.

xlNotYetRouted	The workbook has not yet been routed by the originator (that is, the Route method of the Workbook object has not yet been called).
xlRoutingInProgress	The workbook is somewhere in the middle of a sequential routing list (available only when sequential routing is used).
xlRoutingComplete	The routing process for the workbook has been completed.

Subject: Text string that represents the subject line of the e-mail message in which the routed workbook is embedded.

TrackStatus: If True, an e-mail message is sent to the originator each time a user on the recipient list receives and opens the e-mail message containing the routed workbook. (The e-mail message indicates the user's name.) The property is read/write before the workbook is routed; it is read-only after the routing process begins.

The following method of the RoutingSlip object is also important to the routing process.

Recipients: Use the Recipients method to specify a string (for one user) or array of strings (for multiple users) that lists the e-mail names of all users to whom the workbook will be routed.

When sequential routing is used, the user forwards the workbook to the next user on the list by choosing the Send command from the File menu. Using the Route method of the Workbook object accomplishes the same task. One other method of the RoutingSlip object is also of importance to the routing process: the Reset method, which deletes an existing routing slip.

Proc42, which follows, first checks whether the active workbook has a routing slip; if it does, the routine deletes the routing slip by calling the Reset method. A new routing slip is added, the properties for the routing slip are set, and the Route method of the Workbook object is called to route the workbook.

NOTE   When you add a routing slip to a workbook, Excel starts a MAPI session. To end the MAPI session, you must call the MailLogoff method on the Application object, as is done at the end of Proc42.

```
Sub Chap07bProc42_RoutingSlip()
    If Application.MailSystem = xlMAPI Then
        With ActiveWorkbook
            If .HasRoutingSlip = True Then
                .RoutingSlip.Reset
            End If
```

```
            .HasRoutingSlip = True
        With .RoutingSlip
            .Delivery = xlOneAfterAnother
            .Message = "Please forward comments " & _
                       "on attached file. -Steve"
            .Recipients = Array("Harshbarger, Steve", _
                                "Heft, Jennifer", _
                                "Bonta, Tony")
            .ReturnWhenDone = True
            .Subject = "Fiscal Year Budget"
            .TrackStatus = True
        End With
        .Route
    End With
    Application.MailLogoff
    Else
        MsgBox "Microsoft Mail not installed."
    End If
End Sub
```

The Routed property of the Workbook object can also be useful when routing. It is a read-only property that has a value of either True or False. If True, the workbook has already been routed to the next recipient; if False, the workbook has not yet been routed.

Posting to an Exchange Public Folder with the Post Method

If you are attached to a Microsoft Exchange Server, Excel offers the ability to post a workbook to an Exchange public folder using the Post method of the Workbook object. A public folder is simply a shared location for posting messages, sharing information, and conducting discussions.

Proc43 demonstrates the Post method. Post takes one argument, destination, which refers to the name of the public folder the workbook will be posted to. If you leave this argument blank, a dialog box displays a selection of folders you can post to.

```
Sub Chap07bProc43_PublicFolder()
    If Application.MailSystem <> xlNoMailSystem Then
        ActiveWorkbook.Post
        Application.MailLogoff
    Else
        MsgBox "No mail system installed."
    End If
End Sub
```

Pictured on the following page is a sample dialog box displayed by running Proc43.

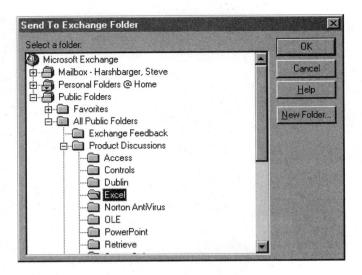

Using OLE Messaging Objects

A separate object model for messaging, OLE Messaging objects, is available from Excel. OLE Messaging is in fact available from any Office 97 application and Visual Basic. With OLE Messaging, you can perform more advanced messaging operations than sending, posting, and routing workbooks. You could, for example, do the following:

- Create and send messages with or without attachments.

- Retrieve and read messages from the inbox or other folders.

- Delete messages.

- Move messages between folders.

- Determine which folders are available and what fields are in each folder.

Figure 7-3 shows the OLE Messaging object model.

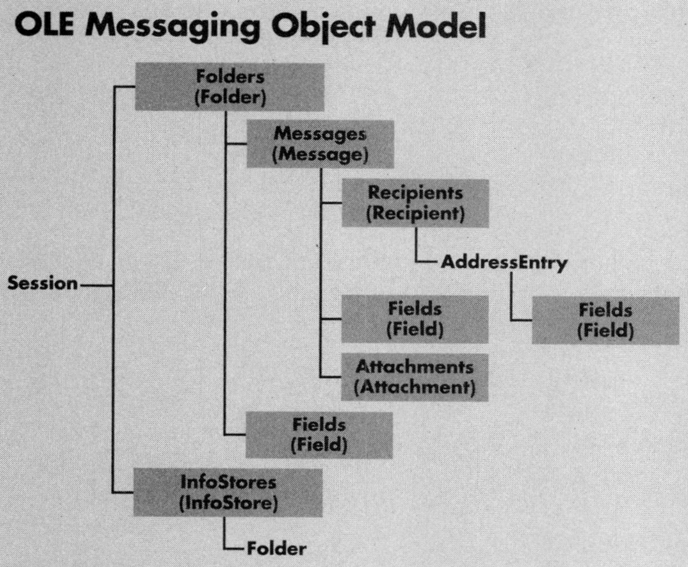

OLE Messaging Object Model

Figure 7-3. *The OLE Messaging object model.*

The OLE Messaging object hierarchy consists of 14 objects. Of these, 6 are objects in collections, 6 are collections (which are objects in their own right), and 2 (Session and AddressEntry) are singular objects.

Before using OLE Messaging, you should carefully consider whether you really need to. Excel's RoutingSlip object, SendMail method, and Post method provide most of the functionality typically required by a spreadsheet application. OLE Messaging is not difficult to use, but Excel's own messaging objects are quicker and simpler to implement if they fulfill the need at hand.

If you decide that you should use OLE Messaging, you will need to establish a reference to the file MDISP32.TLB, which is in the Windows/System directory. This file is installed with Microsoft Exchange clients and will eventually be installed automatically with future versions of Windows and Windows NT.

More information about the OLE Messaging interface is available through the Microsoft Exchange Software Development Kit. (For information, in the United States, contact Microsoft Developer Services at 1-800-426-9400; outside the United States, contact your local Microsoft office.)

SUMMARY

In this chapter, we looked at various ways to get data in and out of Excel through databases and through messaging systems. These are the most important points we covered:

- Excel supports the Open Database Connectivity Standard (ODBC), which allows Excel to share data with any ODBC database easily.

- Excel provides the powerful Data Access Objects (DAO) model for accessing local .MDB data (via Jet DAO) or server-based ODBC data (via ODBCDirect DAO).

- In addition to DAO, Excel provides three other means of accessing external databases:

  - Using Microsoft Query and the QueryTable object

  - Using pivottables

  - Using direct database access

  Pivottables are best suited for applications that involve retrieving data from a database and importing it to Excel for analysis only.

- Excel provides different levels of access to Microsoft Mail and Lotus VIM. In either of these systems, you can embed a workbook and send an e-mail message from Excel.

- Excel's RoutingSlip object, which is available only with Microsoft Mail systems, provides a way to route a workbook—either sequentially or in parallel—to a specified list of users.

- The Workbook object's Post method provides a way to post a workbook to an Exchange public folder.

- By using OLE Messaging, you can perform more advanced messaging operations from within Excel.

8

Taking Full Advantage of Microsoft Excel's Built-In Features

Many regard the Microsoft Excel worksheet as a development environment in and of itself. In fact, many developers have created powerful Excel applications without writing any VBA code; they've done this by taking full advantage of the features and capabilities that the Worksheet and Range objects offer. Worksheets and the cells they contain have a vast amount of built-in intelligence associated with them—more than 200 built-in functions plus roughly another 200 functions available through various add-in files shipped with the product. All of these functions are accessible from any range on the worksheet, and with Excel's built-in calculation engine, such functions often execute much faster than similar routines written in Microsoft Visual Basic for Applications (VBA).

This chapter takes a look at some of Excel's built-in features for manipulating objects and describes the advantages they offer to developers. These topics are covered: formulas, functions, names, calculation settings, hiding and protecting, scenarios, goal seeking, sorting, subtotals, autofiltering, consolidation, application events, range navigating, entering data, data validation, and report printing. Because these topics deal with what is generally considered to be Excel's basic functionality, which is well documented in the manuals shipped with Excel and in several books about Excel, each is discussed only briefly here, with an emphasis on how such features can be accessed from VBA.

NOTE If you are already familiar with Excel's basic functionality, you might want to skim this chapter. If you are new to Excel, however, you should read the whole chapter, and you might also want to look elsewhere for additional information about topics of particular use to you in developing applications.

The routines in this chapter follow the naming convention established earlier in this book and can be found in the CHAP08-1.XLS and CHAP08-2.XLS files on the companion CD.

Formulas, Functions, Names, and Calculation Settings

By using formulas and functions on the Excel worksheet, you can delegate aspects of your application that involve advanced number crunching to the Excel calculation engine, which calculates all formulas entered in cells on the worksheet. Because Excel's calculation engine is much faster than any routines you can write using VBA, it is often to your advantage to use the worksheet for calculating complicated numeric formulas.

The Worksheet Defined

In its simplest definition, an Excel worksheet is a group of 16,777,216 cells arranged in a grid that consists of 256 columns and 65,536 rows. Each cell is capable of holding numbers, text entries, or formulas. When entering formulas in cells, you can use all the traditional arithmetic operators as well as the built-in functions available in Excel—you can even use your own VBA functions. Formulas can be linked to other cells that are on the same worksheet, on different worksheets, or even in different workbooks. Formulas can also be linked to what are known as "named formulas," which are discussed in the section titled "Named formulas," beginning on page 20. Excel's ability to link cells and named formulas in complex formulas that use various functions lets you create powerful models by using only the worksheet.

Worksheet Formulas

The Excel spreadsheet consists of two layers—the value layer and the formula layer. The value layer is active by default so that the results of any formulas entered in cells are displayed. When the formula layer is active, formulas—as opposed to their results—are displayed in cells. To display the formula layer, choose the Options command from the Tools menu, and then click Formulas in the Window Options section of the View tab.

TIP You can press the Ctrl-tilde (~) key combination to toggle between the value and formula layers.

In VBA, the DisplayFormulas property of the Window object controls the display of the formula layer. It is not necessary to display the formula layer to enter formulas; you display the formula layer only to view all formulas on a worksheet. You can also view a formula in an individual cell either by selecting the cell and viewing the cell's formula in the formula bar or by double-clicking the cell, which allows you to edit the formula in place (provided the Edit Directly In Cell option is checked in the Edit tab of the Options dialog box, accessible through the Tools menu).

You enter a formula in Excel by typing an equals operator (=) followed by the expression that contains the elements and operators the formula uses. For example, the following formula in cell A1 can be used to add two integers:

```
=1+2
```

When entered in a cell, this formula displays "3" when the value layer is active or "=1+2" when the formula layer is active. You can reference another cell in a formula by using either A1 or R1C1 notation, depending on the state of Excel. By default, you enter formulas in cells using A1 notation. For example, a formula that multiplies the value in cell B3 by 10 appears as follows:

```
=B3*10
```

To set Excel to accept formulas in R1C1 notation, choose the Options command from the Tools menu, and then select R1C1 Reference Style in the Settings section of the General tab. Doing so is equivalent to setting the ReferenceStyle property of the Application object to xlR1C1. (Use the constant xlA1 to specify A1 notation.) The same formula that multiplies the value in cell B3 by 10 appears as follows if entered in R1C1 notation:

```
=R3C2*10
```

TIP You can tell at a glance which form of notation is being used by looking at the column headings. Column headings are letters when A1 notation is in effect and numbers when R1C1 notation is in effect.

Relative references in A1 notation

Formulas entered in A1 or R1C1 notation behave differently when copied to other cells on the worksheet. For example, set Excel to A1 notation, and enter the following formula in cell B1:

```
=A1+100
```

If you now select cell B1, choose the Copy command from the Edit menu (or press Ctrl-C), select cell C1, and choose the Paste command from the Edit menu (or press Ctrl-V) to paste the formula, the formula appears in cell C1 as shown below:

```
=B1+100
```

When you paste the A1-style formula to another cell, the formula is copied with a relative reference—that is, the new formula in C1 makes a reference to B1 and not to A1.

Absolute references in A1 notation

To copy the formula with an absolute reference, you must preface both the letter and the numeric parts of the cell reference with a dollar sign ($) when you enter the formula.

> **TIP** You can press the F4 key on your keyboard while entering a relative cell reference in A1 notation to change it automatically to an absolute reference.

Delete the formulas entered in cells B1 and C1. Now enter the following formula in cell B1:

```
=$A$1+100
```

Again, copy the formula in cell B1, and paste it to cell C1. The formula in cell C1 now appears as follows:

```
=$A$1+100
```

Because the A1-style reference included dollar signs before both the letter and the numeric references, the formula was copied to cell C1 with an absolute reference to cell A1.

Relative and absolute references in R1C1 notation

R1C1-style formulas are always copied exactly as they are entered. For example, set Excel to R1C1 notation, and enter the following formula in cell B1:

```
=R1C1+100
```

This is an absolute reference. If you copy and paste this formula from cell B1 to cell C1, the formula appears in cell C1 exactly as shown above.

With R1C1 notation, you can also enter formulas that use relative referencing. You specify a relative row or column reference by entering the row or column number offset in brackets. For example, the following formula, when entered in a cell, takes the value from the cell three rows down and one column to the right and divides it by 5:

```
=R[3]C[1]/5
```

Reset Excel to A1 notation for the examples in the next section.

Entering formulas that reference other worksheets and workbooks

A formula can reference a cell that's on a different worksheet or in a different workbook. For example, the following formula takes whatever value is in range A1 on worksheet Sheet2 and multiplies it by 10:

```
=Sheet2!A1*10
```

In a formula, when you reference a range that is on a different worksheet, always specify the name of the worksheet followed by an exclamation point (!) before you specify the range address. You can also use what is known as a "3D reference" in Excel. For example, the following formula uses the SUM function to sum all the values that appear in the range A4 on all worksheets between Sheet2 and Sheet4:

```
=SUM(Sheet2:Sheet4!A4)
```

To reference a range that is in another workbook, you enclose the name of the workbook in brackets ([]) before the reference to the sheet name. For example, the following formula references the range A1 on worksheet Sheet1 in workbook BOOK2.XLS:

```
=[BOOK2.XLS]Sheet1!$A$1
```

NOTE   If the workbook name contains non-alphanumeric characters (such as the hyphen in CHAP08-1.XLS), you must enclose the workbook and sheet name in single quotation marks as follows:

```
='[CHAP08-1.XLS]Sheet3'!D10
```

When you first open a workbook that contains a formula that references a range in another workbook not currently open, Excel displays a message to explain that the workbook contains a formula that is linked to another workbook and asks the user whether the link should be updated. If the user chooses Yes, Excel updates the link to the formula without actually opening the workbook to which the formula is linked.

Entering formulas using VBA

To enter an A1-style formula in a cell through VBA, you set the Formula property of the Range object to a string that represents the formula. Proc01 sets the Formula property of cells B1 and C1. The formula in B1 makes a relative reference to A1, and the formula in C1 makes an absolute reference to A1.

```
Sub Chap08aProc01_EnterA1Formula()
    With Worksheets(1)
        .Select
        .Range("A1").Value = 100
        .Range("B1").Formula = "=A1+100"
        .Range("C1").Formula = "=$A$1+200"
    End With
End Sub
```

Range has another property, named FormulaR1C1, that allows you to enter formulas in R1C1 notation. Even if the formula reference style is set to A1, you can still use the FormulaR1C1 property to enter formulas in R1C1 notation; Excel converts the formulas to A1 notation automatically before entering them in cells. Likewise, even if the formula reference style is set to R1C1, you can still use the Formula property to enter formulas in A1 notation. Proc02 provides an example of setting the FormulaR1C1 properties of cells B2 and C2 to formulas in R1C1 notation:

```
Sub Chap08aProc02_EnterR1C1Formula()
    With Worksheets(1)
        .Select
        .Range("A2").Value = 200
        .Range("B2").FormulaR1C1 = "=R2C1+200"
        .Range("C2").FormulaR1C1 = "=RC[-2]+400"
    End With
End Sub
```

Array formulas

Array formulas are considered to be among Excel's most powerful worksheet features. They allow you to easily enter formulas that perform numeric calculations on columns or rows of data. You write an array formula in the same manner as you do a standard formula; however, after you type the formula, you hold down the Ctrl and Shift keys on your keyboard as you press the Enter key. For example, enter the values *1*, *2*, and *3* in cells A4, A5, and A6 on the worksheet. Next select the range B4:B6. Then enter the following formula, holding down the Ctrl and Shift keys as you press Enter:

```
=A4:A6
```

The values 1, 2, and 3 are now displayed in cells B4:B6. If you display the formula bar and select one of the cells in the range B4:B6, you see the formula shown here:

```
={A4:A6}
```

The curly brackets indicate that this is an array formula. The following screen displays the value layer of the worksheet that contains the above array formula:

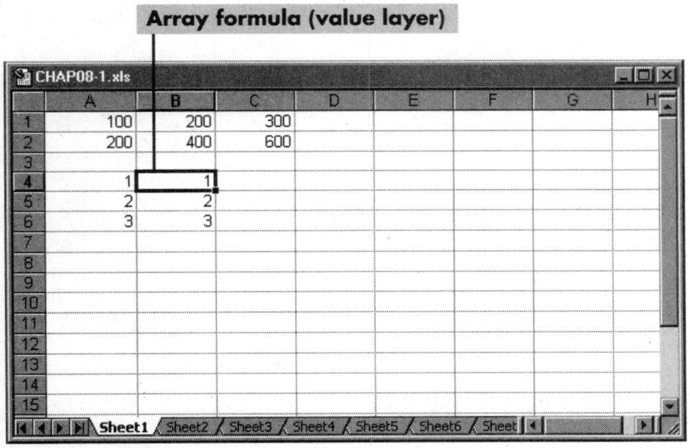

Array formula (value layer)

This screen displays the formula layer of the same worksheet:

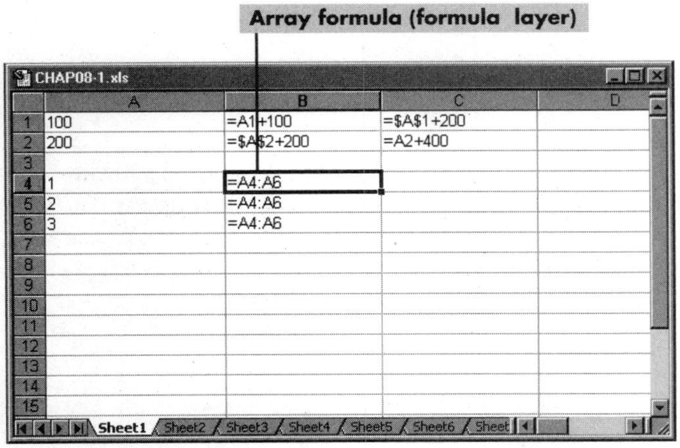

Array formula (formula layer)

Note that you were able to enter this single array formula in three cells, yet you had to type and enter the formula only once. If you try to delete the formula from a single cell, Excel generates an error message; when you delete an array formula, you must delete it from all cells that contain it. Therefore, to delete the formula entered in cells B4:B6 on the previous page, you would have to select cells B4:B6 and then press the Del key (don't delete it now, though).

Let's take the array formula a step further. On the same worksheet, select cells C4:C6. Then enter the following formula, again holding down the Ctrl and Shift keys as you press Enter:

```
=A4:A6*B4:B6
```

In cells C4:C6, you now see the result of multiplying each of the corresponding values in cells A4:A6 and B4:B6. The following example displays the result:

Array formula

Entering array formulas using VBA

Array formulas are extremely powerful in calculating complicated formulas that involve large segments of data. You enter array formulas through VBA using the FormulaArray property of the Range object. Proc03 sets the FormulaArray property of the range C10 on Sheet15.

```
Sub Chap08aProc03_EnterArrayFormula()
    With Worksheets("Sheet15")
        .Select
        .Range("C10").FormulaArray = "=SUM(C4:C8*D4:D8)"
```

```
    End With
    MsgBox "Array formula entered in range C10"
    Range("C10").ShowPrecedents
End Sub
```

> **NOTE**
>
> You might want to analyze the worksheet after this routine runs to be sure you understand what the entered array formula does on the worksheet. The formula calculates a weighted average for a range of cells containing grades. Since we are using an array formula, the entire calculation and result can be entered into a single cell. The array formula "=SUM(C4:C8:*D4:D8)" multiplies each grade by its weight individually, then each result is summed together to produce a final result.

Precedents and dependents

The Range object has two powerful methods that can be used to trace formulas on a worksheet: ShowPrecedents and ShowDependents. When you call either of these methods on a range, blue tracer arrows are displayed on the worksheet to identify to which cells the range is linked. If the ShowPrecedents method is called, tracer arrows are displayed that connect the specified range to the source cells for the formula in the range (this is demonstrated in Proc03). If the ShowDependents method is called, tracer arrows are displayed that connect the specified range to cells that contain formulas that reference the specified range.

The Range object also has a method named ShowErrors that draws red tracer arrows to any precedent cells that contain error values. In addition, Range has properties named Dependents, DirectDependents, Precedents, and DirectPrecedents, all of which are useful in tracing formulas. For more information about these properties and methods, see Excel's online VBA Help.

> **NOTE**
>
> Don't confuse an Excel worksheet array formula with a VBA array. An array formula is an actual formula that you use to perform calculations on rows and columns of cells. As explained in Chapter 2, however, an array is an *n*-dimensional grouping of values that are all of the same data type. If your goal is to enter a two-dimensional VBA array in a range on the worksheet, it is not necessary to use the FormulaArray property; you can use the Value property. (See the "FYI" on the next page.)

FYI

Exchanging Data Between VBA Arrays and Worksheet Ranges

You can assign a VBA array directly to a worksheet range without looping through each element of the array by setting the Value property of the range to equal the array. Likewise, you can easily transfer data from a range directly into a VBA array by setting the array to equal the Value property of the range. Be aware that when you are transferring data from an array to a range, the array can be either a VBA array declared as a specific data type or a variant variable holding an array. However, when you are transferring data from a range to a VBA array, the array must always be a variant variable. (Excel creates the array when the assignment statement is made.) Using VBA arrays provides a high level of performance in transferring large blocks of data between VBA and a range. You can assign a portion of an array to a range. The portion of the array that you assign to the range is governed by the size of the range to which the array is assigned. For example, if you assign a 10 × 10 array to a 5 × 5 range, only the intersection of the first five columns and the first five rows of the array will be assigned to the specified range. Proc04 below provides an example of transferring data between a VBA array and a range:

```
Sub Chap08aProc04_EnterArray()
    Dim Array1(50, 50) As Integer
    Dim Array2 As Variant
    Dim x As Integer
    Dim y As Integer
    For x = 1 To 50
        For y = 1 To 50
            Array1(x, y) = x * y
        Next
    Next
    Worksheets(1).Select
    Range("A9").CurrentRegion.ClearContents
    With Range(Cells(9, 1), Cells(58, 50))
        .Value = Array1
        Msgbox "Entire array entered in range " & _
            .Address & "."
    End With
    Array2 = Range("A9").CurrentRegion.Value
    MsgBox "Data transferred out of range to " & _
        UBound(Array2, 1) & " by " & UBound(Array2, 2) & _
        " array contained in a variant variable."
    Range("F3").CurrentRegion.ClearContents
    With Range("F3:H7")
        .Value = Array2
        MsgBox "Partial array entered in range " & _
            .Address & "."
    End With
End Sub
```

Worksheet Functions

Worksheet functions are predefined formulas that can be entered in a cell in order to perform a calculation. Excel's 200-plus built-in functions fall into these categories:

- Database and list management
- Date and time
- Financial
- Information
- Logical
- Lookup and reference
- Math and trigonometry
- Statistical
- Text

Excel's Analysis ToolPak also provides several advanced statistical and engineering functions. To access the Analysis ToolPak, select Add-Ins from the Tools menu, click the Analysis ToolPak checkbox in the Add-Ins dialog box, and click OK. You can see a list of all of the functions in Excel's online Help under Analysis ToolPak.

Let's take a look at a few examples of functions. Perhaps the most commonly used function in Excel is SUM, which is used to sum a range of cells. On the second worksheet of the CHAP08-1.XLS file, try entering the values *10*, *20*, and *30* in the range A1:A3. Then, in the range A4, enter the following formula:

```
=SUM(A1:A3)
```

Here is the resulting worksheet:

Other functions can be entered in cell A4 in a similar manner. For example, entering the following function returns the average of the value in the range A1:A3, which evaluates to 20:

```
=AVERAGE(A1:A3)
```

And entering the following function returns the maximum of A1:A3, which is 30:

```
=MAX(A1:A3)
```

As you can see, functions are entered as formulas. It's even possible to combine multiple functions in a formula. For example, the following formula adds the average of A1:A3 to the sum of A1:A3 and returns a value of 80:

```
=SUM(A1:A3)+AVERAGE(A1:A3)
```

Any combination of functions can be incorporated in a range formula. Note that functions usually take arguments, and some functions take multiple arguments. It's even possible to embed some functions within others. For example, the following IF function returns one of two text strings; which one it returns depends on the average of the test range being evaluated in the test condition. The first text string is returned if the test condition evaluates to True, and the second text string is returned if the condition evaluates to False:

```
=IF(AVERAGE(A1:A3)>10,"High Average","Low Average")
```

The NPV (Net Present Value) function, which is a bit more complicated, is often used by financial institutions to calculate the present value of a future stream of cash flow. The first argument of NPV is the interest rate that will be applied to the cash flow, and the second through thirtieth arguments (which can be represented by a worksheet range) are periodic payments that form the cash flow. Assuming the values 10, 20, and 30 still exist in the range A1:A3 on the second worksheet, you can enter in A4 the following formula, which uses the NPV function to determine what the present value would be of payments corresponding to 10, 20, and 30 dollars when discounted at an interest rate of 10 percent. This NPV function evaluates to $48.16:

```
=NPV(10%,A1:A3)
```

> **TIP** The Function Wizard offers the easiest way to enter functions in a worksheet. To activate the Function Wizard, choose the Function command from the Insert menu. In the Function Wizard, you can view all of the functions available in Excel and then step through the process of entering a function in the worksheet.

Worksheet database functions

Excel has a set of database functions that you can use to query sets of data in a worksheet. When you are working with small databases, it is often best to store those databases directly on a worksheet and then to use Excel's worksheet database functions to query the data. Excel has 13 database functions in all; all but one begin with the letter "D." For example, the DSUM function takes three arguments: a range that represents a database, a range that contains a field name, and a range that contains a set of criteria. DSUM sums the values in the specified field for all of the records that match the specified criteria. Sheet3 of the CHAP08-1.XLS file contains an eight-record, four-column worksheet database, and a table that contains several database functions that calculate information from the database. Here are the table and the database:

CHAP08-1.xls

	A	B	C	D
1		State	State	State
2		CA	NY	MA
3	DSum	$27,029,022	$4,676,299	$2,281,968
4	DAverage	$5,405,804	$2,338,150	$2,281,968
5	DCount	5	2	1
6	DMax	$9,499,972	$3,328,998	$2,281,968
7	DMin	$2,645,833	$1,347,301	$2,281,968
8				
9	Customer Name	City	State	Sales
10	Atlanta Shipping	Los Angeles	CA	$4,078,050
11	Northgate Systems	San Francisco	CA	$2,645,833
12	American Freight	Los Angeles	CA	$6,845,268
13	Westin-Reed	San Diego	CA	$9,499,972
14	West-Coast Air	New York	NY	$1,347,301
15	National Crane	Los Angeles	CA	$3,959,899
16	SalTec	Boston	MA	$2,281,968
17	Western Systems	New York	NY	$3,328,998

Sheet1 / Sheet2 \ **Sheet3** / Sheet4 / Sheet5 / Sheet6 / Sheet7

The table's five rows contain the DSUM, DAVERAGE, DCOUNT, DMAX, and DMIN functions, which calculate the values shown in the table for the states of California, New York, and Massachusetts. Here is the same worksheet with the formula layer activated, which allows the user to view the database functions; visible in the example are those for the state of California:

CHAP08-1.xls

	A	B
1		
2		
3	DSum	=DSUM(Database,$D$9,B$1:B$2)
4	DAverage	=DAVERAGE(Database,$D$9,B$1:B$2)
5	DCount	=DCOUNT(Database,$D$9,B$1:B$2)
6	DMax	=DMAX(Database,$D$9,B$1:B$2)
7	DMin	=DMIN(Database,$D$9,B$1:B$2)
8		
9	Customer Name	City
10	Atlanta Shipping	Los Angeles
11	Northgate Systems	San Francisco
12	American Freight	Los Angeles
13	Westin-Reed	San Diego
14	West-Coast Air	New York
15	National Crane	Los Angeles
16	SalTec	Boston
17	Western Systems	New York

Sheet1 / Sheet2 \ **Sheet3** / Sheet4 / Sheet5 / Sheet6 / Sheet7

The worksheet on the preceding page shows how five of the worksheet data-base functions can be entered and used to query a worksheet database. The DSUM function for California, for example, appears as follows:

```
=DSUM(Database,$D$9,B$1:B$2)
```

The first argument, Database, is actually the name of the range on the worksheet that contains the data—the range A9:D17. The second argument is the field to be summed; in this case, $D$9 corresponds to the Sales field. And the last argument is the criteria to be used to determine which records are to be summed; the range reference is to B$1:B$2. Range B1 contains the string State, while range B2 contains the string CA, both of which are combined into a criteria statement of State = CA.

The worksheet Sheet1 in the CHAP08-2.XLS file contains an interesting example of using a worksheet database; the next screen example displays that worksheet. The example uses various on-sheet control objects to change the values used by DSUM functions to query a worksheet database, and no VBA code whatso-ever lies behind the functionality of the interface, which is driven entirely by worksheet formulas and functions. You might want to take a close look at the various formulas and functions used in CHAP08-2.XLS to be sure you under-stand how they work. All the controls on the worksheet are linked to worksheet ranges; when the values of the controls change, the values of the ranges to which they are linked change as well, causing Excel to recalculate the linked formu-las on the sheet and to update the numbers in the table.

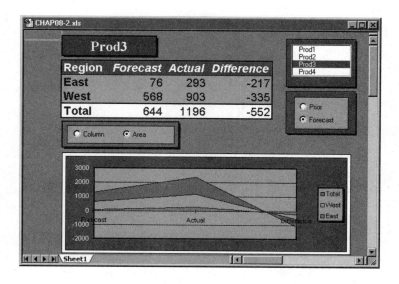

TIP You can link a control to a cell on a worksheet by viewing its Properties window, which can be displayed by clicking the Properties button on the Control Toolbox toolbar. The LinkedCell and ListFillRange properties (for listboxes and comboboxes) are used to establish the link via a cell reference or range name.

Note that by using the two optionbuttons labeled "Column" and "Area," you can change the chart that is displayed in the lower portion of the worksheet. The link between the optionbuttons and the chart was accomplished not with VBA code but with Excel's Camera tool and a named formula. To use the Camera tool, you must add the Camera button to a commandbar. The Camera button is in the Tools category of the Commands tab of the Tools Customize dialog box. Using the Camera tool you can place a picture object on the worksheet, and then write a formula to link the picture to one of the two charts based on which optionbutton is clicked. To view the formula used to link the picture created with the Camera button to the charts, choose the Name command from the Insert menu, and then select Define. In the Define Name dialog box, select the change-chart entry in the listbox; the formula is displayed in the Refers To edit box. (Named formulas are explained in the section titled "Named formulas," beginning on page 20.)

For more detailed information about worksheet database functions, see Excel's online Help.

Entering functions using VBA

You can enter functions through VBA by setting either the Formula or the FormulaR1C1 property of the Range object. Proc05 enters in the range A1:A5 on Sheet4 formulas that use the INT() and RAND() functions to generate five random integers from 0 through 999. The routine then calculates the sum, average, count, maximum, minimum, median, variance, and standard deviation for those five random integers. Finally, Proc05 calls the Calculate method on the worksheet 10 times to recalculate the worksheet and to show that the values returned by the functions are updated every time the random integers that feed into the functions change. A Do-While loop pauses the routine for one second after each recalculation so that you can see the results.

```
Sub Chap08aProc05_EnterFunctions()
    Dim x As Integer
    Dim oldCalc As Integer
    Dim time As Single
    Worksheets("Sheet4").Select
    Range("A1").CurrentRegion.ClearContents
```

(continued)

continued

```
        oldCalc = Application.Calculation
        Application.Calculation = xlManual
        For x = 1 To 5
            Range("A" & x).Formula = "=INT(1000*RAND())"
        Next
        Range("A6").Value = "Sum:"
        Range("B6").Formula = "=SUM(A1:A5)"
        MsgBox "=SUM(A1:A5)"
        Range("A7").Value = "Average:"
        Range("B7").Formula = "=AVERAGE(A1:A5)"
        MsgBox "=AVERAGE(A1:A5)"
        Range("A8").Value = "Count:"
        Range("B8").Formula = "=COUNT(A1:A5)"
        MsgBox "=COUNT(A1:A5)"
        Range("A9").Value = "Max:"
        Range("B9").Formula = "=MAX(A1:A5)"
        MsgBox "=MAX(A1:A5)"
        Range("A10").Value = "Min:"
        Range("B10").Formula = "=MIN(A1:A5)"
        MsgBox "=MIN(A1:A5)"
        Range("A11").Value = "Median:"
        Range("B11").Formula = "=MEDIAN(A1:A5)"
        MsgBox "=MEDIAN(A1:A5)"
        Range("A12").Value = "Variance:"
        Range("B12").Formula = "=VAR(A1:A5)"
        MsgBox "=VAR(A1:A5)"
        Range("A13").Value = "Standard Deviation:"
        Range("B13").Formula = "=STDEV(A1:A5)"
        MsgBox "=STDEV(A1:A5)"
        Range("A1").CurrentRegion.Columns.AutoFit
        MsgBox "The worksheet will now be recalculated 10 times."
        For x = 1 To 10
            Worksheets(4).Calculate
            time = Timer
            Do While Timer < time + 1
                DoEvents
            Loop
        Next
        Application.Calculation = oldCalc
End Sub
```

TIP
You can also call some of the built-in Excel worksheet functions directly from VBA without having to go through the worksheet. For example, certain worksheet functions can be called as methods on the WorksheetFunction object (which is contained within the Application object). Not all worksheet functions can be called in this manner, however; for a complete list of those worksheet functions that can be called on the WorksheetFunction object, use the Object Browser. See the Help topic "List of Worksheet Functions Available to Visual Basic" for more information. Proc06 provides examples of using Excel worksheet functions directly from VBA.

Proc06, which follows, uses several worksheet functions as well as a couple of built-in VBA functions. First the routine creates a five-element array of random integers using the built-in VBA functions Int and Rnd. Then it uses the SUM, AVERAGE, COUNT, MAX, MIN, MEDIAN, VAR, and STDEV worksheet functions to perform various calculations on the array values.

```
Sub Chap08aProc06_CallFunctions()
    Dim RndArray(5) As Integer
    Dim String1 As String
    Dim x As Integer
    For x = 1 To UBound(RndArray)
        RndArray(x) = Int((1000 * Rnd) + 1)
        String1 = String1 & RndArray(x)
        If x <> UBound(RndArray) Then
            String1 = String1 & ", "
        End If
    Next
    With Application.WorksheetFunction
        MsgBox "Numbers:   " & String1 & Chr(13) & Chr(13) & _
                "Sum:       " & .Sum(RndArray) & Chr(13) & _
                "Average:   " & .Average(RndArray) & Chr(13) & _
                "Count:     " & .Count(RndArray) & Chr(13) & _
                "Max:       " & .Max(RndArray) & Chr(13) & _
                "Min:       " & .Min(RndArray) & Chr(13) & _
                "Median:    " & .Median(RndArray) & Chr(13) & _
                "Variance:  " & .Var(RndArray) & Chr(13) & _
                "Standard Deviation: " & .StDev(RndArray)
    End With
End Sub
```

FYI

Creating Your Own Worksheet Functions Using VBA

You can call a VBA function directly from a formula in a range. For example, the following Factorial function can be used to calculate the factorial of a number, and you can call this function directly from a range formula, as shown in this example:

```
=Factorial(5)
```

Entering the above formula in a cell returns the factorial of 5. By writing your own VBA functions and using such functions in range formulas, you can greatly expand the calculation power of the Excel worksheet. Incidentally, the following function calculates factorials; however, Excel has a built-in worksheet function (FACT) that also performs this calculation.

```
Function Factorial(ByVal Int1 As Variant)
    Dim x As Integer
    Application.Volatile True
    Factorial = 1
    If (Not (IsNumeric(Int1)) Or Int(Int1) <> Int1 Or Int1 < 0) Then
        Factorial = "#NUM!"
    Else
        For x = 1 To Int1
            Factorial = Factorial * x
        Next
    End If
End Function
```

Keep in mind when using VBA functions in range formulas that, by default, a function is nonvolatile. That is, the function does not recalculate whenever the worksheet on which the function resides recalculates. It is possible, however, to make a function volatile so that the function recalculates whenever the worksheet on which the function resides recalculates; to do so, call the Volatile method on the Application object in the body of the function, and pass True for the method's only argument (as shown above). For more information about the Volatile method, see Excel's online VBA Help.

The Name Object

A Name object can refer either to a name of a range on a worksheet or to what is known as a "named formula" (or a "named constant"). Range names can exist on two levels: workbook-level range names and worksheet-level range names. No two ranges on the same worksheet can have the same name, although two ranges on different worksheets within a single workbook can have the same name. Before we look at the difference between workbook-level range names and worksheet-level range names, let's look at the process of defining a name for a range.

Defining a range name

Every range on a worksheet can be given a name. Ranges can be given names in one of two ways: via the Name drop-down listbox or via the Define Name dialog box.

■ Using the Name drop-down listbox: Select the range, type the name in the Name drop-down listbox located in the upper left corner of the worksheet, and then press Enter. Here you can see range A1 on worksheet Sheet5 being assigned the name Range1 via the Name drop-down listbox.

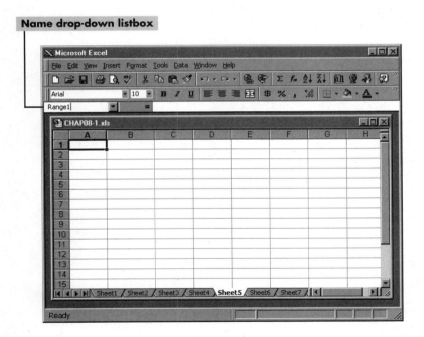

■ Using the Define Name dialog box: First select the range. Then choose the Name command from the Insert menu and select Define. In the Define Name dialog box, enter a name for the selected range as in the example on the following page—the name Range2 is being assigned to range A2 on worksheet Sheet5.

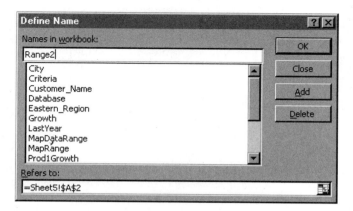

After you have specified a name for a range, you can refer to that range by using its name when calling the Range method. Proc07, for example, assigns the name Range3 to range A3 on the worksheet and then uses the name with the Range object to assign a value to the range and to display the value in a message box:

```
Sub Chap08aProc07_RangeName()
    Worksheets("Sheet5").Select
    Range("A3").Name = "Range3"
    Range("Range3").Value = 5
    MsgBox Range("Range3").Value
End Sub
```

You can also use range names in formulas that you enter directly in cells on the worksheet. For example, the following formula, when entered in any cell on worksheet Sheet5, returns the value of range A3:

```
=Range3
```

FYI

The Difference between Workbook-Level and Worksheet-Level Range Names

Excel makes a distinction between workbook-level and worksheet-level range names. At first this distinction might be a bit difficult to grasp, but one easy rule differentiates workbook-level from worksheet-level range names.

The first time a name is assigned to a range in a workbook, that name is a workbook-level name. Thereafter, each time that same name is assigned to ranges on different worksheets within the original workbook, the name is a worksheet-level name.

This may not make a whole lot of sense at first, but this rule does point to the one difference that distinguishes workbook-level names from worksheet-level names. For example, when you first assigned the name Range1 to range A1 on worksheet Sheet5, Range1 became a workbook-level name. If you now try to assign the name Range1 to range A1 on worksheet Sheet6, one of two things happens, depending on how you try to assign the name:

- If you try to assign the name using the Name drop-down listbox, Excel prevents you from doing so—as you type *Range1* and press Enter, Excel changes the focus to Range1 on Sheet5.

- If you try to assign the name using the Define Name dialog box or by setting the Name property of the range through VBA, Excel assigns the name Range1 to range A1 on Sheet6, replacing the original definition of Range1.

Because Range1 is a workbook-level name, it can reference only one range within the workbook.

To see how worksheet-level names work, let's return to the original scenario in which the name Range1 was assigned to range A1 on worksheet Sheet5. Now try going to worksheet Sheet6 and using the Define Name dialog box to give range A1 the name Sheet6!Range1, as shown here:

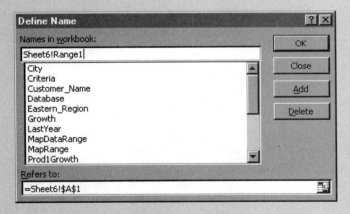

By assigning the name Sheet6!Range1 to range A1 on worksheet Sheet6, you have created a second instance of the name Range1 in the workbook; however, this second instance is actually a worksheet-level name. Proc08 assigns the name Range1 to range A1 on both worksheet Sheet5 and worksheet Sheet6, assigns a different value to each named range, and then activates a third worksheet and displays the two values using the workbook-level name (on Sheet5) and the worksheet-level name (on Sheet6).

(continued)

The Difference Between Workbook-Level and Worksheet-Level Range Names, *continued*

```
Sub Chap08aProc08_RangeName2()
    Worksheets("Sheet5").Select
    Range("A1").Name = "Range1"
    Range("Range1").Value = 5
    Worksheets("Sheet6").Select
    Range("A1").Name = "Sheet6!Range1"
    Range("Range1").Value = 6
    MsgBox Range("Range1").Value
End Sub
```

You can now use Range1 in the Name drop-down listbox or in VBA as an argument for the Range method in order to move directly to Sheet5!A1 from any worksheet except Sheet6. When Sheet6 is active, the Sheet6!A1 definition of Range1 is used.

The Names collection can be accessed through both the Workbook object and the Worksheet object as well. Using the Names collection on the Worksheet object, you can access a collection of worksheet-level names specific to a particular worksheet. Note, however, that the Names collection for a worksheet does not contain workbook-level names that are defined on the particular sheet—such names must be accessed through the Names collection of the Workbook object.

Named formulas

A named formula is actually a name that refers to a particular formula. You can assign a name to a formula in the Define Name dialog box. In the following illustration, a formula named LastYear is being entered and assigned the formula=YEAR(NOW())-1.

Named formula

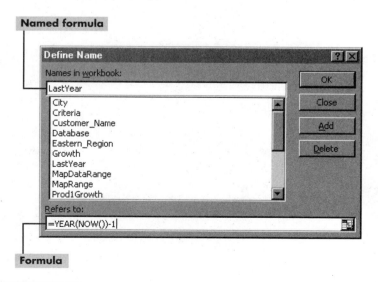

Formula

What does this named formula called LastYear do? Let's step through it. The NOW function returns the current date, and the YEAR function converts the date to a year; YEAR and NOW are combined and then 1 is subtracted. So you have a formula that can be used in a cell to return the previous year—thus, the name LastYear.

You should use named formulas when you want to repeat the same formula in many cells. Named formulas are useful in such situations for two reasons:

- The formula is easy to edit: you only have to edit the formula once to make changes to all cells on the worksheet with that formula.

- A named formula takes up less memory: only one copy of the formula is stored in memory as opposed to multiple copies that might be stored in memory when the formula is entered separately into individual cells on the worksheet.

Name properties and methods

The Names collection contained in the Workbook object is used to refer to all workbook-level and worksheet-level range names as well as to all named formulas. Each of these types of names can be referenced as a Name object. Below are some of the properties of the Name object that you should be familiar with:

Name	Actual text string of the name.
RefersTo	If a range name, range address to which the name refers; if a named formula, formula to which the name refers.
RefersToR1C1	Name reference in R1C1 notation.
Visible	Boolean value. If set to False, the name is hidden from view in the Define Name dialog box and Name drop-down listbox. This property can only be set programmatically.

The Name object also has one method—Delete—which can be used to delete a name from a workbook. Also, you can add a name to a workbook in VBA by calling the Add method on the Names collection. Proc09, which follows, uses a For-Each-Next loop on the Names collection to display (in a series of message boxes) the Name and RefersTo properties of all names in the workbook.

```
Sub Chap08aProc09_DisplayNames()
    Dim String1 As String
    Dim x As Variant
    For Each x In ActiveWorkbook.Names
        String1 = String1 & x.Name & ", " & x.RefersTo & Chr(13)
```

(continued)

continued

```
        If Len(String1) > 220 Then
            MsgBox String1
            String1 = ""
        End If
    Next
    If String1 <> "" Then
        MsgBox String1
    End If
End Sub
```

Here is the first of the resulting message boxes:

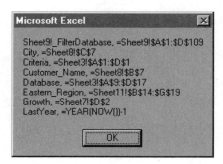

```
Microsoft Excel                    [X]

Sheet9!_FilterDatabase, =Sheet9!$A$1:$D$109
City, =Sheet8!$C$7
Criteria, =Sheet3!$A$1:$D$1
Customer_Name, =Sheet8!$B$7
Database, =Sheet3!$A$9:$D$17
Eastern_Region, =Sheet11!$B$14:$G$19
Growth, =Sheet7!$D$2
LastYear, =YEAR(NOW())-1

                [  OK  ]
```

NOTE You can create named formulas programmatically using the Add method of the Names collection. You can create named formulas that will appear in different categories in the Excel Function Wizard when you create a name with the Add method by passing appropriate values for the macroType and category arguments, allowing the user to add the formulas easily and directly to a worksheet.

Excel's Calculation Setting

To use formulas—and any functions and names they contain—effectively, you need to understand how formulas are calculated. Excel calculates formulas in three different modes:

- **Automatic:** Every time a value, formula, or name is changed, all dependent formulas in a workbook are automatically recalculated.

- **Semiautomatic:** Every time a value, formula, or name is changed, all dependent formulas—except those in data tables—are automatically recalculated. (This book does not include a discussion of data tables. For information about data tables, see Excel's online Help.)

- **Manual:** No formulas are calculated until one of the following occurs:

  - The user presses the F9 key.

  - The user clicks Calc Now on the Calculation tab in the Options dialog box.

  - The Calculate method is called from a VBA Routine. The Calculate method can be called on the Application object to calculate all formulas in all open workbooks or on the Worksheet object to calculate formulas only on a given worksheet. The Range object also has a Calculate method for calculating formulas in a specific range.

You can change the mode of Excel's calculation by setting the Calculation property of the Application object. The Calculation property can take one of three values—xlAutomatic, xlSemiautomatic, or xlManual—which correspond to Excel's three modes of calculating.

> **TIP**
> The Application object has a CalculateBeforeSave property that, if True, forces calculation on a workbook before it is saved on disk.

> **NOTE**
> If you attempt to set the Calculation property when no workbook is open or visible, a run-time error will occur. This can be an issue when your code is delivered as an add-in, which is a hidden workbook containing your application. Always make sure a workbook is visible before setting the Calculation property.

Hiding and Protecting Worksheets and Workbooks

By hiding and protecting worksheets and workbooks, you can greatly limit the user's access to the components of your Excel application. Most professional Excel applications use hiding and protecting features extensively.

Hiding Worksheets

To hide a worksheet manually, you simply choose the Sheet command from the Format menu and then select Hide. To unhide a worksheet, you choose the Sheet command from the Format menu and then select Unhide. In the Unhide dialog box on the following page, you select the worksheet you want to unhide and then click OK.

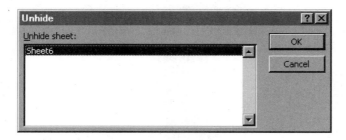

You control a worksheet's visibility in VBA through the Visible property of the Worksheet object. The Visible property can have one of three values:

True	The worksheet is visible.
False	The worksheet is not visible.
xlVeryHidden	The worksheet is not visible, and the user cannot make the worksheet visible again by using the Unhide dialog box. That is, if Visible is xlVeryHidden, Visible can be set back to True only through a VBA routine.

Hiding Workbooks

Manually hiding and unhiding a workbook is similar to hiding and unhiding a worksheet, except that you choose the Hide or Unhide command from the Window menu. To hide a workbook through VBA, you must set the Visible property of all windows in the workbook's Windows collection to False. A Window object's Visible property can be set only to True or False; it cannot be set to xlVeryHidden.

Protecting Worksheets, Charts, and Workbooks

You can protect worksheets, charts, and workbooks. A worksheet can have different levels of protection; at the highest level of protection, no data can be entered in any locked cells, no drawingobjects on the worksheet can be moved or resized, and no scenarios can be changed. (The next section discusses scenarios.) You can implement worksheet protection on a lower level, however, through some combination of protecting cell contents, drawingobjects, and scenarios. You can also take advantage of user-interface–only protection (through the Protect method), in which worksheets and charts are protected from actions taken by the user but not from actions executed through VBA code. To protect a worksheet manually, choose the Protection command from the Tools menu, and then select Protect Sheet. Next you select the appropriate level of protection in the Protect Sheet dialog box and, if you want, also enter a password:

You can use the VBA Protect method to protect a worksheet or chart. Protect takes the following arguments:

password	This is the password used to protect the sheet.
drawingObjects	If True, Shape objects on the sheet are protected.
contents	If True for a worksheet, contents of locked cells are protected; if True for a chart, the whole chart is protected.
scenarios	If True, the scenarios on the worksheet are protected (worksheets only).
userInterfaceOnly	This argument was introduced in Excel 95. If True, the sheet is protected against user actions; however, the sheet is not protected against actions executed from VBA code. If False, the sheet is protected from both user and VBA actions.

You can unprotect a worksheet or chart through VBA by calling the Unprotect method on the Worksheet or Chart object. Unprotect takes one argument—password.

You protect an entire workbook in much the same way as you protect a worksheet. Two aspects of a workbook can be protected—its structure and its windows. The structure of the workbook refers to the ordering of its worksheets, whereas the windows of the workbook refer to the number, size, and placement of workbook windows that are open at the time the workbook is protected. You protect a workbook manually by choosing the Protection command from the Tools menu, selecting Protect Workbook, and in the Protect Workbook dialog box setting the protection level and the password. You protect a workbook through VBA by calling the Protect method on the Workbook object. For the Workbook object, Protect takes the three arguments on the following page.

password	The password used to protect the workbook.
structure	If True, the structure of the workbook is protected.
windows	If True, the windows of the workbook are protected.

The Unprotect method can be called on the Workbook object to unprotect a workbook. As it does with a worksheet, Unprotect takes one argument—password.

F Y I

User-Interface–Only Protection

By passing True for the userInterfaceOnly argument when calling the Protect method on a sheet (worksheet or chart), you can protect the interface from user actions while keeping the interface unprotected from actions taken by VBA code. This provides a tremendous benefit for VBA routines that act on protected sheets. In the past, such routines would have to continually unprotect and protect sheets in a workbook in order to carry out programmatic actions on protected sheets. Excel 97 has three additional properties to fine-tune protection of Worksheet objects against user actions:

EnableAutoFilter: If True, and if user-interface–only protection is implemented, AutoFilter drop-down listboxes are unprotected after the Protect method is called. This allows the user to make use of AutoFilter drop-down listboxes without having to unprotect the sheet. If False, AutoFilter drop-down listboxes are protected.

EnableOutlining: If True, and if user-interface–only protection is implemented, outlining symbols are unprotected after the Protect method is called. This allows the user to expand and contract outline displays without having to unprotect the sheet. If False, outlining symbols are protected.

EnablePivotTable: If True, and if user-interface–only protection is implemented, any pivottables on the worksheet are unprotected after the Protect method is called. This allows the user to fully manipulate a pivottable on a protected worksheet.

NOTE

When you protect the structure of a workbook, the user cannot add new sheets to the workbook. If the user double-clicks in the body of a pivottable in a workbook for which the structure has been protected, an error message will be displayed indicating that the workbook is protected. (Double-clicking in the body of a pivottable normally causes Excel to add a new worksheet that displays the underlying records that make up the pivotitem corresponding to the double-click.) To keep such an error message from being displayed when a user double-clicks, write an event handler routine for the BeforeDoubleClick event of the Worksheet object and include the line "Cancel = True". In this manner, you can have your own error message displayed or no error message at all displayed.

The Scenario Object

By using the Scenario object, you can store multiple values in a single cell. Each unique value in a cell—or each unique group of values for a set of cells—is known as a scenario. The Worksheet object contains the Scenarios collection, which is made up of all the Scenario objects that exist on the worksheet. Scenarios are useful in workgroup applications that allow various people to enter different assumptions for values in a spreadsheet. To add a scenario manually, choose the Scenarios command from the Tools menu, click Add, and fill in the Add Scenario dialog box. In VBA, you can add a scenario to a worksheet by calling the Add method on the Scenarios collection object. The Add method takes the arguments shown here:

name	A text string that represents the name of the scenario
changingCells	A range that specifies the cells to which the scenario applies
values	A single value or an array of values to be applied to the changing cells
comment	A text string that represents a comment to be stored with the scenario
locked	If True and protection for scenarios is turned on for the worksheet, scenario is locked so that changes cannot be made to it
hidden	If True and protection for scenarios is turned on for the worksheet, scenario is hidden and cannot be viewed

After you add a scenario to a worksheet, you can display the results of the scenario by calling the Show method on the Scenario object. Proc10, which follows, adds three scenarios that correspond to the cell named Growth on the seventh worksheet. After adding all three scenarios, Proc10 displays the results of the scenarios by calling the Show method three times:

```
Sub Chap08aProc10_AddScenarios()
    Dim objScenario As Scenario
    With Worksheets("Sheet7")
```

(continued)

continued

```
        .Select
        For Each objScenario In .Scenarios
            objScenario.Delete
        Next objScenario
        .Scenarios.Add Name:="Worst Case", _
                    ChangingCells:=Range("Growth"), _
                    Values:=0.8
        .Scenarios.Add Name:="Likely Case", _
                    ChangingCells:=Range("Growth"), _
                    Values:=1.1
        .Scenarios.Add Name:="Best Case", _
                    ChangingCells:=Range("Growth"), _
                    Values:=1.5
        .Scenarios("Worst Case").Show
        MsgBox "Worst Case scenario."
        .Scenarios("Likely Case").Show
        MsgBox "Likely Case scenario."
        .Scenarios("Best Case").Show
        MsgBox "Best Case scenario."
    End With
End Sub
```

Here is the result of calling the Show method on the Best Case scenario:

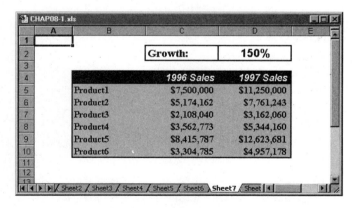

The GoalSeek, Sort, Subtotal, AutoFilter, and Consolidate Methods

The Range object has five methods that offer great power when dealing with data—GoalSeek, Sort, Subtotal, AutoFilter, and Consolidate. The names of these methods tell you the actions they perform:

GoalSeek	Adjusts the inputs to a formula until the formula evaluates to a specified value
Sort	Sorts data in a range based on up to three sort keys
Subtotal	Calculates subtotals for data in a range
AutoFilter	Turns on autofilter drop-down listboxes for data in a range, which can then be used to filter data
Consolidate	Combines data from multiple ranges on multiple worksheets in a single summary range

The following sections take a brief look at each of these methods.

The GoalSeek Method

The GoalSeek method of the Range object adjusts the inputs of a formula in the range until the formula evaluates to a desired goal. To use Excel's Goal Seek feature manually, choose the Goal Seek command from the Tools menu. In VBA, the GoalSeek method takes the following arguments:

| goal | Desired value that the formula will evaluate to |
| changingCell | Cell reference that specifies the input to be changed in the attempt to reach the goal |

Proc11, which follows, calls the GoalSeek method on the range Prod1Growth on worksheet Sheet7, which is the same worksheet used for the scenario example in Proc10. The call to the GoalSeek method in Proc11 adjusts the value in the range Growth until the value in the range Prod1Growth is equal to $75,000,000.

```
Sub Chap08aProc11_GoalSeek()
    Worksheets("Sheet7").Select
    Range("Growth") = 0
    Range("Prod1Growth").GoalSeek 75000000, Range("Growth")
End Sub
```

More advanced modeling and problem-solving functions are also available in the SOLVER.XLA add-in file shipped with Excel. SOLVER.XLA is discussed in Appendix H, "Programming with Solver," on the companion CD.

The Sort Method

Excel supports the sorting of data using up to three sort keys. To sort a range of data manually, choose the Sort command from the Data menu. To sort a range using VBA, call the Sort method on the range to be sorted. Sort takes the major arguments which appear on the following page.

key1	Range that corresponds to first sort key
order1	Sort order for first sort key; can be one of two values: xlAscending (data sorted in ascending order) xlDescending (data sorted in descending order)
key2	Range that corresponds to second sort key
order2	Sort order for second sort key—either xlAscending or xlDescending
key3	Range that corresponds to third sort key
order3	Sort order for third sort key—either xlAscending or xlDescending
header	Can be one of three values: xlYes (first row of data is header row; first row not sorted), xlNo (first row of data not header row; first row sorted), or xlGuess (Excel makes logical guess about whether first row of data is header row)
orderCustom	Integer that represents a custom sort order, which can be specified on Custom Lists tab of the Tools - Options dialog box
matchCase	If True, sort is case sensitive
orientation	Can be one of two values: xlTopToBottom (sort done by row) or xlLeftToRight (sort done by column)

Proc12, which follows, calls the Sort method twice on the range named Table1 on Sheet8. The first time Sort is called, the data in the table is sorted by State, City, and Customer Name. The second time Sort is called, the data is sorted in descending order based on Sales.

```
Sub Chap08aProc12_SortData()
    Worksheets("Sheet8").Select
    Range("Table1").Sort key1:=Range("State"), _
                         order1:=xlAscending, _
                         key2:=Range("City"), _
                         order2:=xlAscending, _
                         key3:=Range("Customer_Name"), _
                         order3:=xlAscending, _
                         header:=xlYes
    MsgBox "Data sorted by State, City, and Customer Name."
    Range("Table1").Sort key1:=Range("Sales"), _
                         order1:=xlDescending, _
                         header:=xlYes
    MsgBox "Data sorted in descending order by Sales."
End Sub
```

Here you see the result of the second call of the Sort method:

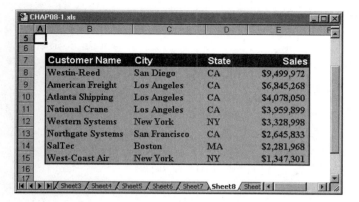

The Subtotal Method

The Subtotal method automatically inserts subtotals in a list of data based on changes in certain fields of the data. It's important that the data be sorted appropriately before the Subtotal method is called. Subtotal looks for changes in values in certain fields. If the data is not sorted before Subtotal is called, the data will not be grouped appropriately and Subtotal will not be able to calculate the true subtotals.

You can apply subtotals to a range of data manually by choosing the Subtotals command from the Data menu. In VBA, you call the Subtotal method on the Range object and pass values for the arguments shown here:

groupBy	Column number of field on which subtotal is to be implemented.
function	One of 11 functions to be used to calculate subtotal. (See Excel's online VBA Help for details.)
totalList	Array of integers that specifies column numbers of fields for which subtotals are to be calculated.
replace	If True, existing subtotals replaced.
pageBreaks	If True, page breaks inserted after each group for printing purposes.
summaryBelowData	If xlBelow, subtotal displayed below data; if xlAbove, subtotal displayed above data.

Proc13 calls the Subtotal method on a range of data on Sheet9. Subtotals are calculated for Product, Category, and Continent—and because False is passed for the replace argument, the subtotals are cumulative. As subtotals are calculated for the range, Excel implements outlining on the range for collapsing and expanding the display of data. Near the end of Proc13 the ShowLevels method is called on the Outline object, and 4 is passed as the rowLevels argument, which collapses the display of the outline to show the Product subtotals. The Outline object is used to control the display of various levels of detail of a range of data that contains totals and subtotals. We do not look at the Outline object in detail here; however, you can get more information about the Outline object in Excel's online VBA Help.

```
Sub Chap08aProc13_Subtotals()
    Worksheets("Sheet9").Select
    Range("A1").CurrentRegion.Subtotal groupBy:=1, _
                                       Function:=xlSum, _
                                       totalList:=4
    MsgBox "Continent subtotal"
    Range("A1").CurrentRegion.Subtotal groupBy:=2, _
                                       Function:=xlSum, _
                                       totalList:=4, _
                                       Replace:=False
    MsgBox "Category subtotal"
    Range("A1").CurrentRegion.Subtotal groupBy:=3, _
                                       Function:=xlSum, _
                                       totalList:=4, _
                                       Replace:=False
    MsgBox "Product subtotal"
    ActiveSheet.Outline.ShowLevels RowLevels:=4
    MsgBox "Outline level 4"
End Sub
```

Here is the result of Proc13:

You can remove subtotals from a range of data by calling the RemoveSubtotal method on the Range object. Here Proc14 removes the subtotals that were created in Proc13:

```
Sub Chap08aProc14_RemoveSubtotals()
    Worksheets("Sheet9").Select
    Range("A1").CurrentRegion.RemoveSubtotal
End Sub
```

The AutoFilter Method

Excel's AutoFilter method provides an easy way to query data on a worksheet. When the autofilter is activated, each column heading of a range-based data set is converted to a drop-down listbox that displays a list of unique values held by the respective field. By selecting a value from a drop-down listbox, you can query the list so that only those records that match the selected criteria are displayed.

You can activate the autofilter manually by choosing the Filter command from the Data menu and then selecting AutoFilter. In VBA, you call the AutoFilter method to toggle the autofilter on and off. Proc15, which follows, first checks the value of the AutoFilterMode property of the Worksheet object for Sheet9. If AutoFilterMode is False, Proc15 turns on the autofilter. It then makes the drop-down listbox invisible for the Revenue column by calling the AutoFilter method again with the following arguments:

field   Number that represents field whose drop-down listbox you want to hide or show

visibleDropDown   A Boolean value representing whether to show (True) or hide (False) the drop-down listbox

```
Sub Chap08aProc15_TurnOnAutoFilter()
    Worksheets("Sheet9").Select
    If ActiveSheet.AutoFilterMode = False Then
        Range("A1").AutoFilter
        Range("A1").AutoFilter field:=4, visibleDropDown:=False
    End If
End Sub
```

After the autofilter is turned on, the user can select unique values from the drop-down listboxes displayed in the field headings. The following example shows a worksheet data set with the autofilter turned on and the user about to apply a filter:

445

In VBA, the AutoFilter method can also be used to select values out of the autofilter drop-down listboxes after they have been activated. When you use the AutoFilter method in this way, you pass the following arguments:

field
: Number that represents field on which filtering is to be performed.

criteria1
: First criterion to be used to filter data.

operator
: Operator used to combine criteria1 and criteria2; operator argument can be one of two values—xlAnd or xlOr. If only one criterion is specified, operator can be used to control how many matching items are displayed (see the online VBA Help for details).

criteria2
: Second criterion to be used to filter data.

Proc16 calls the AutoFilter method to filter the third field (Product) so that only the records for the Titan1 product are displayed:

```
Sub Chap08aProc16_AutoFilter()
    Worksheets("Sheet9").Select
    If ActiveSheet.AutoFilterMode = False Then
        Range("A1").AutoFilter
    End If
    Range("A1").AutoFilter field:=3, criteria1:="Titan1"
End Sub
```

Here is the result of Proc16:

By calling the ShowAllData method on the Worksheet object, you can reset all the autofilter drop-down listboxes to All. To remove the autofilter drop-down listboxes, set the AutoFilterMode property to False by toggling the AutoFilter method of the Range object, as shown in Proc17:

```
Sub Chap08aProc17_TurnOffAutoFilter()
    Worksheets("Sheet9").Select
    If ActiveSheet.AutoFilterMode = True Then
        Range("A1").AutoFilter
    End If
End Sub
```

The Range object has another method, named AdvancedFilter, that provides a way to filter data based on a criteria range on a worksheet. With the Advanced-Filter method, you can copy the results of the filtering to a specified worksheet range. For more information about the AdvancedFilter method, refer to Excel's online VBA Help.

The Consolidate Method

The Consolidate method of the Range object can be used to consolidate data from multiple ranges on multiple worksheets, based on one of 11 functions. Consolidate is useful for totaling values in data tables that exist in different worksheets and is particularly powerful in the way that it combines data. It actually reads and interprets row and column headings and intelligently combines similar data from different worksheets. To consolidate data manually, choose the Consolidate command from the Data menu. When calling the Consolidate method in VBA, you pass the arguments shown here:

sources	Array of text strings specifying worksheet and range addresses in R1C1 notation for the sources of the consolidation.
Function	One of 11 functions that can be used to consolidate tables. (See the "Consolidate Method" topic in Excel's online VBA Help for details.)
topRow	If True, data consolidated based on matching column header titles in data sources.
leftColumn	If True, data consolidated based on matching row titles in left columns of consolidation ranges.
createLinks	If True, consolidation table linked to source data.

Proc18, on the following page, calls the Consolidate method on range B4 of Sheet12. In doing so, it specifies data ranges named Western_Region and Eastern_Region on Sheet10 and Sheet11. Take a look at Sheet10 and Sheet11 in the CHAP08-1.XLS file. You see two different tables at two different positions on the worksheet that will be used as the basis for the consolidation table that Proc18 creates on Sheet12. After creating the consolidation table, Proc18 calls the AutoFormat method to format the consolidation table with the xlClassic2 formatting style.

```
Sub Chap08aProc18_Consolidate()
    Worksheets("Sheet12").Select
    With Range("B4")
        .Consolidate sources:=Array("Sheet10!Western_Region", _
                            "Sheet11!Eastern_Region"), _
                    Function:=xlSum, _
                    topRow:=True, _
                    leftColumn:=True, _
                    createLinks:=True
        .AutoFormat format:=xlClassic2
    End With
End Sub
```

Here is the resulting consolidation table created by Proc18. You will notice that after creating the consolidation table, Excel implements outlining on the table automatically, allowing the user to expand and contract the data:

Range Navigating

Several properties and methods of the Application, Worksheet, and Range objects are useful in navigating and selecting ranges on a worksheet. They are listed here.

Column: Range property that references the first column of the range.

EntireColumn: Range property that references the entire column or columns that contain the specified range. For example, the EntireColumn property of Range("B2") returns a range that contains all the cells in column B.

Columns: Application, Worksheet, and Range method that returns a range representing the collection of columns in the given object. Use the syntax Columns.Count to determine the number of columns in the object.

Row: Range property that references the first row of the range.

EntireRow: Range property that references the entire row or rows that contain the specified range.

Rows: Application, Worksheet, and Range method that returns a range representing the collection of rows in the given object. Use the syntax Rows.Count to determine the number of rows in the object.

CurrentArray: Range property; if the specified range is part of an array, CurrentArray references the range that holds the entire array.

CurrentRegion: Range property; if the specified range is part of a larger range of contiguous cells that contain data, the CurrentRegion property references the entire rectangular range of contiguous cells that contain data.

Dependents: Range property; if the specified range is used in formulas in other ranges, the Dependents property returns the ranges that contain such formulas. The Dependents property returns all ranges that contain formulas that, either directly or indirectly, reference the specified range.

DirectDependents: Range property; if the specified range is used in formulas in other ranges, the DirectDependents property returns only ranges that contain formulas that reference the specified range directly.

Precedents: Range property; if the specified range contains a formula that references other ranges, the Precedents property returns all of the ranges that are referenced, either directly or indirectly, by the formula.

DirectPrecedents: Range property; if the specified range contains a formula that references other ranges, the DirectPrecedents property returns only ranges that are referenced by the formula directly.

Previous: Worksheet and Range property that references the previously selected worksheet or cell.

Areas: Range method that returns a single range or a set of ranges as an Areas collection, each member of which is a Range object representing a selected range or a section from a multiple-selection range.

Cells: Method that can be called on the Application, Worksheet, or Range object. The Cells method takes one argument (index to a cell) or two arguments (a row number and a column number). Cells returns a Range object that references a single cell corresponding to the specified index or row and column number. The Cells method can also be used to return a collection of Cells when called on a multi-cell range.

Offset: Range method that takes two arguments: rowOffset and columnOffset. Offset returns a Range object that matches the row and column offset values you specify.

Resize: Range method that takes two arguments: rowSize and columnSize. The Resize method is used to resize a range to fit the dimensions specified by rowSize and columnSize.

Select: Range method that is used to select a range.

ActiveCell: Application property that references the currently selected cell. If multiple cells are selected, ActiveCell references the first (upper-left) cell in the selection.

Intersect: Application method that takes two or more ranges as arguments. Intersect returns a Range object that references the intersection of all the specified ranges.

Union: Application method that takes two or more ranges as arguments. Union returns a Range object that references the union of all the specified ranges.

UsedRange: Worksheet property that references the range on the worksheet containing data.

The CommandButton1_Click event procedure in Sheet13's code module in the CHAP08-1.XLS file (not shown here) provides access to a dialog box that allows you to view the return values associated with many of the range properties and methods we've just reviewed. To run the routine, first activate worksheet Sheet13. Then select any range on the worksheet, and click the Display Selected Range Properties button located on the sheet. CommandButton1_Click will execute and display the following dialog box. (In this case, the selected range is A2:A3.)

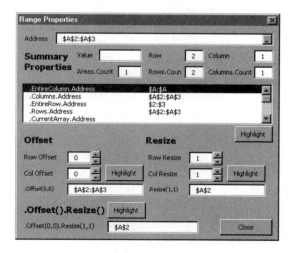

NOTE   This dialog box uses a listbox control with multiple columns. The relevant properties are ColumnCount (which is set to 2 to create a second column) and Column. You can use the Column property to set or get the value in any row/column combination in the listbox. Column is indexed by two arguments: column and row. Both of these arguments are zero-based. Note that the Column property cannot be used to add new rows to the listbox—you must use the AddItem method to establish a row before you can address it with the Column property. Refer to the online VBA Help for more information on multi-column listboxes.

The Range Properties dialog box (UserForm frmRangeProperties) provides information about numerous properties for the selected range. At the top of the dialog box is a refedit box labeled "Address" containing the address of the range. Next, a list of properties provides summary information about the selected range. The middle section of the dialog box displays a list of 12 addresses associated with various range properties. You can scroll through the list by using the scroll bar on the right. Next to the list is a Highlight button. When you click this button, a routine is invoked that sets the ColorIndex property of the interior of the range corresponding to the selected address to 15 (light gray). You might have to move the dialog box out of the way a little to see the highlighted ranges on the worksheet in the background. The following screen shows the Highlight button being clicked in the dialog box as well as the address corresponding to the EntireColumn property of the selected range (A2:A3) colored in light gray on the worksheet in the background.

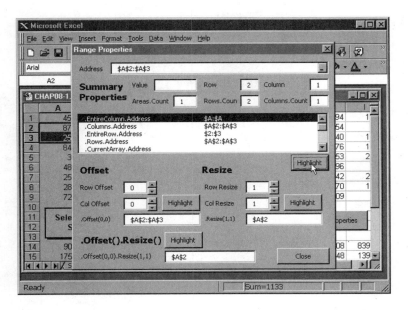

In the lower portion of the dialog box, you can see the results of passing different row and column values to the Offset and Resize methods. Using the spinner controls, you can adjust row and column values for Offset and Resize and view the address that results from calling each method. And at the bottom of the dialog box, you can see the address that results from combining the Offset and Resize methods. As with the property list in the middle of the dialog box, if you click one of the Highlight buttons under Offset or Resize, a routine will run that will color the corresponding address on worksheet Sheet13 light gray. The following screen displays the resulting address when 1 is passed for both the row and column arguments of the Offset method when called on range A2:A3 and after clicking the Highlight button. (The resulting address is displayed in light gray on the worksheet.)

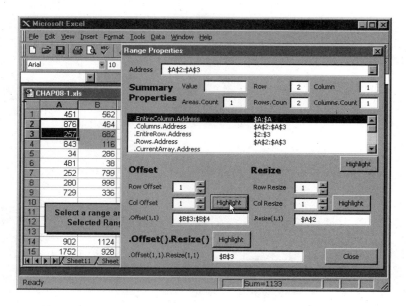

Several routines and event procedures provide the functionality for the Range Properties dialog box, all of which are found in userform frmRangeProperties' code module.

- UserForm_Initialize

- UserForm_Terminate

- GetRangeProperties

- GetOffsetProperties

- GetResizeProperties

- GetOffsetResizeProperties

- HighlightRange

- refRange_Change

- Change event code for SpinButton1, 2, 3, and 4

- Click event code for CommandButton1, 2, 3, 4, and 5

You might want to study the preceding routines in detail to better familiarize yourself with the various properties and methods that enable range navigation.

FYI

Writing a Routine to Select the Last Cell on the Worksheet

Often there is a need to select the last cell containing data on a worksheet. In writing a routine to select the last cell, the first inclination would be to use the UsedRange property of the Worksheet object. Proc19 provides an example of this approach:

```
Sub Chap08aProc19_GotoLastCell1()
    Dim RowNum As Integer
    Dim ColNum As Integer
    With Worksheets("Sheet13")
        .Select
        .Range("AZ200").Value = 1
        RowNum = .UsedRange.Row + .UsedRange.Rows.Count - 1
        ColNum = .UsedRange.Column + .UsedRange.Columns.Count - 1
        Cells(RowNum, ColNum).Select
        MsgBox Cells(RowNum, ColNum).Address & " is the " & _
            "last cell on the worksheet."
        .Range("AZ200").Clear
        RowNum = .UsedRange.Row + .UsedRange.Rows.Count - 1
        ColNum = .UsedRange.Column + .UsedRange.Columns.Count - 1
        Cells(RowNum, ColNum).Select
        MsgBox "After deleting the value from the cell, " & _
            Cells(RowNum, ColNum).Address & " is still the " & _
            "last cell on the worksheet."
    End With
End Sub
```

Proc19 demonstrates a problem with UsedRange. Under certain circumstances, UsedRange can return an address that includes more than the used area of a worksheet. If you have a cell on the periphery of the used area of the worksheet and that cell contains data, UsedRange will include that cell appropriately.

(continued)

Writing a Routine to Select the Last Cell on the Worksheet, *continued*

However, if you clear the data from the cell, UsedRange will continue to recognize the cell as containing data until the workbook file is saved and the worksheet is refreshed.

Proc20, which follows, uses the SpecialCells method instead of UsedRange and provides a routine that will, under all circumstances, select the last cell in the used area of a worksheet:

```
Sub Chap08aProc20_GotoLastCell2()
    Worksheets("Sheet13").Select
    If Range("A1").SpecialCells(xlLastCell).Value = "" Then
        Cells(Cells.Find("*", _
                        ActiveCell.SpecialCells(xlLastCell), _
                        , , xlByRows, xlPrevious).Row, _
            Cells.Find("*", _
                        ActiveCell.SpecialCells(xlLastCell), _
                        , , xlByColumns, _
                        xlPrevious).Column).Select
    Else
        Range("A1").SpecialCells(xlLastCell).Select
    End If
End Sub
```

DocumentProperties

Excel provides two collections that take advantage of the DocumentProperty objects available with Microsoft Office 97. The BuiltinDocumentProperties and CustomDocumentProperties properties of the Workbook object allow you to access general information regarding a workbook as well as to create and store custom properties with a workbook. You can view names and values associated with all built-in DocumentProperty objects by indexing specific objects by name or number or by using a For-Each-Next loop to visit all of the objects in the collection. You can create your own DocumentProperty objects by calling the Add method on the DocumentProperties collection and specifying name, type, value, and whether the property value is linked to an Excel worksheet range. If there is a link, you must also specify the name of a range to which the value is linked. After a DocumentProperty object has been added, it can be accessed through the CustomDocumentProperties collection. DocumentProperty objects are especially useful in creating applications that take advantage of Microsoft Outlook. Through use of the ActiveX Automation interface provided by Microsoft Exchange, you can use DocumentProperty objects to access information about files stored in Outlook folders without having to start host applications to load the files. (For more information, see Chapter 10, "Integrating Other Applications into Excel VBA Solutions.")

NOTE Excel provides a Post method for the Workbook object. The Post method allows you to post an Excel workbook directly to a Microsoft Exchange folder.

TIP Excel offers an AutoCorrect object that provides the functionality to correct user mistakes as data is entered. The AutoCorrect object is a useful tool for users but might be of only minor importance in developing custom applications. See the online VBA Help in Excel 97 for information about the AutoCorrect object and its properties and methods.

Entering Data

Several objects and properties that involve the user entering data are important in designing applications. Two properties of the Worksheet object, EnableSelection and ScrollArea, control what the user can select and where they can scroll. The Validation object (under Range in the object hierarchy) controls what data can be entered into ranges, and one property of the Application object—Interactive—can be used to limit all interaction with Excel. Following are descriptions of these objects and properties.

EnableSelection Property: Takes effect only when the worksheet's contents are protected. It can be set to one of three values:

xlNoRestrictions	User can select any cell
xlUnlockedCells	User can only select cells that are formatted as unlocked
xlNoSelection	User cannot select *any* cells

ScrollArea Property: The ScrollArea property of the Worksheet object determines where the user can scroll to. This property can be set to an address or range name. If your ScrollArea is not visible when you set the ScrollArea property, Excel will automatically scroll to it.

NOTE The ScrollArea and EnableSelection properties are meant to replace the DataEntryMode feature of the Application object available in earlier versions of Excel. These new properties provide more flexibility and control than the DataEntryMode.

Data Validation and the Validation Object: A new feature in Excel 97—called Data Validation—can tightly control what a user is and is not allowed to enter into cells. Using this feature, you can set valid values, ranges, and data types for cells. You can also specify a prompt to display when the user enters the cell and an error message to display when invalid data is entered. You can even create a drop-down list that displays valid values for the cell. The best way to implement validation is manually through the user interface. To do this, select the Validation command from the Data menu. Pictured here is the Data Validation dialog box:

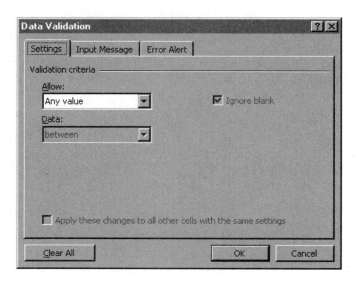

Sheet14 in CHAP08-1.XLS contains examples of data validation. Here is an example of data validation in action—specifically, a drop-down list created for a cell:

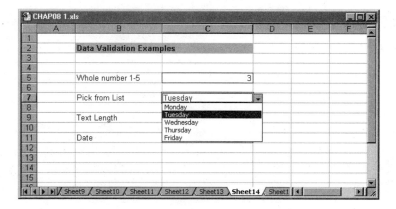

You can control validation programmatically using the Validation object, which is accessed by the Validation property of the Range object. The Validation object lets you create, modify, and delete validation rules.

Interactive Property: Used to block all user interaction with Excel. Interactive can take a value of True or False. If it is False, all user input from the keyboard or the mouse—except input in any dialog boxes that are displayed by your routine—is blocked. (User input remains blocked until Interactive is set to True.) With the Interactive property set to False, you can prevent the user from pressing the Esc key and interfering with routine execution.

> **NOTE**
>
> Take care to always set Interactive back to True at the end of a routine that modifies this property. Otherwise, interaction with Excel cannot be re-established except by closing Excel externally or rebooting your computer.

Report Printing

To create and print reports in Excel, you use the PageSetup object, the PageBreak property of the Range object, and the PrintPreview and PrintOut methods of numerous objects. Briefly, you complete four steps to create and print a report:

1. Set the PageBreak property of the range of data to be printed. By setting PageBreak, you can specify either manual or automatic page breaks.

2. Set various formatting aspects of the report by setting properties of the PageSetup object. These aspects include the report's header, footer, margins, paper size, and orientation.

3. Preview the printed report by calling the PrintPreview method of the object you wish to print.

4. Print the report by calling the PrintOut method of the object.

For more information about creating and printing reports, see Excel's online VBA Help.

SUMMARY

This chapter has touched briefly on a great number of topics, many of which deserve much more discussion. You can find additional discussion in Excel's documentation and in the numerous books that describe Excel's basic functionality. If you are new to Excel, it's a good idea to take the time to find other sources of information for those topics that you want to know more about. Understanding the basic functionality of Excel is integral to developing powerful Excel applications.

The following list summarizes the main points covered in this chapter:

■ The Excel worksheet provides a powerful grid of cells that can contain formulas that can call functions as well as reference other cells or names. In addition, array formulas provide a way to perform advanced calculations on rows and columns of data. These features, combined with Excel's powerful and versatile calculation engine, provide a platform for creating extremely powerful models.

■ The Scenario object provides a way for a range of cells to store multiple values; each set of values is referenced by a particular scenario.

■ The GoalSeek, Sort, Subtotal, AutoFilter, and Consolidate methods of the Range object provide five powerful methods for analyzing and manipulating ranges of data.

■ Several properties and methods of the Application, Worksheet, and Range objects are extremely useful for navigating and selecting ranges.

■ Office 97 DocumentProperty objects can be accessed directly from within Excel by using the BuiltInDocumentProperties and Custom-DocumentProperties collections.

■ The following are useful for creating applications in which the user enters data: the ScrollArea and EnableSelection properties of the Worksheet object; the Interactive property of the Application object; the Data Validation feature and associated Validation object.

■ To create and print reports in Excel, you use the PageSetup object, the PageBreak property, and the PrintPreview and PrintOut methods.

9

Sample Application 3: Setagaya Cycle

In this chapter, we look at a sales entry and forecasting system for another fictitious manufacturer of bicycles—Setagaya Cycle. We use another bicycle company here to reuse the BikeData database included on the companion CD. We'll assume that Setagaya Cycle is the main competitor of Wellington Cycle Works and that all of the products for both companies have the same names. The Setagaya Cycle application can be found in the CHAP09.XLS file on the companion CD.

NOTE In order to successfully run the Setagaya Cycle application contained in CHAP09.XLS, you must be certain that the BIKEDATA-.MDB Access database file is contained in the same folder as the CHAP09.XLS file. The code in CHAP09.XLS makes direct references to the BIKEDATA.MDB file with the assumption that the file is located in the same folder as the CHAP09.XLS file. The file location is thus hard-coded, but it is possible to edit the references in CHAP09.XLS to utilize a Registry- or file-based DSN ODBC data source. In doing so, you could place the BIKEDATA.MDB folder in a completely separate location from CHAP09.XLS and the Setagaya Cycle application would still function properly.

The Setagaya Cycle application is much more complicated than any application covered so far in this book. The main purpose of the application is to provide a tool for making minor adjustments to sales records and to generate and distribute a sales forecast. To provide this functionality, the application uses two pivottables, the Scenario object, the GoalSeek method, array formulas, and numerous other objects that were covered in detail for the Wellington Cycle Works sample application in Chapter 6. The application also uses database access routines that take advantage of the Data Access Object model and messaging functionality exposed by the RoutingSlip object.

The Setagaya Cycle Application

Start Microsoft Excel and open CHAP09.XLS. The main Setagaya Cycle Control form is displayed:

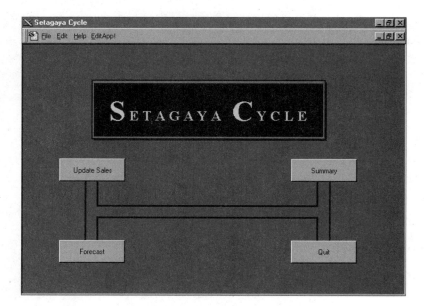

The Control form contains four buttons that allow the user to access the three parts of the application and to quit the application. As in the Wellington Cycle Works application, all aspects of the Excel environment in the Setagaya Cycle application have been customized—the title bar and menus have been modified, and all Excel interface artifacts have been removed. Unlike the Wellington Cycle Works application, the Setagaya application has no custom commandbar, although it does modify the standard menu. You might also have noticed when you first opened the Setagaya Cycle application that a textbox was displayed on the screen indicating that the application was reading data. Two pivottables are used with this application, and because neither has been created with the option to save data with the workbook file, the application must refresh the pivottables when it is first opened.

The Update Form

By clicking the Update Sales button on the Control form, the user can access the Update form, shown here. With the Update form, you can make minor changes to sales data and have the option to export those changes back to the BikeData database.

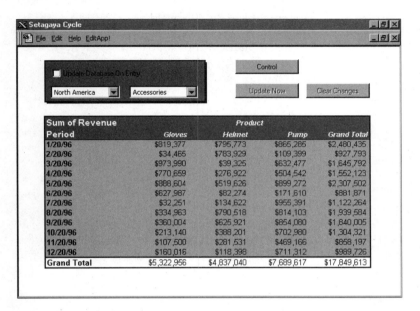

You will notice that in the Setagaya Cycle application, both ActiveX controls as well as older Excel controls from the Forms toolbar have been employed on the various worksheets that make up the application. You may find advantages in using the older Excel controls accessed from the Forms toolbar—in some cases, they exhibit a higher level of performance. In the Setagaya Cycle application, DropDown and Spinner controls from the Forms toolbar have been used instead of their ComboBox and Spinner ActiveX counterparts. This was done primarily for performance reasons.

The table in the Update form bears some resemblance to a pivottable, although it is actually only a standard Excel table in a range on an Excel worksheet. By using the two drop-down controls in the form's upper left corner, you can look at data for different continents and different product categories. After you select a new continent from the leftmost dropdown, Excel displays a message in a textbox indicating that data is being read from an external database. Actually, Excel is reading data into a pivottable named Pivot1, which resides on a different worksheet that the user never views. At any given time, the pivottable holds data for only a single continent so that it can conserve the amount of RAM required by the application. This is accomplished by specifying in the query a continent name that is used to populate the pivottable. After the pivottable is updated, the data is copied to the Update form and displayed as shown in the preceding table—all while the ScreenUpdating property of the Application object is set to False so that the user does not view the new data being pasted and formatted on the Update form. You'll notice that if you select a new product category from the rightmost dropdown, Excel displays the new data almost instantaneously. Excel does not have to requery the database when a new product category is selected because the data set for each continent contains data for all product category sales for that continent.

At this point, you might ask why the Pivot1 pivottable is on another sheet, hidden from the user, rather than on the Update form. There is a good reason behind constructing the Update form in this manner. You might recall from the discussion in Chapter 4 that a user cannot make changes to the data in a pivottable. If a user tries to make entries directly in the cells of a pivottable, Excel generates an error message to inform the user that changes cannot be made to it. On the Update form, however, you can type directly in the cells of the table that display data and actually change the data. For example, try changing some of the dollar amounts in the table on the Update form. For the continent, select Africa, and for the product category, select Accessories. Then enter *$1* for the Gloves product for the months of January, February, March, and April, and notice how the data changes.

The Update Now button

You might have noticed that before you entered data in the Update form, the two buttons labeled "Update Now" and "Clear Changes" were grayed out, indicating that they were disabled. After you typed data in the table, however, the buttons resumed their normal display and became active. A Worksheet_Change event procedure accomplishes this functionality. After data is entered in the table, the Change event fires to activate the Update Now and Clear Changes buttons. When you click Update Now after making changes to the table, your changes are exported to the BikeData database and become permanent. Try clicking the Update Now button.

Database changes are written using the DAO object library. While updating the database, Excel displays a textbox at the bottom of the screen indicating that the database is being updated. After the update is complete, the Update Now and Clear Changes buttons return to their grayed-out state. To verify that the changes were made to the database, select a new continent—thus forcing Excel to refresh the pivottable—and then select Africa again. You'll find that your $1 entries have been saved to the database.

The Clear Changes button

Try making more changes to the table—but don't click the Update Now button. Instead, restore the original values before the database is updated by choosing the Clear Changes button. This button launches a routine that refreshes the table display by copying data from the pivottable and pasting it to the Update form—without updating the database. If you change any values in the table and do not click the Update Now button, the application updates the database automatically whenever you select a new continent or product category from one of the dropdowns or when you exit the Update form by clicking the Control button. The application senses when changes have been made and assumes that the user wants the changes to be permanent unless the Clear Changes button is clicked. Excel also determines when the underlying pivottable should be refreshed with the changed data. Recall that when you select a new product category, the underlying pivottable is not normally refreshed. If you make changes before you select a new product category, however, Excel refreshes the underlying pivottable. The application knows that changes have been made to the database and that the pivottable's current data does not reflect the changes to the underlying data.

The Update Database On Entry checkbox

The upper left corner of the Update form contains the Update Database On Entry checkbox control. If this checkbox is checked, every time you change a value in the table, Excel updates the database automatically. As with the enabling of the Update Now and Clear Changes buttons, the application updates the database through a Worksheet_Change event procedure that runs and updates the values in the selected cells as the change is completed (by pressing Enter or by moving out of the cell using an arrow key). If the checkbox is unchecked, the application allows the user to make multiple changes to the table and to update the database with those changes only when the Update Now or Control button is chosen or when a new product category or continent is selected.

Worksheet protection

The worksheet that makes up the Update form is protected. Although you can enter data in the cells that make up the table in the middle of the screen, you cannot enter data anywhere else on the form. Nor can you manipulate any of the controls on the form other than to click them. Protection has been implemented on the worksheet by setting to False the Locked property of the range that makes up the table and then calling the Protect method on the Worksheet object. The whole worksheet is thus protected, except those ranges for which the Locked property is set to False.

After you spend some time experimenting with the functionality of the Update form, click the Control button to return to the Control form.

Tips for Controlling User Interaction with the Worksheet

You cannot move the cell selector beyond the range that makes up the Update form. The worksheet comes to an abrupt end at the right and bottom borders of the form. To accomplish this effect, the rows and columns outside the form have been hidden. Protecting the worksheet and limiting the scroll area in this manner allows you to transform the worksheet into what might be considered a "true" form.

The Forecast Forms

Clicking the Forecast button on the Control form launches a routine that displays the custom Forecast dialog box, in which you can select either the Summary form or one of five forecast forms that correspond to the five continents on which Setagaya Cycle does business:

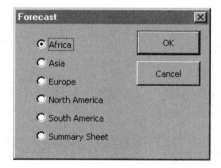

By default, the Forecast dialog box displays a selection that corresponds to the continent for which data was most recently viewed in the Update form. If it is not yet selected, select North America. Then click OK to see the forecast form for North America, as shown in Figure 9-1 on the facing page.

This example forecast form allows the user to look at a summary of 1996 sales, broken down by product category for North America, and to project 1997 sales for each product category. In the middle of the form is a table that displays 1996 actual and 1997 projected sales data for each product category, as well as the percentage difference between the two. Like the Update form, each forecast form is protected. The user can enter data only in the three Percent Growth cells in the table. In addition, the user cannot scroll past the right or bottom border of the form.

Above the table is a textbox that displays in large letters the name of the continent to which the data pertains, and below the table is a chart that displays the 1996 and 1997 sales for the three product categories. At the top of the form

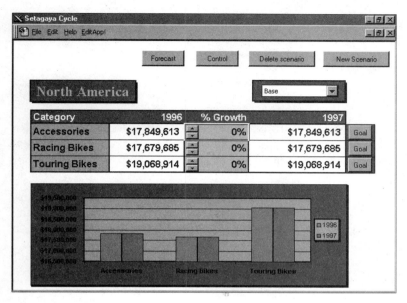

Figure 9-1. *The forecast form for North America.*

are four buttons—Forecast, Control, Delete Scenario, and New Scenario. Clicking Forecast displays the Forecast dialog box, which allows the user to select a forecast form for another continent (or to click Cancel to return to the forecast form). Clicking Control returns the user to the Control form. The remaining two buttons are discussed in the section titled "Adding and deleting a scenario" on page 468.

The second pivottable

The data displayed in the forecast form's table originates from a second pivottable named Pivot2. Like Pivot1, Pivot2 is hidden from the user's view and is used only as a tool for generating queries. When the user activates a particular forecast form, the pivottable is updated to display data for the selected continent. The data is then copied from Pivot2 and pasted to the table in the appropriate forecast form. Handling the data in this way ensures that the data displayed in the forecast form for a particular continent is always current. In fact, if the user makes changes to 1996 sales records in the Update form, those changes are immediately reflected in the forecast form that corresponds to the continent for which the changes were made.

When you select different forecast forms from the Forecast dialog box, the application activates the appropriate form and displays a message stating that data is being read from the database. That data is actually being read into Pivot1 through a call to the RefreshTable method. Because Pivot2 uses the same RAM cache as does Pivot1, calling the RefreshTable method on Pivot1 updates the RAM cache for Pivot2's access as well. By building two pivottables from the same

RAM cache in this manner, you can conserve the amount of memory used by the application and enhance performance.

The Scenario dropdown

The forecast form allows the user to enter and view different scenarios for sales growth for 1997, and the dropdown control above the right side of the table can be used to display names of scenarios that have been entered for 1997 growth. When you first open the forecast form for North America, the entry for the Base scenario is displayed in this dropdown. Base represents 0 percent growth across all product categories.

Click the dropdown, and three additional scenarios are displayed in the list box: Best Case, Worst Case, and Likely Case. If you select any of these other scenarios, the table updates to display the Percent Growth figures for that scenario. In the following screen, you see the Best Case scenario for North America, in which 25 percent growth is projected for all product categories in 1997:

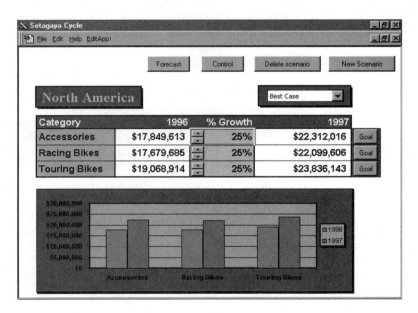

Select the other scenarios, and you will see that the Likely Case scenario represents 10 percent sales growth across all categories whereas the Worst Case scenario represents −25 percent sales growth across all categories. By default, the application offers four built-in scenarios. When a new scenario is selected from the dropdown, the Show method is called on the Scenario object to display it.

Entering percentage growth numbers

Suppose the user of the application is not satisfied with any of the scenarios and instead thinks that the sales growth for Accessories will be –25 percent, the growth of Touring Bikes sales will be 50 percent, and the figure for Racing Bikes sales will remain at 25 percent. With the Best Case scenario displayed, enter –25% for Accessories growth and 50% for Touring Bikes growth. As you change data in the Percent Growth cells, you'll see a new textbox that displays the message "Scenario Changed":

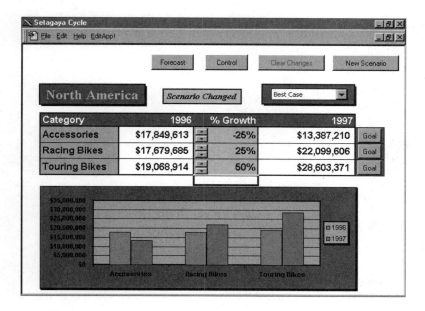

The OnEntry property of the worksheet contains the name of a routine that displays this new textbox to notify the user that the numbers in the table's Percent Growth cells are not indicative of the scenario selected in the scenario dropdown. That is, although "Best Case" is displayed in the scenario dropdown, the Percent Growth numbers in the table do not represent the previously entered Best Case scenario (25 percent growth across all product categories).

As you enter data in the table, another change occurs as well: the name of the Delete Scenario button changes to Clear Changes. Again, this change is accomplished through the OnEntry property of the worksheet. If you click the Clear Changes button, the changes you entered are cleared and the table is restored to the original Best Case scenario. In addition, the Scenario Changed textbox disappears and the caption on the button reverts to Delete Scenario.

TIP	You can also clear changes by selecting a new scenario from the Scenario dropdown.

Adding and deleting a scenario

Suppose the user wants to enter some growth assumptions and save them in a scenario that can be viewed (in the same way that the built-in scenarios can be viewed) at any time by selecting the scenario from the Scenario dropdown. To add a scenario, select the Best Case scenario and change the Percent Growth cell for Accessories to −25% growth and the Percent Growth cell for Touring Bikes to 50% growth. Click the New Scenario button to display the New Scenario dialog box:

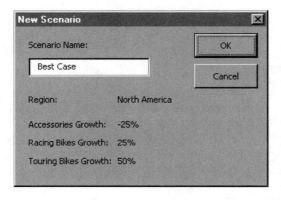

In the New Scenario dialog box, you can either change an existing scenario or add a new one. By default, the Scenario Name editbox displays the name of the scenario currently selected in the Scenario dropdown. Also displayed are the name of the continent and the current percentage growth value for each product category. If you click OK without changing the scenario name, the application displays a message asking whether you are sure you want to change the percentage growth values for a scenario that already exists—in this case, for the Best Case scenario.

Clicking Yes changes the Best Case scenario to reflect the current values in the Percent Growth cells. Clicking No displays the New Scenario dialog box again, enabling you to enter a new name.

For this example, click No, type *Realistic Case* in the Scenario Name editbox, and then click OK. On the forecast form, the Scenario Changed textbox disappears, the Clear Changes button changes to Delete Scenario, and "Realistic Case" is displayed in the scenario dropdown. Click the Scenario dropdown to see that Realistic Case has indeed been added to the list of available scenarios.

Deleting a scenario is a simple process. Click the Delete Scenario button, and when prompted with a message box that asks whether you are sure you want to delete the scenario, click Yes. The currently displayed scenario is deleted from the workbook, and its name is removed from the Scenario dropdown.

If you delete all the scenarios, the Delete Scenario button is disabled (and appears grayed out), the Scenario dropdown disappears, and a "No Scenarios" message is displayed. Note also that after all scenarios are deleted, if you enter new numbers in the Percent Growth cells, the Scenario Changed textbox no longer appears.

The spin button controls and Goal buttons

On the forecast form, you might have noticed the spin button controls in the Percent Growth cells. These controls can be used to make 1 percent adjustments to the values in each of the cells—by using a simple routine attached to each control. You might also have noticed the three Goal buttons next to the cells that correspond to 1997 sales numbers. If you click one of the Goal buttons, a routine executes that displays the custom Goal Seek dialog box shown here. (This is not the built-in Excel Goal Seek dialog box but rather a custom dialog box that uses the GoalSeek method.)

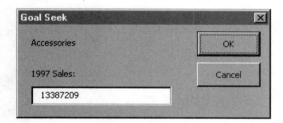

This dialog box displays the currently forecasted 1997 Sales number (for the selected scenario) for the Accessories product category in North America. Although changing percentages provides a way to forecast by percentage growth, the user might want to forecast by an absolute growth number. The Goal Seek dialog box is perfectly suited for the situation in which the user knows what the target sales figure is but does not know what percentage growth that figure represents. Suppose the user has determined that 1997 sales for Accessories in North America will be $80,000,000. If you enter *80,000,000* in the Goal Seek dialog box and click OK, Excel automatically calculates the percentage growth that $80,000,000 represents, as shown in Figure 9-2 on the following page.

Spend some time exploring the functionality of the forecast forms. Select additional forms to view from the Forecast dialog box. After you finish looking at the forecast forms, select the Summary form either from the Forecast dialog box or by clicking Summary on the Control form. The next section describes the Summary form.

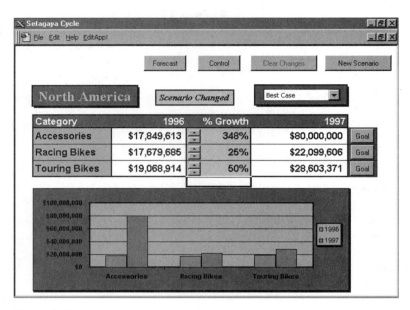

Figure 9-2. *Percentage Growth figures based on $80,000,000 entered in the Goal Seek dialog box.*

The Summary Form

The Summary form summarizes in a table 1996 sales data as well as 1997 sales forecasts and percentage growth for each product category for each continent:

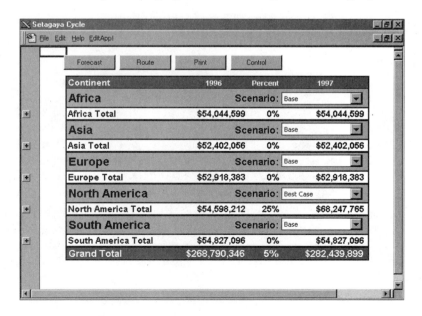

Expanding the display of the Summary table

The table in the Summary form (shown in the preceding illustration) is divided into five sections—one for each continent. Each section contains a scenario dropdown control that you can use to select different scenarios for the different continents. Along the left side of the form is a series of five buttons labeled with plus signs (+). These are outlining buttons. By clicking these buttons, you can expand the display to show data for each continent's product categories. In the next screen, you see the expanded outlines for the continents of Africa and Asia. The Best Case scenario has been selected for Africa, and the Likely Case scenario has been selected for Asia.

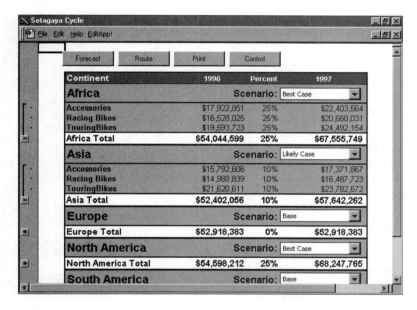

The Summary table and the forecast forms are linked in the following ways:

- By routines attached to the scenario dropdowns on the Summary form so that changing a particular scenario for a particular continent on the Summary table automatically changes to that scenario on the corresponding forecast form

- Through array formulas in the Summary table that link the 1996 sales figures in the Summary table to the sales figures on the corresponding forecast forms so that modifying a displayed scenario on a forecast form automatically updates corresponding data in the Summary table

Routing and printing the Summary form

Above the table on the Summary form are the Forecast, Route, Print, and Control buttons, described on the following page.

- **Forecast:** Clicking Forecast displays the Forecast dialog box through which you can select a forecast form for any of the continents.

- **Route:** Clicking Route copies the Summary form to a new workbook and then displays Excel's Routing Slip dialog box, which allows you to route the new workbook to other users in the company:

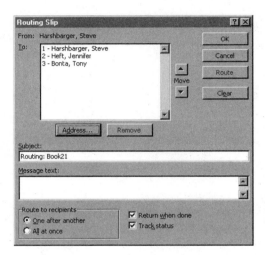

- **Print:** Clicking Print opens the Print Summary Report dialog box in which you enter a title for the printed report. Clicking OK prints the report:

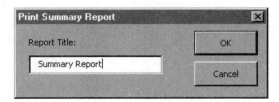

- **Control:** Clicking Control activates the Control form.

After you finish exploring the Summary form, click Control to return to the Control form. Now let's take a look at some of the code behind the application.

Exploring the Setagaya Cycle Application

The flow diagram in Figure 9-3 shows the paths that the *user* can take to navigate through the Setagaya Cycle application.

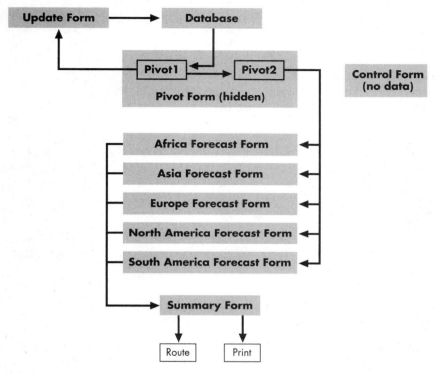

Figure 9-3. *The way the user navigates through the Setagaya Cycle application.*

The route that the user takes, however, is different from the route that the *data* takes. Figure 9-4 shows the actual flow of data in the application.

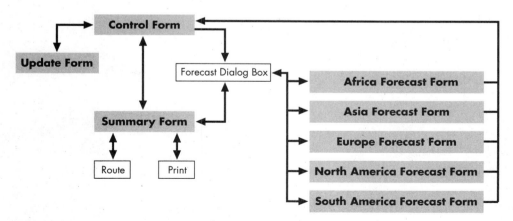

Figure 9-4. *The flow of data in the Setagaya Cycle application.*

Figure 9-4 reveals a rather complicated model for querying, analyzing, and changing the data in the external database, but the application was constructed with this data flow scheme to conserve RAM and improve performance. The application's most significant aspect (as shown in the diagram) is the use of two pivottables—Pivot1 and Pivot2—on the Pivot form, which is hidden from the user's view. You use both pivottables to query and handle data coming in from the external database. Pivot1 is the querying mechanism for the data table displayed on the Update form. Data is brought into Pivot1 and is then copied to the Update form. Changes to the data in the Update form, however, are sent directly back to the external database without going through the pivottable. Pivot2 provides data to the forecast forms and is constructed from the same RAM cache as is Pivot1. Each time the user selects a forecast form from the Forecast dialog box, Pivot2 is updated from the shared RAM cache. The data then flows from Pivot2 into the selected forecast form. The data from all of the forecast forms is consolidated in the Summary form, where it can then be distributed via the e-mail system or in the form of a printed report.

The Components of the Setagaya Cycle Application

You can view the worksheets that make up the Setagaya Cycle application by clicking the EditApp command on the application menu.

> **NOTE** By choosing the RunApp command from the menu when you are in edit mode, you can return to the application's run mode.

The Setagaya Cycle application is made up of nine worksheets: the Control form; the Update form; the five forecast forms (one for each continent); the Summary form; and the hidden Pivot form, which contains the Pivot1 and Pivot2 pivottables.

In the Visual Basic Editor, you can view the modules and userforms used to create the application. These include the following:

ApplicationState	Class module used to save and restore the application state
mMain	General-purpose routines that apply to the whole application
mUpdate	VBA routines for the Update form
mForecast	VBA routines for the forecast forms
mSummary	VBA routines for the Summary form
frmForecast	UserForm implementing the Forecast dialog box
frmNewScenario	UserForm implementing the New Scenario dialog box
frmGoalSeek	UserForm implementing the Goal Seek dialog box
frmSummaryReport	UserForm implementing the Print Summary Report dialog box

SUMMARY

In this chapter, we have looked at a complex and powerful application that can be used to enter data in an external database and to generate multiple scenarios for a sales forecast. Here are the new concepts covered in this chapter:

- Pivottables can be used on a hidden worksheet to query data from an external database.

- Two pivottables can operate from the same RAM cache originating from a common database.

- Implementing full worksheet protection, including limiting the scroll area, can be useful.

- Row and column headings from a table can be used to create SQL query statements for values changed in the table (see the Update-Database routine in the mUpdate code module).

- You can use the Scenario object in combination with dropdown controls.

- You can use array formulas to link data from multiple forms in a table on a single Summary form.

- You can apply outlining to a table so that the user can expand and contract table views.

FOUR

Integrating with Other
Applications, the Web,
and Other Topics

10

Integrating Other Applications into Excel VBA Solutions

Although Microsoft Excel provides a tremendous amount of data analysis functionality, Excel does not provide functionality in a number of other areas, including advanced report and presentation generation and project management. You can build such additional functionality into your Excel Visual Basic for Applications (VBA) solutions by integrating other applications into them. As discussed earlier in this book, Excel supports ActiveX, a technology that essentially breaks down the barriers that separate applications. ActiveX lets you create custom solutions from the objects contained not only in Excel but also in other applications.

ActiveX provides these two powerful features that are of vital importance to development:

- In-place editing (also known as "visual editing"), which allows you to embed an object from one application directly in a document created in another application

- Automation, which allows you to write code in one application to set properties, call methods, and handle events of both embedded objects and objects in external applications

Because Excel supports both of these features of ActiveX, you can easily develop custom Excel VBA solutions that use multiple applications.

FYI

New ActiveX Terminology

With the introduction of ActiveX in 1996, Microsoft implemented new terminology to refer to programmable objects. The term "ActiveX" in many cases now replaces the term "OLE." For example, what was previously known as an "OLE Object" is now known as an "ActiveX Component" or an "ActiveX Object," or even just as a plain "Object." Additionally, what was once called "OLE Automation" is now referred to as "ActiveX Automation" or even just plain "Automation." In this book, we have opted to use the generic terms Object and Automation in most cases.

In this chapter, we look at how to integrate the following Microsoft products into your Excel VBA solutions and how these products support ActiveX:

■ Microsoft Access 97—Microsoft's desktop database application

■ Microsoft PowerPoint 97—Microsoft's presentation graphics program

■ Microsoft Word 97—Microsoft's word processing application

■ Microsoft Outlook 97—Microsoft's desktop information manager

■ Microsoft Office Binder 97—Combined file type provided in Microsoft Office 97

■ Microsoft Visual Basic 5—Microsoft's visual development language for Microsoft Windows

■ Other Office 97 Applications and Objects

Excel, Access, PowerPoint, Word, Outlook, and Office Binder are included in Microsoft Office 97. This chapter does not cover programming in each of these applications in detail; numerous other books are devoted to those topics.

As with previous chapters, you can find the sample routines used in this chapter on the companion CD packaged with this book, in the CHAP10.XLS file. Many of the routines in this chapter cannot be run in Excel, however; some are intended to be run in Word, Project, Access, or Visual Basic. CHAP10.XLS includes two VBA modules—one named ExcelRoutines and the other named NonExcelRoutines. ExcelRoutines contains all of the routines that can be run in Excel, and NonExcelRoutines contains all of the routines that are to be run in other applications. The name of each routine includes the name of the module in which it can be found.

Programming Across Applications

ActiveX is a technology developed by Microsoft that has gained wide acceptance as a standard for sharing data across applications. ActiveX is an open standard. That is, any software vendor has free access to the ActiveX specification and can develop applications to meet ActiveX guidelines. Numerous major software vendors—including IBM/Lotus, and Corel/WordPerfect—have to date developed and released applications that conform to ActiveX technology. Keep in mind that software applications can support ActiveX in varying degrees. For example, a software product can be billed as supporting ActiveX, but it might in fact support only in-place editing, not Automation (or vice versa). If you plan to develop with an ActiveX application, you should first do research to determine the extent to which the application actually supports ActiveX. Because both in-place editing and Automation have proven to be extremely powerful development technologies, more and more software applications are being developed to support them.

The space limitations in this book do not permit us to discuss ActiveX in great detail. As a shortcut to understanding ActiveX, you can think of it as the mechanism that allows you to look at applications such as Excel as a set of programmable objects. When dealing with several applications that all support ActiveX, you're essentially looking at several sets of programmable objects, with each set representing a discrete application. Excel, Access, Word, PowerPoint, Outlook, and Office Binder all have programmable objects.

To access another application via ActiveX, an application must meet these two requirements:

- The application must be written specifically to conform to the ActiveX specification.

- The application must be installed and properly registered in the system Registry. This is usually done automatically when the application is installed.

You will sometimes find, however, that problems associated with accessing an application through ActiveX are related to improper registration of the application. (We do not delve into the details of the Registry or into the registration process in this book.)

Using ActiveX to Integrate Separate Sets of Objects

The real power of ActiveX comes in using Automation to integrate into a single solution separate sets of objects that represent discrete applications. Automation allows you to program with separate sets of objects as though the objects were all part of the same application. For example, because both Excel and Word support Automation, you can write a VBA routine in Excel that can be used to manipulate objects, such as documents and paragraphs, in Word. Likewise, you can write a VBA routine in Word that can be used to manipulate objects, such as worksheets and charts, in Excel. ActiveX renders transparent the boundaries that separate applications, letting you get or set the properties, call the methods, or respond to events of objects that are external to what is referred to as the "host application"—the application in which the routine is running.

In-Place Editing of Embedded Objects

Before we look at in-place editing in detail, we'll need an object to work with, so let's look at the process of embedding an object.

Embedding an object

ActiveX provides a feature that allows you to place—or embed—an object created by one application in a document created by another application. For example, you can embed an Excel worksheet or an Excel chart in a Word document, as shown here:

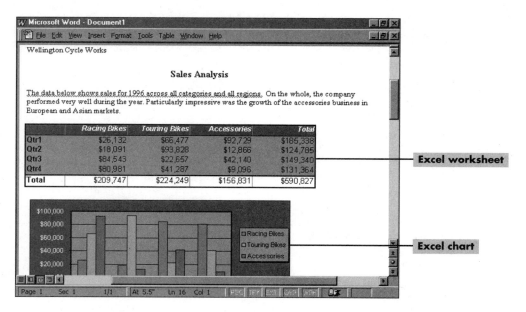

Likewise, you can embed a Word document within an Excel spreadsheet, as shown in the screen at the top of the facing page.

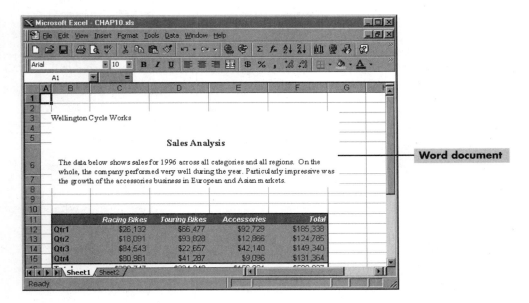

Word document

In Office 97, the process of embedding an object in an application's document is the same across all Office applications—you first choose the Insert Object command, which displays the Object dialog box, select any of the objects in the Object Type list on the Create New tab, and click OK.

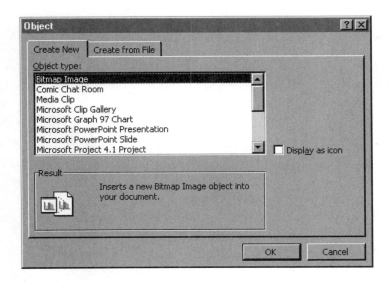

When an object is embedded in a document, all data associated with that object is stored with the object in the document. For example, when you embed an Excel worksheet in a Word document, you are saving an entire Excel workbook file with the Word document. You can also embed an object that is linked to an external file. For example, let's assume you use an Excel worksheet to track sales data. Let's also assume you want to incorporate this worksheet data in a Word document that you print and distribute once a week to supply updated sales data to others in your company. If you embedded the entire file in the Word document, you would have to change the Word document every week to update the Excel numbers. But if you linked an embedded Excel worksheet in the Word document to an external Excel file, you would have to change the numbers only in the external Excel file each week; the link would cause the embedded object in the Word document to be updated automatically when the Word document was opened.

To embed an object with a link to an external file, you select the Create From File tab in the Object dialog box, select a file from which to create the object in the File Name edit box, and then check the Link To File check box. Click OK to complete the process.

CAUTION Take care when linking an object to a file because an absolute path for the file is stored with the object. If you move the file on the disk, the link to the object is broken.

In-place editing

After an object is embedded in a form, you can double-click the object to edit it without having to start the application associated with the object in a separate window. For example, if you double-click an Excel worksheet embedded in a Word document, you can edit that worksheet entirely in the context of the Word document. In-place editing gives you access to all the menus and toolbars in the associated application. If you double-click an embedded Word object in a Excel document, for example, Word's menus and toolbars appear automatically, giving you access to all the features and functionality of Word while you are still in the context of the Excel document. You can see this in the screen on the facing page.

NOTE Word, Excel, PowerPoint, Access, and Outlook all support in-place editing.

In-place editing on its own provides a powerful interface for editing embedded objects. Automation can be used to control both embedded and external ActiveX objects using VBA routines, as you'll see in the next few sections.

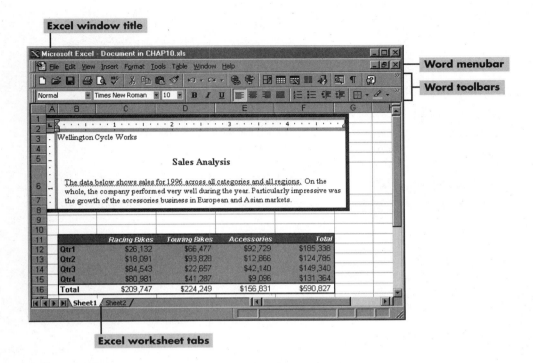

Excel window title

Word menubar

Word toolbars

Excel worksheet tabs

Automation

Automation is one of the most important features of ActiveX. When used to integrate different applications, it allows you to write a routine in one application that controls the objects in another. In the past, a technology known as Dynamic Data Exchange (DDE) was used to integrate multiple applications into a single solution. When used for this purpose, DDE was often considered slow and difficult to work with. Automation provides a much faster and easier method of programming across applications.

Automation exposes the object model of an application to the outside world, allowing you to write routines in a different application that takes advantage of the exposed objects.

An application can support Automation by serving as one of the following:

- An "Automation object application" ("object application," for short), which has its object model exposed to the outside world and through that exposure allows itself to be controlled by controller applications. An object application receives commands from a controller application.

■ An "Automation controller application" ("controller application," for short), which controls Automation objects. A controller application sends commands to an object application.

Some applications are designed to serve only as object applications, some only as controller applications, and others as both object and controller applications. An application that is both can receive commands from other controller applications and send commands to other object applications. Microsoft Office applications support Automation to varying degrees, as shown in the following table:

Office 97 Applications Supporting Automation	Object Application	Controller Application
Access 97	X	X
Excel 97	X	X
Office Binder	X	
Outlook 97	X	
PowerPoint 97	X	X
Project 97	X	X
Team Manager 97	X	
Word 97	X	X

Developers often question the reasoning behind Automation support—why is one application an object, another a controller, and a third both an object and a controller? Different levels of Automation support in applications provide flexibility for designing custom solutions. When you write a custom solution, you usually choose a single application in which to base it, and that choice rests on the type of functionality the custom solution requires. For example, if you wanted to write an application that analyzed data and crunched numbers, you would likely base the solution in Excel. If you wanted to write an order entry and lookup system that involved a lot of database access, however, you would do best to base the solution in Microsoft Access. And if you wanted to integrate multiple applications into a custom solution through Automation, you would base the solution in an application that is an Automation controller. Access, Excel, PowerPoint, Project, and Word are Automation controllers—that makes sense because each application provides an area of specialty that might lead a developer to base a custom solution in that application.

The 97 versions of all Office applications are Automation objects. An application makes a good Automation object application if it contains functionality that might be useful in custom solutions based in other applications. The following table summarizes the functionality provided through the objects of Office applications:

Office 97 Application	Object Functionality
Access 97	Data entry/lookup, forms, reports
Excel 97	Data analysis, data viewing
Office Binder	File storage and retrieval
Outlook 97	E-mail, group scheduling, contacts database, and task management
PowerPoint 97	Presenting data
Project 97	Critical-path project management and scheduling
Team Manager 97	Resource group management
Word 97	Reporting data

NOTE   Many other products, from Microsoft and other companies, also can be used in Automation. Throughout the chapter we include examples of using Visual Basic 5, which produces stand-alone executables, as a controller application.

NOTE   You can find additional information about developing with Microsoft applications in the Microsoft Office 97 Developer Edition and Microsoft Developer Network CDs. Contact Microsoft for details. In the United States, call 1-800-360-7561; outside the United States, contact your local Microsoft office.

Programmatic Control of Automation Objects

Now that we've looked at the different ways in which Office products support Automation, let's take a look at how you can write code to control an Automation object. You program through Automation in a unidirectional manner. That is, code contained in an Automation controller application can control Automation object applications and the objects within them. Five of the applications we have discussed are controllers: Access, Excel, PowerPoint, Project, and Word. All five of these applications use the same coding techniques to control Automation objects and the same language—Visual Basic for Applications (VBA).

To control an Automation object through a VBA routine, follow these steps (which are described in greater detail in the sections that follow):

1. Create a variable to represent the Automation object.

2. Use the variable to access the object model that falls under the Automation object when you get or set properties and call methods.

3. Relinquish the Automation object when it is no longer needed.

Establishing a Reference to the Object

By far the most efficient way to control an external or embedded Automation object is to establish a reference to it. (See the FYI titled "Early Binding and Late Binding" on pages 497 through 499 for a description of why this is the most efficient.) As you saw in Chapter 7, you can use the Tools References command in the Visual Basic Editor to refer to object models not intrinsic to the host application itself. In Chapter 7, we established a reference to the DAO object library. The same technique can be used to refer to other Automation objects. For example, the following graphic shows references established to the Word, Access, Outlook, and PowerPoint object libraries from Excel (with the Word library selected):

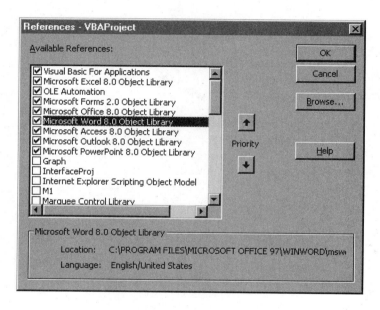

Once the reference is established, you need to create a variable to reference a specific object in that application's object model. (This is typically accomplished with only a few select objects for each application—more details on this in a minute.) So for example, you would use the following variable declaration to refer to Word:

```
Dim objWord as New Word.Application
```

The New keyword tells VBA to launch a new instance of the application and point the object variable to it. The data type or class—Word.Application in this case—tells VBA what type of object application to create. The following table lists the references for each Office application and examples of some of the classes exposed by each reference. The Auto List Members feature of the Visual Basic

Editor provides a comprehensive list of available exposed classes in each object library.

Reference	Class	Description
Microsoft Excel 8.0 Object Library	Excel.Application	Excel application
	Excel.Workbook	Excel workbook
	Excel.Worksheet	Excel worksheet
	Excel.Chart	Excel chart
Microsoft Access 8.0 Object Library	Access.Application	Access application
Microsoft PowerPoint 8.0 Object Library	PowerPoint.Application	PowerPoint application
Microsoft Word 8.0 Object Library	Word.Application	Word application
Microsoft Binder 8.0 Object Library	OfficeBinder.Binder	Office Binder application
Microsoft Outlook 8.0 Object Model	Outlook.Application	Outlook application

Once declared this way, the variable can be used to communicate with any other object that falls within the hierarchy of the object to which it refers. While this method is the best way to refer to external objects, it does present one disadvantage. If code written this way is distributed to a machine that does not have the referred object application installed, the reference will "break" and no code in the application will run. For example, if you establish a reference to Word from your Excel application and distribute that application to users without Word installed, they will not be able to run VBA code in your application and they will receive the following compiler error message if they try:

Using the CreateObject function

You can use the CreateObject function in a controller application to access an Automation object in an object application without establishing a reference to it. CreateObject takes one argument, named class, which is a string that represents the name of the Automation object to be controlled (in most cases the same class names described above); CreateObject returns the specified Automation object.

FYI

Creating Application Objects vs. Other Objects

All the applications we have discussed (except Microsoft Binder) provide an Application object that can be referenced or created using the CreateObject statement. (In Binder, the Binder object provides equivalent functionality.) Just as in the Excel object model, the Application object is the topmost object in Access, Word, PowerPoint, and Outlook. Of course, hundreds of other objects also fall under the Application object in each of the object models. Only a few of these objects can be created directly through the Dim As New syntax or CreateObject function, however. Instead, they are referenced through the Application object, as we'll see in the code samples throughout the chapter.

Examples of objects other than Application that can be directly created include the Excel Chart and Excel Workbook. Each of these objects has a corresponding exposed class that lets you create an instance of the object directly through VBA code. This capability is provided for the Chart and Workbook objects because they are so common.

Following are code fragments that show how you would use CreateObject to create an object of the specified type and assign it to a variable in a controller application.

Excel 97

- Application object: "Excel.Application"

```
Dim XLApp As Object
Set XLApp = CreateObject("Excel.Application")
```

- Workbook object: "Excel.Sheet" (a misnomer—this actually returns a workbook)

```
Dim XLBook As Object
Set XLBook = CreateObject("Excel.Sheet")
```

- Chart object: "Excel.Chart"

```
Dim XLChart As Object
Set XLChart = CreateObject("Excel.Chart")
```

Access 97

- Application object: "Access.Application"

```
Dim AccApp As Object
Set AccApp = CreateObject("Access.Application")
```

PowerPoint 97
- Application object: "PowerPoint.Application"

```
Dim PPTApp As Object
Set PPTApp = CreateObject("PowerPoint.Application")
```

Word 97
- Application object: "Word.Application"

```
Dim WordApp As Object
Set WordApp = CreateObject("Word.Application")
```

- WordBasic object: "Word.Basic" (This is provided only for compatibility with previous versions of Word and the old WordBasic language.)

```
Dim WordBasic As Object
Set WordBasic = CreateObject("Word.Basic")
```

Office Binder
- Binder object: "OfficeBinder.Binder"

```
Dim OfcBind As Object
Set OfcBind = CreateObject("OfficeBinder.Binder")
```

Outlook 97
- Application object: "Outlook.Application"

```
Dim OutlookApp As Object
Set OutlookApp = CreateObject("Outlook.Application")
```

An object variable set using the CreateObject function can be used just like a variable declared with the New keyword as described in the previous section. For example, when you use the CreateObject function in Word to obtain an object for Excel.Application, you can use the returned object to access the entire Excel object model that falls under the Application object.

> **NOTE** You can start or activate any Microsoft Office application programmatically by calling the ActivateMicrosoftApp method on the Application object in Excel. You specify which application to start or activate by passing the appropriate constant: xlMicrosoftWord, xlMicrosoftPowerPoint, xlMicrosoftAccess, xlMicrosoftProject, xlMicrosoftMail, xlMicrosoftSchedulePlus, and even xlMicrosoftFoxPro.

Proc01, which we'll examine in a moment, shows how CreateObject can be used in Access, Word, PowerPoint, Project, or Visual Basic to access the Excel Application object. Proc01 activates Excel with the CreateObject function, opens a new workbook with the Workbook.Add method, and places random numbers in the cells in Range("A1:D5") on the first worksheet. It then closes Excel after asking if you want to save the workbook. If you have a copy of one of these other applications, you might want to try running this routine. Open the CHAP10.XLS file in Excel, select the module named NonExcelRoutines, select all of Proc01, and then choose the Copy command from the Edit menu (or press Ctrl-C). Because CreateObject will start another instance of Excel, you might want to close Excel before executing the routine. To run the routine in another controller application, do one of the following (depending on the application).

- **Word or PowerPoint:** Start the application (in PowerPoint, create a new document) and select the Macro, Visual Basic Editor command from the Tools menu. (This will launch the same Visual Basic Editor we've been using from Excel.) Insert a new module. Choose the Paste command from the Edit menu (or press Ctrl-V) to paste the routine into the new module. To execute the code, click the Run Sub/UserForm button on the Standard toolbar.

- **Access:** Start Access, create a new database, click New on the Modules tab, and then choose the Paste command from the Edit menu (or press Ctrl-V) to paste the routine into the new module. To execute the code in Access, click the Go/Continue button on the Visual Basic toolbar.

- **Visual Basic:** Start Visual Basic, open a new project, add a button to Form1, and paste the routine code into the Click event handler for the button. You will have to remove the old Sub and End Sub lines from the routine after you paste it. Run the form, and then click the button to execute the routine code.

- **Project:** Start Project and open the Macros dialog box with the Tools Macros command. Click New to create a new macro, and click OK to accept the default macro name and description. Delete the default Sub and End Sub lines in the code window, and paste the routine code by using the Edit Paste command or by pressing Ctrl-V. Run the routine using the Run Start command.

```
Sub NonExcelRoutines_Proc01_TalkToExcel()
    Dim XLObj As Object
    Dim RangeVar As Object
    Set XLObj = CreateObject("Excel.Application")
    With XLObj
        .Visible = True
        .Workbooks.Add
        With .ActiveWorkbook.Worksheets(1)
```

```
            For Each RangeVar In .Range("A1:D5")
                RangeVar = 1000 * Rnd
            Next
        End With
    End With
    XLObj.Quit
End Sub
```

Proc02 can be used to access the Excel.Sheet object (which returns a workbook object). This routine performs essentially the same function as does Proc01, but it uses the Excel.Sheet object instead of Excel.Application. Try running Proc02 by copying and pasting the routine from Excel into one of the host applications we discussed:

```
Sub NonExcelRoutines_Proc02_TalkToExcelSheet()
    Dim XLSheet As Object
    Dim RangeVar As Object
    Set XLSheet = CreateObject("Excel.Sheet").ActiveSheet
    With XLSheet
        XLSheet.Application.Visible = True
            For Each RangeVar In .Range("A1:D5")
                RangeVar = 1000 * Rnd
            Next
    End With
    XLSheet.Application.Quit
End Sub
```

And Proc03, which follows, can be used to access the Word.Application object from Excel. The routine opens a new file in Word; enters a title ("Sales Report"); and then formats the title, making it boldface, setting the font size to 32, and centering it horizontally on the page. Notice that this procedure must define the wdAlignParagraphCenter constant because, due to late binding, this code does not have access to the Word object library. This routine can be found in the ExcelRoutines module.

```
Dim WordApp As Object

Sub ExcelRoutines_Proc03_TalkToWord()
    Const wdAlignParagraphCenter = 1
    Set WordApp = CreateObject("Word.Application")
    With WordApp
        .Visible = True
        .Documents.Add
        With .Selection.Font
            .Bold = True
            .Size = 32
        End With
```

(continued)

continued

```
        With .Selection
            .TypeText "Sales Report"
            .ParagraphFormat.Alignment = wdAlignParagraphCenter
        End With
        .Quit
    End With
End Sub
```

Using the GetObject function to access Excel files

The GetObject function is similar to CreateObject. The only difference is that GetObject can be used to access existing documents stored in files—for example, Excel.Sheet objects and Excel.Chart objects. The GetObject function takes two arguments: pathname and class. The pathname argument takes a string that specifies the path of the file that contains the object, and the class argument takes a string that specifies the type of object—e.g., "Excel.Sheet" or "Excel.Chart".

Proc04, which follows, can be run in any controller application to display in a message box the contents of Range("A1") on the first worksheet of the specified Excel file. Note that in the last Set statement in the routine, the value Nothing is assigned to the XLSheet variable to relinquish the Excel.Sheet object. Save a workbook as BOOK1.XLS in the root of your C drive before running this routine. Otherwise, if the file does not exist, a dialog box is displayed indicating that the file cannot be found, and then an "Automation Error" message is displayed. Notice that the Excel.Sheet object actually returns a workbook object, so the ActiveSheet property must be appended to the GetObject call to access the worksheet.

```
Sub NonExcelRoutines_Proc04_RetrieveExcelSheet()
    Dim XLSheet As Object
    Set XLSheet = _
        GetObject("C:\BOOK1.XLS", "Excel.Sheet").ActiveSheet
    MsgBox XLSheet.Range("A1").Value
    Set XLSheet = Nothing
End Sub
```

> **TIP**   After you have an object that references an individual worksheet or chart sheet, you can access other sheets in the same file by referencing the Parent property of the object. Parent returns the Workbook object that contains either the worksheet or the chart sheet.

When GetObject accesses Excel.Sheet or Excel.Chart, objects contained in files, the object application need not be running. GetObject starts the object application when an object file reference is specified.

Using the GetObject function to access running instances of Application objects

GetObject can also be used, however, to access the Application object of any *running* Office application. This is useful when you do not want to start a new instance of the application (which is what CreateObject does). When you want to use GetObject to access any running Office Application object, nothing must be passed for the first argument of GetObject. If the requested Application object is not running, the operation will produce a runtime error.

Proc05, which follows, can be run in a controller application to get the Application object of an instance of Excel that is already running. If Excel is not running when Proc06 is executed, the routine fails.

```
Sub NonExcelRoutines_Proc05_GetXLObject()
    Dim XLObj As Object
    Set XLObj = GetObject(, "Excel.Application")
    MsgBox XLObj.ActiveWorkbook.ActiveSheet.Name
    Set XLObj = Nothing
End Sub
```

FYI

Single Instance Applications

As stated, CreateObject typically creates a new instance of the application to which it is referring (as does the Dim As New method). There is one exception to this rule, however. Some applications register themselves as "single instance" applications, meaning that you cannot run more than one instance of an application at a time. For this type of application, CreateObject or Dim As New would simply reference a running instance instead of creating a new instance. PowerPoint and Word, for example, are single instance applications.

Using Automation to Control an Embedded Object

In a controller application such as Excel, you can activate an embedded object through the OLEObjects collection and then control that object in place through Automation. This process is essentially in-place editing through programming; it combines programming features of Automation with those of in-place editing. For example, let's assume that you are building an application that contains a Word document object embedded in an Excel worksheet. You can use VBA in Excel to activate the Word object and then use Automation to get a Word.Application object to control the embedded Word document. Proc06 uses the OLEObject object in Excel to activate an embedded Word document on the first worksheet and then uses GetObject to access a Word.Application object and format the first line of the embedded document.

```
Dim WordApp As Object

Sub ExcelRoutines_Proc06_ControlWordObject()
    Const wdAlignParagraphCenter = 1
    Const wdLine = 5
    Const wdStory = 6
    Const wdExtend = 1
    With Worksheets(1)
        .Select
        .OLEObjects(1).Activate
        Set WordApp = GetObject(, "Word.Application")
        With WordApp.Selection
            .HomeKey
            .MoveDown wdLine, 1, wdExtend
            With .Font
                .Bold = True
                .Size = 16
                .Name = "Arial"
            End With
            .ParagraphFormat.Alignment = wdAlignParagraphCenter
        End With
        Set WordApp = Nothing
        .Range("A1").Select
    End With
End Sub
```

Here you see the embedded object before Proc06 is run:

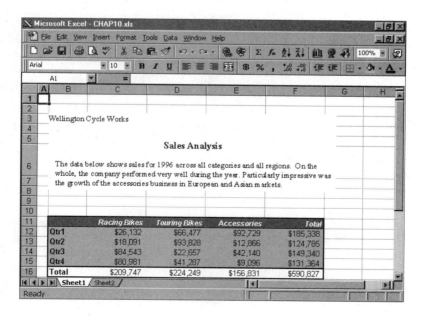

And here you see the embedded object after Proc06 is run:

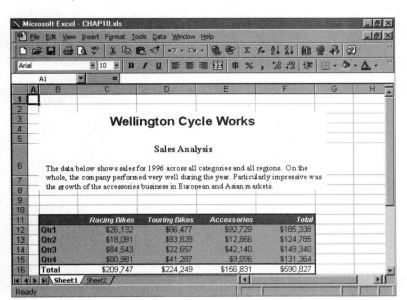

Now that we have covered in-place editing and Automation and have shown how the two can be used together, let's take a look at several other Microsoft applications: Access, PowerPoint, Word, Office Binder, and Visual Basic. The pages that follow focus on the functionality of these applications and provide examples of how that functionality can be incorporated in an Excel VBA solution.

FYI

Early Binding and Late Binding

When you work with objects through Automation, it is important to understand the concepts of "early binding" and "late binding." Early binding provides better performance, but if you want to use early binding, the object application you want to access must provide a special file called an "object library," also called a "type library."

Most object applications come with an object library (.OLB) file that contains information about the various objects and the associated properties and methods provided by the application. If an object application provides a type library, you can establish a reference to the application and take advantage of early binding. For example, assume you are running Excel 97 and Access 97 on the

(continued)

Early Binding and Late Binding, *continued*

same computer. You can establish a reference to the Access type library by first switching to the VBE window and then selecting References from the Tools menu and selecting Microsoft Access 8.0 Object Library from the Available References list. When you establish a reference to a type library in this way, you can take advantage of the two main benefits that early binding provides.

Early binding allows you to declare variables for objects in the external type library using the specific object type. For example, after establishing a reference to Access, you can declare an object variable in Excel of the Form type to represent an Access form:

```
Dim Form1 As Form
```

By allowing you to declare variables of a specific object type available in a referenced type library, early binding provides a mechanism for increasing the performance of your code. You might recall from the discussion in Chapter 2 on declaring object variables that you can enhance performance by using the specific object type when declaring object variables. Early binding resolves object references "early," increasing performance of your code.

Early binding allows you to take advantage of many of the VBE tools that make writing and debugging code easier. These include browsing external objects with the Object Browser and using Auto Syntax Checking, Auto List Members, and Auto QuickInfo in the code editor. You can even access help topics on the objects, properties, events, and methods in the referenced library from within the Object Browser.

Early binding also allows you to use defined constants that are provided by the application. Excel provides numerous defined constants (all of which begin with the letters "xl"). Such constants are provided by other applications as well. For example, Microsoft Access has several defined constants (all of which begin with the letters "ac"). With early binding, you can use defined constants provided by external type libraries, making applications easier to maintain, as well as more readable. As new versions of type libraries for Microsoft applications are released, it is highly likely that values for some defined constants will change. By referencing such constants by name in your code, you need not worry about values of constants changing when you migrate to new versions of Microsoft applications.

It is possible to access objects in a type library of another application without first establishing a reference to the type library—by a process known as late binding. With late binding, when object variables are declared for accessing objects in external type libraries, such variables must be declared as the generic Object type, and not by using the specific object type, as in the following example:

```
Dim Form1 As Object
```

Additionally, with late binding, you cannot access defined constants in an external type library. You must either define such constants yourself or use absolute values in their place. (This forces you to update constant values when new versions of Microsoft applications are released.) By establishing references, you can take advantage of early binding, improve the performance of your code, and make your code easier to maintain. However, when you establish a reference to an external type library as a part of your application, the users of your application must have access to the referenced external type library. If the referenced external type library is absent from the machine of a user, the user might encounter an error message when attempting to run your application. Therefore, you should establish references and take advantage of early binding only when you are absolutely certain that your users will have the referenced type libraries installed on their machines. If you are uncertain, do not establish references and rely on late binding (and declare object variables using the Object type).

> **NOTE** If the type library for an object application installed on your machine does not appear in the list of available references in the Tools References dialog box, you can search for the type library by clicking the Browse button and then selecting the .OLB file associated with the application (usually found in the same directory as the executable file for the application). For example, the type library for Microsoft PowerPoint is stored in the MSPPT8.OLB file found in the same directory as the POWERPNT.EXE file.

As an example, let's assume that you are developing an application in Excel 97 that takes advantage of objects in Access 97 and Word 97. You are absolutely certain that all of your users will have a copy of Access 97 on their machines, but you are uncertain that all users will have Word 97. Under such circumstances, you should establish a reference to Access 97 in your application and take advantage of early binding with Access objects, but you should not establish a reference to Word 97. (You should rely on late binding for referencing Word objects.)

Because the readers of this book are unlikely to have all the Office 97 applications installed on their machines, the CHAP10.XLS sample file does not contain references to external object type libraries but relies on late binding to manipulate objects in other Office applications.

Programming with Microsoft Access 97

Like Excel, Access 97 is an Automation controller and object. You can write VBA applications in Excel 97 that control Access 97 objects or vice versa. Objects that are generally used within Microsoft Access can be divided into two categories:

■ **Access objects:** Those objects contained within the Microsoft Access 97 object library and used for creating user-interface elements of an Access application (forms, reports, controls, and so on).

■ **DAO objects:** Data Access Objects that are used to access the Jet engine as well as other ODBC data sources. (DAO is discussed extensively in Chapter 7 and is not covered here.)

The Access 97 Object Model

The Access object model is shown in Figure 10-1. (Objects in collections appear in boxes; singular objects are not enclosed in boxes.)

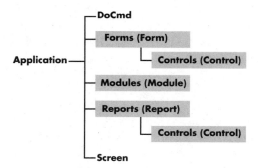

Figure 10-1. *The Microsoft Access object model.*

The Application object is used to access various properties and methods that deal with the Access interface as a whole. The Forms and Reports collections are used to reference forms or reports that are open or displayed. To access forms or reports that are not displayed, you must use a DAO container object (discussed in Chapter 7). There are actually several types of Control objects in Access, including the following: BoundObjectFrame, CheckBox, ComboBox, CommandButton, CustomControl, Image, Label, Line, ListBox, ObjectFrame, OptionButton, OptionGroup, Page, PageBreak, Rectangle, SubForm, TabControl, TextBox, and ToggleButton. The Screen object is used for manipulating various screen display elements; the DoCmd object is used to execute Access macro actions. (Note that Microsoft Access has a macro language that is separate from Visual Basic for Applications. Certain processes in Access require the use of macro actions.)

NOTE Object indexing in Access starts at 0 rather than 1. This is similar to DAO (which begins indexing at 0), but differs from Excel, Power-Point, Word, Outlook, and Project (which begin indexing at 1).

Controlling Access 97 from Excel

Because Access 97 is both an Automation object application and a controller application, you can control Access 97 from a controller application (such as Excel). Proc07, which follows, uses DAO to create a new database and to create a TableDef object that is attached to the Sales table in the BIKEDATA.MDB database. (The BikeData database must be in the same directory as the CHAP10.XLS file in order for the routine to execute properly. Also, you must have established a reference to the DAO 3.5 object library in the Visual Basic editor—a process that is described in detail in Chapter 7.) The routine uses the CreateObject function to obtain a Microsoft Access object. The new database is then opened, and a form that displays all fields from the attached table is created. At the end of the routine, the form is displayed and maximized in the visible Access window. Note that due to late binding, Access constants are defined at the beginning of the routine, and all object variables that refer to Access objects are declared using the generic object type. If you have a copy of Access 97, you can establish a reference to the Microsoft Access 97 type library and remove the defined constants at the beginning of the routine.

```
Dim AccApp As Object

Sub ExcelRoutines_Proc07_CreateAnAccessForm()

'Because this module relies on late binding, various
'Access constants must be declared.
    Const acTextBox As Integer = 109
    Const acLabel As Integer = 100
    Const acDetail As Integer = 0
    Const acCommandButton As Integer = 104
    Const acForm As Integer = 2
    Const acSaveNo As Integer = 2

'Variable declarations
    Dim DB1 As Object
    Dim TB1 As Object
    Dim Form1 As Object
    Dim Control1 As Object
    Dim Label1 As Object
    Dim x As Integer
    Dim y As Variant
```

(continued)

continued

```
'The routine first uses DAO to create a new database.
'Then a TableDef object that is an attached table pointing
'to the BikeData database is created. BikeData
'must be in the same directory as this file, or
'this code will fail.
    On Error Resume Next
    Dim DBEng As New DAO.DBEngine
    Set DB1 = DBEng.Workspaces(0).CreateDatabase( _
            ThisWorkbook.Path & "\SAMPDB.MDB", _
            DBLangGeneral, _
            DBVersion30)
    Set TB1 = DB1.CreateTableDef("Sales", _
                    DBAttachExclusive, _
                    "Sales", _
                    "; Database=" & _
                    ThisWorkbook.Path & "\BIKEDATA.MDB")
    DB1.TableDefs.Append TB1
    DB1.Close

'CreateObject is then used to start Access. The Access
'window is made visible by setting the Visible property,
'and the newly created database is opened.
    Set AccApp = CreateObject("Access.Application")
    With AccApp
        .Visible = True
        .OpenCurrentDatabase ThisWorkbook.Path & "\SAMPDB.MDB"
    End With
    Set DB1 = AccApp.CurrentDB

'The CreateForm method is called to create a new form,
'and the recordsource for the form is set to the
'Sales table.
    Set Form1 = AccApp.CreateForm(DB1.Name, "Normal")
    With Form1
        .RecordSource = "Sales"
        .Width = 2
    End With

'A label and a textbox are then added to the form
'for each field in the table. Adding controls to
'the form might take some time to execute, resulting
'in a slight delay.
    x = 100
    For Each y In DB1.TableDefs("Sales").Fields
        Set Label1 = AccApp.CreateControl(Form1.Name, _
                            acLabel, acDetail, , , _
```

```
                            300, x, 1500, 230)
        Set Control1 = AccApp.CreateControl(Form1.Name, _
                            acTextBox, acDetail, , , _
                            1100, x, 1500, 230)
        Label1.Caption = y.Name
        Control1.ControlSource = y.Name
        x = x + 400
    Next

'A command button is then added to the form. Using the
'InsertText method, a string is assigned to the button as a
'VBA procedure. The button, when clicked, closes the form.
    Set Control1 = AccApp.CreateControl(Form1.Name, _
                            acCommandButton, acDetail, , , _
                            3500, 300, 1000, 400)
    Form1.Module.InsertText "Sub " & Control1.Name & _
        "_Click" & Chr(13) & "Application.DoCmd.Close " & _
        acForm & ", " & """" & Form1.Name & """" & ", " & _
        acSaveNo & Chr(13) & "End Sub"
    With Control1
        .Caption = "Close"
        .OnClick = "[Event Procedure]"
    End With

'Last the active window is maximized, and the
'form is displayed.
    With AccApp.Docmd
    .Save acForm, Form1.Name
        .Maximize
        .OpenForm Form1.Name
    End With
End Sub
```

NOTE	The AccApp object used in Proc07 for controlling Access 97 was declared as a module-level variable. Declaring AccApp as a module-level variable ensures that Access will continue to run after Proc07 ends execution. Variables declared at the procedure level lose their values as soon as routine execution stops. Had AccApp been declared as a procedure-level variable, Access would cease to run after Proc07 finished executing. You will notice that module-level object variables are used to control object applications in most of the sample routines in this chapter.

After executing Proc07, you should see the Microsoft Access 97 window with a form displaying the fields from the Sales table of the BikeData database, as shown at the top of the following page.

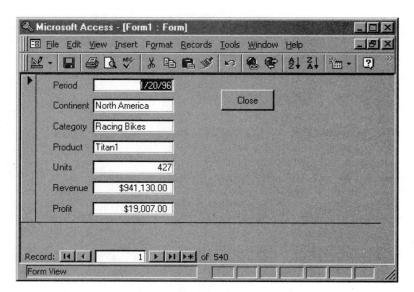

After closing the Access form, you have to manually quit the Access application. However, if you do not interact with Access while it is running, you can quit Access by running Proc08 (shown here), which sets the AccApp variable to Nothing:

```
Sub ExcelRoutines_Proc08_SetAccAppToNothing()
    Set AccApp = Nothing
End Sub
```

Controlling Excel from Access

Access 97 is an Automation controller, allowing you to control Excel 97 from VBA code hosted in Access. Proc09 (the next routine we look at) is an example of an Access procedure that can be used to control Excel. The procedure takes data from an Access form and places it in an Excel worksheet using Automation. A sample database with a form that includes the same code as in Proc09 has been included in the CHAP10.MDB file on this book's companion CD. You can view the code associated with Proc09 in the CHAP10.MDB file by opening the file in Access 97 and then editing Form1. To edit the form, select Form1 under the Form tab of the Database window and click Design. The code for Proc09 is contained in an Access module assigned to the Click event for the Export To Excel button. Close the form to exit design mode. You can execute the following code by opening Form1 and clicking the Export To Excel button.

```
Sub NonExcelRoutines_Proc09_ControlExcelFromAccess()
    Dim xlObj As Object
    Dim RegVar As String
    Dim CouVar As String
    Dim CatVar As String
    Dim SalVar As Double
    RegVar = Forms(0)("Region").Value
    CouVar = Forms(0)("Country").Value
    CatVar = Forms(0)("Category").Value
    SalVar = Forms(0)("Sales").Value
    Set xlObj = CreateObject("Excel.Application")
    With xlObj
        .Visible = True
        .Workbooks.Add
        With .Workbooks(1).Worksheets(1)
            .Range("A1").Value = "Region"
            .Range("A2").Value = "Country"
            .Range("A3").Value = "Category"
            .Range("A4").Value = "Sales"
            .Range("B1").Value = RegVar
            .Range("B2").Value = CouVar
            .Range("B3").Value = CatVar
            .Range("B4").Value = SalVar
            .Range("A1:B1").ColumnWidth = 15
            .Range("B4").NumberFormat = "$#,##0"
        End With
    End With
End Sub
```

The first screen below shows the Access form with which Proc09 is associated, and the second screen (on the following page) shows the results after Proc09 takes data out of the Region, Country, Category, and Sales textboxes and places the data in an Excel worksheet:

Controlling Embedded Excel Objects in Access Forms

You can embed an Excel Worksheet object or a Chart object directly in an Access form and then control that object via Automation. Proc10 provides an example of an Access procedure that does this. Instead of transferring data to a separate Excel worksheet as Proc09 did, Proc10 transfers data from editboxes on the form to an Excel Worksheet object embedded in the form. Form2 in the CHAP10.MDB file contains an embedded Excel worksheet. The code from Proc10 is contained in a module assigned to the Click event for the Place Data In Table button. You can execute this code by opening Form2 and clicking the Place Data In Table button.

```
Sub NonExcelRoutines_Proc10_ControlExcelObjectEmbeddedInAccess()
    Dim xlObj As Object
    Dim RegVar As String
    Dim CouVar As String
    Dim CatVar As String
    Dim SalVar As Double
    RegVar = Forms(0)("Region").Value
    CouVar = Forms(0)("Country").Value
    CatVar = Forms(0)("Category").Value
    SalVar = Forms(0)("Sales").Value
    Forms(0)("Embedded24").Action = acOLEActivate
    Set xlObj = GetObject(, "Excel.Application")
    With xlObj
        .Range("A1").Value = "Region"
        .Range("A2").Value = "Country"
        .Range("A3").Value = "Category"
        .Range("A4").Value = "Sales"
        .Range("B1").Value = RegVar
        .Range("B2").Value = CouVar
        .Range("B3").Value = CatVar
        .Range("B4").Value = SalVar
```

```
        .Range("A1:B1").ColumnWidth = 15
        .Range("B4").NumberFormat = "$#,##0_);($#,##0)"
    End With
    Forms(0)("Embedded24").Action = acOLEUpdate
    Forms(0)("Embedded24").Action = acOLEClose
End Sub
```

Here is the form before Proc10 is executed:

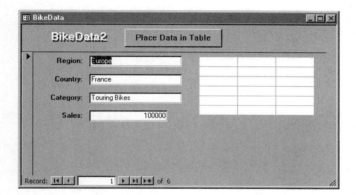

The next example screen shows the form after Proc10 has finished executing and the data has been transferred to the embedded Excel Worksheet object:

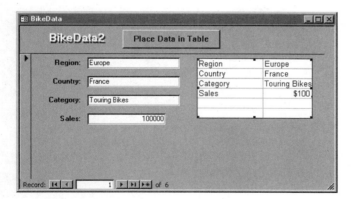

Programming with Microsoft PowerPoint 97

PowerPoint 97 provides a powerful object model for creating graphical presentations that can be used for displaying or reporting data in slide format. In this section, we will look at controlling PowerPoint 97 through Automation. Note also that PowerPoint 97 is an Automation controller and hosts the same VBA environment as Excel 97.

The PowerPoint 97 Object Model

A portion of the PowerPoint 97 object model is shown in Figure 10-2. To view the complete object model, see the Microsoft PowerPoint Visual Basic Reference topic in PowerPoint online Help.

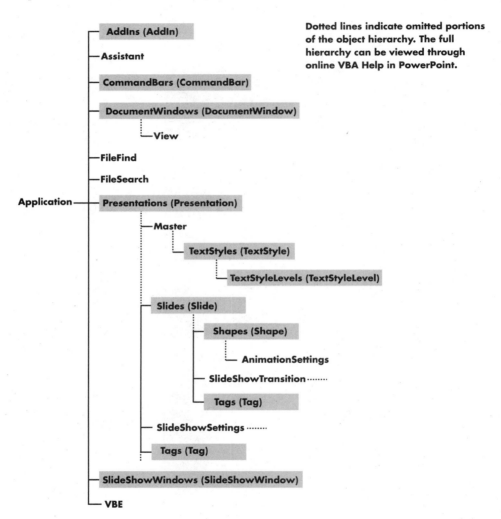

Figure 10-2. *The Microsoft PowerPoint 97 object model (partial reproduction).*

The PowerPoint 97 object model contains numerous objects, and on the surface the model can appear to be quite complex. However, it does bear some similarity to Excel's object model in its hierarchical structure as well as in its use of collections. Space does not permit an in-depth discussion of the PowerPoint 97 object model here, but we will briefly review some of the main objects and take a look at a rather complicated routine that is used to build a PowerPoint presentation. Following are descriptions of some of the more important objects found in the PowerPoint 97 object model.

Application: Sits at the top of the PowerPoint 97 object model hierarchy. It is the object that is returned from CreateObject. With the Application object, you can do the following (this is a partial list of functionality accessible through the Application object):

- Add a new presentation (by calling the Add method on the Presentations collection).

- Access the Slides collection. By calling the GotoSlide method on the View object contained in a Document Window object, you can activate a specific slide.

- Call the Quit method to quit PowerPoint.

Presentation: Accessed through the Presentations collection contained within the Application object. The Presentation object represents the PowerPoint file. Each presentation contains a series of Slide objects that make up the presentation. With the Presentations collection, you can add a new presentation or open an existing presentation. With the Presentation object, you can do the following, among other tasks:

- Add new slides by calling the Add method on the Slides collection contained in the Presentation object.

- Save a presentation file.

- Access the SlideShowSettings object to set various parameters that will govern the showing of the presentation.

- Create and set Tags (custom properties) for the presentation.

Slide: Accessed through the Slides collection contained within the Presentation object. Using the Slides collection, you can add, find, or insert slides. A slide represents a single "page" of a presentation. A series of slides make up the entire presentation. Using the Slide object, you can do the following:

- Add background fills to your slide through the Background property.

- Add Shape objects (nearly identical to the shape object in Excel). These include textboxes as well as various other graphical objects, embedded ActiveX objects, or video clips. Also be aware that there are several methods that can be used to add various kinds of Shape objects to a slide. All of these methods are called on the Shapes collection.

- Set the layout of the slide through the Layout property.

- Add text to the slide's notes page through the NotesPage property.

Use the Master object (accessible through the Master property of a Slide object) to set background fills, build-effects, and other parameters that will be applied to each slide in your presentation.

Shape: Used to represent various graphical elements on a Slide object. Shape objects are accessed through each slide's Shapes collection and can be used to manipulate the size, position, and formatting of shapes. The fundamentals of Shape objects covered in Chapter 3 apply to PowerPoint shape objects as well.

AnimationSettings: A property of the Shape object that lets you control various animation settings for the shape. These can include the EntryEffect (such as ppEffectBlindsHorizontal or ppEffectFlyFromLeft), SoundEffect, and AfterEffect. For text within shapes, you can also specify subeffects such as word-level or character-level builds.

SlideShowTransition: Used to specify slide-show effects for advancing individual slides. SlideShowTransition can also be used to hide slides or to specify the AdvanceTime property, which is used when a slide show is run using slide timings.

SlideShowSettings: Used in actually running the slide show or displaying the slides of the presentation. The only method of the SlideShowSettings object is the Run method, which will run the slide show once. Note that if you set the LoopUntilStopped property to True, the slide show will run continuously when the Run method is called.

TextStyle: Used to specify various parameters for styles of text used within the presentation.

TextStyleLevel: The TextStyleLevel object, accessed through the TextStyle-Levels collection, is used to reference different text levels within textboxes in a presentation and, through such text levels, to set various parameters of the text style for a particular level.

Tag: Essentially a custom property. You access a Tag through the Tags collection. You can create custom Tag objects for various PowerPoint objects, allowing you to specify custom information regarding such objects.

A Sample PowerPoint 97 Application

The object model provided by PowerPoint 97 is quite extensive and provides advanced capabilities for creating multimedia presentations. In this section, we look at a sample routine that takes advantage of many of the objects we've just examined to create a PowerPoint 97 presentation from data contained within an Excel spreadsheet. Proc11, which we look at next, is rather long, but it contains comments throughout explaining the various segments of code within the routine. Note that in the CHAP10.XLS sample file included on the companion CD, there is no established reference to the PowerPoint 97 object library. Proc11 relies on late binding in working with PowerPoint 97 objects. In the sample file, you will find numerous declarations for PowerPoint 97 constants in Proc11. (These declarations are not displayed here in order to conserve space.) If you have access to a copy of PowerPoint 97, you can establish a reference to the PowerPoint 97 object library to take advantage of early binding. You will find that after establishing such a reference, you can delete the constant declarations and still run Proc11 successfully.

Proc11 creates three slides that make up a presentation for Setagaya Cycle. The resulting presentation might not be all that visually appealing—numerous fill, transition, and build effects have been incorporated purely for the sake of demonstrating some of the capabilities of PowerPoint 97. Slides are created one at a time. At the end of the presentation, the Run method is called on the Slide-ShowSettings object to run the presentation. (Note that because the Advance-Mode property is set to use slide timings, the presentation runs on its own.) You might want to run this routine as you analyze it in this book in order to better familiarize yourself with the various PowerPoint 97 objects it uses.

```
Dim PPTApp As Object

Sub ExcelRoutines_Proc11_CreatePowerPointPresentation()

'Variable Declarations:
    Dim Pres1 As Object
    Dim Slide1 As Object
    Dim Shape1 As Object
    Dim Shape2 As Object
    Dim Shape3 As Object
    Dim Shape4 As Object
    Dim Shape5 As Object
    Dim Picture1 As Object
    Dim SlideNum As Integer
    Dim x As Variant
```

(continued)

continued

```
'The routine starts by using CreateObject to get
'an object that points to PowerPoint.
    Set PPTApp = CreateObject("PowerPoint.Application")

'The PowerPoint window is then maximized and a
'new presentation is added.
    With PPTApp
        .Visible = True
        .WindowState = ppWindowMaximized
        Set Pres1 = PPTApp.Presentations.Add
    End With

'The first slide is added -- the title slide.
        Set Slide1 = Pres1.Slides.Add(1, ppLayoutTitleOnly)
        Pres1.SlideMaster.Background.Fill.PresetTextured _
            msoTextureFishFossil

'Then various properties of the first shape
'on the title slide are set.
    With Slide1
        With .Shapes(1)
            .Top = 120
            With .TextFrame.TextRange
                .Text = "Setagaya Cycle" & Chr(13) & _
                    "Annual Sales Report"
                .Font.Size = 54
            End With
            With .AnimationSettings
                .EntryEffect = ppEffectCheckerboardDown
                .AdvanceMode = ppAdvanceOnTime
            End With
        End With
    End With

'Three graphic objects representing a bicycle are added to
'the slide. The objects are assigned one-color shades
'and random build effects.
        With Slide1.Shapes
            Set Shape1 = .AddShape(msoShapeOval, _
                100, 300, 200, 200)
            With Shape1.Fill
                .ForeColor.RGB = RGB(255, 0, 0)
                .BackColor.RGB = RGB(255, 255, 255)
                .OneColorGradient msoGradientHorizontal, 1, 1
            End With
            With Shape1.AnimationSettings
```

```
                .EntryEffect = ppEffectRandom
                .AdvanceMode = ppAdvanceOnTime
            End With
            Set Shape2 = .AddShape(msoShapeOval, _
                400, 300, 200, 200)
            With Shape2.Fill
                .ForeColor.RGB = RGB(0, 255, 0)
                .BackColor.RGB = RGB(255, 255, 255)
                .OneColorGradient msoGradientHorizontal, 1, 1
            End With
            With Shape2.AnimationSettings
                .EntryEffect = ppEffectRandom
                .AdvanceMode = ppAdvanceOnTime
            End With
            Set Shape3 = .AddShape(msoShapeParallelogram, _
                Shape1.Left + (Shape1.Width * 0.5), _
                Shape1.Top + (Shape1.Height * 0.33), _
                (Shape2.Left + (Shape2.Width * 0.5)) - _
                (Shape1.Left + (Shape1.Width * 0.5)), _
                Shape1.Height * 0.25)
            With Shape3.Fill
                .ForeColor.RGB = RGB(0, 0, 255)
                .BackColor.RGB = RGB(255, 255, 255)
                .OneColorGradient msoGradientHorizontal, 1, 1
            End With
            With Shape3.AnimationSettings
                .EntryEffect = ppEffectRandom
                .AdvanceMode = ppAdvanceOnTime
            End With
        End With

'Before moving to the second slide, the first slide
'is assigned an advance time of 1 second and a random
'entry effect.
        With .SlideShowTransition
            .AdvanceOnTime = True
            .AdvanceTime = 1
            .EntryEffect = ppEffectRandom
        End With
    End With

'The second slide is added and activated.
    SlideNum = Pres1.Slides.Count + 1
    Set Slide1 = Pres1.Slides.Add(SlideNum, ppLayoutText)
    PPTApp.ActiveWindow.View.GotoSlide SlideNum
```

(continued)

continued

```
'As a text slide, the second slide contains two shapes
'that can hold text.  Text strings are assigned to both.
'The second slide object holds bulleted points. A
'continuous text string with line-feed characters--chr(13)--
'is assigned to the shape and used to create the bulleted points.
    With Slide1
        .Background.Fill.PresetTextured msoTextureBouquet
        .Shapes(1).TextFrame.TextRange.Text = _
            "Revenue Growth by Region"
        With .Shapes(2)
            .TextFrame.TextRange.Text = "North" & Chr(13) & _
                    "Sales are getting Stronger every day." & _
                    Chr(13) & "South" & Chr(13) & _
                    "Revenue is at a record high." & _
                    Chr(13) & "East" & Chr(13) & _
                    "We can't grow any faster." & _
                    Chr(13) & "West" & Chr(13) & _
                    "This is by far the best year ever."

'Through use of IndentLevel, even lines are indented.
            For x = 1 To 8
                If x Mod 2 = 0 Then
                  .TextFrame.TextRange.Lines(x, 1).IndentLevel = 2
                Else
                  .TextFrame.TextRange.Lines(x, 1).IndentLevel = 1
                End If
              Next
            .Left = 100

'A character fly-from-top build effect is then assigned
'to the shape.
            With .AnimationSettings
                .EntryEffect = ppEffectFlyFromTop
                .TextUnitEffect = ppAnimateByWord
                .TextLevelEffect = ppAnimateByFirstLevel
                .AdvanceMode = ppAdvanceOnTime
            End With
        End With

'And lastly, advance time and entry effects are set
'for the second slide.
        With .SlideShowTransition
            .AdvancedOnTime = True
            .AdvanceTime = 1
            .EntryEffect = ppEffectRandom
        End With
    End With
```

```
'The third slide is added to the presentation and activated.
    SlideNum = Pres1.Slides.Count + 1
    Set Slide1 = Pres1.Slides.Add(SlideNum, ppLayoutTitleOnly)
    PPTApp.ActiveWindow.View.GotoSlide SlideNum
    With Slide1
        .Shapes(1).TextFrame.TextRange.Text = _
            "Quarterly Sales Summary"
        With .SlideShowTransition
            .AdvanceOnTime = True
            .AdvanceTime = 1
            .EntryEffect = ppEffectRandom
        End With
    End With

'After setting various effects for the slide, a worksheet
'is copied from Sheet1 and pasted into the slide.  The routine
'then adjusts the size of the embedded Excel worksheet object
'and assigns build effects.
    Worksheets("Sheet1").Range("SalesTable").Copy
    PPTApp.ActiveWindow.View.Paste
    Set Shape4 = Slide1.Shapes(2)
    With Shape4
        .Top = .Top * 0.6
        .Left = .Left * 0.4
        .Width = .Width * 1.2
        .Height = .Height * 1.2
        With .AnimationSettings
            .EntryEffect = ppEffectBoxOut
            .AdvanceMode = ppAdvanceOnTime
        End With
    End With

'Likewise, a chart is copied and pasted into the slide.
    Worksheets("Sheet1").ChartObjects("SalesChart").Copy
    PPTApp.ActiveWindow.View.Paste
    Set Shape5 = Slide1.Shapes(3)
    With Shape5
        .Top = Shape4.Top + Shape4.Height + 20
        .Left = Shape4.Left
        .Width = Shape4.Width
        .Height = .Height * 1.2
        With .AnimationSettings
            .EntryEffect = ppEffectBoxIn
            .AdvanceMode = ppAdvanceOnTime
        End With
    End With
```

(continued)

continued

```
'When all slides are built, the first slide is
'activated, various parameters of the SlideShowSettings
'object are set, and the Run method is called
'on the SlideShowSettings object to start the show.
    PPTApp.ActiveWindow.View.GotoSlide 1
    With Pres1.SlideShowSettings
        .StartingSlide = 1
        .EndingSlide = 3
        .AdvanceMode = ppSlideShowUseSlideTimings
        .Run
    End With
End Sub
```

> **NOTE** PowerPoint 97 will continue to run even after you set an object variable representing PowerPoint 97 to Nothing. This allows you to start a slide show and leave it running. To exit PowerPoint, call the Quit method on the PowerPoint Application object.

After running Proc11, a PowerPoint 97 presentation is created that contains the following three slides:

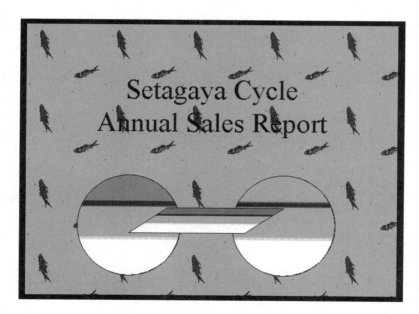

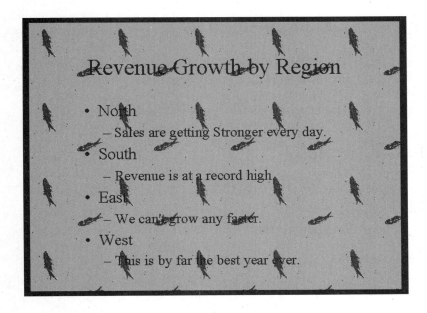

Programming with Microsoft Word 97

Microsoft Word provides advanced report generation functionality. For an Excel VBA solution designed to include advanced reporting, consider Word as an appropriate programmable reporting tool. Word serves as both an Automation object and controller, meaning it can be controlled via VBA code and can control other applications. This chapter will focus on controlling Word as an Automation object.

The Word 97 Object Model

A portion of the Word 97 object model is shown in Figure 10-3. To view the complete object model, see the Microsoft Word Visual Basic Reference topic in Word online Help.

The Word 97 object model contains numerous objects, and on the surface the model can appear to be quite complex. However, it does bear some similarity to Excel's object model in its hierarchical structure as well as in its use of collections. Space does not permit an in-depth discussion of the Word 97 object model here, but we will briefly review some of the main objects and take a look at a sample routine that is used to build a Word report. Following are descriptions of some of the more important objects found in the Word 97 object model.

Application: Sits at the top of the Word 97 object model hierarchy. It is the object that is returned from CreateObject.

Document: Represents a Word document file. It is contained in the Documents collection of the Application object. You can create a new document with the Add method of the Documents collection or open an existing one with the Open method of the Documents collection. You can also save and close documents with the Save and Close methods.

Selection: Represents the currently selected area of the active document. This could be as small as an insertion point or as large as the entire document. The Selection object provides methods to insert text; move the cursor throughout the document; and perform cut, copy, and paste operations. This object is typically accessed using the Selection property of the Application object.

Methods to insert text include InsertBefore and InsertAfter, which insert text before or after the selection (without replacing the selection); and TypeText (which, if the Replace Selection property is True, replaces the current selection). InsertParagraphBefore and InsertParagraphAfter insert a paragraph without replacing the selection, whereas TypeParagraph does replace the selection.

The MoveLeft, MoveRight, MoveUp, MoveDown, HomeKey, and EndKey methods all move the insertion point relative to the current selection. They can all operate in different units such as a character, word, sentence, line, paragraph, or section.

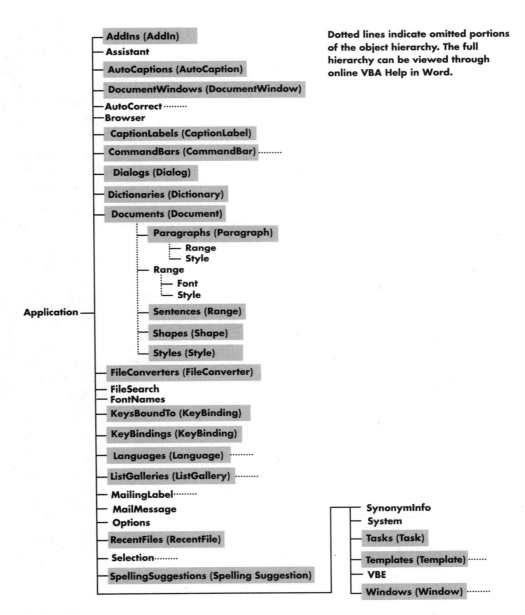

Figure 10-3. *The Microsoft Word 97 object model (partial reproduction).*

Range: Very similar to the Selection object in terms of the properties and methods it offers. A Range object is different because it represents a contiguous range of a document *independent* of the current selection. It is, in fact, analogous to Excel's Range object. You can set variables to refer to Word Range objects and manipulate their formatting and other properties just as if they were selected.

Range objects have a Select method to force their selection, and they have a Text property to return a string representing the text contained in the Range.

The Document object has a Range method that lets you specify as arguments a start and end point for the range. The Characters method of the Document object returns a characters collection object which allows you to access individual characters as Range objects by specifying an index in the collection (with the first character in the document being index 1). You can also get Range objects in larger units such as paragraphs and sentences.

Paragraph: Represents a single paragraph of text in a document. It is accessed through the Paragraphs collection of the Document object via an index. Paragraphs are numbered sequentially, with the first paragraph in the document being index 1.

The Paragraph object contains a Range object that you can use to treat the paragraph as a range. It also contains a set of properties under its ParagraphFormat object that control paragraph-level formatting such as Alignment, SpaceBefore, SpaceAfter, and LeftIndent.

Sentences Collection: A collection of Range objects; each represents a single sentence of text in a document. Sentences are numbered sequentially; the first sentence in the document is index 1.

Font: The Font object groups properties that control formatting such as the font name, size, and bold attribute. It can be accessed as a property of the Style and Range objects.

Style: Represents a named group of formatting properties that can be applied to a paragraph in one step.

Shape: Word implements a Shapes collection of Shape objects nearly identical to the collection we have already seen in Excel and PowerPoint.

A Sample Word 97 Application

The object model provided by Word 97 is quite extensive and provides advanced capabilities for creating complex reports from data stored in Excel and in many other sources. In this section, we look at a sample routine that takes advantage of the Word object model to create a simple sales report. Proc12, which follows, shows how Word can be called from an Excel VBA routine to create a report. In the sample file, there are numerous declarations for Word 97 constants in Proc12—these declarations are omitted here.

```
Dim WordApp As Object

Sub ExcelRoutines_Proc12_CreateWordReport()
    Dim WordDoc As Object
    Set WordApp = CreateObject("Word.Application")
    With WordApp
        .Visible = True
        .WindowState = wdWindowStateMaximize
        .Documents.Add
        Set WordDoc = .ActiveDocument
    End With
    WordDoc.ActiveWindow.View = wdNormalView
    With WordApp.Selection
        .InsertAfter "Wellington Cycle Works"
        .InsertParagraphAfter
        .InsertAfter "Sales Report"
        .InsertParagraphAfter
        .InsertAfter "Presented below are sales results for the " _
            & "current year:"
        .InsertParagraphAfter
        .MoveRight
    End With
    With WordDoc.Paragraphs(1).Range
        .ParagraphFormat.Alignment = wdAlignParagraphCenter
        With .Font
            .Name = "Arial"
            .Size = 20
            .Bold = True
            .Animation = wdAnimationShimmer
        End With
    End With
    With WordDoc.Paragraphs(2).Range
        With .ParagraphFormat
            .SpaceAfter = 12
            .Alignment = wdAlignParagraphCenter
        End With
        With .Font
            .Name = "Arial"
            .Size = 14
        End With
    End With
    WordDoc.Paragraphs(3).Range.ParagraphFormat.SpaceAfter = 30
    Range("SalesTable").Copy
    With WordApp.Selection
        .Paste
        .TypeParagraph
    End With
```

(continued)

continued

```
Worksheets("Sheet1").ChartObjects("SalesChart").Copy
With WordApp
    .Selection.PasteSpecial Link:=False, _
        DataType:=wdPasteMetafilePicture, _
        Placement:=wdInLine, DisplayAsIcon:=False
    .Selection.ParagraphFormat.Alignment = _
        wdAlignParagraphCenter
    .Selection.GoTo What:=wdGoToLine, Which:=wdGoToAbsolute, _
        Count:=1
End With
End Sub
```

The following screen shows the Word document created by running Proc12:

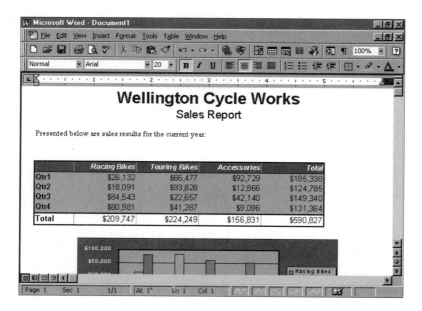

As stated earlier in this chapter, a routine can control a Word document object embedded in an Excel worksheet. Refer to Proc06 on page 496 for an example of how to select and modify an embedded Word object.

Programming with Microsoft Outlook 97

Microsoft Outlook is a "Desktop Information Manager" with built-in e-mail, group scheduling, contact management, to-do lists, notes, and journaling. It can work with many back-end mail systems and groupware products including Microsoft

Exchange and Microsoft Mail. As a programmable application, Outlook provides an extensive object model with which you can fully manipulate all its features. We'll take a brief look at how to navigate through Outlook folders and create different types of items. You can learn more about Outlook through the Outlook VBA Help file (which is available in the ValuPack folder on the Office 97 CD) and through the Object Browser.

The Outlook Object Model

The Outlook object model is shown in Figure 10-4.

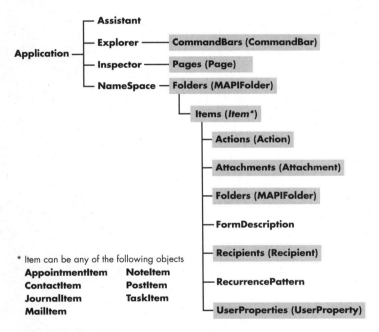

Figure 10-4. *The Microsoft Outlook object model.*

The hierarchy of the Outlook object model is straightforward and corresponds to the folder/subfolder structure that is visible in the Outlook user interface. The most common objects are described as follows.

Application: At the top level is the Application object, which represents Outlook itself.

NameSpace: Below the application is the NameSpace object, which represents a particular messaging layer. Currently, MAPI is the only type of NameSpace supported. This object is accessed through the GetNameSpace method of the Application object.

MAPIFolder: The NameSpace object contains a Folders collection that is made up of one or more MAPIFolder objects. These objects correspond to the folders that are displayed in Outlook. Any MAPIFolder object can also contain a Folders collection of additional MAPIFolder objects. In this manner, folders can be nested ad infinitum. Proc13 iterates through each folder in the Name-Space object, and recursively calls Proc14 to iterate through any subfolders which may exist:

```
Sub ExcelRoutines_Proc13_ListFolders()
    Dim OutlookApp As Object
    Dim NS As Object
    Dim Folder As Object
    Set OutlookApp = CreateObject("Outlook.Application")
    Set NS = OutlookApp.GetNamespace("MAPI")
    For Each Folder In NS.Folders
        If MsgBox(Folder.Name, vbOKCancel) = vbCancel Then End
        If Folder.Folders.Count > 0 Then
            ExcelRoutines_Proc14_ListSubFolders Folder
        End If
    Next Folder
End Sub

Sub ExcelRoutines_Proc14_ListSubFolders(Folder As Object)
    Dim Subfolder As Object
    For Each Subfolder In Folder.Folders
        If MsgBox(Folder.Name & ": " & Subfolder.Name, vbOKCancel) _
            = vbCancel Then End
        If Subfolder.Folders.Count > 0 Then
            ExcelRoutines_Proc14_ListSubFolders Subfolder
        End If
    Next Subfolder
End Sub
```

Item Objects (7 Different Types): In Outlook, a MAPIFolder object can contain items of different types: tasks, contacts, appointments, journal entries, notes, posts, and messages. All these different types of items can be accessed through the Items collection of the MAPIFolder object.

To create a new item, call the CreateItem method of the Application object. This method takes one argument, called type, which determines which type of item is created. Depending on the value of type, one of the following objects will be created: MailItem, ContactItem, AppointmentItem, TaskItem, JournalItem, PostItem, or NoteItem.

NOTE An alternative way to create an item is to call the Add method of the Items collection of a specific Folder to create a new item in that folder.

Each of the item objects has common methods like Save (used to save an item in a folder), Display (used to display an item in a window), and Copy (used to create a duplicate of an item). Common properties like Subject are available as well. Each item object type also has a set of unique properties that correspond to the fields specific to the particular object. For example, LastName and First-Name are properties of the ContactItem object.

Proc15, which follows, demonstrates creating one of each type of the item objects available. Note that when you run this routine, the items are created in the appropriate folder—Outlook automatically creates each item in the folder that makes logical sense. When this routine is finished, open Outlook and look at the various items that were created.

```
Sub ExcelRoutines_Proc15_AddOutlookItems()
    Dim OutlookApp As Object
    Const olMailItem = 0
    Const olAppointmentItem = 1
    Const olContactItem = 2
    Const olTaskItem = 3
    Const olJournalItem = 4
    Const olNoteItem = 5
    Const olPostItem = 6
    Const olPink = 2
    Set OutlookApp = CreateObject("Outlook.Application")
    With OutlookApp.CreateItem(olTaskItem)
        .Subject = "New Task from Excel"
        .DueDate = Now()
        .Save
    End With
    With OutlookApp.CreateItem(olContactItem)
        .Save
        .LastName = "Jones"
        .FirstName = "Robert"
        .BusinessTelephoneNumber = "(703) 555-1212"
        .Save
    End With
    With OutlookApp.CreateItem(olNoteItem)
        .Body = "Learn the Outlook object model!"
        .Color = olPink
        .Save
    End With
```

(continued)

continued

```
With OutlookApp.CreateItem(olAppointmentItem)
    .Start = Date & " 2:00 pm"
    .End = Date & " 3:00 pm"
    .Subject = "Meet with staff re Outlook object model."
    .Save
End With
With OutlookApp.CreateItem(olJournalItem)
    .Subject = "Entry made by Excel."
    .Type = "Excel 97 Developer's Handbook"
    .Start = Now
    .Save
End With
With OutlookApp.CreateItem(olMailItem)
    .Subject = "Test message"
    .Body = "This is a test message."
    .To = "Steve"
    .Save
    ' Since the addressee will not be recognized,
    ' we just save the message into
    ' a folder instead of calling the send method
    '.Send
End With
With OutlookApp.CreateItem(olPostItem)
    .Subject = "Test posting"
    .Body = "This is a test posting."
    .Save
    'Since we don't want to actually post
    'this message, we just save it into
    'a folder instead of calling the post method
    '.Post
End With
End Sub
```

Programming with Microsoft Office Binder 97

Microsoft Office Binder, a feature of Office 97, provides a common file type for storing multiple Office documents within a single file (the .OBD file). Excel 97, Word 97, and PowerPoint 97 all support Office Binder. (Access does not support the Office Binder.) You can store documents from all three of these applications in a single file. In addition, several third-party products that are compatible with Office support Office Binder, including TriSpectives by 3D/Eye, Designer and Picture Publisher by MicroGrafx, and Visio by Visio Corporation.

As an object application (not a controller application), Office Binder provides a very simple object model that can be used for saving, retrieving, and printing documents in an office binder. (We'll take only a brief look at Office Binder objects here.) Office Binder objects are documented in a help file that can be found in the ValuPack folder of the Office 97 install CD. You can access help topics on the various properties and methods associated with Office Binder objects through the Object Browser: first establish a reference to the Office Binder 8.0 object library, and then use the Object Browser to access the various Office Binder objects. Office Binder is rather simple in its structure and in the actions it can perform.

The Office Binder Object Model and Objects

The Office Binder object model is shown in Figure 10-5.

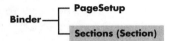

Figure 10-5. *The Microsoft Office Binder object model.*

As you can see in Figure 10-5, Office Binder is characterized by three objects: Binder, PageSetup, and Section. The Object property of the Section object represents objects that are not actually a part of the Office Binder object model. Instead, the Object property is used as an entry point to object models of files contained within a binder. For example, if you have an Excel file as the first section of a Binder object, you could access the Excel object model for that particular file by referencing the following:

```
Binder.Sections(1).Object
```

Following are brief descriptions of Binder objects.

Binder: Used to reference a binder file. With the Binder object, you can open binder files, add sections to a Binder object (by calling the Add method on the Sections collection), print sections, and save binder files.

Section: Used to reference an embedded file that makes up a section of the binder. As mentioned, Excel 97, Word 97, and PowerPoint 97 support Office Binder, and therefore files from these applications can be included as sections of a Binder object. You add a new section to a Binder object by calling the Add method on the Sections collection. You can reference a specific section in the Binder object by indexing the Sections collection by number or by the name of the section. With the Section object, you can activate, delete, and move sections. Through the Section object, you can also access the Object property to access the object model of an embedded file.

The object returned by the Object property is not really a part of the Binder object model, but it serves as an entry point for accessing the object models of files embedded within a Binder object. Proc16 on page 528 provides an example of using the Object property to manipulate an Excel workbook file embedded in a Binder object.

Controlling Office Binder from Excel

Using VBA in Excel, you can create and manipulate Binder objects as well as gain access to the object models associated with files stored within a Binder object. Office Binder provides a type library when you install Office 97. This allows you to establish a reference to the type library from a VBA module and then view Binder objects using the Object Browser as well as take advantage of early binding (by declaring object variables of Binder object types and accessing Office Binder–specific constants). The CHAP10.XLS file included on the companion CD does not contain a reference to the Office Binder object library, so the file relies on late binding to access Binder objects. Also note (as stated previously) that complete help is provided on Binder objects when you install the Binder Visual Basic Help file from the Office 97 install CD. (The help topics are accessible from the Object Browser.)

Proc16, which follows, provides an example of an Office binder being created. The routine starts out by creating and saving three files: a Word file, a PowerPoint file, and an Excel file. A new Binder object is then created by calling the Create-Object function and passing "OfficeBinder.Binder". The three files are then added as sections to the Binder object, and the Binder object is displayed by setting the Visible property of the Binder object to True:

```
Sub ExcelRoutines_Proc16_CreateOfficeBinder()
    Const ppLayoutTitleOnly As Integer = 11
    Dim WordApp As Object
    Dim PPTApp As Object
    Dim Pres1 As Object
    Dim Slide1 As Object
    Dim Book1 As Workbook
    Dim WordPath As String
    Dim PPTPath As String
    Dim XLPath As String
    WordPath = ThisWorkbook.Path & "\WordDoc1.doc"
    PPTPath = ThisWorkbook.Path & "\PPTPres1.ppt"
    XLPath = ThisWorkbook.Path & "\XLWkBk1.xls"
    Set WordApp = CreateObject("Word.Application")
    With WordApp
        .Visible = True
        .Documents.Add
        .Selection.InsertAfter "This is a Binder Document."
        .ActiveDocument.SaveAs ThisWorkbook.Path _
            & "\WordDoc1.doc"
        .ActiveDocument.Close
    End With
    WordApp.Quit
    Set WordApp = Nothing
    Set PPTApp = CreateObject("PowerPoint.Application")
    With PPTApp
        .Visible = True
```

```
        Set Pres1 = .Presentations.Add
        Set Slide1 = Pres1.Slides.Add(1, ppLayoutTitleOnly)
        Slide1.Shapes(1).TextFrame.TextRange.Text = _
            "Binder Presentation"
        Pres1.SaveAs PPTPath
    End With
    PPTApp.Quit
    Set PPTApp = Nothing
    Set Book1 = Workbooks.Add
    With Book1.Worksheets(1)
        With .Range("A1")
            .Value = "Binder Data"
            .Font.Size = 18
            .Font.Bold = True
        End With
        .Range("A2:E10").Formula = "=Int(10000*Rand())"
    End With
    Application.DisplayAlerts = False
    Book1.SaveAs XLPath
    Book1.Close
    Set OfcBind = CreateObject("OfficeBinder.Binder")
    With OfcBind
        .Sections.Add Filename:=WordPath
        .Sections.Add Filename:=PPTPath
        .Sections.Add Filename:=XLPath
        .Visible = True
    End With
End Sub
```

The resulting Office binder from Proc16 appears as follows:

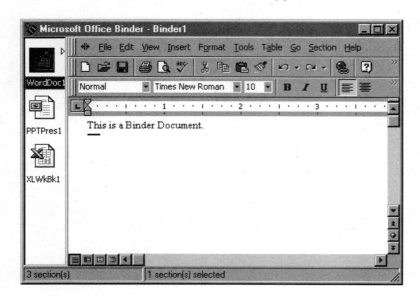

Proc17 provides an example of accessing the object model associated with an Excel workbook file embedded in a Binder object. The routine starts out by creating and saving an Excel file. A Binder object is then created and the Excel file is added as a section. By indexing the Sections collection and accessing the Object property, the routine gains entry to the Excel object model for the embedded file at the worksheet level—in this case, the active sheet. New data is entered into a range on the active sheet. In accessing other sheets contained within the embedded Excel file, the Parent property is used to gain a reference to the workbook file, and then the Worksheets collection of the Workbook object is indexed to access the second sheet (on which data is then entered):

```vb
Sub ExcelRoutines_Proc17_ControlExcelInBinder()
    On Error Resume Next
    Dim Book1 As Workbook
    Dim XLPath As String
    XLPath = ThisWorkbook.Path & "\XLWkBk1.xls"
    Set Book1 = Workbooks.Add
    With Book1.Worksheets(1)
        With .Range("A1")
            .Value = "Binder Data"
            .Font.Size = 18
            .Font.Bold = True
        End With
        .Range("A2:E10").Formula = "=Int(10000 * Rand())"
    End With
    Application.DisplayAlerts = False
    Book1.SaveAs XLPath
    Book1.Close
    Set OfcBind = CreateObject("OfficeBinder.Binder")
    With OfcBind
        .Sections.Add Filename:=XLPath
        .Visible = True
        With .Sections("XLWkBk1").Object
            .Range("A1:E10").Value = "NewData"
            With .Parent.Worksheets(2)
                .Range("A1:Z256").Value = "Sheet2"
                .Select
            End With
        End With
    End With
End Sub
```

Programming with Microsoft Visual Basic

Visual Basic 4 and 5 are both Automation objects and controllers. As such, you can control Excel from Visual Basic executables or use Excel to control Visual Basic executables through ActiveX. Note that Visual Basic 3 is an Automation controller only. (With Visual Basic 3, you can write applications that can control Excel but not vice versa.) Because VBA serves as the language engine for Visual Basic 4 and 5, many of the code samples that we have already looked at in this chapter could easily be adapted to run in Visual Basic.

Controlling Excel from Visual Basic

The process of controlling Excel from Visual Basic is the same as the process used for controlling Excel from Access, PowerPoint, or Word. From Visual Basic, you establish a reference and declare a variable that references Excel with the New keyword, or you use the CreateObject or GetObject function to obtain an Application object for Excel. You can then access the Excel object model directly through the obtained object. Proc18 (which we examine next) shows an example of a Visual Basic procedure that can be used to control Excel. Via the Excel.Sheet object, the procedure inserts formulas that use the RAND( ) function in a range on a worksheet. The procedure then creates a chart of the data and adjusts the Rotation and Elevation properties of the chart while periodically calling the Calculate method to change the values in the range on the worksheet.

To run Proc18 do the following:

1. Start Visual Basic, open a new project, and double-click the form to display the Form_Load routine.

2. Switch to Excel; select the code in Proc18 (but not the Sub and End Sub lines).

3. Choose the Copy command from the Edit menu (or press Ctrl-C) to copy the code.

4. Close Excel and switch back to Visual Basic.

5. Be sure that the cursor is in the body of the Form_Load routine, and then choose the Paste command from the Edit menu (or press Ctrl-V) to paste the code into the Visual Basic routine.

6. To run the program, either choose the Start command from the Run menu, click the Start button on the Standard toolbar, or press F5. If you do not close Excel before running the program, the Excel window in which the program runs might be hidden by any open Visual Basic windows.

7. After the program finishes executing, choose the End command from the Run menu, or click the End button on the Standard toolbar.

Note that Proc18 has been written so that it can be executed from Visual Basic 5, 4, or 3—use of VBA-specific features such as the With statement have been avoided to ensure compatibility.

```
Sub NonExcelRoutines_Proc18_CallExcelFromVisualBasic()
    Const xlFillDefault = 0
    Dim xlSht As Object
    Dim Chart1 As Object
    Set xlSht = CreateObject("Excel.Sheet").ActiveSheet
    xlSht.Application.Visible = True
    xlSht.Range("B1").Value = "Q1"
    xlSht.Range("B1").AutoFill xlSht.Range("B1:E1"), xlFillDefault
    xlSht.Range("A2").Value = "Prod1"
    xlSht.Range("A2").AutoFill xlSht.Range("A2:A5"), xlFillDefault
    xlSht.Range("B2:E5").Formula = "=INT(1000 * RAND())"
    xlSht.Range("B2:E5").Copy
    xlSht.Application.Charts.Add
    Set Chart1 = xlSht.Application.ActiveChart
    Chart1.ChartWizard xlSht.Range("B2:E5"), 14
    For x = 1 To 9
        If Chart1.Rotation + 10 > 360 Then
            Chart1.Rotation = Chart1.Rotation + 10 - 360
        Else
            Chart1.Rotation = Chart1.Rotation + 10
        End If
        xlSht.Calculate
    Next
    For x = 1 To 7
        Chart1.Elevation = Chart1.Elevation + 10
        xlSht.Calculate
    Next
    For x = 1 To 16
        Chart1.Elevation = Chart1.Elevation - 10
        xlSht.Calculate
    Next
    For x = 1 To 9
        Chart1.Elevation = Chart1.Elevation + 10
        xlSht.Calculate
    Next
    xlSht.Application.Quit
    Set xlSht = Nothing
End Sub
```

Controlling Embedded Excel Objects in Visual Basic Forms

As with Access, you can control an Excel Worksheet object or a Chart object that has been embedded in a Visual Basic form via Automation, although the process differs slightly from that used for Access. Instead of using the Create-Object or GetObject function, you can directly set a variable equal to an active embedded Excel object. Proc19, which follows, provides a simple example. The procedure activates the object represented by the object named OLE1 and then sums the values in Range("A1:A3") and displays the result in a message box. Controls on a Visual Basic form are treated as individual objects that are referenced directly by name; in this case, the name of the embedded Excel workbook object is OLE1. To activate an embedded object, you set the Action property of the object to 7, and to deactivate an embedded object, you set the Action property of the object to 9.

Before running Proc19, insert an Excel worksheet in the Visual Basic form by performing the following steps.

1. In the Form Design mode, double-click the OLE button in the Visual Basic Toolbox.

2. In the Insert Object dialog box, select Microsoft Excel Worksheet and click OK. An Excel workbook with one worksheet will be displayed.

3. Enter numbers in the cells in the range A1:A3.

4. Double-click the form to display the Form_Load routine.

5. Delete the code you added earlier, and replace it with the code from Proc19 (but not the Sub and End Sub lines) by cutting and pasting.

6. Choose the Start command from the Run menu, or click the Start button. This routine simply displays a message box showing the sum of the values you entered in the embedded worksheets.

7. After the program finishes executing, choose the End command from the Run menu or click the End button.

```
Sub NonExcelRoutines_Proc19_ControlExcelObjectFromVisualBasic()
    Dim xlSht As Object
    Dim SumVar As Integer
    Dim x As Integer
    Form1.OLE1.Action = 7
    Set xlSht = Form1.OLE1.Object.ActiveSheet
    For x = 1 To 3
        SumVar = SumVar + xlSht.Range("A" & x).Value
    Next
    OLE1.Action = 6
    OLE1.Action = 9
    MsgBox "The sum is " & SumVar & "."
End Sub
```

Other Office 97 Objects

In addition to the Access, PowerPoint, Word, Binder, and Visual Basic objects we have discussed, several other object models are available through Office 97 and related products. While space limitations prevent us from going into these object models in depth, a brief overview is provided for each.

Microsoft Office 97 Common Objects

Microsoft Office 97 provides a set of objects that are common to all Office 97 applications through the Microsoft Office 8.0 object library. One of these sets was already covered earlier in this book—CommandBars. The Shapes (OfficeArt) object model is also shared between applications, but each application actually implements its own slightly different version. (Therefore, no reference to the Office 8.0 object library is required.) Shapes are substantially the same between applications, but each application adds its own unique features to the core set of functionality. For example, PowerPoint alone adds AnimationSettings to the Shape object. A reference to the Office 8.0 object library is automatically established when Excel 97 is installed.

Two other object models, OfficeAssistant and FileSearch, which are shared among applications through the Office 8.0 object library, are discussed in the following sections.

OfficeAssistant object model

The OfficeAssistant object model lets you take programmatic control of the new Office 97 Assistant (the animated character that provides help to the user). Using this object model, you can display messages from the assistant (complete with embedded checkboxes and labels) and run specific character animations. You cannot, however, create new characters or animations programmatically. Figure 10-6 shows the OfficeAssistant object model.

Figure 10-6. *The Microsoft OfficeAssistant object model.*

The Assistant object represents the animated character which is the Office Assistant. The Balloon object represents the "balloon," which contains the text of messages the assistant delivers to the user. The Balloon object can contain BalloonLabel and BalloonCheckBox objects that let the user make choices and select options in the balloon.

Proc20 shows how to use the Assistant object to display the assistant and run a particular animation. Note that the Visible property is used to display the assistant:

```
Sub ExcelRoutines_Proc20_ShowAssistant()
    With Assistant
        .Visible = True
        .Animation = msoAnimationWritingNotingSomething
    End With
End Sub
```

Proc21, which follows, shows how to display the assistant with a balloon that prompts for user input. This involves creating a Balloon object and setting properties that control the object's appearance; showing the balloon; and then determining what input the user provided through the balloon.

Since the Balloon object is not actually contained in a collection, you must declare a variable as Balloon, and then use the NewBallon property of the Assistant object to set the variable. Once this is done, you can use the Heading, Text, and CheckBoxes properties to control the title, text, and checkboxes displayed in the Balloon. The Mode property determines whether the balloon will display modally or modelessly, and the Button property determines what button(s) are present.

Calling the Balloon's Show method will display the balloon along with the assistant. The Show method returns a constant representing the button clicked. Once closed, you can use the Checked property to determine which checkboxes were checked.

```
Sub ExcelRoutines_Proc21_Balloons()
    Dim Msg As String
    Dim BalloonVar As Balloon
    Set BalloonVar = Assistant.NewBalloon
    With BalloonVar
        .Heading = "Report Options"
        .Text = "Which report(s) would you like to view?"
        .CheckBoxes(1).Text = "Sales Summary"
        .CheckBoxes(2).Text = "Regional Analysis"
        .CheckBoxes(3).Text = "Audit Report"
        .BalloonType = msoBalloonTypeButtons
        .Mode = msoModeModal
        .Button = msoButtonSetOkCancel
        If .Show() = msoBalloonButtonOK Then
            Msg = "Reports Selected:" & Chr(13) & Chr(13)
```

(continued)

continued

```
            If .CheckBoxes(1).Checked Then
                Msg = Msg & "    Sales Summary" & Chr(13)
            End If
            If .CheckBoxes(2).Checked Then
                Msg = Msg & "    Regional Analysis" & Chr(13)
            End If
            If .CheckBoxes(3).Checked Then
                Msg = Msg & "    Audit Report" & Chr(13)
            End If
            MsgBox Msg
        Else
            MsgBox "Cancel clicked."
        End If
    End With
End Sub
```

Pictured below is the balloon created by running Proc21. (The illustration shows the default character, "Clippit"—your screen might show a different character.)

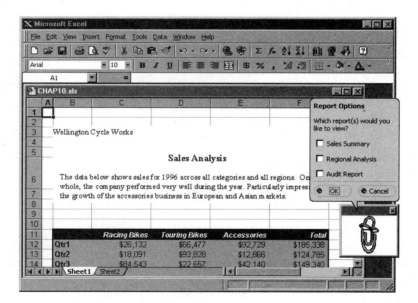

FileSearch object model

The FileSearch object model provides all the searching power of the Advanced Find feature of the File Open dialog box in all Office 97 applications. Figure 10-7 shows the FileSearch object hierarchy.

Figure 10-7. *The Microsoft FileSearch object model.*

The FoundFiles object represents a list of all the files returned from a file search. PropertyTests is a collection of objects representing the search criteria of a file search.

Proc22, which follows, searches for all Access database files in the same directory as the sample workbook file. If files are found, a count is displayed and then each filename is displayed in turn. Otherwise, a message is displayed indicating that no files were found.

```
Sub ExcelRoutines_Proc22_FileSearch()
    Dim x As Integer
    With Application.FileSearch
        .LookIn = ThisWorkbook.Path
        .FileName = "*.mdb"
        If .Execute > 0 Then
            MsgBox .FoundFiles.Count & " databases were found."
            For x = 1 To .FoundFiles.Count
                MsgBox .FoundFiles(x)
            Next x
        Else
            MsgBox "No databases were found."
        End If
    End With
End Sub
```

Microsoft Project 97

Project 97 is a project management application. It is intended to schedule tasks and resources on complex projects using the critical path method of project management. At the time of the writing of this book, Project 97 was in an early alpha state and not ready to build sample applications with. When Project 97 is released, it will serve as both an Automation object and controller as well as a host to the full VBA environment. Figure 10-8 on the following page shows the Project 97 object model.

Project's object model has a similar structure to Excel's. At the top of the hierarchy is the Application object, which represents Project itself. Below the Application object, the object of most significance is the Project object; this is an object in a collection that represents Project files. Each Project object is used for project planning and project management. Task, Resource, and Calendar are the primary objects contained in the Project object; these are objects in collections that represent the component parts of a project.

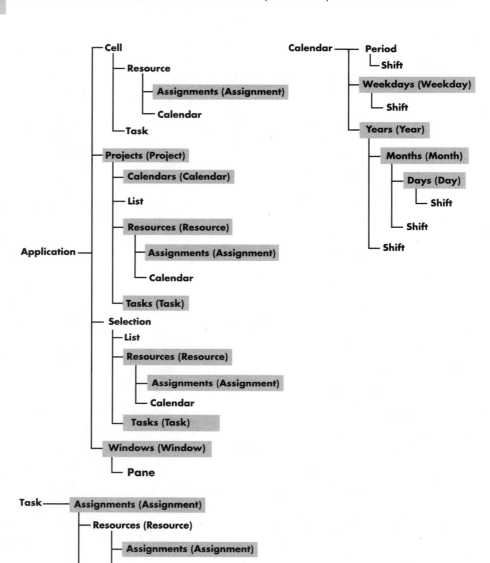

Figure 10-8. *The Microsoft Project 97 object model.*

Microsoft Team Manager 97

Team Manager 97 is a resource management application. It is intended to help managers manage the work and milestones of their staff. It is different from Project in that the focus is on assessing and scheduling continuing work without regard to critical path scheduling. At the time of the writing of this book, Team Manager 97 was in an early alpha state and not ready to be used to build sample applications. When Team Manager 97 is released, it will serve as an Automation object but not as a controller. Figure 10-9 shows the Team Manager 97 object model.

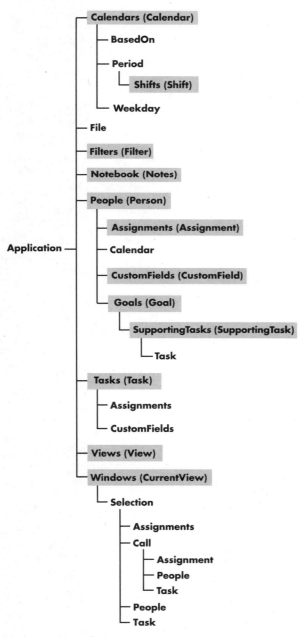

Figure 10-9. *The Microsoft Team Manager 97 object model.*

SUMMARY

In this chapter, we've looked at a number of ways to incorporate other applications in Excel VBA solutions. Here are this chapter's major points:

- Although Excel has a tremendous amount of advanced data analysis functionality, it is lacking in other areas of functionality—for example, in the areas of presentation, report creation, and data entry. Instead of trying to write advanced VBA routines in Excel that attempt to provide this additional functionality, consider integrating a separate application that has been designed specifically to provide such functionality. Doing so saves you time and energy and will result in higher-quality solutions.

- Other areas of functionality can be incorporated in Excel VBA solutions by integrating other Microsoft products: Access, PowerPoint, Word, Office Binder, Visual Basic, Outlook, Project, and Team Manager.

- ActiveX, a technology developed by Microsoft, provides two important features for programming across applications: in-place editing and Automation.

  - In-place editing allows you to embed an object from one application in another application's form or document.

  - Automation allows you to write procedures in a controller application that can control Automation objects in an object application or, used in combination with in-place editing, allows you to control an object that is embedded in a form.

- Excel, Access, PowerPoint, Word, Project, and Visual Basic can behave as Automation controllers.

- Excel, Access, PowerPoint, Word, Office Binder, Project, Team Manager, Outlook, and Visual Basic can behave as Automation objects.

- The CreateObject function can be used to access an Automation object while either initiating an instance of or using an already running instance of the application that contains the Automation object.

- The GetObject function can be used to reference an Automation object stored in a file.

- Common object models for the Office Assistant and FileSearch are provided by the Microsoft Office 97 object library.

Excel and the Web

Recently, activity and interest in the Internet has exploded. Microsoft Excel 97 offers a host of new features—including hyperlinks, HTML document support (with several useful Excel-specific extensions), and Web queries—to help people interact with the Internet and World Wide Web, and to enable application developers to build corporate *intranets* that facilitate the gathering, analysis, and sharing of information. Intranets are networks based on Internet technologies but maintained privately within an organization for internal use. Excel, and indeed all of Microsoft Office 97, enable developers to create true interactive intranet applications that provide far more value than static Web pages.

Let's briefly look at a few of the features we'll be examining in this chapter. Hyperlinks let users click a cell or an object and jump to an Internet/intranet Web page, another Excel worksheet, or Office document. By using hyperlinks and a new technology called ActiveX Documents, you can view Excel and other Office documents directly within Microsoft Internet Explorer. In addition, hyperlinks can be managed either manually through the User Interface or programmatically through VBA using the Hyperlink object.

Much of the information presented to Internet and World Wide Web users today is in the form of HTML documents. Many of these documents contain tables, which display information effectively and attractively. Microsoft Excel 97 is able to import HTML documents directly and is especially effective at importing HTML tables. Excel supports some HTML extensions that allow tables to display normally in a browser but automatically import into Excel with formulas, pivottables, and filters. Finally, Excel can save workbooks as HTML documents with a simple menu command.

The Web queries feature retrieves data from a specific Web page and then inserts the data in an Excel worksheet. Worksheets can use Web queries to pull live data from the Internet/intranet, and then perform calculations and analysis on that data. Information can be refreshed as often as needed while maintaining worksheet layout and formulas, even if the amount of data returned changes.

This chapter will explain how each of Excel's Internet features works and how to apply it to an Internet/intranet solution. Bear in mind that these features do not stand alone; they are intended to extend Excel's functionality. Any custom Internet/intranet solution you write in Excel will likely involve functionality discussed earlier in this book (e.g., pivottables, charts, custom interfaces) that is working in concert with the new Internet features. Also bear in mind that many other tools could contribute to an Internet/intranet solution, including Microsoft Office 97, Microsoft FrontPage 97, Microsoft BackOffice (including Microsoft Internet Information Server), Microsoft Visual Basic Script, and custom ActiveX controls. (For an excellent discussion of these tools in an intranet context, refer to the book *Microsoft Intranet Solutions*, which is available from Microsoft Press.)

Hyperlinks

Hyperlinks are cells or objects in Excel worksheets that, when clicked, can jump the user to another location in the current worksheet, to another worksheet, to another Microsoft Office document, to an Internet/intranet URL, or to a file at a separate network address. You can create a hyperlink in two ways:

- By selecting the cell or object and then selecting Hyperlink from the Insert menu

- By using a hyperlink formula in this form:
  =HYPERLINK (link_location, friendly_name)

The Insert Hyperlink Command

To create a simple hyperlink, type an entry in a cell. This is the text the user clicks on to follow the hyperlink. Select that cell, and then choose Hyperlink from the Insert menu (or click the Insert Hyperlink button on the standard toolbar). If you have not saved your workbook, you will be prompted to do so. At that point, you will see the Insert Hyperlink dialog box. In the following graphic, we see that a link is being established to another Excel file—the sample application from Chapter 3:

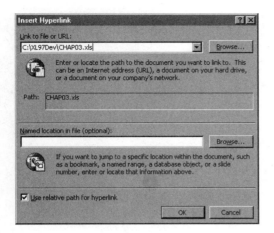

Once you choose a target file for the link, you can connect the hyperlink to a specific location in the file by filling in the Named Location In File box on the Insert Hyperlink dialog box. For Excel workbooks, a named location can refer to a particular sheet, a cell reference, or a named range—if you're linking to an Excel workbook, clicking the Browse button next to the Named Location In File box will display a list of named locations in the workbook. Here we see a link being established to a sheet:

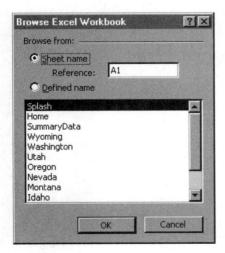

The type of document you link to affects the type of component—or location—within the document that you can link to. For example, if your hyperlink is to a Word document, the location of the link can be anything you create a bookmark for, such as a paragraph or a heading. For Microsoft PowerPoint presentations, you can link to a graphic or to a particular slide. With Excel workbooks, you can link to a specific worksheet, a cell, or a range of cells by row/column labels or by defined name ranges. In Microsoft Access, you can link to a table, a query, a report, or a form.

Once you have established the link, it is displayed as underlined in blue until you click it, at which point it changes to magenta. Should you want to edit the hyperlink later, simply right-click it and on the pop-up menu choose Hyperlink, and then click the Edit Hyperlink command. Here's what a completed hyperlink looks like in an Excel workbook:

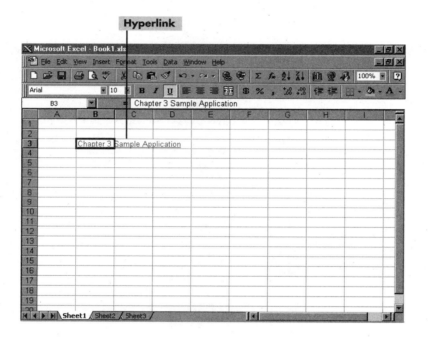

FYI

Tips and Tricks for Creating Hyperlinks

If you want to create a hyperlink from a cell or range in one Excel worksheet to a cell or range of another worksheet (or to a location within the same Excel worksheet), you can take advantage of some built-in shortcuts.

Shortcut #1: Using the Copy Command

1. Select the destination cell or range and select the Copy command from the Edit menu.

2. Select the cell or range that will contain the hyperlink and then select the Paste As Hyperlink command from the Edit menu. This will place the hyperlink in your selected cell. You can edit the text of the hyperlink by selecting the cell and editing its contents in the Formula Bar.

3. Go back to the destination cell. You can edit the text and keep the hyperlink intact. The text appears underlined and in blue, indicating that it is a hyperlink. Once you click this hyperlink, the text will turn magenta automatically.

Shortcut #2: Using Drag-and-Drop

Note: For this method to work, the Allow Cell Drag And Drop option must be checked on the Edit tab of the Options dialog box (accessible through the Tools Options command).

1. Select the cell or range for which you want to establish a link (called the destination cell or range).

2. With the mouse cursor, point to the border of the selected element you want linked and press the right mouse button, which enables you to drag the selection.

3. If the source cell and destination cell are on the same sheet, drag the selection to the area that will contain the hyperlink and let go of the right mouse button.

   If the source and destination locations are on different sheets, drag your selection toward the sheet tabs at the bottom of the screen. Hold down the Alt key as you drag your selection over the desired sheet tab and then let go of the Alt key. Now navigate to the area on the new sheet that will contain the hyperlink and let go of the right mouse button.

4. From the shortcut menu that appears, select the Create Hyperlink Here command.

5. As with Shortcut #1, you can edit the text of the hyperlink in the Formula Bar.

The Hyperlink Formula

Another way of inserting a hyperlink in a worksheet is with the HYPERLINK formula. Why would you choose to use a formula instead of the Insert Hyperlink command? Using a formula allows you to customize the link based on changing conditions. The HYPERLINK formula allows you to change the destination of a hyperlink by modifying the contents of cells in your worksheet.

To create a hyperlink using a formula, use the following syntax, where link_location is the file/URL reference and friendly_name is the text you would like displayed in the cell.

```
= HYPERLINK(link_location,friendly_name)
```

For example, if you typed the following formula, you would create a link to Microsoft's home page.

```
= HYPERLINK("http://www.microsoft.com","Microsoft")
```

The hyperlink causes the word "Microsoft" to be displayed in the cell in blue underline:

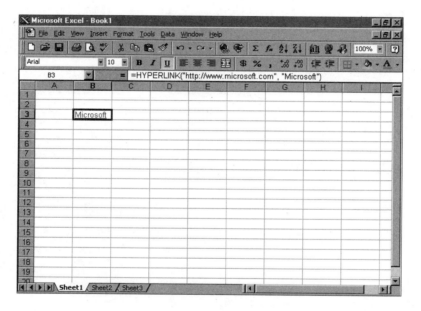

Both of the arguments to the HYPERLINK formula can be cell references. Therefore, you can dynamically change either the hyperlink destination or the text that appears in the cell by changing the corresponding cell value. Sheet1 in CHAP11.XLS contains an example of this:

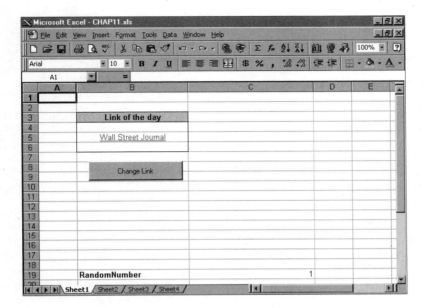

In this example, a table of Web site URLs and names appears starting in row 21 of the worksheet. By combining the OFFSET and RAND worksheet formulas, a different Web site is selected from the table each time the sheet recalculates. The selected site is referenced by the HYPERLINK formula in cell B5.

```
:=HYPERLINK(URL, DisplayName)
```

The command button control on this sheet calls a one-line VBA routine to re-calculate the sheet:

```
Private Sub CommandButton1_Click()
    Application.Calculate
End Sub
```

Recalculating causes the random number in cell C19 to change, which in turn causes the values referred to by URL and DisplayName to change.

Browsing Excel and Office Documents

So far, we have been viewing Excel workbooks in Excel. However, all Office 97 documents, including Excel workbooks, can also be viewed using Microsoft Internet Explorer (IE). ActiveX provides the technology that allows you to open Office documents in the Internet Explorer browser. Office documents viewed in this manner are known as ActiveX Documents. This aspect of ActiveX allows

Web masters to expand intranets to include not only HTML documents but Office documents and other ActiveX documents as well. Users can navigate using the browser and move from document to document without switching applications because the application activates in place within the browser window. Pictured here is the same hyperlink example we just looked at but viewed using IE. Note that Excel's menus and toolbars appear along with IE's own. All of Excel's toolbars are accessible through the View menu or by clicking the Tools button on the IE toolbar.

Excel also provides a Web Toolbar that turns Excel into a virtual browser.

You can test the navigation of your hyperlinks without having to open the file in Internet Explorer because the Web Toolbar provides the following features of standard browser functionality:

- The navigation buttons—Forward, Back, Stop Current Jump, Refresh Current Page, Start Page, and Search The Web—function just as they do in a "real" browser.

- A Favorites list enables you to easily link to frequently visited Web sites. Users can easily add new favorite entries to the list or edit existing entries.

- The Go button provides access to a menu that contains commands that essentially offer the same functionality as the other buttons on the Web toolbar. However, additional functionality is provided in commands that allow you to set Web start and search pages.

- The last toolbar button hides all other toolbars in the application except the Web toolbar, completing the virtual browser effect.

- The History list tracks the 25 most recently visited sites. The list updates universally across the Office suite and in Internet Explorer. For example, if the last site you jumped to in Excel was http:// www.micromodeling.com, that same site would also appear at the top of the History lists in Microsoft Word, Access, PowerPoint, and Internet Explorer.

Each Office application has its own Web toolbar, but only the toolbar belonging to the active application is displayed at any given time, keeping the screen display uncluttered. You can customize the Web toolbar in the same way you customize any Office toolbar; as with all toolbars that are common among Office applications, customizations to the toolbar of a particular application remain local to that application. A button you add to the Access Web toolbar, for example, won't appear on the Excel Web toolbar.

The Office 97 Web Object Model

The Web object model for Office 97 applications is based on two fundamental elements:

- The Hyperlinks collection and Hyperlink object
- New Internet methods specific to the document format of the application (for example, there are different methods for Excel workbooks and Word documents)

The Hyperlink Object and Hyperlinks Collection

Hyperlinks in Excel are represented by the Hyperlink object, which is contained in a Hyperlinks collection owned by the Chart, Range, and Worksheet objects. You can use the standard properties and methods of collections—such as the Item and Count properties—on Hyperlink collections. To create a Hyperlink programmatically, you call the Add method on the collection.

NOTE The Hyperlinks collection does not include hyperlinks created using the HYPERLINK formula. Only hyperlinks created with the Insert Hyperlink command or created programmatically using VBA are represented in the Hyperlinks collection.

The Hyperlinks collection methods

Add: Takes three arguments:

anchor	Determines the hyperlink's location (can be either a range or a shape)
address	Determines the destination path and filename for the hyperlink; the address also becomes the display text which the user clicks on to follow the link
subAddress	The only optional argument, determines the specific area in the target file to jump to

Proc01, which follows, adds two new hyperlinks to Sheet2 that point to Microsoft's Web site. One is attached to a Range object and the other to a Shape object:

```
Sub Chap11aProc01_AddHyperlink()
    With ThisWorkbook.Sheets(2)
        .Activate
        .Hyperlinks.Add Range("A1"), "http://www.microsoft.com"
        .Shapes.AddShape msoShapeExplosion2, 45, 55, 90, 45
        .Hyperlinks.Add .Shapes(1), "http://www.microsoft.com"
    End With
End Sub
```

Delete: Deletes all hyperlinks in the collection. Takes no arguments.

Hyperlink object properties

Following are selected properties of the Hyperlink object.

Address: Sets or returns the destination file or URL of the hyperlink.

SubAddress: Sets or returns the subaddress—such as a bookmark or cell range—within the hyperlink's destination file.

Name: Returns the display text of the hyperlink. Read-only.

Range: Returns the Range object to which the hyperlink is attached. Read-only.

Shape: Returns the Shape object to which the hyperlink is attached. Read-only.

Type: Indicates whether the hyperlink is attached to a Range object or a Shape object. Read-only. This property can return one of the following msoHyperlinkType constants:

- msoHyperlinkInlineShape

- msoHyperlinkRange

- msoHyperlinkShape

Proc02, which follows, displays the properties of each of the hyperlinks in Sheet2 that were created by Proc1:

```
Sub Chap11aProc02_GetHyperlinkInfo()
    Dim LinkVar As Hyperlink
    Dim sLinkInfo As String
    With Sheets(2)
        .Activate
        For Each LinkVar In .Hyperlinks
            With LinkVar
                sLinkInfo = "Name: " & .Name & Chr(13)
                sLinkInfo = sLinkInfo & "Address: " & _
                    .Address & Chr(13)
                sLinkInfo = sLinkInfo & "Subaddress: " & _
                    .SubAddress & Chr(13)
                If .Type = msoHyperlinkRange Then
                    sLinkInfo = sLinkInfo & "Range: " & _
                        .Range.Address & Chr(13)
                Else
                    sLinkInfo = sLinkInfo & "Shape: " & _
                        .Shape.Name & Chr(13)
                End If
            End With
            MsgBox sLinkInfo
        Next LinkVar
    End With
End Sub
```

Hyperlink object methods
Following are all the methods of the Hyperlink object.

AddToFavorites: Adds to the Favorites folder a shortcut to a specified hyperlink.

Follow: Executes the hyperlink as if the user clicked on it. The Follow method can take five optional arguments:

newWindow	If set to True, displays the target file in a new window
addHistory	Reserved for future use
extraInfo	A string or byte array that supplies additional information to resolve the link
method	A variant that tells how the extraInfo argument should be used—it can be one of the following: the msoMethodGet value, which appends the information to the URL address; the msoMethodPost value, which supplies the extra information as a string or byte array after the address has been resolved. (For further information, see the discussion of GET and POST parameters under "Web query fields" on page 568.)
headerInfo	Supplies header info for the HTTP request (as defined by the HTTP protocol specification)

Proc03 follows the first hyperlink that was created in Sheet2 by Proc1, opening the hyperlink's target in a new window. (You must have an active Internet connection for this routine to work.)

```
Sub Chap11aProc03_FollowHyperlink()
    With Sheets(2)
        .Activate
        .Hyperlinks(1).Follow NewWindow:=True
    End With
End Sub
```

Delete: Deletes the hyperlink from the Hyperlinks collection of which it is a member. Proc04, which follows, deletes the first hyperlink from Sheet2. Notice that the display text remains on the worksheet even after the hyperlink is deleted.

```
Sub Chap11aProc04_DeleteHyperlink()
    With Sheets(2)
        .Activate
        .Hyperlinks(1).Delete
    End With
End Sub
```

Hyperlink object as a property of a Shape object

In addition to being a member of a Hyperlinks collection, an individual Hyperlink object can be a property of a Shape object. (As described earlier, you can determine whether a hyperlink is attached to a shape object by examining the hyperlink's Type property.) Proc05 demonstrates use of the Hyperlink property of a Shape object:

```
Sub Chap11aProc05_HyperlinkFromShape()
    MsgBox Sheets(2).Shapes(1).Hyperlink.Name
End Sub
```

Workbook Object Web Methods

Excel 97 offers intranet-oriented methods that apply to the Workbook object. Two handy methods for working with hyperlinks are AddToFavorites and FollowHyperlink.

AddToFavorites: Allows you to add to your Favorites folder a shortcut to the workbook. Proc06 adds the active workbook to the Favorites folder:

```
Sub Chap11aProc06_AddWorkbookToFavorites()
    ActiveWorkbook.AddToFavorites
End Sub
```

FollowHyperLink: Allows you to follow a hyperlink that you supply in the address and subAddress arguments to the method. Takes the following arguments:

address, subAddress	Same as the address and subAddress arguments of the Hyperlinks collection's Add method
newWindow, addHistory, extraInfo, method, headerInfo	Same as the arguments described for the Follow method of the Hyperlink object, discussed on page 552

When you click the commandbutton control on Sheet3 of CHAP11.XLS it calls the following routine, which links to the Microsoft Web site using the FollowHyperlink method of the workbook. (You must have an active connection to the Internet for this routine to work.)

```
Private Sub CommandButton1_Click()
    ThisWorkbook.FollowHyperlink "http://www.microsoft.com"
End Sub
```

HTML Support and Extensions

Excel 97 provides support for HTML in several ways:

- Excel can save a workbook as an HTML document, making Excel itself an HTML authoring tool.

- Excel can read HTML documents and display them as Excel workbooks—especially useful for HTML tables.

- Excel supports a series of HTML extensions for tables that allow you to create HTML tables that actually include formulas, filters, and pivottables. When such tables are viewed in a Web browser, they appear as normal tables. However, when the tables are opened in Excel, Excel takes advantage of the HTML extensions stored with the file to implement formulas, filters, and pivottables.

FYI

New to HTML?

To get the most out of this section, you should be familiar with HTML. Space constraints prevent a discussion of HTML syntax and usage here, but the following web sites provide good information on HTML:

- The Microsoft Internet Center:

  `http://www.microsoft.com/internet/html.htm`

- Microsoft's HTML guide:

  `http://www.microsoft.com/workshop/author/newhtml/default.htm`

- A quick HTML tutorial for the novice:

  `http://www.microsoft.com/workshop/author/plan/novice-f.htm`

- The popular Beginner's Guide to HTML from NCSA:

  `http://www.ncsa.uiuc.edu/General/Internet/WWW/HTMLPrimer.html`

- An HTML library in compiled online help format:

  `http://subnet.virtual-pc.com/~le387818/`

Saving as HTML

Excel 97 ships with the Internet Assistant Wizard add-in, which enables you to save your Excel spreadsheet as an HTML document. To use the Wizard, select the Save As HTML command from the File menu to initiate a series of steps in which you select specific charts and/or data ranges to export to HTML and format your HTML document to have the look and feel you desire. The Save As HTML command also lets you export charts and/or data to an existing HTML document, making it one of the easier ways to add a table to a Web document.

> **TIP**　　If you don't have the Save as HTML command as an option on your File menu, the Internet Assistant Wizard add-in is not installed and selected. To display the list of installed add-ins, select Add-Ins from the Tools menu. If the Internet Assistant add-in is not listed, you will need to install the Web Page Authoring component from the Microsoft Office 97 installation CD.

Displaying HTML Documents in Excel

Microsoft Excel 97 offers good support for HTML table and general formatting tags, but limited or no support of other tags such as those having to do with forms and graphics. Tables 11-1 below and 11-2 on page 558 list some of the major non-table and table HTML tags and attributes and briefly describe how they are handled when imported into Excel through the File Open command.

Behavior of HTML Non-Table Tags and Attributes When Viewed in Excel

Tag or Attribute	Description
General and structural elements	
HTML, HEAD, BODY, BACKGROUND=	Ignored.
TITLE, COMMENT	Places text or item in the Title edit box on the Summary tab in File Properties.
Text	
P	Places text or item two rows down in the worksheet.
BR	Places text or item one row down in the worksheet.
LISTING, PRE, PLAIN-TEXT, TT, KBD, XMP	Formats text as Courier.

Table 11-1. *A description of how Excel handles the importing of non-table tags and attributes. Attributes are distinguished from tags by the presence of an equals sign (=). The sample file CHAP11A.HTM can be used to view many of these tags in Excel and in your browser.* *(continued)*

Table 11-1 *continued*

Tag or Attribute	Description
BLOCKQUOTE	Treats text as paragraph, but indent level is set to 4 and the merge cell feature omits the rightmost cell in the row that is displayed on the screen.
B, STRONG	Boldfaces text.
I, DFN, CITE, EM	Italicizes text.
U	Underlines text.
CODE, SAMP	Sets the font 1 point size smaller than the default.
VAR	Formats text as Courier and sets the font 1 point size smaller than the default.
ADDRESS	Places text in a cell and italicizes it.
CENTER	Centers text across the page.
NOBR	Places text in cell with wrapped text turned off.
Anchors	
A	Places a hypertext link into a cell and formats the cell with the hypertext style.
HREF=, NAME=	Attributes of anchor tags that are supported, though a graphic link won't import into Excel. Anchors are placed on their own row, so a sentence with an anchor in the middle of it will end up on three separate rows in Excel.
Headers	
H1 through H6	Uses heading styles equivalent to Excel's.
Lists	
DL/DT/DD	Places items as two-column list setting the indent level of DD entries to 2.
UL/LI, OL/LI, MENU/LI, DIR/LI	Treats items as a single string of text and places them on one row.
Miscellaneous	
IMG, AREA, MAP	Not supported.
HR	Inserts a blank row with a lower border across the width of the page; does not merge the cells.
SIZE=	As attribute of HR tag, represents border size; can be 1, 2, or 3 pixels. As attribute of FONT tag, represents font size.
Internet-Explorer-Specific	
FONT, COLOR=, FACE=, SIZE=	Supported. Displays text in the specified color, typeface and point size.
MARQUEE	Centers text.

Figures 11-1 and 11-2 illustrate how non-table tags affect presentation when viewed in Excel and Internet Explorer, respectively. Note how the fonts differ slightly. (Sample screens are from CHAP11A.HTM.)

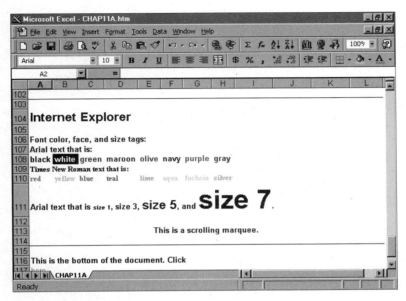

Figure 11-1. *HTML document with non-table tags, viewed in Excel.*

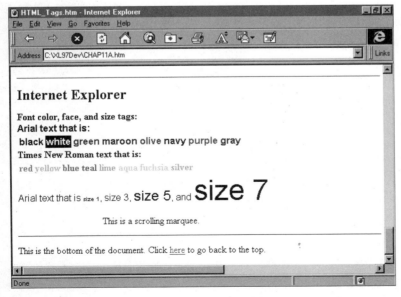

Figure 11-2. *HTML document with non-table tags, viewed in Internet Explorer.*

Behavior of HTML Table Tags and Attributes When Viewed in Excel

Tag or Attribute	Description
Table alignment	
ALIGN=	Affects placement of table on page. Takes the values LEFT, RIGHT, CENTER, and JUSTIFY.
WIDTH=	Controls width of entire table relative to the screen— usually as percentage of the screen.
Borders	
BORDER=	Sets border width around entire table.
FRAME=	Specifies which sides of table have borders.
RULES=	Controls internal table borders (cell borders) within a cell range.
Columns	
COLGROUP	Specifies attributes that apply to groups of columns, though only ALIGN and VALIGN are supported.
COLSPAN=	Controls cells spanning columns.
COL ALIGN=	Tag/attribute pair that sets horizontal and vertical alignment of columns.
Caption	
CAPTION	Places caption in row directly above or below table.
ALIGN=	CAPTION attribute; the default value is CENTER, but LEFT and RIGHT are also valid—text is placed relative to table.
VALIGN=	CAPTION attribute; places text at the top or bottom of the table.
Internal table elements	
TR	Identifies a table row.
TH	Identifies a table header.
TD	Identifies an individual cell.
BGCOLOR=	Color of cells (TH and TD). BORDERCOLOR attribute is not supported.
Miscellaneous	
CELLPADDING=, CELL-SPACING=, CLASS=, CHAR=, CHAROFF=, CLEAR=, COLS=, ID=, LANG=, NOFLOW=	Not supported.

Table 11-2. *A description of how HTML table tags are handled when viewed in Excel. Attributes are distinguished from tags by the presence of an equals sign (=). The sample file CHAP11B.HTM can be used to view many of these table tags in Excel and in your browser.*

Figures 11-3 and 11-4 illustrate how table tags affect presentation in Excel and Internet Explorer, respectively. Notice how differently the tables are formatted. (Use the sample file CHAP11B.HTM to view many of these tags.)

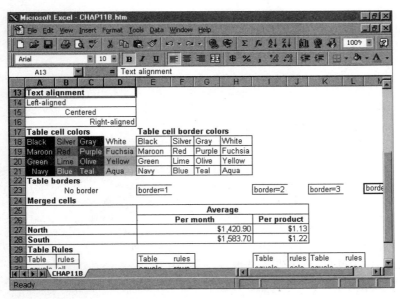

Figure 11-3. *HTML document with table tags, viewed in Excel.*

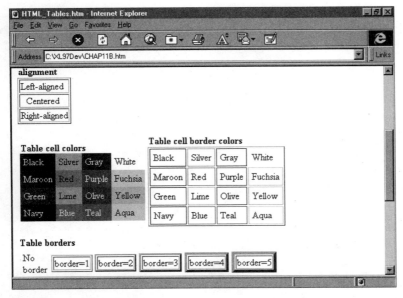

Figure 11-4. *HTML document with table tags, viewed in Internet Explorer.*

HTML Table Tag Extensions in Excel 97

Microsoft Excel 97 supports several HTML table tag extensions that will let you exploit some of Excel's best features when creating HTML tables. These extensions are especially powerful when built into tables that are dynamically generated through server-based programs such as Common Gateway Interface (CGI) scripts and Internet Server API (ISAPI) applications. For example, you could write a server-based program to search a database and, using these extensions, produce an HTML table that displays as a pivottable when viewed in Excel 97. Because browsers ignore any unrecognized tags or attributes, tables that make use of these Excel-specific extensions will still display as normal tables when viewed in a browser.

Formulas

FORMULA is an attribute of TH and TD table elements. It allows a function or formula to be placed in a specific cell when the HTML table is opened in Excel. The advantage, of course, is that the data is imported as a worksheet, which can be easily changed and automatically updated. When inserting a function, you use Excel syntax; any Excel function or formula can be used. In creating a formula, you specify references in the formula relative to the top left cell of the table (cell A1). References can only refer to the current table. Cell references will be adjusted in Excel according to the placement of the table. Note that even if you include a FORMULA attribute, if the table element itself has no value included with it, the cell will come into Excel blank without the formula. The presence of the value triggers insertion of the formula in Excel, but Excel does not display the value.

For example, to subtract expenses from sales to get a profit figure, the following tags and formula could be used:

```
<TABLE>
<TR>
    <TH>Sales
    <TH>Expenses
    <TH>Profit
<TR>
    <TD>100
    <TD>85
    <TD FORMULA="A2-B2">15
</TABLE>
```

This produces a table that looks the same both in Excel and in your browser, though in Excel the actual contents of the Profit cell are "=A2-B2":

Sales	Expenses	Profit
100	85	15

The example is simple, but it demonstrates that by using formulas in HTML tables, you ensure that changes to the data in Excel are dynamic—that is, data automatically recalculates. This provides a great advantage over data viewed in a browser, which would be static.

Syntax   When using Excel's built-in functions, be sure to place the equals sign (=) in front of the function as well as after the FORMULA attribute, as in the following two examples:

```
<TD FORMULA="=SUM(B2:B5)">1500
<TD FORMULA="=AVERAGE(D3:D10)">43.25
```

If you need to use quotation marks within the function itself, then you have to enter them as "&quot" or the browser will interpret the quote as the end of the formula attribute. For example, if you are using the concatenate function to join two strings, in Excel you would enter this:

```
=CONCATENATE("The ","Best")
```

But in HTML, you would enter this:

```
<TD FORMULA="=CONCATENATE(&quotThe &quot,&quotBest&quot)">The Best
```

The file CHAP11C.HTM demonstrates use of the FORMULA attribute. Pictured here is how this HTML document is represented in Excel:

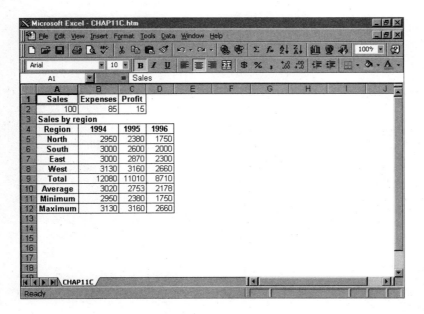

Filters

The FILTER extension in an HTML table causes Excel to display filter drop-down listboxes on the column headers. Selecting values from the drop-down listboxes allows the user to limit the rows displayed in the table to those matching the values selected in the drop-down listboxes. The table is displayed in its entirety in the browser.

Syntax   FILTER is an attribute that can be used with TD, TH, TABLE, or TR tags. Here's an example of the syntax:

```
<TABLE>
<TR>
    <TD FILTER=ALL>Store #
    <TD FILTER=NONBLANKS>Date
    <TD FILTER=ALL>Channel
    <TD FILTER=ALL>Division
<TR><TD>Store 2<TD>1/1/95<TD>Wholesale<TD>Brass
<TR><TD>Store 6<TD>1/8/95<TD>Wholesale<TD>Electronic
<TR><TD>Store 5<TD>1/15/95<TD>Wholesale<TD>Brass
. . .
</TABLE>
```

The FILTER extension accepts the following values:

- ALL

- BLANKS

- NONBLANKS

- *"VALUE"* (variable; a text string)

Using any of these values determines what is displayed when the table is first opened in Excel, but the user can subsequently change the display using the drop-down listboxes on the heading row. For instance, in the above example, the table shows all stores with nonblank dates in all channels and all divisions.

The file CHAP11D.HTM demonstrates use of the FILTER attribute. Pictured here is how this HTML document is represented in Excel:

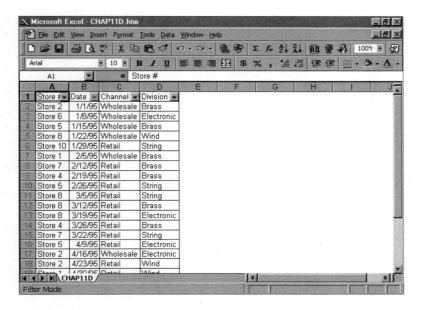

Pivottables

By using the CROSSTAB attribute when creating an HTML table, you can generate a pivottable when the data is brought into Microsoft Excel 97. Please note that this will only work when doing a file open of the HTML document. This will not work when you open an HTML document from the Web toolbar.

Two HTML table tag extensions are associated with pivottables—the attributes CROSSTAB and CROSSTABGRAND—as are six TH and TD extensions (all attributes): ROWFIELD, COLFIELD, DATAFIELD, PAGEFIELD, AGGREGATOR, and SUBTOTAL. You can reference each extension that we examine in the example file CHAP11E.HTM, a portion of which is shown here:

```
. . .
<TABLE border CROSSTAB CROSSTABGRAND=ROWCOLUMN>
<TR>
    <TH ROWFIELD>Store #
    <TH>Date
    <TH PAGEFIELD>Channel
    <TH COLFIELD>Division
    <TH>Product
    <TH DATAFIELD AGGREGATOR="SUM">Units
    <TH>Price
. . .
</table>
```

The next screen shows how this file looks in Excel. Note that the source data range for the pivottable has been automatically hidden from view. (Rows 1 through 25 are hidden; if you unhide them, you will see the source data.)

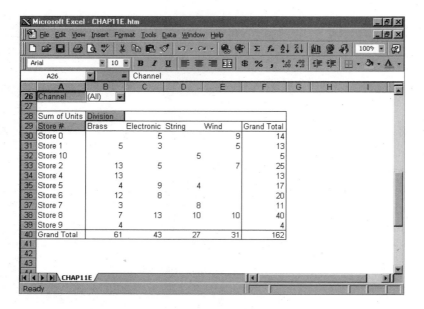

Extensions affecting pivottables   The following extensions affect the formatting and display of information in a pivottable.

CROSSTAB: An attribute of the TABLE tag, CROSSTAB instructs Excel to display the data as a pivottable. If this attribute is used, then ROWFIELD, COLFIELD, DATAFIELD, PAGEFIELD, AGGREGATOR, and SUBTOTAL attributes (if specified) must appear in the first row of the table definition as attributes of TH or TD. At least one DATAFIELD attribute must be present for the pivottable to contain data.

CROSSTABGRAND: An optional attribute that works with CROSSTAB to designate whether and how grand totals should be displayed. Four values are possible: NONE, ROW, COLUMN, and ROWCOLUMN (the default).

ROWFIELD, COLFIELD, DATAFIELD, and PAGEFIELD: Each indicates how a column of data (e.g., a field in the source database) should be treated in the Excel pivottable. These attributes must be in the first data row of the table—any columns without these attributes are not displayed in the pivottable.

AGGREGATOR: Lets you select one of the following aggregator options for the DATAFIELD:

AVERAGE	Average of the data items
COUNT	Count of the data items (the default for non-numeric data)
COUNTNUMS	Number of rows with data
MAX	Maximum value of the data items
MIN	Minimum value of the data items
PRODUCT	Product of the data items
STDDEV	Estimate of the standard deviation of a population, where the underlying data is the sample
STDDEVP	Standard deviation of the population, where the underlying data is the entire population
SUM	Sum of the data items (the default for numeric data fields)
VAR	Estimate of the variance of the population, where the underlying data is the sample
VARP	Variance of a population of data, where the underlying data is the entire population

To display multiple aggregators for a single data field, separate the options with commas, as shown in this example:

```
<TH DATAFIELD AGGREGATOR="SUM,AVERAGE">Sales
```

SUBTOTAL: Controls which row, column, and page field values are subtotaled. It applies to TH and TD elements with ROWFIELD, COLFIELD, and PAGEFIELD attributes. When SUBTOTAL is specified for a field, subtotal rows (for a ROWFIELD) or columns (for a COLFIELD) or values (for a PAGEFIELD) are inserted in the pivottable for each grouping of that field. SUBTOTAL only has an effect if more than one field of the given orientation exist in the table (e.g., two ROWFIELDS).

The options for SUBTOTAL are the same as for the AGGREGATOR attribute (see the table above), and you can use a comma-separated list to display multiple subtotal rows, columns, and page values for a data field.

NOTE These HTML table extensions can only be read by Excel. Excel will not insert these extensions into an HTML document that is being created with the File Save As HTML command.

Web Queries

Web queries allow you to query data in Excel from an Internet or intranet site. Web queries are, in essence, text files with an .IQY extension that consist of three or four lines of text separated by carriage returns. Web queries rely on Internet/intranet technology such as HTML forms and CGI scripts to retrieve data and return results to Excel in the form of an HTML document or tab-delimited ASCII text. In Excel, the information can then be stored, manipulated, analyzed, and published.

You can create a Web query easily despite knowing little more than the URL, but you'll get the best results by creating Web queries that draw data from Web pages specifically designed to support them.

FYI

Creating Web Queries from Scratch

To create a Web query, you need to know what information the server is requiring and the URL where it needs to be sent. Typically, the Web query and the server application are designed to work together. Designing and building Internet server applications is beyond the scope of this book. For more information on how to create your own Web queries and integrate them with server applications, refer to the Microsoft Office Resource Kit. This kit is available at http://www.microsoft.com/msoffice/ork/.

> **NOTE**   Microsoft Excel 97 includes a few sample Web queries. More are available on the Excel page of Microsoft's Web site (http://www.microsoft.com/msexcel).

Running a Web Query

Running a Web query is easy for a typical user. Before you try creating a Web query in the next section, try running one of the sample queries that come with Excel. Here are the steps (you must have an active connection to the Internet for this procedure to work):

1. From the Data menu, select Get External Data and then Run Web Query. The Run Query dialog box appears:

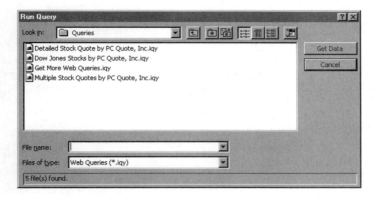

2. Select a Web query and click Get Data. The following dialog box appears:

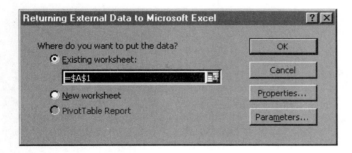

3. To place the query results in the current cell of the active worksheet, click OK. Or, if desired, select a different location. If the query is designed to prompt for parameters, you will be prompted for each parameter in a dialog box similar to the following:

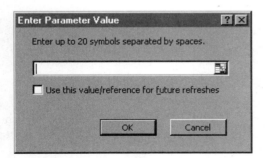

4. Enter the desired value or values, and click OK. The query is transmitted to the Web server and results of the query are displayed in the worksheet at the location you specified.

Understanding Web Query (.IQY) Files

As noted earlier, a Web query is a text file with an .IQY extension. You can create a Web query file using any text editor such as Notepad. A Web query consists of three or four lines of text (depending on the type of parameters you supply) separated by carriage returns. (Carriage returns are indicated by [CR] in the examples below.) Here is the structure of a Web query.

Type of Query [CR]	(optional)
Version of Query [CR]	(optional)
URL [CR]	(required)
POST Parameters [CR]	(required for queries referencing POST forms/data)

Two sample Web queries are included here and on the companion CD provided with this book:

- CHAP11A.IQY

```
WEB
1
http://webservices.pcquote.com/cgi-bin/excelget.exe?TICKER=msft
```

- CHAP11B.IQY

```
WEB
1
http://webservices.pcquote.com/cgi-bin/excel.exe
QUOTE0=["QUOTE0","Enter up to 20 symbols separated by spaces."]
```

You might want to refer back to these sample queries as you read the following discussion of Web query fields.

Web query fields

You can indicate four types of information when writing a Web query: the query type, the query version, the URL, and the GET or POST parameters. In the following four sections, we look at each of the four Web query fields in the context of the CHAP11A.IQY and CHAP11B.IQY example files shown above.

Type Of Query field   This field is optional unless a Version Of Query value is specified—Type Of Query and Version Of Query fields must be used together or not at all. If a value is omitted, Excel assumes the value is WEB, which currently is the only valid value for the Type Of Query field.

Version Of Query field   This field is optional unless a Type Of Query value is specified—Type Of Query and Version Of Query fields must be used together or not at all. The only valid value for the Version Of Query field is 1.

URL field   The URL is the file location to which the query will be sent and is the only required field unless the Web page being queried is a POST type. (See the description of POST parameters, which follows.) The URL has three formats, depending on where the query is being sent:

- To a Web site—http://server/file

- To a local file—drive:\directory\file

- To a network share—\\server\share\directory\file

In both examples, the URL is http://webservices.pcquote.com. In CHAP11A.IQY a GET parameter is appended to the URL after a question mark. GET parameters are discussed in the next section.

POST Parameters field   You can send data to a Web server using an Internet/intranet form using either GET or POST parameters. The server application and creator of the HTML form determine which type of parameter should be used. Excel distinguishes between GET and POST parameters by where the query parameters are placed. If the parameters are included as part of the URL, they are GET parameters. Parameters placed on a separate line following the URL—in the POST parameters field—are considered POST parameters. In our example files on page 568, CHAP11A.IQY uses a GET parameter, and CHAP11B.IQY uses a POST parameter. The following table compares these two methods:

GET parameters	POST parameters
Used to send smaller amounts of data	Used to send larger amounts of data (usually more than 200 characters)
Appends data to the URL itself after a question mark	Sends data as a separate line of text
Default	Used when queries are referencing POST forms/data
In an Excel Web query, parameters indicated immediately after the URL and question mark: http://server/file?parameters	In an Excel Web query, parameters indicated on line immediately following the URL; [CR] indicates the carriage return: http://server/file[CR] POST parameters

Static and Dynamic Parameters: In Web queries, static parameters send query data that is stored in the query file without prompting the user, whereas dynamic parameters prompt the user for one or more values and use those values in the query. Both GET and POST parameters can be either static or dynamic. Static queries include the parameter name(s) and the value(s) to be passed to the server. (Parameter names are determined by the HTML form.) Multiple parameters are separated by an ampersand character (&):

```
parameter_name1=value1&parameter_name2=value2
```

Note that some forms accept multiple values for a single parameter, so the values for each parameter would be separated by a plus sign (+):

```
parameter_name1=
    value1+value2+value3+value4&parameter_name2=value5+value6
```

(Although this string is shown here on two lines, it would appear as a single line in a Web query file.) Rather than values following the parameter name and equals sign, dynamic queries specify two arguments contained in square brackets. Each of the two arguments must be enclosed in quotation marks; the first one is the name of the value (this can be any name of your choosing), and the second is the text of the prompt that appears in the dialog box. The brackets cue Excel to build a dialog box that prompts the user for the parameter values. In the next example, two dialog boxes will be generated when the query is run— one each for parameter_name1 and parameter_name2.

```
parameter_name1=["value1","Prompt for first value"]
    &parameter_name2=["value2","Prompt for second value"]
```

(This would appear as one line in a Web query field.) The following two examples illustrate the difference between static and dynamic queries. Here is CHAP11A.IQY, which is a static query with a single parameter specified as a GET parameter:

```
WEB[CR]
1[CR]
http://webservices.pcquote.com/cgi-bin/excelget.exe?TICKER=msft
```

This same query could be written as a dynamic query. In this example, it prompts the user for the company symbol (the URL field should be all one line—it is broken up here in order to fit on the page):

```
WEB[CR]
1[CR]
http://webservices.pcquote.com/cgi-bin/excelget.exe?TICKER=
    ["stock1","Enter a ticker symbol:"]
```

The dynamic query would produce the following parameter dialog box:

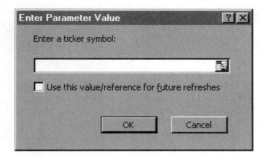

Getting Dynamic Parameters from a Worksheet

If the query is dynamic, you can manage its parameters and prompts through the Parameters dialog box. You access this dialog box through the Parameters button on the Returning External Data To Excel dialog box which appears after you have chosen the Web query you want to run from the Run Query dialog box. The Parameters button is available only when the query is dynamic.

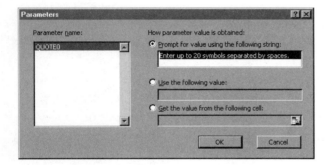

Using this dialog box, you can prompt for a value, establish a specific value to be used in the future, or retrieve a value from a cell reference. If you choose to get the value from a cell reference, you can build applications that use data from worksheet-based or dialog-box-based forms to refresh a dynamic query saved with the form.

Sheet4 in CHAP11.XLS demonstrates a simple example of this. In this example, the user can enter up to 20 stock symbols directly into the worksheet, and then click the Refresh button to run a saved Web query and import the results into the worksheet, as shown on the following page.

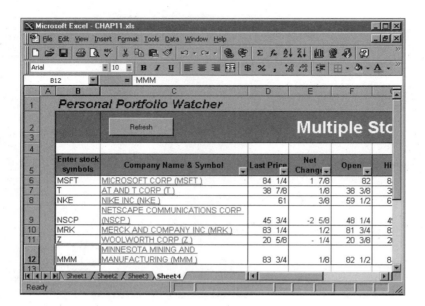

This sample form has three components:

- A Web query ("Multiple Stock Quotes by PC Quote, Inc.") is used to supply the stock price data.

- This query's parameter values are being supplied by the cell B26, which contains a formula to concatenate each stock symbol (separated by spaces) entered on the sheet.

- A commandbutton control calls a VBA routine that refreshes the query via the QueryTables collection object.

How does this work? Web queries are represented by the same QueryTable object that we examined in Chapter 7. The QueryTable object has several properties that represent portions of a Web query: Connection, representing the URL and GET parameters, if any; Parameters, representing a collection of parameter names and prompts for dynamic queries; PostText, representing the POST parameter data, if any; and others. The QueryTable object also has a Refresh method that will execute the query to retrieve the latest data. The commandbutton's Click event procedure uses this Refresh method to refresh the saved Web query:

```
Private Sub CommandButton1_Click()
    Sheets(4).QueryTables(1).Refresh BackgroundQuery:=False
End Sub
```

SUMMARY

In this chapter, we looked at new features of Excel 97 that can help you build Internet or intranet solutions. Here are some of the key points we covered:

- Excel's Internet features are used in conjunction with its other features to create Internet and intranet applications.

- Excel now supports hyperlinks, which enable you to link to a cell or object in the same workbook, a separate workbook, an Office document, a World Wide Web site, or another document on a network. Hyperlinks can be attached directly to cells or shapes or can be represented by the HYPERLINK worksheet formula.

- The Hyperlinks collection (of the Chart, Range, and Worksheet objects) and Hyperlink object can be used to control hyperlinks programmatically. Additionally, the Shape object has a Hyperlink property.

- Internet Explorer can view many types of documents such as HTML and Office 97 files (including Excel workbooks) through a technology called ActiveX Documents.

- The Workbook object provides two methods—FollowHyperlink and AddToFavorites—that are useful for Web applications.

- Excel can save workbooks as HTML documents, thus making it an HTML authoring tool.

- Excel can read HTML documents and display them as workbooks. This feature works particularly well with HTML tables.

- Excel provides several HTML table tag extensions that allow HTML tables to contain formulas, filters, and pivottables. Ordinary browsers ignore these tag extensions.

- Excel can only read the table tag extensions; it will not create them when using the File Save As HTML command.

- Web queries are a powerful way to pull data from an Internet or intranet server application into an Excel workbook.

- A Web query is really just a three to four line text file with an .IQY extension that tells Excel which URL to retrieve data from and what parameters to pass.

- You can write your own custom .IQY files to interact with server applications.

- Web queries can get parameters from cells on a worksheet.

- Web queries are represented in VBA by the QueryTable object. Using this object, Web queries can be refreshed programmatically.

12

Sample Application 4: Pacific Industries

In this chapter, we'll walk through a custom intranet application for a fictitious company named Pacific Industries. The Pacific Industries application combines HTML documents with an Excel application running in Microsoft Internet Explorer. It integrates with several other Microsoft Office 97 products including Microsoft Access 97, Microsoft Word 97, and Microsoft PowerPoint 97. Access and Word provide report generation services; PowerPoint generates presentations. The application even uses the Office Assistant to guide the user through requesting reports. As an Excel-based intranet application, it incorporates many of the objects and techniques covered throughout the book. The most notable of these are querying external databases, charts, and chart events.

You will need Microsoft Internet Explorer, Access 97, Word 97, and PowerPoint 97 installed on your machine to run all parts of the application. Also, the following files, supplied on the companion CD, must be together in the same directory on your hard disk:

CHAP12.HTM	HTML document that constitutes the main menu of the application
CHAP12A.HTM	HTML document that represents a sample submenu of the application
CHAP12.XLS	Microsoft Excel 97 workbook containing all the VBA code for the application
CHAP12.POT	Microsoft PowerPoint 97 template
EXPENSES.MDB	Microsoft Access 97 database
IMAGEx.GIF	Nine image files used by the web pages

The Pacific Industries Application

Like most corporations, Pacific Industries has developed an internal web, or intranet, to facilitate the analysis, presentation, dissemination, and sharing of business information. Pacific Industries employees can access the intranet from their computers using Microsoft Internet Explorer (IE). The intranet has a home page that serves as a directory to the various sections of the site. Although much of the site is stored in the form of HTML documents, certain documents and applications are stored in the form of Microsoft Office (Excel, Access, PowerPoint, and Word) documents. Since Pacific Industries has standardized IE and Office 97 on the desktop, users can browse all these document types from within IE.

The part of Pacific Industries' intranet that we are interested in is the Expense Analysis application, which is used by managers to compare budgeted and actual expenses. It is an interactive application that enables users to drill down through two dimensions of the company's finances: organization and expense account. Pacific Industries is divided into divisions, then departments within divisions. The application displays expense data at the department, division, or corporate-wide level. Account expenses are classified into categories and subcategories— for example, one category is Travel, which has various subcategories such as Hotel, Meals, and Tickets. The application can display expenses at either the category or subcategory level. In addition to the interactive drill-down features, the application also produces reports and presentations, and even provides hyperlinks for the department and divisions it displays; these hyperlinks jump users back to home pages on Pacific's intranet.

The Intranet Home Page

A small subset of documents from Pacific's intranet is included on the companion CD, and you can view these documents using IE. Let's start by opening the Pacific Industries home page. To do this, launch IE and choose the File Open command. Click the Browse button on the Open dialog box, and locate and open the file CHAP12.HTM. You should see a screen like Figure 12-1 (on the facing page) in the browser.

The Expense Analysis Form

The home page contains a link to an Expense Analysis application. (The link is actually to an Excel workbook file, CHAP12.XLS.) Click the link so that IE loads the workbook into its own application window. If macro virus protection is enabled in Excel, you will have to respond to a dialog box warning that the workbook you are opening contains macros. After the workbook is loaded, your browser should look like Figure 12-2 (note that the Excel menus have been merged with IE's menus).

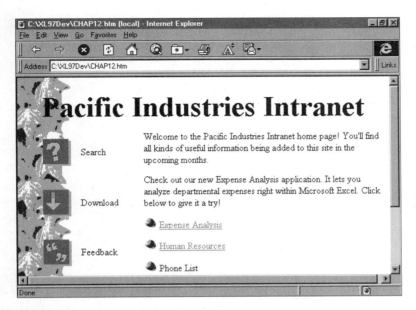

Figure 12-1. *The Pacific Industries home page.*

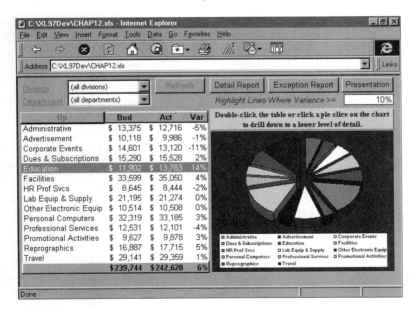

Figure 12-2. *The Expense Analysis form, loaded in Internet Explorer.*

FYI

Excel Commandbars and Internet Explorer

You manipulate commandbars when your application runs in Internet Explorer (IE) a little differently than when Excel runs alone. Whereas you can show and hide toolbar-style commandbars through code (this application hides toolbars using the Workbook_Open event), you cannot change or hide Excel's built-in worksheet and chart menu commandbars that display in the browser. (This has to do with how IE merges its menus with Excel's.) Take care to use appropriate workbook and sheet protection properties to maintain the integrity of your application since all menu commands will be available to the user through the browser.

The Expense Analysis form contains several design elements and Excel objects. The table of expense data on the left side of the form is actually populated with data from an external database (programmatically referred to as the QueryTable object). When you first enter the application, data is retrieved at the highest summary level—corporate-wide by broad expense category—from the Expenses database. Two properties of the QueryTable object have been used to control how the data is presented:

- FillAdjacentFormulas has been set to True to copy the formula that calculates the percentage over or under budget for the incoming data.

- RefreshStyle has been set to xlInsertDeleteCells to cause the totals line to move up and down to accommodate whatever number of rows come back from the database.

Note that one of the lines is highlighted in red (it appears dark gray in the illustration). The application is actually using conditional formatting on the cells in the table to accomplish this. If the variance percentage in a given row is 10 percent or greater, the background color of that row is set to dark red and the text color is set to white. Otherwise, no special format is applied. You can change the variance threshold by entering a value in the cell labeled "Highlight Lines Where Variance >=". None of this dynamic formatting requires any code whatsoever. It is accomplished using the new Conditional Formatting features in Excel 97 (accessed by selecting the Conditional Formatting command from the Format menu).

As explained in the following section, the data in the table is refreshed whenever a value in one of the dropdowns changes. Since the table is the source data range for the pie chart beside it, users can be confident that the chart always reflects current data.

Retrieving information about all levels of the organization

The dropdown controls at the top of the Expense Analysis form control the display of data for Pacific's divisions and departments. Note that these are *not* the same ActiveX combobox controls (from the Control Toolbox toolbar) that we have been using throughout the book. When you view an Excel document within IE, ActiveX controls cannot be activated or interacted with. However, the set of controls available on the Forms toolbar *can* be used within IE. The Forms toolbar controls are actually from earlier versions of Excel; because they are built into Excel and are not shared ActiveX controls, IE can use them normally.

FYI

Using Forms Toolbar Controls

The controls on the Forms toolbar work differently than the ActiveX controls on the Control Toolbox in two primary ways:

- First, they do not have a set of events but rather one event—OnAction. To link this event to a VBA routine, you right-click the control and choose the Assign Macro command from the popup menu.

- Second, they do not have an associated Properties window. To set the few properties these controls have, you right-click the control and choose the Format Control command from the popup menu.

When you select a division from the first dropdown, two things happen. The table data is refreshed from the external database, with the selected division passed in as a parameter via the Query Table object's SQL property. This causes the application to "drill down" for data from the corporate-wide level to the division level. The other thing that happens is that another query is run that retrieves the department names that fall within the selected division and places them into the second dropdown control.

You can also select a department in the second dropdown; this will refresh the data yet again. This time both the division and department are passed in as parameters in the SQL property of the QueryTable object, so the application drills down to the lowest level of the organization. Figure 12-3 on the following page shows the results of selecting the Administration division and then the Human Resources department.

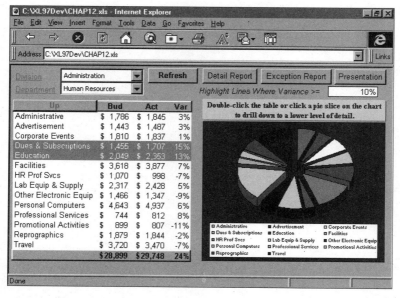

Figure 12-3. *New table data based on specific division and department parameters selected in the dropdowns.*

Retrieving levels of account information

You can also increase the level of detail of expense account information from the category level to the subcategory level. This can be accomplished in two different ways:

- You can either double-click a particular row in the table so that the DoubleClick event handler for the sheet refreshes the query, passing the selected category in as a parameter.

- You can click a particular pie slice on the chart so that the chart's MouseUp event procedure selects the corresponding row in the table and then refreshes the query, passing the selected category in as a parameter.

Figure 12-4 shows the effect of the drill-down process in the Travel expense category (for the Human Resources department in the Administration division).

Hyperlinks to Organization Home Pages

You might have noticed that the captions for the Division and Department dropdowns have a blue underline format. That is because they are hyperlinks that jump to the home page for the selected organization. This link is accomplished through the HYPERLINK formula, which looks up a URL on a separate worksheet based on the value in the adjacent dropdown.

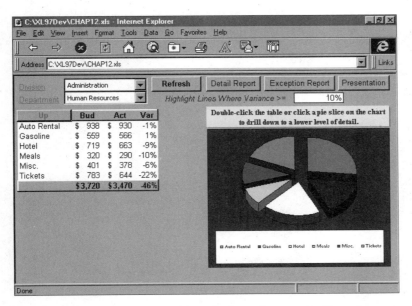

Figure 12-4. *Information displayed after selecting the Travel expense category.*

Click the Department hyperlink when the Human Resources department is displayed (in the Administration division). This Web page (Figure 12-5) appears:

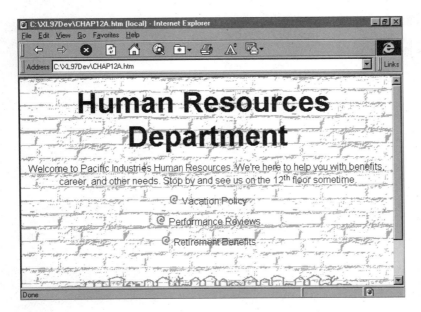

Figure 12-5. *The Human Resources Department Web page.*

Note that if you select other departments or divisions, you will link to various sites on the World Wide Web.

The Four Button Controls

Use the browser to return to the Expense Analysis workbook. Notice the four command buttons at the top of the screen—these allow you to refresh the data or create a report or presentation using another Microsoft Office product. (These controls are also from the Forms toolbar, not from the Control Toolbox toolbar.)

The Detail report

This button produces a detailed expense analysis report in Microsoft Word. When you click the button, the application uses the Office Assistant to prompt you to identify which division you would like included in the report (Figure 12-6 below).

Figure 12-6. *An Office Assistant prompt.*

This prompt is activated using the Office Assistant; the routine activated by the button uses the Assistant, Balloon, and BalloonCheckBox objects. (This prompt cannot be activated through a userform because like ActiveX controls, userforms cannot be used from within Internet Explorer.)

When you select a division and click the OK button on the Assistant prompt, data from the Expense Analysis form is pasted into Word and formatted via Automation. Specifically, the CreateObject function launches an instance of the Word application. The resulting application object is then manipulated through VBA code to create a new document, add and format the report title, and paste into the document a copy of the expense data table and corresponding pie chart for the selected division. Figure 12-7 shows a Detail report for the Administration division:

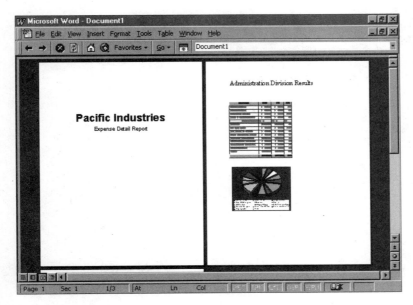

Figure 12-7. *A Detail report for the Administration division.*

After the report is produced, you remain in Word—you must return to Excel to continue running the application (you can do this by closing Word or by task-switching to Excel).

The Exception report

The Exception Report button on the Expense Analysis form produces an Exception report that lists any department whose total budget has been exceeded by 10 percent or more. The report is actually produced by Microsoft Access through a VBA routine attached to the button. Automation is used to format the report in a manner similar to that described for the Detail report. Try clicking the Exception Report button. Figure 12-8 on the following page appears.

After the report is produced, you remain in Access—you must return to Excel to continue running the application (you can do this by closing Access or by task-switching to Excel).

Generating a presentation

The Presentation button on the Expense Analysis form creates a PowerPoint slide show that summarizes the expense analysis for all divisions. When you click this button, a routine creates the presentation via Automation. Figure 12-9 on the following page shows the slides from the presentation.

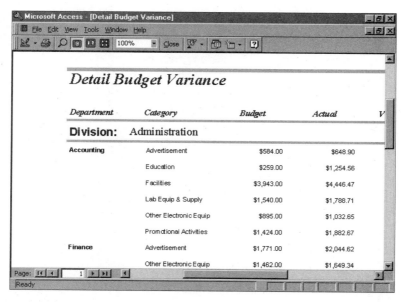

Figure 12-8. *The Exception report.*

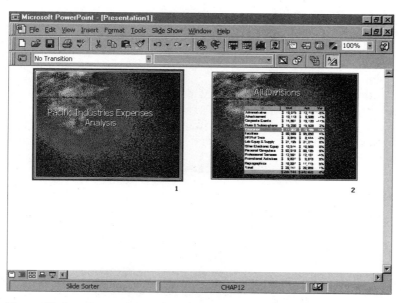

Figure 12-9. *Slides from a presentation created by PowerPoint and Automation.*

> **NOTE**
>
> At the time of the writing of this book, we encountered some problems in controlling PowerPoint 97 using Automation. Specifically, it was discovered that if you pasted an Excel object into a PowerPoint presentation via Automation, PowerPoint actually activated the object when the paste operation was executed, which caused the Workbook_Open event in the pasted Excel workbook to fire. Therefore, you should take care to either paste Excel objects into PowerPoint 97 as bitmaps (this can be accomplished by using the CopyPicture method in Excel) or paste only Excel objects that do not contain VBA code responding to the Workbook_Open event.

> **FYI**
>
> **Using Code in Excel Workbooks Activated in the IE Browser**
>
> You should be careful when using VBA code in Excel workbooks that are to be activated in the Internet Explorer (IE) browser. As has been shown in the Pacific Industries sample application, certain programmable features of Excel do not work when Excel is activated in the IE browser. For example, it is not possible to use ActiveX controls or userforms, nor is it possible to customize built-in commandbars. Additionally, you may find that certain memory-intensive VBA operations may not execute when an Excel workbook is activated in the IE browser. You should extensively test any VBA application that you anticipate will be activated in the IE browser to ensure your code runs appropriately.

Exploring the Pacific Industries Application

The application is made up of two worksheets including the Expense Analysis form and one supporting form that holds a list of URLs for the two dropdown control labels. You can view the worksheets that make up the Pacific Industries application by opening CHAP12.XLS directly in Excel and using the Tools Options command to display sheet tabs.

In the Visual Basic Editor, you can view the modules used to create the application, including those listed on the following page.

Module	Description
mAccess	VBA routines for production of the report in Access
mAnalysis	VBA routines for drill-down and other functionality of the Expense Analysis form
mDSNCreator	VBA routine that creates the ODBC data source for the Expenses database
mMain	General-purpose VBA routines that apply to the whole application
mPowerPoint	VBA routines for production of the presentation in PowerPoint
mWord	VBA routines for production of the report in Word

SUMMARY

This chapter examined a simple application that performs interactive data analysis using Excel within the context of a corporate intranet. Here are the main points of this chapter:

■ Excel applications can run within the Microsoft Internet Explorer, but this affects their functionality. For example, ActiveX controls embedded in a sheet or user form will not operate. You can, however, use controls from the old Forms toolbar and the Office Assistant to prompt users for input.

■ The worksheet and chart menu commandbars cannot be changed when an Excel application is running in the browser.

■ The functionality of Excel can be extended by integrating with other applications using Automation. The Pacific Industries application takes advantage of Automation to manipulate Word, Access, and PowerPoint for advanced reporting and presentation features.

■ By exhibiting the capabilities of these applications through Automation rather than by using only the objects in Excel, we have been able to save a tremendous amount of time and effort in expanding the functionality of this application.

13

Distributing Applications and Enhancing Performance

In this chapter, you'll find recommendations for distributing applications and enhancing their performance.

Distributing Applications

So far we have not touched on the area of distributing applications—several issues are apparent the moment you take a Microsoft Excel VBA solution off your development machine and try to run it on a user's machine. For example, any VBA application developed in Microsoft Excel 97 requires that Excel 97 be installed on the user's machine. Consider these other issues as well, which are discussed in detail on the following pages:

- Using add-ins

- Distributing applications that contain multiple files

- Distributing applications that use objects from other OLE applications (such as DAO, Microsoft Access, Microsoft Word, Microsoft PowerPoint, Microsoft Outlook, Microsoft Binder, and Microsoft Project)

- Maintaining references to add-in files

- Maintaining pivottable data sources

- Setting up an ODBC data source on the user's computer

- Establishing custom commandbars

- Hiding and protecting worksheets

- Checking for mail installation

- Changing and restoring Excel workspace settings

- Using a custom installation routine

FYI

Hardware Recommendations

When distributing an Excel 97 VBA application for the Microsoft Windows 95 environment, be sure that your users have at least a 486/66 with 16 megabytes (MB) of RAM. (For even better performance, they should have a Pentium-90 or higher computer with more RAM.) When distributing applications on the Microsoft Windows NT Workstation 4.0 platform, be sure your users have at least a Pentium-90 computer with 32 MB of RAM. (For better performance with Windows NT Workstation, you should consider a higher Pentium-class processor—Pentium Pro 200 being perhaps the best at the time of the writing of this book—and more memory.)

Using Add-Ins

An add-in is an Excel workbook with attributes that are ideal for applications that will be distributed. An add-in is typically distributed along with other workbooks as part of a complete application. Most attributes of add-ins are activated when you set a special property of the Workbook object—IsAddIn—to True. Other attributes must be set manually before you create the add-in. The following list describes the special attributes of add-ins.

The add-in code is fully compiled: Because the code of an add-in is fully compiled, you'll see a slight improvement in performance over normal workbooks. Here's why: each VBA module in a workbook can exist in one of a number of stages of compilation. When a module is edited, it becomes uncompiled; when a routine is run in an uncompiled module, Excel automatically compiles it. When a workbook is saved with an uncompiled module and the user tries to run a VBA routine in that module, the user will experience a slight delay in performance while the module is compiled. (You must manually force compilation before you save an add-in; the IsAddIn object does not do this for you. See step 1 in the procedure on page 589.)

Code modules and userforms are protected from view: This attribute is critical as it prevents users from unintentionally modifying your application. (You must create the password protection for the project manually—the IsAddIn property does not do this for you. See step 2 in the procedure on page 590.)

The workbook window is hidden: The workbook window cannot be made visible, which allows you to use the worksheets in the .XLA file for storing lists or calculations that you want to keep hidden from the user. However, it also poses certain problems for distributing worksheet-based forms in an add-in. Although you can include worksheets in an add-in and access all worksheet functionality, using VBA to display a worksheet contained in an .XLA file is difficult. If you want to use add-ins, you should store any worksheet-based forms for your application in a separate workbook file and keep your VBA code in the add-in file. You then open both files when your application is first started so that the code executes from the add-in file while the user interacts with the forms in the workbook file. No problems are associated with the display of userforms in an add-in file.

Users cannot bypass automatic events: When opening an add-in, a user cannot bypass Workbook_Open or any other automatic events by holding down the Shift key. This ensures that any initialization code you write is run at the correct time.

Unwanted user prompts are not generated: When quitting an application stored in an add-in, the user won't be prompted to save the workbook if changes have been made while the workbook is open. This frees you to let your code "dirty" worksheets in the add-in file without having to worry about generating unwanted prompts when your application is closed.

Invisible routines can still be run: When the user opens the Macro dialog box (by selecting Macros from the Macro submenu on the Tools menu), any routines in the add-in won't be visible. However, these routines can still be run from the Macro dialog box. Routine names don't need to be qualified with the workbook name.

Add-ins have an .XLA extension: By convention, add-ins typically have an .XLA extension to differentiate them from normal workbook files.

Creating add-ins

The process for creating add-ins has changed dramatically in Excel 97. (Microsoft Excel 95 and 5, for example, had a Tools Make Add-In command that created an add-in file that couldn't be directly debugged or modified.) The new add-in model provides many new benefits—for example, the developer can debug and modify the code directly in the add-in as well as extend the add-in concept to other Office applications.

To create and distribute an add-in that contributes to the overall professional quality of your application, follow these steps.

1. **Compile the project.** To ensure that the project is fully compiled, select the Compile VBAProject command from the Debug menu in the Visual Basic Editor. (See the screen on the following page.)

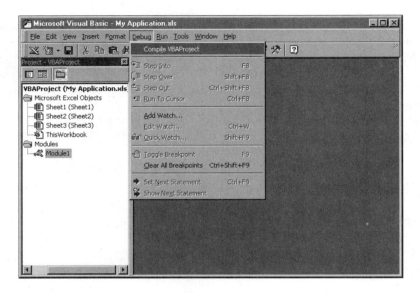

2. Protect the project from viewing. In the Visual Basic Editor, select
the VBAProject Properties command from the Tools menu. From the
Project Properties dialog box, select the Protection tab. Check the Lock
Project For Viewing option and assign a protection password. Keep in
mind that this password is case-sensitive.

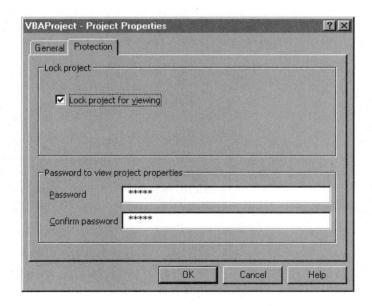

Once protection is set, the user will be unable to view the objects in the project without supplying the password, but will be able to launch the Visual Basic Editor and see the name of the project in the Project Explorer window (the name is at the top level of the project tree). If the user attempts to expand the tree, however, the user will be prompted for the password.

3. **Set the IsAddIn property of the workbook to True and save the workbook with an .XLA extension.** Switch to the Excel window and select Save As from the File menu. Save the file as type Microsoft Excel Add-In (*.XLA), which is the last file type in the list.

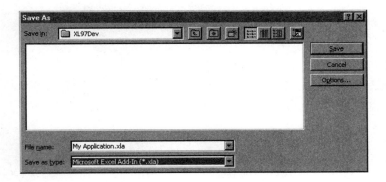

This save method sets the IsAddIn property to True and saves a copy of the workbook with the .XLA extension, leaving the original .XLS file open.

Testing and debugging an add-in

To test the add-in, first close the source .XLS workbook, and then open the add-in to run your application. If you encounter errors and need to debug the code in your add-in, you can make the add-in visible and view the code provided you supply the proper project password. To do this, open the Visual Basic Editor and double-click the project name in the Project Explorer window. Then enter the password when prompted.

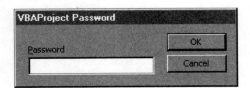

Once the project is unprotected, you can freely view and debug the code.

To make the add-in workbook visible, change the IsAddIn property to False using the Properties window for the ThisWorkbook object, as pictured on the following page.

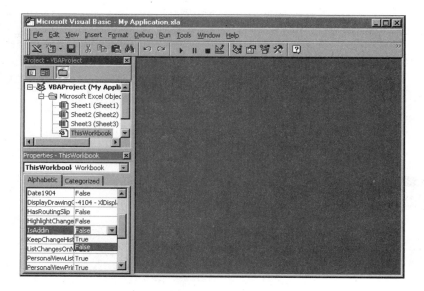

FYI

The Break On All Errors Option

Excel add-in files ignore settings for Break On All Errors, whereas normal workbooks do not. When you turn on the Break On All Errors option by checking the appropriate check box in the General tab of the Options dialog box (accessible through the Tools Options command in the Visual Basic Editor), routines in .XLS files halt execution if an error is encountered, even when an On Error statement is used. However, .XLA files ignore Break On All Errors settings and execute On Error statements even when Break On All Errors is on.

FYI

Referencing the Add-In Workbook

In several examples in this book, we have used ActiveWorkbook to reference the current workbook rather than index the Workbooks collection by name. But because an add-in file is hidden, it can never be referenced by using ActiveWorkbook. Instead, you must either use ThisWorkbook to reference an add-in or index the Workbooks collection by using the name of the file.

Distributing Applications That Contain Multiple Files

To take advantage of performance enhancements offered by an .XLA file and to keep your application organized in manageable, logical parts, it is best to distribute VBA applications in multiple files rather than in a single file. When you create multiple files, however, you must decide where the .XLS or .XLA files will be stored on the user's hard disk and how they will be located.

Ideally, all files of an application are installed in a single folder on the user's hard disk, which ensures that at any time during the execution of the application, the path to the folder can be identified using the Path property of the Workbook object. The Path property holds a string that specifies the path for the specified workbook. For example, let's suppose your application contains two .XLS files. As your application starts executing, one .XLS file is loaded. If the user decides at a certain point to access a particular piece of the functionality of the application that the second .XLS file contains, your application can open the second .XLS file by calling the Open method on the Workbooks collection and specifying for the filename argument the name of the second .XLS file, preceded by the string that the Path property of the first .XLS file contains. This method is far preferable to using hard-coded paths.

Distributing Applications That Use Objects from Other Applications

In Chapter 10, we saw how it is possible to establish references to type libraries of external applications. Doing so allows you to take advantage of the benefits of early binding: increased performance through declaring object variables that point to external objects using the specific object type, and less work in code maintenance through use of constants provided by external type libraries. However, when you reference an external object library in an Excel file and the user attempts to run a routine in the file on a system that does not contain the referenced object library, Excel will generate an error message and halt execution.

Unless you are absolutely positive that all your users will have the correct external applications and object libraries installed, you should not establish references to external type libraries in the Excel file containing your application. Instead, you should rely on late binding and access external object models through use of the CreateObject and GetObject functions. Doing so will allow you to implement your own error checking in warning users who don't have the appropriate type libraries installed and, therefore, bypass Excel's runtime errors. Examples of using late binding are provided in the CHAP10.XLS and CHAP12.XLS files included on the companion CD. Be aware that when using late binding, you must declare object variables that reference external objects using the generic Object data type (as opposed to the specific object type). In addition, with late binding, you cannot access constants provided by external type libraries. Therefore, you must declare and assign such constants locally in your application.

Maintaining References to Add-In Files

To access subroutines and functions in another add-in file, you must establish a reference to the add-in by choosing the References command from the Tools menu in the Visual Basic Editor and then locating the add-in file using the Browse button. Certain problems arise when you save a VBA application with a reference to an add-in file—namely, that Excel hard-codes the path of the add-in file when the reference is established and the file that contains the reference is saved. When you open an Excel file that has a saved add-in reference on another computer, Excel searches the hard-coded path for the add-in file. In addition, Excel searches the path of the file that contains the reference (e.g, the working folder). If Excel finds the referenced add-in in either of these locations, Excel successfully re-establishes the reference. Therefore, the following rule is imperative when you distribute an application that has a saved reference to an add-in—otherwise, Excel fails to find the add-in file, and the reference is not established on the user's machine.

RULE The relevant add-in file must be saved in the same folder as the Excel file that contains the reference.

An alternative to establishing references to add-ins is to use the Run method of the Application object to call routines in the add-in. The Run method will run the requested routine without a reference assuming the file containing the routine is in memory. Using this approach, you could open the add-in file through code from whatever location it is in, then call the Run method. This method takes the name of the routine or function to run as a string argument, and then takes any arguments to the routine being called as additional optional string arguments. For example:

```
Application.Run "MyRoutine", "Argument1", "Argument2"
```

The drawbacks of this approach are that the arguments must be converted to text and that pass by reference arguments cannot return values (since arguments are converted to pass by value automatically).

Maintaining Pivottable Data Sources

If you write applications that use pivottables that access data in local external databases (Microsoft Access, Microsoft FoxPro, dBASE, and so on), you might have a problem related to the pivottable data source when you distribute your applications to users. When you create a pivottable on a worksheet manually from a local external database using the PivotTable Wizard, Excel stores the hard-coded path for the local database in the pivottable's data source definition. Excel searches the hard-coded path for the database when you call the RefreshTable method on the pivottable. The problem occurs when you try to distribute the application that contains the pivottable to a user who might not have the local database in the same hard-coded path as on your development machine. The only way you can avoid storing this hard-coded path with the pivottable is to use the PivotTableWizard method of the Worksheet object to create the pivot-table from within a subroutine.

NOTE   You can create the pivottable using a routine at design time; you do not have to create it at runtime.

Remember that an array is passed for the sourceData argument when the Pivot-TableWizard method is called to create a pivottable from an external data source. The first element of the array is an ODBC data source name, and the second element is a SQL query string. The following is an example of an ODBC data source definition that contains a hard-coded path to an Access database:

```
DSN=BikeData;DBQ=C:\EXCEL\BIKEDATA.MDB;FIL=RedISAM;
```

To avoid saving a hard-coded path with the pivottable's data source, specify only the DSN portion of the ODBC data source name in the array's first element for the sourceData argument, as in the following:

```
DSN=BikeData
```

The following code is an example of a call to the PivotTableWizard method that could be used to create a pivottable that contains an ODBC data source with-out a hard-coded path:

```
Worksheets(1).PivotTableWizard _
        sourceType:=xlExternal, _
        sourceData:=Array("DSN=BikeData", _
                    "SELECT * FROM Sales"), _
        tableDestination:=Worksheets(3).Range("B10"), _
        tableName:="Pivot1"
```

After you create the pivottable in this manner, you can use the PivotTable Wizard to design the pivottable manually. (Again, this process of programmatically creating the pivottable without the hard-coded path to the local data source can be done during design time.) After the pivottable is saved in a workbook file, the workbook file that contains the pivottable can be distributed to any user, and the pivottable will function without relying on a hard-coded path.

FYI

Setting Up an ODBC Data Source on the User's Computer

For any application that uses a pivottable with an external data source or uses DAO to access an external database, issues arise in regard to whether the appropriate ODBC data sources (DSNs) exist on the user's machine. For example, if you use an ODBC data source named BikeData that is established on your development computer, how can you be sure that your user will also have a BikeData DSN? You can provide instructions to the user for setting up the appropriate data source manually, although this approach might prove to be difficult for the user. If you are using Excel 95 or Excel 97, you can use the RegisterDatabase function of the DBEngine object supplied in the DAO object model to establish a Windows Registry-based DSN at runtime.

File DSNs (covered in Chapter 5) can also help alleviate this problem. Recall that a File DSN is simply a file containing the data source information. This file can be distributed with your application, thus preventing the need to set up a DSN on the target machine. However, if the data source is a local database such as an Access MDB file, this approach may be problematic as well. Since the File DSN would contain a hard-coded path to the MDB file, the database would need to reside in that specific path on the target machine.

NOTE   As a general rule, it is recommended that you consider use of a Registry-based DSN as opposed to the new file-based DSNs that are provided with Excel 97. Once you familiarize yourself with the RegisterDatabase function provided by DAO, you will find that Registry-based DSNs are easier to manage than are file-based DSNs. Additionally, Registry DSNs can be shared among multiple solutions developed in other products (such as Microsoft Visual Basic or Microsoft Access). The one drawback of using Registry DSNs is that in the initial release of Excel 97, users cannot view Registry DSNs from Microsoft Query. This is new to Excel 97. (In past versions of Excel, users could view Registry DSNs from Microsoft Query). You should take this into account when determining whether to employ Registry or file-based DSNs.

Establishing Custom CommandBars

As discussed in Chapter 5, you can establish custom commandbars either through VBA code or by using the Tools Customize command and attaching the custom commandbars to your workbook file. To maintain the integrity of the user's workspace, take care to reset Excel's commandbars after your application has finished executing. The sample applications in Chapters 6, 9, and 12 provide examples of how to do so.

Hiding and Protecting Worksheets

To protect the internal workings of your application from access by the user, protect and hide worksheets whenever possible. Doing so limits the user's access to Excel while your application is running, preventing the user from wandering into an area of your application that you don't want the user to see.

Checking for Mail Installation

For any applications that involve integration with MAPI or another messaging system, be sure to check for installation of a mail system before calling routines that act on the mail system. Use the MailSystem property of the Application object to check this. The MailSystem property will hold one of three values: xlNoMailSystem, xlMAPI, or xlPowerTalk.

Changing and Restoring Excel Workspace Settings

To maintain the integrity of the Excel workspace on the user's machine, be sure to restore all original workspace settings after your application finishes executing. The sample applications in Chapters 6, 9, and 12 show examples of how the Workbook_Open event can be used to save the user's original workspace settings and how the Workbook_BeforeClose event can be used to restore those settings. You should be concerned about workspace settings for visible commandbars, the formula bar display, the status bar display, the application caption, and the application window state. The following routines can be used in any application to save and restore all of these settings. Simply call SetEnvironment from the Workbook_Open event procedure and RestoreEnvironment from Workbook_BeforeClose. Note that SetEnvironment also changes the application caption and turns off display of the status bar and the formula bar. This code is included in the CHAP13.BAS file on the companion CD.

```
Option Explicit
Public VisibleCommandBars() As String
Public AppWindowState As Variant
Public AppFormulaBar As Boolean
Public AppStatusBar As Boolean

Sub SetEnvironment()
    Dim CBar As CommandBar
    Dim Counter As Integer
    Application.ScreenUpdating = False
    Counter = 0
    For Each CBar In Application.CommandBars
```

(continued)

continued

```
            If CBar.Visible And CBar.Type <> msoBarTypeMenuBar Then
                ReDim Preserve VisibleCommandBars(Counter)
                VisibleCommandBars(Counter) = CBar.Name
                CBar.Visible = False
                Counter = Counter + 1
            End If
        Next
        With Application
            If UCase(Left(.OperatingSystem, 3)) <> "MAC" Then
                AppWindowState = .WindowState
                .WindowState = xlMaximized
                .Caption = "Pacific Industries"
                ActiveWindow.Caption = ""
            Else
                ActiveWindow.Caption = "Pacific Industries"
            End If
            AppFormulaBar = .DisplayFormulaBar
            AppStatusBar = .DisplayStatusBar
            .DisplayFormulaBar = False
            .DisplayStatusBar = False
        End With
    End Sub

    Sub RestoreEnvironment()
        Dim CBar As Variant
        With Application
            .ScreenUpdating = False
            If UCase(Left(.OperatingSystem, 3)) <> "MAC" Then
                .WindowState = AppWindowState
                .Caption = Empty
            End If
            ActiveWindow.Caption = ActiveWorkbook.Name
            .DisplayFormulaBar = AppFormulaBar
            .DisplayStatusBar = AppStatusBar
            .CommandBars("Worksheet Menu Bar").Reset
            .CommandBars("Chart Menu Bar").Reset
        End With
        For Each CBar In VisibleCommandBars
            Application.CommandBars(CBar).Visible = True
        Next
    End Sub
```

Using a Custom Installation Routine

To make your VBA application appear more professional and to make it easy for users to install the application on their systems properly, you might want to use a custom installation routine. For information about how to create such routines for the Windows platform, see the Windows Software Development Kit or obtain a copy of Office Developers Edition, both of which contain utilities for developing custom installation routines. (Contact Microsoft Developer Services for details. In the United States, call 1-800-426-9400; outside the United States, contact your local Microsoft office.)

Enhancing Performance

Throughout this book, we've looked at some of the ways you can improve the speed at which your Excel VBA code executes. The speed of any VBA application in Excel is governed largely by the manner in which the application accesses Excel objects. You can, therefore, enhance the performance of your applications by learning all you can about Excel objects and how best to use them. In addition, you should follow a few general guidelines to ensure that your VBA code will execute at its highest level of performance.

Declare variables with the appropriate data type: When a variable is declared as a Variant, Excel must coerce the variable to the appropriate data type whenever a value is assigned to the variable. This coercion takes a certain amount of time, which has a negative impact on performance. Variables that are not declared and that default to the Variant data type degrade performance for the same reason. To avoid this situation, you should place Option Explicit statements at the top of all your VBA modules to force yourself to always declare variables.

Declare object variables with the appropriate object type: You can declare an object variable using the generic Object data type, which is similar to declaring a standard variable as a Variant. As with Variants, declaring an object variable using the generic Object data type forces Excel to coerce the variable whenever an object is assigned to the variable, resulting in a negative impact on performance. To avoid this problem, use the actual name of the object to be assigned to the object variable when you declare the variable.

Use early binding if possible: If you are absolutely sure that your users will have external applications and object libraries installed, you should use early binding by establishing references to the object libraries. Early binding is significantly faster than late binding when automating external objects. Of course, early binding is a luxury that many applications cannot afford. If you do not know the exact configuration of the target platform (the object models installed on the target machine) to which your application is being distributed, then you should be very cautious in using early binding. If you attempt to early bind to an object model that is not installed on the user's machine, an error message will result. Late binding allows you to handle this error situation and keep Excel-generated error messages from appearing to the user.

Use object variables in place of long hierarchical object references: When you work with object references, it is often more efficient to use an object variable than to use a hierarchical object reference to reference the object. Think of the dot operator (.) used in a hierarchical object reference as representing a unit of time—time required by Excel to evaluate the reference. For example, a hierarchical object reference that contains four dots will require four units of time, but a single object variable that refers to the same object will contain no dots and so represents a positive impact on performance. This improvement in performance will be especially evident when an object is referenced in a loop that executes many times.

Use With statements to set properties of or call methods on an object: When you are setting multiple properties of or calling multiple methods on an object, it is always more efficient to use a With statement. As mentioned, if you think of every instance of the dot operator (.) as representing a unit of time, you'll see that With statements reduce the number of dot operators required to reference the properties and methods of an object and therefore can have a positive impact on performance.

Force VBA modules to compile before you save add-in and .XLS files: Be sure that all the VBA modules are compiled before any file to be distributed (add-in or normal workbook) is saved. To do so, use the Compile command on the Tools menu in the Visual Basic Editor.

When possible, use VBA arrays instead of worksheet ranges to manipulate data: You can manipulate matrices of data at a much higher level of performance if the data is manipulated in a VBA array instead of in a worksheet range. To manipulate data in a range, VBA must read and write data to the range constantly, which has a negative impact on performance. By manipulating data in an array, you do not experience this negative impact; however, certain features of worksheet ranges cannot be duplicated in an array. You can easily exchange data between a range and a Variant variable holding an array. For example, setting a Variant variable to the Value property of a multi-cell range will cause the range to be read into the variable as an array. Likewise, you can assign an array variable (or an array held in a Variant) directly to a range by setting the Value property of the range equal to the variable.

Use Array formulas: For formulas that affect large ranges of data, you will see an improvement in performance if you use array formulas rather than standard worksheet formulas. As a result, you should familiarize yourself with array formulas and use them whenever possible.

Don't link controls to worksheet ranges: Several controls, including checkboxes, dropdowns, scrollbars, and spinbuttons, can be linked to worksheet ranges. These controls can also be accessed directly through VBA without linking them to worksheets. You will see a marked improvement in performance if you access controls directly from VBA rather than link them to a worksheet range. Therefore, you should avoid linking controls to worksheet ranges whenever possible.

Set the ScreenUpdating property of the Application object to False: For any subroutine that requires numerous changes to the currently displayed worksheet or chart, set the ScreenUpdating property of the Application object to False at the start of the routine. If ScreenUpdating is set to True, the graphics display is updated each time a change is made to the currently displayed worksheet or chart, which has a negative impact on performance because updating the graphics display requires a certain amount of time. If it is not necessary to update the display every time a change is made while a routine is executing, set ScreenUpdating to False to improve performance.

SUMMARY

In this chapter, we've taken a brief look at several issues related to distributing and enhancing the performance of Excel VBA applications. Keep the following key points in mind:

■ You should test any special accommodations that you make for distributing applications on different computer configurations to be sure they work properly before you distribute your applications.

■ You will be able to enhance the performance of your VBA applications most effectively by learning all you can about the Excel object model.

INDEX

ABOUT THE AUTHORS

Eric Wells was formerly a Microsoft Group Product Manager for Microsoft Office and Microsoft Excel and has lectured worldwide on developing with Microsoft Excel and Microsoft Visual Basic for Applications. Eric works as an independent consultant in Seattle, WA, specializing in development and marketing of VBA and Web-based solutions.

Eric earned a B.S. in kinesiology and an M.B.A. from the University of California at Los Angeles. He also completed two years of master's level course work in computer science at the University of California at Santa Barbara. Prior to joining Microsoft, Eric was a product manager for Dynamic Solutions, a division of Millipore Corporation, developing marketing programs for its leading line of chromatography software applications.

Eric can be reached at ericwell@msn.com.

Steve Harshbarger is a Director at Micro Modeling Associates, Inc., an application development consulting firm specializing in delivering custom business applications to Fortune 1000 clients using Microsoft tools and technologies.

Steve joined MMA in March of 1994 and is responsible for its Washington, DC practice. He oversees a team of developers implementing business applications and using the entire suite of Microsoft development tools for clients in public accounting, telecommunications, insurance, and other industries.

Steve is a contributing author of several books including *Official Microsoft Intranet Solutions* (Microsoft Press, 1997), *The Intranet Data Warehouse* (Wiley, 1997), and *Excel Professional Techniques* (Que, 1994). He is a frequent speaker at Microsoft-sponsored events including Tech-Ed, VBITS, Developer Days, and various product launches. Steve is also a Certified Public Accountant, which gives him a unique perspective on business solutions.

Prior to joining Micro Modeling, Steve was a senior consultant at KPMG Peat Marwick in Washington, DC and earned his degree in Accounting Information Systems from Virginia Tech.

Steve can be contacted via email at harshbargers@micromodeling.com or through MMA's web site at http:\\www.micromodeling.com.

The manuscript for this book was submitted to Microsoft Press in electronic form. Galleys were prepared using Microsoft Word 7.0 for Windows 95. Pages were composed by Microsoft Press using Adobe PageMaker 6.0 for Windows, with text type in Garamond and display type in Futura Medium. Composed pages were delivered to the printer as electronic prepress files.

Cover Graphic Designers
Greg Erickson, Robin Hjellen

Cover Illustrator
Landor and Associates

Interior Graphic Designer
Kim Eggleston

Interior Graphic Artists
Michael Victor, Joel Panchot

Compositors
Sandra Haynes, Sue Prettyman

Principal Proofreader/Copy Editor
Patricia Masserman

Indexer
Julie Kawabata

Think of it as a turbocharger for your spreadsheets.

Microsoft® Excel 97 is loaded with functions— ready-made "building blocks" with which you can easily assemble powerful formulas to go in your most sophisticated spreadsheets. And this book puts all those functions at your fingertips. Here you'll find a clear, easily referenced guide to the hundreds of functions offered in Microsoft Excel 97—mathematical, statistical, trigonometric, engineering, and financial. So put more power into your spreadsheets. Get MICROSOFT EXCEL 97 WORKSHEET FUNCTION REFERENCE.

U.S.A.	**$24.95**
U.K.	£22.99
Canada	$34.95
ISBN 1-57231-341-2	

Microsoft Press® products are available worldwide wherever quality computer books are sold. For more information, contact your book retailer, computer reseller, or local Microsoft Sales Office.

To locate your nearest source for Microsoft Press products, reach us at mspress.microsoft.com, or call 1-800-MSPRESS in the U.S. (in Canada: 1-800-667-1115 or 416-293-8464).

To order Microsoft Press products, call 1-800-MSPRESS in the U.S. (in Canada: 1-800-667-1115 or 416-293-8464).

Prices and availability dates are subject to change.

Microsoft Press

Make *professional-quality* *data-access* and *decision-making* tools *fast!*

U.S.A. **$39.99**
U.K.   £37.49 [V.A.T. included]
Canada $53.99
ISBN 1-57231-358-7

New in the *Solution Developer* series, this title brings a wealth of information to power users and developers who want to build effective information systems in less time and at lower cost. MICROSOFT ACCESS 97 DEVELOPER'S HANDBOOK covers:

- Working in the VBA environment
- Designing easy-to-use interfaces
- Creating applications that look and feel like Windows®-based products
- Easily automating tasks based in Microsoft Access
- Using ActiveX™ with Microsoft Access
- Integrating intranets and the Internet into your database application

No matter how you use Microsoft Access 97—in the stand-alone edition, in the Microsoft Office Developer Edition, or in any other edition of Microsoft Office—this is your essential one-stop development resource.

Microsoft Press® products are available worldwide wherever quality computer books are sold. For more information, contact your book retailer, computer reseller, or local Microsoft Sales Office.

To locate your nearest source for Microsoft Press products, reach us at mspress.microsoft.com, or call 1-800-MSPRESS in the U.S. (in Canada: 1-800-667-1115 or 416-293-8464).

To order Microsoft Press products, call 1-800-MSPRESS in the U.S. (in Canada: 1-800-667-1115 or 416-293-8464).

Prices and availability dates are subject to change.

Microsoft®*Press*

The most popular office suite—and the top development platform.

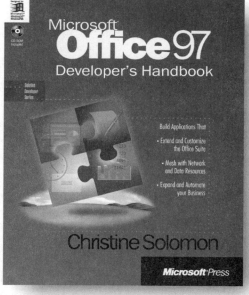

Microsoft Office 97 Developer's Handbook

Build Applications That
- Extend and Customize the Office Suite
- Mesh with Network and Data Resources
- Expand and Automate your Business

Christine Solomon

Microsoft Press

In this thoroughly revised edition, well-known author and experienced consultant Christine Solomon shows systems professionals and developers how to automate and re-engineer a wide assortment of businesses on the powerful Microsoft® Office 97 platform. You'll find plenty of information on new features and technologies. And everything is clarified with detailed explanations, sample applications, anecdotes, examples, and case studies. Plus, the enclosed CD-ROM contains source code and files for sample applications. Get MICROSOFT OFFICE 97 DEVELOPER'S HANDBOOK. And find out why Microsoft Office 97 is a whole new development.

U.S.A.	**$39.99**
U.K.	£37.49 [V.A.T. included]
Canada	$53.99
ISBN 1-57231-440-0	

Microsoft Press® products are available worldwide wherever quality computer books are sold. For more information, contact your book retailer, computer reseller, or local Microsoft Sales Office.

To locate your nearest source for Microsoft Press products, reach us at mspress.microsoft.com, or call 1-800-MSPRESS in the U.S. (in Canada: 1-800-667-1115 or 416-293-8464).

To order Microsoft Press products, call 1-800-MSPRESS in the U.S. (in Canada: 1-800-667-1115 or 416-293-8464).

Prices and availability dates are subject to change.

Microsoft Press

Industrial-strength
information
for developing with
Microsoft®
Excel 97.

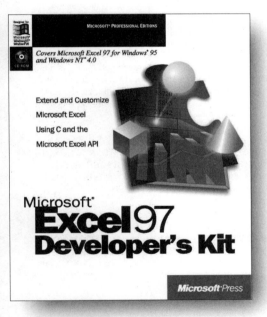

U.S.A. **$49.99**
U.K. £46.99 [V.A.T. included]
Canada $66.99
ISBN 1-57231-498-2

This is *the* technical reference you need for creating extremely robust custom applications that extend and work with Microsoft Excel. It's for developers who need to work directly with the Microsoft Excel Application Programming Interface (API) using Microsoft C/C++. And it's for everyone who needs full details about the file format of Microsoft Excel. The MICROSOFT EXCEL 97 DEVELOPER'S KIT is filled with specific—and valuable—information. It's not a guide to the Microsoft Excel macro language or to Visual Basic® for Applications (VBA). Instead, this is the only book that:

- Contains everything a C programmer needs for creating applications that extend and work with Microsoft Excel
- Shows C programmers how to extend Microsoft Excel to create custom applications using the Microsoft Excel API
- Provides file format and extension information for Microsoft Excel

Plus, you get a CD-ROM filled with valuable sample code and additional documentation not found in the book. In short, if you're a high-level developer who wants to customize Microsoft Excel in specific and unique ways, this is the handbook you need.

Microsoft Press® products are available worldwide wherever quality computer books are sold. For more information, contact your book retailer, computer reseller, or local Microsoft Sales Office.

To locate your nearest source for Microsoft Press products, reach us at mspress.microsoft.com, or call 1-800-MSPRESS in the U.S. (in Canada: 1-800-667-1115 or 416-293-8464).

To order Microsoft Press products, call 1-800-MSPRESS in the U.S. (in Canada: 1-800-667-1115 or 416-293-8464).

Prices and availability dates are subject to change.

Microsoft®Press

IMPORTANT—READ CAREFULLY BEFORE OPENING SOFTWARE PACKET(S). By opening the sealed packet(s) containing the software, you indicate your acceptance of the following Microsoft License Agreement.

MICROSOFT LICENSE AGREEMENT

(Book Companion CD)

This is a legal agreement between you (either an individual or an entity) and Microsoft Corporation. By opening the sealed software packet(s) you are agreeing to be bound by the terms of this agreement. If you do not agree to the terms of this agreement, promptly return the unopened software packet(s) and any accompanying written materials to the place you obtained them for a full refund.

MICROSOFT SOFTWARE LICENSE

1. GRANT OF LICENSE. Microsoft grants to you the right to use one copy of the Microsoft software program included with this book (the "SOFTWARE") on a single terminal connected to a single computer. The SOFTWARE is in "use" on a computer when it is loaded into the temporary memory (i.e., RAM) or installed into the permanent memory (e.g., hard disk, CD-ROM, or other storage device) of that computer. You may not network the SOFTWARE or otherwise use it on more than one computer or computer terminal at the same time.

2. COPYRIGHT. The SOFTWARE is owned by Microsoft or its suppliers and is protected by United States copyright laws and international treaty provisions. Therefore, you must treat the SOFTWARE like any other copyrighted material (e.g., a book or musical recording) except that you may either (a) make one copy of the SOFTWARE solely for backup or archival purposes, or (b) transfer the SOFTWARE to a single hard disk provided you keep the original solely for backup or archival purposes. You may not copy the written materials accompanying the SOFTWARE.

3. OTHER RESTRICTIONS. You may not rent or lease the SOFTWARE, but you may transfer the SOFTWARE and accompanying written materials on a permanent basis provided you retain no copies and the recipient agrees to the terms of this Agreement. You may not reverse engineer, decompile, or disassemble the SOFTWARE. If the SOFTWARE is an update or has been updated, any transfer must include the most recent update and all prior versions.

4. DUAL MEDIA SOFTWARE. If the SOFTWARE package contains more than one kind of disk (3.5", 5.25", and CD-ROM), then you may use only the disks appropriate for your single-user computer. You may not use the other disks on another computer or loan, rent, lease, or transfer them to another user except as part of the permanent transfer (as provided above) of all SOFTWARE and written materials.

5. SAMPLE CODE. If the SOFTWARE includes Sample Code, then Microsoft grants you a royalty-free right to reproduce and distribute the sample code of the SOFTWARE provided that you: (a) distribute the sample code only in conjunction with and as a part of your software product; (b) do not use Microsoft's or its authors' names, logos, or trademarks to market your software product; (c) include the copyright notice that appears on the SOFTWARE on your product label and as a part of the sign-on message for your software product; and (d) agree to indemnify, hold harmless, and defend Microsoft and its authors from and against any claims or lawsuits, including attorneys' fees, that arise or result from the use or distribution of your software product.

DISCLAIMER OF WARRANTY

The SOFTWARE (including instructions for its use) is provided "AS IS" WITHOUT WARRANTY OF ANY KIND. MICROSOFT FURTHER DISCLAIMS ALL IMPLIED WARRANTIES INCLUDING WITHOUT LIMITATION ANY IMPLIED WARRANTIES OF MERCHANTABILITY OR OF FITNESS FOR A PARTICULAR PURPOSE. THE ENTIRE RISK ARISING OUT OF THE USE OR PERFORMANCE OF THE SOFTWARE AND DOCUMENTATION REMAINS WITH YOU.

IN NO EVENT SHALL MICROSOFT, ITS AUTHORS, OR ANYONE ELSE INVOLVED IN THE CREATION, PRODUCTION, OR DELIVERY OF THE SOFTWARE BE LIABLE FOR ANY DAMAGES WHATSOEVER (INCLUDING, WITHOUT LIMITATION, DAMAGES FOR LOSS OF BUSINESS PROFITS, BUSINESS INTERRUPTION, LOSS OF BUSINESS INFORMATION, OR OTHER PECUNIARY LOSS) ARISING OUT OF THE USE OF OR INABILITY TO USE THE SOFTWARE OR DOCUMENTATION, EVEN IF MICROSOFT HAS BEEN ADVISED OF THE POSSIBILITY OF SUCH DAMAGES. BECAUSE SOME STATES/COUNTRIES DO NOT ALLOW THE EXCLUSION OR LIMITATION OF LIABILITY FOR CONSEQUENTIAL OR INCIDENTAL DAMAGES, THE ABOVE LIMITATION MAY NOT APPLY TO YOU.

U.S. GOVERNMENT RESTRICTED RIGHTS

The SOFTWARE and documentation are provided with RESTRICTED RIGHTS. Use, duplication, or disclosure by the Government is subject to restrictions as set forth in subparagraph (c)(1)(ii) of The Rights in Technical Data and Computer Software clause at DFARS 252.227-7013 or subparagraphs (c)(1) and (2) of the Commercial Computer Software — Restricted Rights 48 CFR 52.227-19, as applicable. Manufacturer is Microsoft Corporation, One Microsoft Way, Redmond, WA 98052-6399.

If you acquired this product in the United States, this Agreement is governed by the laws of the State of Washington. Should you have any questions concerning this Agreement, or if you desire to contact Microsoft Press for any reason, please write: Microsoft Press, One Microsoft Way, Redmond, WA 98052-6399.

Register Today!

Return this
Microsoft® Excel 97 Developer's Handbook
registration card for
a Microsoft Press® catalog

U.S. and Canada addresses only. Fill in information below and mail postage-free. Please mail only the bottom half of this page.

1-57231-359-5A | ***MICROSOFT® EXCEL 97*** | *Owner Registration Card*
| ***DEVELOPER'S HANDBOOK*** |

NAME

INSTITUTION OR COMPANY NAME

ADDRESS

CITY   STATE   ZIP

Microsoft Press
Quality Computer Books

**For a free catalog of
Microsoft Press® products, call
1-800-MSPRESS**

BUSINESS REPLY MAIL
FIRST-CLASS MAIL   PERMIT NO. 53   BOTHELL, WA

POSTAGE WILL BE PAID BY ADDRESSEE

NO POSTAGE
NECESSARY
IF MAILED
IN THE
UNITED STATES

MICROSOFT PRESS REGISTRATION
MICROSOFT® EXCEL 97 DEVELOPER'S
HANDBOOK
PO BOX 3019
BOTHELL   WA   98041-9946